ALSO BY STEPHEN S. HALL

Invisible Frontiers: The Race to Synthesize a Human Gene

MAPPING
THE NEXT
MILLENNIUM

Random House 🏠 New York

MAPPING THE NEXT MILLENNIUM

THE DISCOVERY OF NEW GEOGRAPHIES

STEPHEN S. HALL

All rights reserved under International and Pan-American
Copyright Conventions. Published in the United States
by Random House, Inc., New York, and simultaneously in Canada by Random House
of Canada Limited, Toronto.

Library of Congress Cataloging-in-Publication Data

Hall, Stephen S.
Mapping the next millennium : the discovery of new geographies /
Stephen S. Hall.—1st ed.
    p.   cm.
Includes bibliographical references and index.
ISBN 0-394-57635-7
1. Science—Popular works.   I. Title.
Q162.H315 1991
500—dc20   91-52667

Grateful acknowledgment is made to the following for
permission to reprint previously published material:

Farrar, Straus & Giroux, Inc. and Faber & Faber Ltd.: Ten lines from "The Birthplace"
from *Station Island* by Seamus Heaney. Copyright © 1985 by Seamus Heaney. Rights
throughout the world excluding the United States are controlled by Faber & Faber Ltd.
Reprinted by permission of Farrar, Straus & Giroux, Inc. and Faber & Faber Ltd.

Macmillan Publishing Company: Three lines from "Byzantium" from *The Poems of
W. B. Yeats: A New Edition,* edited by Richard J. Finneran. Copyright 1933 by
Macmillan Publishing Company. Copyright renewed 1961 by Betha Georgie Yeats.
Reprinted by permission.

Manufactured in the United States of America
24689753
First Edition
Set in Times Roman

Endpapers: Radar maps of the surface of Venus,
recorded by the *Magellan* space probe (NASA).

Book design by Oksana Kushnir

For NATHAN ROBERT HALL,
who has more of a future
than anyone else I know

"It must have been at such an early age that I decided I would be a scientist. But I foresaw one snag. By the time I grew up—and how far away that seemed!—everything would have been discovered. I confided my fears to my mother, who reassured me. 'Don't worry, Ducky,' she said. 'There will be plenty left for you to find out.'"

—Francis Crick,
What Mad Pursuit

THE FIRST ATLAS

There came a moment some months ago when, while reading the journals of Lewis and Clark and tracing their route on my dog-eared Rand McNally road atlas (1979 edition, coverless and thumbed unto decrepitude, easily the most used and abused book in my entire library), I realized with sudden annoyance that I had wasted *hours* poking my finger at that damn map. How could I justify such a profligate waste of time? Deadlines loomed, editors demanded, letters reminding magazines of tardy payments awaited composition. Then just as suddenly it occurred to me that this was in fact no waste of time at all, for in traveling from text to map and back to text, imagining that naked line sketched by Lewis and Clark and following it across the northern plains, I was acting out one of the supreme joys of map-reading: every map outlines, in its boundaries and water gaps and mountain passes, a wonderful human story.

The story of this book, though not the book itself, began quite unbeknownst to me in Providence, Rhode Island, in the beginning of 1982. I was engaged in one of the archetypal rituals of the free-lance writing profession—researching an article that was never published, for a magazine that never appeared. My mission was to describe the historical contribution of Italian cartographers, and that brought me to the map collection of the John Carter Brown Library at Brown University. There it was my exquisite good fortune to inspect, at a range so close that my breath would have fogged a mirror, some of the most beautiful maps to survive from the great age of discovery.

I recall the deep cobalt blue of the ocean surrounding a fifteenth-century version of the Ptolemaic universe; indeed, I recall the quality of the color more than the quality of the map itself. But even more I remember an atlas assembled by the Italian mapmaker Battista Agnese, its *mappa mundi* a glorious explosion of vivid colors on vellum, billowing clouds and exhaling cherubs (the twelve winds) in the margins, the continents green with promise, the oceans tamed by lines marking the historic voyages of discovery. Perhaps it was my privileged proximity, perhaps it was coming to such splendor with such ignorance; whatever, I felt certain I beheld one of the most beautiful objects ever crafted by human hands. By that I do mean *hands,* plural and metaphoric; for as I think back on that experience, I realize that every map is the sum not only of the cartographer's skills, but of the many explorers who win the territory in the first place. Thus the map is both aesthetic and informational, as individual as any work of art but also communal and consensual, the product of cultural values (especially the value of exploration itself) and accumulated wisdoms. And perhaps in that moment the germ of an idea unconsciously took root, the idea of the map as an object that straddles the worlds of art and science, one of the few bridges linking the two cultures.

The idea continued to germinate, even though in those days my assignments wandered far from the concerns of cartography: boomerangs and pigs and paper airplanes and mosquitoes and Italian baseball were my beat. Several years ago, however, I became fascinated by the revolution in contemporary biology, especially molecular biology and genetic engineering. As far as I can surmise, looking back now, the other penny dropped when I began to hear about, then write about, chromosome mapping. Suddenly the idea of mapping, at least in my mind, began to spill beyond the customary bounds of geography and the earth sciences. Once the mind is tuned to the idea of maps, the eye finds them everywhere, and over the course of several years, I indeed found them everywhere, in journals and at scientific meetings and on laboratory walls. Scientists, too, had the mapping bug.

Not that it was something new. Maps have always formed a part of the scientific discourse. But something *was* different. Satellites, new instruments of measurement, computer graphics software, the advent of the computer itself, used for the first time in 1950 to create a weather map—they all contributed to a qualitative *and* quantitative change in cartography, a change dating from about the middle of the twentieth century. No period in history rivals the sheer sophistication and extent of the mapping that is occurring right now.

I won't say I reached that conclusion reluctantly, but it would be fair to say that I reached it tentatively. When I began this project in earnest, it was unclear to me if there was enough scientific mapping going on to justify the premise; or, put more bluntly, I didn't know if I could come up with enough maps, of sufficient variety, to fill a book.

Two years later that dilemma has evolved into something entirely different. I am keenly aware, as will be the astute reader, of how much is missing. Many deserving mapping projects are omitted or mentioned only in passing. The aim was not to be comprehensive, but to use maps to illustrate many of science's most interesting frontiers. To that end, I have selected a sample that covers many *kinds* of mapping, and I have tried to select maps that not only are informational, but that speak the second language of cartography, which is aesthetic beauty. And in describing each map, I have attempted to follow the example of map historian Lloyd Brown, who in *The Story of Maps* set out to tell the story of "the men [and women, I'm sure he meant] who made them and the methods they employed, what can be found on them and the devious ways by which the information required for their compilation was obtained." Each map, each *effort* to map, is its own unique tale.

But maps, as I began to realize that winter day in Providence, do not belong to the mapmakers. When we look at a map, when its lines and borders and colors impinge on the retina, visual information riding on light waves enters the mind. Little has been written about the transformation that occurs when we look at a map, a process that begins with physiology and perception but ends up as knowledge and worldview. Yet maps represent one of the fundamental tools by which we make sense of the world around us. So powerfully do maps stamp out their spatial signature in the memory that the mere shape of Africa or North America becomes fixed in our minds, instantly recognizable upright or upside down, detailed or in the fuzziest of outlines, shaded green or Day-Glo red. When we begin to interpret those shapes, associate them with other memories (trips, romances, wars, tragedy) and other forms of knowledge, we move beyond visual perception to something quite different, something requiring imagination. This wonderful moment suggests that invisible, elusive border between science and culture, and that transitory movement from the cartography of maps to that more personal and interior cartography, never far off, of one's place in the larger universe, which in fact is the map each one of us constructs and carries and emends in the course of a lifetime, the map in which the overlays of scientific discovery commingle with the obverse meridians, uneven and sporadic though they be, of personal history—what we think and believe, and how we act on the basis of those beliefs.

I think the late Italian writer Primo Levi had something like that in mind when he wrote a poem called "The First Atlas." "Not one of the lands written into your destiny," Levi wrote, "will speak to you the language of your first Atlas." It is a lovely insight not simply because it acknowledges the role of imagination in geography, but because it therefore acknowledges the role of the imaginer in the quintessential human activity of making a place for oneself, *orienting* oneself, in that larger environment we call the world. I would like to think of *Mapping the Next Millennium* as a kind of first atlas: a new collection of maps, a new way of looking at the world, a new way of imagining one's place in it. As Levi realized, maps most of all speak the language of possibility.

When we look now at the very first atlas ever published, a loose collection of maps assembled by Abraham Ortelius in 1570 and called *Theatrum Orbis Terrarum,* we are impressed by its accuracy and charmed by its flaws. As is the case with other early atlases, too, I suspect many of the maps in this collection will be superseded by better knowledge, more data, new insights, more sophisticated imaging. The 1990s are likely to see the greatest explosion of cartography in the history of the world, thanks to projects as various as the Hubble Space Telescope (even with its damaged eye), the National Aeronautics and Space Administration's ensemble of earth-orbiting satellites known collectively as Mission to Planet Earth, NASA's Magellan and Galileo missions to survey parts of our solar system, the project in biology to map the human genome, the superconducting super collider and its attempt to reveal the innermost sanctum of the atom, to say nothing of international consortiums that are mounting large-scale projects in astronomy, geophysics, climatology, atmospheric science, and other areas of science.

Every one of those maps will become part of our burgeoning new atlases; every one a new form of orientation, every one speaking a new dialect of possibility. And possibility, after all, is what makes any new world truly New.

—February 1991
New York

CONTENTS

MAPPING
THE NEXT
MILLENNIUM

Latitude, Longitude, Infinitude:

SCIENTIFIC MAPPING AND
THE REINVENTION OF GEOGRAPHY

||||||||||

> Those who explore an unknown world are
> travelers without a map; the map is the
> result of the exploration. The position
> of their destination is not known to
> them, and the direct path that leads to
> it is not yet made.
>
> —Hideki Yukawa,
> Japanese physicist

If I had to select one object to put in a time capsule, one single artifact of human hands and minds that might explain who we were and where we lived, what we thought about the physical world around us and how we visually organized those thoughts, an object that said something about our scientific sophistication in taking the measure of the world and something about our aesthetics, too, in rendering that knowledge in an eye-pleasing way and something even about our industrial arts and technological skill in reproducing and disseminating that knowledge as widely as possible, an object that revealed as much about what we didn't know as what we did, I wouldn't take a lot of time to decide: I would pick a map. Maps are "art with a purpose," as map historian Lloyd Brown once wrote; beautiful objects revealing layer upon layer of meaning and information, not the least of which is a self-portrait of the cultures that create them.

But if I were forced to select one single map to stand for all we know (and don't know) in the late twentieth century, the task would assume illuminating difficulty. As I write this, the National Aeronautics and Space Administration's Magellan space probe has finished its first pass at mapping the surface of Venus with radar, and the Gamma Ray Orbiting Observatory has just been unfurled; three other man-made spacecraft, *Voyager 1, Voyager 2,* and *Pioneer 11,* are speeding outward from the sun after their spectacular tours of the planets, and with any luck they will reach and define the outer boundary of our solar system, a vacuum wilderness known as the heliopause, for the first time; a gene related to breast cancer in humans has just been mapped to chromosome 17; neurologists at the Institute of Medicine announced a plan to create an atlas of the human brain; the exact atomic landscape of germanium, its chemistry suggested in the pattern of electron clouds, was recently mapped by scientists at IBM; mathematicians at the University of Maryland are trying to make sense of a mathematical chart that suggests how certain physical fates are inherently unpredictable; astronomers at Princeton and the University of Chicago have set out to map the location of a million galaxies, while the faintest, farthest echo of the Big Bang appeared in the recent map procured by the Cosmic Background Explorer; and a transcendently beautiful map of the ocean floor, made possible by a satellite that does nothing more than bounce microwaves off the surface of the sea, has revealed a hidden landscape shaped by aeons of tectonic tumult.

Never before in human history has so much diverse territory succumbed to the march and measure of discoverers and cartographers—not the sixteenth century of Columbus and Magellan and Vesalius and Copernicus, not the seventeenth century of Galileo and van Leeuwenhoek, or the grand age of mapping and classification led by von Humboldt and Darwin and other great eighteenth- and nineteenth-century explorers. It is tempting to proclaim a new revolution in cartography (it is always tempting to announce a revolution), but renaissance seems a more appropriate term for the changes under way. The real breakthrough—messy and beyond category, a chain reaction rather than a single explosion—is in twentieth-century science's ability to measure, and therefore to map, a breathtaking range of spatial domains. Scientists, our latter-day explorers, are charting worlds that Magellan and Columbus, in their most homesick and delirious moments, could never have imagined. With stunningly precise new instruments of measurement developed over the last half century and with the tremendous graphic powers provided by computers over the last two decades, everyone from archaeologists to zoologists has been able

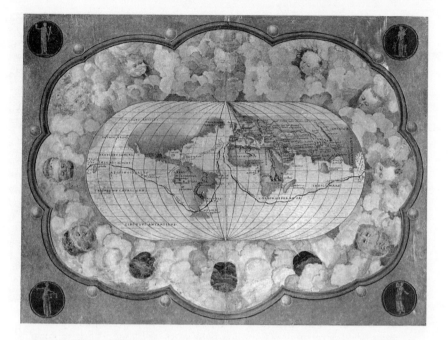

Map of the universe, circa 1544: Battista Agnese's world map, with Spain's route to its South American silver mines and Magellan's circumnavigation marked in dark lines. North America is still a fuzzy, borderless figment of the cartographer's imagination. (John Carter Brown Library, Brown University)

to discover, explore, chart, and visualize physical domains so remote and fantastic that the effort involves nothing less than the reinvention of the idiom of geography.

To get an idea of how far the "map idea" has traveled in the twentieth century, consider the definition of "map" in the famous eleventh edition of the *Encyclopaedia Britannica,* published in 1910 and the ultimate word in turn-of-the-century scholarship. A map, it begins, is "a representation, on a plane and a reduced scale, of part or the whole of the earth's surface." That narrow land-based definition of map, like the geocentric myth of the earth itself, has been conceptually overwhelmed and ultimately retired by scientific advances since the end of World War II. Understandably, the *Britannica*'s editors could never have foreseen the discovery of territories that scientists continue even now to roam and reconnoiter: chromosomes, zygotes, atomic surfaces, star-forming regions in the Milky Way, the large-scale galactic structure of the universe.

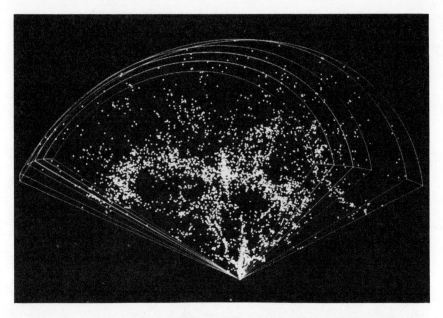

Map of the universe, circa 1990: galaxies mapped in the celestial sky form a "Great Wall" stretching 500 million light-years, the largest "geographical" feature ever to appear in a map. (Smithsonian Astrophysical Observatory)

Here, as we are poised to enter the next millennium, we find ourselves in the midst of what is arguably the greatest explosion in mapping, and perhaps the greatest reconsideration of "space" (in every sense of that word), since an anonymous Babylonian first attempted to organize human knowledge of the physical world by drawing a map of the world on a clay tablet twenty-six centuries ago. This evolving use of high technology has in part forced a redefinition of mapping so fundamentally different, and so perversely broad, that cartographers Arthur Robinson and Barbara Bartz Petchenik, in their thoughtful 1976 book *The Nature of Maps,* were reduced to defining a map as "a graphic representation of the milieu." The definition at first seems vague, almost evasive, denuded of all the usual criteria such as latitude, longitude, scale, legend, projection. But it is a definition both supple and wise, accommodating a new reality: science, with its invasive curiosities and ever-more-powerful modes of measurement, has completely stolen cartography from the purely terrestrial domain.

One might venture another, less official definition. If a scientist calls it a map, it probably is a map. The urge to map animates every quadrant of the modern scientific enterprise, just as the map idea is everywhere apparent in the desire for spatial understanding: Where do genes go on the chromosome? How big is the hole in the ozone layer? Where does the shrapnel fly when an electron collides with a positron? The answer in all cases is "geographic," and therefore the answers can be learned and recorded and stored cartographically, in maps. Those maps might not all provide ultimate answers, but they almost surely suggest where to look for those answers.

A whirlwind tour of the world captured by modern mapping extends from the atomic and microscopic to the cosmic. Planetary geologists have mapped the hills and dales of Venus by radar, Mars by magnetometer, Jupiter with photopolarimeters, the moon in person. Paleoecologists have mapped the location of lakes that dotted the Sahara until disappearing four thousand years ago, and climate modelers are mapping the climate as it will appear one hundred years hence. From 590 miles up in space, satellites can determine the average income of a neighborhood, follow wandering ice bergs, track the Wandering Albatross; from instruments resting on the surface of the earth, physicists can see into the heart of the planet, into the heart of the atom, into the heart of the Big Bang. Astronomy's new telescopes chart the cosmos in all its multiple electromagnetic personalities: optical of course, but also X ray, gamma ray, infrared, radio, and ultraviolet. Biologists have mapped the location of proteins in cells, atoms in proteins, electrons in atoms. Neurobiologists have mapped areas of the brain that light up when we dream. Where Aeneas may once have trod, the smoldering Phlegrean Fields now glow in aerial infrared maps. No earthly or celestial or even artistic territory has been spared this rampant cartography: experts not long ago scanned the *Mona Lisa*'s sublime and mysterious face with a microdensitometer, measuring and mapping the topography of pigments in La Gioconda's smile.

Exactly four hundred years ago, near the end of a century that experienced tumultuous scientific discovery and convulsive intellectual change much like our own, Gerhardus Mercator published a work whose frontispiece featured the Greek titan Atlas and whose title reflected its purpose: "Atlas, or cosmographical meditations upon the creation of the universe, and the universe as created." Ever since, the word "atlas" has been used to characterize a collection of maps. Just as those old atlases portrayed a world at once larger and startling and disquietingly different to citizens of the sixteenth century, a new atlas is aborning in the maps churned out by contemporary scientists; just as the world looks back to celebrate and ponder the quincentennial feats of Columbus, science is making and mapping discoveries of entirely new and equally momentous geographies.

Staggering in volume, stunning in their beauty, almost arrogant in the sheer extent of territory they presume to conquer, these new maps are charting the world all over again. They reinvent our idea of frontier. They push back the boundaries of what we know and where we might explore. They are changing our notions not only of what the future may hold, but where we are likely to find that future, which in some ways is the most important geographical question of all.

THE POSSIBLE AND THE ACTUAL

Mapmaking is the process of winning data points from nature. During the first great age of discovery, those points were won with compass and astrolabe and sextant, to say nothing of the courage and curiosity of adventurers who plunged without maps into the unknown. The vessels of exploration were ships—Columbus discovered the New World in 1492, da Gama discovered the Cape of Good Hope and pressed on into the Indian Ocean for the first time in 1497, Cabral discovered Brazil in 1500, and, culminating three decades of exhilarating exploration, Magellan and his crew between 1519 and 1522 circumnavigated the globe. The data "won" in those great voyages resulted in the sixteenth-century maps that literally redrew the world, maps as beautiful as Battista Agnese's 1544 *mappa mundi* and as mathematically rigorous and utilitarian as Mercator's famous 1569 projection.

If "geography is facts," as the French navigator Louis Antoine de Bougainville proclaimed, then new facts, new spatial measurements, produce new landscapes and new kinds of geography. Instrumentation has been the silent partner of all cartographic revolutions. Longitude and latitude, the x and y of terrestrial coordinates, have given way to entirely new units of measure and spatial definition: angstroms on the atomic scale, base pairs in molecular biology, megaparsecs on a cosmological scale. To the x and y of latitude and longitude has been added the z of a third dimension, whether red shifts in astronomy or angstrom-sensitive voltages in scanning probe microscopes. As a result, these new maps still abide by cartography's traditional demand for a calibrated space, with quantifiable coordinates and symbols and legends and scale; but they avail themselves of such sensitive new instrumentation that the terrestrial reach of latitude and longitude has been expanded to the infinitely large and infinitely small.

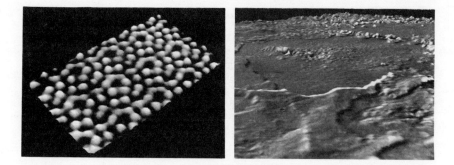

New technologies, new terrains: landscape of silicon *(left)*, its surface pattern of atoms revealed by the scanning tunneling microscope, and computer-enhanced topography of a caldera on the Neptunian moon Triton *(right)*, visited by *Voyager 2.* (IBM Research; NASA/JPL)

It is ironic that physicist Werner Heisenberg, whose Uncertainty Principle replaced scientific certainties with quantum probabilities, perhaps best discerned the crucial process by which theory becomes converted into universally accepted physical fact. "The transition from the 'possible' to the actual," he said, "takes place during the act of measurement." Measurement is the first act of mapmaking, intrinsically bound to exploration, and so rapid have the advances been in the last three or four decades, and on so broad a front, that it is easy to forget that science has discovered, and taken the measure of, an extraordinary range of new domains in a historical eye blink of time. Science's twentieth-century revolutions are hardly news to the well-informed reader, but reconsider them for a moment with the idea of mapping in mind:

Until the 1940s biologists did not know that genetic information was stored in and imparted by molecules of deoxyribonucleic acid (or DNA), and it wasn't until 1953 that the double-helix structure of DNA (and thus its intimate molecular geography) became known; now molecular biologists have crashed the landscape of chromosomes, and they, too, are being mapped. Only in 1973 did neuroscientists isolate the first brain receptor, a molecule that permits mood-altering drugs like opium to enter brain cells and effectively alter mood; now the field has a burgeoning atlas of brain receptor maps (to say nothing of PET scans, CT scans, magnetic resonance images, and other measuring devices that have redrawn twentieth-century anatomy as much as

Vesalius's seminal *De Humani Corporis Fabrica* changed sixteenth-century medicine).

Until the sudden appearance of Sputnik in 1957, no satellite circled the earth; now the skies are thick with orbiting electronic eyes and ears. In 1972 Landsat 1 became the first of many remote-sensing satellites to provide an information-rich spectral-band portrait of the planet, and during a three-month period in 1978, an oceanographic satellite called Seasat provided data about the lay of the ocean floor that would have taken a surface ship more than a century to collect.

Particle accelerators did not come into widespread use until the late 1940s; now, massive detectors developed over the last two decades of high-energy physics have so precisely defined a three-dimensional space known as the Interaction Point that the passage of evanescent subatomic particles, traveling less than a millimeter in a trillionth of a trillionth of a second before decaying into quantum buckshot, can nonetheless be detected; and with another sensitive instrumental probe, the scanning tunneling microscope and related imaging devices of the 1980s, the topography of physical surfaces has been revealed, the outline of electrons appearing as rounded and misty as the moors of Scotland.

Before 1950 there simply were no computers with which to assess complex interactive systems related to the physical world, such as weather or fluid dynamics; now, supercomputers can model the future of the earth's climate, or collate millions of earthquake measurements in order to reveal the hidden topography of the planet's interior. In the newly computerized world of mathematics, imaginary pendulums have been set aswinging inside desktop computers, allowing mathematicians to measure and chart processes like chaos and the topological nature of boundaries.

Astronomers have always mapped the heavens, but now they are doing so with unprecedented precision. Until 1924 galaxies outside our own Milky Way were not believed to exist; now, their existence firmly established, astronomers for the past decade have scrambled to map the three-dimensional structure of the universe. We had never detected the hiss of radio signals from space until the 1930s, or systematically scanned the heavens for those signals until the 1950s; now, massive radio telescopes have mapped giant molecular clouds, hot jets spewing out of galaxies, pulsars, and quasars with X rays, ultraviolet rays, and infrared radiation.

In the spirit of Mercator, who gathered maps of "the universe as created," scientific mapping in the twentieth century represents newer, more intimate glimpses of that same universe. And yet all of these new spatial domains have revealed themselves to human scrutiny since 1950, and most of them have become reliably measurable, and thus truly mappable, in only the last quarter century.

One voyage of discovery above all others seems to typify the transition from traditional modes of exploration and measurement to the new. It is the "Grand Tour" mission of *Voyager 2* through the solar system. Like Columbus's caravels and Magellan's galleons, *Voyager 2* was a vessel of discovery; in visiting Jupiter, Saturn, Uranus, and Neptune, it provided glimpses of new worlds for the first time. Yet *Voyager 2* was a *robot,* a surrogate vessel, its small and fussy computer digitally stoked again and again by human engineers from nearly 3 billion miles away; the reports it sent back—occultations, bow-shock measurements, most of all computer-enhanced pictures—made vicarious sightseers out of an entire civilization, and it is ironic that twentieth-century explorers resort to a timeless, centuries-old Columbian vocabulary to express their wonder. The late Tim Mutch of NASA, speaking of *Voyager 2* as it sailed past Jupiter, remarked: "It was like being in the crow's nest of a ship during landfall and passage through an archipelago of strange islands."

Modern instruments of measurement have become the "ships" of twentieth-century science. So, too, by analogy are scientists our most adventuresome contemporary explorers, traversing strange and sometimes dangerous frontiers. The measures they lay against the physical world are calibrated in femtoseconds, picograms, nanometers, gigaflops, megaparsecs—a quadrillionth of a second, a trillionth of a gram, a billionth of a meter, a billion calculations per second, three million light-years. Modern telescopes scoop light from galaxies 15 billion light-years away; modern physicists annotate events of nature down to a distance of 10^{-16} centimeters, a thousand times smaller than a proton. Biologists can read heredity's text one letter at a time, even though there are 3 billion biochemical letters stuffed into each and every one of the 100 trillion or so cells that we drag out of bed each morning to contemplate the eternal mysteries.

If, as biologist Francis Crick has remarked, the front line of research is "almost always in a fog," it is instruments that function as our eyes, allowing us to gather map-points in the fog, to construct a picture of the world in the form of a map and ultimately to penetrate those obscuring mists.

ONE INSTRUMENT MORE EQUAL THAN OTHERS

One instrument, however, is more equal than all the others, because it is the electronic ganglion that sifts and assesses and shuffles all those hard-won data points, much as the brain assesses the information collected by sensory organs. Occasionally this instrument is used to conduct experiments. More often, it handles and merges and makes sense of the data, and then creates maps out of numbers. That instrument is the computer.

When John von Neumann and colleagues at the Institute for Advanced Study published weather maps generated by the original ENIAC numerical calculator in 1950 in *Tellus,* they produced what is believed to be the first computer-assisted map to appear in a scientific journal. It was a modest, almost homely, hand-drawn black-and-white map, but it was the forerunner of all the maps and charts to come: multidimensional, nonterrestrial, false color or phase space, in every projection and every hue. Although the first primitive computers like ENIAC came into use in the late 1940s, it has been only in the last ten to fifteen years that powerful desktop machines have become available for routine visualization of data—visualization in the sense that data is converted into a cartographic image of a spatial domain with distinct regions, contours, and patterns that allow scientists to derive insight and meaning from the "visual display of quantitative information" (to purloin the title of one of Edward Tufte's illuminating treatises on visualization of data).

The widespread availability of computers with specialized graphics software puts the equivalent of a cartographer inside every computer, and therefore inside every laboratory group. Where cartographers of the sixteenth century sat in their Lisbon studios, patiently debriefing mariners returning from their voyages, weighing the credibility of each report and each measurement, piecing it all together into a single, coherent, consistent picture of the geographic world, computers collate information from a number of sources before plotting out the result in a map. They routinely manage and merge multiple data sets totaling billions of bits of information. They can be programmed to assess the relative credibility of various measurements. Perhaps most important, they can process more information and do it more rapidly than any single human cartographer. As a result, not only are more scientific "explorers" producing more maps, but they are doing so at an unprecedented pace. In the 1870s, the British *Challenger* mission took about 350 ocean soundings during its three-year expedition; in 1978, Seasat made 25 million radar altimeter readings of the ocean in three months; in 1990, using a technology tested on Seasat, *Magellan* generated 18.2 billion bits of radar data with each orbit around Venus; and mappers have been forewarned that when the Earth Observing System satellite of the late 1990s begins operation, the sensors will generate information equivalent to the entire contents of the Library of Congress each month. It would be impossible to make cartographic sense out of so much data without a computer.

By relying on computers to plot data points with "geographic" integrity, scientists have learned to convert almost any kind of data into a landscape, whether it is the position of galaxies in the northern celestial hemisphere or the position of hydrogen atoms in a bacterial enzyme. If variations in a physical property are being mapped, such as the density of brain receptors in various regions of the brain, the computer will assign colors according to intensity (red for the highest density, blue for the lowest); the data is made instantaneously thematic. These brilliant-hued maps, called "false-color" because the computer arbitrarily assigns color where it does not exist in nature, predate the computer, of course, but the ease with which they can now be created has produced a dazzling atlas of images from the worlds of astronomy, biology, and chemistry, readily apparent in almost any recent issue of *Science* or *Nature*. False-color maps, in addition to their beauty, take advantage of an evolutionary gift of vision: color itself conveys information, and humans are among the few mammals capable of perceiving color. Color allows another layer of information to be squeezed into the same limited amount of space. Looking at these new maps, many of them exquisite in their electronic pattern and color, one is reminded of a recent comment by British mathematician Roger Penrose. "Aesthetic qualities are important in science," he said, "and necessary, I think, for great science."

The *speed* of computers in manipulating data allows modern mappers to introduce an even more revealing variable: time. By measuring quantitative changes in a well-defined landscape over time, such as the appearance and disappearance of gene-controlling proteins in an embryo as it develops or the geographic migration of spruce forests in paleoclimatic maps, scientists have begun to create what might be called time-lapse cartography. Superimposed values *move* across fixed, well-defined geographies, and there is information in the movement. In the past several years, movies have become an increasingly frequent feature of meetings, symposia, even congressional presentations. (Ironically, movie maps suffer a problem that only highlights the utility of old-fashioned maps: they can't be easily stored, shared, archived, or consulted.)

The culmination of computer manipulation is the map as printed or, increasingly, televised object. Once it is an object, we can hold it and look at it. Light waves reflected by the black of its borders, the blue of its oceans, the greens and browns of its mottled continents, and the imaginary electronic hues of landscapes too distant or too tiny to see, enter the eye and rustle the cells of the retina, itself a mapmaking instrument of exquisite precision. Through the process of perception, the information from the two-dimensional page enters the wily dimensions of the human mind; maps, in the words of historian J. B. Harley, are "mediators between an inner mental world and an outer physical world." After perception creates an internal map of the world, the mind takes hold of it and transforms it into a tool of thought, and we begin to think about the world in a different way.

MAPS AND THE EDUCATED EYE

The eye and the brain seem to be particularly felicitous partners in the act of map-reading. It is almost as if we are physiologically disposed to extract information from maps more rapidly, more intuitively, more *globally* than from, for example, a text or a visual scene. That process of visual mining begins with perception—a process that touches on both the physiological and the conceptual processing of map knowledge. Bearing that in mind, we might take a walk with astronomer Patrick Thaddeus, removing him from his preferred cartographical milieu, which is mapping carbon monoxide molecules in the Milky Way with a radio telescope at Harvard University, and placing him in a rather less exotic environment—namely the woods surrounding his country home in upstate New York.

"The forest goes on for miles and miles," Thaddeus explains. "And I love just walking through the woods by myself. You're not alone, in the sense that the forest is crisscrossed with deer trails. These deer trails are quite imperceptible. But after a while you know how to recognize them, and you can see them. They're just very faint patterns that generally tend to go in a straight line. Now I followed one of these trails for a mile through the woods. And I suddenly stopped and asked myself, 'How do I know I'm on this trail?' But I *am* on it, and I suddenly get shaken off. The signal-to-noise ratio [that is, the relevant information, or 'signal,' compared to irrelevant information, or noise] must be one in a thousand, or much less than that. That is, I know I'm on the trail because of a little leaf here, a very faint linear line. But there are much *stronger* sources of noise. Trees across the path, great rocks, and things like that—no computer in the world could possibly filter out that path from all of the conflicting signals around."

Thaddeus can do this, he believes, because of evolution. "Finding your way home, getting back to your babies, your families, is something which we and our ancestors, both human and animal, have had to do for not just millions but *tens* of millions of years," he continues. "Animals are *astonishingly* adept at that, following both visual traces and smell. Smell in humans is a very atrophied sense, but we're particularly good at visual recognition. So it is technically true that I can follow these trails with a high degree of confidence, where I don't think any computer in the world has ever been constructed, or could be programmed, to filter out all the noise and not lock onto the tree trunk or things like that. The point is, human beings think in terms of images, and they know what they are looking for. The educated eye knows what it's looking for, can see things that are, in the technical sense of signal to noise, way, way below one. A very weak, astonishingly weak signal. That is, the human brain is an *incredible* filter for extracting information from confusion."

Confusion is another name for the world unfiltered, and maps are external, man-made filters that make sense of the confusion, just as the eye and brain are internal, physiological filters that cut through the bewildering mix of signal and noise in a visual scene. By breaking down the graphic or pictorial vocabulary to a bare minimum, maps achieve a visual minimalism that, physiologically speaking, is easy on the eyes. They turn numbers into visual images, create pattern out of measurements, and thus engage the highly evolved human capacity for pattern recognition. Some of the most intense research in the neurosciences today is devoted to elucidating what are described as maps of perception: how perception filters and maps the relentless torrent of information provided by the sense organs, our biotic instruments of measurement. Maps *enable* humans to use inherent biological skills of perception, their "educated" eyes to separate the message from the static, to see the story line running through random pattern.

More than half the human cortex is involved in vision, and much of vision and perception is built upon the ability to distinguish borders and outlines (what more, in both the geographical and visual sense, is a map than borders and outlines?). "Mathematical equations and literary phrases are useful," Arthur Robinson has written, "but they are no substitute for the spatial eloquence of the map." Indeed, maps speak subtle and surprising truths, and many scientists have remarked upon their ability to spot patterns and derive new insights from the simplified graphic image of the map, patterns that elude them in the mass of unfiltered data.

Borders and outlines have long been known to be essential to perception. Richard L. Gregory writes in his book *Eye and Brain*: "Large areas of constant intensity provide no information. They seem to be 'inferred' from the signalled borders: the central visual system makes up the missing signals." The mind keys on boundaries and, literally, fills in the blank spots. Experiments by Anne Treisman of the University of California-Berkeley and others describe how, as we visually process a scene, the mind instantaneously—and, even more fascinating, *unconsciously*—creates what she calls "feature maps," an instant series of "primal sketches," each built around a particular visual element: color, size, contrast, tilt, curvature, and movement. It is remarkable how closely these elements reflect the symbolic vocabulary of maps, as if the mind *needs* a rough map of boundaries and borders to reach a visual conclusion about what it is looking at.

Neurobiologists continue to push the cartographic idea deep into the brain. John Allman of Caltech has been instrumental in showing that primate brains have evolved about twenty separate regions of cells in the neocortex, the "new" outer layer of the brain, each of which maps certain aspects of the visual field. Indeed, Allman argues that the visual cortex is organized topographically, as a series of adjacent but highly specialized mapmaking domains that identify and then collate features of the outer physical world. Moreover, he believes that at least one form of learning, called perceptual memory, is stored within maps in the neocortex—a hypothesis that places more emphasis on memory storage in the peripheral districts of the brain than on its processing by central switchboards such as the hippocampus. Intriguing support for this notion comes from the well-known amnesia patient H.M., who, lacking a hippocampus, cannot encode everyday experiences as memories, but nonetheless seems able to recall visual solutions to maplike puzzles.

"We live in a noisy environment, with too much information," Allman says, "and the main task is to pull information out of that. The brain does that by making maps that accentuate the useful information. And once you do that, it makes sense to store it." "Storage" is another word for memory, and humans appear to have evolved an inordinately large cerebral warehouse for precisely these maplike mem-

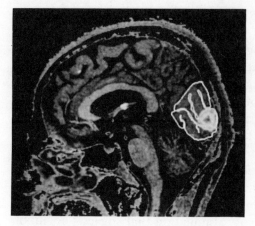

Mapping perception: by superimposing a PET scan of his brain upon an MRI map of the same territory, Caltech scientist John Allman pinpoints the area of the visual cortex (small circle at right) that is metabolically active during perception. (John Allman/George J. Carman, *Mappings of the Cerebral Cortex,* Ann Arbor, Mich., University Microfilms, 1990)

ories: the neocortex. "We don't have a huge amount more of hippocampus than other animals," Allman points out, "but we have a huge amount more in the neocortex. It's the maplike structures in the neocortex of the brain that seem to have undergone this amazing expansion." So it may be that the human brain not only perceives but stores the essentials of a visual scene using the same geometrical, quasi-symbolic, minimalist vocabulary found in maps.

Embedding maps as a kind of memory in the visual brain gives animals an evolutionary advantage. Geography is essential to survival—to finding food, to migration, to reproduction and nurturing—and geographic orientation underlies the movements of birds that migrate to winter nesting spots they have never before seen, of butterflies that find their way to winter grounds three generations after leaving (which suggests a genetic component to geographic orientation), of turtles and bats and bees. Natural selection seems to have nudged the primate brain toward the process of making and retaining maps (humans are unique, though, in externalizing the process and in making maps as objects). Perceptual maps not only show us how we derive information from the maps we make, but they begin to suggest the next big step in the processing of map knowledge. What happens to the map once it enters the warp and weave of human consciousness? That process, too, is being charted, and the emerging cartography suggests why maps, riding into the brain on mere light waves, can have such profound effects on social, intellectual, cultural, and personal worldviews.

FROM PERCEPTION TO WORLDVIEW

How does a map effect thought? What happens to a map when the pattern of its borders and outlines has been etched in the perceptual chambers of the brain and begins to influence thought? The answer is by no means clear, but neurobiologists are again making headway.

John Allman, for example, has combined two powerful new technologies—positron emission tomography (PET) scans and magnetic resonance imaging (MRI)—to pinpoint areas of the brain that are active during visual stimulation. Those maps, in turn, become the starting point for a branch of neurobiology that is attempting to map how neural areas of perception interact with other regions of the brain, an outward spreading of sensory stimulation that suggests cognition and thought. Researchers at EEG Systems Laboratory, a private research lab in San Francisco, have combined MRI with traditional electrical measurements of brain wave activity (EEGs) to create maps of what they call "shadows of thought." Initial work, according to director Alan Gevins, indicates that "our brains seem to devote a very large portion of their activity to continuously forming, maintaining, and revising detailed simulations, or models, of what we imagine our self- and world-states to be." Another way of putting it might be that the neocortex retains flexible maps of expected reality, working copies of the physical world, against which the maps of perception are compared and incorporated again and again, almost on a minute-by-minute basis. Notions of reality may be primarily a process of interior cartographic revision.

If thought begins with the comparison of sensory information to past experience, then encoding both entities, perception and memory, as maps would make the process faster and easier, and thus evolutionarily more useful to organisms needing to distinguish prey from predator in a split second. The mind seems to traffic in a multitude of similar maplike representations. As research by Walter J. Freeman's team at UC-Berkeley has shown, olfactory perception registers in the brain as a set of electrical waves that the cortex translates into a contour map; the map in turn sets off other clumps of cells in complex patterns of interaction that suggest those same "shadows of thought." If the shadows of thoughts are indeed map-related, we might speculate that looking at a map initiates squalls of thought-shadows bouncing around the cognitive centers of the brain. "We have found," Freeman wrote recently, "that perception depends on the simultaneous coopera-

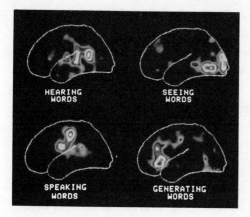

HEARING
WORDS

SEEING
WORDS

SPEAKING
WORDS

GENERATING
WORDS

"Shadows of thought":
PET scans map increases of
blood flow to different regions of
the brain as it performs cognitive
tasks, such as hearing, seeing,
speaking, or generating words.
(M. Raichle, *Mapping the Brain
and Its Functions,* Washington,
National Academy Press, 1991)

tive activity of millions of neurons spread throughout the expanses of
the cortex."

Let us speculate further. Perhaps the map embedded in the brain
becomes a set of grid points upon which cognitive associations can
arise. The associative power of a simple geometrical shape, once it has
lodged in the memory, is a good example. Once we have learned the
outline of the United States, we recognize it instantly in all sorts of
contexts, whether the shape has been created by a Rand McNally
cartographer or Landsat or Jasper Johns (even though no one except
a few astronauts has actually seen that shape in the "real" world).
Once the original maplike memory has been embedded, we recognize
it in other scales and contexts. We associate. And perhaps it is in that
global play of map associations within the mind that, like a photocopying machine, human thought can blow up the image or reduce it. As
Hannah Arendt and others suggest, once the brain has embraced an
image (or map), the conceptualized image becomes plastic, intellectually malleable. Arendt writes in *The Human Condition,* inferring a
process that begins with perception but quickly transcends it, "there is
the infinitely greater and more effective shrinkage which comes about
through the surveying capacity of the human mind, whose use of
numbers, symbols, and models can condense and scale earthly physical
distance down to the size of the human body's natural sense and
understanding."

The brain shrinks territory like a map, but astronomer Alan
Dressler would argue that maps also stretch the brain. In creating or

looking at a map, scale is not brought down to human dimension, but rather human thought inflates or shrinks in order to inhabit the size of the newly accessible geographic domain—cosmologists think big and molecular biologists think small, because those are the dimensions of the domains they think about all the time. The process demands not only intellect, but creativity and imagination. Dressler describes it this way:

> My approach is to try to get people to *drop* human scale completely. And when they think of something, they go into *that* scale. If you're going to think galaxies, you've got to be galaxy-like. You've got to be God-like. You better be able to move, you better be able to think, "I can travel from this galaxy to the next and hold one in my hands." And that you can do. But if you don't expand yourself to that scale, I think it's hopeless.

Dressler seems to suggest that humans project themselves into the worlds around them by some mysterious process of geographic (or spatial) imagination; the map is the launching pad for that act of imagination. The interior merges with the exterior, the personal with the physical, the conscious with the quantitative. Map-readers enter the world of the map, and in that process become changed by it. The map in the mind provides the grid points of cognition; and our new maps of distant and abstract landscapes promote new geometries of thought—new associations and therefore new ways of thinking about the world "out there."

Even though maps have historically been commissioned by monarchs and popes, governments and industries, they are perceived by cultures at large, and in that simple act of popular and collective perception there begins the construction of a conceptual link between scientific knowledge and social worldview. If you happened to be an ordinary burgher of Renaissance Europe, born in 1480 perhaps and, if fortunate, schooled in the geography passed down from Ptolemy with nary an emendation for ten centuries, you would see in Battista Agnese's beautiful 1544 map an image of the world that contradicts and overthrows everything you have ever been taught, and everything you thought you knew, about the geographic world. Just as maps have the power to tyrannize beliefs, as did Ptolemy's atlas for ten centuries, so do maps have the power to overthrow beliefs. Maps that emerge from ambitious periods of exploration and discovery have the power to convulse not just scientific theory, but the belief systems of cultures at large.

Finally, one could view the history of cartography, from the crudest clay tablet to yesterday's survey of galaxies, as the story of civilization shedding a succession of untenable centrisms. The terracentric world of Aristotle and the ancients, which erroneously presumed that the knowable world stopped at the shoreline of the encircling sea, gave way to Ptolemy's geocentric view, which erroneously placed the earth at the center of the solar system; the heliocentric view of the solar system, first proposed by Copernicus in 1543, overturned the earth-centered notions of the solar system, but erroneously made the sun the center of the universe; the galactocentric view of the universe, which placed the Milky Way ("our" galaxy) at the center of the astrophysical world, turned out to be an erroneous centrism that gave way only in the 1920s, when Edwin Hubble proved that the Milky Way is not the only galaxy in the universe. Each one of these centrisms died hard, and each demise was aided and celebrated by maps. The current mapping work in astronomy, and the problems it poses for cosmology, seems to be moving us to the verge of another great historical juncture, forcing us to molt yet other centrisms. One possibility is that ours is not the only universe. A distant and improbable notion, to be sure, but in our brief historical passage on the planet the finest minds of earlier eras could not conceive of a world with more than one continent, one ocean, one planet, one galaxy.

That is why we continue to map. As Edwin Hubble himself remarked in his last scientific paper, "Our immediate neighborhood we know rather intimately. But with increasing distance our knowledge fades . . . until at the last dim horizon we search among ghostly errors of observations for landmarks that are scarcely more substantial. The search will continue. The urge is older than history. It is not satisfied and it will not be suppressed."

Abiding that imperative, scientists are in the midst of another great period of discovery. It is too soon to tell just how broad and universal the intellectual convulsions will be. Like the best of old maps, however, these new maps are surprising, beautiful, revelatory, disquieting. They orient us not only spatially, but conceptually, culturally, historically, philosophically. They provide a record of where we have been and what we have believed, an inspiration to visit places we have not yet explored. A map, above all, is a worldview committed to paper, a worldview endlessly challenged and ultimately forced into retirement by the next extraordinary map, of which there are likely to be many in the coming decades.

THE REINVENTION OF TERRA INCOGNITA

There persists the notion in some quarters that modern science is too invasive of the eternal mysteries, that to explicate the unknown is to somehow violate or merely banalize. Yet one of the reassuring lessons of twentieth-century mapping is that science merely positions itself on the boundary between the known and the unknown. That boundary may shift, retreat, and change location, but it never vanishes. The unknown remains a province of every map.

In the twenty-first century, geography may better serve as metaphor than scientific discipline in suggesting the multitude of boundaries that science continually bumps up against, boundaries that abut our collective ignorance. No concept of geography is blanker on the map, yet richer with both invitation and peril, than terra incognita. It is why humans continue to map, and why as a civilization we *need* to map. Maps serve as a visual shorthand for how we conceptualize and integrate the unknown.

More mapping of more domains by more nations will probably occur in the next decade than has occurred at any time since Alexander von Humboldt "rediscovered" the earth in the eighteenth century, and more terra incognita will be charted than ever before in history. Biologists should have a complete map of human genes within twenty years, and neurologists hope to have their brain atlas by then, too. New telescopes are already charting the heavens with unprecedented precision: to complement NASA's Magellan and Galileo planetary probes and the Hubble Space Telescope (despite its limitations), international scientists recently completed an all-sky X ray survey with the Roentgen Orbiting Satellite, or Rosat, the Soviets and French are collaborating on the Granat gamma-ray satellite, and the Europeans in the European Southern Observatory have on the drawing board a ground-based Very Large Telescope (VLT), scheduled for completion in 1998, which, if it performs up to design specifications, will far exceed the space-based Hubble telescope in resolution. Construction of the superconducting super collider, if it wins political approval, will bring the subatomic landscape to a new level of resolution by the year 2000. NASA and other agencies are preparing two dozen new sensors for the

Mission to Planet Earth project, scheduled to begin in the 1990s. Where will this ambitious agenda of mapping take us, and what can we hope to learn from it? What will these new maps tell us?

As has historically been the case, new maps have contradicted, and will continue to contradict, expectation; in the best of situations, they unambiguously resolve controversy. Maps hold up a quantitative picture of data that can be compared with the predictions of theory. In the case of brain receptor maps, the fact that the location of receptor molecules does not always match the location of the brain cells that would be expected to signal them illustrates a contradiction in synaptic theory that only now is beginning to be addressed. The galactic mapping done by Alan Dressler and his "Seven Samurai" colleagues highlighted departures from the predicted smooth expansion of the universe, which led to the discovery of the Great Attractor and, with it, of serious flaws in several long-cherished tenets of modern cosmological thought. In the continuous dialogue between theory and experimentation, maps arising from experimental data often provide incontrovertible visual evidence that theory must be revised or reassessed. In astronomy alone surveys published in the last five years have so undermined theory that some are beginning to reexamine the very notion of the Big Bang.

Maps, moreover, can be seen as diagrams showing the evolution of our collective thought about a particular spatial domain, and as archival images documenting states of knowledge, they help us appreciate those who attempted to explore the same terrain in earlier epochs with less adequate instruments of measurement. All maps have precedents. We can always find examples of explorers or scientists who intuited the importance of the same terrain but—and this is one of the little-appreciated dramas of intellectual endeavor, and certainly a central drama of any scientist's life— did not have access to the technology that would reward the intuition. No matter how enamored we are with the elegance and precision of contemporary technology, we can always find earlier examples that remind us that science resides as much in the *art* of measurement as in the technology of measurement. In 1671, the French Jesuits who charted Lake Superior relied for their "unit of measure" upon the canoe stroke, yet produced a map that was not surpassed in accuracy for a hundred years.

The galactic surveys undertaken in the 1980s supplant the sky surveys conducted at Mount Palomar in the 1960s. The idea of a chromosome map became implicit from the discovery in 1911 that only men were color-blind, and that thus the genetic cause of color blind-

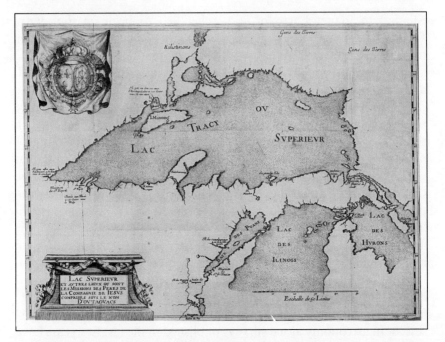

Measurement is an art as well as a science: French Jesuits, using only canoe strokes to gauge distance, produced this map of Lake Superior in 1671; it remained the most accurate map for at least a century. (Edward E. Ayer Collection, Newberry Library)

---

ness must be somehow attached to the male's single X chromosome, just as the promise of chromosomes as mappable domains became explicit in 1935, when Calvin Bridges of Caltech published maps of the gigantic salivary chromosomes of fruit flies and showed they had distinct and recognizable topography. The detailed genetic maps of developmental biology derive from the fate maps that Theodor Boveri and other embryologists struggled to chart in the nineteenth century. The maps created by Landsat and the French SPOT remote-sensing satellite derive from, and refine, systematic efforts to triangulate and map the earth's topography dating back at least to Cassini in the seventeenth century and continuing through the aerial photogrammetry of the twentieth century; William Haxby's stunning map of the ocean floor has as predecessors not only the famous Heezen and Tharp maps of the 1950s, but Matthew Maury's early and unsystematic nineteenth-century soundings. The mathematical maps of James Yorke reexamine the same topological ground originally explored by a Japanese mathematician early in the twentieth century. Contemporary scientists would argue that recent maps are more accurate, more comprehensive, more detailed, and more credible, but only time will attest to their ultimate accuracy and worthiness. Without a doubt, they are more rapidly produced because of the efficiency with which data is acquired, and that alone speeds up the process of exploration, discovery, and mapmaking. Interpretation, understanding, and, of course, revision soon follow.

Maps surprise. If there is a persistent theme that emerges from the chronicles of contemporary scientific cartography, it is that the creation of a map almost inevitably leads to unexpected revelations. Any large-scale effort to map or survey a physical milieu, be it the ocean floor or a slice of the cosmological pie, results in a picture of the unexpected. Maps are data-driven. They are not entirely free of bias (no map is), but experimentalists tend to undertake their explorations with a minimum of theoretical baggage; surveyors let the chips—the data points, if you will—fall where they may, and the pictures that emerge often confound theory and expectation. Perhaps the most vivid example of this involves the discovery by astronomers of a sudsy, bubblelike texture of galaxies in the northern celestial hemisphere, defying all conventional theoretical prediction. So confident were Margaret Geller, John Huchra, and Valérie de Lapparent that their map of galaxies would reflect the predicted random distribution in the sky that they did not bother looking at the data until nearly eleven hundred galaxies had been measured, catalogued, and plotted. Only then, in a kind of push-button epiphany unique to our computer age, did they produce a picture of their data in the form of a map, and saw, with surprise bordering on stupefaction, that contrary to theory galaxies bunched up in bubbles and other large-scale structures.

Such unexpected results carry an implicit, cautionary, and counterbalancing message to the conservative impulses of legislative auditors who insist on knowing the results ahead of time before embarking on large, expensive, and somewhat speculative mapping projects, such as the proposed initiative to map the human genome. While it is difficult to petition a Senate committee and seek the trifling sum of $3 billion with the argument that the results are likely to provide some unanticipated surprise, the recent history of large-scale mapping in fields as disparate as biology and astronomy argues persuasively that, with able scientists and proven technology and at least modest and attainable goals at the outset, the results are almost guaranteed to produce revelations of the most unpredictable and transforming sort. Less recent history argues the same: Galileo's discovery of the moons of Jupiter in 1610 appeared to be of no practical value, yet by the end of that same century they proved crucial to determining longitude and thus to the creation of the first truly accurate modern maps of the earth. Societies, like individuals, need the courage to test their belief systems by undertaking such commitments; the exploration of new frontiers, and the mapping that symbolizes and distills such exploration, typifies the kind of society willing to risk its familiar and comforting intellectual certainties in order to discover new, contradictory, potentially alarming, but ultimately liberating truths.

Indeed, scientists—especially the theorists—need maps to recalibrate their professional humility. Carolyn Porco, an astronomer at the University of Arizona and expert on planetary ring systems, responded to the surprises of Neptune in the following way: "The solar system, each *planet,* is so damned different! I love this. I like the idea that Voyager is going out with a bang. It's going to blow our minds, again. How could we be so ignorant or cocky to guess what planets are going to look like outside the solar system? About the best you can say is that they're probably going to be round."

Maps make discovery real. A classic example is perhaps the greatest geographical discovery *not* to benefit by the subsequent creation of a map: the Norse discovery of North America around 1000 A.D. "An unmapped discovery is of little value to succeeding generations," writes John Noble Wilford, and because there is no credible map to accompany the Vinland discovery, it is almost as if it never took place. No one parades down Fifth Avenue for Leif Ericson. Every map of the New World, on the other hand, visually validated Columbus's discovery in a way that could not be accomplished by ten thousand books. The map not only makes the territory tangible; it invites a kind of symbolic possession. Ferdinand and Isabella never visited the New World, but they were able to possess it vicariously through the map (to the everlasting woe of indigenous populations, but that touches upon a different theme, one that is explored in the concluding essay). In a similar way, lay citizens intuitively discern the message conveyed by a map, even though we may not (and probably do not) understand the technology that allowed the knowledge to be acquired in the first place.

Maps make the world, even its complexities and uncertainties, approachable and understandable. You don't need to be a cosmologist to understand the intrinsic question posed by a "Great Wall" of galaxies arranged in space: how did it get there? Nor do you need to be a geophysicist to discern and appreciate patterns that vividly paint the movement of hot material in a vast convection cell beneath the Pacific Ocean floor, a cell that powers the jostling movement of plates on the surface of the earth. You do not need to be a planetary geologist or astronomer to gasp in wonder and awe as images of new worlds, revealed for the first time by our robotic eyes, are sent back by our post-Columbian vessels of exploration and reconnaissance, from the early Surveyors and Mariners and Pioneers and Apollos to the recent Grand Tour of the solar system by *Voyager 2.* In reducing the massive scale of the cosmos to a page in a book, in blowing up the tiny geography of a chromosome or atom to the size of a page in a journal, maps bring every precinct of the physical world within the grasp of our dumb, curious hands and the comprehension of our eager and insatiable human eyes.

Finally, and perhaps most important, maps goad us on, prick us out of our occasional world-weariness, draw us out of historical doldrums, and lure us on to that next inevitable frontier. In its gaps as well as its details, a map focuses our thinking, incites our curiosities, tempts us to peek over that line dividing the known and the unknown. Who can look at "Terra Incognita" on a map and fail to at least entertain the thought, "I wonder what is there"? Who can think about the example of Columbus, scrutinizing Pierre d'Ailly's *Imago Mundi,* or perusing the sea chart sent to him by Paolo dal Pozzo Toscanelli around 1470, and not be moved by the way maps intersect with human curiosity, belief, destiny? The very best scientists share with Joseph Conrad's Marlowe in *Heart of Darkness* that fascination with terra incognita:

> Now when I was a little chap I had a passion for maps. I would look for hours at South America, or Africa, or Australia, and lose myself in all the glories of exploration. At that time there were many blank spaces on the earth, and when I saw one that looked particularly inviting on a map (but they all look that) I would put my finger on it and say, "When I grow up I will go there."

South America, Africa, and Australia hold precious few blank spaces at this late juncture of the twentieth century, but it is the triumph of the modern scientific imagination to push Conrad's metaphor into new realms, to see inviting blank spaces in exotic and inferred and previously unattainable terrains. In so doing, modern scientists are creating maps that reinvent the world we inhabit, maps that are—and this is a point we ignore only at our great peril—a composite picture of the world all of us will inhabit in the millennium to come.

PLANETARY
LANDSCAPES,
OURS AND OTHERS

1. "We Do Precision Guesswork"

THE NAVIGATIONAL CHART OF VOYAGER 2
AND THE GRAND TOUR OF
THE SOLAR SYSTEM

‖‖‖‖‖‖‖‖

> Then felt I like some watcher of the skies
> When a new planet swims into his ken;
> Or like stout Cortez when with eagle eyes
> He star'd at the Pacific—and all his men
> Look'd at each other with a wild surmise—
> Silent, upon a peak in Darien.
>
> —John Keats,
> "On First Looking into Chapman's Homer"

The heroic deeds of Peralonso Niño and Juan Sebastián del Cano are buried in forgotten graves and academic footnotes; we know of their work through the fame of their respective employers, Christopher Columbus and Ferdinand Magellan. Niño and del Cano served as pilots on several of the historic voyages of discovery in the fifteenth and sixteenth centuries, and they have latter-day counterparts in anonymity—Don Gray, Anthony (Tony) Taylor, Bob Cesarone, Christopher Potts, Mark Ryne, and of course Gary Flandro—who have kept the navigator's ancient art alive, though the seas they sail are interplanetary and their vessel is a rickety robotic spacecraft known as *Voyager 2*.

Shortly before 9 P.M. on the evening of August 19, 1989, as a waning three-quarter moon rose over the San Gabriel foothills in Pasadena, California, a dozen or so of these postmodern helmsmen gathered down in their second-floor enclave in Building 264 of

NASA's Jet Propulsion Laboratory. They gathered to make one final review of their navigational plots. Outside, scientists working late that Saturday night hurried across the campuslike grounds, ignoring a large billboard that reported the progress of *Voyager 2*; that geriatric spacecraft, about as aerodynamic as a toaster with its booms and cameras and flying elbows, had already sailed flawlessly by Jupiter, Saturn, and Uranus, and now, twelve years into its journey and five days hence, it would brush the treetops of Neptune and hurtle past Triton—"a most intriguing moon," in the opinion of the project's chief scientist and certainly among the most interesting objects in the solar system.

If it got there. If the navigators laid the spacecraft on target, adjusting the rudder by radio wave from 2.7 billion miles away. Which is just what they planned to discuss this Saturday night.

A robotic hedgehog with instruments for bristles, *Voyager 2* and its brethren—*Voyager 1, Pioneer 10,* and *Pioneer 11*—have served as the eyes and ears of an entire civilization. We have all marveled at the images sent back over the years by those spacecraft from distant, solitary landmarks in the solar system. The imaging scientists get the lion's share of attention, for they produce the pictures—pictures which, among other virtues, qualify as the first photomaps of previously unseen worlds. But you can't get to unseen worlds without turning the dream into geographical possibility, and that requires a map, some sort of navigational chart. And you can't get there without navigators, who merely drop the spacecraft on target, in the right position, at the right time, so that when *Voyager 2* snaps its shutter, you do not get the robotic equivalent of a thumb over the lens. The astronomer Carl Sagan has said, "I think it's a great pity that the engineers responsible for this spacecraft are not better known . . . they should be on postage stamps." This is a modest commemorative to the men and women who anonymously guided *Voyager 2* on the greatest exploratory voyage humankind has ever undertaken.

In earlier centuries, on other vessels, navigation seemed hopelessly crude. In Columbus's day, the makers of compass cards did not even bother to mark them with the traditional *E, S, W,* and *N*; most seamen were illiterate and couldn't distinguish the difference. According to biographer Samuel Eliot Morison, Columbus never even figured out how to use an astrolabe on his first crossing. Magellan, for his part, practiced an early version of the kind of redundancy we associate with the space program; he packed thirty-five precious compass needles for his circumnavigation of the globe. The bare essential was the chart, a

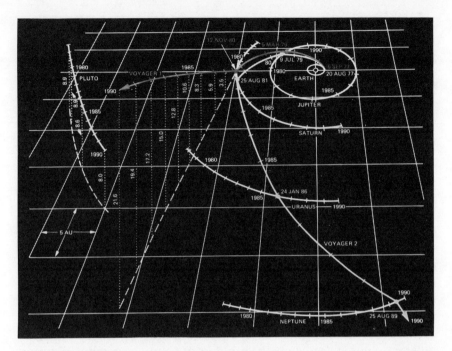

Map of the solar system shows the intersection of *Voyager 1* and *Voyager 2* with the outer planets (each square measures five astronomical units, roughly 465 million miles, on a side). Once *Voyager 1* passed by Saturn's moon Titan in 1980, it left the plane of the planets for good. (NASA/JPL)

large piece of sheepskin nailed to a timber, perhaps, or a gorgeous watermarked portolan, crisscrossed by rhumb lines and spread out on a table atop a heaving sea.

But in the late twentieth century, the navigational chart is a different beast. It resides inside computers and constantly revises itself as a journey proceeds. All the raw data, all the possibilities and parameters, become numbers that interweave like a writhing brood of newborn serpents, numbers tangled and teeming and in digital flux, numbers ("ephemeris," a perfect word) updated on a daily, even hourly, basis, until the computer sorts through threads of movement out there near the edge of the planetary plain and spits out an answer—a "solution," it is called, one of many possible trajectories. Then the navigators take a colored adhesive dot and place it on a large sheet of grid paper, about a yard wide and two feet high, with cross hairs at its very center. This map, pinned to the wall, is called the B-plane. It represents a very particular section of interplanetary space, a vertical slice of the solar system out near Neptune; a large red dot marks the "aim point." This is where Neptune, traveling at 12,000 miles per hour around the sun, and *Voyager 2,* traveling around 61,000 miles an hour, are expected to meet. A small sign on that same wall reads WE DO PRECISION GUESSWORK.

Someone—a congressman, for example—might be unnerved to wander into the navigation room someday and see how the navigators make sport of their own uncertainty. They have turned hundreds of millions of taxpayer dollars into a dart board (not for nothing is the insignia of the group the character Albert the Alligator from the comic strip "Pogo," grasping a dart). On the floor they have laid several white stripes, marking successively closer distances to the far wall; there, next to the B-plane, is a small quiver of darts. Yet this inside joke offers as serviceable and simple a metaphor as any for navigation: the closer you get to your target, the easier it is to hit the bull's-eye. As the spacecraft nears its encounter with Neptune, the navigators' darts, which is to say their computer projections, edge closer to the bull's-eye. On this latest B-plane chart, on this particular Saturday night, different-colored dots show the progress of solutions computed during the previous weeks and months. The dots wander like an indecisive ant toward the aim point; as they get closer to the target, the dots change color—blue for approximate solutions, orange for getting close, red for closing in. The last solution run through the computer prior to the meeting, called "Nav H," is a red dot. Around nine o'clock they head up to the fourth floor for a meeting both pivotal and, oddly, elegiac. This will be the last time NASA engineers steer the spacecraft. Ever.

To judge by newspaper accounts, *Voyager 2* faced uncertain dangers during this final approach. Mission scientists knew, for example, that Neptune possessed a potentially large magnetic field (with potentially damaging radiation), and eight days earlier, on August 11, Voyager had also detected two partial rings, or "ring arcs," circling the planet. Lovely at a distance, the ring material could knock out an instrument and possibly even the spacecraft. "There's some risk of collisions," one scientist told the *New York Times.* "I'm not predicting doom, but it's going to be an anxious moment when we fly through the equatorial plane."

No air of doom or gloom surfaced at the meeting; the navigational team had satisfied their angst about rings and radiation by adjusting course several years earlier. If anything, the gathering had all the drama of an operating room during open-heart surgery, by which is suggested not the tension-filled theater of life and death that many mistakenly presume, but rather a calm, routinized, almost bored conclave of specialists who, having thought through every possible scenario, seem incapable of surprise. One by one, members of the Voyager team filed into Room 461-B: the project manager, Norman Haynes; Edward Stone, the chief scientist; mission engineer Lanny Miller; and deputy science director Ellis Miner, chomping on an apple. Images of the planet flashed on the three TV monitors against the far wall. Already, the images were spellbinding: a big blue ball of cerulean gases, serene in color but not in temperament, judging by the angry dark spot swirling in its southern latitudes. Someone passed out a sheaf of documents and data. It bore the title "NAV H TCM B20 Tweak Results Meeting." Their final navigational whisper to *Voyager 2* would be, in engineers' parlance, a tweak.

Donald Gray, chief of the navigation team, rose to say a few words. A red-faced, sandy-haired man of punctilious speech, Gray reminded the scientists in attendance that Neptune had proved an elusive target. Its exact mass and exact distance from the sun were unknown, and if you know anything about Newtonian physics, where mass and distance are the legs on which equations stand, you will understand how that ignorance made wobbly their every attempt to pinpoint *Voyager 2*'s exact location in space. Not that they would miss the planet; they knew where the spacecraft was headed. But several key scientific experiments required precision to within six miles or so of the aim point, and any last-minute maneuvers had to take place days in advance. "We really diddled around for a while," Gray confessed. "I watched the guys do a lot of breast-beating and soul-searching as they would try a value and see how it worked out." The navigators were too tired to laugh much that Saturday night: disheveled, red-eyed, in need of shaves and sleep, they slouched in clothes that had an unmistakable lived-in look. "Now," said Gray, "it looks like maybe things are settling down."

It fell to Tony Taylor, head of orbit determination ("OD" in the interminably acronymed world of NASA), to report the latest results. As it approached its target, *Voyager 2* snapped pictures of Neptune and several of its moons against background stars, and these optical navigation (opnav) pictures were used to calculate its location in space. The navigators would plug the data into computers, the computers would belch out an inch-thick document of computations, and the

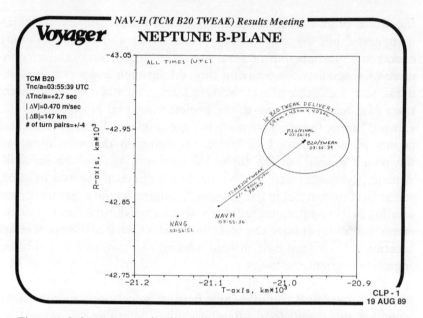

The twentieth-century navigational chart: a "tweak" maneuver on Aug. 21, 1989, nudged *Voyager 2* from its projected arrival point (Nav H) to the optimal zone (circle) for scientific experiments. (NASA/JPL)

---

results would be plotted on the B-plane—that two-dimensional bull's-eye in space where the spacecraft was supposed to be in exactly five days.

"I have bad news and good news," Taylor announced. A handsome man with a genteel South Carolina accent and a set of California bangs, Taylor said, "The bad news is that we shifted ahead seventy-six seconds in arrival time, and the good news is that the B-plane shift is compensating for that." They talk like this; theirs is the dialect of error ellipses, shrinking error bars, Doppler signatures. They don't predict; they "advertise." "We're going to advertise forty seconds' uncertainty in time of flight," Taylor said. Every appointment in *Voyager 2*'s agenda—instructions on where to point its cameras, when to point, when to take magnetic field measurements, where to aim its radio waves during the crucial experiments known as occultations—every twitch and pivot and blink of this robotic messenger depended on an absolutely precise determination of its location in time. When it passed closest to Neptune, the probe would be traveling 61,000 miles an hour. A 120-second error in arrival time could mean a 2,000-mile error in location, jeopardizing experiments a decade in the planning.

To nudge *Voyager 2* back on course, Taylor had proposed something called a roll maneuver. They would tweak the spacecraft, roll it back and forth like a spinning bullet four or five times, to change its velocity by a minuscule amount. Slight velocity changes had tormented the navigators in the early years when they were the unwanted side effect of spacecraft roll maneuvers; now they could be used, and for the best of reasons. The tweak could be accomplished without firing the main maneuvering rockets. The heat of those rockets knocked out *Voyager 2*'s delicate radio receiver two days. Like all good scientific ideas, Taylor admitted later, the idea for this maneuver came to him one night in bed.

The only disagreement during the entire meeting—and it was minor, hardly debated, never in raised voices—concerned whether the maneuver should be four or five turns. No one mentioned ring arcs; no one fretted about the magnetic field. Thirty-four minutes after the meeting began, Ed Stone, *Voyager 2*'s chief scientist, said simply, "Okay, so it's four rolls." If he had been ordering breakfast, the tone could not have been a whit different.

The following Monday morning, the navigators "tweaked" *Voyager 2*. Short puffs of hydrazine gas rocked the spacecraft back and forth four times. It took 100 minutes to complete, and this rockabye roll imparted a negligible change in velocity of 0.47 meter per second— about 1 mile an hour in a vehicle doing close to 45,000 miles an hour at the time. It was enough. That gentle rightward nudge would carry the spacecraft 91 miles farther from Neptune, 439 miles closer to Triton, within whispering distance of the most distant targets ever visited by human exploration, setting the stage for what Ed Stone would later call "the final movement of the Voyager symphony." "This is the last maneuver we will do on *Voyager 2,*" project manager Haynes told reporters that Monday. "In fact, it's probably the last maneuver we'll do on any of the Voyager spacecraft." So they said sayonara with a tweak, which may be as close as engineers get to affection on the job.

The meeting a success, their work nearly done, the navigators returned to their warren of work stations on the second floor. As people stood around, someone asked Bob Cesarone, one of the navigators, if he had ever met a fellow named Gary Flandro. "No," said Cesarone, "but if you happen to run into him, tell him there are a lot of guys over here who would like to meet him."

Of all the anonymous engineers and technicians involved in *Voyager 2*'s Grand Tour of the solar system, perhaps the most uncelebrated is Gary A. Flandro. Asked to do a make-work project one summer while working at JPL, he imagined a map in his mind, sketched it out as the first route to the outer regions of the solar system, and called it the Grand Tour. Maps are the product of measurement, but also imagination.

In the spring of 1965, Flandro was a burr-headed graduate student at the California Institute of Technology specializing in aeronautics. A trim young man just turned thirty, wearing his hair and shirt sleeves short, Flandro possessed intense curiosity and immense confidence, the latter of which leaked out then—as it still does today—in the form of a wry, self-satisfied smile. He worked under Elliott Cutting, who asked Flandro to figure out if exploration of the outer solar system—the giant gaseous planets of Jupiter, Saturn, Uranus, and Neptune—was at all feasible. This was the summer of 1965. Cassius Clay was the heavyweight champ, Adlai Stevenson had just died, and Lyndon Johnson gravely announced that the United States would commit its troops against Viet Cong soldiers "if the South Vietnamese army requested such assistance." Flandro undertook his project with few illusions. As he recalls, "I thought they'd just given me something to do so I'd stay out of their hair." He was asked once if it was just a glorified summer job, and he replied, "I'm afraid that that's what it was."

Space exploration was so new in 1965 that there was hardly time for any conventional wisdom to set in, but what little there was argued strongly against a Grand Tour. The U.S. space program was exactly eight years old in the spring of 1965. NASA was lobbing Ranger probes at the moon, and the first half dozen never got there. The moon was five days away; Jupiter was two years. Looking out the window of his third-floor office in Building 180 (now JPL's administration building), staring past pine trees to the sere foothills beyond, Flandro contemplated the absurdity of a mission to the distant planets. He did the standard calculations and discovered, as had everyone before him, that it would take thirty to forty years to get to Neptune (this at a time when some of the Ranger spacecraft didn't last the sixty-six hours to the moon). He had heard all the standard objections. You couldn't get to Jupiter because you couldn't safely pass through the gravelly gauntlet of asteroids between Mars and Jupiter, and even if you could, Jupiter's intense radiation would poach any spacecraft flying close by. You couldn't communicate over those long distances. And Uranus or Neptune or Pluto? Forget it. The flight time to Neptune would take longer than the average productive lifetime of a working scientist.

Gary Flandro during
the summer he worked at the
Jet Propulsion Laboratory.
(G. Flandro)

So Flandro had few illusions. But he explored ways of cutting down the flight time, and as he followed his fancy down seemingly arcane paths of celestial mechanics, he discovered, as often happens, the footprints of scientists who had been there before him. A *long* time before him, as it turned out.

First, Flandro considered the idea of using the gravitational pull of a large planet like Jupiter, thirteen hundred times the size of earth, to fling a spacecraft farther into space with a boost in energy. Another JPL scientist, Michael A. Minovitch, had pioneered this concept, previously showing the potential of using gravity to reach the outer planets. During a close pass, the mass of Jupiter and the mass of a spacecraft will influence each other. The spacecraft would ever so slightly perturb the orbit of Jupiter, but "perturb" is not quite the right word to describe what Jupiter would do to the orbit of an 1,819-pound midge like *Voyager 2*. It would yank it like a small dog on a leash, sending it into a new trajectory and—relative to the sun—giving it a goodly kick of speed in the exchange. Gravity assist, it was called.

The idea was not new. When Flandro later searched through old technical papers from the nineteenth century, he was surprised to discover that the French astronomer Urbain Jean Joseph Leverrier— the same astronomer who, with John Couch Adams, had predicted the existence of Neptune by analyzing oddities in Uranus's orbit—had troubled to calculate exactly such effects. As early as the seventeenth century, astronomers were keenly interested in the dynamics of comets and how their speed and trajectories were affected by large planets like Jupiter. It bespeaks the shelf life of classical physics that Flandro unknowingly dusted off Leverrier's cometary equations when he showed that such a gravity-assist mechanism could actually save time. "They had already done all the mathematics," Flandro says, "but nobody in the space flight community knew that." Instead of taking thirty years to Neptune, it could be done in twelve. This was one of two crucial insights that made a Grand Tour mission possible.

"We realized that you can gain energy in that process," Flandro recalls, "and by that means shorten the flight time." Minovitch had published papers in 1963 and 1965 showing that gravity-assist could speed up or slow down a spacecraft, depending on whether it approached the planet from the front or back, and he also speculated on a mission to the outer planets. But Minovitch devoted his considerable imagination primarily to routes between the inner planets; at a 1967 symposium in Boston, he described a delightfully futuristic scenario using gravity-assist to keep a fleet of spacecraft commuting between Mars, Earth, and Jupiter. A certain rivalry for credit has developed over the years between Flandro and Minovitch, who both worked at JPL at the same time. In Flandro's opinion, they were as different as night and day. "He was around, but he liked to work at night," Flandro recalls. "He really was a computer type, so he had access to the computer, and that was his way. I don't think I saw him more than two or three times that whole summer."

Flandro's other great insight, mirroring the great strength of the space program itself, reflected his ability to think ahead. In what might facetiously be called conjectural cartography, he projected his evolving flight plan one and even two decades into the future. The outer five planets of the solar system, circling around the sun at their petty or hectic pace, happened to all be on one side of the solar system in the 1980s, aligned in a special configuration that occurs but once every 175 years. Flandro toppled onto that realization in June of 1965, and the discovery quickened the blood of any space scientist who understood its significance.

"The thing that really set it off was when I began to draw pictures of the solar system at *different* times," Flandro says. "I did what other people weren't doing. They were thinking of missions in the sixties. That was their time frame. And I think I was the first person to go beyond the sixties. I needed to see what the seventies looked like, and the eighties, and I started drawing pictures of the outer solar system. I made plots. Probably the key plot was a drawing of the celestial

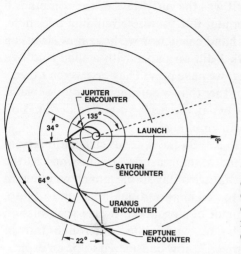

JUPITER
ENCOUNTER
135°
34°
LAUNCH
φ
SATURN
ENCOUNTER
64°
URANUS
ENCOUNTER
NEPTUNE
ENCOUNTER
22°

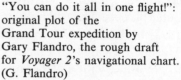

"You can do it all in one flight!":
original plot of the
Grand Tour expedition by
Gary Flandro, the rough draft
for *Voyager 2*'s navigational chart.
(G. Flandro)

longitude of all the outer planets as a function of time. I made that graph very, very carefully. I had it on a big piece of paper, showing the track of each of these planets. So it's longitude versus time, and the planets had different slopes. I saw all these outer planets, and I noticed something very interesting: that Neptune and Uranus and Saturn and Jupiter all had their longitude tracks *crossing*! I thought, 'Wow!' No one had ever seen that before. I saw that first! And there it was. And that happens, of course, in 1981. You know, that's the flash of insight, that picture right there. I said, 'That's it! They're all over on the same side. That means you can do it all in one flight. *You can do it all in one flight!*' " The last time the alignment occurred, in roughly 1806, Thomas Jefferson was president, Lewis and Clark were heading back from the Pacific Northwest, and Napoleon Bonaparte was contemplating the use of a daring new technology, the hot-air balloon, to cross the English Channel. Neptune itself would not be discovered for another forty years.

With these two crucial insights in hand—the gravity-assist method and the unique planetary alignment—Flandro went back to his calculations. The exercise was a bit like hitting four moving targets with one shot, or firing a bullet through a slalom. When would you have to launch a spacecraft, and where would you point it, and at what velocity would you fire it, in order to intersect all four of the outer planets? Flandro estimates that he worked out two-to-three thousand solutions; and perhaps the most amazing thing is that he worked out these computations by hand. "It was the early days of the computer," Flandro points out. "Our computer filled a whole building over here, and it was about as good as a hand calculator we have now. It was a different era. Most of the work I did on paper with a slide rule. We didn't have the kind of tools that we have now. They just weren't there. I think maybe that was a help rather than a detriment in a lot of ways. It made you really understand what the heck you were doing. You couldn't let the machine do your thinking."

Space engineers love "options." By the time his calculations were complete, Flandro had prepared a smorgasbord of missions to the outer planets. They all took advantage of favorable launch windows in 1977, 1978, and 1979; he even tossed in an optional mission to Pluto. The ink drawing that Flandro made of a proposed twelve-year mission to Neptune, with a 1977 launch date, was in effect the rough draft of the journey undertaken by *Voyager 2,* now considered to be an exploratory voyage every bit as grand and transforming as those of Columbus, Magellan, and Cook. Flandro borrowed the name for such a mission from an Italian aviation pioneer named Gaetano Arturo Crocco, who in the 1950s, as a hobby, figured out a self-perpetuating, gravity-assisted trajectory between Mars, Earth, and Venus. Crocco called it the "Grand Tour," and Flandro adopted the term when he published a paper about this ambitious exploratory journey in *Astronautica Acta* (it appeared in 1966). At the end of the summer of 1965, his work completed, Flandro returned to Caltech, hopeful about the mission. But those were different days. A group calling itself the Pasadena Society for the Preservation of Jupiter's Orbit promptly mounted demonstrations to protest any perturbation of Jupiter's orbit by the gravity-assist method.

Impressed by Flandro's work, NASA issued a press release about the Grand Tour the day after he presented it to JPL's Advanced Concepts group. By 1970 the space agency had plans for a grandiose mission involving four sophisticated spacecraft capable of repairing themselves in flight. The first two, to be launched in 1976 and 1977, were targeted for Jupiter, Saturn, and Pluto; the second pair, to be launched in 1979, would fly by Jupiter, Uranus, and Neptune. Then Congress—which had spent the equivalent of $100 billion getting a man to the moon, was spending $165 billion on the Vietnam War, and would spend tens of billions on the notoriously flawed space shuttle— balked as the estimated cost inched toward $1 billion. The mission was canceled in December 1971.

But even crew-cut engineers with plastic shirt-pocket penguards can be a little subversive when they believe in a project. "Just a few days elapsed," recalls Andrey Sergeyevsky, one of the early Voyager navigators, "and then slowly, from grass roots, the project resurrected itself as a *cheap* mission." The JPL engineers proposed using two stripped-down spacecraft for a bare-bones trip to Jupiter and Saturn. The mission would cost about $360 million. On July 1, 1972, this not-so-grand tour won congressional approval. The mission was smaller, cheaper, leaner. But if all went well, the scientists reasoned, there was no reason to stop at Saturn. They had seen Flandro's charts. They knew how rare the opportunity was. They kept the so-called hip-pocket option alive.

Gary Flandro did some follow-up trajectory work, including an ingenious plan to fly solar-powered spacecraft toward the sun, pick up extra energy, and scoot out to Neptune in as little as five years. But he never did more work on the Grand Tour project (he now teaches aeronautics at Georgia Tech and runs a private company in his native Utah). His rival, Michael Minovitch, has become an independent inventor and obtained a patent in 1989 for a 1,000-mile-long, 46-mile-deep vacuum tunnel through the earth that would use electromagnetic force to hurl rockets into space. Still different as night and day.

At the time Flandro left JPL, he doubted the United States would capitalize on the opportunity provided by the rare planetary alignment. But both Voyagers ultimately flew. *Voyager 1,* launched on September 5, 1977, reached Jupiter in 1979, Saturn in 1980, and, hooking around Saturn, shot past its moon Titan while being flung up out of the plane of the planets. *Voyager 2* was launched two weeks earlier but followed a longer, slower flight path to Jupiter. "If *Voyager 1* had failed to see Titan for whatever reason, like a camera broke down or you name it, then *Voyager 2* would never go to Uranus and Neptune," says Andrey Sergeyevsky, one of several navigators who designed the original flight plan. "Instead, it would go to Titan, too. And of course once you go past Titan, you have used up your degree of freedom. Now you're going out to the black sky."

Voyager 2 did not have to repeat this itinerary. With the success of *Voyager 1,* NASA engineers dusted off their long-secret agenda: on to Uranus and Neptune.

At one point in *The Odyssey,* the sorceress Circe pledges to help Odysseus avoid the perils of navigation, to protect him from "some black sack of trouble." To get from here to there, and to do so while avoiding that "black sack of trouble," is the fundamental challenge of navigation. Yet as late as March 1989, six months before the Neptune encounter, the Voyager navigators seemed headed for trouble. The spacecraft had drifted 1,500 kilometers (more than 900 miles) off course.

All the planning up to that point had been as perfect as can be expected in the imperfect world of pioneering interplanetary voyages. It took years of work by dozens of engineers to convert Gary Flandro's primitive navigational chart into a precise set of spacecraft instructions. Between 1974 and 1976, JPL engineers evaluated some ten thousand Voyager trajectories. They wanted to get to Neptune, of course, and they especially wanted a close look at the moon Triton. But how exactly did they map out this epic journey? It is not exactly dead reckoning. Voyager navigators often speak of their "knowledge," by which they often mean their ignorance. As Andrey Sergeyevsky puts it, "You never really return to where you thought you ought to be."

Robert J. Cesarone, who was a high school student in Chicago, Illinois, when the original mission was designed, began working with Sergeyevsky as a trajectory engineer in June of 1977, two months before the *Voyager 2* launch; he would serve as "traj" chief for the Neptune encounter twelve years later. "If everything just goes exactly smooth as it ought to, and you had really good knowledge of everything you wanted to do before you set out, you would just fly one of your predesigned trajectories," Cesarone explained, pausing to smile at this point. "But I've never seen it work out that way."

Even by the standards of unpleasant surprises, *Voyager 2* threw some real curves at the navigators. The thruster rockets used to maneuver the spacecraft did not perform as expected, and engineers soon discovered that the five-foot struts holding *Voyager 2* to its booster rocket motor had failed to fall away as designed, so the metal struts partially blocked and reduced the thrust of the maneuvering rockets. "What that meant," Cesarone recalls, "was that if you wanted to make it all the way to Neptune, you weren't going to have enough propellant unless you started making some changes in your designs." And so as early as 1978, the navigators began rewriting *Voyager 2*'s script for a denouement eleven years in the future. They speeded up the arrival of the spacecraft at Saturn, Uranus, and Neptune. With each change, of course, they had to recompute the location of Neptune, its moons, all the aim points.

Those problems compounded the everyday headaches of interplanetary exploration. Just as marine navigators worry about hidden shoals and reefs, *Voyager 2*'s navigators worried about ring material in the path of the spacecraft. Just as mariners worry about currents and gales, *Voyager 2*'s navigators worried about the strong radiation "winds" caused by the magnetic field around Neptune (Jupiter's strong magnetic field knocked out part of *Voyager 1*'s operation). "So then you launch," Cesarone continued, "and then you find that because you didn't have perfect knowledge of the physical world in space, you're off course. Well, the process to find out how far you're on or off course is called 'orbit determination.' "

Orbit determination places the spacecraft in a distinct three-dimensional section of space. Navigators could determine the distance to *Voyager 2*'s location to within thirty to sixty feet by measuring the time it took for a radio signal to reach the spacecraft, and then dividing that time by the speed of light. They could determine the speed at which it moved away from earth to within a millimeter per second by a change of frequency in that same radio signal, known as the Doppler shift. And they could determine its position relative to the planets by taking pictures, for example, of Neptune and its moons, principally Triton and the newly discovered N1; these opnav landmarks are as essential to navigators bringing a spacecraft to its aim point as the statue of the Virgin or a lighthouse are to mariners bringing a ship into an unknown harbor.

"When you know where you want to be from the trajectory," Cesarone continues, "and you've found out where you *are* from the orbit determination, it's 'What am I going to do to get back?' And then once you get back, you find that new errors creep in or new knowledge came in that cause you to refine your original line, so you just keep iterating that process all the way." The interplanetary navigational chart is not a fixed piece of paper. It is sheaves of revisions, laminate approximations, a constant sculpting of numbers, from rough to roughly accurate to smooth; the knowledge at first is not bad and then gets better and finally quite good. The navigators speak of the solutions "settling down."

It wasn't until 1980, more than two years after launch, that Andrey Sergeyevsky figured out a trajectory that would hit both Neptune and Triton. Yet as *Voyager 2* approached Uranus in January of 1986, the final flight plan for Neptune had not been decided. The original scheme called for the spacecraft to pass close over the cloud tops of Neptune at its north pole; such a close pass would bend the craft's path, by dint of gravity, and send it scooting down to within 10,000 kilometers (about 6,000 miles) of Triton. "We got a new, updated orbit of Triton around Neptune in late 1985," Cesarone recalls. "See, our

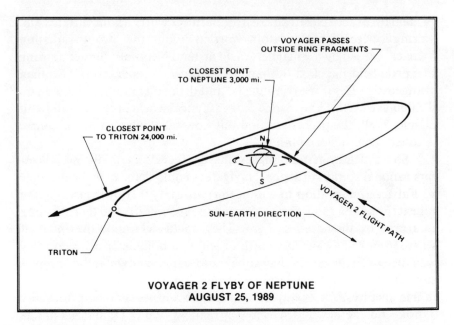

VOYAGER 2 FLYBY OF NEPTUNE
AUGUST 25, 1989

To avoid any "black sack of trouble" such as ring material, Andrey Sergeyevsky and colleagues designed *Voyager 2*'s trajectory to approach Neptune just outside the ring arcs, pass over its north pole, and, using a bit of "gravity-assist," shoot down to Triton. (NASA/JPL)

knowledge of it was pretty poor. And as that was being worked out, as we refined the knowledge of it and did a better orbit solution, we found that in order to retain the 10,000-kilometer trajectory, we had to go much closer to Neptune than we had originally thought." That incurred potential perils. There might be "sensible atmosphere"—the thin, near-vacuum layer of Neptune's atmosphere with just enough molecules of nitrogen, say, or hydrogen to slow the spacecraft down. More ominously, there might be rings.

Beautiful and alluring as sirens from a distance, rings were every navigator's nightmare. Submillimeter dust, small as salt or pepper, and millimeter-sized particles on the order of BBs would sandblast the spacecraft, with likely damage to the antennae, propellant tank, and the precious cameras; it would be like throwing sand in *Voyager 2*'s eyes at supersonic speed. Grape-sized particles in the centimeter range would strike the spacecraft with a force equivalent to a baseball traveling 27,000 miles per hour, nearly three hundred times the speed of a

Nolan Ryan fastball. An actual rock or boulder would be catastrophic. As ring expert Rex Ridenoure would put it, "One particle in the wrong place can completely wipe out the encounter." So they sweated out the ring problem years in advance. After extensive study, mission planners changed course. *Voyager 2* would pass only within 40,000 kilometers (25,000 miles) of Triton—four times more distant than originally planned. "That bought us a little more protection from the atmosphere, and for any possible ring hazard," Cesarone says.

So everything seemed fine until March 21, 1989, when the navigators ran their Nav 9 orbit determination and discovered to their considerable surprise that they had wandered 1,500 kilometers, or 930 miles, to the left and below the aim point. One navigator called it "alarming." "At that point, it wasn't anything critical to the mission," Tony Taylor says. "The only thing critical about it was our credibility." What they were learning, slowly, was that Neptune wasn't where they thought it would be. On August 1 they executed a trajectory-course maneuver to bring *Voyager 2* back on line. Then their calculations kept showing them arriving sooner than anticipated. Again, their knowledge wasn't perfect. Neptune, it turned out, lay about 2,800 miles closer to the sun than they had thought. That tiny wrinkle flexed through every calculation.

One other recurring navigational headache came back to bother them days before the final approach. A sequence of human and mechanical follies early in the mission had reduced *Voyager 2*'s capability to receive instructions from the earth; in terms of radio signals, the result was the difference between hitting the broad side of a barn with a dart or hitting one particular vertical plank in the barn wall, a task that of course becomes ever more difficult as the barn speeds away from you at 40,000 miles per hour. Engineers were able to compensate for this, but at a price; firing *Voyager 2*'s maneuvering rockets generated heat, and that heat made the radio receiver bandwidth shaky—made that narrow plank wobble back and forth. As a result, each rocket burn had to be followed by a forty-eight-hour moratorium on all signals sent to *Voyager 2*. That didn't present much of a problem while the spacecraft was on its years-long cruises between planets, but during the last-minute adjustments of an encounter, it knocked out radio communication at a crucial time.

That trade-off was much on the minds of mission planners when they gathered that Saturday night, August 19, to discuss the final maneuver. Tony Taylor's idea to tweak the spacecraft without firing the main thrusters, an idea first broached several years earlier, was very good news because it didn't cost them two days of radio silence. And so *Voyager 2,* poked ever so gently to the right, zoomed through its final hours of approach toward Neptune, trying to skate close enough to the planet for a good look and an optimal turn toward Triton, but not so close that it would sandblast itself into blind silence. On Wednesday, August 23, as expectations for the encounter grew, the navigators delivered three more solutions. "They've nailed it right down the middle," Norman Haynes told the assembled press. A good thing, too. For all his hardships, Columbus never had a thousand journalists crowded on the bridge to see if he would hit Hispaniola. But as even the navigators admit, knowledge is never perfect. "Now we hold our breath for the occultations," Tony Taylor would say.

Behind him, on the B-plane chart on the wall, three small red dots, one atop the other, marked the final three orbit solutions. From their red center, like a bouquet of celebratory flowers, sprouted three red-tailed darts.

Late in the evening of Thursday, August 24, 1989, *Voyager 2* made its final approach to Neptune. Members of the navigational team, exhilarated and nervous, gathered in their second-floor work area to monitor this final event, fortified with soft drinks, beer, chips, and the adrenaline of a thirty-six-hour shift just completed. They had done all they could do. Their knowledge was as good as it was going to get; they had run the last solutions; the calculations, each one an inch or two thick, filled an entire floor-to-ceiling cabinet. Now all they could do was watch television like everyone else. As images scrolled up on the television monitors, pictures whose accuracy depended on *Voyager 2*'s being exactly where the navigators said it should be, each well-centered image became the most public of report cards. A picture of the Neptunian moon 1989 N2 popped up, square in the middle of the TV screen, prompting oohs and aahs and the obligatory California "Awesome!" Tony Taylor bolted out of his office for a look and yelped, "Jesus, right in the middle!" The pictures were spectacular.

One final passage of high anxiety remained. It occurred around midnight local time when signals from *Voyager 2,* requiring four hours and six minutes to travel back to earth, brought news of the spacecraft plunging through the plane of Neptune's rings. It made for an eerie sensation of displacement, as if we were eavesdropping on some incident of distress yet were powerless to intercede; and a Voyager scientist narrating the passage on TV sounded palpably shaken by the intensity and duration of the impacts, later measured at three hundred per

Photomosaic images like these of Triton are used to make maps; *Voyager,* having traveled 4 billion miles to take the pictures, achieved a resolution of 0.5 mile. (NASA/JPL)

---

second and sounding like frenzied insects trapped in a can. After many nervous seconds, the racket finally subsided, and *Voyager 2* leaned into its downward dogleg turn over Neptune's north pole and made for Triton.

All through the night, borne on radio signals limping back to earth on $\frac{1}{10,000,000,000,000,000}$ of a watt, came one arresting image after another, electronic postcards of new worlds (see color illustrations): the great blue gaseous planet itself, with its enigmatic dark spot and thin ethereal rings, its swirling winds and its high cirrus clouds looking like welts from a lashing, welling up from the skin of clouds below; rocky and pyramidal N1; and of course Triton, with its pink methane snows and ice geysers, its frozen calderas and veined, cantaloupelike polar plains, "a big sloppy bog of hydrocarbons," as one scientist later put it. These photographs, like the ones from Jupiter and Saturn and Uranus, were photomaps in and of themselves, the first cartographic sketches of previously unseen worlds; and each photo was a page in a book on the new geology yet to be written. They were all the more remarkable at Neptune because, as JPL astronomer Richard Terrile pointed out, *Voyager 2* took its pictures in $\frac{1}{900}$ the amount of light

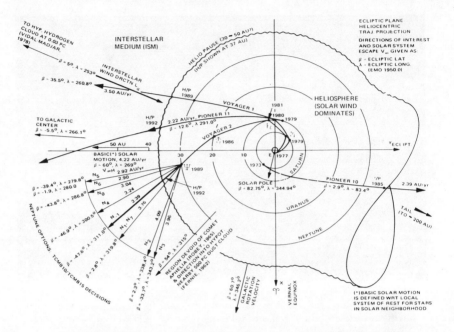

Each good map begets another: Voyager's "final tour de force" may be the discovery of the outer boundary of the solar system, known as the heliopause. JPL scientists have already mapped out the possibilities. (NASA/JPL; AAS Publications, Advances in the Astronautical Sciences, 1981)

that falls on earth, traveling at a speed of 27 kilometers per second, holding exposures lasting fifteen *minutes,* with a camera that had a focal length of 1,500 mm and an ASA of about 10. Its Neptune rendezvous complete, the robotic spacecraft set off to map one final boundary, where the outward million-mile-an-hour flow of the solar wind is overcome by the inward flow of cosmic rays from interstellar space. That is where the solar system technically ends; and the two Voyagers may tell us where this border, called the heliopause, is before they risk running out of power around 2010. "That would be the final tour de force," said one engineer, "for Voyager to survive to interstellar space." That would also be a new line on a new map.

When it was all over, when *Voyager 2* had dumped the last of its five trillion bits of data and wonder into our laps, we were all left speechless in the Keatsian sense, that special and rare silence that derives from the sense of privilege each one of us feels at having glimpsed new worlds for the first time. As the final, spectacular images of Triton appeared on TV monitors on the morning of August 25, 1989, a trim short-haired man with a wry, self-satisfied smile sat in the cafeteria at the Jet Propulsion Laboratory, marveling at the immensity of the achievement. "I must tell you," Gary Flandro admitted, "I expected the opportunity to be wasted." After twelve years on the road, after piling up 4,429,508,700 miles on the odometer, its hearing impaired and its computer brain addled by old age, *Voyager 2* was guided by its navigators to within twenty miles of its intended aim point. It arrived about five minutes ahead of a schedule made years earlier, 0.6 second later than advertised in the last navigational solution.

2. Ground Truth

|||||||||

We perceive no beauties that are
not sharpened, prinked out, and
inflated by artifice. Such as
appear in their pure and natural
simplicity easily escape a vision
as coarse as ours. Theirs is a
delicate and hidden beauty; it
needs clear and purified sight
to discover their secret
brightness.

—Montaigne,
Essays

On a warm August night in 1972, a barge burdened with the vilest of industrial wastes made its way slowly from the mid-Atlantic coast of the United States toward a watery refuse dump located about twelve miles offshore and known as the New York Bight. With the anonymity conferred by dark of night on open sea, the barge stopped short of its designated dumping area and proceeded to flush thousands of gallons of acid iron wastes into the Atlantic Ocean. The dumping took a matter of minutes. Then, with a tight hairpin turn and with the complicity of that same darkness, the barge chugged back to shore, leaving the scene without a trace. Or so it seemed. At approximately nine o'clock the following morning, August 16, a satellite launched only a few weeks earlier glided silently over the East Coast of the United States at an altitude of about 570 miles. With the satellite traveling at more than 14,000 miles per hour, its instruments made thirteen sweeps a second over the still waters of the New York Bight, canvassing 13,000 square miles of ocean and land in a mere twenty seconds or so, forming a picture in the morning light. There was no trace of the barge by then, of course. But there remained a map of its bad intent. Instruments aboard the satellite revealed a smear of white acid on the dark and pristine sea. The satellite showed that the dumping had occurred too close to shore; indeed, it even revealed the composition of the wastes as 8.5 percent sulfuric acid and 10 percent iron sulfates. Tugged by currents, the trail of acid curled back and forth. From space, it took on the appearance of a sinuous question mark.

The question it posed, then and now, is how attentively we wish to monitor the ongoing abuse of our planet. One of the earliest replies came in the form of that satellite. Known at the time as the Earth Resources Technology Satellite (or by its technological oink of an acronym, ERTS), it would eventually adopt the name Landsat, and that photomosaic of the New York Bight was one of its very first pictures sent back to earth. The image of mankind's polluting auto-graph, scribbled recklessly on the continental shelf, captured in one blink of the technological eye all the power of mapping from space, formally called "remote sensing." Now, nearly twenty years after Landsat's spectacular debut, we can look back at that image of the acid dump in the New York Bight and see how it anticipates the crucial role remote-sensing devices are destined to play in the future as we struggle to map and monitor and manage resources on earth that seem, with each passing decade, ever more precious, ever more finite, and, alas, ever more identifiable to exploiters as well as conservators because of those same satellites.

Long before Mission to Planet Earth, there was Landsat. The first remote-sensing satellite in this series was launched in July of 1972. Within days it had stunned geologists, rewritten the textbooks of forestry and land use, and revolutionized cartography. Its earliest transmissions revealed several dozen earthquake faults near Lake Tahoe and Monterey Bay in California, faults that had escaped the notice of geologists who had crawled over that same shifting seismic terrain for decades. Undiscovered lakes winked up at the camera. One early image of Alaska showed a forest fire eating through a forest north of Fairbanks; nothing unusual about that, except people in Fairbanks didn't know about it. A ship stranded by chance in the Arctic Ocean received Landsat's satellite maps of the ice pack and picked its way to freedom. Previously unseen terrestrial patterns took on the beauty of modern art and modern metaphor: there were peeling fragments of landscape around Elephant Butte, Montana, that reminded one of Clyfford Still,

Like a jagged surgical scar,
the Grand Canyon cuts through
the northern Arizona landscape
in this 1980 Landsat image.
(USGS/EROS Data Center)

Cairo as it might be imagined by Helen Frankenthaler, a network of
Russian roads imitating astrocytes in the mammalian brain. From
those first heady days, Landsat images have graduated to the level of
cultural artifacts with coffee-table status: the posters hang in offices
and homes, the maps have generated entire atlases, the images fill year
after year of calendars. The satellite taught us, NASA administrator
James C. Fletcher said at the time, "a new way to look."

The maps generated by Landsat, perhaps more than any other
type of map discussed in this book, bridge the gap between old and new
cartography. Landsat images cover common ground. They represent
the ultimate refinement of fifty years of aerial photography and mapping, albeit in grander and more sophisticated terms; they are photographs and maps at the same time, and so they speak the age-old
cartographic vernacular of hill and valley, basin and range, fault line
and fracture zone, with perhaps crisper, more precise optical pronunci-
ation. On the other hand, many Landsat images mark a qualitative
breakthrough in mapmaking. The Landsat map showed not just the
lay of the land, but—through a happy convergence of technical tricks,
computer enhancement, and interpretation—the *quality* of the land:
how it was used, what grew on it, whether the soil was dry or moist.
Since the launch of *Landsat 4* in 1982, there has even been an instrument circling the planet whose very name sums up this new qualitative
cartography. It is called the Thematic Mapper (see color illustration).

Perhaps most important, Landsat has provided us with the most
obvious and accessible benefits of remote sensing from space. Remote

sensing refers to the use of robotic instrumentation, an eye in the sky in this case, to replace or enhance the human senses, and thus can be seen as a metaphor for how we explore and chart the physical world in the late twentieth century. Just as *Voyager 2* is a robotic eye wandering through the solar system, just as radio telescopes are huge metallic ears listening for the dry rattle of radio waves in the cosmos, just as radioactive DNA probes poke like fingers through the maze of chromosomes; just so, the late-twentieth-century explorer need not stand on the bridge of a heaving ship or traipse dry, uncharted wastelands like explorers in earlier epochs. He (or she) more likely can be found at a computer terminal, manipulating data sent by a far-flung probe surfing the solar wind, by a quantum subatomic stylus riding the grooves of atoms like a phonograph needle on an LP. In the world of remote sensing, the vessels of discovery are instruments; our eyepiece is the computer. No enterprise of mapping has made that more apparent to more people than Landsat.

And no enterprise had to overcome more obstacles to prove the point. Landsat almost never happened.

The folklore surrounding the project and its origins offers up plenty of heroes and plenty of obstructionist villainy. Certainly one of the most visionary of the scientific pioneers was Robert N. Colwell, a native of Star, Idaho, and professor of forestry at the University of California at Berkeley. It was not simply that Colwell was one of the early experts in aerial photo interpretation, nor that he'd worked with Lockheed engineers on a secret Air Force satellite project called SAMOS in the mid-1950s. It was his premonitional realization that scientists could peer from a privileged, elevated perch—a balloon, an airplane, ultimately a satellite—and eavesdrop on all the electromagnetic chatter reflected or emitted by objects on the earth's surface, a chorus of voices ranging from X rays and infrared to radar microwaves. "Certainly, lots of people had the same kind of thoughts," Colwell said recently in his careful, erect manner of speaking, "though maybe not so gung-ho as me."

How gung-ho? Colwell, who would go on to head remote-sensing research at the Space Sciences Laboratory at UC-Berkeley, was willing to buzz the California state capitol building in Sacramento to make his point. Actually, he made low passes over both the capital and agricultural test plots in the 1950s in a Cessna 180 to prove the value of remote sensing. Peering down on the landscape from several thousand feet, he showed that by photographing a scene in several different wavelengths and later combining the images, you could distinguish grass from soil, even cement from asphalt, in black-and-white photographs. Colwell and others had shown that agricultural crops, trees, even different soils possess a telltale electromagnetic signature, as distinct as the handwriting of different individuals. This signature depended on how each type of plant reflected radiation in the near-infrared region of the spectrum, which is a frequency of electromagnetic radiation just beyond the gathering capacity of the human eye.

If we could see the world with infrared eyes, vegetation would appear to us not green but red (infrared detectors gained great importance during World War II precisely because of their ability to distinguish between real vegetation, which creates an infrared signal, and green plastic camouflage covering a tank, which does not). With instruments known as spectrometers, researchers could image a field of corn, for example, in a particular infrared wavelength; the image differed quite significantly from a regular black-and-white photograph. A Soviet scientist named E. L. Krinov had measured the spectral signatures of some 370 natural and man-made objects in the 1940s; he, too, had aerial mapping in mind. By the early 1960s, researchers had demonstrated that corn could be distinguished from wheat solely on the basis of its spectrographic signature, whether viewed from two thousand feet or five hundred miles above ground; soils heavy in clay could similarly be distinguished from sandy soil. Colwell even managed to show that diseased or stressed plants, like pale and infirm humans, had a different spectral tone than healthy plants, and that you could discern the difference more easily, and earlier, with an infrared sensor in space than if you inspected the plants at ground level and rolled the diseased leaves between your fingers. In the early literature of remote sensing, one detects a growing cockiness in the pioneers as they muse about distinguishing pigweed from soybeans, even a fat pig from a calf.

In a prescient article that appeared in *American Scientist* in 1961, Colwell described not only his own work along these lines; he intuitively grasped that emerging technologies in other fields would forever change humankind's ability to measure—and therefore to map—the physical universe. He cited the use of fluorescent and radiographic techniques to map biological objects microscopically small and nearby, the use of radio waves to detect celestial objects astronomically large and distant. Each different wavelength spoke to us in a different language, contained different information, if only we had the electronic ears to hear. "Just as our musical appreciation is increased greatly when more than one or two octaves are exploited," Colwell wrote, "so

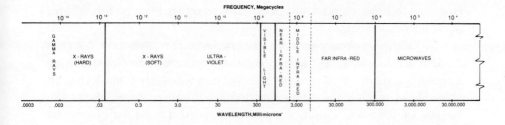

FREQUENCY, Megacycles

| 10^{14} | 10^{13} | 10^{12} | 10^{11} | 10^{10} | 10^{9} | 10^{8} | 10^{7} | 10^{6} | 10^{5} | 10^{4} |

GAMMA RAYS | X - RAYS (HARD) | X - RAYS (SOFT) | ULTRA - VIOLET | VISIBLE LIGHT | NEAR INFRARED | MIDDLE INFRARED | FAR INFRA -RED | MICROWAVES

| .0003 | .003 | .03 | 0.3 | 3.0 | 30 | 300 | 3,000 | 30,000 | 300.000 | 3.000.000 | 30.000.000 |

WAVELENGTH,Millimicrons'

Spectral portraits: remote-sensing satellites detect different spectral signatures from the same terrain, a principle equally applicable to anatomic imaging (X rays) and astronomical mapping (X-ray telescopes).

---

also is our appreciation of the physical universe, through multiband spectral reconnaissance, which already can exploit more than forty 'octaves.' " The first Landsat went up with just such a multiband spectrograph, thanks to a persuasive effort by Colwell and colleagues at the University of Michigan and Purdue, and its extra octaves have given scientific cartography the richness and tonal nuances that have emerged in the past thirty years.

But it was a Russian development that speeded up remote sensing from space. Even before October 4, 1957, that infamous date when the Soviets launched *Sputnik 1,* scientists—especially agricultural scientists—had been aware that aerial surveys revealed features of the earth that were either too hard to obtain on the ground or too costly and time-consuming. The space race merely stepped up the pace.

Satellites represented the other main stream of research at the time. Shortly after World War II, U.S. Army scientists obtained the first photographs of earth from space—shots of White Sands, New Mexico, and environs taken by captured German V-2 rockets, and so even before Sputnik, scientists had prepared wish-lists of possible applications for space satellites. What remained unclear in the initial days of remote sensing was the "platform," as they liked to call it—the vehicle from which to peer down at the earth. Airplanes and balloons were the obvious candidates in the 1950s, but as early as 1955 the air force began planning what it called a Strategic Satellite System. Remote imaging of the *atmosphere* from space began in 1959 with the launch of the *Explorer VI* satellite, which sent back televised pictures of meteorological conditions; the first Tiros weather satellites, launched in 1960, used television cameras to return even better pictures of cloud movements.

A satellite's ability to take in very large, or "synoptic," scenes made it economically attractive. With sophisticated spectral-detecting technology, its power to convey information was truly remarkable. In principle, a mechanical device located five hundred miles above the surface of the earth could, with several spectral wave bands, reveal everything from nuclear missiles in Cuba to the average household income in any given neighborhood on earth. That is why people like Colwell wanted it; it is also why people in the military did not want civilians to have it. As early as 1783, when as ambassador to France Benjamin Franklin observed the first Montgolfier balloons in flight over Paris and predicted their use in "conveying Intelligence" about "an Enemy's Army," generals and spies have understood the power of aerial reconnaissance; the high-altitude surveillance possible from satellites promised both a revolution in surveillance and insurance against political embarrassments like the downing of U-2 spy pilot Gary Powers in 1960.

The two streams converged in February of 1962, when the Institute of Science and Technology at the University of Michigan, a research organization funded by the military, invited seventy agronomists, agriculturalists, foresters, geologists, hydrologists, land-use experts, photogrammetrists, and of course cartographers to the First Symposium on Remote Sensing of Environment. From that date, civilian remote sensing as a discipline began to come of age. On that same date, the two converging streams began to back up behind a dam of security and secrecy. Scientists at that very first symposium did not bemoan the technical impediments that lay in their path; scientists rarely do. They complained about how the military scrambled to classify information about remote sensing.

"This came up over, and over, and over again," one symposium participant remarked, "and it was the one single wet blanket on the whole conference." All this was duly noted by William Fischer, a photogeologist from the United States Geological Survey, who attended that first meeting. Fischer returned to Washington and suggested to his boss at the Department of the Interior, William T. Pecora, that the time might be right for a remote-sensing satellite.

The fact that Landsat almost never happened is a reminder that maps—from Columbus's chart of the New World to that satellite view of the New York Bight—depend to some degree on political resolve;

Landsat's most persevering bureaucratic angel was Bill Pecora of the U.S. Geological Survey. He not only overcame military obstructionists but, it now appears, bluffed the National Aeronautics and Space Administration into reluctant cooperation, too.

NASA's participation was critical. If there were any lingering questions about the promise of space observation, they were dispelled—to everyone's considerable surprise—by John Glenn, Wally Schirra, and Gordon Cooper. Despite cramped conditions, these astronauts took large-format cameras aboard America's early space flights and came back with breathtaking photographs of the earth shot through the window of their Mercury and Gemini spacecraft. These were ordinary photos using visible light, not the information-rich spectral images pushed by the remote-sensing crowd, but the surprising amount of clarity and detail excited geologists. More important, the images excited the public.

Probably the most heralded episode occurred during the twenty-two orbits of *Mercury 9* in May of 1963, when astronaut L. Gordon Cooper, endowed with extraordinarily acute 20/12 vision, peered through a 70-mm Hasselblad camera and reported seeing individual houses in the plains of Tibet, even smoke curling out of chimneys. If that didn't strain credulity, there was his claim to have seen dust clouds kicked up by a vehicle traveling on a road in the southwestern United States. As John Noble Wilford writes in *The Mapmakers,* "Since the physiological effects of space flight were at that time largely unknown, a number of scientists suspected that Cooper, under the influence of prolonged weightlessness, had suffered hallucinations." But his claims were later substantiated. If the engineers could come up with a detector as sensitive as Gordon Cooper's eyes, remote sensing would have a great future.

But NASA administrators were not interested in a civilian satellite program, and the most generous interpretation for their reluctance is that it would have distracted time and resources from their mandate to put a man on the moon. A less generous interpretation would be that NASA cocked too willing and deferential an ear in the direction of the intelligence community. And so from the very beginning, Landsat was a political stepchild, sought by scientists but shunned by the military, claimed by the Interior Department but coveted by Agriculture, a nuisance to NASA and undermined at almost every step of the way by the Bureau of Budget (later the Office of Management and Budget). "There was a lot of pressure *not* to get it off," says Alden Colvocoresses, a senior cartographic expert at the U.S. Geological Survey and, in the 1960s, a military officer on loan to NASA. "The military and the National Security Council didn't like the idea of the civilian community looking at the earth at all. That was *their* prerogative. They wanted to keep this classified." Landsat historian Pamela E. Mack goes so far as to suggest that "NASA may have had a secret agreement with the Department of Defense or the National Security Council to go slowly on earth resources satellites."

Colvocoresses, and many others, credit William Pecora with forcing the issue. Born near Newark, educated at Princeton, and a member of the U.S. fencing team at the 1936 Olympics in Berlin, Pecora was a big-eared, balding, blunt-spoken man with a genial smile. A respected geologist, he joined the USGS in 1939, discovered a new mineral—pecoraite—in Brazil, intended to teach, but got waylaid by the federal bureaucracy; he ended up as director of the U.S. Geological Survey in 1965. From the moment Sputnik went up in 1957, Pecora wanted a satellite to monitor the earth and its resources; when his close aide William Fischer returned with reports from the first Michigan symposium, the desire became an obsession. And when higher-ups in NASA and the government didn't seem to share his enthusiasm, after several years of feasibility studies, Pecora decided to take matters into his own hands. He set up an impromptu and now-legendary press conference on September 20, 1966, at which his boss, Interior Secretary Stewart Udall, announced Interior's plans for the Earth Resources Observation Satellites. The EROS program, Udall said, would be run in cooperation with NASA. This came as a big surprise to NASA, which was pushing a plan for a *manned* observation platform and had little prior warning, apparently, about the press conference. The space agency was committed to manned missions and trying to put a man on the moon, and had no taste for receiving, storing, and analyzing data from an earth-monitoring satellite. Pecora announced that the first satellite could be launched by 1969 at a wildly optimistic cost of only $20 million. The story made the front page of the *New York Times* the following morning. Pecora was delighted. He was also convinced, he told his wife, that he would be fired the following day.

"The next day all hell broke loose," recalls his widow, Wynn Pecora. "The White House was ready to kill him, the Pentagon was ready to kill him, and the State Department was ready to kill him." "NASA and the military intelligence community were furious," confirms Colvocoresses. "The intelligence community felt it could keep a strong handle on NASA, but they were shocked when Interior got involved in this. Pecora nearly got fired, but President Johnson supported his action and so did Congress." Once the idea received an enthusiastic public response, NASA's policymakers decided they wanted a satellite, too, and geared up to coordinate the construction and operation of EROS in 1967 ("That the initials form the name of the Greek god of love and fertility," the *Times* article noted, "is a coincidence"). As Richard Mroczynski, who has worked on Landsat since the first launch, bluntly puts it: "NASA was the reluctant benefactor of a great thing."

Responding to continuing pressure from Interior, NASA began planning for a small unmanned satellite in early 1967. Then, just as the political waters began to calm, a technological dispute erupted. It would turn out to be another example of how a small piece of hardware—a ball bearing, an O-ring, a fan-jet part—can determine the success or failure of a machine, a mission, an entire program.

The argument was all about the mirror. In 1968, out of the blue, NASA received an unsolicited bid from a group of scientists at the Hughes Aircraft Company in El Segundo, California. NASA and the Department of the Interior planned to use television cameras as the main sensors. The Hughes group, headed by a woman named Virginia T. Norwood, wanted to put a different type of mapping device on the proposed satellite. Known as a scanner, it featured that bête noire of aerospace engineers—a moving part. The part that moved was the notorious "banging mirror." It measured nine by thirteen inches, and was designed to slam back and forth thirteen times a second. The Hughes team argued that it would perform better than television cameras.

"We were pushing a scanner because a scanner gives you some advantages," Virginia Norwood explained one day in her office. She is a handsome, robust woman with a hearty smile and a tan that takes longer than a vacation to get; pictures on her office wall established that she was a grandmother, just as technical papers in the literature have long established her crisp competence as an engineer, and you could hear both qualities, the sweetness and the toughness, in her voice. A self-described "Army brat," she was born in Fort Totten, an army base tucked away in a corner of Queens, New York. One of seventy women among five thousand undergraduate and graduate students at the Massachusetts Institute of Technology, she graduated in 1947 with a degree in mathematical physics and sought a job in private industry, only to get a rude introduction to the realities of the American workplace; her salary requirement stunned one prospective employer, who howled, "No woman in our *plant* has ever gotten that kind of money!" So she took a job with the U.S. Army Signal Corps, and worked her way up the electromagnetic ladder, as she puts it, specializing first in antennas, moving up to communications, and finally graduating to optics. Norwood joined Hughes Aircraft in 1954, where she worked for thirty-five years. She contributed to the Surveyor missions to the moon as well as on the microwave circuitry for Falcon missiles. By 1968 she had for many years worked in the space and communications division, where the design for the Landsat scanner was developed.

Norwood and Hughes entered the game late. By 1968 the Interior Department had formally requested congressional money for its Earth Resources Observation Satellites program, and NASA planned to adapt one of the Nimbus weather satellites for the job. The key mapping instrument aboard the satellite would be three RCA television-type cameras known as return beam vidicons, or RBVs. These detectors operated like a camera: they took whole-frame snapshots of the earth from airplanes, and each "saw" a different wavelength of light (green, red, and infrared). "People thought it would be straightforward to adapt that to remote sensing," Virginia Norwood recalls, "but it wasn't so darned straightforward."

In April of 1968, Norwood's group at Hughes first made its unsolicited bid to NASA. The company had developed a different type of meteorological sensor, called a scanner, for the early advanced technology satellite (ATS) weather satellites; this type of detector did not take snapshots of an entire scene. Rather, it scanned the landscape, line by line in rapid succession, as the spacecraft moved over it; computers back on the ground later assembled the complete scene out of the digitized data in each line. "We were an afterthought," Norwood admits. "NASA was planning to use the vidicons, but some of us just felt the scanner was the way to go, so we pounded. We visited people, showed them the idea, demonstrated it."

Since the satellite was destined to be rather small, the Hughes mapping device had to squeeze into what little room was left. The device was a compact, 120-pound package that looked like a telescope that never quite got removed from its packing crate. It possessed a nine-inch mirror much like a Cassegrain telescope; as the satellite flew over the earth and light reflected up from the surface, the infamous moving mirror scanned the landscape underneath it, sweeping back and forth in a motion likened to a person sweeping with a broom while

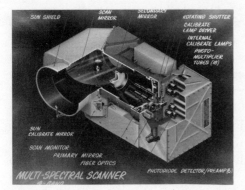

"People were so *emotionally* opposed to a mechanical device," says Virginia Norwood, whose team at Hughes Aircraft Co. designed the first multispectral scanner (MSS), shown here in a promotional illustration. (Hughes Aircraft Co.)

walking across a room; its movement directed lines of light onto a focal point in rapid west-to-east scans that covered approximately 115 miles. They called it the multispectral scanner.

The scanner took big, quick swallows of data. In twenty seconds, the MSS could map a patch of land 100 nautical miles by 100 miles, and in so doing generate 7.6 million digitized picture elements, or pixels, for later visual display. It could swallow all of New Jersey in little more than thirty seconds; it could survey the coastline from Maine to Miami in about six minutes. The scanner resolved objects about 79 meters, a bit smaller than a football field.

But that kind of resolution was not the instrument's strong suit. The scanner, a four-eyed creature, embodied all the research done by the agricultural researchers—Colwell, J. Ralph Shay at Purdue, and Archibald Park at the Department of Agriculture among others; it distinguished four different spectral wave bands of light. The scanner optics directed filtered light over four different detectors; these separated the incoming light waves just as a change separator distinguishes coins, but instead of nickels and dimes and pennies and quarters slipping into their respective slots, different wavelengths of reflected light fit into the separate spectral detectors. Two were for visible light; two were in the near infrared. Not only did each different wavelength create a different picture of the same landscape; analysts back on the ground could mix two, three, or four of those wavelengths together in one map, providing different information about the same landscape. Norwood's group knew how to build a scanner, but they didn't know what spectral bands would convey the best information about the earth, which is why, on one occasion, they carted bags of groceries (tomatoes, bell peppers, brussels sprouts, broccoli, and strawberries) from a market in Santa Barbara back to the lab to measure their spectral signatures.

Each spectral slot had been carefully chosen to tell something unique about the ground it covered. The wavelengths varied by as little .1 micron, or $\frac{1}{10,000}$ of a millimeter, yet divined a rainbow of colors and a pot of gold in terms of information. Norwood quickly learned the immense versatility of the instrument. "The blue band, around .5 micron, is good for water quality," she explains. "The band between .5 and .6 micron gives an indication of the growth stage and vigor of crops. The band from .63 to .69 micron measures chlorophyll absorption. The band from .79 to .90 micron measures the water content of plants; we call that the 'blooming band.' That's where mature plants are brightest in the infrared spectrum, and it's a measure that can be used to assess biomass and stress. That is why false-color maps of vegetation are so red even though they're showing something green. And the band from 1.55 to 1.75 microns measures soil moisture. This is also the band that distinguishes clouds from snow and is used to measure the snowpack." The Hughes group crammed all this into an ambitious, six-band scanner. Then NASA, short of space on a satellite that was designed only to house the TV cameras, sent Norwood back to the drawing board. In 1971 the Hughes team came back with the more modest four-band multispectral scanner (a seven-band Thematic Mapper went up on *Landsat 4* and *Landsat 5*).

The Hughes scanner triggered quite a debate. It was one of those behind-the-scenes, nitty-gritty, technical contretemps to which the general public is completely oblivious; yet, decades later, anyone who has marveled at the images from space can be grateful that the debate turned out the way it did. NASA scientists and mappers from the U.S. Geological Survey favored the vidicon cameras. Critics of the scanner expressed grave concern about that banging mirror and about the reliability of the mapping information it would provide. "Mapmakers like myself were very suspicious of the multispectral scanner, which we could not believe would have geometric integrity," admits Colvocoresses. "We were wrong on that one." "People were so *emotionally* opposed to a mechanical device," Norwood recalls. One wonders if the MSS might have gotten a slightly warmer reception if the engineer arguing its merits had been a man and not a woman.

In any event, the argument raged for well over a year and turned out to be unexpectedly crucial. "When Landsat was being conceived, the argument was: should we use RBVs or these newfangled, untested instruments on this satellite?" recalls David Landgrebe of Purdue University, an expert in the agricultural applications of remote sensing and an early advocate of the controversial scanner. "The whole community felt much stronger about a framing type of instrument than a line-by-line instrument, because their background was in aerial photography. Naturally, that was something they were more comfortable with. The government, in its usual fashion, decided to compromise and put on both."

So on July 23, 1972, a gloomy, overcast day in California, dignitaries and scientists (including Virginia Norwood) gathered at Vandenberg Air Force Base near Lompoc to watch as a Delta rocket lifted a refitted weather satellite, now bureaucratically burdened with both the vidicon cameras and the multispectral scanner, through the low cloud deck and into what science writer Boyce Rensberger called "a new era of earth exploration." This first Earth Resources Technology Satellite (later renamed *Landsat 1*) settled into an orbit over the poles approximately 570 miles above the earth. The orbit design itself was an unheralded work of art: as the satellite descended from North Pole to South over North America, for example, the earth would be spinning, so that the satellite's mapping instruments would cut diagonal swaths, and in such a manner the satellite could cover the entire planet every eighteen days. Moreover, every time the satellite crossed the equator, the local time was approximately 9:30 A.M., so each location was always photographed under identical lighting conditions. So great was the pressure to launch that there was an improvised quality to it—the initial data, for example, would be beamed down to a computer originally designed to write checks.

The raging debate over the mirror resolved itself within hours of the launch. The TV cameras became afflicted with what officials later described as an "unexplained electrical problem"; within a month of launch, mission controllers quietly shut down all three vidicons. The scanner, on the other hand, worked perfectly; designed to last one year, it was operating ten years later. David Landgrebe, an advocate for the scanner, would later remark: "If they had decided to go just with the RBVs, I don't know that we'd have heard any more about this enterprise." Allen H. Watkins, who heads the EROS Data Center in Sioux Falls, South Dakota, where Landsat data and images are archived, says that would not have terminated the project. "But if ERTS had not functioned, if the multispectral scanner had not been on board," he admits, "it would have been very damaging."

The gloomiest thing about the launch was that it had been delayed

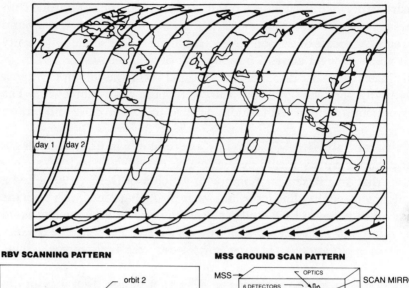

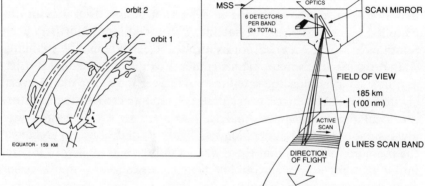

RBV SCANNING PATTERN

MSS GROUND SCAN PATTERN

Orbit design as a work of art: *(above)* Every eighteen days, the north-to-south polar orbit of *Landsat 1* passed over the same territory at the same time of day, assuring identical light conditions for all the images. The return beam vidicons *(below, left)* took snapshot-like frames of the ground; line by line, the multispectral scanner's "banging mirror" *(below, right)* composed scenes of 10,000 square nautical miles. The controversial MSS outperformed the RBVs on *Landsat 1,* ending a pitched technological debate. (Based on NASA diagrams)

---

for several months because of technical problems, and just four days before the successful lift-off, William Pecora died in a Washington hospital of surgical complications at the age of fifty-nine. He never saw his bird off, but one prediction he made would come true within a matter of days. "Sophisticated in program execution it is indeed," he promised, "but the products of its efforts are practical and wide-ranging—and *understandable*."

One of the most powerful benefits of a map is its sheer "under-standability." The human eye seems to have an aptitude, an under-standing, of what a map conveys, and what makes it beautiful, and that seems especially true of Landsat images, which were immediately understood and appreciated by an immensely large audience. The first image from *Landsat 1* came down two days after launch. It showed the Lake Texoma area on the Oklahoma-Texas border, about seventy-five miles north of Dallas. David Landgrebe compared the image with what mappers call "ground truth"—knowledge about the types of trees and crops in a given region of land, for example. *Landsat 1* passed muster. In its first three months of operation, the satellite showered fifty-three thousand photomaps down to earth.

No one could have predicted in 1972 just how versatile *Landsat 1* and its successors would prove to be, or how many unexpected and sometimes profound insights they would fire down to us in their eighty-four-megabits-per-second cataract of data. The most straightforward Landsat images belong to the grand tradition of geographical and topographic maps; in the crisp folds and wrinkles of mountain ranges, the shimmer of shallow seas, the traditional iconography of mapmak-ing is preserved. Photomaps of this precision virtually merged the ancient cartographic skill of scaled illustration with the photograph: by calibrating with ground coordinates, the picture becomes the map. Paul D. Lowman, Jr., a research scientist at NASA's Goddard Space Flight Center, remarked, "Our first discovery from ERTS is that all our maps, topographic as well as geographic, are out of date." Even the defense establishment, once a bitter adversary, had to agree: the CIA and the Defense Mapping Agency began to use Landsat data because it was cheaper than data acquired by classified satellite, and the military has ultimately become Landsat's heaviest user.

Landsat stood traditional cartography on its ear. By seeing the world in electromagnetic increments beyond the normal range of human vision, Landsat revealed whole new worlds hidden within the folds of a familiar world we thought we knew so well. It was no great surprise that Landsat, from 570 miles up in space, could discern the health of corn plants on a half-acre plot of land in Iowa, could deter-mine which were suffering from corn blight and where a fungal infesta-

The Sierra Nevada range of California separates Mono Lake *(top)* from the agriculturally rich Central Valley *(lower left)* in a Landsat scene composed by the multispectral scanner in October 1979. (USGS/EROS Data Center)

tion appeared to be gaining a foothold. That is exactly what it was designed to do.

But even the most visionary and optimistic were surprised at how well it could detect a pink bollworm infestation in the cotton crops of California's Imperial Valley; that it would show the extent of defoliation by gypsy moths in a Pennsylvania forest; that it would outline the perimeter of grizzly bear habitats in Montana; that its infrared sensors would detect the ominous glow of the damaged reactor at the Chernobyl nuclear plant in 1986 and by similar means predict the imminent eruption of a Guatemalan volcano; that it could detect skid marks left by jets at the ends of airport runways and the morning shadow cast by the Washington Monument; that conservation groups would use its data to map the habitats of waterfowl in North America, and that states would use those photogenic stains of pollution, like the slick spotted in the New York Bight in 1972, to sue private industry for illegal chemical discharge; that entomologists could predict mosquito populations in inland Florida and epidemiologists could predict outbreaks of *Fasciola hepatica,* a liver fluke afflicting cattle, in the coastal zones of Louisiana; that a satellite could be used to gauge the affluence of urban and suburban neighborhoods (by measuring the amount of green space) and to chart the spread of that suburban fungus, the shopping mall; that it could look down at a stretch of coastline, in New York or Florida, and show us the stains of careless modern industrialism upon our waters. For a relatively modest cost, roughly $1.5 billion spread over twenty years, we have procured 2.5 million pictures, the most comprehensive and informative photo album of the planet ever assembled. And, military objections notwithstanding, the most democratic. Any citizen from any nation could obtain one of the original Landsat images of any spot on earth for $1.25.

With the success of *Landsat 1,* NASA managed to find funding for additional satellites. *Landsat 2* went up in January 1975, *Landsat 3* in March 1978. The improved Thematic Mapper, again engineered and built by Virginia Norwood's group at Hughes, went up with *Landsat 4* (in July 1982) and *Landsat 5* (in March 1984), providing even more sparkling images. But the administration of Jimmy Carter instituted a phased plan to privatize Landsat, and that operation was accelerated, with perhaps ruthless dispatch, by the Reagan administration, which transferred operational responsibility for the satellites in 1985 to the Earth Observation Satellite Company, or EOSAT. Landsat was an orphan once again. John Pike, a space analyst for the Federation of American Scientists, says the "mania for commercialization in the early 1980s represented the triumph of ideology over common sense," and in the case of Landsat was "like throwing the thing into the deep end of a swimming pool and telling it to sink or swim, without even checking to see if there was any water in the pool."

An administrative orphan since inception, Landsat faces an even more hostile and indifferent world now. There is competition from abroad, in the form of the French SPOT remote-sensing satellite (which provides ten-meter resolution using an American-developed solid-state detector called a multilinear array), and there is indifference at home, in the form of a Congress that tried to shut down *Landsat 4* and *Landsat 5* in 1989 to save money, to say nothing of a blasé public that has perhaps seen too many calendars and posters. Echoing its birthing pains, Landsat's very existence is again at the mercy of the political process. Only those people with long memories appreciated the irony in a short story about Landsat in the *New York Times* in November of 1989; the item reported that government officials were considering a proposal that would place the greatest civilian mapping enterprise in the history of civilization under the control and jurisdiction of the Department of Defense, whose interest has only increased since the Persian Gulf War. While Landsat's fate remains uncertain, the scientists—as they always do—are dreaming the next big cartographic dream: a stereo mapping satellite that can make three-dimensional maps of the earth.

Despite its many well-documented problems, Landsat was a spectacular vindication of remote sensing. One could argue that the greatest benefits of the space program have come not from hurling a few men and women into space for a few spectacular photo ops and long-distance sound bites, but from those satellites that, year in and year out, steadily and unspectacularly help us understand our planet better, improve lives, and, as in a recent program to identify breeding areas of the insect that causes sleeping sickness, even save lives. There is a place for manned flight, but over the long haul it can't compete with the satellites. Former astronaut Walter Schirra admitted as much back in 1972, when he said, "We should start looking down instead of up."

"We should send a man up when he can do something that an unmanned thing cannot do, or a robot cannot do," Virginia Norwood lamented one afternoon in her office. "Manned missions are *so* expensive, but they seem to stimulate greater interest in the public. The man on the street is not the least bit interested in Landsat. He doesn't even know what it is." That public indifference may be the most unfortunate thing of all, because as two decades' worth of remarkable images attest, Landsat has always had the right stuff, and we can now see that, compared with the space shuttle, it has the right stuff at the right price.

3. The Hidden Crucible

GRAVITY ANOMALIES AND
A MAP OF THE OCEAN FLOOR

||||||||||

Those images that yet
Fresh images beget,
That dolphin-torn, that gong-tormented
  sea.

—William Butler Yeats,
"Byzantium"

The current revolution in the mapping of the ocean floor began one day around 1976, when Donald Turcotte, a geophysicist at Cornell University, returned from a meeting at the National Aeronautics and Space Administration with a two-inch-thick pile of photocopies. Looking like a series of electrocardiogram lines with latitude and longitude, the xeroxes represented data compiled by a NASA satellite called *Geos 3.* Launched in 1975, in the afterglow of the Apollo moon missions and Skylab, *Geodetic Earth Observing Satellite 3* was a mere hiccup in the space program, but during its three years of service the satellite nonetheless cast an unusual technological eye upon the earth's surface, especially the earth's oceans.

The satellite carried an instrument known as a radar altimeter, which bounced short pulses called microwaves off the surface of the sea. Knowing the satellite's exact orbit and measuring the amount of time it took for the radio waves to bounce back up to within a thousandth of a second, scientists could calculate the height of the sea surface at any given spot. Common sense suggests that, wind and waves notwithstanding, the altitude of the ocean at any given point is going to be—no surprise—sea level. Geophysicists, however, have long known of subtle but significant variations in the sea surface—upswellings and depressions of as much as a hundred meters. They knew, too, that these variations are clues about the topography of the ocean floor underneath. And so Turcotte dumped the mass of satellite data on the desk of one of his graduate students, a tall, lanky, and laconic midwesterner named William F. Haxby, and said, "What can we do with these?"

Haxby's immediate impression was, not much. And in the cartographic sense, he was right. *Geos 3* represented the leading edge of a new technology that promised to cut through the opaque window of seawater obscuring the seafloor below, but it still offered a rather dull blade. This was a young revolution, beginning with the first crude altimeter that went up with Skylab in 1972. With the launch of *Geos 3* three years later, the instrumentation on the satellite, crude as it was, represented a tenfold improvement in accuracy over the Skylab altimeter.

None of this seemed especially intriguing to Haxby, whose interest in projects tended to evolve in rather glacial time frames. This was a fellow who waited until his fifth year as an undergraduate at the University of Minnesota to settle on a major. It turned out to be geology. Extremely bright and maddeningly modest, he began to establish a reputation as one of those researchers who love to do creative work and hate the chore of writing it up. He had until then focused primarily on the forces that wrinkle and upheave the crust of the earth on the continents, which have the deceptively misleading advantage of leaving their signature above water and thus being easily accessible to study. Haxby knew that those same forces buckle and bruise the ocean floor as well, and he began to realize that studying those forces under water, oddly enough, might be simpler with the newer technologies of measurement. Now, four years into a graduate school career that was already a hodgepodge of projects, he agreed to take a look at the *Geos 3* data.

He concentrated on the North Atlantic, but he never produced a map out of the data. He merely convinced himself that there was a mathematical relationship between the height of the sea surface and the density, the gravity pull, of the sea surface below, which, run through a series of calculations called a "power series expansion," produced an extraordinary result: you could infer ocean floor topography from variations in the sea surface. By carefully measuring and analyzing surface variations as small as a foot or two, you could infer entire mountain ranges, valleys, subtle seafloor undulations. It was a very useful exercise in working out ways to handle altimeter data. By the time he was done, Haxby had, in the grand tradition of graduate studies, acquired a skill for which there was neither practical demand nor pending application. He was among a handful of people in the world who were capable of converting satellite microwave altimeter data into useful form. Unfortunately, there were no satellites with radar altimeters, and no crying need for altimeter maps.

Then, in 1978, NASA launched another satellite, called Seasat. It lasted barely as long as a June bug before blinking out. For Bill Haxby's purposes, however, it lasted long enough.

The bird's-eye view, paradoxically enough, has often afforded an important scientific crow's nest to geologists curious about the sea, and it was while gazing out the window of an airplane in the late 1950s, looking down upon the Hawaiian Islands, that a geophysicist named J. Tuzo Wilson saw in their strange erosion patterns the final piece in a jigsaw puzzle the size of the globe. It was an insight built on centuries of patient mapmaking of the ocean floor.

To say that 70 percent of the earth's surface is covered by water is simply another way of saying that 70 percent of the clues about the geological processes shaping the planet have been hidden from scientific scrutiny. Limpid and transparent when cupped by the hand, the ocean's waters become stubbornly opaque at a depth of two hundred meters, impervious to light and the nosy inquisitions of oceanographers and geophysicists. Imagining what the seafloor looks like has been, to the scientists who study it, a bit like trying to decipher a fingerprint while looking through ten feet of smoked glass.

For centuries those clues remained buried under a mile or more of water and sedimentary muck. Nor, to be honest, was there much compelling reason to determine the topography and structure of the ocean floor. From the earliest days of antiquity, it was commerce, not science, that defined interest about the oceans, and thus curiosity about it tended to have a bottom-line practicality. True, Ferdinand Magellan did try to measure the bottom of the Pacific Ocean in 1521 (he declared it "immeasurably deep"), but measurements of the ocean depths did not much improve upon the traditional "heaving the lead"—dropping a weighted line of hemp into the water to determine its depth—for the next three hundred years. In any event, sailors concerned themselves mostly with the coastal margins and harbors of continents, for this was where a ship was likely to get into trouble. Only in 1840 did James Clark Ross inaugurate the era of deep-sea sounding when he took a depth reading of 4,365 meters in the South Atlantic; he also, alas, inaugurated the era of errors in deep-sea soundings by exaggerating the depth by about 600 meters.

It was not until the middle of the nineteenth century that scientists attempted to measure the mid-ocean depths in any systematic way. In 1854, Matthew Fontaine Maury of the United States produced the first contour map of the floor of the Atlantic Ocean. With a paucity of data and a surfeit of self-promotion, Maury's map nonetheless provided the first hint of an underwater mountain range running north to south down the middle of the Atlantic. The next generation of charts took advantage of a technical revolution in measurement. In 1922, acoustic methods of measuring depth were first tested; sound waves could be bounced off the ocean floor, and the travel time could be mathematically computed to reveal the depth. The advent of submarine warfare gave this information military as well as commercial import; and the submarine era in turn ushered in an atmosphere of military secrecy about seafloor cartography that would haunt William Haxby and other would-be mappers of his generation. The acoustic maps, too, showed that same large, curious underwater mountain range running down through the Atlantic.

It wasn't until after World War II that deep-sea echo sounders of sufficient precision became available for use by geophysicists to map the bottom of the sea. They provided ever-greater accuracy, but at a price. It took a long time to make the measurements. Lumbering armadas of research vessels chummed the sea with sound, passing back and forth over the ocean floor much as computer printers trace lines on a page, though of course much more slowly; and just as slowly, a picture began to crystallize into one of the great theoretical insights of twentieth-century science.

The theory, known as plate tectonics, took visual seed in the minds of scientists as a result of maps published during exploration's first great age of discovery. The seventeenth-century English philosopher Francis Bacon had remarked upon the great complementarity— the "fit"—of the eastern coastline of South America and western coastline of Africa. This remained more an item of curiosity than an avenue of research until 1912, when a German meteorologist named Alfred Wegener advanced the argument—skimpy in fact and detail,

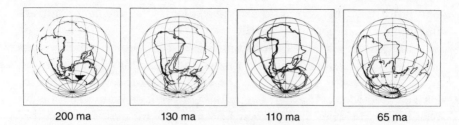

200 ma   130 ma   110 ma   65 ma

"An explanation which explains nothing that we want to explain": Alfred
Wegener's theory of continental drift inspired skepticism, but geophysicists
now estimate that the breakup of the supercontinent Pangaea (200 million
years ago) began about 130 million years ago. By 65 million years ago South
America and Africa had separated, Antarctica had spun over the South Pole,
and India *(lower right)* had begun its epic tectonic journey to Asia. (John L.
LaBrecque, Lamont-Doherty Geological Observatory)

---

correct in its intuition and thrust—that continents were not fixed, but
moved like huge ponderous rafts upon the crust of the planet; tens of
millions of years earlier, much of the earth's land mass had been
grouped in one great supercontinent that Wegener called Pangaea, but
over geologic time the continents had drifted apart and floated over the
oceans, occasionally bumping into other land masses with cataclysmic
upheavals of terrain. The French geophysicist Xavier Le Pichon has
handily summarized Wegener's thesis thus: "The continents would
plow through the ocean floor, generating mountain belts on their bows
and disseminating small pieces as island arcs behind their sterns." The
Himalayas, extending Le Pichon's analogy, were titanic waves piled up
on the bow of India, which according to plate tectonics slammed into
the Asian subcontinent about 50 million years ago.

Wegener had observed intriguing geologic and paleobotanical
similarities between parts of Africa and South America, but his
"mobilist" theory suffered from the absence of a credible force that
could move such massive slabs of crust. To many, the theory suffered
even more from sheer implausibility. Just as Einstein dismissed the
probabilistic nature of quantum physics by asserting "God does not
play dice," geologists seemed to reject Wegener's mobilist ideas by
saying "God does not do jigsaw puzzles." One leading geologist dismissed continental drift in the 1920s as an "explanation which explains
nothing that we want to explain." It was an idea not only ahead of its
time, but, more unfortunately for its creator, an idea well ahead of the
technology that could confirm it. When Wegener died in 1930, the

obituaries cited his reputation as an explorer of Greenland, not as the originator of continental drift.

But just as a map can sometimes lead to a theory, a theory can sometimes guide the creation of a map, and something like that happened in the 1940s and 1950s in the work of Maurice Ewing, Bruce Heezen, and Marie Tharp at Columbia University's Lamont-Doherty Observatory. Ewing and Heezen had mapped the Atlantic seafloor using shipboard sonar measurements. When Tharp began to plot the data, she not only confirmed the long, thin underwater mountain chain first seen by Maury a century earlier; she noticed a small depression, almost like a gutter or jagged aqueduct, that ran down its middle. This so-called "rift valley" coincided with unusually heavy submarine earthquake and volcano activity, and in 1956 Heezen and Tharp concluded that this structure was not unique to the Atlantic. They made the startling proposal that such a mid-ocean ridge, as they called it, bisected all the world's oceans—it ran down the Atlantic, south of Africa, up the Indian Ocean, and across the Pacific, like the curved seam of a baseball. Heezen and Tharp claimed the mid-ocean ridge was the largest structure on earth, a mountain range that ran some 65,000 kilometers (nearly 40,000 miles). Heezen went a little further: he believed that these seams marked the place where the earth's hot interior mantle issued out to form a constant, self-renewing, expanding crust. Heezen later described it as "a wound that never heals."

An explanation for this feature awaited the famous self-described "essay in geopoetry" ventured by Princeton geophysicist Harry Hess. In 1960, Hess integrated several theoretical strands into an astounding idea: the mid-ocean ridges, he suggested, formed over rising convective currents in the earth's hot mantle, which brought hot lava to the seams and caused the underwater volcanos and earthquakes. Moreover, the lava would be extruded—squeezed out like a flat plane of lasagna— from the rift valleys and would spread in both directions, paving the ocean floor with fresh crust (another scientist, Robert Dietz, later labeled this "seafloor spreading"). Hess's thesis in turn awaited experimental confirmation, and indeed two Cambridge geophysicists, Fred Vine and Drummond Matthews, presented paleomagnetic evidence in 1963 proving that the mid-ocean seams marked the boundaries between vast "plates" of crust, that new crust slowly emerged from these seams in conveyor-belt fashion, and that the plates steadily edged away from the seams. Unfortunately, as one contemporary recalls, this paper was "completely ignored." Not until 1968 did the doubts dissipate.

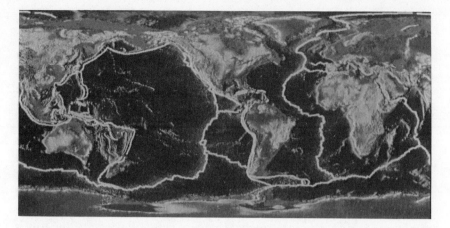

The earth's surface is divided into crustal plates, the boundaries of which appear as white lines. (NOAA/National Geophysical Data Center)

Seafloor spreading took Wegener's notion of continental drift a step further. It wasn't the continents per se that moved; they were just passive passengers atop vast sheets of ocean crust, exuded at a steady pace. This motion, this *tectonic* movement of plates, led to significant geologic jostlings, which nature brings to our attention in the form of volcanoes and earthquakes. Which brings us back to the young Canadian geophysicist named J. Tuzo Wilson who, peering out his airplane window at the Hawaiian Islands, realized that the easternmost islands appeared less eroded, and thus younger, than the islands that lay to the northwest. "It was very obvious that Oahu was deeply eroded and gullied," Wilson recalls. "The main volcano was deeply eroded, whereas the main volcanos on the newer islands were *not* deeply eroded." He realized that the entire Hawaiian archipelago sat on a gigantic Pacific plate, which crept in a northwesterly direction and passed over a hot spot deep in the earth's mantle. That hot spot acted like a blowtorch that volcanically coughed up islands every now and then, a Maui here, a Molokai there. From this insight Wilson went on to spell out the rules of plate tectonics, showing that as the plate in the Pacific crept eastward, it collided with the plate upon which North America floats and deflected underneath it in a deep underwater trench. We now realize that the coastal mountains, from the Cascades in the Pacific Northwest to the Coast Range in California, as well as coastal volcanoes like Mount St. Helens and coastal earthquakes like the ones that almost monthly rattle the windows and nerves of Southern California—all these geologic grindings and grunts reflect the enormous pressure and friction of two huge plates rubbing against each other. Tuzo Wilson went so far as to predict a regular cycle, requiring about 200 million years, during which the continents would separate, drift apart, and float back together, reuniting in a supercontinent comprising North America, South America, Africa, and Europe.

It soon became obvious that the tectonic borders of the planet, a more enduring and significant set of boundaries than any political demarcation, lay buried under seawater many fathoms deep. Much of this territory had been mapped by the plodding ships dragging their microphones over the "gong-tormented sea." By the 1970s the theory of plate tectonics, though widely accepted, was still warm to the touch after a decade of hot debate. But since it was apparent that the ocean floor was the crucible in which the earth remade itself, great anticipation attended the June 26, 1978 launch of the Seasat satellite from Vandenberg Air Force Base in California. Equipped with five ocean-monitoring sensors, including a state-of-the-art microwave altimeter, Seasat promised to provide the most wide-ranging and accurate mapping data of the seafloor ever obtained.

Then early in October of 1978, barely three months into its mission, the satellite experienced a system failure and died.

Almost to the day that Seasat died, William Haxby reported to his new job as a research scientist at the Lamont-Doherty Geological Observatory, a cluster of buildings observing, among other things, the Hudson River in Palisades, New York. The previous year he had received his Ph.D. from Cornell and had just completed a one-year postdoctoral fellowship at Oxford University. An admirer of Ewing, Heezen, and Tharp, he hadn't the slightest inkling that he would follow in their rather ample footsteps, or that Seasat's skeletal data set would give him the opportunity.

It was Ewing's philosophy that the earth revealed its geophysical secrets only with global research, and no instrument offered a more global data set than Seasat. The satellite was equipped with a microwave altimeter that was about twice as sensitive as the one in Geos 3. From an altitude of five hundred miles, Seasat could measure variations with a sensitivity down to five centimeters—about the length of a pen cap. Seasat managed to log 25 million kilometers of tracks across the ocean; it would have taken a ship like the one used by Ewing and Heezen 142 years to cover the same territory that the satellite scanned

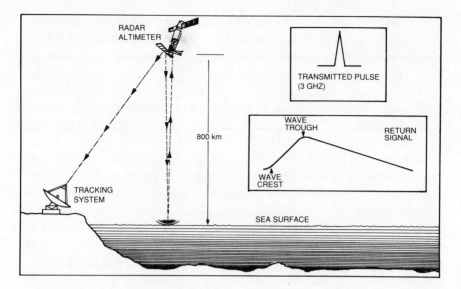

During its short-lived summer of 1978, Seasat's altimeter fired one thousand radar pulses at the sea surface every second and detected variations of 1 to 2 inches.

in three months. Every second, Seasat fired off a thousand pulses of radar at the sea below, generating 25-to-30 million measurements of the ocean surface. Then, three months into its projected three-to-five-year mission, it simply stopped sending signals back to earth. There were anguished meetings and bureaucratic breast-beating and retrospective analyses, and, as Haxby recalls, the consensus emerged that "everything worked beautifully, except the power supply." When the batteries in Seasat died, Haxby says, so did interest in funding the analysis of what little information it did manage to collect. And so the data that would ultimately produce one of the most detailed, not to mention beautiful, maps of the ocean floor in the history of cartography languished in cans for lack of money.

Nor was that the only complication. Just as intelligence officials opposed a civilian satellite like Landsat, military officials did not want Seasat data released at all. In measuring the gravity effect of the ocean floor, the altimeter aboard the satellite also measured areas that could affect inertial guidance systems, and thus the accuracy, of ballistic missiles. In addition, accurate seafloor maps of the U.S. coastline, it was argued, would allow hostile vessels to track American submarines better as they left their ports. This debate, initiated even before the launch of Seasat, continued several years after its demise. It fell to a former naval officer named Jimmy Carter to release the Seasat data. In late 1979, Seasat's meager gleanings—fourteen computer tapes—arrived in Haxby's office at Lamont. No one, not even Haxby, expected much to come of it. "I simply expected an incremental improvement over the *Geos 3* data," he recalls. The last thing he expected to come out of the incomplete jumble of data was a map.

Any map that emerges from the use of radar altimeter data is philosophically akin to the famous René Magritte painting of a pipe, which is entitled *This Is Not a Pipe*. Haxby's map, which appears to show contours of ocean floor topography, in reality shows something entirely different. It shows variations in the gravity field. "The shape of the ocean surface is determined by gravity," Haxby explains, and thus fluctuations in the height of the ocean surface, measured by the microwave altimeter, reflect underlying variations in the gravity field of the ocean floor. An underwater volcano, known as a seamount, generates a strong gravity field and can cause the sea surface to rise thirty feet above average; deep valleys in the seafloor, with their low gravity fields, can cause smooth dips to a similar degree. If the measurements are sensitive enough, and uniform enough, every little variation in the ocean surface will reflect some significant wrinkle or berm or majestic underwater tor on the seafloor. With Seasat's accuracy Haxby figured he could manipulate the data to spot features as small as three thousand feet in height and perhaps twelve miles long.

The influence that gravity exerts on sea surface height is counterintuitive—that is, not what we would intuitively expect. We think of gravity as an attractive force, one that pulls, so you would think that a large underwater gravity field would pull down in a way that causes a depression—a drop in altitude—of the sea surface. That is not quite the case. Gravity tugs in a direction that is perpendicular to the surface of its mass, and so above a seamount, water is slightly tugged straight down not only from the small area directly above the peak of the underwater mountain, but tugged in perpendicularly to the much more massive flanks of the hill, and it is especially the broad flanks of underwater mountains that gather water over the seamount and cause a slight bulge. Similarly, a rift in the seafloor would cause a slight drop in sea surface. The variations suggested underlying "gravity anomalies" because they depart from what would be a uniform gravity field. "There are gravity anomalies everywhere," Haxby says. "They're not so anomalous. But they're all different."

At first, Haxby intended only to examine a remote area in the southernmost South Atlantic around Antarctica, which was not routinely accessible to ships. John L. LaBrecque, a research scientist at Lamont, had been assigned to create an atlas for scientific ocean drilling around Antarctica, and early in 1981 he asked Haxby to make a gravity map of the area. Haxby spent nearly a year just tidying up the data. He had to average out numbers and smooth in the gaps where the satellite tracks did not overlap, gaps that sometimes ranged ninety miles across. He had to account for possible distortions in sea surface height introduced by winds, waves, currents, tides, and barometric pressure. Using a DEC Vax computer in the geoscience building, grabbing computer time whenever he could (which was often late at night), he refined each data point. Then he plotted this initial data as a series of black-and-white "profiles" on his computer screen—an old-fashioned contour map, as it were, on an electronic piece of paper.

Late one night in the spring of 1982, around 1 A.M., John LaBrecque was working in the computer room when Haxby stuck his head in the door and said, "Why don't you take a look at what I've got?"

"He produced a map of the Agulhas Basin, just south of Africa," LaBrecque recalls. It was an area of intense geological interest, for it featured a series of ridges showing where the continent of Africa had pulled away from South America. "Bill showed me a contoured gravity field of that area, and I was astounded. The gravity field looked a *lot* like the morphology that we had been expecting to see." LaBrecque asked him to crank up the resolution of the contours. "He went off for ten minutes and came back and said, 'Look at this.' The ridge structure was just popping out of the data set. It was really looking good." LaBrecque asked him to try one more time. Haxby went off to his computer for a few more minutes and increased the resolution a little bit more. "We could actually see structure," LaBrecque recalls; eight years after that singular night, there is still wonder in his voice. "It was just a miracle. It was like he had drained the water out of the ocean."

Within three or four days, Haxby had produced a black-and-white map of the Agulhas Basin. Next he assigned colors to the contours of the Agulhas map. Having figured out the resolution and color scheme, he managed to produce a color map of the entire ocean floor within two or three months (see color illustration on cover). "Suddenly, we had a map of the world's ocean basins, something we'd never had before," LaBrecque says. Haxby presented the map in public for the first time at a meeting of the American Geophysical Union in San

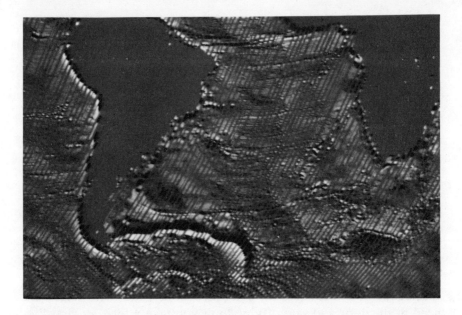

A map emerges: in what he calls the "venetian blind effect," William F. Haxby began to detect hints of topography in the profiles measured by Seasat, even though there were obvious gaps in the coverage. (W. Haxby)

Francisco in December of 1982; as the *New York Times* reported, the map "created a sensation." It was indeed, as LaBrecque suggests, the cartographic equivalent of pulling a plug and letting all the water drain out of the oceans. Most of all, it was beautiful.

There is a tendency to view it as a lovely extension of Heezen and Tharp's superb maps of the 1950s, but Charles Drake of Dartmouth University, one of geophysics' elder statesmen, makes the point that the earlier maps, because of insufficient data, were "extremely subjective" and that Heezen and Tharp "filled in the gaps according to how they thought it must look." The Haxby map truly represents a new way of mapping. "First of all," Drake says, "you could get a picture of the seafloor just by measuring small changes in the level of the sea surface. That's remarkable. It used to take us a hundred years to come up with maps of the seafloor. Now, data from a couple of satellites flying around for a couple of months show the same thing. *That's* remarkable. Secondly, it showed us some things that we didn't know about, especially in the southern hemisphere, which we might never have found out about because it's expensive to do. So it filled in parts of the map."

"The progress toward the mapping was accidental," Haxby says in retrospect. "I began to derive information about the two-dimensional gravity field. There was actually not a mistake, but a *surprise* when, trying different ways of displaying the data, I discovered that it looked very much like an image. It was not so much that I saw unexpected features. It was mainly that I could see everything in a way that I could interpret with a minimum amount of effort. It was like seeing a picture. And displaying data as images is much easier than drawing contour maps. I didn't set out to make beautiful maps of the earth's gravitational field. Before then I was making mainly just contour maps, black-and-white contour maps. Which showed the same information, but you had to work harder to perceive it. Once I started generating the images, it was an obvious extension to derive a global map, and add color. Suddenly you didn't have to work hard at all. It made everything very simple."

The great virtue of a map is its ability to tell a complex story in a single visual swallow. The Haxby map told at a glance the theory of plate tectonics. This theory didn't need the Haxby map for scientific proof, but this map may well be the loveliest, most detailed, visually richest confirmation of the theory, and it is important not least because it so beautifully reaffirms the fact that the engine driving dynamic geologic change on earth does not lie on land, so convenient to geophysical measurement, but in those deep hot spots first noticed by Tuzo Wilson. Haxby's map thematically reversed centuries of terrestrial bias. The continents faded into flat, dark monotones, just as the oceans had been blued into featureless anonymity on so many maps of centuries past. It was the seafloor that stood out in relief.

To look at this map is to see geology as a movie caught in freeze-frame. With just a little imagination, you can see the earth's twenty-odd plates in motion. It is a theater of activity normally hidden from view, where the dueling scars measure hundreds of miles in length, where beneath a mile or so of sediment, the seafloor is grooved and wrinkled like elephant hide, resilient yet traumatized by cataclysmic forces reshaping the planet, the skin registering each gouge mark and fracture zone as tectonic memory.

With just a little knowledge of geology, the picture manages to explain even more. During a recent visit I made to Lamont-Doherty,

Bill Haxby invited me back to his office. He is in the oceanography building now, which enjoys the most privileged site, on a highpoint of the Palisades overlooking the Hudson River (its position is so prominent that when it was first built, a wealthy family living across the river complained that the yellow brick building marred the view, so it has ever since been painted green on the side facing the river). But the only view from Haxby's office is into his nineteen-inch computer screen. It is a small, windowless room with orange carpeting, an old oak armchair in one corner, the computer screen in the other, a rack full of the Seasat tapes, and a sign on the door: GRAVITY. IT ISN'T JUST A GOOD IDEA. IT'S THE LAW.

He called up an image of the seafloor map. Its orange-and-blue features, astonishingly sharp, appear especially realistic because Haxby, with Olympian imagination and computer dexterity, has electronically fixed a permanent sun in the northern sky, so that the geologic ridges and valleys are all lit as if in the afternoon light. All the stitchwork of plate tectonics shows up on the globe. There is the long mid-Atlantic ridge, the boundary line separating the plates of North America and Africa. These two plates are moving apart at a speed of about two centimeters a year. In a million years, they will have have moved about 12½ miles apart; or, considered another way, they've moved 33 feet since Columbus first set sail for the New World, 25 feet since the Pilgrims arrived at Plymouth Rock, about 4½ feet since the Boston Red Sox last won a World Series, not quite 27 inches since the Dodgers left Brooklyn.

There are the deep trenches, such as the one off the coast of Oregon and Washington, where the eastward-creeping Pacific Ocean crust dives under North America. And throughout the ocean basin, there are fracture zones, a kind of seismic track left behind by continents in motion. Haxby discovered another interesting feature in the Agulhas Basin, that area in the South Atlantic off the southwestern tip of Africa. Through it runs a thin line resembling a mid-ocean ridge. It is now believed to be the scar left in the crust about 130 million years ago as Africa, South America, and Antarctica, once all clumped together in the supercontinent known as Pangaea, began to pull apart. This primordial seam, buried under hundreds of feet of sediment, had never been seen before. It showed up as a gravity anomaly.

The Indian Ocean, too, reveals itself as a theater of violent activity. The crust is wrinkled like an accordion in the seafloor south of India and Sri Lanka, visually suggestive of the power of the Indian plate as it smashes into the Indian subcontinent. Farther south a fracture zone hints at the time when present-day India separated from Antarctica, perhaps 150 million years ago. Its ten-thousand-mile journey left a kind of tire track in the seafloor until India plowed into Asia some 50 million years ago. Haxby has also looked for evidence of a huge submarine crater that might mark the spot where an asteroid struck the earth 65 million years ago, according to a popular theory, and knocked out the dinosaurs. "Nothing earth-shattering" is how he describes the preliminary results.

Finally, there are hints of the invisible engines driving the movement of the earth's massive plates. "In this part of the world," Haxby explains, pointing to an area in the central Pacific, "there's an impression of lineations in this east-southeasterly direction. The direction we would *expect* lineations to be in is the east-northeast direction. These are very prominent ridges related to fracture zones. The ridges are fairly well understood, but this subtle texture in the central Pacific was a surprise." Haxby and colleague Jeffrey Weissel now suspect that these fine gravity patterns mark the location of what are called "convective cells." These are powerful upwellings of hot, partly liquid rock from perhaps thirty to ninety miles beneath the ocean floor. (The following chapter describes efforts to map convection in the earth's interior.)

Haxby makes no extraordinary claims for the map. Geologists saw just about what they expected to see in 90 percent of the seafloor, he says; it is the 10 percent that departed from expectation that has generated the most interest from colleagues, and the most enthusiasm from Haxby. As he puts it, "Generating maps was rewarding in and of itself, both aesthetically and, as you can imagine, I was looking at parts of the world that had never been seen clearly before. I was the first person in the world to see a *lot* of striking physiography."

Every map, no matter how accurate, is a rough draft constantly being rewritten and improved by technological change. In the spring of 1985, the Navy launched a satellite called Geosat. Just as Seasat was more than twice as sensitive as *Geos 3,* Geosat is about twice as sensitive as Seasat, and although the data acquired during the first eighteen months of operation remains classified, the satellite—which looks like a high-tech swizzle stick—now traverses an orbit that repeats itself every seventeen days. The extremely accurate data from this phase of operation, known as the Exact Repeat Mission (ERM), became available to researchers beginning in the fall of 1986.

The most interesting and unexpected site in this new data turned out to be the Weddell Sea, an area of vigorous and enigmatic tectonic

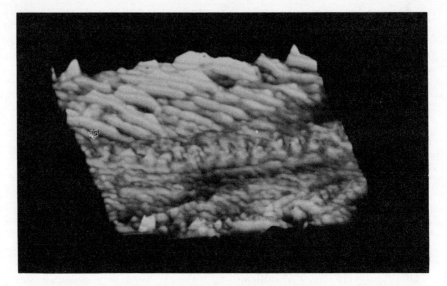

With more recent Geosat data, Haxby has created this three-dimensional topographical view of the "fishbone" structure in the Weddell Sea, where Wegener's supercontinent began to pull apart 130 million years ago. (W. Haxby)

activity between the South American plate and the Antarctic plate. "This is the tip of South America and the Antarctic Peninsula," Haxby explains, calling up the image on his computer screen. For a small ocean basin, it fairly explodes with features that Haxby says are "distinct in character from any other known seafloor structures." Foremost is a series of about fifteen prominent ridges running north-south in the Weddell Sea, each about ninety miles long and four thousand feet high, each separated by a distance of about thirty-five miles. At its southernmost end runs a long east-west ridge measuring some five hundred miles in length. Haxby refers to it as the "fish-bone structure," though the whole thing also resembles a comb with slanted teeth. It represents something that happened 100 million years ago, and not only is it unique to the ocean floor, it had been impossible to detect before, its sharp teeth buried under a mile of sediment. "When you see something like that, you know it has to be telling you something about the mechanical nature of the crust," Haxby says. "But I don't know *what!*"

Explaining any confluence of geophysical contradictions is like stumbling upon the scene of a hit-and-run accident that occurred millions of years ago and trying to piece together from the remaining clues—skid marks, ruts in the grass, heaved earth—what may have happened. When continents collide, fortunately, they leave big clues.

Using the Geosat data, Haxby has created a spectacular three-dimensional map of the fishbone structure in the Weddell Sea. Haxby and others are also using the more comprehensive Geosat data to create new global maps. Like the Seasat map, the new Geosat maps don't answer any questions, but they frame them beautifully. "In the last ten years in geophysics, we've posed some very nice problems," Haxby says, "but we're a long way from answering any of them."

4. A Particular Discontinuity

A MAP OF THE
EARTH'S CORE AND MANTLE

▐▌▌▐▌▌▐▌

Centuries passed by like days. I went
back through the long series of terrestrial
changes. The plants disappeared; the
granite rocks softened; solid matter
turned to liquid under the action of
intense heat; water covered the surface of the
globe, boiling and volitilizing; steam
enveloped the earth, which gradually turned
into a gaseous mass, white-hot, as big
and bright as the sun.

—Jules Verne,
Journey to the Center of the Earth,
Axel's dream

Seismologists generally refer to them as "events." By quirk of birth
and mother tongue, Adam Dziewonski refers to them as "earsequakes," and the bigger the better. When the Loma Prieta earthquake
hit the San Francisco Bay Area with a jolt registering 7.1 on the
Richter scale in October of 1989, Dziewonski was saying one day in his
office at Harvard University, many geophysicists viewed it as pretty
much of a yawner. Not strong enough, not in an exotic enough locale,
not sufficiently *informative,* as they like to say. If you ask members of
the geophysics community about the most interesting earthquake of
1989, Dziewonski and many others will instead mention a place most
people have never heard of, and an event hardly anyone except seismologists seems to recall.

On May 23, 1989, a portion of the Indian plate pushed against the
Pacific plate in the remote southwestern corner of the Pacific Ocean,
resulting in a massive underwater seismic event centered about 230

kilometers (140 miles) north of Macquarie Island, a sliver of uninhabited land located about equidistant from Australia, New Zealand, and Antarctica. So remote was the site that there were no casualties and no damage, no toppled domiciles, no collapsed freeways. Yet the few people who felt it, including fourteen very startled researchers from the Australian National Antarctic Research Expedition encamped on the island, happened to experience the strongest earthquake to hit the planet in a dozen years, an 8.2 shake of the Richter scale that unleashed about thirty times more energy than Loma Prieta. To a growing group of geophysicists interested in mapping the interior of our planet, it was a wonderful earthquake, a gloriously informative earthquake, an event during which the earth itself becomes the laboratory and all the experiments are unplanned.

The earthquake took place along the Macquarie Ridge, a seismically active submarine area where the Indian plate, creeping in a northeasterly direction at a rate of about one inch per year, butts up against the Pacific plate. As these two massive shoulders of the earth's crust pushed against each other, they suddenly slipped sideways. Just as a bow sliding across the stretched gut of a cello creates sound waves that travel through the air to our appreciative ears, vast slabs of rock sliding against each other along a fault line create acoustic vibrations known as compressional waves that travel through the earth to the appreciative instrumental ears of geophysicists. On May 23 these waves moved outward from the epicenter near Macquarie Island at a speed of about thirteen thousand miles per hour.

Called P (or primary) waves, because they travel quickly and are the first to be felt at a distance, they are capable of passing through both solid and liquid material; within a few minutes, the P waves spreading outward from the Macquarie event had set seismometers askitter in monitoring stations belonging to the French Geoscope network—first in nearby Canberra, then Papeete in Tahiti, then Réunion in the Indian Ocean, then Kipapa station in Hawaii. Some of the P waves traveled downward about eighteen hundred miles to the boundary marking the beginning of the earth's core before bouncing up to the surface; others actually penetrated farther down into the liquid outer portion of the core, bending through it before they bounced back up to the surface; still other P waves traveled straight through the core and reached the other side of the planet about twenty minutes later. Because the Macquarie event was particularly powerful, the earth vibrated like a bell. The acoustic waves set off detectors all over the planet.

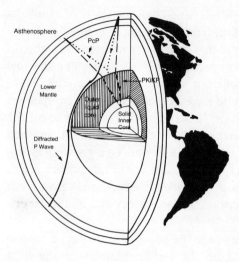

Seismic probes: primary
(P) waves from earthquakes
can penetrate the mantle,
liquid outer core, and metallic
inner core of the earth, while
shear (S) waves (not shown) travel
more slowly through the mantle.
By measuring the time it takes for
the waves to arrive at distant
seismological observatories,
geophysicists can obtain a
CT scan–like image of the
planet's interior. (from *The Fine
Structure of the Earth's Interior*
by Bruce Bolt. Copyright © by
Scientific American, Inc.
All rights reserved.)

Now it so happens that in the mid-1970s several groups of mathematically astute geophysicists, Adam Dziewonski among them, thought up a complicated computational method to use those sound waves much like the X rays that doctors use in computed tomography, or CT scans, to image the internal structure of the human body. In CT scans, a portion of the body is examined by encircling it with a measuring device and firing X rays through it from all 360 degrees of the circle, so that slight variations in the time it takes for X rays to travel through the anatomical region under study may pinpoint the three-dimensional location of dense masses such as tumors.

Earthquake waves traveling through the earth change speed on the basis of the material they travel through, and indeed the technique has become known as seismic tomography. Powerful earthquakes like the one near Macquarie Island in effect perform an enormously useful, if unscheduled, CT scan on the planet itself. By analyzing these waves, by carefully calibrating the time it takes for them to reach various seismic stations on earth, geophysicists have been able to journey inferentially to the center of the earth, using a technology Jules Verne could never have imagined. They have been able to map the subterranean landscape where mantle meets core, and in so doing are nearing an answer to the very question so beautifully posed by the maps of William Haxby and his predecessors: What is the engine driving the machine of plate tectonics? What force propels those massive bergs of planetary crust to creep slowly but inexorably, one or two confrontational inches a year, until they collide in the course of millions of years and throw up mountains in the process?

The path to an answer begins with those rare powerful earthquakes, which occur perhaps once a year. That is why Adam Dziewonski likes "earsequakes." On the snowy afternoon when I interviewed him in his office at Harvard's Department of Earth and Planetary Sciences in Cambridge, he was on the phone, complaining with courtly exasperation about a gravimeter—an instrument used to measure these vibrations—that had arrived damaged in the mail that morning. His face was long, with black peppery hair sticking out a little, and a big, straight nose. There is a husky, hedgehoggish bulk to Dziewonski—the high, hunched shoulders, bushy eyebrows, a bristly fire in his eyes—but he moved more like a ballerina, on small feet and in running shoes, than like the linebacker he physically resembles; his language tiptoes, too, fond as he is of "maybe" and "I guess." It is his curse—a mild one, but an amusing one, given his line of work—that he has devoted his entire academic life to studying the innermost geography of a planet that possesses a fricative for which there is no equivalent in the language of his native Poland. Nevertheless, he has very shrewdly plotted those processes affecting the "earse" with colleagues at Harvard University in a series of maps that attempt to reveal the precise internal structure of the planet.

"See, that's the point!" Dziewonski was saying, extolling the virtues of the Macquarie event. "Its energy was sort of a decent order of magnitude greater than that of the earsequake in California. I am interested in earsequakes occurring in *new* places. An earsequake in an area where there were no earsequakes before essentially contributes in a remarkably important fashion, I guess, to our ability to map the discontinuities.

"Of course, I like the big earsequakes," he added. "There aren't too many of those."

On April 18, 1889, a very big earthquake hit Tokyo, Japan. As jarring as this event was for the residents of Tokyo, it shook up the science of seismology even more, for thousands of miles away, on the other side of the world, a German scientist named E. von Rebeur Paschwitz took note of the fact that horizontal pendulums in both Potsdam and Wilhelmshaven were set aquiver by some powerful seismic force shortly before 6 P.M. on April 17. Upon further investigation, Paschwitz later concluded, "The disturbances noticed in Germany

All the experiments are unplanned: dark spots on this map denote earthquakes greater than magnitude 5 on the Richter scale that occurred between
1980 and 1990. (NOAA/National Geophysical Data Center)

were really due to the earthquake in Tokyo," and thus was the principle established that earthquakes generate waves that can be detected at
a great distance from the event. Every classical seismograph, whose
skittering needles have become a sight-bite accompanying every middling temblor reported on the evening news, traces its lineage back to
those two German pendulums, and to theoretical lines sketched out
several years earlier by the English seismologist John Milne, who
predicted in 1883, "It is not unlikely that every large earthquake might
with proper appliances be recorded at any point of the globe."

Owing to these "proper appliances," or instruments, modern seismology began to take shape in the last decade of the nineteenth century. As von Rebeur Paschwitz noticed in 1889, earthquakes generate
three types of waves, each arriving one after another. The fast-moving
are the primary, or P, waves, which travel through both the solid and
liquid portions of the interior; the secondary, or S (or shear), waves
travel half as fast. Because both P and S waves penetrate the interior,
they are also known as "body waves." The last waves to arrive at
distant seismographs, and the least interesting to seismic tomographers, are the surface waves, for they do not penetrate deeply into the
earth and thus bear no information about that inaccessible terrain.

By measuring the intervals between the arrival times of these
waves, and triangulating the measurements among three geological

observatories, turn-of-the-century seismologists were able to determine systematically the surface location, or epicenter, of large earthquakes anywhere on the earth (and, incidentally, to create the first
maps of the world's active seismic zones). Then, by measuring the
travel times of the body waves, they began to peel the oblate onion,
determining the layers and boundaries of the earth's interior from its
thin skin down to its very pip.

"Of all regions of the earth," Richard Dixon Oldham observed in
1906, "none invites speculation more than that which lies beneath our
feet, and in none is speculation more dangerous. . . ." And yet Oldham,
a brilliant seismologist, was the first to realize that, by measuring the
fast-moving P waves and their slower-moving cousins, the S waves,
seismologists could begin to detect layers deep below the surface.
These layers revealed themselves in subtle variations in the time it took
for seismic waves to travel through them.

The typical velocity of a P wave through the earth's crust, for
example, is 6 kilometers per second—more than 13,000 miles an hour.
As these waves travel deeper into the earth, however, they encounter
what are called "discontinuities," and their velocity changes. A discontinuity represents some sort of boundary, marked by an abrupt change
in temperature, or pressure, or composition of rock; and at every
major boundary, the velocity of earthquake waves fluctuates slightly.
When a P wave hits the denser mantle, some 35 kilometers below
continental crust (rather less beneath the oceans), its speed jumps from
6 to 8 and then to 13.7 kilometers per second (about 30,000 miles per
hour); then it abruptly slows down to 8 kilometers a second where it
encounters the mushy material of the outer core. This last velocity
change is not unlike what sometimes happens in a baseball game after
a rain delay; a crisply stroked ground ball travels swiftly through the
dry infield, which has benefited from the protection of a tarp, but the
moment it hits the soggy outfield grass, it visibly slows down.

In a similar way, seismologists have detected velocity changes in
earthquake waves and have inferred boundaries where those velocities
make a noticeable change. Beneath continents, at a depth of about
thirty or thirty-five kilometers, the so-called Mohorovičić discontinuity marks the boundary between crust and mantle. It is a significant *chemical* boundary, because the mantle is much richer in iron, and
about 30 percent denser, so waves travel more rapidly through it.
Imagine wiggling your finger in a bowl of water, and then wiggling it
in a bowl of whipped cream. Waves travel more rapidly through water,
which is dense, compared to whipped cream, which is buoyant; a

P wave traveling from crust to mantle encounters a similarly qualitative change in density, with the resulting effect on velocity. With each subtle change in density or temperature, deeper and deeper toward the center of the earth, there is a corresponding change in the velocity of the waves. And geophysicists were remarkably successful in the first half of this century in interpreting those variations.

As early as 1906, Richard D. Oldham used the principle of multiple perspectives—many disparate measurements of the same seismic event, a kind of *Rashomon* with seismometers—to suggest the general dimensions of the earth's core, which he inferred, correctly, to have a liquid center. Nearly 2,000 miles of solid rock lie between us and the outermost boundary of the earth's core, yet by carefully timing earthquake waves we have been able to calculate the radius of the core to within 200 meters. By 1936 geophysicists had identified and roughly mapped all the major internal boundaries, and by the time they finished these calculations, seismologists figured that the mantle, a thick spherical blanket of dense rock, is nearly 2,900 kilometers (about 1,800 miles) thick. Next came the outer core, another 2,200 kilometers (or 1,350 miles thick); mostly iron, it is liquid, of about the fluidity of water. And finally, at the heart of that layer, at the steely pith of the planet, there lies a solid core of iron with a radius measuring about 1,200 kilometers (roughly 750 miles). The journey from any point on the earth's surface—say, Jules Verne's study in his home outside Paris—to the center of the earth traverses about 6,371 kilometers (3,950 miles). A compressional wave triggered by any earthquake travels that distance in about ten minutes.

Much of the work in the first three-quarters of this century established the near-perfect symmetry of the earth's internal structure; the layers appeared as spherically symmetrical as an onion's, and the boundaries sketched out in the previous paragraphs hold true for 99 percent of the planet as a whole. The mapping that has taken place in the last decade, however, marks a dramatic departure from pure sphericity, a mapping made possible by increasingly sensitive instrumentation and more sophisticated data analysis. Geophysicists can now detect and map *very slight* departures from the average readings, tiny fluctuations in the expected boundaries. Theirs are maps of *anomalies,* of the 1 percent that strays from perfect symmetry, and at each spherical boundary layer within the earth, it has been possible to plot very distinct topographies, interior borderlands that are marked by subtle rises and valleys and ridges.

One could view the current clamor in geophysics, in fact, as a transition of focus from the symmetrical view of the earth to an asymmetrical one. Those subtle imperfections, it now appears, are linked to the processes that make our planet, almost alone in the only solar system we know, alive and dynamic and capable of reinventing itself. As Dziewonski and his principal colleague, John Woodhouse (formerly of Harvard and now at Oxford University), wrote recently, "If the internal properties of the earth were spherically symmetric, our planet would be tectonically dead." Asymmetry breathes life into the heart of the planet, perhaps explaining how lava flows through its veins to the surface and how the crust, like skin, grows and perishes and is replenished, perhaps explaining how the earth's magnetic field shifts and changes, perhaps even explaining why a day is as long as it is.

The interior of the earth is so remote from direct measurement, Richard Oldham also wrote, that it is "a playground for mathematicians," and it was in the mid-1970s that Adam Dziewonski, working at what is now the University of Texas at Dallas as an assistant professor, began playing with the math. He had the idea of taking decades worth of seismic wave data and shaping them mathematically to achieve exceptional three-dimensional precision. By focusing on those enlightening anomalies, hundreds of miles below the surface, he began his own late-twentieth-century journey to the center of the earth.

The vehicle for this journey was called a "functional"—a mathematical formula that allowed one to work backward, or "inversely," from the travel times of the earthquake waves to a three-dimensional model of the earth's interior. Dziewonski and J. Freeman Gilbert of the University of California at San Diego developed a mathematical filter, as it were, through which to shape the data generated by earthquakes and determine if, at for example a depth of 670 kilometers, the boundary was symmetrical and stable or if there were local variations, hills and valleys, along the border.

The idea had been kicking around since the 1960s, but it took an improvement in seismic networks to bring it to fruition. It's inviting to think, in this celebritized age of ours, that scientific revolutions begin only with profound thinkers and powerful ideas; but this revolution in mapping the interior of the earth may be better characterized as a good idea that became truly powerful when seismologists got more organized about analyzing the data they already had in hand.

Prior to the 1960s, information gathered at seismological stations throughout the world tended to be spotty, nonstandardized, and—surprisingly enough—not always shared among peers. There was no central clearinghouse of information. There was no dissemination of data without a formal request made to an individual seismological station. And there was precious little sharing anyway, because as one paper puts it, seismological stations "often lacked copying facilities and were reluctant to lend the original records."

That began to change with the establishment of a global network of 125 seismic stations, called the World-wide Standard Seismograph Network, in 1965 (part of the impetus for setting up this network, it should be noted, was the detection of underground nuclear tests). The establishment of networks was accompanied, beginning in the 1970s, by the phased retirement of old analog seismographs, the machines that recorded earthquakes as skittering lines on graph paper, to make room for the less graphic but more useful digital instruments. They are not only more sensitive but encode seismic data in numbers that can be instantaneously transmitted and shared by modem or satellite. The system is far from perfect: certain data on the Macquarie earthquake limped back to Paris by ship several months after the event. Like many other modern maps, seismic tomographic maps benefited from a quantum jump in the amount of available data, thanks to the networks, and a quantum jump in the power of computers, which were used for processing and analysis. Don L. Anderson of the California Institute of Technology has referred to seismic networks as "an inward-looking telescope."

But it fell to Gilbert and Dziewonski to work out the math. With a tremendous mass of data (5 million raw data points to sift through) and with measurements of unprecedented sensitivity (variations in wave velocities down to a thousandth of a second), Dziewonski and his colleagues at Harvard made the first attempt to convert velocity variations into a topographic view of boundaries inside the earth. "And then I think I probably was the first one who tried to map this in a sort of systematic fashion," Dziewonski says.

There is hesitation in his voice, and it seems to recall the controversy that attended this first foray into seismic tomography. Dziewonski presented a first, tentative tomographic map of the earth's mantle in 1974 at Harvard and went public with a paper delivered at the spring meeting of the American Geophysical Union in 1975. His first full-blown paper, with coauthors Bradford Hager and Richard O'Connell, appeared in the *Journal of Geophysical Research* in 1977. It met, Dziewonski recalls, with "large doses of skepticism." Only several years later, when a group at Caltech produced similar results, did interest perk up considerably. "For the first time, I guess, sort of a majority . . . I don't know exactly how opinions form in a large body of scientists"—his inflection suggests that this process is at least as mysterious as the processes that govern the interior of the earth—"but all of a sudden it was all right and it was very exciting."

Since then Dziewonski and John Woodhouse have created maps. They have created a new color vocabulary for geophysical maps, too, where qualities of the earth's interior are depicted in vivid blues and oranges. Not surprisingly, these maps have appeared on the covers of scientific journals all over the world. Whereas maps made at the turn of the century showed static boundaries, the maps made in the 1980s show movement at those boundaries, and movement implies the process known as convection—the rising and falling of material within the earth.

"To the first order," says Raymond Jeanloz, a geophysicist at the University of California at Berkeley, "one can look at these cartoons, these maps, that the seismologists have put together, and where you see red—that is, the slower regions—you can imagine material coming up *toward* the surface. The bluer region is material that's tending to sink towards the bottom. And all of a sudden you have this *visualization* of the underlying forces that tend to drive geological processes as we see them at the surface. That's been a tremendous breakthrough."

To test their earliest ideas, one of the initial maps by Dziewonski and Woodhouse attempted to see if a shallow seismic map reflected what geophysicists already knew about the surface. They mapped the velocity of shear waves at a modest depth of 150 kilometers (about 90 miles), and the map corresponded beautifully to known features on the surface of the planet. At the East Pacific Rise in the Pacific, where mantle is exuded to form new crust, shear waves moved slower than average—just what you'd expect in a hot area where mushy material is rising toward the surface. Conversely, deep blue regions, indicating faster velocities and thus colder rock, matched the vast cold lumps of continents. The Canadian Shield, the Brazilian Shield, western Australia, Scandinavia, the Siberian Shield, even Africa—all these large, deep-rooted land masses appeared blue on the map after a computer assessed the data and assigned color values. To a depth of 200 kilometers or so, the velocity anomalies very closely matched the tectonic expression on the surface. The maps, apparently, were telling Dziewonski and Woodhouse about the *dynamics* of the earth's interior.

Burrowing straight down from meridian 110 West *(top figure),* a cross-sectional map of the upper mantle—from a depth of 26 kilometers *(top of cross-section)* to 670 kilometers *(bottom)*—shows deep cold roots beneath the continents and warmer material below the Pacific's mid-ocean ridge. (A. Dziewonski and J. Woodhouse/© 1987 AAAS)

Part of the job description of a map-reader is to drop old poses, to look at familiar materials in unfamiliar ways. In order to appreciate these maps, it helps to look at a piece of granite, for example, and see it not in its familiar role as pillar and post, staircase and doorsill, but rather as something counterintuitive, something that goes against common sense. We must think of that hard rock as a liquid, as something that actually *flows.*

In the course of geological time, with pressures in the mantle and core up to 3.5 million times atmospheric pressure on the surface and temperatures reaching 6,000 degrees Centigrade, rock *does* flow. It becomes fluid and plastic. People who own older homes may have seen this flow in windowpanes, where with the passage of time glass becomes thicker at the bottom of the window. "The rock is like rock in mountains," explains Jeanloz, who attempts to recreate the pressures and temperatures of the earth's interior in his Berkeley lab in order to study the physical qualities of minerals. "It's hard. It's solid. Almost none of it is molten; it's all crystalline. But on a geological time scale, it actually behaves like a fluid."

If you have a fluid, you can have flow, or movement. And if there

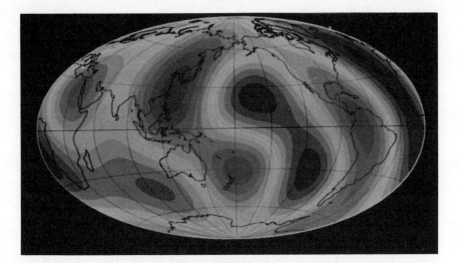

"The most dramatic discontinuity in the earth's internal structure": hills and valleys at the rugged core-mantle boundary *(above)* may affect everything from the earth's geomagnetic field to the length of the day. (A. Morelli and A. Dziewonski/© 1987 Macmillan Magazines Ltd.)

is movement, you can probably detect its overall direction. That is what Dziewonski and his colleagues have done. They figured out how to look at any stratum of the interior, any horizontal layer, and map the *direction* of the movements of this fluid rock in the interior of the earth. Taken together, those movements look for all the world like the physical phenomenon known as convection.

The physics inherent in a pot of boiling water, in broad brush, provides all the rules needed to look at the interior of the earth. Simply put, warm material rises, cold material sinks. Buoyant material rises, dense material sinks. When you heat water in a pan, even before the water comes to a boil, the warm—and therefore less dense—water rises to the surface, while the cold, denser water on top sinks to the bottom of the pan. If you could take a horizontal slice of a boiling pot of water, you could pinpoint the areas where hot water was rising and where cooler water was sinking; seismic tomographic maps paint the same kind of convection at various horizontal slices of the earth's interior. The seismic waves tell researchers whether the mantle at any given depth is more or less dense than average, hotter or cooler than average, and—this is the crucial interpolation—therefore whether it is rising or sinking. With enough precise measurements, enough global data, you gain the power to set the rock in motion, detect its flow, and then you see actual topography, cross-sections of convection cells.

"Then you might ask yourself, 'Well, what is it that drives this convection?' " adds Jeanloz. "And now it so happens, there's an underlying physical connection that's theoretically understood. Let's just say if you go into the laboratory and measure the seismic wave velocity, the sound velocity, through rocks or metals or ceramics or most materials, as you heat up the material, the sound velocity goes down with increasing temperature. Basically, the material gets a little bit mushier. So now you can start seeing there's a correlation, and it's a very good one in the laboratory. There's quite a bit of theoretical underpinning to this, whereby whenever you have slower-than-average wave velocity, it corresponds to *hotter*-than-average rock, and vice versa. Faster-than-average velocities would be slightly colder rock. And so the colder rock is denser. It's the stuff that tends to sink. The hot rock is less dense. It's the stuff that tends to come up." In the maps, color thus encodes information about *movement*—blue suggests downward movement, orange upward.

When asked if, as they burrowed deeper, they saw things they hadn't expected to see, Dziewonski looked puzzled. "We did not expect to see—" he began to say, then cut himself off with a shrug. "Frankly, sometimes there wasn't really terribly good reason to expect *anything*, I guess."

Once they had established at least a tentative correlation between their mapping idea and surface features, the seismic tomographers journeyed deeper into the earth. They mapped into the mantle and reached what Dziewonski calls "a particular discontinuity" where the upper mantle meets the lower mantle. In doing so they ventured, 670 kilometers below the surface, into one of the most disputed territories on or in the earth, at least in the view of contemporary geophysics.

"This argument has been going on for so long that one begins to wonder whether we are ever going to resolve it, and how," Dziewonski says a bit wearily. "The debate is whether convection is a two-layer convection—that is, that the upper mantle is separated from the lower mantle—or whether they mix. It has a fairly profound significance in terms of the internal composition of the earth and its evolution. This particular discontinuity is the subject of debate, or has been subject to debate, for roughly the last quarter century."

Technically, the debate revolves around the chemical and thermal boundary between upper and lower mantle; more generally it speaks to the mechanism with which the earth keeps its tectonic plates in motion. The issue, again, centers on convection.

Is the mantle, according to the view championed most vigorously by Don Anderson of Caltech, divided into two convective chambers, somewhat like a parboiler, where the lower chamber heats the upper chamber and only convection in the upper chamber moves the plates? Or does the mantle function as one big convection cell, as Thomas Jordan of the Massachusetts Institute of Technology (and another prominent seismic tomographer) argues, meaning that minerals from deep within the earth can be transported to the surface? As Dziewonski and Woodhouse mapped deeper into the earth, they uncovered evidence—hardly unambiguous evidence, but evidence all the same—that the mantle operates as a large, single, indivisible convective cell.

Nothing makes the point more vividly than a map. Dziewonski turns to two of them on his office wall; one shows shear wave velocities in the upper mantle, and the other one shows compressional wave velocities in the lower mantle. In both maps the vast expanse of the Pacific Ocean is orange. Orange indicates that seismic waves traveling through that layer move at a speed slower than average; velocities slow down, again, when material is hotter or less dense. And hot, less dense material tends to rise. Though measured at different scales and dealing with different types of waves, the maps concur in color from the surface down to the core-mantle boundary. Both show a great upward swelling movement of mantle material, which happens to coincide with the bulge of the mid-ocean ridge in the Pacific, where fresh crust is extruded. "I would say that, if anything, our results seem to support the idea of whole mantle convection," Dziewonski says.

The circumference of the Pacific is infamous, from the Macquarie Ridge to Tokyo to Alaska to the denizens tensely perched along the San Andreas fault, as an area rich in volcanoes and earthquakes. It is known more familiarly as the "Ring of Fire," and along its edges, according to the theory of plate tectonics, plates moving outward from the East Pacific Rise collide with continental plates in North America and Asia, for example, and plunge down into the mantle, a frictious geological encounter known as subduction. Do these subduction zones show up on seismic maps? "The Pacific Basin, which is by far the largest feature on the surface of the earth, nearly one-third of the total surface, is surrounded by—this is if you look at the lower mantle, at a depth of two thousand or even twenty-five hundred kilometers—by a ring of fast velocities," Dziewonski explains. Fast velocities mean

The "Ring of Fire"
encircling the Pacific Ocean:
seismic tomographers detect
warm material rising and spreading
from the center of the Pacific
seafloor, while cool, denser material
dives back down into the earth at the
continental margins, where almost
all the earthquakes (dark spots
on map) occur. (NOAA/National
Geophysical Data Center)

cold, sinking rock; this ring is marked by a deep, cool blue. So the
"Ring of Fire" is essentially associated with relatively high velocities,
while the center of the Pacific is slow. "And if you think about it, it sort
of makes sense because it actually delineates, perhaps, a large-scale
convection in the earth. In some sense the Pacific is a large convective
cell, and maybe these can actually exist and be stable over very long
periods of time. Because we know that while the Atlantic Ocean
opened and closed, and opened and closed, the Pacific was essentially
empty throughout this time."

In that blue ring girding the Pacific, perhaps, lies the resolution of
the mantle controversy. According to a recent proposal by Peter Olson
of Johns Hopkins University, and Paul G. Silver and Richard W.
Carlson of the Carnegie Institution of Washington, the blue regions on
the seismic tomography maps represent subducted slabs—slabs of
crust fifty miles thick and perhaps a thousand miles long—that dive
into trenches at the subduction zones where plates meet and descend
into the earth. Olson argues that not only do these slabs sink nearly
to the core-mantle boundary, but that in so doing, they essentially
drag the plates behind them and set in motion the convection that
involves the entire mantle. "Everyone now agrees that convection
occurs throughout the mantle," Olson says. "That may sound obvious,
but the importance of that can't be overemphasized. The maps represent the first time people have seen three-dimensional structure that
deep in the mantle." And convection causes the seafloor to spread,

creates ocean basins, builds mountains, moves continents, ignites volcanoes, and triggers earthquakes; it is the pulse of a living planet.

Deeper and deeper did Dziewonski and his colleagues journey
toward the center of the earth, reaching that enigmatic border between
mantle and core in the mid-1980s. It turned out to be, as they described
it in a 1987 paper, the "most dramatic" discontinuity in the earth's
interior. "It's a very remote thing," Dziewonski says, "but more and
more people believe that processes *critical* to the dynamics of the earth
actually take place there." Indeed, surface volcanoes, the earth's magnetic field, even the length of a day seem in thrall to forces connected
to this invisible subterranean boundary.

First of all, they discovered an "enormous coincidence" between
the topography just above the core-mantle boundary (often abbreviated as CMB) and the surface fireworks of geophysics—the volcanoes, the hot springs, and so on. They superimposed the location of
volcanoes and other so-called hot spots on the earth's surface over a
map showing seismic wave velocities at a level about 140 kilometers
(roughly 87 miles) above the core-mantle boundary. Some 85 percent
of the hot spots, represented by white circles, hovered above orange
regions of the core-mantle map, suggesting that the hot plumes that
carry rock to the surface may in fact originate at the very basement of
the mantle.

In 1987, Dziewonski and Andrea Morelli published more detailed
maps of the core-mantle boundary. They found significant topography—fingers of the solid mantle dipping down like stalactites, some of
them five kilometers long, into the liquid iron of the outer core. It is
now argued that these fingers of mantle stir the liquid and create flows
that cause minor fluctuations in the earth's rotation, shaving a few
microseconds off the twenty-four-hour day. The flows may also influence periodic changes in the earth's magnetic field. Raymond Jeanloz,
for example, believes the chemical interaction between the liquid iron
core and the silicate- and oxide-rich lower mantle create "blobs" of
metallic alloys that influence the geomagnetic field. And Jeremy Bloxham, a colleague of Dziewonski's at Harvard, has created maps of the
earth's wandering magnetic field that, in addition to being beautiful
and informative in their own right, complement the seismic maps
nicely. "What Jeremy noticed," Dziewonski says, "is that wherever the
seismic velocities are slow at the core-mantle boundary, there is also a
region in which the magnetic field changes rather rapidly. . . . So again,
an additional perhaps indication that there is some link between the

properties of the earth *just* at the core-mantle boundary and what we see at the surface. Some possibility of communication and flow of some sort."

Using data from all the analyses, John Woodhouse has gone on to prepare truly Verne-like, three-dimensional cutaways of the earth, as if he were slicing into a spherical orange-and-blue layer cake (see color illustrations). One cutaway, carved in incisions ten thousand kilometers long, covers the area of the mid-Atlantic ridge, while the other explores the Pacific around the East Pacific Rise, between Mexico and Hawaii. They are maps that discourage hopes of general principles.

"If we compare these pictures of the Pacific and the Atlantic at a depth of five hundred fifty kilometers, they are completely different," Dziewonski observes. Deeper down, at the core-mantle boundary, the Pacific is very slow, the Atlantic rather fast. "So we have two oceans, completely different." The lesson being: "You have to consider each piece of the earth on its own merits."

"Once you get close to the core-mantle boundary," Dziewonski says, "things change very dramatically." All of a sudden, there is a "tremendous asymmetry" between hemispheres. The northern hemisphere becomes significantly faster than average and the southern hemisphere significantly slower, or hotter. The meaning is unclear; the temptation to speculate irresistible. "In some sense perhaps the thermal state at the core-mantle boundary might have some major implications on the plate tectonics of the surface. Or vice versa. What we see at the core-mantle boundary is in part the result of, for example, some dead subduction zones."

The uncertainty betrays the major drawback of seismic tomographic images. In recording tiny variations, the subtlety of the information is such that the initial maps are best regarded as rough sketches, not finely crafted portraits. Friendly critics, like Jeanloz at UC-Berkeley, believe that the large-scale features revealed by seismic tomography, such as the "Ring of Fire" image, appear to be "quite robust." The problem with the technique—a problem Dziewonski readily concedes—is that seismic wave variations are so subtle and sensitive that they are barely distinguishable from statistical "noise"; the reliable data rise so slightly above the background that it is difficult to say whether they are real or statistical illusions. "First of all, in resolution, they can only look at very large-scale features," says Jeanloz. "They can look at something the size of the Pacific. But anything less than a thousand kilometers or so, forget it. There's so much noise in the data, they have to do a lot of smoothing and averaging."

Dziewonski is aware of the problem. Dziewonski concedes the problem. "There's probably some good work that can be done with existing data. And I hope that we are doing part of it. But it's rather clear that in order to increase the overall resolution, we need data from many more seismographic stations."

Seismologists are tackling this problem as much logistically as technologically. Dziewonski is attempting to organize a new network of some one hundred modernized seismographic stations, capable not only of recording seismic waves digitally, but also of transmitting the data instantly via satellite to researchers throughout the world. The National Science Foundation is supporting sixty-some U.S. universities, jointly known as the Incorporated Research Institutions for Seismology (IRIS), in developing this state-of-the-art global network of stations. The French-organized array known as Geoscope, using a similar approach of modernization and standardization, already has twenty stations in operation.

The Macquarie event of 1989, surprisingly enough, was the first large earthquake from which digital seismic data in the IRIS network was instantaneously shared. This came twenty years after the moon was digitally imaged, and just three months before digitized images of the outermost planet on the Grand Tour of the solar system, Neptune, would appear on home television sets in real time. The irony is not lost on Dziewonski and Morelli. As they remarked in their 1987 *Nature* paper: "While it may take hundreds of millions of dollars to map the surface of Venus, the mapping of the more inaccessible interior of our planet could progress much more rapidly at negligible cost."

"It's true that perhaps solid earth geophysics does not get as much attention and interest as other branches closer to the surface, like oceanography," Dziewonski would admit later. "But when earsequakes happen," he added slyly, "people sort of get *very* interested."

5. Plausible Fortunes

PALEOCLIMATE MAPS AND
COMPUTER MODELS OF
GLOBAL WARMING

|||||||||||

From a drop of water, a logician could infer
the possibility of an Atlantic or a Niagara without
having seen or heard of one or the other. So all
life is a great chain, the nature of which is
known whenever we are shown a single link of it.

—Sherlock Holmes,
quoted in A. Conan Doyle,
A Study in Scarlet

Of all the simulations of future climates that have been spit out by computers over the last forty years, some of them looking twenty-four hours in advance and some of them twenty-five years, not a single one has managed to predict the heaviest weather of all: the fierce storms and crackling atmospherics that have roiled the political and scientific landscape over the reliability of the simulations themselves. And no one could have predicted that the scientists known as climate modelers, weathermen of the ultimate long-range forecast, would become so beleaguered by controversy that they would shy away from the very responsibility for which their counsel is sought: prediction. Yet here is Warren M. Washington, who heads the Climate Research Section at the National Center for Atmospheric Research (NCAR) in Boulder, Colorado, and has modeled climate for twenty-seven years, saying, "We don't call them predictions. Other people call them predictions. We call them 'sensitivity experiments.' There's a difference," he insists.

Yes, there is. It's right there in the textbooks, including one coauthored by Washington, one of the most accomplished black scientists in the country. But the semantic dance away from even the appearance of prediction only serves to illustrate a scientific community traumatized by public attention.

Rarely has scientific work proceeded under such intense public scrutiny, and rarely have scientists felt so many kibitzers looking over their shoulders—congressmen and presidential advisers, blue-ribbon panelists and environmentalists, journalists and urban planners, philosophers and gadflies—as they do now, at the end of civilization's first gas-guzzling century, as climate modelers take imperfect steps toward understanding the greenhouse effect and predicting (or rather, *suggesting*) what impact global warming will have on the planet fifty or one hundred years down the road. History argues that all mapmaking transpires in a politicized environment, where social or cultural biases creep in from the margins, but the danger seems especially true of the work on what are called general circulation models (or GCMs), an unusually, even unpleasantly vivid example of rhetorical atmospherics adding an extra dimension of confusion to a scientific mapping problem that is difficult enough in four dimensions.

While climate modelers toil to improve their simulations, public debate has generated its own kind of global-warming trend. One writer has recounted the more ominous scenarios of the greenhouse effect and concluded that the "end of nature" is at hand; an episode in the television series *The Infinite Voyage* illustrated one possible outcome of global warming, a dramatic rise in sea level, by showing the U.S. Capitol disappearing under water (a comment, perhaps, as suggestive of political indecision as environmental degradation); and scientists like Daniel Lashof of the National Resources Defense Council fearlessly forecast "more powerful hurricanes, more frequent severe droughts, pest outbreaks, forest diebacks, millions of environmental refugees fleeing their flooded homelands and other impacts we cannot now imagine." On the other side of this occluded front, one needn't look much further than the December 25, 1989 issue of *Forbes* magazine, with its cover headline THE GLOBAL WARMING PANIC: A CLASSIC CASE OF OVERREACTION, its gleeful tweaking of the "calamitarians," and its overheated economic apocalypticism (". . . just as Marxism is giving way to markets," moaned the voice of capitalism, "the political 'greens' seem determined to put the world economy back into the red, using the greenhouse effect to stop unfettered market-based economic expansion"). Enacting legislation to reduce carbon dioxide emissions,

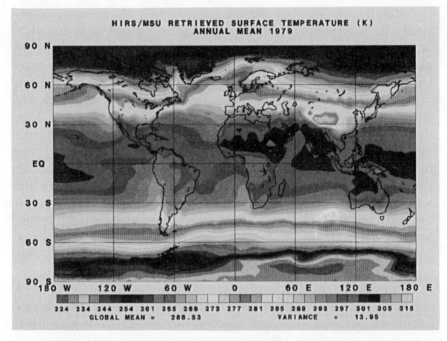

HIRS/MSU RETRIEVED SURFACE TEMPERATURE (K)
ANNUAL MEAN 1979

Global warming? Temperatures in recent years have been among the highest in a century, as tracked by "skin temperature" maps of the earth's surface like this example from 1979. Computer models of the greenhouse effect need to be tested, and one way is by paleoclimate models of past climate. (J. Susskind, NASA/GSFC)

the article warned, "could well spell the end of the American dream for us and the world." Ironically, the rhetoric from both sides seems to confirm what the computer models have so far shown about global warming, which is that the most pronounced increases of heat tend to occur at the polar extremes.

Caught in the middle are the handful of scientists who actually build and run these models. They are the first to admit considerable limitations and uncertainty in their results. The climate record, which is the data base they all use to run their simulations, is, according to a recent commentary in the journal *Nature,* "painfully short" and "heavily flawed." What's a scientific mapmaker to do?

To a small cohort of researchers, the answer has been to do something that almost sounds like the punchline to a joke. They have chosen to predict yesterday's weather.

Two singular developments in the 1950s and '60s laid the groundwork for what has become known as paleoclimatic modeling: scientists at the Institute for Advanced Study in Princeton attempted the first general circulation models of the earth's climate, and a young man named John Kutzbach paid frequent visits to the caves of Lascaux in central France on his days off.

An army meteorologist stationed in Châteauroux, Kutzbach came from a family of German immigrants who had settled in Reedsburg, Wisconsin, in the nineteenth century. Having recently obtained a master's degree from the University of Wisconsin, he experienced that eye-widening taste of the world that happens to people who grow up in a dairy town of forty-five hundred in the Wisconsin Dells, then suddenly find themselves living in the Loire Valley. In France, Kutzbach worked as a weather forecaster for three days straight, then took four days off. On those days off, he would often travel south to Lascaux, where a small and resilient community of Late Paleolithic humans had managed to live in a network of limestone caves, just beyond reach of the white fingers of ice sheets that covered Europe during the last ice age twenty thousand years ago. Since 1963 those caves have been closed to the public, but Kutzbach was stationed in France between 1961 and 1963, and he spent many hours examining the paintings on the cave walls, of red deer and stags and big-horned aurochs (protomaps of a sort, as it is believed at least some of the paintings were intended to indicate the location of nearby hunting grounds). As a curious twenty-four-year-old, Kutzbach wondered how primitive tribes could survive such rugged circumstances, and as a meteorologist, he naturally wondered about the weather. "This was a cave inhabited by real people, who left these paintings and these handprints on the cave walls," he recalls, "and it brought that ancient period alive in a way that I certainly hadn't gotten out of a textbook."

He felt a "strong personal identification" with that past. He tried to imagine what the Dordogne Valley must have been like during the ice ages. It was something he always seemed to do: visualize what a place must have looked like. That curiosity marked the beginnings of a mature scientific sensibility, and from those first crude and impromptu mental images emerged, almost three decades later, what are now called paleoclimatologic maps.

Back at Madison and back in graduate school, Kutzbach fell under the sway of Reid Bryson, a teacher renowned not simply for his expertise in climatology (then, as now, a specialty at the University of Wisconsin) but for his interest, even insistence, on an interdisciplinary approach to science. He got Kutzbach thinking about more than mere weather. He pushed him to draw upon archaeology, and geology, and ecology, and biology, even art history and medicine. The mild-mannered Kutzbach quietly paid visits to all those scientific neighbor-hoods in the interest of paleoclimatology. In the course of a career rather eclectic by the standards of ordinary meteorology, he would go on to chart the circulation of "megamonsoons" on Pangaea, the massive supercontinent that existed about 200 million years ago, and recently studied, with William F. Ruddiman of Columbia University, how the dramatic formation of the Rocky Mountains, some 10 million years ago, changed the climate of North America. Yet because of that background in meteorology, he always thought in terms of maps.

Kutzbach's curiosities coincided with a number of new and important technologies of measurement that allowed accurate reconstructions of ancient climates. Carbon-14 dating, developed in the 1940s, allowed scientists to date ancient sediments and once-organic material back thousands of years. Drill bits fetched core samples from the seafloor and lake bottoms. From the fields of archaeology and paleoecology came evidence of ancient communities, and the environments that surrounded them. As all these sophisticated measuring techniques became available, the pieces lay ready to be assembled into a picture of past climate. Not only did Kutzbach and a few colleagues understand, as they discussed the idea in the mid-1970s, that this was a golden opportunity to see what the earth's climate had been like in the past. Beneath it all was the seed of a bigger idea: that you could look at the past to predict the climate of the future.

While Kutzbach and other paleoclimatologists sifted clues about the past, mathematicians began chasing the future, embarking on a separate track in climatological research that, two decades later, would converge with that of the paleoclimatologists. This was the use of computers to model, or simulate, atmospheric conditions. The very first attempts predated the computer and were undertaken by a volunteer ambulance driver during World War I. Lewis Fry Richardson, an English scientist serving in the Red Cross, took advantage of the lulls between battles to plug some basic equations about atmospheric motions into a mechanical calculator in an attempt to predict the weather. Establishing a precedent that in some respects remains unbroken, he failed to achieve realistic results. Indeed, Richardson concluded in his 1922 book *Weather Prediction by Numerical Process* that it would take sixty-four thousand people—"computers," he called them, in that pre-

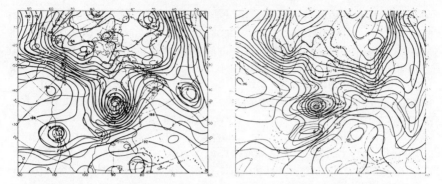

The first computer-assisted weather maps: John von Neumann's group compared the actual weather of Jan. 5, 1949 *(left)*, with ENIAC's predictions *(right)*. It took twenty-four hours to compute a twenty-four-hour forecast. (Tellus)

silicon-chip era—calculating around the clock to predict the following day's global weather.

Richardson's book, but not his pessimism, was picked up by John von Neumann, the legendary mathematician at the Institute for Advanced Study in Princeton. Just as a meteorologist gave birth to plate tectonics, so an outsider would pioneer predictive atmospheric meteorology. As early as 1945, von Neumann realized that "numerical calculations"—the kind of work performed by electronic computers— were particularly well suited to tackle weather prediction. As Richardson had learned, the laws of physics that explain interactions in the atmosphere require a particular genre of solution known as nonlinear partial differential equations, and von Neumann knew only too well that these equations were "disproportionately cumbersome and time-consuming compared with calculations in other fields of mathematical physics." But not for computers. Immediately after World War II, von Neumann set up the Electronic Computer Project at the institute and "was searching around," as one of his junior colleagues, Joseph Smagorinsky, recalls, "for a problem area that might be revolutionized by the use of computers." That problem turned out to be weather prediction.

Von Neumann launched the Meteorological Group, and in March of 1950, von Neumann and his principal colleague, Jule Charney, journeyed down to the U.S. Army Aberdeen Proving Ground in Maryland on a mission of truly historic, though largely uncelebrated, cartographic significance. Not only were they the first scientists to use a computer, the Army Signal Corps' primitive ENIAC computer (all 100 feet and 18,000 bulbs of its vacuum-tube circuitry), to make a twenty-four-hour weather forecast; they were the first researchers in any field to create a map out of computer-generated data. They attempted four forecasts in all, two for North America and two for Europe; and although they achieved mixed success, they discovered some serious drawbacks. As Charney, von Neumann, and Ragnar Fjörtoft slyly noted in the report they wrote up for the journal *Tellus,* "It may be of interest to remark that the computation time for a 24-hour forecast was about 24 hours. . . ."

The group continued to refine its technique, using the controversial computer von Neumann got running at the institute in 1952, and another protégé in the Meteorological Group, Norman Phillips, completed an experiment in 1955 that would forever link computer and climate. He used numerical operations to simulate atmospheric conditions for an entire month. When he published the results in 1956, he entitled the paper "The General Circulation of the Atmosphere: A Numerical Experiment," and ever since such computer simulations have been known as general circulation models, or GCMs. For better or for worse, right and mostly wrong, the era of long-range weather prediction was under way. Von Neumann would later refer to general circulation models as "the infinite forecast."

Despite its initial successes, the Princeton group suffered an intellectual diaspora in the mid-1950s. Von Neumann went to Washington to serve on the Atomic Energy Commission, Charney and others in the meteorology group moved to MIT (where one meteorologist, Edward Lorenz, began to see chaos in his computer simulations), and Smagorinsky returned to the U.S. Weather Bureau to head its General Circulation Research Section outside Washington, D.C. After several name and venue changes, this would become the Geophysical Fluid Dynamics Laboratory (GFDL), and living up to von Neumann's extraordinary vision, the lab managed to anticipate all the major issues and developments that currently dominate climate research, from the dangers of carbon dioxide to general circulation models. Syukuro Manabe joined the group in 1958, and he and Smagorinsky published the results of one of the first GCMs in which both atmosphere and oceans are included, in 1963 and 1965.

Even the crudest climate model posed an archetypally thorny cartographic problem that bedevils much of science in the latter half of the twentieth century: how do you show three and four dimensions of

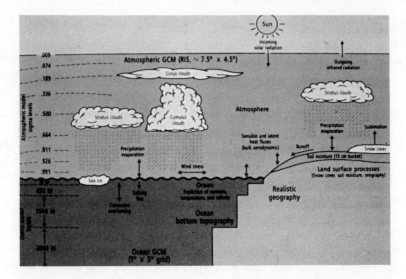

"We don't call them predictions; we call them sensitivity experiments . . .": in sophisticated general circulation models, a dozen key physical equations are used, again and again and again, to simulate climatic interactions between layers of atmosphere and ocean, winds, sea ice, and other factors. (W. M. Washington)

---

information on a two-dimensional plane, be it a piece of paper or a flat computer screen? In this type of cartography, you are in effect superimposing a map of climate-related variables—temperature, barometric pressure, moisture, wind direction, ice sheets, and vegetation, to mention the most rudimentary of contours—upon the same geography that Magellan circumnavigated and Mercator flattened. You must calculate interactions among up to nine layers of atmosphere and four layers of ocean depth, and for the sea ice that influences both. You must account for the fact that heat exchange in the atmosphere fluctuates by the hour while temperature change at the bottom of the sea is measured in centuries. And to extract true meaning, to peer into the future and identify trends, you must set these three-dimensional maps into motion, let the winds howl and the clouds roil, propelling the whole picture through a fourth dimension, time; you must show how the variables interact and evolve over a period of years, decades, centuries. Because it is such a complex system, played out on a gameboard originally mapped and ordered in earlier ages of discovery, sophisticated climate modeling awaited the development of highly powerful supercomputers.

In 1968 the GFDL "returned" to Princeton. It has since been joined by NASA, which established its own climate-modeling group at the Goddard Institute for Space Studies in New York in 1974, and the National Science Foundation, which established the NCAR group at Boulder in 1964. With a direct pipeline to federal funding, these three groups received the sizable grants needed to buy and operate the huge state-of-the-art computers needed to model the climate. They remain the preeminent "Big Three" groups in the United States and, with the United Kingdom Meteorological Office and the European Center for Medium-Range Weather Forecast in Reading, England, probably represent the top climate-modeling centers in the world.

Carbon dioxide first entered atmospheric equations in 1961, when Syukuro Manabe and Fritz Möller at GFDL added CO_2 into a simulated atmosphere and observed its effect on climate. Measurements recorded since 1958 have shown a troubling increase in carbon dioxide concentrations in the atmosphere (in 1990 the concentration measured 355 parts per million, up from 315 ppm in 1958 and up from 280 ppm at the end of the nineteenth century). Scientists invoke an incriminating word to describe this jump: anthropogenic, or "man-caused." Earth's atmosphere had become the flue for a century's worth of consumed fossil fuels, smoldering rain forests, all the coal and gas and oil that powered the Industrial Revolution. Curious about its possible effects, Manabe and Richard T. Wetherald plugged a twofold rise in CO_2 into their climate model, turned the crank, and in 1975 sounded the first modern greenhouse alarm. Within a century, according to their computer simulation, these gases would gather in the atmosphere and act like the glass of a proverbial greenhouse, allowing solar heat in but blocking its escape. Average global temperature, the GFDL model suggested, would soar 3 degrees Centigrade—in climatic terms, a phenomenal increase. So in the late 1970s, there arose much talk about the greenhouse effect.

But not without confusion. Simulations run on other computers produced results that generally agreed with Manabe and Wetherald, but the precise amount of the predicted rise did not, and there was hardly unanimity about future trends. One well-known atmospheric scientist suggested the possibility of a new ice age. And since climatologists had had, in the words of National Academy of Engineering president Robert M. White, a "cry-wolf history" dating back to the 1920s, a legacy of dismal predictions including the inability to forecast monsoons and the inability to create rain, people were understandably sensitive about getting it right. The problem was summed up best, as

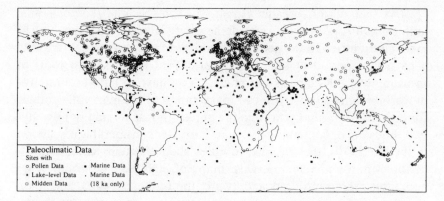

Familiar maps, like the Mercator projection above, become the starting point for new maps when novel data is superimposed on the territory. This one shows sources of data used in COHMAP's paleoclimate modeling. (COH-MAP Project Members/© 1988 AAAS)

usual, by John von Neumann, who paused one day in the 1950s to stare at a few passing clouds in the Princeton sky and remarked to his colleagues, "Do you think we will ever be able to predict that?"

While all this was going on, John Kutzbach was behind the times—about twelve thousand years behind the times. It wasn't that he hadn't thought about global warming; it was just that his scientific worldview remained strictly midwestern. He and several key colleagues—Herbert E. Wright, Jr., of the University of Minnesota and Thompson Webb III of Brown University—began talking in 1974 about understanding the climate history of central North America.

"We in a sense dreamed up this project about fifteen years ago," Kutzbach recalled recently. He was sitting in his light and airy office, eleven floors above the glacial moraine of Madison, Wisconsin; thin and narrow-featured, with a boyish flip of brown hair, he spoke with a nasal earnestness one associates with the Midwest. "It started out just trying to understand, and map, the climate history of the central part of North America. We thought we could do that, from the mapping point of view. But then my involvement in the project led me to say, 'We can't model what's happening in one region. We have to look at the global physics. Because what's happening here in the Midwest is caused by things that are happening elsewhere.' We fairly quickly realized we had to do it for the globe if we were going to do it at all."

As their vision became global, so, too, became their scientific ambitions. From every corner of the earth, they would assemble climate clues buried in the geologic record, each of those clues dated to a particular period of the recent past. "That involved new tools of measurement," Kutzbach continued. "You have to have accurate radiocarbon dates so that you can make sure that the map you produce for eighteen thousand years ago is eighteen thousand, and not twenty-two thousand or something like that." So after considerable discussion in the late 1970s, they decided to take "slices through geologic time" at three-thousand-year intervals: maps of eighteeen thousand years ago, fifteen thousand years ago, twelve thousand years ago, and so on to the present, at each time-horizon plotting the location of ice sheets, sea ice, vegetation, moisture, and sea level. "That was one track of our dream," Kutzbach said. "The other track was to do computer simulations of the climate, using the laws of physics. And then the synthesis was to compare the two and see how well they agreed. Or understand why they didn't."

In some respects this new mapping project represented a terrestrial version of a landmark oceanographic group effort called CLIMAP (Climate: Modeling and Prediction). In the 1970s the CLIMAP group gathered paleoceanographic data, primarily from marine plankton core samples, to reconstruct the climate as it existed at the height of the last ice age, eighteen thousand years ago. In 1976 CLIMAP members published results suggesting a periodic pattern of global cooling and warming that showed three different cycles lasting twenty thousand, forty thousand, and one hundred thousand years; those results were further tested against a computer model. One of the CLIMAP members was Tom Webb, who needed no convincing from Kutzbach or others that a more ambitious mapping project could be attempted. By 1977 discussions were well under way, and the National Science Foundation approved an initial grant application.

If there was a single moment when this subsequent project began to crystallize, it probably occurred in the spring of 1978. Kutzbach was on sabbatical in Germany and Webb was at Cambridge, where they met for lunch one day with F. A. (Alayne) Street-Perrott of Oxford University. "She's got some fantastic maps of lake levels from the past," Webb had promised Kutzbach.

Street-Perrott's work typified the ingenuity that scientists brought to paleoclimatic studies. Borrowing on decades of studies and her own fieldwork in Africa, examining existing sediments, tracing the faint paleoshorelines of now-arid lakes, scientifically conjuring villages out of the dust of the Sahel, she put together a series of maps showing the migration of wet weather from central Africa up into the Sahara, which was dotted with lakes ten thousand years ago; Lake Chad, one of these so-called paleolakes, covered as much area as the present-day Caspian Sea. Street-Perrott's maps showed how moisture swept up the continent twelve thousand years ago, then receded until, about four thousand years ago, all the lakes had dried, the terrain reverting to the desert conditions that prevail in modern times.

At that moment, Kutzbach and Webb realized that Street-Perrott's data mapped areas of the earth that their vegetation and climate studies did not, and by merging her coverage of Africa and southwestern Asia with their coverage of North America and Europe, they were well on their way to mapping the entire globe. "Right around that time," Kutzbach said, "we really began to realize that we *could,* with the help of a lot of people, map what was going on in the world, and hope to try and explain it with these climate models."

Perhaps most important from the cartographic point of view, these three researchers were all disciples of the map as an idea. It was not, Webb insists, a widely held sentiment in the geologic and paleo-ecologic communities at the time. In the early 1970s almost all palynologists—the scientists who study pollen—presented their findings in a stratified, nonspatial plot of data known as a time-series diagram. Out of habit and custom, everyone used them. "Mapping was second nature to me as a meteorologist," Webb recalls. "Alayne was trained as a geographer, and John was always saying, 'Think spatially, think meteorologically.' That allowed for an almost immediate meeting of the minds." Webb rather quickly assembled a network of researchers from around the world, and they began to gather and collate paleoclimatological data sets stretching back eighteen thousand years. They called their project COHMAP—the Cooperative Holocene Mapping Project (Holocene referring to the last ten thousand years). Out of earshot of the global-warming debates, too paleo-ecologic to catch the eye of politicians, too removed from incipient apocalypse to scare calamitarians into interest, they set to work.

Assembling paleoclimatological maps of the world requires an inferential and creative kind of science of the type that Sherlock Holmes could appreciate and would undoubtedly endorse. You had to perceive temperature, rainfall, and ice cover in the shadows cast by other, seemingly unrelated, data.

Microscopic bits of fossilized pollen provided some of the best clues. Each type of pollen has a distinct shape: pine has two bulging pods like a fly's eye, ragweed looks like a spiny meteor, sagebrush like a fertilized egg about to divide. Just as apples can come only from apple and not lemon trees, spruce pollen—as distinct in its shape as are apples among fruit—can come only from a spruce tree. When scientists extract cores of sediment from the bottom of a lake, each year compressed into a millimeter or two of mud, they can date each layer with carbon dating to within three hundred years; then, by picking through each layer of sediment and identifying the type and abundance of pollen, they can deduce the past vegetation and therefore past summer and winter temperatures as well as the amount of moisture necessary to support those populations. The presence of spruce pollen, for example, indicates a northern mid-continental climate. Moreover, by comparing these maps from different time slices—eighteen thousand years ago to nine thousand years ago to the present—they in a sense created a flip movie showing nearly twenty millennia of climate.

The past data on lake levels, compiled by Alayne Street-Perrott and others, was especially valuable because it provided clues in arid regions where vegetation, and therefore pollen, was sparse. Indeed, one of the great mysteries of past climate was how the American Southwest and North Africa, now so arid, had once been inundated by water. The location of Late Paleolithic villages, and the fishhooks recovered from them, placed dots on maps; joined together, they formed the paleo-shorelines of long-extinct lakes. In the absence of moisture and lakes, as in much of the American West, the collaborators resorted to another ingenious source of information: the fossilized middens of pack rats. Middens are hardened biological collages of feces, fossilized plants, pollens, and other informative debris scavenged by rodents and archived for the ages by the unlikely mechanism of their urine, which coats the middens with a glistening, protective sheen that seals the contents for millennia. They, too, could be carbon-dated.

To a lesser extent, ocean core samples offered a variation on the pollen mapping. The presence of different kinds of marine plankton tipped off researchers to variations in sea surface temperatures and water chemistry. More recently, sensitive instruments have plucked astounding results out of ice cores: tests of "fossil air" trapped in ice crystals have revealed the composition of the atmosphere, including the amount of CO_2, from thousands of years in the past.

When all the data was collected, the COHMAP map became in fact a rich, multilayered, laminated map, a kind of cartographic *sfogliatella*. Vegetation superimposed on geography. Temperature super-

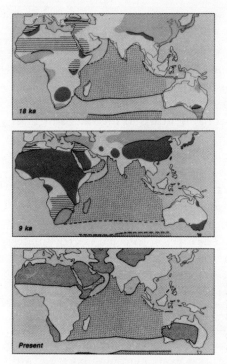

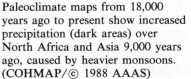

Paleoclimate maps from 18,000
years ago to present show increased
precipitation (dark areas) over
North Africa and Asia 9,000 years
ago, caused by heavier monsoons.
(COHMAP/© 1988 AAAS)

imposed on geography. Ice sheets superimposed on geography. Prevailing winds. Sea ice. Layer by layer, influence by influence, clue by
clue, the evidence piled up into a compelling picture of the world's
ancient climates. "It really is a time machine," Kutzbach would say
later, "that allows us to look as carefully at the past as we can look at
the present." Asked to take an imaginary ride over the earth eighteen
thousand years ago in that time machine, here is the planet as it
appeared to him.

"You'd see the huge ice sheet that covered North America, from
Labrador to the Rockies, and then there were mountain glaciers on the
Rockies and Cascades. The ice extended all the way from the Arctic
archipelago down to Madison. That was a *huge* thing, on the order of
two miles high in the middle near Hudson Bay. And of course that
gradually depressed the crust, and these low lakes or low-lying boggy
areas of the North are still responding to the fact that they were
pressed down so low by the weight of the ice. They're still rebounding.

"With all that water frozen onto the land surface," he continued,
"it meant that the ocean was lower, so that the continental shelf

extended out pretty much wherever there's a broad continental shelf, like on the East Coast or around Florida. You could *see* it! The sea level was a hundred meters lower. And certain areas of silt in the ocean were not ocean at all. They were land. There were land bridges between Siberia and Alaska, and from Southeast Asia all the way down into Indonesia. Most of that was land. And there was a lot more sea ice extending into middle latitudes, probably down to the English Channel. And of course in Europe the ice extended down into southern England, too. Scotland and northern England were glaciated, and all of Scandinavia, and into the Baltic area. The Baltic was covered with ice, and on over east into the western part of the Soviet Union. France was tundra, and it was just on the southern edge of that tundra, in the Dordogne, where some of these deep river valleys cut into the limestone and where these caves were. They were protected microclimates where the Late Paleolithic hunters lived, and painted the wonderful caves of Lascaux." That was also where Kutzbach, in a sense, had become interested in this whole business in the first place. Even time machines take the circle route.

"If you visualize running the clock fast-forward," Kutzbach went on, setting the maps in motion, "you'd see the ice beginning to melt, sea levels beginning to rise, the spruce forests marching back toward the north. And then you'd see this *unusual* thing: lakes forming in Africa between twelve thousand and six thousand years ago." The lakes, they would soon learn, formed as a result of unusually intense monsoons sweeping over North Africa and South Asia (see color illustration).

Even as these paleoclimatic maps were being assembled, the COHMAP group moved on simultaneously to the second stage of their project. Kutzbach began testing computer models as early as 1980. But the most interesting results emerged when they tapped into the same supercomputer and the same modeling program used by scientists at the National Center for Atmospheric Research to predict future climate trends. What they found, to compress many years of results, was that the NCAR computer simulation matched to a surprising degree the maps they had so painstakingly assembled from pollen, lake cores, and pack-rat middens. To be sure, there were some discrepancies. They watched in computerized time-lapse aeons as the huge North American ice sheet split the jet stream, diverting storm tracks to the south and thus creating the ancient lakes in the Southwest that had so puzzled climatologists. Spruce forests migrated north to Hudson Bay. Temperatures grew warmer, setting up sharp thermal boundaries

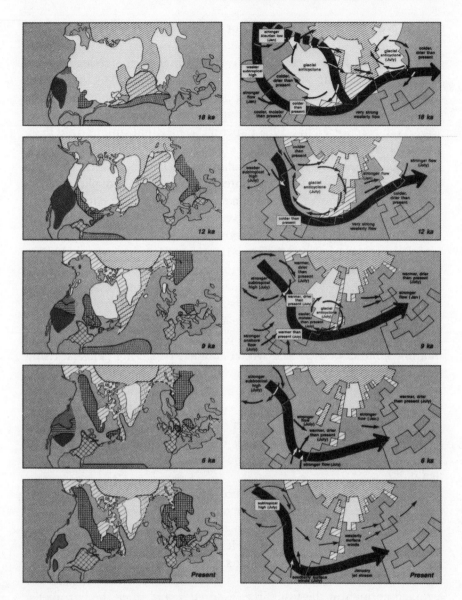

Comparison of paleoclimate data maps (*left,* at 18,000, 12,000, 9,000, 6,000 years ago, and present) with computerized climate models of same data *(right).* As glacial ice sheet recedes, the computer model suggests that the jet stream was deflected farther south about 12,000 years ago, producing increased precipitation in the now-arid American Southwest. (COHMAP/© 1988 AAAS)

where hot continental and cold oceanic air collided, creating fierce monsoons that would form off the western coast of Africa and inundate the continent, leaving mushy footprints in the form of lakes dotting sub-Sahelian Africa.

Maps almost always make explicit and visual certain features that remain implicit and hidden in the data. These maps had their surprises, too. As they reported in a 1988 paper in *Science* that summarized these findings, the COHMAP collaborators concluded that one variable above all others tested in the simulations best mimicked the changes they had mapped over the last eighteen thousand years of climate, best matched the tempo of these changes. It was not the circulation of ocean currents, as some had believed, nor did it appear connected to increasing concentrations of carbon dioxide in the atmosphere. It wasn't sunspots or shifting winds. It was a slight, periodic wobble in the earth's elliptical orbit around the sun, a prolonged shudder that, once every twenty-two thousand years or so, brought the sun closer to the earth in July instead of December. This results in a subtle variation in the amount of solar radiation reaching the earth, on the order of 5 to 10 percent, but that was enough to initiate massive cycles in climate, making summers hotter and winters colder, triggering glaciers, rising oceans, more intense monsoons, even global warming. Nor was this a new idea. As a theory, it had been proposed originally in 1864, championed early in the twentieth century by a Yugoslav mathematician named Milutin Milankovitch, and substantially proven by the CLIMAP group. "Everything else being equal," Kutzbach predicts, "ten thousand years from now the Sahara is going to be blooming again."

The COHMAP project has provided perhaps the most sophisticated check to date on the climate models that have aroused so much controversy. "It's the only way to test what you might call 'ground truth,' " says COHMAP member Herbert Wright. "There's no ground truth in the future." Kutzbach adds: "Our ability to chart the course of climate from instrumental records is very limited. The climate hasn't changed enough in the last three hundred years, since the barometer and thermometer were invented. Yet we're aware by looking at the landscape—in geology, archaeology, and so on—that there have been *huge* changes in climate in the more distant past. Because of a concern that there may be *big* climatic changes in the future, we have to leapfrog back beyond the period of instrumental records to try to visualize what it was really like a thousand years ago or a million years ago, both from data and from computer models that try to simulate those

worlds and explain them. We're applying our concepts and our supercomputer models to explain the past. And if we can do that successfully, when we *know* the answer, that gives us a leg up on looking
toward the future, when we don't know the answers."

No one denies that present-day climate models possess, like the
earth's orbit itself, a disconcerting bit of wobble. No description of
simulated climate, in scientific or popular forums, comes without tor-
tured qualifications from its creators. The models oversimplify ocean
circulation and precipitation. They oversimplify the moisture exchange
that occurs where ocean, land, and atmosphere meet. They don't even
include interactive clouds. As NCAR scientist Stephen Schneider
noted in 1987: "Mathematical climate models cannot simulate the full
complexity of reality." Less gentle is the judgment of Robert Cess, who
heads the Institute for Atmospheric Studies at the State University of
New York at Stony Brook and who recently assessed the reliability of
a dozen such greenhouse models. Asked to assess the best, he replied,
"We're all in shambles. It's not who does the best. It's who does the
least worst." The contradictory results have grown so striking that
Cess believes atmospheric scientists may be missing a fundamental
element in their models. "It's not a cloud problem," Cess said. "It's a
problem of understanding the physics."
    The NCAR model, used both by John Kutzbach's group to test
the past and Warren Washington's group to imagine the future, is
typical of state-of-the-art computer simulations, both in its strengths
and in its weaknesses. Water has covered 70 percent of the earth's
surface for eternity, but only in the last fifteen years or so have modelers been able to incorporate oceans into their climate models, and only
then in the crudest of terms. Predicting climate in the absence of oceans
is like predicting weather in the absence of realistic clouds, which has
been another shortcoming in modeling systems. The resolution of
these simulations is roughly 300-by-300-mile squares of the grid—
rather larger than your average cloud. It takes time. Even with powerful supercomputers, such as NCAR's recently retired Cray-1 at
Boulder, it takes 110 seconds of computer time to simulate one day;
running two nineteen-year simulations required more than 400 hours,
and improving the resolution by two would require 4,000 hours. And
although the actual terrain of continents can affect climate, these features have been incorporated only in the roughest, most amorphous
sense. "The Rocky Mountains are in there," Washington explains,
"but things like the Alleghenies are not." At current resolution, the

Rockies appear in the simulations as a vast lump, not unlike a log under a white blanket that stretches from the Plains nearly to the California coast.

In one of their most recent experiments, Washington and his principal collaborators, Thomas W. Bettge and Gerald A. Meehl, asked the question that most preoccupies us: what would happen to the climate if the amount of carbon dioxide in the atmosphere doubled? They ran their simulation nineteen years into the future, and they discovered that the planet warmed considerably, averaging an increase of 4 to 4.5 degrees Centigrade after two decades. However, this warming occurs primarily in the polar region of the northern hemisphere, and primarily during the winter. The model also suggests milder winters and wetter interiors. This forecast comes with the usual disclaimers. "No 'smoking gun' evidence exists, however," the authors noted recently, "to prove that the Earth's global climate is warming (versus a natural climate variability), or, if it is warming, whether that warming is caused by the increase in CO_2."

That cautious interpretation is at odds, in tone if not conclusion, with the statements of another prominent climate modeler, James Hansen of NASA. Hansen told a congressional committee in 1988 that the greenhouse effect is already here. Most other climatologists, while stressing the potential gravity of atmospheric changes already under way, have backed off from that conclusion, and the disagreement merely points out the very real conflicts that arise when urgent public policy needs meet imperfect science, a conflict summarized succinctly by Stephen Schneider in a *Scientific American* article: "Climate models do not yield definitive forecasts of what the future will bring; they provide only a dirty crystal ball in which a range of plausible fortunes can be glimpsed. They thereby pose a dilemma: we are forced to decide how long to keep cleaning the glass before acting on what we see inside."

Perhaps the least-appreciated aspect of the present greenhouse "crisis" is not that the climate will change and become warmer, for there have been many greenhouse episodes during the earth's climatic past. It is the *speed* with which the current warming appears to be occurring. According to some projections, the concentration of atmospheric carbon dioxide will have doubled by the year 2100, to say nothing of other greenhouse gases like methane, chlorofluorocarbons, nitrous oxide, and ozone. The temperature increase predicted by Warren Washington's group for 2010 is nearly equal to the entire global warming that occurred between eighteen thousand and six thousand

Spruce Observed

Spruce Simulated by CCM Output

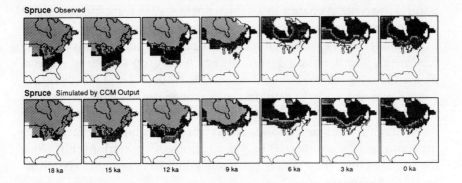

18 ka   15 ka   12 ka   9 ka   6 ka   3 ka   0 ka

Trees on the march: analysis of fossil pollen indicated the northward movement of spruce forests as the ice pack receded *(top)*, a phenomenon predicted
quite well by the NCAR general circulation model *(bottom)* used by Warren
Washington. (COHMAP/© 1988 AAAS)

---

years ago. To put it more bluntly, they see twelve millennia of change
squeezed into two decades. As a scientist who, from those very first
visits to the caverns at Lascaux, has been fascinated by the crucial yet
tenuous relationship between climate and human life, John Kutzbach
has thought a lot about the human ramifications of these changes.

He has thought about the spruce forests of his native Midwest.
Some eighteen thousand years ago, these forests lay in southern Illinois
and, as the climate warmed, they inched 500 miles to the north at a rate
of migration that has been calculated at approximately five miles per
century. According to the projected warming trend for the next century, these trees would have to move 250 miles per century. Only in
computer simulations and in Shakespeare's Birnam Wood do forests
move that fast. "You can argue that humans have survived this long
because we *are* adaptable, and there's a lot of resiliency built into the
earth," Kutzbach says. "But there's probably a normal pace at which
we usually adapt to change, and if the change comes too quickly, it's
hard to adapt."

The race between change and adaptation triggers a thousand
questions: Where are we going to grow food in the next century?
Where are the water resources of North America going to be? Will
there be enough? Will coastal waters lap at new seaports like Tallahas-
see and San Antonio? Are there going to be tropical rain forests left?
And even if we don't slash and burn them into extinction, will these

natural ecosystems change in a catastrophic way in response to climate change? Every answer lies on a map yet to be created.

Finally, the impact of climatic change may ultimately involve one final overlay to the many layers already piled atop terrestrial geography, and that is the geopolitical map of the future. "In an ideal world," John Kutzbach says, "it wouldn't make much difference whether corn was grown in the United States or in Canada. But in the real world, where there are political boundaries, it can make a big difference where the ecotones [the boundaries between regions of vegetation] shift. And the *rate* at which they shift is probably going to compound the problems. And opportunities."

Opportunities? It is a word heard hardly at all in the apocalyptic discussions of global warming. Kutzbach, in that measured and quiet midwestern way, is just trying to keep an equatorial frame of mind in a highly polarized debate. "My sense here is that it's important to have as good a road map as we can have as to what the likely changes are going to be. Not that they're going to be bad, necessarily," he says. "It's just going to be different."

6. The Hole in the Roof of the Sky

ULTRAVIOLET SPECTROMETERS
AND A MAP OF
THE OZONE LAYER

||||||||||

> It had ceased to be a blank space of
> delightful mystery—a white patch for a
> boy to dream gloriously over. It had
> become a place of darkness.
> —Joseph Conrad,
> *Heart of Darkness*

When the National Oceanic and Atmospheric Administration launched its *Nimbus 4* weather satellite in 1970, one of the less-heralded sensors aboard the spacecraft was something called a backscatter ultraviolet instrument, known to the few engineers aware of its existence as the BUV. Circling the earth thirteen and a half times a day, the BUV measured how much ultraviolet radiation, showering down on the earth from the sun, bounced back up off the atmosphere. The amount of backscatter provided a clue to part of the atmosphere's chemistry, because one particular component forms a thin, shifting, waxing and waning molecular shield which absorbs ultraviolet wavelengths of light; the deeper the penetration of sunlight, the more ultraviolet that is absorbed as it bounces back off molecules of air, resulting in less ultraviolet backscatter. That absorbent molecule was a chemical cousin of regular oxygen. Where molecules of oxygen are formed out of two oxygen atoms (O_2), this one is formed out of three. It is called ozone (O_3).

In 1970 when *Nimbus 4* went up, "ozone" was not the environmental buzzword it has subsequently become, and no one outside a small circle of atmospheric chemists cared much about the BUV instrument. Ozone, however, did interest scientists, not only because it formed a small but important component of the atmosphere's chemical makeup, but also because it was a molecule with biological implications; for in the absence of ozone, the potentially lethal rain of ultraviolet radiation reaching the surface of the earth could affect everything from marine plankton populations (and thus the food chain) to the incidence of skin cancer and the performance of the immune system.

But within a year of *Nimbus 4*'s launch, "ozone" entered the vocabulary of global concern. In 1971 an international debate over the use of supersonic transport planes, or SSTs, sensitized the public to the importance of the ozone layer and the dangers associated with its possible degradation, and three years later, two scientists at the University of California-Irvine dropped a bomb on atmospheric chemistry by predicting that the presence of man-made chlorine-based chemicals in the atmosphere (known collectively as chlorofluorocarbons) could have a devastating effect on the protective ozone layer. F. Sherwood Rowland and Mario J. Molina described laboratory experiments foreshadowing this effect in a famous 1974 *Nature* article, and in a much-quoted remark, Rowland later explained the implications of the work in a salutatory comment made to his wife when he returned home from the lab one night: "The work is going very well, but it looks like the end of the world." That was the bigger message of the experiments.

Measurements of the ozone layer suddenly became very important, just as the limitations of the BUV instrument on *Nimbus 4* became very obvious, and that's when Arlin J. Krueger and a group of scientists and engineers at NASA's Goddard Space Flight Center in Greenbelt, Maryland, sat down to design a new instrument. The BUV recorder looked straight down at the earth as the satellite made its multiple passes, from South Pole to North, during the course of twenty-four hours. But the ozone is not a static entity, not truly a "layer" in the sense of a blanket or a veil. Rather, if you had a thick straw measuring fifty kilometers (about thirty miles) long, stretching from the ground up to the upper reaches of the atmosphere, and you took all the ozone molecules enclosed by that straw and gathered them at sea-level pressure and temperature, you would end up with a three-millimeter thickness of molecules, a layer about as thick as this line of

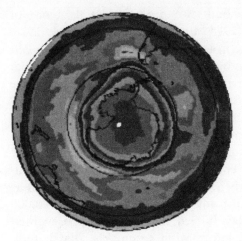

Anatomy of a hole: false-color map of Antarctic spring over the South Pole shows the extent of the hole in the ozone layer on Oct. 3, 1990. The map was created by the total ozone mapping spectrometer (TOMS). (NASA/GSFC)

type is tall; but that "layer" is actually a threadbare mist of molecules diffused through all fifty kilometers of the atmosphere. It swirls, thickens, and thins depending on time of day, time of year, and location, a dynamic and shifting marble cake of gas mixing, massing, and eddying through the stratosphere, and Arlin Krueger knew that there was an awful lot of variation they were missing outside those thirteen and a half passes. "It was as if you took two slices of a marble cake at two different locations," he says now, "and threw away the rest of the cake, and tried to guess what was in between the slices. We just couldn't tell what the structure was. That's when I proposed the Total Ozone Mapping Spectrometer (TOMS)," Krueger says.

They needed a new instrument, so Krueger and his colleagues at NASA-Goddard came up with this sophisticated spectrometer. Like the BUV, it measured the degree of ultraviolet reflection off the ozone layer in something called Dobson units, which express the total thickness of ozone from the ground up to an altitude of fifty kilometers; a value of 296 Dobson units over the South Pole during the austral spring, for example, meant that the total thickness of the ozone layer at that time was 2.96 millimeters. Unlike the old instrument, TOMS had a scanner that measured the ozone over a much broader area. The new instrument, according to Krueger, was "able to map all of the structure in the total ozone."

It would prove to be a remarkably powerful mapping tool. Beck-man Instruments in California built two prototype models, one of which was ready as early as 1975. Finally, on October 24, 1978, NOAA, which manages all meteorological satellites, launched *Nimbus 7* with the TOMS instrument on board. One week later, on November 1, 1978, they switched on the mapper. In order to streamline the handling of an unprecedented amount of data, NASA's data-production group for TOMS programmed their computers to accept a predicted range of ozone measurements. The range limited the data to values from a high of 650 Dobson units to a low of 180 Dobson units; anything higher or lower, they concluded, would be unlikely, unreliable, and would contradict all their computer predictions. As soon as it was turned on, TOMS began firing down something like 190,000 ozone readings each and every day. Indeed, the TOMS mapper worked so well, and gathered so much information so quickly, that it took years to figure out exactly what that information suggested. It suggested nothing less than a hole in the roof of the sky. But it wasn't the people at NASA who saw it first, and therein lies a cautionary tale about mapping in the age of computers.

Joseph Farman, a British atmospheric scientist, made his first trip to the Antarctic Circle in 1956. He and his colleagues at the British Antarctic Survey in Cambridge have been measuring ozone levels above Antarctica ever since, and they haven't come anywhere close to handling 190,000 measurements in those three and half decades.

The very efficiency of satellites introduces a mapping problem that is all too often overshadowed by the pretty pictures they generate. With the increasing use of space as an observation platform, and with increasingly sophisticated and prolix instruments of measure, satellites generate staggering amounts of information. If you do not have the means and the manpower to analyze all that data, to throw out the chaff and keep the wheat of the information, you may well miss the message in the data. Even with powerful computers and a state-of-the-art spectrometer, you may end up worse off than if you were one person analyzing one modest subset of data from one creaky old instrument. That is what happened with TOMS, that and perhaps less than optimum interoffice communication.

All this came to light because of work at the British Antarctic Survey. Joe Farman, a member of the survey staff, belonged to a British team that, as part of the International Geophysical Year in 1957 (the same year as Sputnik), placed ozone-measuring spectrophotometers on the ground at the survey's two Antarctic scientific stations at Halley Bay and the Argentine Islands. Unlike satellite instruments, ground-based spectrometers measure the amount of ultraviolet radiation that reaches the earth, and the thickness and robustness of the ozone layer can be inferred from variations in the amount of ultraviolet rays that slip through.

Around 1982, Farman and his colleagues began to notice that the amount of ultraviolet radiation reaching their instrument at Halley Bay toward winter's end had been steadily rising, meaning that ozone levels must just as steadily be dropping. The trend was not apparent before the early 1970s, and the degradation appeared to be both steep and steady. As so often occurs in science (and healthily so), the immediate response in Cambridge was that something was wrong with the equipment.

"It was a fairly old instrument," Farman recalls, "so we sent in a new instrument and placed the two side by side for a year to see if there was any difference. And there wasn't. As it turned out, this was a new effect indeed." The new spectrometer was deployed in January of 1984. After a year of operation, both instruments showed that the ozone levels became exceptionally low at the end of winter. Indeed, the decline in the ozone layer was nothing short of astonishing: as the data built up, the British measurements indicated that between 1977 and 1984 the springtime ozone layer had decreased by 40 percent. And yet the British scientists felt stymied, too, because the more numerous and global (and presumably more reliable) values reported by TOMS showed no such decrease.

By 1984, as Farman recalls, "things were getting so painful" that one of the British scientists wrote a letter to the ozone mapping team at Goddard reporting this precipitate decline in ozone. "But we didn't get an answer," Farman recalls. Nor was that surprising. He knew the NASA staff was busy revising their definitive three-volume "Blue Book" on the atmosphere. What he didn't know is that data analysts at NASA, poring through tons of TOMS data, had begun to "flag" ozone measurements over the South Pole that were lower than any of NASA's computer models had predicted. These values simply fell outside the parameters set up by NASA's scientists. Unfortunately, the data analysts did not bring this trend to the attention of scientists like Arlin Krueger, and the computer in effect had been programmed to discount the data. "Satellites get so much data that you really have to do something of the sort," Farman acknowledges. "You really need to sort out the information. What they did wrong, toward the end, was that they were throwing away so much data that it should have told them something was wrong." "That should have tipped us off," Krueger agreed recently. Ultimately, it did, but not right away, not until the British group brought it to their attention again, in the most public of ways.

As the data continued to point toward an actual hole in the ozone layer, Farman was especially well positioned to offer a possible explanation for what was happening. James Lovelock, the British atmospheric scientist and author of the Gaia theory, has suggested that "the least complex and most accessible part of a planet is its atmosphere," but the phenomenon over the South Pole suggested exactly the opposite. It was very complex, most inaccessible, and it took some enterprising chemistry to come up with the scenario that Farman and others, notably Richard S. Stolarski of NASA-Goddard and Susan Solomon of NOAA, eventually developed—a scenario that incorporated and expanded the theory originally proposed by Rowland and Molina in 1974. The hypothesis went like this:

Chlorofluorocarbons were invented in 1930, and after half a century of use in everything from the Freon in cooling units and automobile air conditioners to the Styrofoam in packing crates and fast-food packaging, increasing amounts of CFCs had found their way into the atmosphere. CFC molecules are remarkably stable. Indeed, their very stability allowed them to circulate higher and higher in the atmosphere. They were not broken down in the troposphere, the layer of the atmosphere that extends from the surface of the earth to an altitude of about ten kilometers (roughly thirty-three thousand feet, or the cruising altitude of many commercial airliners). Ozone molecules are widely diffused at higher altitudes, from ten to fifty kilometers, with a peak in the layer at about twenty-five kilometers. Because of their stubborn chemical disposition, their unwillingness to mix with other elements, CFCs rise like lazy, indifferent, wayward balloons higher and higher up into the atmosphere above the ozone layer. Here they no longer enjoy the protective layer of ozone, and the intense, unscreened ultraviolet radiation contains enough energy to shear them apart. The result is the creation of chemical monsters: highly reactive rogue chlorine atoms known as free radicals, which dart and diffuse through the atmosphere, looking for reactions almost in the way bullies look to pick fights. A single chlorine atom can decimate up to a hundred thousand ozone molecules, briefly forming chlorine monoxide (ClO), then breaking apart again, to rove about wreaking more destruction. Virtually that entire chemical scenario had been anticipated by Rowland and Molina.

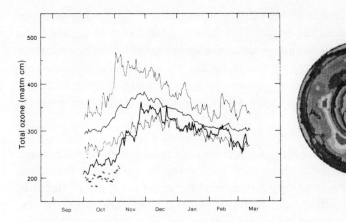

The graph convinced the scientists, but the map convinced the public: compare Joseph Farman's graph of the springtime drop in ozone over Antarctica during October *(left)* with the false-color map by TOMS in 1987. (J. Farman/© 1985 Macmillan Magazines Ltd.; NASA/GSFC)

What they didn't anticipate was *where* those reactions would take place. It fell to Farman and others with expertise in polar regions to suggest the final twist. Since the Antarctic ozone hole appeared only during the austral spring, from roughly August to November, Farman argued that it was probably related to something called the "polar vertex," an intensely cold bubble of air (about 80 degrees Centigrade below zero) boxed over the South Pole during the austral winter. Current theory argues that the cold and dark of the Antarctic winter acts, paradoxically, as an incubator, where chemical reactions occur on ice crystals in the atmosphere to produce a large reservoir of chlorine-based molecules; with the light and warmth of spring, those chlorine atoms are loosed all at once, creating the hole that continued to show up in the Halley Bay ozone data.

When the evidence could no longer be ignored, Farman and colleagues Brian G. Gardiner and Jonathan D. Shanklin wrote up their results documenting the decline of ozone over Antarctica from 1977 to 1984 and sent it off to the British journal *Nature*. As is customary, the journal promptly forwarded the report to expert reviewers. "Because of the reviewing system," Farman remembers, "word had begun to get out. There was a lull when the TOMS people dove into their data and analyzed it. Clearly, there was a measurable effect there, too, so that everyone could accept it. One of our reviewers was a bit argumentative about details, but said, 'Publish it immediately!' The other reviewer had written across his copy, 'This is impossible! But of course if it's true, we can't wait twenty years to find out that it's true, so publish it immediately!' " The report was published more or less immediately, in the May 16, 1985 issue of *Nature*. And, as subsequent measurements have shown, it *was* true: there was a hole in the ozone layer over the Antarctic.

There was not, however, an *image* of that hole. Farman's group published graphs showing the decreasing levels of Antarctic ozone (they also took the opportunity to advert to the "inadequacy" of computer models in setting parameters for acceptable data). But they did not produce their data in the form of a map. And if the *Nature* paper made the ozone hole real and troubling to scientists, NASA's maps of the ozone hole made the phenomenon real and troubling for the world at large.

"Why did Joe Farman catch it before we did?" Arlin Krueger laments these days. "That's easily explained. Joe had only two sets of data, one of them from the Antarctic station since 1957. It was a very long record. Joe was also interested in polar night chemistry. When he saw ozone values getting lower and lower, at some point it became obvious that that had not happened before."

There were other reasons. The ozone decrease was bigger than predicted; if a computer can be likened to a colander in its handling of data, then it is the programmers who decide how big the holes in the colander will be, and if the data you are looking for turns out to be smaller than suspected, it will slip through the holes in your program, as the low ozone values did. In addition, the NASA team was looking at global ozone values, not just over one spot in Antarctica, so they had a lot more information to sift through the colander. In 1982 they were still digging out of the data sent down in 1978 and 1979. "There was this wealth of new data," Krueger says. "You couldn't focus on anything. You have to realize, we're kind of in the Stone Age in terms of earth observation from space."

Once the data was fetched out of the computer archives, however, the Total Ozone Mapping Spectrometer could do what it was designed to do: make maps. And those maps, first produced in 1986 and released by NASA, had a dramatic effect on the perception of the ozone problem (see color illustration). "Most of us were fairly convinced that there was a problem from the ground-based data of Joe Farman," says Robert Watson, NASA's leading ozone expert, "but as soon as we

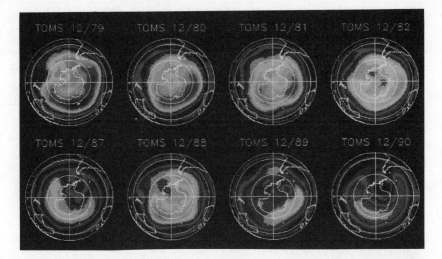

"As soon as we made images," says NASA's Robert Watson, "we could see it wasn't a small, isolated hole." By recording data digitally and storing it in computers, atmospheric scientists can compare yearly Antarctic ozone maps to detect long-term trends. (NASA/GSFC)

looked at the satellite data and made images, we could suddenly see that it wasn't a small, isolated hole. We could see that it was at least as large as the United States, if not larger. It allowed us to see the sheer scale and dimension of the thing. It was an image that allowed scientists, policymakers, and the lay public to see that human activity could perturb the environment and create a hole in a way that you could not *see* in any other way." The indisputable message inherent in those maps, atmospheric scientists believe, created an international political climate that, in 1987, made possible the first Montreal Protocol, in which some forty nations agreed to a 50 percent cut in the use of chlorofluorocarbons by 1999.

It bears repeating, for all the data analysts who will have to cull meaningful information from all future mapping projects, that the burgeoning hole in the ozone layer escaped detection for at least five years because ground-based computers were in effect programmatically blinded from seeing the essential information. Is there a scientific moral to the story? "Well," says Arlin Krueger, "I suppose one lesson is that there should be more funding for the analysis and interpretation of data. In the past many data sets have gone into the archives without being analyzed. A lot of information in the data is not being utilized."

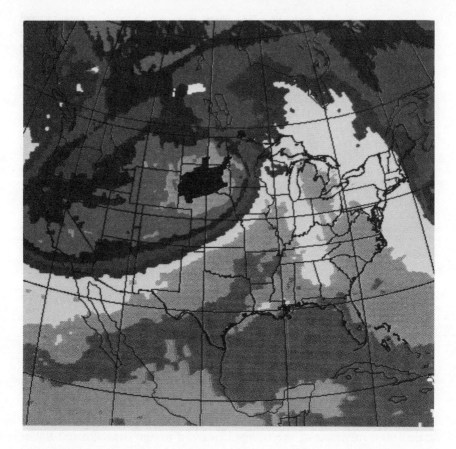

Indeed, a recent report by the General Accounting Office suggests one more grim legacy of the Reagan era: NOAA's plans to manage the data from its climate and weather satellites were vetoed by Department of Commerce officials, who adopted the Reagan philosophy that such data management should be undertaken by the private sector. The private sector saw no commercial potential in the weather data, and consequently thousands of cans of archival climate data have literally rotted from neglect. And any attempt to map trends, especially in meteorology and atmospheric science, depends on having reliable archival data. All this is especially important to remember because, beginning in the mid-1990s, NASA's Earth Observing System, with nearly two dozen new instruments aboard an earth-orbiting satellite, will begin raining billions of bits of information down to data analysts.

The other moral of the story reiterates one of the emerging tri-

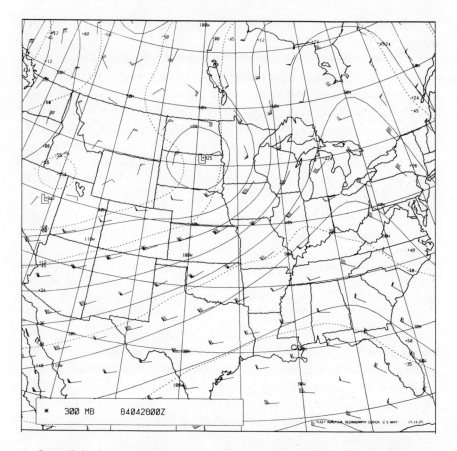

Serendipity in mapping: you start out with a TOMS map of the ozone layer over North America *(opposite page)*, as Arlin Krueger of the Goddard Space Flight Center discovered, and end up with a map that traces, like a biological stain, the contours of the jet stream *(above)*. (NASA/*Planetary Space Science*)

umphs of modern instrumental mapmaking. The TOMS instrument, unexpectedly and serendipitously, has turned out to be able to map two other completely unrelated and unexpected physical domains. First, Krueger and his colleagues at NASA discovered that, by chance, molecules of ozone have turned out to be extremely accurate markers, almost like a biological stain, to movements and shifts in the jet stream, and since the jet stream is probably the single most important determinant in the evolution of mid-latitude weather patterns, this is of enormous interest to meteorologists. With a geostationary satellite positioned over the United States, Krueger believes, maps of the jet stream could instantaneously document changes, leading to more accurate weather forecasts.

The second surprise turned out to be sulfur dioxide (SO_2). In April of 1982, ozone mappers picked up surprisingly strong ozone signals from central Mexico. What they were picking up was not ozone, but sulfur dioxide, which reflects ultraviolet radiation at the same wavelength as ozone. And what they were seeing was the eruption of El Chichón, since sulfur dioxide is produced in copious amounts by volcanoes. Thus TOMS, quite unexpectedly, has become one of the most powerful ways of tracing the movement of volcanic clouds. It enabled Krueger to monitor the massive, multimillion-ton plume of sulfur dioxide belched out in the June 1991 eruption of Mount Pinatubo in the Philippines, a cloud that may deplete the ozone layer even more.

Ozone remains the main job of TOMS, because depletion of ozone is probably the main preoccupation of atmospheric chemists. So much chlorine has been expelled into the atmosphere over the last fifty years, and so slowly is it chemically disarmed, that even with legislative remedies like the Montreal accord, there may still await some nasty chemical surprises for the atmosphere, and for us. "We still have ten years in which chlorine levels will be increasing in the atmosphere, and right now we're breaking records every minute," says Joe Farman. "We may not like what we see in the year 2000. What we are doing now is to give us more options in 2005 or 2010. Otherwise, we won't have any options left at all."

THE
ANIMATE
LANDSCAPE

7. Vesalius Revisited

COMPUTED TOMOGRAPHY, MAGNETIC RESONANCE, AND THE REVOLUTION IN DIAGNOSTIC IMAGING

||||||||||

Whilst my Physitians by their love are growne
  Cosmographers, and I their Mapp, who lie
Flat on this bed, that by them may be showne
  That this is my South-west discoverie
  Per fretum febris, by these streights to die,

I joy, that in these straits, I see my West;
  For, though theire currants yeeld returne to
    none
What shall my West hurt me? As West and East
  In all flatt Maps (and I am one) are one,
  So death doth touch the Resurrection.

       —John Donne,
       "Hymne to God My God, in My Sicknesse"

The temptation has always been irresistible. In the last months of 1895, while toying with a cathode-ray tube in his laboratory, Wilhelm Roentgen could not resist holding his hand—and that of Frau Roentgen—between a stream of mysterious "X rays" and a piece of photographic film, and soon after he was enclosing the bony, ghostly images in letters to friends. In the 1940s and '50s, according to medical folklore, the pioneers of magnetic resonance could not resist sticking their thumbs and feet and even heads into strong magnetic fields to test the effects, just as an obsessed physicist named Raymond Damadian, strapped into his machine and wearing the look of a man about to go over Niagara Falls in a barrel, posed in front of a nuclear magnetic resonance device in 1977. James Prichard, a physician at Yale University, has watched the effects of champagne change the chemistry of his own brain using a related technique known as magnetic resonance spectroscopy, and John Allman, a psychobiologist at Caltech, has mapped his

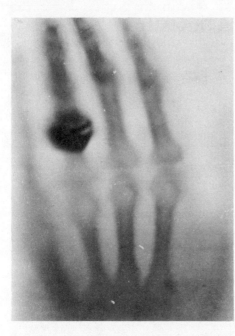

Frau Roentgen's hand,
with ring: the first X ray
of human anatomy. (Francis
A. Countway Library of
Medicine, Boston)

own brain during the process of perception using both magnetic resonance and positron emission tomography (PET) scans. In one of the
classic folktales of magnetic-resonance-imaging (MRI) technology, a
young General Electric technician taking a training course volunteered
to undergo a scan and experienced the thoroughly twentieth-century
trauma of discovering a tumor in his own brain. The pioneers of
anatomic cartography have chosen to follow the Socratic imperative to
"know thyself" by *mapping* themselves.

For much of the twentieth century, the X ray has been the technology of choice—indeed, almost the only choice—for creating images
with which doctors could make rough geographic plots of the human
body, identifying pockets of disease or potential trouble spots. But as
in so many other fields, new technologies of measurement began to
emerge immediately after World War II and entered clinical use in the
1970s and '80s, conferring upon physicians the ability to visualize, to
categorize, to resolve, and to map the interior of the human body with
unprecedented detail and resolution. To underscore the overall success
of CT scans, MRI images, ultrasound, and other technologies, it suf-
fices to invoke a medical term used ever more infrequently: exploratory

surgery. There is diminishing need for invasive surgical exploration when the new technology allows a more artful and less painful reconnaissance.

The new technologies of diagnostic imaging are not limited to the well-publicized virtues of CT scans and MRI images. Video thermography, which measures variations in temperature, can scan the skull and pinpoint areas of elevated temperature where migraine headaches have nested, setting off waves of pain. A sonar device, encased in a catheter measuring 1.64 millimeters in diameter (slightly wider than a pencil lead), uses ultrasound vibrations to map the inner topography of blood vessels and arteries, showing the location and extent of blockages (like devices used outside the body to reveal fetuses and heart function), and has been referred to as an acoustic microscope. With a different application of the same Doppler techniques used by astronomers to measure the outward rush of galaxies, cardiologists can measure and map the rush of blood through the heart. By adapting the technique of stereophotogrammetry, which has been used to create three-dimensional maps from satellite imagery, orthopedists have mapped every hill and dale of cartilage and bone, charting topographic variations of as little as fifty-millionths of a meter.

Even more spectacular technology is on the way. In another variation on the theme of thematic mapping, some devices map changes in tissues over time; tiny changes in the brain's magnetic field, provoked by auditory signals, can be picked up by measuring instruments known as superconducting quantum interference devices (or "squids"), which produce a "tone map" of neurons as they respond to sound. Experiments with monoclonal antibodies suggest that doctors will be able to dress up specific antibodies with radioactive isotopes, so that the antibodies that seek out and seize the protein myosin in heart muscle, for example, will reveal a precise map of the dead cardiac tissue following a heart attack. Maps of brain tumors and of gallstones concealed in the coves of the bladder, the rugged coastlines of cartilage in a joint or the plaque-crusty lumen (interior lining) of blood vessels, rogue cancer cells circulating throughout the body or the eyelids and fingers of a burgeoning, fetal being—all these are features of the anatomical landscape, all can be plotted against fixed anatomic coordinates, and all are suddenly, sensationally within reach of nonphotographic, human vision.

It is an approximate cartography, just as each human body is approximately similar, a landscape dotted with familiar landmarks, the heart reliably at one latitude and the brain at its customary pole, but not always of the same shape or dimension or location. Each diagnostic image shares the general coordinates of the species while retaining the unique coordinates of the individual. These are maps of health and maps of disease, of the body in disarray and in repair, landscapes mortal and remedial.

That there is a connection between anatomy and cartography is perhaps most historically explicit in an anecdote about the intersecting destinies of two brilliant sixteenth-century intellects. It is well known in the annals of cartography that Gerhardus Mercator, the most accomplished mapmaker of his age, toiled at his trade in the Flemish town of Louvain between 1534 and 1552. Less known perhaps is the fact that the preeminent cartographer of a different, biological terrain simultaneously worked in Louvain, and also revolutionized the scientific discipline at which he practiced. His name was Andreas Vesalius, and just as Mercator was drawing and engraving his first map, Vesalius reintroduced the study of human anatomy in Louvain in 1537. Within a few years, he would redraw the world of the human body in much the same way that Mercator would reconfigure the globe.

To find a period comparable in change to today's dramatic advances in medical cartography and diagnostic imaging, one would have to return to the days when Vesalius extended the Renaissance to human anatomy. Just as Ptolemy's geography dominated and constrained geographical thought during the Dark Ages, the medical doctrine of the Roman physician Galen had similarly tyrannized anatomical thought for a thousand years. As an example of how great minds can go wrong without a map, both Hippocrates and Aristotle—neither of whom ever dissected a human body and thus never "explored" the territory—believed the heart was the seat of intellect. Though human dissections began in the medieval period, both religious pressure and academic prejudice assured a furtive quality to the practice, creating an atmosphere in which lectures were delivered by candlelight in cramped, crowded rooms and trapdoors were built beneath the dissecting table so that cadavers, usually of executed criminals and often robbed from graves, could be hastily removed from sight.

When Vesalius attended the university at Paris between 1533 and 1536, authorities permitted only two dissections a year. Partly for that reason, Vesalius eventually moved on to the university at Padua in Italy, where his contributions were not only medical (he successfully lobbied for more frequent dissections) but also political (he convinced

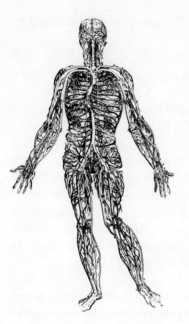

"Venous man": the veins
of the human body as they
appeared in Vesalius's *Fabrica*,
1543 edition. (Francis A. Countway
Library of Medicine, Boston)

local magistrates not to draw and quarter criminals, thus preserving
them as specimens). With the increased number of dissections came the
first "tables," or maps, of human anatomy. Vesalius published *Tabulae
Anatomicae Sex* in 1538, and in 1543 (the same year that Copernicus
published his heliocentric theory of the solar system), he published
what is regarded as one of the great books of the sixteenth century, the
masterpiece known as *De Humani Corporis Fabrica*. It was the first
atlas of human anatomy, and in the words of medical historian Sherwin B. Nuland, it "epitomizes the confluence of science, technology,
and culture in a way that few, perhaps no, other books have ever
done."

Unlike the maps of Mercator, which still resemble the geographical world we know, the new anatomical maps that have emerged in the
past two decades render Vesalius's noble effort almost unrecognizable
except in the grossest details. The heart, and other "soft" tissues, can
now be mapped and imaged by an impressive assortment of diagnostic
tools—magnetic resonance imaging, ultrasound, digital subtraction
angiography (DSA), computed tomography scans, and positron emission tomography scans. Most impressive of all, this knowledge has
been won without knife or saw, with neither massive disfigurement nor

permanent harm. The new technology is, to use the term preferred by so many physicians, "noninvasive."

Every diagnostic-imaging technique developed over the past two or three decades answers one or another of the shortcomings associated with X rays, whose days as a preeminent screening technique may be numbered. X rays create pictures, of course, because bones and other dense structures of the body absorb them, while softer tissues allow them to pass through, creating a "shadowgram" on film. Those images come at a price, however. Standard X rays do not distinguish between soft tissues such as the heart or liver; they produce only a two-dimensional view of the anatomical terrain; and they subject an individual to ionizing radiation. And so researchers began to consider more sophisticated uses of X rays, and one new application began to emerge in the 1950s: computed tomography (CT).

The notion of computed tomography as an imaging technology began to be explored in the 1950s and '60s. Allan M. Cormack, a South African physicist who later moved to Tufts University, did experiments in 1956 and 1963 demonstrating the validity of the fundamental physical idea underlying the technique. He started out with a prototype machine that cost less than a hundred dollars to build and with an inanimate hunk of aluminum and wood as his first "specimen." Cormack realized that by encircling the specimen and firing pencil-thin beams of gamma rays at it from various points of the circle, internal variations of density—and thus structure—could be inferred. The inference, however, was mathematical, requiring a computer to assess tens of thousands of equations to reconstruct a three-dimensional cross section of tissue. (In yet another wonderful example of the long reach of mathematics, the computational equations used to recreate CT images were initially explicated in 1917 by the Austrian mathematician Johann Radon in an attempt to understand gravitational fields.)

Cormack published his results in the physics literature, where they predictably escaped the attention of the medical community. It took an engineer at Britain's Electro-Musical Instruments (EMI) Ltd. to make the technology safe and practical. Working at EMI's Central Research Laboratories and apparently unaware of Cormack's work, Godfrey Hounsfield switched from gamma rays to X rays and realized that "attenuation coefficients"—variations in the amount of time it took for these X rays to penetrate any specimen, be they crankcases or craniums—could be computed so accurately that the resulting images were a hundred times as sensitive as conventional X rays. Of equal

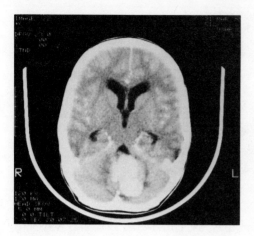

Computed tomography
(CT) scans reveal soft tissues,
including the brain tumor
that appears as a white mass
(bottom) in this patient's scan.
(J. Weinreb/NYU Medical
Center)

importance, he claimed the process could be accomplished without exposing humans to excessive radiation. After computed tomography's feasibility had been demonstrated on such biological samples as a preserved human brain and the carcass of a pig, the first CT scanner was installed in a Wimbledon, England, hospital in 1971, with the express purpose of taking images of the head (a region for which CT scans remain among the preeminent imaging devices). By the summer of 1973, five commercial CT scanners were in operation in the United Kingdom and the United States, arriving with what medical writer William Hendee has called "an impact that is perhaps unparalleled" in the history of radiology. Cormack and Hounsfield shared a Nobel Prize in 1979.

Within a year, whole-body CT scans arrived in the clinic. What ultimately made the CT scan a map is that the device automatically divided the anatomical territory being studied into a grid of some 35,000 squares, each 1.5 millimeters by 1.5 millimeters; the computer determined the density of each square by collating all the rays that had passed through it, assigned a shade of gray to the value, and thus created a highly resolved black-and-white image. CT scans reveal a covert landscape of malignancy, particularly in the brain, where tumors invisible to ordinary X rays (because they are hidden behind the curtain of skull) are suddenly visible. CT scans also excel at revealing the liver, spleen, pancreas, and structures surrounding the heart. They are not, however, good for images of developing fetuses, or for measuring the interior landscape of blood vessels. Those two areas required other types of technology: echoradiography and angiography.

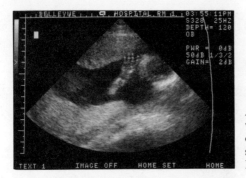

Achieving exquisite detail with sound waves, echoradiograms intrude on such private moments as a fetus sucking its thumb. (J. Weinreb/NYU Medical Center)

Ultrasound, as the name implies, uses high-energy sound waves to probe biological structures and topographies. It evolved out of the technologies of sonar and radar that were developed during World War II; indeed, the first primitive applications in the clinic, during the 1950s, used war-surplus radar and sonar equipment. When instant "real-time" images became available, beginning in the mid-1970s, ultrasound became a staple of obstetrics and gynecology, not least because it afforded a view of the developing fetus without the use of needles, ionizing radiation like X rays, or the injection of chemicals. It also provides one of the best ways to produce images of the heart and gallstones. Like sonar or radar, it recreates an image by measuring the intensity of sound waves bouncing up off an object; a computer, instantly assigning shades of gray (and more recently, color) to those intensity levels, creates an image: a fetal hand, a beating heart.

Angiography is the next best thing to inserting a microscopic camera inside the blood vessels for an up-close look (a development, incidentally, that with fiber optics is no longer inconceivable). During the procedure called cardiac catheterization—one of the most widely practiced techniques—a catheter is threaded from the femoral artery in the leg up into the heart, where a high-contrast dye is released; with X rays or a sensitive detector, it is possible to pick up the presence of the dye as it flows through the tributaries of veins that nourish the heart, and this most critical of cardiac landscapes can be examined for evidence of blockages or sufficient circulation. In digital subtraction angiography, two sets of images are made, and one is "subtracted" from the other to offer a different kind of resolution (see color illustration).

Yet another subdiscipline is nuclear medicine (nuclear because it depends on the injection into the body of radioactively labeled markers, which migrate to specific locations and emit signals that can be

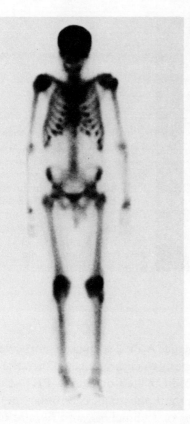

Concentrations of radioactive
drugs absorbed by bone reveal
the human skeleton: metastasized
cancers appear as dark spots in
full-body gamma camera bone
scans. (J. Weinreb/NYU
Medical Center)

picked up by detectors outside the body). Although the use of
nuclear medicine declined in the 1980s, in part because patients balked
at the use of radioactive tracers, some physicians believe it will re-
bound in the 1990s with the use of more specific and more sophisticated markers. Monoclonal antibodies, for example, are
custom-made antibodies, tailored to seek out and grasp onto such
specific targets as cancer cells or, in the case of heart attacks, the
cardiac muscle protein myosin; they can create whole-body maps of
metastatic cancer or dead cardiac tissue following a heart attack. Similarly, gamma cameras take full-body images of the skeleton with the
use of a radioactive pharmaceutical that migrates preferentially to
bone; physicians use it to check for the spread of cancer from primary
sites to the bone.

Perhaps the best-known, and certainly one of the most powerful,
of the *emitting* technologies is positron emission tomography, which

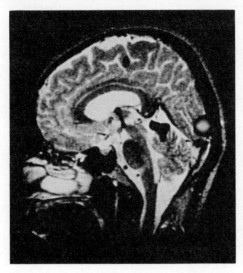

Two maps are more than the sum of their parts: by superimposing a PET scan (small circle at right) on top of a magnetic resonance image of his brain, neuroscientist John Allman maps the location in his brain that is active during visual perception. The combined maps have a spatial accuracy greater than either an MRI or a PET scan alone. (John Allman/© 1989 TINS)

has been in use for about fifteen years. A PET scan uses short-lived but powerful positron-emitting isotopes, which are injected into the body and then can be picked up by sophisticated detectors. PET scanners have several logistical drawbacks (and one major economic one): they are expensive, require large teams of technicians, and require no less than a cyclotron on the site to prepare the short-lived isotopes. Most ominous from the physician's point of view, the procedure is not reimbursed by either the government's Medicare program or by most private medical insurers, which is why the technique is more widely established overseas.

But they offer sensational dynamic maps. They provide views of the anatomy in action. Brain metabolism can be observed to change in PET scans, for example, when a subject thinks about ice cream or wiggles a finger. Michael Kuhar and Henry N. Wagner, Jr., of Johns Hopkins pioneered the use of PET scans to create brain-receptor maps in living people, including schizophrenics (see the next chapter for a discussion of brain-receptor maps). In one recent experiment at the University of Montreal, researchers began to map the domains of pain by watching three specific regions of the cerebral cortex light up in PET scans when brief pulses of heat were applied to the arms of human volunteers. Brain maps of the senses, of language, of memories being logged and stored are now possible, thanks to this new technology.

III

Not all medical cartography charts such a benign landscape. On a rainy Friday not long ago, there was a young woman in Brooklyn with a mysterious, worrisome pain in her back, and two physicians in Manhattan, one of the old school and one of the new, looking at dozens of images of the woman's midsection on a light box. "That's all outside the spinal canal," Jeffrey Weinreb was saying. Weinreb, professor of radiology at New York University Medical Center, was analyzing a series of vertical cross-sectional pictures of the young woman's midsection made by magnetic resonance imaging.

"I can't tell how far it's extended," he told the woman's physician. Like a series of vertical slices, the images showed planes of anatomy around the spinal column, and there was a gathering darkness, like a small pool of oil, leaking out of the backbone. "You see the black stuff there?" Weinreb explained to his older colleague. "That's the tumor, extending up to the fifth lumbar section." The older physician seemed torn about thanking Weinreb for such expert interpretation of such bad news.

If there is one imaging technology that appears to have captured the medical community to a degree that exceeds all others, it is probably this one: magnetic resonance imaging. The very first living creature to have been imaged with magnetic resonance was a four-millimeter clam. It just managed to fit into a five-millimeter-wide cavity, intended for small chemical samples, of the nuclear-magnetic-resonance (NMR) device set up in the laboratory of Paul Lauterbur at the State University of New York at Stony Brook. The year was 1973, the device penetrated the shell to show the structure within, and the clam survived. In less than a decade, humans would go where only bivalves had gone before.

The phenomenon underlying nuclear magnetic resonance, as the technique was originally called, was independently observed by Felix Bloch of Stanford University and Edward Purcell of Harvard University in 1946. It was intended as a tool for analytic chemistry and physics, not for medicine, and it worked in general like this:

Every spinning sphere, be it the planet earth or subatomic particles known as protons in the nucleus of atoms, can create a magnetic field around it, with an axis and a north-south orientation called a magnetic dipole. Bloch and Purcell both realized that subtle but significant differences in the atomic properties of matter—solids and solutions in those pioneering days, brains and backbones in later applications—could be detected by first rigorously aligning and then perturbing those magnetic fields in a controlled way. To make a very long technological story short, researchers discovered early in the 1970s, using biopsy samples from rats, that organic tissues possessed a magnetic resonance signature as distinct as a fingerprint. If you placed a rat liver, for example, in a powerful magnet, the tiny magnetic fields of each hydrogen atom in each molecule of water within the liver would snap to and line up in "agreement"; all the magnetic fields would uniformly align themselves in the same north-south polar orientation. Then you would perturb that orientation by shooting a pulse of radio energy at the tissue. The radio waves would knock all the tiny atomic magnets off the north-south plumb, and they would emit small but discernible radio signals as they reoriented themselves to the north-south axis, little atomic chirps picked up by sensitive receivers surrounding the sample.

This period of reorientation was known technically as the "relaxation time," as each atomic magnet in each atom "relaxed" back to the unperturbed orientation. Remarkably, the hydrogen atoms of water in certain tissues relaxed more quickly than the hydrogen atoms in other tissues. Even more remarkably, as Raymond Damadian first suggested in a 1971 article in *Science,* the hydrogen atoms in the water of cancerous tissues seemed to relax at a different rate from healthy tissue. No one knew why then, and they still don't know why now. But if nuclear magnetic resonance could distinguish between biopsy samples in a pathology lab, the next question was obvious: why not try it in intact human beings as a diagnostic tool?

Both Raymond Damadian and Paul Lauterbur asked that question in the early 1970s; the field is still divided over who answered the question first, and more effectively. Damadian apparently foresaw NMR imaging in a 1972 patent application, but Lauterbur was the first to produce an NMR image, and many radiologists seem to feel that Lauterbur was the first one to see the possibilities of using magnetic resonance to create diagnostic images. Lauterbur perceived, correctly, that the world didn't need a fancy technology for showing the difference between healthy and tumorous tissues in the pathology lab. "However, even normal tissues differed markedly among themselves in NMR relaxation times," he remarked in a 1985 talk, "and I wondered whether there might be some way to noninvasively map out such quantities within the body."

By 1973, Lauterbur used magnetic resonance to produce a deceptively unimpressive image of two thin tubes of water and published it in *Nature.* Interestingly, the journal originally turned down the paper,

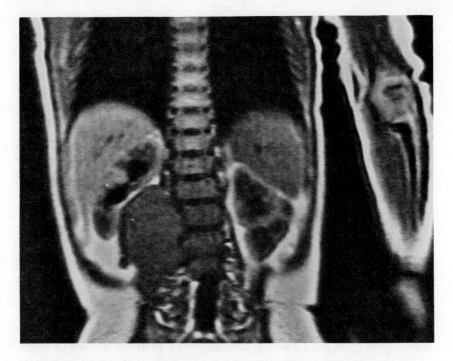

Malignant landscape, benign outcome: the precision of this MRI image, showing the tumorous bulge of a neuroblastoma *(left center)* invading the spinal canal of a six-month-old girl, convinced doctors in 1985 to treat her with chemotherapy rather than surgery. Six years later, physicians report, the child is perfectly healthy. (R. Dietrich/UC-Irvine Medical Center)

apparently because Lauterbur was reluctant to make extravagant claims for the technique; yet as early as 1972, he had sketched out the architecture of the first crude whole-body imaging system. In 1976, Lauterbur established NMR's ability to image cancerous tissue in a live animal when he published a contour map of a tumor-bearing mouse; unfortunately, he published it as an abstract in an exceedingly obscure forum, *Physics in Canada.* In July 1977, meanwhile, Damadian held a press conference to announce that his imaging machine, called Indomitable, had produced the first image of a human being. The contrasting styles of modesty and self-promotion have left a legacy of rivalry, disputed credit, and (on Damadian's part) animosity; fortunately, the controversy has not extended to the credibility of the technique. By 1981 three-dimensional imaging techniques had been developed. In 1982 there were three or four commercial NMR units in the United States; by the end of 1990, there were more than two thousand.

"In general," Jeffrey Weinreb says, "the advantages of MR are that it doesn't use ionizing radiation, it's felt to be very safe, and like CT scans, it makes cross-sectional images. But with MR, we can cut the body any way we want. That's a big advantage, particularly for things like the head. Unlike CT, in magnetic resonance there is a natural contrast between things that are flowing and things that are static, which has led to MR angiography. Magnetic resonance has better contrast resolution between diseased and normal tissue, better than CT or ultrasound. And you can see the difference earlier." Each month, it seems, the power of magnetic resonance zeroes in on new anatomical regions: its virtues already evident in the study of head and brain, MR is now being used to detect abnormalities in the heart, the liver, the prostate, the musculoskeletal system, the spinal cord, and the joints. So successful is the technique at so many levels that Weinreb and many other physicians believe that it is only a matter of time before the chest X ray, a standard part of the annual checkup for virtually all living Americans, will be supplanted by the whole-body magnetic-resonance-imaging map, a map that can be digitally stored and compared with cartographic updates years later.

"Assuming cost does not become a limiting factor," Weinreb says (invoking what might be called medicine's First Amendment to the Hippocratic Oath), "you may end up seeing something not unlike what you saw on *Star Trek,* like the device that you run up and down the body that gives you a readout of everything going on inside. Basically, everyone will come into the hospital, or in for the annual checkup, and get their whole body studied and digitized and kept on permanent record, and you'll be able to look for problems in any part of the body. It's something that sounds futuristic," Weinreb says, "but the future is coming on faster than we think."

Perhaps the greatest irony about magnetic resonance imaging is that, unlike the messy hands-on, seeing-is-believing approach to dissection practiced by Vesalius and all the anatomists that followed him over the centuries, modern science does not understand why MRI works. Hospitals happily spend up to $3 million for an MRI suite, even though the instruments are based on a principle of measurement that remains a complete mystery. "Nobody," smiles Jeffrey Weinreb, blissfully ignorant but gratefully so, "has a clue."

8. "The Brain Is Wet"

MAPS OF PEPTIDE
RECEPTORS IN THE BRAIN

|||||||||||

Like the entomologist catching colorful
butterflies, my attention pursued, in the
garden of gray matter, the delicately and
gracefully shaped cells, the mysterious
butterflies whose wingbeats might someday
reveal the secret of mental life.

—Santiago Ramón y Cajal,
Historia de Mi Labor Científica

Of all the building blocks in that ramshackle, add-on edifice of thought
and consciousness known as the human brain, none is better known or
more freely purloined as an all-purpose metaphor for our mental
acuity (or lack thereof) than the synapse. People who don't know a
neuron from a proton have heard morning disc jockeys bemoan the
mysterious disappearance of their synapses after a night on the town.
The synapse is the place where one nerve cell talks to another in a
snappy biochemical conversation that lasts but a thousandth of a
second and traverses all of two-millionths of a centimeter. Though the
mere suggestion that this conversation was chemical occasioned howls
of opposition only fifty years ago, the synapse has since become such
a commonplace of neurology that no science or medical textbook is
complete without the obligatory cartoon depicting a nerve cell expec-
torating powerful chemicals, called neurotransmitters, across a tiny
gap to the cell next door. The synapse is the basic unit of architecture

in the brain; and in an architecture whose central motif is connection, possibly as many as 100 trillion connections, the synapse is the quintessential junction. As British scientist Steven Rose has written, "It is not too strong to say that the evolution of humanity followed the evolution of the synapse."

Which is why people get a little touchy when Miles Herkenham starts talking about the *myth* of the synapse.

When I visited Herkenham in his laboratory at the National Institutes of Health in Bethesda, Maryland, he was seated in front of a nineteen-inch color monitor connected to a Macintosh II computer. Hardly a fire-breathing *enfant terrible* of neuroanatomy, as the initial controversy surrounding his work might suggest, he looked more the brooding artist, with a long face, dark hair, and a voice both husky and tentative. The image on the computer screen was a false-color map of a guinea pig's brain. It showed a part of the brain known as the hippocampus, a sea-horse swirl of neurons where sensory experiences become encoded into long-term memory. Herkenham tinkered and experimented with what he called his *Miami Vice* palette of colors. He inserted a bright teal blue for the background, daubed in faint shadows of violet and pink within the folds of the hippocampus, and heightened the intensity of the dominant color, a vibrant red. Although he picked the colors, the computer assigned them to the proper regions of the map; these colors, he explained, corresponded to the density of a particular type of molecule, called a receptor, in the hippocampus of guinea pigs. It was the receptor for a class of molecules known as the cannabinoids, a scientific term that looks like "cannabis," which is exactly what it is: marijuana. Like all psychoactive drugs, cannabis works because its active ingredient—delta-9 tetrahydrocannabinol, or THC—can find receptors, or molecular docking berths, on the surface of brain cells; Herkenham's map, to put it bluntly, showed all the places where marijuana can dock in the brain.

In this "Just say no" era, the picture was a shocker (see color illustration). The hippocampus on the computer screen was as red as a tomato, signifying the densest concentration of receptors; the cortex, where higher cognitive functions occur, also showed widespread receptor populations. The same specific pattern appeared in the brains of rats, dogs, a rhesus monkey, and several humans. Herkenham, who is among the preeminent cartographers of brain receptors, remarked that the cannabinoid receptor appeared to have the highest overall density of any of the fifty or so substances that have been mapped in the mammalian brain. The work scored a rare media trifecta, appearing in

Proceedings of the National Academy of Sciences, Science News, and
High Times.

It would be quite enough that the map provided a picture showing
how literally receptive the brain is to the active ingredient in marijuana—how molecularly inclined we are to get high. But in a broader
sense, it reiterated a decade's worth of research showing that the brain
can be mapped in a way that illustrates how and where psychoactive
substances—not just drugs like marijuana, but tranquilizers, anti-
depressants, and even powerful compounds made by the body itself—
interact with parts of the brain, making us giddy or grim or anxious or
morose. Indeed, the presence of the cannabinoid receptor implies the
presence of a marijuanalike chemical in our body that interacts with it,
and one possible interpretation of its role, according to research by
neurobiologist Sam Deadwyler of Wake Forest University, is that
there may be a naturally occurring chemical in the brain "that facilitates forgetting." This natural cannabinoid, Deadwyler speculates,
may help the hippocampus select between significant and insignificant
experiences. "If you remembered everything," he says, "you would
actually remember nothing. If the hippocampus was not selective, it
would encode everything and wouldn't be able to sculpt significant
events into memory at selective times."

Herkenham has been making maps like this for about ten years,
with an artisan's care for craft and beauty as well as the scientist's zeal
for precision, and they have helped to undermine (though there remains much controversy here) the notion of the synapse as the single
fundamental brick of neuroanatomy. The brain's actual geography
doesn't always mimic the textbook cartoon, and Herkenham was
among the first to notice the discrepancy. He has meticulously created
and analyzed maps of various receptors (there are dozens of neuroactive transmitters, each with molecular notches as distinct as a key and
each with a receptor that will accommodate just those notches); he has
studied the pictures made by himself and other neuroanatomists; and
he has been in the forefront in concluding that those pictures do not
show what he and others expected them to show. Many receptors
simply aren't where they are supposed to be, across a narrow strait
from the point of neurotransmitter release. In some cases they are a
neural ocean away. These are maps that contradict expectation.

In their attempts to explain these so-called "mismatches," Herkenham and others have begun to rethink the entire communications
network of the brain, and these new maps stake out the exciting
territory they have begun to explore. They see a brain not simply

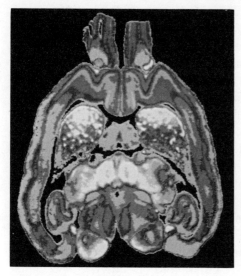

The distribution of opiate receptor molecules in the brain of a rat, revealed by radioactively tagged molecules that mimic the neuroactive substance in opium, morphine, and brain chemicals known as opiates. View is a horizontal slice, showing olfactory bulbs *(top)* and brain stem *(bottom)*. (M. Herkenham/NIMH).

hard-wired with synaptic circuits but awash with chemical gossip and background noise as well, a brain where "parasynaptic" communication may occur and where emotions and mood may modulate, or color, that communication. They see a brain that is complex, hormonal, in conversation with itself. "We still don't have much of a handle on synaptic events other than the classic neurophysiology," Herkenham was saying. "I don't mean to diminish that in any way. It's just that when you study a single neuron in a particular location, you can find out quite a lot about it, but it always leaves you with kind of a sick feeling that you will never get to a complete understanding of, say, something like consciousness."

The field of neuroscience has all sorts of idiosyncratic schisms; one of the most peculiar and enduring may fall on either side of that two-millionths-of-a-centimeter gulf that is the synapse. Scientists who stand on the presynaptic side tend to be interested in anatomy, wiring diagrams, *Cause*; those on the post-synaptic side concern themselves with behavior, consciousness, *Effect*. Herkenham started out as a neuroanatomist on the presynaptic side, and in order to appreciate the great conceptual distance he and others have traveled, it helps to understand the geography of that tiny space.

How did the synapse come to monopolize all notions of neurolog-

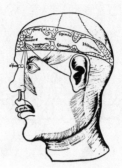

In Aristotelian maps of the brain, areas related to the senses were localized to a vague band, as indicated in Gregory Reisch's 1508 *Margarita philosophica.* (Francis A. Countway Library of Medicine, Boston)

ical connection? The answer begins with an earlier technical break-through that led to an earlier map, of sorts. The Italian anatomist Camillo Golgi discovered in the 1870s that neurons could be made visible when stained with silver salts. Using Golgi's staining method, the Spanish anatomist Santiago Ramón y Cajal visualized networks of brain cells and demonstrated for the first time that the brain was indeed composed of these cells, called neurons; he discovered, too, that neurons did not join together in a solid web of tissue, as previously believed, but grazed each other, formed networks, and touched at points marked by little bulbs at the ends of the nerve cells. In 1897 the British physiologist Charles Sherrington referred to those touching points as "synapses," Greek for "I join together" (although one ac-count has it that his editor coined the term after consulting with a Euripides scholar in the classics department at Trinity College, Ox-ford). A network begged a diagram, and once the cells could be stained, Cajal courageously set out to create a wiring diagram of the brain. Neuroanatomists have been doing wiring diagrams ever since.

While these early neuroscientists had a name for this junction, they did not have good experimental access to it—no way to study it, no hands-on way to learn how it worked. They needed what is called a "model system"—an organism that, for unique and usually seren-dipitous reasons, would provide a window on the biology of the ner-vous system. They ultimately found one in the sea squid. That creature won the job because it possesses an unusually large nerve fiber, or axon, through which the nerve cell imparts messages to the synapse, which in turn orders a muscle to move. It appeared to be the archetypal nervous system junction, and in 1939, Alan Hodgkin and Andrew Huxley managed to slip an electrode into this extraordinarily large

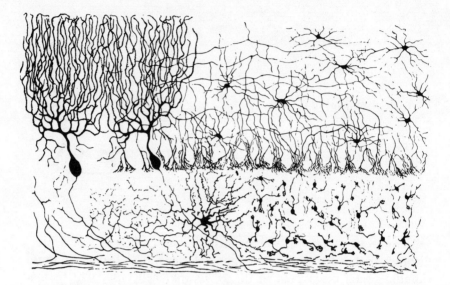

Neuronal maps: at the turn of the century, Spanish neuroanatomist Santiago Ramón y Cajal used new staining techniques to map different neurons, in the cerebellar cortex *(above)* and elsewhere, showing that neurons are not connected tissues but communicate chemically across gaps called synapses.

axon and in so doing discovered that electrical impulses traveled the length of the fiber to the nerve ending; here, at the bulbs first spotted by Ramón y Cajal, they apparently triggered some form of communication to the neighboring nerve cell. It wasn't until the 1950s that John Eccles and Bernard Katz elucidated the nature of the communication. It involved the synapse, and it seemed to work like this: A nerve cell, in its grosser particulars, resembles a tree. It receives communication primarily in its branches and limbs, which are known as dendrites; it collates and assesses this information in the cell body, which corresponds roughly to the point where all the limbs join the trunk; when the cell "fires," it sends an electrical impulse down the length of its trunk, which is the axon; and the axon ends in a tangle of roots, which resemble the nerve terminals that communicate impulses on to the dendrites of other cells. The synapses lie at the very tip of the roots and intersect the branches of nearby nerve cells.

Now we must mix metaphors, for although the structure of the nerve cell is arboreal, its synaptic function more closely resembles a naval exercise. When one cell fires—that is, when its internal chemistry

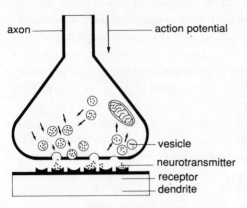

axon — action potential

vesicle
neurotransmitter
receptor
dendrite

The synapse in action: when an excitatory electrical impulse known as the action potential reaches the end of a nerve cell, it triggers the release of neurotransmitters, which diffuse across the gap between nerve cells and "dock" at receptors on the nearby cell. (from *The Amazing Brain* by Robert Ornstein and Richard F. Thompson, illustrations by David Macaulay. Illustrations copyright © 1984 by David A. Macaulay. Reprinted by permission of Houghton Mifflin Company. All rights reserved)

gets suddenly and swiftly reorganized by a shudder of electricity—the impulse travels the length of the axon, where it provokes the release of a packet of neurotransmitters. The release occurs at the very tip of the nerve cell, at its headland, as it were, in closest proximity to the adjoining cell with which it will communicate, and like a tiny flotilla of boats, these small neurotransmitter molecules—serotonin in some cells, dopamine in others, to cite two typical examples—traverse that narrow strait known as the synaptic cleft. When they reach the far shore, these molecules do not simply flop onto the beach; rather, they fit snugly and very particularly into berths called receptors that line the surface of the receiving cell—dopamine into dopamine receptors only, serotonin into serotonin receptors, and so on. When enough molecules of neurotransmitter fill enough berths, the cell on the far side may undergo a sudden storm of chemical change, followed shortly thereafter by an electrical storm that passes the conversation along even further; some neurotransmitters inhibit communication, and since the postsynaptic cell may receive information from a thousand sources at once, it simultaneously sums up the chemical information. If the excitatory messages outnumber the inhibitory messages, it flips an electrical switch and passes the message along to the next cell. Each nerve cell works like a quorum, quick go or no-go votes at each step in a chain of connections. If it took as long to accomplish as to describe, we would starve to death eating breakfast; but in fact each nerve cell can talk to up to 100,000 others in half a millisecond by way of the synapse, and there are 100 billion of those talking cells in our brains.

No less than a dozen Nobel prizes were awarded over the years to acknowledge neuroscience's splendid elucidation of the synapse and related mechanisms; all the glory, though, may have distracted from some intrinsic drawbacks. The much-studied sea-squid axon has its limitations, the foremost of which is that it resides *outside* the brain. At this particular nerve ending, the cell squirts little packets of acetylcholine, a neurotransmitter, across the synaptic gap, inducing a muscle to twitch. That particular synapse, known as the neuromuscular junction, marks the point where the brain tells a muscle what to do. It was natural to generalize the neuromuscular junction to reflect *all* junctions, to assume that it mirrored the way *all* nerve cells spoke to each other. The synapse, it seemed, could explain everything from a wink to a haymaker. Vast numbers of synapses could explain both our admiration of real irises in a vase and our admiration of Vincent van Gogh's *Irises*; they could explain our ability to understand the conceptual difference between the two kinds of irises; they presumably could even explain our ability to rationalize the fact that a painting deemed worth not a penny to its creator during his lifetime could assume a value of $53 million later in time. Everything from perception to rationalization had its roots, somehow, in the synapse.

When Miles Herkenham embarked on his scientific education, the synapse thus prevailed as the keystone of neurobiology. Born in 1949 and raised in Yosemite National Park, where his father worked as a park naturalist, Herkenham would have you believe that his decision to enter the neurosciences was almost a matter of intellectual desperation, of following the path of least resistance. "I would hate to admit that I became a psychology major because I went to Amherst College, and it was so hard for me that I had to look for a major that was easy," he says. He ended up in "physiological psychology," or what might loosely be defined as studying the brain's hardware as it pertained to behavior. That thread of work continued at graduate school at Northeastern University in Boston, where Herkenham earned his Ph.D. in 1975.

"I was sort of a hard-core neuroanatomist, which is a person who looks very closely at synaptic connections and the wiring diagrams," he says. But an important conceptual transition prepared him for what was to follow. He became interested in studying the cortex, the layer of the brain which, though barely thicker than a fluffy hand towel, is the seat of consciousness, of sensory and motor processes, of thought; he was looking for nerve pathways—literally, threads of nerves—that branched out into the cortex and seemed to have wide-ranging, global effects on the mechanisms of attention and memory. "I became interested in the neuroanatomy which might underlie such mechanisms, mainly the pathways to cortex that are not focused but rather diffuse and widespread. They might influence cortical activity in a more holistic manner, which would affect our levels of arousal and the basis for attention." Herkenham began to take on this more global worldview when he worked as a postdoctoral fellow in the laboratory of Walle Nauta at the Massachusetts Institute of Technology and, after 1977, at the National Institute of Mental Health (NIMH).

Herkenham's apprenticeship coincided with a parallel revolution in the field known as psychopharmacology, which studied the effects of drugs on the brain and behavior. In the early 1970s, researchers were hot in pursuit of something called the opiate receptor. The existence of this elusive molecule had teased scientists for as long as opium had customers, but no one had succeeded in finding it. Psychopharmacologists assumed that in order to have an effect on the brain, natural painkilling substances such as morphine and related opium derivatives (known collectively as opiates) needed some kind of portal or doorway to interact with brain cells. What they needed, more precisely, was that keyholelike molecule on the surface of nerve cells that would accommodate the drug. Hardly anyone doubted the existence of the opiate receptor, but it was something of a molecular unicorn; it remained a mythical beast until somebody could find one and prove its existence. In 1973 researchers at Johns Hopkins University—principally Solomon Snyder and Candace Pert—found the much-sought opiate receptor.

Like all important discoveries, this one inspired a new round of inquiry. As the inimitably brash Pert later put it, "God presumably did not put an opiate receptor in our brains so that we could eventually discover how to get high with opium." If the body naturally made opiate receptors, the inescapable implication was that the body made opiates, too—natural "in-house" morphinelike molecules that resembled outside, or exogenous, painkilling molecules like opium, morphine, and other drugs. The implicit question posed by the opiate receptor was answered in 1976 by British researchers John Hughes and Hans Kosterlitz, who reported the discovery of the first of these inhouse opiates, enkephalin. Brain researchers had a new synaptic junction to explore, and an especially intriguing one, too, for the opiate receptor clearly played a key role in such mood states as euphoria, relaxation, pain, and pleasure.

By 1975, Pert and Michael Kuhar at Johns Hopkins had produced the first crude map showing the distribution of opiate receptors in the mammalian brain. Then, in 1979, Kuhar and W. Scott Young III provided the key technical breakthrough in the field: they developed a technique that allowed scientists to map these receptors very precisely. You would prepare a thin slice of frozen rat brain (as pale and pink as a slice of ginger on a sushi plate, though quite a bit thinner), mount it on a slide, and wash it with radioactive molecules that mimicked a particular neurotransmitter and stuck to the receptor. Slapped against a sheet of sensitive film and left at room temperature for up to eight weeks, the radioactive molecules clinging to the brain slice signaled both the location and density of the receptor being studied. "This allowed us to look at large numbers of receptors," Kuhar explained recently. "It was easier. It was more accurate. And it was certainly cheaper. In 1979 I would guess about twenty-five labs were doing receptor mapping. Now I would guess it's five hundred." Neurosurveyors poured into the field.

So, suddenly, they had receptor density maps. And in the grand tradition of unprepared minds, they looked at those maps and managed not to see the message.

Herkenham had moved on to the NIMH by this time, still on the presynaptic side of the gulf, still doing what "hard-core" neuroanatomists do: tracing nerve fibers through the tangle of the brain. In this case he was studying a small bundle of nerve fibers in the mammalian brain. These fibers ran from the thalamus, a kind of anteroom to the cortex where sensory information gets screened, to the cortex itself and to the striatum, a part of the forebrain. Nerve fibers can resemble garden hoses in that they snake through the brain for some distance and only at their very tip, their terminal field, do they spurt their neurotransmitters like a chemical sprinkler; each terminal field is typically associated with one particular flavor of neurotransmitter, be it serotonin or epinephrine or others. In this case, Herkenham kept finding holes in the hose. The nerve path looked discontinuous, which was unusual; then he recalled the patchy mosaic of opiate receptors in the primitive map Pert and Kuhar had made in 1975 and wondered aloud, in a speculation that has become famous, if "my holes fit her patches."

This was in 1979; Pert, too, had moved to the National Institute of Mental Health by then. Intimidated by her reputation, Herkenham at first put off asking her. Pert was in equal parts famous for her codiscovery of the opiate receptor and infamous for complaining loudly that she hadn't received recognition commensurate with that accorded her male peers; she was also energetic, inventive, and—perhaps because of her long-standing interest in literature and Freudian psychology—more willing than her male peers to speculate about consciousness and the brain.

In any event, Herkenham finally worked up the nerve to get in touch. "I called her up and asked her to come to a seminar that I was giving on my connections, and she did, and she saw that . . . this again gets back to mapping, because it was the map that did it. I showed the map, the picture of the pathway, and I said, 'Does this map look like it would be in perfect negative register with your map?' " In other words, Herkenham wondered if his nerve fibers disappeared at precisely the same spots where Pert's map glowed, dense with receptors. "She said, 'It sure does.' And I said, 'How would we go about proving that?' And she said, 'Well, you'd have to develop a technique for visualizing receptors.' " They were unaware that Kuhar and Young at Johns Hopkins had developed just such a technique. "So Candace and I very independently developed a technique. And I think one of the things that marked our technique is that I always *insisted* on perfection of histology, of tissues, so that the map in the end would be beautiful. And that's one thing, I think, that our work is noted for. The technique that evolved from that insistence is one of really gorgeous pictures."

From 1979 to 1984, Herkenham churned out gorgeous pictures showing the distribution of opiate receptors in the mammalian brain. Many scientists merely marveled at the brilliant color of Herkenham's maps when they appeared on the covers of *Nature* in 1981 (with Pert as co-author) and *Science* in 1982 (with Steven Wise); one brain map even ended up as the logo on the T-shirts of Herkenham's NIMH softball team. But to experts these lovely maps posed a very pretty problem. To neuroanatomists familiar with the brain, the receptors did not always match the densest concentration of opiate-secreting nerve cells. Even Pert and Herkenham, regarded in some circles as trigger-happy theorists for pushing unorthodox notions, were so indoctrinated with the traditional synaptic approach that, as often happens, they initially managed to ignore the dissonance in their own data. In their first mapping paper in 1980, they heralded the "striking concordance" of peptide to receptor, even though there were obvious discrepancies.

Herkenham merely hinted at the problem in his papers; in scientific talks, however, like one he gave to the Potomac chapter of the Society for Neuroscience in the fall of 1980, the discrepancies were harder to ignore. In fact, it was one of those lovely moments when a

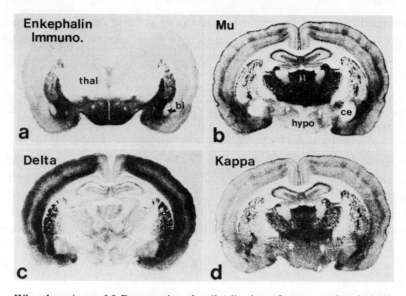

Why the mismatch? By mapping the distribution of receptor sites in brain slices, neuroanatomists such as Miles Herkenham have discovered surprisingly large distances between secreting neurons and receptors. Powerful opiates known as enkephalins are produced and secreted in one part of the rat brain *(dark areas of a),* but the densest concentrations of receptors for mu enkephalin *(b),* delta enkephalin *(c),* and kappa enkephalin *(d)* lie elsewhere. (M. Herkenham/NIMH)

map, a picture rooted not in theory but data, contradicted everyone's theoretical expectations. No one quite knew what to make of it.

It was a typical Pert and Herkenham production. Pert talked for the first thirty minutes, showed all her slides in black and white, then concluded by showing a poppy field abloom in color, a still from *The Wizard of Oz.* Herkenham then spoke for the final half hour, illustrating his talk with the spectacular all-color brain maps. In terms of neurological landscapes, we weren't in Kansas anymore.

"There were immunochemists in the audience," Herkenham remembers, "and some of them noted what I had noted. They said, 'This is interesting. You're failing to see receptors in places like the globus pallidus [a part of the brain rich in opiate-producing nerve cells]. It's the most intensive terminal field in the whole brain, and you're hardly seeing any opiate receptors there at all. And then conversely you have dense opiate receptors in places where we see very few terminals. How can you explain that?' I was very haughty and arrogant and I said, 'I'm sure you guys will work out the flaws in your technique. There can't be flaws in our technique because we validated the binding and this is the receptor. This is *the* receptor that mediates the action of opiates. It can't be our problem. It must be your problem.' "

It became everybody's problem. Herkenham, as tentative and self-deprecating in private as he seemed haughty and arrogant in public, modestly characterized these startling misalignments as "a new concern" in a 1982 paper. But it was a problem. "And to some people it's still a problem. To me, it was an observation and not a problem at all. It was quite exciting. I would start giving talks and people would come away very discouraged, throw up their arms, and say, 'What are we to do?' The general response of the community was to ignore one set of data or the other. It was impossible to embrace both sets. And that's the way it stood for a long time. And explanations for 'the problem' abounded for many years."

While the problem remain unresolved, Herkenham continued to use the new mapping technique to survey this suddenly unpredictable terrain. He wondered, for example, if the distribution of opiate receptors varied from one species to the next, so he and his lab group mapped the hippocampi of four different rodents: rat, squirrel, guinea pig, and hamster. In all four species, the brain regions that churned out opiates were essentially identical; yet in each of the four species the map of opiate *receptors* was different, as particular as a fingerprint. "It's hard to imagine, with such precision and complexity, that there wouldn't be functional significance to that," Herkenham says. "It means something to the animal." He also wondered if maps of other neurotransmitter receptors would show patterns similarly out of register. With Pert, Richard Rothman, and workers at the Merck Institute for Therapeutic Research in Rahway, New Jersey, he mapped the receptors of substance P, a powerful peptide involved in the perception of pain; much of this map, too, showed "poor correlation" with the parts of the brain where substance P was known to be produced. The displacement was as disconcerting as if, knowing that most of the major forests lay in the Pacific Northwest, you saw dense concentrations of lumber mills in the Nevada desert. Herkenham and colleagues reported the findings in a 1984 *Brain Research* paper that for the first time used the word "mismatch" to describe the phenomenon.

By this time many other workers were churning out receptor maps (working with Herkenham, Rémi Quirion of Pert's lab went on to produce receptor maps of many other brain peptides). The mismatch

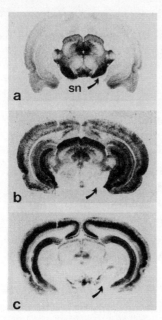

Painful discrepancies: substantia
nigra (SN) secretes the greatest amount of
substance P, a powerful neuropeptide
linked to the perception of pain *(a)*; but the
densest receptors for substance P, as mapped
by Herkenham *(b and c),* lie far from the
source. Such mismatches suggest that
the brain communicates hormonally as well
as synaptically. (M. Herkenham/NIMH)

problem refused to go away. "Maps were published at a furious rate
in the literature," Herkenham recalls, "and so every time one would
come out, I would look at it. Usually, the authors of those maps were
pharmacologists who didn't have a strong anatomy background, so I
was better able to interpret them than they were, basically. So I would
rush to the corresponding immunohistochemistry maps, gather every
bit of evidence together, and start making a list of examples of noncor-
respondence."

The inventory of mismatches grew. The degree of displacement
sounds small, but was biologically significant. "We're talking millimeters, and we could be talking centimeters," Herkenham says. A centimeter is a *very* long distance for a molecule to swim, almost a million
times as far as at a neuromuscular synapse. "There's no evidence for
function beyond microns [a micron is one-thousandth of a millimeter].
Which makes it hormonal." The evidence ultimately became so immense that the notion of the synapse as the single unit of neurological
communication in the brain didn't seem nearly as persuasive. As even
the journal *Science* acknowledged in a 1988 news item, "until recently,
many in the field dismissed Herkenham's data, but he now has so much
anatomical evidence supporting the mismatch phenomenon that it is

impossible to ignore." In recent years, results from another field, electron microscopy, have bolstered the mismatch theory.

"It took me *years* to realize that the maps were really not in register with the neuroanatomy," Herkenham says now. "I was one of the only neuroanatomists to go over to the postsynaptic side, so to speak, and look at the receptors, as opposed to the presynaptic side, which would be the axons that are stained and marked to show the transmitter. And I think in retrospect I know why I did that. I had a psychology background, and I was trying to understand how the brain works as opposed to more or less how it's wired. So I could appreciate better than some the global manifestations."

Still, the implications emerged only slowly. Herkenham began to think that neurotransmitters lead a double life. At synapses, they acted like neurotransmitters, hopping across the narrow gap and instantaneously triggering a nearby nerve cell. But they also seemed to act like hormones—that is, like biochemicals that diffuse through the bloodstream and act on cells from a distance. In the brain they could diffuse through the fluid that circulates in cavities called ventricles. Five hundred years earlier, Leonardo da Vinci had "mapped" these very same cavities by making wax castings of their structure, but no one had offered much of an explanation for their function. Herkenham repeated earlier studies to confirm that fluid circulates rather vigorously through these cavities and could deliver hormonal messages throughout the brain. The brain began to look like a target of its own hormones.

Herkenham would argue that the historical focus on the synapse has attained an obscuring mythology, so that neuroscientists have been reluctant to accept any challenge to its hegemony. "It's the myth of the neuromuscular junction, which has been *extensively* studied," Herkenham says. "And the myth is that what happens at the neuromuscular junction ought also to happen in the brain because you have a perfect match of release, quantal release, of neurotransmitter only at the terminals. Then you have these receptors, and 99.7 percent of them are *right there,* on the postsynaptic side, at the synapse. It was shocking to find that such arrangements virtually do not exist anywhere in the brain for any system. Most people don't realize that." Herkenham stops short, and succumbs to a sudden, born-again laugh. "It shocks *me!*"

What do those mismatches mean? Herkenham didn't quite know, but he was intuitively groping toward one possible hypothesis during a television interview in 1981. He had been asked to refute certain assertions made by the astronomer and writer Robert Jastrow in his book *The Enchanted Loom*. Jastrow, reflecting the increasingly anachronistic view that neuronal communication is based solely in electricity, argued that brains and computers are so similar in structure and function that they ultimately could be wired together, directly communicating with each other. Herkenham thought the idea preposterous. "I said that there was one huge difference between a brain and a computer," he recalls, "and that's that a computer, if you poured a bucket of water on it, would short out, whereas the brain *is* wet, and lives in that kind of environment. I didn't even realize what I was saying at the time."

The remark zeroed in on a crucial difference between a purely synaptic, wired brain, and what has come to be considered a more fluid, hormonal, "parasynaptic" brain. Not a brain that works exclusive of synapses, of course, but a brain that complements point-to-point synaptic communication with a kind of holistic priming. And "holistic," despite its gooey, New Age connotations, is precisely the word used by Francis O. Schmitt, an eminent old-school neurobiologist at MIT, to describe this type of communication.

Schmitt published a pioneering article in 1984 in the journal *Neuroscience* called "Molecular Regulators of Brain Function: A New View." In it he argues that many molecules in the brain act at a distance rather than directly at the synapse; he proposes the term "parasynaptic" to describe this type of long-distance chemical signaling. It is a remarkable paper, for Schmitt sought nothing less than a systematic reorganization of the body's chemical vocabulary.

Rather than artificially categorizing these biochemicals as hormones, neuropeptides, growth factors, or lymphokines (the latter being molecules secreted by immune cells), Schmitt suggested that it was more useful to think of all of them as "informational substances": biochemical messengers able to carry news between, say, the endocrine system and the central nervous system and the immune system. In their ability to convey information over a distance (and across boundaries erected, it sometimes seems, more rigidly in textbooks and medical classrooms than in actual human anatomy), these molecules suggested a network of information exchange that eroded the very notion of separate and distinct systems in the body. The Schmitt paper did not cite Herkenham's work, and Schmitt says he prefers to emphasize the action of informational substances over the location of receptors, but he does not contest the reality of mismatches or the suggestion that Herkenham's maps complement his parasynaptic theories. Schmitt believes the marketplace for informational exchange occurs in the wet marshes between brain cells, and that is where he has started to look. "You have the opportunity for a whole lot of communication to go on there," Schmitt says.

The Schmitt paper shocked Herkenham, not least because it preempted some of the very conclusions toward which he and his colleagues were moving. The NIMH group has nonetheless pushed the concept in a different, more controversial direction. Having demonstrated heavy and overlapping concentrations of peptide receptors in parts of the brain associated with emotions (the thalamus, hypothalamus, and amygdala), the NIMH researchers boldly suggested that molecules diffusing through the brain could account for mood, behavior, and attitude—could in fact account for what they call a "psychosomatic network" linking the mind to the rest of the body not by the traditional nerve fibers or point-to-point synapses, but by diffuse chemical conversation. With this rich vocabulary of neuroactive go-between molecules—"perhaps hundreds," Schmitt speculated—the human body had the chemical means that enabled the mind to talk to the body, and for the body to reply to the mind. In effect, they were saying that the brain is bathed in a rich broth of mood-affecting molecules, conferring a background tone to our cerebral activities much as background color in a painting—such as the menacing sky of Giorgione's *The Tempest*—conditions and colors the human activity taking place in the foreground.

This psychosomatic network—the brain receptor maps form only a part of this much grander picture—represents one of the most intriguing and fertile areas of contemporary medical research. In the past decade, researchers have found, for example, that white blood cells— the roving bodyguards of the immune system—not only possess receptors for opiate molecules, but can themselves manufacture "brain chemicals" such as neurotransmitters. Similarly confounding and no less extraordinary, brain cells make and communicate with insulin, a hormone whose production has historically been associated only with the pancreas. Many of these informational substances—what are conventionally called neuropeptides, hormones, and so on—have a powerful influence on mood and behavior. In a 1985 paper in the *Journal of Immunology* coauthored by Herkenham, Pert, Michael R. Ruff, and Richard J. Weber, the authors wrote, "Neuropeptides and their receptors thus join the brain, glands and immune system in a network of communication between brain and body, probably representing the biochemical substrate of emotion." Using evanescent molecules, they claim to have identified the forming and dissolving girders that link body and mind. As neurosurgeon and writer Richard Bergland puts it: "Can thinking go on outside the brain? Much scientific evidence points to that disturbing, previously unthinkable possibility."

These ruminations are not without problems, or without detractors. One of the paradoxes of the mismatch phenomenon, for example, is that when neurotransmitters or drugs are experimentally introduced a short distance from the mismatched receptors, they fail to elicit a response, suggesting either that they do not diffuse over distance or are broken down before they arrive. Furthermore, the psychosomatic network must overcome a serious communications problem: the inability of many substances to pass an anatomical border crossing known as the blood-brain barrier. For those and other reasons, Herkenham maintains a polite distance from this alternative theory. "I would like to subscribe to it," he says, "but I'd like there to be more evidence."

This emerging parasynaptic view of the mind nonetheless has significance for therapeutic treatment of brain disorders. "I'm in the mental health institute," says Herkenham, "and we're trying to understand such phenomena as depression. It's a universal, global change, and the drug serves to bring the system back to some state of equilibrium, as if the system had gone haywire in a global way to begin with. To understand that the brain, by itself, probably works in a manner similar to what we do when we manipulate it through drug therapy is a great step forward," Herkenham believes. "It means we're not as invasive as we thought we were. We're not doing such strange things after all. And it might suggest that there are ways to naturally induce those changes. People have thought it might be outside the realm of science to explain how mystics or transcendentals could alter their brain physiology and brain chemistry so completely. I don't have as much problem with that as I used to. At least I have an understanding as a scientist that these are inside the realm of science now."

The mismatch maps, beautiful and instructive, suggest that the synapse is not the only feature on the neural landscape, and they do so with rare power. "You could publish tables, graphs, plots, all of which were satisfying the essential criteria for the establishment of the receptor," Herkenham says. "But then you show one picture. And the heterogeneity which is unique to that receptor and which conforms to what we already know about brain structure is just . . . just the crowning glory and the single most convincing piece of evidence. And people can see that immediately. At a glance, you *know* there's something there because it's a striking, unique pattern that could not have come about through any form of artifact. It's believable in an instant. You don't need to be an expert to know that this is something real."

9. A Most Unsatisfactory Organism

"RIFLIPS" AND MAPS
OF HUMAN GENES

|||||||||||

Before the infinite can be thine
You must first break it down
and then recombine.

—Goethe

The year was 1978, and the place was a ski resort located in the Wasatch Mountains southeast of Salt Lake City. In April of that year, a University of Utah professor named Mark Skolnick, along with other members of the Utah faculty and their graduate students, re- treated to the mountains for their annual spring seminar, and exercis- ing the time-tested sybaritism with which biologists choose their gathering spots, they convened in the lovely setting of Alta. According to the informal agenda, students would describe aspects of their re- search, and faculty members would comment on it. Out of this modest and free-form scenario would emerge, over the course of a day or two, one of the most powerful technologies in modern biology, a theoretical and yet also cartographic innovation that would forever change the possibility and indeed the likelihood of creating a complete map of human genes. Like many discoveries in science, the Alta breakthrough was built upon a rickety and amusing scaffold of coincidence.

In some ways the coincidences stretch all the way back to Mark Skolnick's childhood in San Mateo, California. It just so happened that Skolnick's father was a social acquaintance of Joshua Lederberg, the biologist who won a Nobel Prize in 1958 for showing that bacteria "conjugate" (a technical term for the exchange of genetic material between biological individuals that in higher organisms goes by other names), so even as a schoolboy Skolnick developed an early fascination for genetics. It just so happened that Lederberg made this discovery about bacteria at about the same time as his colleague Luca Cavalli-Sforza, a prominent geneticist who divided his time between Stanford University and his native Italy; and so it was Lederberg who introduced Skolnick to Cavalli-Sforza when the young man, trained in demographics but enamored of computers, decided to pursue population genetics as a career. It just so happened that Skolnick was living in Italy in the early 1970s, working with Cavalli-Sforza to develop a computer model for population genetics, when he learned by chance about the rich genealogical (and therefore genetic) records of the Mormon population in Utah—a trove of information on family size, births, deaths, and cause of death unrivaled anywhere in the world. It just so happened that the University of Utah turned to Cavalli-Sforza for recommendations when they began looking for someone to manage a program using the Mormon resource; Cavalli-Sforza of course recommended Skolnick, who moved to Salt Lake City in 1974 with the ambition of using those Mormon records to explore the genetic mysteries of carcinogenesis—specifically that of breast cancer.

And finally, it just so happened that in the spring of 1978, when the Utah researchers headed up to Alta for their annual meeting, another of the Utah faculty members had invited along two "yeast men," two high-powered protagonists of the East Coast and West Coast molecular biology establishments, David Botstein from the Massachusetts Institute of Technology and Ronald Davis of Stanford, to sit in on the meetings. In that one conference room would gather all the crucial ingredients for insight: expertise in classical genetics and population genetics, a population to study (the Mormons) with diseases to trace, these two outsiders with their brusque expertise in the powerful new molecular techniques of recombinant DNA, and, no less important, personalities on all sides willing to talk out ideas in rough-draft form and mix it up intellectually. It could have happened, and *would* have happened, somewhere else sooner or later; because of all those coincidences, though, and because of one particular student presentation, it happened at Alta.

During an afternoon session on the second day (as well as anyone recalls), one of Skolnick's graduate students, Kerry Kravitz, presented the results of an extensive investigation into an inherited disease known as hemochromatosis. It is a metabolic disorder in which the body absorbs and retains dangerous levels of iron in key organs and tissues; at least one doctor has marched a patient through a metal detector and set it off, simply to demonstrate how much iron can accumulate. Geneticists knew that hemochromatosis occurred when an individual inherited a defective gene from his or her parents. What they didn't know was whether the gene was *dominant,* meaning a single defective copy inherited from either parent could cause the disease, or *recessive,* meaning defective copies had to be inherited from both parents. And indeed, University of Utah researchers led by George Cartwright and Corwin Edwards had undertaken a classic type of genetic investigation to determine the pattern of inherited disease in an extended, five-generation Mormon family. Then Kerry Kravitz mathematically analyzed that pattern and argued that the data best fit with the hypothesis that the disease gene was an "autosomal recessive." A defective copy had to be inherited from both parents in order for hemochromatosis to develop.

Kravitz and his Utah colleagues helped resolve this long-standing medical controversy with the help of an intriguing fellow traveler to the hemochromatosis gene. As French biologists had reported in 1975, people with hemochromatosis seemed to inherit only one among several possible biochemical "fingerprints" typical of the immune system. It is not critical to understand this system, known as the major histocompatibility complex (or HLA, for human leukocyte antigen); it is only important to remember that these two genetic factors, the hemochromatosis gene and one particular type of HLA fingerprint, seemed to travel together from generation to generation. And on that April day Kravitz described how that HLA protein "marker" had helped the Utah team to identify 20 people with hemochromatosis and approximately 145 others with a single copy of the gene. The "marker," like a red tag or blue ribbon, tipped off the presence of the defective gene that caused the disease. And that gene, Kravitz's analysis showed, was recessive.

As Kravitz explained the statistics used to reach this conclusion, the discussion grew spirited, even loud. The scientists jawed back and forth about the statistical necessity for such complicated analysis. As he followed the argument, David Botstein instinctively found himself thinking about where this information fit in a somewhat bigger picture.

His is an especially capacious and eclectic intellect, and so it is not surprising that his thoughts turned to the history of genetic research, to why it was so difficult to study human genetics, and why the Kravitz discovery provided a clue that suddenly, improbably, magnificently promised a way to overcome more than a century of scientific frustration.

"Man," wrote A. H. Sturtevant in 1954, "is one of the most unsatisfactory of all organisms for genetic study."

That is why it has been other organisms—Mendel's peas and Morgan's vinegar flies, Avery's slick-skinned bacteria and molecular biology's viruses and yeast and wriggling nematodes—that have been used to pry out the biochemical secrets of inheritance. For the most universal and obvious of reasons, geneticists cannot put human beings in stoppered flasks, arrange forced matings, create white-eyed mutants, and study the passage of the defective gene through subsequent generations. It would take too long, and geneticists are impatient.

Actually, the secrets culled from lilliputian creatures have a biochemical universality that applies to all organisms, up and down the line. And during the past century, the unstated long-term aim running through genetics has been spatial, if not downright geographic: to plot out inheritance by discovering its organic terrain, surveying it, measuring it, staking out landmarks, and then painstakingly assigning genes to specific regions. Little more than a century after the first fleeting glimpse of that abstract and hidden realm known as heredity, biologists are on the verge of mapping it in its entirety, down to every zip code, every neighborhood, every house, every room.

"It requires indeed some courage to undertake a labor of such far-reaching extent; this appears, however, to be the only right way by which we can finally reach the solution of a question the importance of which cannot be overestimated in connection with the history of the evolution of organic forms." Those words, biology's twentieth-century marching orders, were buried in a paper published the same year that America's Civil War came to an end, words written in German and largely unread (even by Germans) for nearly half a century. They come from Gregor Mendel's classic 1865 paper, "Experiments in Plant-Hybridization."

Mendel, an Austrian monk, was the first to espy biology's Holy Land. During eight patient years experimenting with *Pisum,* the common pea plant, he followed certain physical traits—round or wrinkled seeds, white or dark seed coats, color of pod, length of stem—from generation to generation and discerned that these "constantly differentiating characters," as he called them, seemed influenced by "factors" contributed by the parents. Each parent plant contributed one of these factors in the germ cells, and their combination in offspring occurred as "purely a matter of chance." What he was seeing, in those combinations, was the genetic lottery that leads to round seeds, towering height, blue eyes, mortal diseases like hemochromatosis. Genes were the "factors"; combinations of genes *created* traits. An underappreciated aspect of Mendelian inheritance is the simple but crucial role of *counting*—that is, quantitative thinking based on numbers large enough to be statistically significant. Plotting the percentage of traits from generation to generation allowed Mendel to see the nuts-and-bolts mechanism of heredity. But what exactly were these "factors," and—more important from the geographic point of view—where were they located? What was the domain of the gene?

One of the first hints emerged in 1877, when a German scientist named Walther Flemming visualized chromosomes for the first time in tumor cells, but it wasn't until two stellar intellects congregated at Columbia University shortly after the turn of the century that the picture began to assume some coherence. Thomas Hunt Morgan noticed that mutations in fruit flies—a white-eyed male, to cite his most famous mutant—were inherited in telltale patterns in subsequent generations, depending on the matings (or "crosses") of the parents; in a short 1910 paper in *Science,* Morgan noted that the white-eye trait seemed to be linked to maleness, a seemingly modest conclusion with enormous geographical implications. Maleness in fruit flies, as in humans, is linked to one specific chromosome. Hence, this specific gene was tentatively mapped for the first time to a specific chromosome. One year later, in 1911, Morgan's colleague E. B. Wilson showed that a disease trait in humans, color blindness, occurred only in males, too. It, too, must be associated with the domain that determined sex. Thus was the first human gene, loosely speaking, mapped to the X chromosome (males inherit only one copy of this chromosome while females inherit two).

But it was a sophomore in Morgan's laboratory, the aforementioned A. H. Sturtevant, who discovered the cartographic principle that guides even today's gene mappers. Like Morgan, he realized that certain genetic traits seemed to be inherited in pairs, or linked; unlike Morgan, he went on to examine this linkage statistically and discovered that one could reasonably infer the relative proximity of two genes on a landscape by analyzing patterns of inheritance. That landscape

```
O
B C                              P R                                M
├─┼─────────────────────────────┼─┼────────────────────────────────┤
0.0 1.0                        30.7 33.7                          57.6
```

In 1913, a Columbia undergraduate named A. H. Sturtevant inferred the relative position of genes on a chromosome merely by statistical analysis and published this scrawny gene map, the first ever. (© 1913, *Journal of Experimental Zoology*, reprinted by permission of Wiley-Liss, a division of John Wiley and Sons, Inc.)

was the chromosome, and the key word in the entire paper was "linear." Sturtevant was saying that the statistical frequency with which two traits appeared together in an organism contained a message about how close the two genes lay next to each other on this linear landscape. Indeed, his 1913 paper explaining this principle contained what can be considered the first genetic map, a short inferential stretch of *Drosophila* chromosome. "As a sophomore in college," David Botstein is fond of saying, "Sturtevant wrote *the* fundamental paper in genetics."

Fundamental, perhaps. All-encompassing? Not by a long shot. It took half a century of superb biology to put some flesh on that thread of insight. In 1944, Oswald Avery's team at Rockefeller University proved that the biochemical substance that transmitted genetic information from generation to generation was deoxyribonucleic acid, or DNA; in 1953, James Watson and Francis Crick showed that DNA assumed the form of a double helix, its genetic information encoded in the sequence of biochemical letters arranged like rungs along the spiraling ladder, its transmission to sex cells (and thus to subsequent generations) facilitated by the unique double helix structure that could chemically separate and unravel down the middle like a zipper; in the 1960s, the genetic code was cracked, showing that each three-letter unit (or codon) of the genetic alphabet spelled out an amino acid, and each gene spelled out a string of amino acids that formed a protein; and between the 1950s and '70s, in a parallel line of research, cell biologists learned to separate and identify all twenty-three pairs of human chromosomes (twenty-four different entities in all, when the X and Y sex chromosomes are counted), lay them out on a page in what is called a karyotype, and stain them to produce unique banding patterns. Each chromosome pair—the twenty-two autosomes shared by men and women, the female XX and the male XY—possessed a distinct size, a distinct pattern of bands, a particular and unique topography.

And so, by the mid-1970s, the heirs of Mendel made landfall on

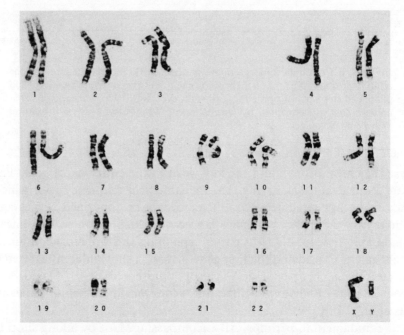

Landfall for human genetics: the territory awaiting exploration lies buried in the folds of each individual's chromosomes. Humans possess twenty-three pairs: twenty-two "autosomes" (1–22), plus the X and Y sex chromosomes (women have XX, men have XY). (U. Francke, Stanford University School of Medicine)

a genetic New World. This New World had a territory, the chromosome. Each of the twenty-four chromosomes, like states in a nation, represented a separate domain, with its own population of genes. Sprinkled throughout the twenty-four chromosomes were 50,000 to 100,000 genes, ranging in size from about 1,500 letters (or "base pairs" of DNA, to use the technical term) to as many as 2 million letters. And those letters of DNA—typically abbreviated as A, C, G, and T for the biochemicals they represent—became a form of measurement, as reliable a yardstick for determining genetic distance as meters or miles on a larger map. Medical geneticists compiled a growing list of inherited disorders that clearly had their origin in genes.

What they *didn't* have up to that point, however, was surveying tools. They didn't have the biological equivalent of theodolite and compass. With almost traumatic swiftness, those tools became available.

||||

If scientific earthquakes could occur in a ski lodge, why not in a delicatessen? In 1972 two biologists broke bread in a Waikiki Beach deli and talked about their work, and by the time Stanley Cohen of Stanford and Herbert Boyer of the University of California-San Francisco finished their sandwiches and their conversation, they had agreed on the outlines of a collaborative experiment that, by 1973, would allow biologists to cut DNA, insert it into bacteria, and copy it. The process became known as cloning. All the elements began to fall into place.

To the molecular cartographer, the tools of the trade include cloning, sequencing, and hybridization, all at the service of several forms of mapping. The first tool available was a kind of biochemical cutting agent known collectively as "restriction enzymes" (chapter 11 describes a series of mapping experiments that explained how those enzymes work). Each of the enzymes, culled from bacteria, cut DNA with what might be called alphabetical precision; *Eco* RI, perhaps the most famous of these enzymes, cut DNA wherever it found the six-letter sequence GAATTC. You could tell where you were on any given piece of DNA by the locations where *Eco* RI cut it, just as you could tell where you were on a state highway by the location of the county roads that intersected it. Indeed, the literature began to fill up with these so-called "restriction maps." Furthermore, different restriction enzymes cut DNA in different places and with different frequencies, providing something like triangulation and scale; whereas *Eco* RI on average made a cut every four thousand letters or so and was good for high-resolution work, another enzyme, such as *Not* I, cut DNA much less frequently, roughly every 250,000 bases, and thus was better for resolving the large-scale structure of an entire chromosome.

Restriction enzymes did something else, too. They allowed biologists to cut out little pieces of DNA and splice them into the DNA of bacteria, which dutifully reproduced the inserted DNA like a genetic document inserted into a biochemical photocopying machine. Cloning was crucial because biological mappers need copious amounts of the same stretch of DNA to parse out its letter-by-letter sequence and be able to fit it into the larger topography of the chromosome. Finally, in the mid-1970s, Frederick Sanger in England and Walter Gilbert and Allan Maxam of Harvard University independently developed ways to *rapidly* sequence pieces of DNA. With cloning and sequencing, biologists could take any piece of DNA, replicate it, and read the biochemical message of the gene. And since everyone—black and white, man

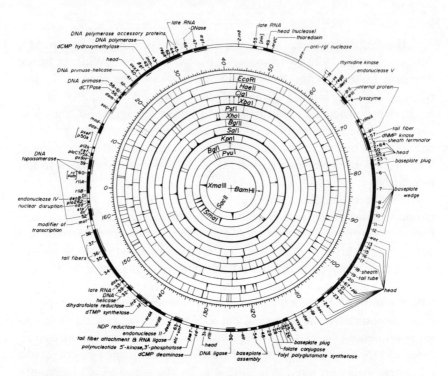

Genomic map of a virus: mapped genes form the outer ring, while inner concentric rings indicate where the virus's DNA is cut, or "intersected," by different restriction enzymes. (Reprinted with permission from Stephen J. O'Brien, ed., *Genetic Maps 1987,* vol. 4, Cold Spring Harbor, N.Y., Cold Spring Harbor Laboratory, 1987)

and woman, Bo Jackson and Pee-Wee Herman—possesses the same essential sequence for, say, the insulin gene in his or her chromosomes, each identified gene became a tiny but unvarying piece of the landscape, as distinctive and unique as a genetic mesa, if you will, that appeared in the same place on the same chromosome of every human being. All you had to do was find that place.

We might pause here to propose an extended metaphor that suggests not only the genetic landscape, but the various ways in which mappers attempted to make sense of it. Both the interstate highway system and DNA are double-stranded structures that run through the landscape. Both are *linear* landscapes. An interstate in New York looks about the same as one in California, just as DNA looks essentially the same in chromosome 1 and chromosome 22. So how do you begin to map it and distinguish one part from another?

One way, of course, is to look at the surrounding landscape. Genetic markers can be likened to roadside markers that intersect or lie just off the highway. Restriction enzymes provide another set of markers; they intersect DNA the way exits intersect a toll road, providing one form of geographic precision. Some markers lie near genes, sticking out like mountains or lakes along the roadway, and those form what are called linkage maps. And then the genes themselves form landmarks, which appear large and small along the interstate just like cities and towns; moreover, just as cities reveal their location on the landscape at night with the glow of their lights, genes and other informative stretches of DNA can be made to glow biochemically in experiments to reveal their location in, say, California rather than New York. That becomes a gene map. By this piecemeal, patient, overlapping kind of mapping, using the powerful surveying tools of modern biology, geneticists can slowly but surely break down the genetic highway system to states, then regions, and finally locate genes between particular markers and particular exits, until all the genes are mapped.

That surveying ability is what molecular biologists brought to the party—a party that, in the sociology of science, they seemed always to be crashing. Flush with the success of their new technological prowess, they would meet scientists from other biological disciplines, tell them how to do their work, and act surprised when they didn't. Yet those new technologies could change the way genetics was done. That is what David Botstein was thinking about—that and the geography of human chromosomes—on the afternoon in Alta when the argument about disease genes and mapping swirled around the room.

"So I listened to the argument," Botstein recalled, "and finally I got in the middle of it." For anyone who knows Botstein, this is not an uncharacteristic set of conversational coordinates. Well spoken, good-humored, with sardonic and refreshing opinions on almost everything, he had early on established a reputation as a leading light in molecular biology, although his first love was music and he had intended to pursue a career in choral music or as a conductor. (He comes from a family of polymaths; both parents are physicians, and his brother Leon, currently professor of history and president of Bard College in New York, was recently named conductor of the American Symphony Orchestra.)

Botstein heard Kerry Kravitz's comments with the ears of a molecular biologist; but he also heard them with the ears of someone steeped in the history of genetics. The early work of Sturtevant and

Thomas Hunt Morgan, who had begun to infer the spatial arrangement of genes in fruit flies by studying patterns of inheritance, was
"mother's milk" to geneticists, as he put it later. The discussion at Alta
became too complex to report here, but it would be fair to say that
Botstein immediately realized that the paired appearance of hemochromatosis and its HLA "flags" could—*could*—serve as a new way of
establishing recognizable landmarks on all the human chromosomes,
landmarks almost as regular as mileage markers along a highway. And
the key to finding those landmarks was something called polymorphisms.

"Polymorphism" is one of biology's less friendly words of jargon.
But the concept is quite simple. It refers to a patch of genetic landscape—the fringe of a gene, a random stretch of letters, part of the gene
itself—that contains generally insignificant but discernible variations.
A classic example is blood type. Everyone has the same human genes
for hemoglobin, but small variations result in one of four standard
blood types: A, B, AB, and O. Those are polymorphisms—slightly
different forms of the same thing. If people with O-type blood happened to be the only people to develop hemochromatosis (which is not
the case), then geneticists would say the genes for the disease and the
O polymorphism were "linked," implying that they lay in the same
genetic neighborhood.

Now Botstein knew that inheritance wasn't quite as neat and
clean as Mendel's pea plants implied. Just to confuse matters more, the
landscape of heredity rearranges itself a bit. Chromosomes swap and
exchange segments during the formation of sex cells. Just prior to
migrating into sperm or egg sex cells, while they are lying side by side,
chromosome strands often cross over each other, the way lovers sometimes cross legs while asleep at night; unlike the legs of lovers, those
chromosomal limbs switch places, merging onto the adjoining strands.
This obviously confuses both landscape and linkage. The farther apart
two genes are, the likelier they are to become separated at some point
during this process, known as "recombination."

Botstein didn't need to explain all this to the Utah group. But he
talked about how mathematical analysis could penetrate that confusion. "And then I said—and this I'm sure I said exactly this way—I
said, 'If you had things as polymorphic as HLA all over the genome,
then you could map anything.' And just as I said that, I was looking
at Ron Davis. Ron Davis is looking at me. And as the words come out
of my mouth, we both realize that in fact we *have* a way of doing that,
because we're working on it!"

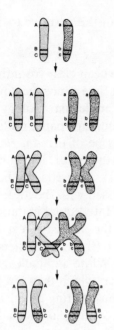

Linkage maps and "riflips" are detectable because during the separation of chromosomes into sex cells (meiosis), chromosome strands duplicate themselves and then often "cross over"—portions formerly on one limb switch places with neighboring chromosome limbs (recombination). The closer two genes are linked, the higher the likelihood that they will survive crossovers and appear together from one generation to the next.

Molecular biology, in short, offered an end run to this problem. Polymorphisms don't occur only in genes. Working with yeast, Botstein and Davis had seen polymorphisms pop up on the fringe of yeast genes, and the variations revealed themselves when you cut the yeast DNA with restriction enzymes. Some of the fragments were long, as if they had tails; others were short. If a long-tailed marker came from father, for example, then the defective gene linked to it came from father, too, and patterns of inheritance suddenly, magically became clear. The idea would become known as restriction fragment length polymorphism, or RFLP, denoted by the neologism "riflip." These "riflip" tails, of varying lengths attached to genes, flagged genes in a way that allowed them, and genetic diseases, to be traced through generations.

All during the day, they talked out the idea. Davis, soft-spoken and highly respected, agreed that the technique should work. As Skolnick remembers it, "It took a while before the ideas gelled." But in Botstein's memory, the genetic seas parted then and there. "By dinner that night," as he puts it, "we had laid out the whole business of how you would make a map—Skolnick and Davis and myself, with kibitzing from a few others. So this idea—for *us,* in any case—was generated at that moment. And basically the development of the next five to ten years was clear."

The future of genetic cartography may have been clear from that moment, but not until two years later—a lapse of time almost geologic given the pace of discovery during that period of molecular biology— did Botstein, Davis, and Skolnick publish the landmark paper outlining this strategy. It appeared in the May 1980 issue of the *American Journal of Human Genetics,* and there was a fourth author, Raymond L. White. A researcher at the University of Massachusetts Medical School at the time, White was not initially impressed with the idea; as he recalled later, "My initial response was one of intellectual irritation at the grandiose and presumptuous scale" of the strategy. Yet he volunteered to take on the task of proving that RFLPs could indeed serve as useful markers. The others waited until White and colleague Arlene Wyman found their first mappable marker, which they did by late 1979. White then moved to Utah to begin constructing an RFLP map with Skolnick, with the Mormon resource providing an unusually rich lode of potential landmarks.

In the uncharted terrain of chromosomes, "riflip" markers revolutionized the mapping of that landscape. Botstein sent a preprint of the RFLP paper to several prominent human geneticists, including Victor A. McKusick of Johns Hopkins University School of Medicine. McKusick, author of *Mendelian Inheritance in Man* and unofficial Mercator of the human genetics community since the 1950s, realized that RFLPs gave to gene mappers what the longitudinal clock gave to old geographers: precise meridians marking the landscape. The technique "opened up tremendous possibilities. It was a very exciting, landmark, watershed paper." In 1980, when the paper was published, McKusick's genetic gazetteer consisted of "at most two dozen markers. Now," he added, speaking in 1991, "we have twenty-four hundred markers. That gives an idea of what sort of explosion we've had, and it's been not only a quantitative explosion but a qualitative one."

That was the productive aspect of the RFLP paper. Unfortunately, the opening of a new territory, not for the first time in the history of cartography, led to territorial skirmishes, commercial competition, and political disputes, the effects of which are still evident within the biological community. Or, as Botstein puts it, "The history thereafter is a little bit less . . . attractive."

With the powerful surveying tool of polymorphic markers, the question arose: should biologists try to find specific, high-profile genes related to human disease, or should they take a more systematic approach, create markers throughout the genome (the total of all human genetic terrain), and in effect lay down a preliminary grid of genetic coordinates? In 1983 that question seemed to be decisively answered when James Gusella and his coresearchers at MIT located an RFLP marker for Huntington's disease. This devastating neurological disorder unfolds in a particularly tragic manner, for it reveals itself only in the fourth, fifth, or sixth decade of life, after the childbearing years when the mortal dominant gene may already have been passed on to children.

The marker wasn't the gene, mind you. It simply indicated the right genetic neighborhood. Nonetheless, the Huntington's discovery set off a gold rush for disease genes. "People reacted the same way they do in Las Vegas when they see a slot machine pay out lots of money," says David Botstein, who had been arguing for years that a modest RFLP map of all human chromosomes could be made for about $5 million. "What they do is they *cluster* around the machine and put more money in—a phenomenon that the people who *own* the casinos have exploited to their eternal, endless profit. That's what happened to human geneticists. They started to play the slot machine."

A few hit the jackpot. In the 1980s, genes linked to such prominent disorders as muscular dystrophy, cystic fibrosis, and chronic granulomatous disease were discovered and mapped. But at the beginning of 1991, the Huntington's gene still eludes researchers, who have been wandering in the wilderness at the very tip of chromosome 4, where the gene is believed to lie. Between 1983 and 1990, the National Institutes of Health (NIH) spent $15.2 million on the search for this one gene; for $15 million, Botstein has argued, a reasonably detailed RFLP map of *all* the chromosomes, with landmarks closer together than researchers currently are to the Huntington's gene, could be made. With each passing year, the argument grows more persuasive, the approach certainly more systematic and cost-effective.

There was another, more political barrier to speedy progress. The push to map human genes emerged not from the human-genetics community, but from those pushy molecular biologists. But the human-genetics community—through its funding section at the NIH—was slow to grasp the cartographic power of markers, according to several key biologists. "What they were particularly skeptical about—and this skepticism remains—is the value of a *map* as opposed to just individual markers," Botstein says. And that skepticism accounts for the rather unusual fact that the two earliest mapping initiatives were supported not by the NIH's customarily astute funding mechanisms, but by private enterprises: a philanthropic organization in one case, a small biotechnology company in the other. And it was the French who most successfully pushed for a cooperative international mapping effort. In 1984, Nobel biologist Jean Dausset formed the Centre d'Etude de Polymorphisme Humain (CEPH) as a central clearinghouse for genetic landmarks; researchers would deposit markers and cell lines from families, such as the Mormon families in Utah, and any researcher could then request DNA from the CEPH collection in the interest of creating a linkage map of human genes.

When it became apparent that the NIH balked at supporting a mapping project—it looked like "a fishing expedition" at the time, McKusick admits—Botstein and others "shopped the idea" to outside sources of funding. The Howard Hughes Medical Institute ultimately agreed to fund a group at the University of Utah—an obvious place because it had the Mormon resource at its fingertips, the acknowledged pioneer of RFLP mapping in Ray White, and Mark Skolnick's expertise in population genetics (White and Skolnick, however, would later have a falling-out). White's group promptly set out to map individual chromosomes, beginning with the short arm of chromosome 11, while taking productive detours to study interesting disease genes.

Meanwhile, Botstein and others pushed an effort in the private sector, and that is how the first overall map of markers and genes on human chromosomes began to take shape on a corkboard office wall in the suburbs of Boston. It was there, at a small biotechnology company called Collaborative Research, that Helen Donis-Keller and a team that would ultimately number thirty-three biologists began to attach little flags of blue, yellow, and orange paper to long vertical strands of blue and red yarn pinned to the wall; each strand of yarn represented one of the twenty-four human chromosomes, male and female, and the tags represented genes and RFLP markers. Starting with 12 useful markers in 1981, the Collaborative Research team gathered 403 markers, including 393 "riflips," and began plotting them. Eric Lander of MIT invented a computer algorithm called MAP-MAKER that translated statistical linkage into genetic geography.

In October of 1987, the Collaborative team announced it had completed the first map of the human genome. The map appeared on the cover of the journal *Cell,* the undisputed Bible of molecular biology, and was greeted by a tremendous reaction ranging from praise to censure. Praise because it was a first draft of human genetics, however crude and full of gaps (which it was). Censure because some claimed

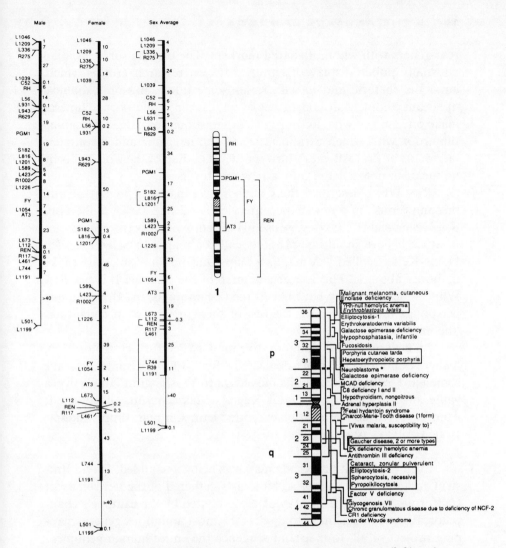

Two maps of the same territory: linkage maps of chromosome 1 *(left),* published in *Cell* in 1987, shows the location of RFLP markers, while map of "morbid anatomy" compiled by Victor McKusick *(right)* show the location of genes related to human disease. Linkage maps help researchers find the genes related to diseases. (H. Donis-Keller/© 1987 *Cell*; V. McKusick/ *Mendelian Inheritance in Man*)

---

it was too incomplete and borrowed heavily on the work of others—specifically markers donated to CEPH by the Utah group. Another undercurrent of discontent stemmed from the fact that because Collaborative Research wanted to patent some of its markers for genetic-testing kits, the company stood to benefit commercially from researchers with whom it shared markers. The dispute surfaced in an unusually public display of enmity between research groups which, amid the rhetoric and ill will, raises some interesting philosophical questions about what constitutes a map, when is the proper time to make one, and by what authority its utility should be judged. Recalling the ardor with which Strabo attacked the irregular and incomplete meridians of Eratosthenes' third century B.C. map of the world, it is by no means a new debate, only a new territory.

Ray White described the Collaborative map as "premature and presumptuous" in a newspaper interview, and told Leslie Roberts of *Science* magazine, "It is a very useful collection of markers, but it is not what we believe should be properly called a map." In *Science,* Helen Donis-Keller replied, "A map is a map. Our map has holes, we make no bones about it. This is *a* genetic map of the genome. It is not Ray White's ideal, but so what? This is the beginning for us. How can one person set the standard for the rest of the world on what constitutes 'the map'?"

Like all maps, the Collaborative map invited further exploration, higher resolution, and more dedicated effort. But the dispute did leave some hard feelings. Before she moved on to Washington University, a white sweatshirt hung in Donis-Keller's Massachusetts office, a gift from her research team. In black gothic letters, it read simply PREMATURE AND PRESUMPTUOUS.

Even while that first crude map was being assembled, David Botstein and another dozen or so biologists gathered at the University of California-Santa Cruz in May of 1985, invited by the campus's chancellor, Robert Sinsheimer, to discuss the most ambitious genetic mapping project of all: to map and sequence the entire human genome.

Botstein was there, and Donis-Keller, and Leroy Hood of Caltech, and Walter Gilbert of Harvard—heavy hitters all. Unlike many scientific meetings, this one began with a consensus. "Most people thought the idea was crazy," Botstein recalls. But as the reports of technical progress came out during the informal two-day meeting, the mood shifted. As Sinsheimer later summed it up, "There was perhaps a consensus that it could be done, but not that it *should* be done."

From that moment on, after the leading lights of the field convinced themselves of its feasibility, the project gained the kind of intellectual bona fides that carry tremendous weight in the scientific community. This is not the occasion to describe the many meetings and workshops, technical arguments and battles over turf, that ensued; the story is only now beginning to unfold. But by October 1, 1989, barely a decade after the original RFLP paper appeared in the literature, the $3 billion Human Genome Project was officially up and running.

The genome project will unfold in a series of maps of ever-increasing resolution. The first crude RFLP map, its four hundred or so markers spread over twenty-four chromosomes, represents little more than a hand-drawn sketch of the territory, divided by forlorn and infrequent intervals similar to lines of latitude and longitude. A physical map, currently being assembled, is also a map of broad brush, but it might be likened to breaking up the chromosomal territory—the interstate genetic highway, if you will—into smaller, self-contained segments, such as the part of Interstate 80 that runs through Iowa. The genetic map, more particular still, provides the exact location of genes—pinpointing the exact location of Des Moines and Davenport, for example, along that particular stretch of I-80. The color map illustrating this chapter shows a technique developed by workers at Yale University by which biologists can assign a small physical part of the map, a "segment" of the genetic highway, to its exact location on its particular chromosome. The final map, the map providing ultimate resolution, is the equivalent of a street map of Des Moines or Davenport. This is the sequence—the fine-scale topography of the genes, as spelled out in the sequence of biochemical letters in the genetic code. As information increases, diagnostic tests will be developed, genes will be studied, disease mechanisms explored, and—it is hoped, but by no means guaranteed—cures may be discovered.

Mark Skolnick, it will be remembered, moved to Utah with the dream of finding the genetic causes underlying breast cancer. In 1974, before the molecular surveying tools were in place, that may have seemed little more than a pipe dream. Finally, in 1990, Skolnick and his team converted the dream into partial reality; they published a paper strengthening the case for a genetic predisposition to breast cancer in women, which raised hopes that such inherited tendencies might be identified ahead of time. It was merely the latest crest in what he calls a "tidal wave" of change in the way human heredity is being charted and understood. Over the next decade or two, those changes will affect the way we think about having children and the way pregnancies proceed, the way we make decisions about our long-term health and the way we apply for health insurance (and why we may be turned down).

In that future, as Skolnick sees it, "clinicians doing diagnoses will request sequence testing the way they do allergy tests today. On a chip-sized blot, one centimeter by one centimeter, just like an integrated circuit, you'll be able to test for ten thousand genetic sequences. We'll know so much sequence information by then, so much about normal and so-called abnormal sequences, that we'll be able to identify tendencies to disease before they occur. And then all of medicine will be completely different. You'll be born, you will have your sequences tested, and if there are sequences associated with disease, we'll try to counter those before there are symptoms or cell degradation."

And how far away is this?

"Not that far," says the forty-five-year-old Skolnick. "I think I'll see it in my lifetime."

10. Head Stuff and Tail Stuff

FATE MAPS AND

THE GEOGRAPHY OF THE

FERTILIZED EGG

Am not I
A fly like thee?
Or art not thou
A man like me?

—William Blake,
"The Fly"

To step into Room 303 of Kerckhoff Laboratories, a wood-paneled corner office in the biology wing at the California Institute of Technology, is to inhale the musty, venerable air of nineteenth-century science. With its high, generous ceilings and rust-brown, foot-weary linoleum floor, its faint sweet-sour smell of fruit flies stoppered in their glass bottles, it is as if you had been transported back in a time machine to a kinder and gentler epoch in the history of science. This is the biology of the old school, mapmaking executed with familiar tools and according to familiar rules; there in the corner the Zeiss microscope, next to the classical music cassettes and the tape deck; there the stodgy old textbooks with dull gray spines, their pages dense with small print and inchoate ideas; there the old blackboard, still sporting a dark, varnished chalk tray and, propped up on the chalk tray, old photographs of Thomas Hunt Morgan, the legendary geneticist who initiated the study of fruit-fly genetics in 1908, and Alfred H. Sturtevant, his student, who mapped the first fruit-fly genes in 1913, and even one of William Bateson, the argumentative turn-of-the-century British geneticist who coined the term "homeosis" to hint at the mysterious process by which a fertilized egg "knows" what to become; and finally, up on the wall, like a commemorative section of decorative frieze surviving from Pompeii, one of biology's earliest and most influential maps, showing the three giant chromosomes of the fruit fly, their zebralike bands having been meticulously pinpointed and reproduced in the 1930s, their cartographer, Calvin Bridges, never imagining to what degree the key to Bateson's mystery lay buried in the bands and folds of those chromosomes. Even the office itself has bloodlines, for it was occupied for many years by the wife of Thomas Hunt Morgan, until her death, whereupon Room 303 passed on, like the germ of an idea or a gene itself, to a serious, self-contained, elfin young man from Pennsylvania named Edward B. Lewis.

Lewis did not invite immediate comparison with the giants who preceded him. Morgan looked imperious and scowled; his students, in their stiff Edwardian collars, looked sober and dignified. Lewis—small, bespectacled, as reserved as a church usher—came across as unfailingly polite. Indeed, his very politeness and patience have a museum quality to them in the rude if productive world of modern biology. But patience, in retrospect, was the key. Being smart is important in the study of genetics; being patient is essential. Working for the most part alone, studying his fruit flies for half a century, the map on the wall merely a ground plan for bigger and better things, Ed Lewis quietly (there is no other word for him) drew up the blueprint for a revolution that has completely overturned a field that was called embryology when he started out and now goes by the less suggestive name of developmental biology. More than any other biologist in this half century, working in Room 303 and in the labs down the hall, Ed Lewis has mapped out the process by which living creatures—fruit flies, certainly, and probably human beings as well—take the information in a single cell and transform it into the complex, highly specific three-dimensional organism we all become. Both genetic and geographical, this information serves to initiate the greatest mystery and miracle of life.

"The early experimenters used big words to cover up for the things that were intractable experimentally," Lewis was saying, sitting in Room 303 not long ago. He said it with a twinkle in his eye; it's not his style to boast. Soft-voiced and silver-haired, now an emeritus pro-

fessor at seventy-two, he still puts in twelve-hour days. "Bateson invented the term 'homeosis'; he was very mystical, he didn't believe in
chromosomes. Sturtevant once quoted Bateson's wife as saying, 'The
only thing that came between us were chromosomes.' But the word
'homeosis' doesn't mean anything." A mischievous smile. "It conveyed
an aura of mysticism. Developmental biology has been plagued by
words that *seem* to explain things, but don't really provide any fundamental understanding. There's always a tendency to go for the catchy
phrase."

The irony is that "homeotic" has become the trendiest word in
developmental biology, and Ed Lewis—who obviously doesn't care
much for the term—is widely acknowledged as the father of homeotic
genes. The term refers to genes that switch on in the embryo and, like
foremen at a construction site, oversee the orderly spatial organization
and segmentation of a lump of cells into head, gut, tail, and everything
in between; many of them share an intriguing, if enigmatic, element
known as the "homeobox," which may play a central role in this
control. In the past decade, biologists have identified several dozen
genes crucial to the embryo, and their unusual, idiosyncratic names dot
the literature like italicized buckshot: *bicoid, swallow, oskar, torso,
hunchback, knirps, runt, hairy, even-skipped, odd-paired, gooseberry,
sevenless, Toll, zen, twist, snail,* and *single-minded,* to name a few.
These genes, as they turn on at specific times and places, all nudge
fruit-fly embryos toward maturity, and they all in a sense are progeny
of Ed Lewis's rich scientific imagination. "If one of us died," says
Michael Levine, a molecular biologist now at the University of California at San Diego, "the field would be set back maybe one or two weeks.
If there were no Ed Lewis, I wouldn't say we wouldn't have found the
homeobox, but the work would have been set back *years.*"

The clarity of Lewis's thought is such that, years before molecular
biology existed as a discipline, a few years even before the structure of
DNA was discovered and the physical nature of genes became clear,
Lewis predicted the existence of a hierarchical class of related genes
that seemed to control the development of body segments in the embryo of fruit flies.

It was not a new idea. Indeed, Lewis brandishes a recent British
book called *Mechanisms of Segmentation.* It is not the contents that
make him so excited; it is the illustration on the cover, a drawing made
by William Blake in 1793. It shows a segmented caterpillar lounging on
one leaf of a leafy plant and a human face nestled cocoonlike inside a

or What is Man !

"What Is Man!" William Blake suggested in 1793, and Edward Lewis has shown in recent years, that insect and human embryos seem to develop by using the same set of master genes. (Trustees of the British Museum)

segmented, caterpillarlike form on a lower leaf. The title is *What Is Man!* The drawing excites Lewis because it shows both insect and human with multiple body segments.

"It's an incredible idea, this illustration!" Lewis cries. "This is very much like the vertebrate and invertebrate segmentation pattern, which we now know is controlled essentially by the same mechanism. It's amazing he could make the connection. Another mystic!"

The compartments of a fruit fly's body—a head, followed by three thoracic segments, followed by about eight abdominal segments—turned out to be the critical clue to understanding development. The power of Lewis's intellect is such that he could study the body plan of insects and, almost in his mind's eye, visualize the location and purpose of the genes that control the development of those segments. He predicted where these genes lay on the fruit-fly chromosome. He predicted which gene was next door to which. It was great science, but in the period before molecular biology, it bordered on the mystical: It was like intuiting the floor plan of a house one had never visited. Moreover, the architect, in the view of Charles Darwin, had drawn that plan in invisible ink.

"The fertilized germ of one of the higher animals . . . is perhaps the most wonderful object in nature," Darwin wrote. ". . . besides the visible changes which it undergoes, we must believe that it is crowded with invisible characters . . . separated by hundreds or even thousands of generations from the present time: and these characters, like those written on paper with invisible ink, lie ready to be evolved when the organism is disturbed by certain known or unknown conditions."

It was impossible for nineteenth-century embryologists to see the "invisible characters," but they could chart the more visible changes in the fertilized egg, and by the turn of the century Theodor Heinrich Boveri and others began to see in the fertilized egg a "fate map"—an organic geography where certain regions of the egg were destined to develop into particular structures, brain or gut or limb. The frustration of this approach can be inferred from Thomas Hunt Morgan's fitful career in embryology. A bearded man of high forehead, eaves for eyebrows, dark intent eyes, and a mouth built for skepticism, Morgan spent nearly twenty years studying the spatial orientation of frog eggs. He did not learn much. In a very colloquial turn-of-the-century confession of his lack of progress, he spoke of "a sort of stuff that is more or less abundant in different parts of the body." He referred to this as "head stuff" and "tail stuff."

It wasn't mystical, but it wasn't exactly quantitative either, and in 1908, Morgan switched to studying genetics in the vinegar fly, *Drosophila*. Not, interestingly, in the belief that flies would provide better answers. The man now viewed as one of the towering figures in twentieth-century genetics began to study fruit flies in the belief that Mendelian theory was wrong, that Darwinian natural selection was wrong, and that "particulate bodies"—what we now call genes—did not even exist. Instead, Morgan and a legendary cohort of undergraduates at Columbia University detected mutations in their flies and ultimately proved both the existence of genes and their existence as discrete physical elements arranged along chromosomes. (It has been said that Morgan's three greatest discoveries in science were his three star students: Alfred Sturtevant, Calvin Bridges, and Hermann Muller.) Unlike the frustrating spatial geography of frog eggs, the genetic geography implicit in a stretch of chromosome paved the way for the earliest gene mapping to occur.

Mutations are the windows through which geneticists view development, and by comparison with other creatures, the fruit fly provides a veritable picture window of embryological change because its external skeleton—known as the cuticle—is transparent. All the glitches in segmentation are plain to see. This is the egg as time-lapse architecture, sketching out the ground plan, marking off partitions, walling off parts

"Homeotic," or embryological, mutations create freaks of the fruit fly world. When the *Antennapedia* gene misfires, fruit flies grow legs out of their heads *(left)*; if the *bithorax* gene misfires, they grow two sets of wings instead of one. (E. B. Lewis)

of the embryo into the first body segments. Even humans are suscepti-ble to the same kind of segmental mutations, although we rarely see them because they hardly ever survive gestation; a classic, grotesque example is the occasional woman with multiple sets of breasts, or polymastia. "You see, primitive mammals had multiple mammary glands, like the dog," Lewis explains. "We have suppressed those, but there are mutants where you fail to suppress the gene. There are body segments for every rib and every vertebral segment. Mammary glands start under the armpits, come down the front, and continue down as far as the groin. You can develop mammary glands at any one of those segments, and it has happened." The occasional human mutation occurs in the womb and often vanishes with miscarriage. The mistakes of the fruit fly are there for all to see.

William Bateson, credited with founding the science of genetics, was among the first to see them. In 1894 he described bizarre mutants in which legs, of all things, projected out of the heads of sawflies and "humblebees" where the antennae were supposed to be, and this muta-tion came to be called *Antennapedia* (see note that explains the peculiar rules governing the spelling of mutations). In other anomalous cases, wings popped out of the thorax in place of important ballasting struc-tures called halteres; this mutation became known as *bithorax*. Some-times the embryos developed as one long thorax, with no abdomen, the symphony of life stuck on a single note. Sometimes a fly had four wings, or two; four legs, or eight.

Bateson had no way of explaining these peculiarities, but clearly something went dramatically awry in the early embryonic formation of the insects. The matter would have remained a minor curiosity of the animal kingdom except for one thing: such mistakes occurred in other creatures as well, including humans.

Fruit flies were easier to study, but Ed Lewis almost didn't get the chance. He came from a relatively poor family, with no tradition of science ("No books, practically," he recalled); his father, a watch-maker, never finished high school. A promising flutist, he went off to college in 1937 on a music scholarship, and later married a scientific illustrator (his wife, Pamela, occasionally illustrates the posters an-nouncing scientific meetings). According to one biologist, Lewis was unique in possessing "much more of an artist's temperament than your standard sort of scientist. He just sees the problem in such a different way. He doesn't construct brilliant arguments. He really relies on intuition, on his sense of smell, in doing things. He's very creative. He really reflects [Nobel Prize–winning geneticist] Barbara McClintock's notion of the organism talking to you if you pay attention." By paying attention Lewis in effect answered the question that Thomas Hunt Morgan died with: how do genes affect development?

The flies started talking to Ed Lewis during his high school years in Wilkes-Barre, Pennsylvania. He was a gifted student who, in addi-tion to his aptitude for music, showed considerable talent in the sciences. The biology teacher at Meyers High School happened also to be the football coach, which meant that after school, while the coach was tutoring the Grabowskis out in the mud, Lewis and his close friend Edward Novitski had the run of the lab. What did they study? Fruit flies.

For anyone who has ever had to do battle with fruit flies in a high school or college biology course, who has tried to scrub that gagging sour smell from memory, who has lunged in frustration as parts of your experimental control (not to mention your grade for the semester) fly out the window: *there is a reason.* First and foremost, fruit flies are among those creatures that reproduce and reach maturity the fastest. From the moment of fertilization, a fruit-fly egg divides every ten minutes (bacteria by comparison are deadbeats, taking twenty to thirty minutes per cell division). Within five or six hours, identifiable body segments begin to form. Within twenty-four hours, the larva is fully developed. Within ten days, that larva has transformed into a fully mature, reproductively fecund adult capable of making a nuisance of itself around any fruit bowl. At each step of this process, the body plan takes shape like a slow-motion, sometimes jittery movie. The cuticle provides a picture window; the embryo provides a constantly changing scene.

Lewis and Novitski kicked off their precocious scientific careers with the kind of unbelievable stroke of good luck that could spoil one for a scientific lifetime. Around 1935, while still high school students, Novitski sent off letters to several prominent "fly men," including Sumner A. Rifenburgh of Purdue and Calvin Bridges of Caltech, asking for a supply of flies. That same year Bridges published a discovery in the *Journal of Heredity* that would forever change genetics: the fruit fly's three polytene chromosomes, isolated from their salivary glands, proved to be unusually large, so large that, with landmark bands dark and prominent, it was an obvious step to see them as a geographical terrain waiting to be mapped. Bridges, along with Thomas Hunt Morgan, was also the first to observe that ill-formed class of mutants, called *bithorax,* in 1923; these were flies that possessed an extra pair of wings. Little did Lewis suspect that he would devote half a century of his scientific life to this one genetic glitch.

But that was not the stroke of luck. To the great surprise of the high school boys, when they began mating their flies, they discovered an exceedingly rare and previously undiscovered mutant. Fruit flies with this mutation developed a tiny, diamond-shaped eye, and so they named it *star.* This one-in-a-million misfit made Lewis's career. He abandoned the creature briefly while pursuing his musical studies at Bucknell University. But after one year, he transferred to the University of Minnesota, taking *star* with him; and with him went this valuable mutant again in 1939 when he headed west to do his graduate work at Caltech under Alfred Sturtevant; and with him also at Caltech was his old high school friend Novitski, who had made his way to Pasadena to study population genetics. Science was a small world then.

The *star* mutant got Lewis to thinking about the position of these genes on Bridges's chromosome maps. For the next half century, Ed Lewis studied these mutations, first *star* and then the *bithorax* mutation. It was thought at the time that certain genes could have a bewildering number of different forms, literally hundreds or thousands of variants known as multiple alleles. Lewis set out on the monumental task of sorting through all those variations, with the hunch that these variants were in fact clusters of related but distinct genes, genes that had important ramifications for the developing fly.

With only World War II and service as an air force meteorologist

Portrait of the artist as a
young fly man: E. B. Lewis with
flasks of fruit flies at Caltech.
(California Institute of Technology)

interrupting, Lewis retreated into that bewildering, patient, logical
process of sorting known as classical genetics. Just as Gregor Mendel
had teased out the laws of heredity in 1865 by pairing pea plants and
observing the statistical patterns of inherited traits in subsequent generations, Lewis arranged specific matings of fruit-fly stocks. Just as
Mendel paired plants with smooth or wrinkled peas to study their
offspring, Lewis paired wild-type (or normal) flies with mutant flies,
and looked for patterns of inheritance. "The whole basis of genetics
has always been that you try to study wild-type through removing one
or more genes at a time and seeing what happens," Lewis would
explain. "The rest of biology tries to study wild-type by hitting it with
a sledgehammer. And that principle just pervades all of biology, still.
People who can understand that the genes really are sort of units that
control everything will realize that you have to have mutants, and use
them effectively and properly."

No sledgehammers for Lewis. Tweezers, rather: in certain experiments, he says, he could check ten flies a second in his search for
mutants. As he would be the first to admit, genetics is a complicated
and dizzying discipline that does not lend itself to snappy exegesis. The
papers are dense distillations of back crosses, "lozenge" phenotypes,
and so on. Lewis himself tends to wander off into digressions that get
swiftly technical, and there are few things in science more perplexing
than a geneticist who gets rolling about wild types and crosses and A +

and B + in a rush, as does Lewis, who characteristically catches himself at some point and apologetically mumbles, "But that's probably more detail than you're interested in."

He began to focus on mutations that occurred about one hundred minutes into the development of the fruit-fly embryo, when the cells first began to organize themselves into segments like rooms in a house, later to be furnished with organs, nerves, and so on. He began to correlate mutations in the thorax and abdomen with a set of related genes. He noticed that certain mutations occurred together, and he shrewdly intuited this as a message about physical geography down at the level of chromosomes, that the two genes responsible for the two mutations were inherited together and thus probably lay close together on the same chromosome. Lewis compiled a thicket of statistics to analyze these so-called "pseudoalleles," or "linked" genes. The genetics of this work, spanning decades and involving tens of thousands of matings and offspring, of Lewis peering into his microscope and picking through millions of flies, each barely larger than a poppy seed, searching for their oddball and telltale mutations, would in any event represent an incredible feat of perseverance. But it was truly heroic because fruit flies had fallen out of favor as a model organism.

In 1946, Lewis was offered a job at Cold Spring Harbor Laboratory. The man at Cold Spring Harbor, Lewis recalls, wanted him to work on bacterial genetics because everyone seemed to feel that *Drosophila* would no longer be of importance. Lewis turned down the job, preferring to stick with fruit flies. In 1951 he published a paper suggesting how these linked genes might have developed in evolution, and where that insight might lead. Two years later Watson and Crick discovered the structure of DNA. You could practically hear the whoosh of biologists rushing to study DNA in bacteria and viruses.

But Lewis didn't chase fads. He was of the old school. "It was quite nice, you know. In those days the professor didn't have to put his name on every paper. See that paper there?" He motioned at the 1951 article. "Well, in those days you could have your name on a paper if you did all the work. Nowadays . . ."

Lewis stuck it out with the flies. He and a few colleagues almost single-handedly kept the mutant stocks alive. Faithful to his vision, working alone, sorting through an estimated 10 million flies over the years, he pursued the insight outlined in that 1951 paper. The work came together, brilliantly. In an age when biologists have been known to milk two or three publications out of a single set of experiments,

Lewis summarized three decades of work in a single six-page paper that appeared in 1978 in the British journal *Nature*.

It is a famous paper, an astonishing paper, although it does exactly what exemplary science is supposed to do: it gathers up a body of data, joins it with firmly based intuition, and makes predictions about the future. In this case Lewis provided a map of embryological development in fruit flies that was so well reasoned and complete that, loosely speaking, it served as a template for all other organisms, including humans.

What was so remarkable and intuitive about the map was that it sketched out a territory yet to be discovered. In his decades of observation, Lewis noticed that the development of the fruit fly abided by certain rules. He had concentrated on the *bithorax* mutation and related genes (an ensemble known as the Bithorax complex), which controlled formation of the third thoracic segment and all nine abdominal segments that followed. He theorized that at each step of development, from one segment to the next, a master switch had to be thrown in the embryo—the fate of the cells had to be channeled into becoming, for example, a thoracic segment (which could sprout wings) or an abdominal segment (which could not). What served as the master switch? What could prod cells toward one fate or another?

The answer was hierarchical genes. Lewis suggested that about eight genes functioned as master switches in the Bithorax complex (it now looks like there are eleven regulatory switches in all). Like railroad switches, they would shuttle a collection of cells down one biological track or another, hurtling toward one morphological destination or another. As the massive genetic data built up, he began, like all mapmakers, to see pattern. These genes did not act randomly. They appeared to kick in one after another, like dominoes, from head to foot, and if a mutation occurred at any point, if the master switch malfunctioned for any reason, development—indeed, the destiny of that particular ill-fated fly-in-the-making—jammed at that point. When the entire Bithorax complex was knocked out, for example, it was like a bomb going off in the switchyard; the fly embryo got stuck, reiterating itself as an endless, exaggerated thorax, never developing an abdomen. If a mutation occurred in the second abdominal section, the rest of the abdomen repeated this segment the rest of the way, a morphological stutter.

Lewis's next great insight was to correlate this domino effect with microscopic geography. He predicted, quite simply, that these eight genes must lie next to each other on the same chromosome, in the same

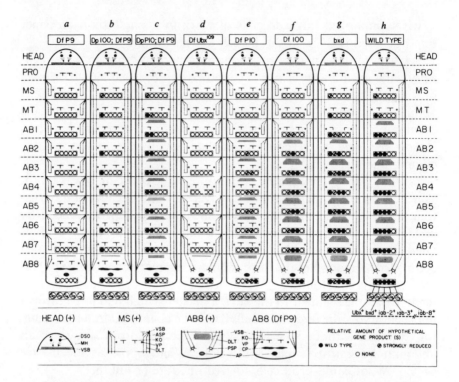

"A neat little story": by reducing the elaborate pattern of mutations in the head, thorax, and abdomen of *Drosophila* to one chart, Lewis deduced the relative locations of genes and predicted their geographical position on a map *(lower right corner)*—a map subsequently confirmed by molecular biologists. (E. B. Lewis/© 1978 Macmillan Magazines Ltd.)

sequence in which they kicked in. This prediction came at an opportune moment, for in the late 1970s molecular biology suddenly offered new tools to confirm this cheek-to-jowl alignment if it indeed existed.

The suspected proximity of these genes suggested the final prediction, resuming a theme Lewis had played throughout his career and first suggested in his doctoral thesis in 1945. These related genes, bunched closely together, positively symphonic in their power to control and influence the embryo, had all derived from a single, ancestral gene. During the normal cycle of cell replication, organisms constantly make mistakes in which a gene is accidentally duplicated, and Lewis argued that over hundreds of millions of years, these duplications can be stored and refined by the organism.

Duplicate genes give organisms the luxury of rewriting and im-

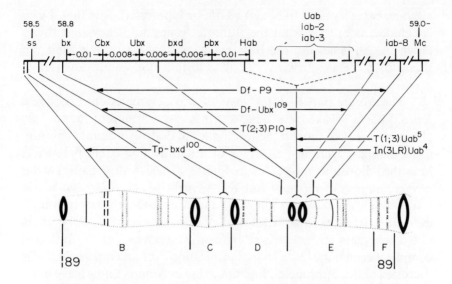

The giant fruit fly chromosomes *(below)* form the landscape upon which schematic gene maps *(above,* and derived from map on opposite page) denote the location of hierarchical genes that control development. (E. B. Lewis/ © 1978 Macmillan Magazines Ltd.)

proving their genetic script. The original gene continues to perform its regular function; if it were lost or changed by mutation, the organism might perish. But the second, duplicate gene is like a rough draft upon which random mutation can daydream, doodle, ad lib, jam, scribble genetic digressions and riffs. Most of the changes will not be useful. But a few will be, and after a sufficient amount of rewriting, over a sufficiently long period of time, these duplicate genes become sufficiently different from their ancestor to assume a new function. And if that new function enhances the chances of survival for the organism, natural selection plucks it out and keeps it. It was in precisely this way, Ed Lewis concluded, that evolution selected these duplicated fruit-fly genes and gave them hierarchical importance. He took the whole scheme even further. He imagined how it must have happened. He pictured a simple arthropod, something like a millipede, prowling the planet some 600 million years ago. It possessed many legs, and in the laboratory of its own chromosomes, its progeny cooked up the Bithorax complex and became an insect, with two wings and six legs. To evolve into a fly, the ancestral genes that created the extra wings and all those extra legs had to be turned off, or suppressed. And that, Lewis concluded, is exactly what the Bithorax genes did. They shut things down. As all genes do, the Bithorax genes make a protein, and this group of proteins—Lewis called it "substance S"—shut down other genes.

The *Nature* paper—forty years of work crammed into six dense journal pages—was a tour de force. It laid out a map of the fruit-fly chromosome even though the techniques to do truly accurate chromosome mapping were just emerging at the time. You could practically hear the whoosh as molecular biologists, armed with the spectacular new techniques of recombinant DNA, rushed back to *Drosophila* to test Lewis's predictions. They produced ever-more-accurate maps, ever-more-startling discoveries. But as British biologist P. W. Ingham noted ten years later, Lewis's "innovative analysis" of the Bithorax complex became the "intellectual inspiration" for an entire field. "The successes of this approach," Ingham wrote in *Nature,* "now leave us on the threshold of a new era in the study of development." That new era belonged to molecular biologists, the Young Turks of biology.

"Molecular biology put the fruit fly back on the map."

The speaker, not surprisingly, is one of those Young Turks, a biologist who wears black high-topped tennis shoes and, on occasion, an L.A. Dodger cap—Michael Levine, late of Columbia, now at UC-San Diego, one of many molecular embryologists who have traveled the road paved by Ed Lewis. In the early 1980s, shortly after Lewis's seminal paper, molecular biologists began to apply their powerful techniques of cellular visualization to peer inside the egg and watch the embryo at its earliest moments of unfurling. They were able to map the earliest geography of the egg by using radioactive antibodies to light up protein-rich regions, and the journals began to fill up with dazzling images of glowing red stripes, zebra patterns, and brilliant star bursts. They were able to map specific cells in the embryo where certain homeotic genes turned on. They were able to clone, or replicate, these genes and decipher them according to the genetic code; they could "map," or locate, these genes to precise spots on chromosomes; and they could use parts of the genes as "probes," which can pull out related genes just as a magnet can pull a needle out of a haystack. For a century the egg had been historically studied like a globe, with its poles and equator and strange, swirling currents of cytoplasm, its "head stuff" and "tail stuff." Now, with Lewis's genes blazing the path and molecular biology providing the vehicle, old-fashioned embryology became a new type of molecular geography. This new breed of molecular geographers were finally able to journey to the center of the egg.

The first molecular landmark was sighted by workers in the Stanford laboratory of David Hogness. As early as 1979 (though they published the results much later), Welcome Bender and Pierre Spierer invented a technique called "chromosome walking," and in so doing happened upon the entire Bithorax complex and discovered one of its specific genes, called *Ultrabithorax*. This gene controlled the orderly transition from thorax to abdomen in the fly. Another postdoc, Michael Akam, began studying the way the *Ultrabithorax* gene worked. Not long after the Hogness group made their discoveries, Michael Levine began to work as a postdoctoral fellow in the Basel laboratory of Walter Gehring. It would be hard to imagine a more dramatic contrast in personal, if not scientific, style with Ed Lewis; Hollywood-born-and-bred, Levine arrived in Switzerland in Hawaiian shirts and big straw hats, and was soon heard complaining loudly about the finite pleasures of bratwurst. As he puts it, "Somehow I lost whatever vestige of inhibition I had when I got to Europe. I felt even more anonymous, and got even crazier."

But the times were crazy with excitement, too, as hordes of biologists closed in on the elusive genes that created the freaks of the fruit-fly world, and Basel was one of the best places to be. In 1982, Richard Garber of Gehring's lab blazed a second molecular path into this world by isolating and identifying the homeotic gene called *Antennapedia*. When this gene misfired, fruit flies sprouted legs out of their heads, the same kind of mutation that William Bateson had observed nearly a century earlier. Within five years of Lewis's paper, the first two homeotic genes were on the map.

What good did a gene do them? A gene is a stretch of deoxyribonucleic acid, or DNA, and the order of chemical subunits in the DNA—its "sequence"—tells a cell how to make a protein. In a developing organism, homeotic genes made critically important proteins. These proteins had the power to determine a cell's fate.

Moreover, these proteins could be mapped in a way that clearly illustrated, to use geopolitical argot, their spheres of influence. Like all genes, homeotic genes convey these instructions when information in the DNA is transcribed into a go-between molecule called messenger RNA, which carries the job order, as it were, out to the protein-making precincts of the cell. Using sophisticated techniques of molecular tagging, researchers can pinpoint dense congregations of these messenger

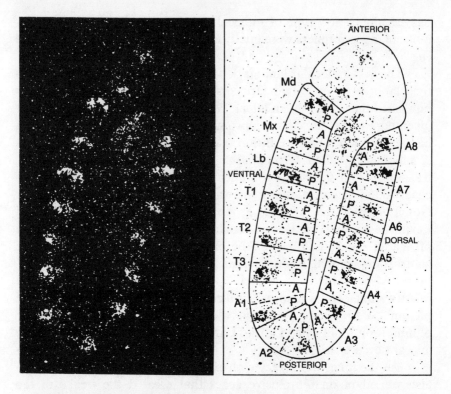

As a fruit fly embryo develops, molecular biologists can watch genes turn on (*left*); spots mark locations that develop into the head, three thoracic segments (T1–T3), and eight abdominal segments (A1–A8). (W. Gehring)

molecules as they build up in certain parts of the cellular landscape. In fact, they can map their location in the body plan of a developing fruit fly, which tells them exactly where and when the gene is turned on and active. By pinpointing heavy populations of the messenger, you could pinpoint the cells where the gene had turned on and was imparting, or "expressing," the message. Both Gehring's group and Akam's group in England raced to identify these regions in the embryo.

The true magnitude of this emerging picture, this embryological map, began to take shape in early 1983, when Michael Akam passed through Basel and gave a seminar on his *Ultrabithorax* work. Levine recalls it as a highly charged encounter. The Basel group—Levine, Garber, and Ernst Hafen at the time, William McGinnis later—exchanged ideas and data with Akam; and as they talked, they stumbled upon the realization that their two homeotic genes seemed to be cut from the same cloth. They behaved almost exactly the same. "What was striking," Levine recalls, "is that patterns of expression for the two genes were *remarkably* similar. The genes turned on about three hours after fertilization. They both showed this funny accordion effect, where genes initially expressed in a very sharp domain, sort of a swath of cells that encircle the circumference of the embryo, within ten to twenty minutes of each other. They were expressed in different segments, *Ultrabithorax* being expressed in regions posterior to [behind] the primary domain of *Antennapedia* expression. But if you ignore that detail, the overall patterns of expression were remarkably similar." "To see molecules that corresponded to Lewis's model was fantastic," McGinnis says now.

"That really left a strong impact on our thinking," Levine remembers. "We immediately ran to Lewis's 1978 paper and reread that more carefully and saw, yes, that he explicitly states that these genes arose from a common ancestor. We saw the very similar expression patterns for two of the genes that were in separate complexes, and we just reasoned that maybe these genes shared sequence similarity." In other words, the Lewis paper suggested that genes from the same family had similar function. Molecular biology provided a quick way to find out. With the *Antennapedia* gene in hand, William McGinnis used it as a "probe" to search through every smidgen of DNA in all the fruit-fly chromosomes; if there were sibling genes with a similar chemical identity, the probe would find them and attach to them, light them up radioactively, and give researchers a visual clue as to their location. In a feverish burst of activity, McGinnis found no less than eight related regulatory genes. Using more molecular tricks, they took these genes and discovered their proper niches on the fruit-fly chromosome, like putting jigsaw pieces of a map into their correct locations. Then came the surprise. "They were predominantly mapping to two places," Levine remembers. One was the Bithorax complex, the other the Antennapedia complex. Just as Ed Lewis had predicted, these hierarchical genes lay bunched together, physically adjacent on the chromosomes.

Not even Lewis had foreseen the next twist in the story, however. It emerged simultaneously in Gehring's lab in Switzerland and at Indiana University. In Basel, McGinnis, Levine, and Hafen discovered that all eight genes shared a section of DNA that was incredibly similar. Similarity of sequence in a gene is like an inherited physical trait—a big nose, red hair—that runs through a family; it suggests relatedness. The odds against such similarity was astronomical. Bearing in mind that genes carry instructions for the manufacture of a particular protein, all these funny-sounding homeotic genes contained a clause in the instructions that was exactly the same from gene to gene, and the resulting protein, it was presumed, possessed a three-dimensional shape—a hook, an arm, some telltale structure—that was exactly the same. Matthew Scott, a biologist then at Indiana University, independently discovered this segment in the Antennapedia complex, and with great fanfare this little segment came to be known as the homeobox. How universal was this element? William McGinnis went on to find homeoboxes—this curiously ubiquitous genetic clause—in toads and mice, earthworms and chickens. Mike Levine completed the family portrait in 1984 when, with Gerald M. Rubin and Robert Tjian, he showed that human beings possess homeoboxes in their DNA, too.

Once again, Ed Lewis had beaten them all to the prize. As he predicted with his mysterious substance S, experiments have shown that all the proteins with homeoboxes have a similar function: they regulate other genes. They attach to DNA and either goose a gene into heightened activity or simply flop down on the gene like a wet blanket, completely smothering its activity. As these genes turn on and off, as they excite and suppress other genes, they create or modulate the geography of the embryo, just as sudden upwellings of lava can suddenly change the topography of the earth. As Levine explains: "These are the genes that make the fate map. These genes *set* the fate map, no question about it. You can superimpose the patterns of expression of these genes *snugly* onto the big map, and say that the expression of homeobox gene A in this region of the embryo is responsible for that region of the embryo giving rise to the head."

The knowledge that continues to pour out about these genes has been astonishing, but no less so than Ed Lewis's visionary ability to map out these gene complexes in his head before molecular biology provided the technical fireworks to light up the landscape in all its glory. "It was just his intuition," says Michael Levine. "He was trying to devise an integrated model that took into account both the development of fly segmentation as well as the evolution of diverse body segments. And this was the simplest proposal to accommodate both constraints. Now a lot of people would not have been at all concerned about the evolutionary angle. The notion of ontogeny recapitulating phylogeny had been pretty much ousted. But in a way Ed was resuscitating that concept in his model-building. In a way. That notion of duplication of an ancestral gene is just one of the incredible intuitions that he had gained by playing with the material for so long. If he had been a big operator with a giant lab, he might never have come up with that notion. I personally would give Ed Lewis *full* credit for the development and discovery of the homeobox because, again, it's *explicitly* predicted and proposed in his 1978 paper, which is a paper we *all* read. To varying degrees of understanding, you know. But we all read it."

The ability to map the location of crucial chemicals in the fertilized egg and developing embryo has begun to tame the egg just as circumnavigations of the earth in the sixteenth century clarified the relationship of land masses to ocean. Again, molecular biology's ability to tag and trace molecules—much as wildlife biologists, for example, tag and trace the movement of birds and bears with their bands and beepers—has made this possible. As the techniques have grown more sensitive, scientists have been able to explore the primordial geography of the early egg.

Christiane Nüsslein-Volhard, a German biologist based at the Max Planck Institut in Tübingen, has been perhaps the foremost geographer of early development. She has looked at the early egg as a paleogeophysicist would look at, and map, the distribution of continents on earth in its early history. Nüsslein-Volhard's work has focused on a gene called *bicoid,* which possesses a homeobox and is active moments after fertilization. Her lab has shown, in exquisitely beautiful false-color maps, that geography is destiny, even before an egg is fertilized (see color illustration). Prior to insemination, fruit-fly eggs nestle in the ovaries of the mother. The maternal landscape surrounding each egg provides the very first cues about the ultimate fate of the egg: how the location of the head is determined (known technically as the anterior-posterior axis) and how front and back (the ventral-dorsal axis) is determined. This is the pattern, the grid, upon which the genes identified by Ed Lewis sketch in the specialized structures of the embryo.

How does a fertilized egg *know* north from south, or head from tail? For the fruit fly, at least, we finally have answers. The female surrounds one end, one pole, of her egg with nourishing sentinel cells known as nurse cells. In a lovely set of experiments, Nüsslein-Volhard has demonstrated that the mother fly slips biochemical messages from the nurse cells into the egg. These maternal love notes, in the form of messenger RNA molecules, do not spread through the entire egg. They get tangled up almost as soon as they pass through microscopic canals and enter the egg, and thus the message is confined to a small geographic area of the egg—a region that might be likened to the North Pole. That polar region, where they get tangled up, without fail becomes the head.

Like all messenger RNAs, these molecules instruct the developing egg to manufacture a very particular protein known as *bicoid.* Nüsslein-Volhard has mapped the geographic distribution and amount of this protein in the egg and demonstrated that it is most highly concentrated in the north, or anterior, pole of the egg—the hemisphere where the head develops—and gradually decreases in amount as it diffuses toward the equator. This type of phenomenon is known as a gradient or, more geographically, as a "concentration landscape." It appears that the *bicoid* RNA makes a protein that regulates other genes in the egg, either turning them on or shutting them down. To show how powerful these inaugurating proteins are, Nüsslein-Volhard has tampered with the early geography and literally turned this single-celled world upside down. She has injected the *bicoid* protein into the south pole of an egg; those eggs develop into flies with two heads, one at each end of the body. Conversely, when she inserted cytoplasm from the south pole of an egg in the north, anterior pole, the resulting flies have no head and, as it were, arses fore and aft. She had identified nothing less than the "head stuff" and "tail stuff" envisioned by Thomas Hunt Morgan at the turn of the century.

Though the overall story is far from clear, the emerging picture suggests that the egg uses the messages passed on from the mother to create a chemical landscape upon which the structure of the organism is built. Those maternal messages kick off a series of self-organizations, each stage of which is presided over by its own ensemble of genes, each gene ensemble not only accomplishing its own tasks (such as establishing the head-tail axis, sketching in the rough metastructures of thorax and abdomen, and creating specialization within each segment), but also setting the table for the next stage by leaving a hand-me-down message in the form of a protein gradient.

Embryology, according to this view, is a dialogue between protein and gene. The proteins, like those first maternal messages, turn genes in the egg on and off; those activated genes make new proteins; those second-generation proteins turn on new genes or shut down existing ones; and as the dialogue cascades, like one of those extravagantly ramifying arrays of tumbling dominoes, the embryo organizes itself into greater and greater complexity. First, it assembles a thin wall of cells around the outside of the egg, then it etches in the location of segments, then it creates head, thorax, abdomen, and all the specialization within each region, the entire job essentially completed in 24 hours. We tend to think of fruit flies, if we think of them at all, as pests; but think of them as the genetic text made flesh, that in 240 hours a suite of genes as frenetic and precise as any Bach concerto harmonize into a creature that can fly, eat, reproduce, *exist*. It is a final, spectacular vindication of Ed Lewis's vision.

The ability to generalize from a six-legged nuisance to a human being has patent limitations, but as Michael Levine observes, "Our justification for working on flies is that there will be fundamental mechanisms of development that are more *easily* seen in flies that will apply to the systems we're intrinsically, inherently more interested in, namely ourselves." And indeed, that is exactly what has happened. Researchers have recently discovered that mammals like humans and mice possess a strip of regulatory genes that lie next to each other on one chromosome, that turn on one after another, and that control body segmentation in the exact same linear, spatial order in which they are arrayed on the chromosome. Coming full circle, William McGinnis recently substituted a human homeobox gene for its analogous fruit fly gene and watched as the insect embryo developed normally. "The proteins are similar enough that they work in *Drosophila* embryos," says McGinnis, "even though they've been separated for six hundred million years."

The complexity of the entire system—the growing number of hierarchical genes, their funny and peculiar names—can make the casual observer despair of biology's ever emerging with a clear, simple, concise explanation of how one single cell, the egg, unfurls into a creature of such specialized functions, appearances, and taste. I once remarked to Ed Lewis that putting homeotic genes on the map did not seem to satisfy one of science's unofficial criteria for the worthiness of a theory: namely that it be beautiful and elegant and, with any luck, simple. Ed Lewis is too polite to express anger, but he was not friendly to the suggestion.

"It's remarkable how simple in a way it's turned out to be!" he replied. "You don't have a million ways to make an organism. You only have one or two. The development of the early embryo in fruit flies and humans is very similar, remarkably similar. These master control genes may well have evolved from one or two primordial genes, and they remained linked for a long time. There's a certain simplicity and beauty to that. It may take only eight or twelve genes to control our overall body plan. In our bodies, we have segments in the form of cervical vertebrae and lumbar vertebrae and thoracic vertebrae. The idea that an embryo can build all that structure with a small number of genes, all related in function and presumably from a common ancestor"—he paused, drawing himself up to full height, launching into understatement—"it seems to me that's a neat little story."

11. A Saga of Low Cunning

MAPPING THE ATOMIC
INTERACTIONS OF DNA AND PROTEINS

||||||||||||

This place is known as the Abode
of the Accursed. . . . Sisyphus now
pursues, now pushes the stone that
always comes rolling back.

—Ovid,
Metamorphoses

In a world of hostilities large and cruel, microscopic acts of violence do
not cry out much for our attention, and yet it was just such a modest
little episode of biological *mano a mano,* invisible to even the most
powerful microscopes, that began to obsess a small segment of the
biological community about two decades ago. Indeed, one group of
biologists had nothing better to do than ponder how a common,
run-of-the-mill bacterium defended itself against the occasional depre-
dations of viruses. The organism in question was called *Escherichia
coli,* a Babbitt in the world of bacteria, an utterly routine burgher of
the gut that browses upon our dietary whims and multiplies in the
warmth and murk of our intestines, usually causing neither offense nor
harm. What piqued the interest of researchers was the success with
which *E. coli* fended off the occasional viral invader.

Viruses typically pick on bacteria, up to one thousand times their
size, by injecting a slender but subversive strand of their genetic mate-

rial, deoxyribonucleic acid (DNA), into the bacterial cell; this viral DNA exerts hierarchical control over the bacteria's own DNA, effecting a kind of genetic coup d'état within the singled-celled bacterium and taking over its machinery. Since DNA is little more than encoded instructions for making proteins, the virus orders the bacterium to make, say, 100 copies of the virus's modular parts—its threads of DNA, its protein coat—and finally, in a blaze of pathogenic glory, new viruses burst from the cell (whose debut, alas, coincides with the rupture and demise of the bacterium). This grisly if invisible little scenario, played against our Baghdads and our Beiruts, seems so insignificant as to merit barely a nanogram of concern. But in the case of *E. coli,* the scenario took an odd twist, and odd twists in science often reward the curious. When these marauding viruses infected certain strains of *E. coli,* nothing happened. The viruses became benign, as if suddenly and mysteriously disarmed. Why?

It was one of those questions so particular, so abstruse, that it promised no practical value whatsoever, and of course the few biologists who did pursue it tumbled upon a jackpot of unimaginable riches, both intellectual and financial, to say nothing of launching one of the most glamorous and significant new industries of the twentieth century. Back in 1971 two scientists at the University of California at San Francisco, Herbert W. Boyer and Howard Goodman, decided to investigate this little mystery. They discovered that the RY13 strain of *E. coli,* like other bacteria, fended off invading viruses with the use of an enzyme. They painstakingly isolated this enzyme and called it *Eco* RI. It belonged to a newly emerging class of proteins called restriction enzymes. Not only did these enzymes recognize viral DNA as foreign, they seized onto that foreign DNA and chopped through it with the lethal dispatch of a sword, aborting the genetic coup in a fraction of a second and chemically beheading the insurgents. The first restriction enzyme was discovered by researchers at Harvard University in 1968. But the particular enzyme studied by Boyer and Goodman, *Eco* RI, just happened to produce sticky little flaps when it sliced through DNA, and those flaps could later be rejoined like splice points in a film. That is what put the splice in gene splicing. Thus did genetic engineering obtain its first scissors and pastepot, all rolled up in one convenient enzyme.

The rest is much-chronicled entrepreneurial legend. Herb Boyer went on to cofound Genentech, considered the premier biotechnology start-up company, and many other biologists became uncharacteristically wealthy on the basis of cutting and pasting DNA in a way first made possible by *Eco* RI. Less well known is the fact that Boyer and his UCSF colleague Patricia Greene continued to be curious about how the enzyme worked. How did it target, out of long stretches of DNA, a very precise stretch of chemical letters to cut (a process called "recognition")? How did it grab onto the DNA at that particular spot? How did it slice through the twin cables of the spiraling helix? What mechanism allowed it to do this without making mistakes, including the instantly lethal mistake of cutting its own DNA in two?

In order to answer these questions, Boyer and Greene needed to find a "structure person." More formally known as X-ray crystallographers, structure people belong to a small tribe of scientists who straddle the fields of biology and chemistry and physics; they parse proteins and nucleic acids like DNA down to the level of atoms and in so doing create a three-dimensional atomic map of their exact shape. Boyer and company ultimately found their man in John M. Rosenberg.

Like most practitioners of X-ray crystallography, Rosenberg tends to take the long view. At this time, around 1977, he was finishing up a postdoctoral fellowship at the California Institute of Technology, and the *Eco* RI problem intrigued him. While Wall Street throbbed with excitement over the potential of biotechnology, while biologists from Harvard to Stanford cut deals with venture capitalists, Rosenberg set out to make a map of the mysterious mechanism that was making everybody else rich. He intended to map the position of each and every atom involved in the interaction between *Eco* RI and DNA. And he decided to do so knowing full well that the solution might take, and probably would take, years and perhaps even decades. At the time he started, Rosenberg in fact knew it was not unusual for an X-ray crystallographer to spend an entire career trying to obtain and interpret one decent picture of one single substance.

Despite those daunting time frames, Rosenberg set up his new laboratory at the University of Pittsburgh and, with a supply of enzymes and advice from Boyer and Greene in San Francisco, began to map this important atomic landscape. What they did, to profane years of effort and sweat, was to pluck out this tiny piece of DNA with a protein clinging to it, pose it before a very unusual camera, get it to say "Cheese" for about four years, and produce one of the most detailed, highly resolved snapshots science has yet managed of the interaction between atoms on a molecular scale.

"Almost all aspects of life are engineered at the molecular level," Francis Crick noted in his book *What Mad Pursuit,* "and without

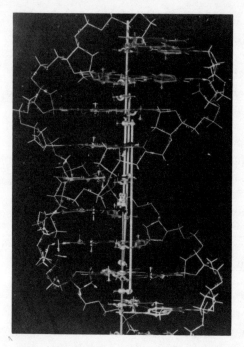

Compare the original structure
of DNA's double helix *(left)*
with the computer-generated
images created by Rosenberg,
in the color section. (Cold Spring
Harbor Laboratory Archives, from
J. D. Watson, *The Double Helix,*
New York, Atheneum, 1968)

understanding molecules we can only have a very sketchy understanding of life itself." There is no better, no more taxing, way to understand
molecules than by the use of X-ray crystallography, as Crick well
knows, since he and James Watson used crystallographic data in 1953
to figure out that DNA assumes the structure of a double helix. Without a doubt, that discovery ranks as the field's greatest success, and it
garnered Nobel prizes for Watson and Crick.

In attempting to compose a picture of a protein clinging to the
double helix, Rosenberg in a sense merged the two great historical
themes that run through X-ray crystallography: the study of proteins
and the study of nucleic acids, such as DNA. Indeed, in attempting a
double portrait, Rosenberg was venturing into unexplored terrain. No
one had managed to solve the structure of a cocrystal before.

X-ray crystallography began as a lifeless discipline—lifeless in the
sense that the pioneering crystallographers studied minerals, not biological molecules. And with the exception of Linus Pauling at Caltech
(a gigantic exception, to be sure), the field was essentially a British
invention, deriving much intellectual vigor in the 1930s from the grand
old men of structure—Sir William Bragg, his son Lawrence Bragg,

J. D. Bernal, and the students they coaxed and cajoled into the field (X-ray crystallography is so difficult and demanding, with such delayed and esoteric payoffs, that its mentors draw on rare evangelical skills to recruit new martyrs to the discipline). It is a field driven by one fundamental dictum: if you can construct the three-dimensional structure of a molecule, you can understand what it does. Structure suggests function. And in order to get a peek at structure, you need a map. As Sir Lawrence Bragg succinctly put it, "The object is to get as accurate a map as possible of the positions of the atoms in a structure."

The shift to biological molecules began in the 1930s. Rosalind Franklin, who did first-rate crystallographic studies of coal, produced the X-ray pictures of DNA that helped Watson and Crick solve the molecule's structure in 1953. On the protein side, John Kendrew first solved the structure of a biological protein, myoglobin, in 1957, and Max Perutz, the legendary protein chemist, got his prized molecule, hemoglobin, in 1959, after a Job-like quest that began in 1937; both received Nobel Prizes for their work in 1962. Typical of the field's rarefied frustrations, Perutz devoted fourteen years trying to solve the hemoglobin problem using an equation that turned out to be inadequate to the task. John Rosenberg approvingly quotes Perutz on the difficulty of X-ray crystallography. "It's a bit like hunting," Perutz reportedly said. "It requires good knowledge of your prey, and a certain amount of low cunning."

In the clone-or-die ethic that increasingly pervades biology, X-ray crystallographers are an anachronism. It can easily take five or ten years to do the work necessary to produce a paper, and since only the most mathematically inclined of colleagues outside the field understand the subtleties of their work—their diffraction patterns, their "heavy atom derivatives," their Fourier transforms—crystallographers tend to form a small, esoteric enclave. There are only a handful of top-notch labs in the United States, at places like Harvard, MIT, Yale, Johns Hopkins, UCLA, Caltech, and the universities of Pittsburgh, Oregon, and Chicago. Despite suspicions in other quarters of science, however, X-ray crystallographers are not necessarily an owl-eyed guild of compulsives. It's just that the experiments take an inordinate amount of time and therefore require a certain patience and emotional tenacity not always conspicuous in other disciplines. It thus attracts workers of a particularly steadfast temperament.

Born and raised in Denver, Colorado, son of a businessman father and a mother active in local politics, Rosenberg attended Case Western Reserve University in Cleveland as an undergraduate in physics and intended to do graduate work in theoretical astrophysics at MIT. But while visiting relatives in Colorado during a vacation break in the late 1960s, he got a hard-sell on biology from a Colorado State professor named Ted Puck. "He was very evangelical, and really snowed me under as to molecular biology as a way of life," Rosenberg recalls. "And he said that when I got back to MIT, I should give Alex Rich a call." Rich, a world-renowned X-ray crystallographer, turned out to be even more evangelical. "You have to be bright, persistent, and motivated," says Rich, recalling his campaign to recruit Rosenberg. "He was all those things." At the time, when Rosenberg decided to switch from physics to this most physical wing of biology, he had just placed first on the qualifying exam among that year's graduate students in theoretical physics. "And there he was, doing a project in biology!" Rich recalls. Converted by the evangelists, Rosenberg joined the small fraternal order of frustration.

"For a very long time, I had this feeling that I was like the kid who'd been told that if he beat his head against the wall long enough, the wall would fall down," Rosenberg said one day in his office. "But in the meantime, it *hurts*!" He is a subtly tall man, with thick rimless glasses and dark frizzy hair, not too long, combed straight back. He dresses informally, tending to the brown and the baggy. At first, he appears to have a sober manner; ask a question, and there is a slight delay, as if someone accustomed to swimming around in deep waters has to make his way back to the surface before responding. But the comments are regularly, almost ritually, punctuated by a laugh that adverts to a deep understanding of the absurd. You don't have to have a sense of humor to be an X-ray crystallographer, Rosenberg intimates, but it helps.

"What keeps you going," he says, "is the knowledge of what you're going to get when you get your answer."

X-ray crystallography is like a lopsided concerto: the first movement, growing the crystals, goes on forever. The rest of the piece—taking the X-ray pictures and interpreting the data—flashes by with sudden, edifying swiftness, which is to say as little as three or four years. The long prelude is due to the most difficult part of the entire procedure: growing crystals that can be photographed with X rays. That step alone can take many years, and historian of science Horace Judson notes that those who are good at it are said to have "glass thumbs." Not many do, prompting Rosenberg to add, "Sisyphus is the patron saint of those who would grow crystals."

"Three-dimensional wallpaper": like the fish in an illustration of M. C. Escher *(above),* molecules in a crystal line up in a repetitive three-dimensional order. (© 1962 M. C. Escher/Cordon Art, Baarn, Holland)

A crystal, Rosenberg explains, is "something like three-dimensional wallpaper. "Another way of thinking about it is that molecules in solution are like fish darting about in a pond—they are pointed every which way and assume no regular pattern. In order to get at the fundamental shape and structure of the molecule, just as one might want to identify an elusive species of fish deep in the sea, crystallographers need to see their prey organized into regular patterns—swimming in schools, as it were. In effect, the crystals freeze the fish into an organized school. Only in a crystal do all the atoms in a molecule snap to attention, become arranged in a regular, repetitive pattern—patterns similar to the drawings by M. C. Escher, which Rosenberg employs to teach the concepts of X-ray crystallography. Only by creating crystals can scientists figure out what DNA and protein molecules look like and, more important, what they look like when they hold on to each other. Rosenberg's first step in taking a picture was to get *Eco* RI and DNA to join together in a single crystalline conjunction known as a cocrystal.

Over many seasons, you would often see Rosenberg's students— usually John Grable or Cleopas Samudzi—wandering around the third floor of Langley Hall, even during the hottest of summer days, as if they were about to pose for an ad in L. L. Bean's winter catalogue.

That is because crystals grow in a cold room, maintained at 4 degrees Centigrade, just above freezing. The technique Rosenberg and his confederates use is in principle similar to what happens if you leave a glass of water saturated with sugar or salt out in the open air. As the water evaporates, the remaining molecules organize themselves in a rigid, regular, crystalline structure. In the case of sugar, you get rock candy; in the case of salt, you get salt crystals.

Growing crystals of the DNA-protein complex is a much trickier proposition. Both the DNA and the protein must be exceedingly pure; impurities on the order of parts per million can effectively thwart crystal formation. In little plastic boxes that resemble novelty ice-cube trays, crystallographers mix a solution containing highly purified DNA, *Eco* RI, and chemical solutions known as buffers, which promote evaporation. Hundreds of these trays, each with nine concave wells, are stacked inside a refrigerator (superfluously, it would seem) inside the cold room. "You have to have a lot of experiments going at one time," explains John Grable, "because it's so rare to get a good protein crystal."

Twice a week, week after week, bundled up in goose down, Grable would go into the cold room and check all the plastic boxes, maneuvering each of several hundred wells under a microscope, looking for something no larger than a grain of salt, a glint of a sign that a crystal might have formed. It usually takes one or two weeks for the DNA and protein atoms to organize themselves into a rigid, three-dimensional pattern. Often they don't grow correctly, and the crystals look spindly or cracked. More often, they simply don't grow at all. No one knows why crystals grow or not, why one takes hold while all the wells around it hold small cold puddles of failure.

Rosenberg doesn't mention it, but the glaring success of his chief collaborator's entrepreneurial venture could not have made these setbacks any easier. Genentech enjoyed a spectacular debut on Wall Street in October of 1980, and Boyer became a paper millionaire overnight. Rosenberg and his group kept staring at those little puddles of failure.

When grown just right, a good crystal appears hexagonal—like a slab-thick stop sign. "They don't all grow that big, that beautiful," says Grable, showing one to a visitor. "Unfortunately." In 1981, Grable discovered one of those thick hexagonal crystals after weeks of fruitless reconnaissance. With this crystal, the group could get back on track. According to the gentle, reverent, almost superstitious rituals of X-ray crystallography, the crystal was delicately suctioned, along with a little bit of its "mother liquor" (as the liquid in which it has grown is called), into a thin, hollow glass filament known as a capillary tube. Sealed in this thin tube of glass, it was then hustled off to have its picture taken.

That was the first movement. It took four years. During that time, Rosenberg didn't produce a single paper on the crystal work. There was a bit of grumbling, he remembers; structure laboratories can cost up to $2 million to set up, and the universities that fund them naturally like to see evidence of progress, but there is no cookbook for growing crystals, no way to speed up one of nature's most mysterious and fickle processes. "Everybody copes with the prelude in their own way," Rosenberg says. "I think what really motivates everybody is the recognition that the payoff is sufficiently bounteous that it's worth the wait. Especially now that things toward the latter stages have really accelerated. I mean, it used to be that it would take the better part of a lifetime to do a single structure. Now the main hang-up is getting the right kind of crystals."

Nevertheless, they graduated to another sizable hang-up as soon as they took a picture of the crystal. It was called the phase problem.

"Growing a crystal for molecular structure," Rosenberg explains, "is like preparing a slide for a cell biologist. What we are talking about is very analogous to the microscope. The object in both cases is to see something very small. In our case, we want to see something very small indeed, because we're talking about molecules. Now the real question is: why do you have to make a crystal? The answer is that in order to see on a molecular scale, you have to illuminate the object with light that has a wavelength on a molecular scale. That forces you to use X rays."

To put things in perspective, Rosenberg was attempting to illuminate the beams and joints of a molecule at a scale of 2.5 angstroms. One angstrom equals $1/250,000,000$ of an inch; another way to think of this is to look at a standard ruler and realize that 250 million angstroms fit in one inch. *That* small. By contrast, in our everyday world, we see objects—a red barn, a blue sky—in wavelengths of visible light that measure 4,000 to 6,000 angstroms when they strike our eyes. Attempting to capture molecules with visible light would be like trying to capture gold dust with a colander; the apertures of the strainer are much too big to intercept the smaller particles, and visually speaking, you'd come up empty.

And here we reach some fundamental problems with trying to

"see" molecules with X rays. When researchers fire X rays at the tiny crystal, the X rays cannot be gathered into a coherent image; X rays have a wavelength of 1.5 angstroms, which in practical terms means they are so small that you can't use a lens to focus the image. Rather, the X rays diffract, or skip like flat stones on a pond, when they hit certain dense patches in the crystal. A piece of X-ray film (or, more recently, a computerized electronic detector), placed behind the crystal like a backstop on a ball field, catches all the caroms, and the resulting collection of sharp spots is called a diffraction pattern. Since the crystal is arrayed like that three-dimensional wallpaper with a repeating pattern of atoms, these skipping and scattering X-ray beams tend to pile up more at some points of the film than others. The relative intensity of each diffracted beam depends on the internal atomic arrangement of the crystal. The trick is to figure out from which face of the crystal the spot is reflecting. "Then, if you are very clever," Rosenberg explains, "you can go back and use a computer to create an image of the object that the X rays go through."

The machine that generates the X rays is called a Rigaku RU200. It has the look of a small minicomputer except for a square, totemic, foot-high protuberance on top from which the X rays emerge in a narrow, invisible stream. One of Rosenberg's postdocs, a Korean named Youngchang Kim, will typically spend half an hour adjusting dozens of small screws to line up the crystal correctly; in his running shoes, blue jeans, and ski jacket, Youngchang could pass for a gas station attendant or pizza delivery boy, but that is not unusual in the world of biology. After each incremental adjustment is made, the X-ray machine is turned on. Each crystal must be photographed many times. Since researchers have no idea if they have posed the crystal face forward or in profile, up or down, they shoot it at a series of angles or profiles. Powered by forty killivolts, the camera will beam X rays anywhere from forty to ninety minutes per exposure. If they shoot too long, the crystal will begin to degrade and melt under the onslaught of X rays. It is one of the ironies of X-ray crystallography—a cruel one, of course—that those crystals, four years in the making, rarely survive more than a few hours of experimental use.

The diffraction pictures that emerge are circular and, to the untrained (or irreverent) eye, appear like gauzy, out-of-focus photos of UFOs. They are marked by a series of spots, and the more intense spots represent places where X rays have "puddled." Since the X rays are scattered by *electrons* (and not nuclei), crystallographers use the location and intensity of these dots to infer the location of electrons in

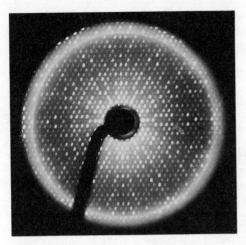

Sisyphus rewarded:
once crystals are grown, an
X-ray diffraction picture records
the pattern of X rays deflected
off clouds of electrons within
the molecule. (J. Rosenberg)

the crystals; and since electrons are like atmospheres that surround the nuclei of atoms, they tip off the location of the nuclei themselves. In the early days of crystallography, weary-eyed researchers would gauge the intensity of each dot, on a scale of one to a hundred, by sight; would assess thousands of spots per film; would need to take perhaps a dozen films of a single crystal to get all the alignments correct. Thanks to the cottage industry that has sprung up around X-ray crystallography, diffraction patterns can now be placed in a high-tech electronic detector that has no purpose in life other than to divide these bleary images into a million quadrants and measure the X-ray intensity in each quadrant; the newer diffraction machines make instant measurements as the crystal is being bombarded. This information is shuttled directly into a computer, which attempts to make sense of the various patterns.

The intensity of the spots is mathematically related to the three-dimensional structure of the molecules, and it would be nice if the computer could work directly back from the diffraction pattern to the structure itself. But that would be too easy. First they had to solve the "phase problem."

At this point X-ray crystallography becomes a mathematical thicket of fractional coordinates and periodic functions, full of what Rosenberg cheerfully admits is "incomprehensible Greek stuff." But he offers this analogy. "On a conventional microscope," he explains, "you have one or two knobs to adjust and focus the image. Think of the phase problem as if you had one knob for each spot of the diffraction pattern, thousands and thousands of knobs, all of which had to be turned to the right position to get it in focus. I think sometimes my students sort of feel like I've left them in this room with this microscope with ten thousand knobs and said, 'Call me when you've got it focused.' "

Well, they didn't call for about three years. During this time, Rosenberg's collaborator Herb Boyer appeared on the cover of *Time* magazine as guru of biotechnology, and Genentech scored one page-one discovery after another. Boyer was touted in some circles for a Nobel Prize for his pioneering gene-splicing work. Rosenberg toiled in the fuzzy, unfocused obscurity of a structure problem stuck in the second movement.

They resolved the problem by resorting to a rather clever trick of the trade: a heavy-atom derivative. They created a separate cocrystal with an extra atom aboard, an atom of platinum, which is considered "heavy" because it attracts a thick cloud of seventy-eight electrons around it; within each subunit of the crystal, there would now be one extra-dense cloud of platinum electrons scattering the X rays in a different way. A comparison of the regular cocrystal with this so-called heavy-atom derivative provided a kind of X-ray parallax. Photographs of the same crystal were taken again and again and again, perhaps 150 films for fifteen crystals. This produced 150 million bits of information. Given that slight edge of perspective, sophisticated computers could compare the two data sets, resolve the phase problem, and predict the exact three-dimensional location of electrons. Those locations gave them a map. Once you had plotted the location of electrons in three-dimensional space, you could begin to assign the location of the atoms that lay at their core. Christin A. Frederick, a graduate student in the lab, spent three years finding a heavy-atom derivative that worked. By the time she was finished, they had an electron density map.

Imagine an apple through which a worm has eaten its way. The task is to trace the path of the worm, and in X-ray crystallography, the method is to take horizontal slices of the apple and treat each slice as a map—where each slice is a flat plane, and the worm's path is a circle somewhere on that plane. Slice by slice, layer by horizontal layer, the circles will begin to line up and carve a path, or hole, through the entire three-dimensional structure, until the path of the worm becomes clear. X-ray crystallographers adopt the same philosophy, except those circles are formed not by worms but by dense clouds of electrons, and the maps are not slices of apple but thick plates of Plexiglas upon which

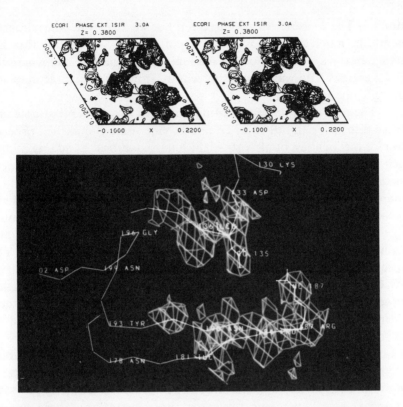

"The object is to get as accurate a map as possible": computers interpret X-ray diffraction patterns and produce electron density maps. The old style *(above)* look like contour maps; the new style *(below)* resemble neon chicken wire. (J. Rosenberg)

each slice through the DNA-protein unit leaves a distinctive map of spidery, almost topographic electron densities.

The hole left by the worm is nothing less than the spiraling, curving, cork-screwing shape of DNA, with the protein *Eco* RI wrapped around it. The protein is composed of 276 amino acids linked together in a long chain, and it is the path of this chain that becomes apparent when you look down through twelve milky inches of Plexiglas. This is a first, tentative, out-of-focus blowup of a remarkably tiny molecular interaction. Finally, they got enough data plotted to see the first rough outlines in late 1983. "That was a very high emotional moment," Rosenberg recalls. "We knew we had slain the second great dragon. The treasure wasn't there yet, but we knew the other dragons would be much smaller. Within a couple of weeks of getting this first image out, we could see where the DNA molecule was and where the polypeptide chain was interacting with it. It meant the whole map was going to be interpretable."

The next step, the culminating step, was to transfer that hole to a three-dimensional, full-color computer video screen and then proceed to plot the location of all forty-eight hundred atoms (excluding hydrogen atoms) of the complex. The electron density map, in three dimensions, looked a bit like an odd, neon-blue, chicken-wire construct; the map told them where the densest clouds of electrons were, and the Rosenberg group proceeded to fit atoms into their proper niches until they had an approximate structure consistent both with the data and with established chemical rules about bond angles and distances. The spectacular details began to come to life on an Evans and Sutherland PS300 monitor, with the help of an exceedingly clever program called Frodo. Each time they adjusted the location of a single atom, it took their old computer four hours to realign the other forty-eight hundred or so atoms according to physiochemical laws (speedier computers do it now in less than ten minutes). In all, it took another three years.

When they finally peeled away the chicken wire, what they saw, in glorious Technicolor, was the structure of the DNA–*Eco* RI cocrystal, and what a thrilling image it was (see color illustration). There, in cool electric blues and greens, was the double helix, curling up in one lovely corkscrew turn, and there, too, was the enzyme, its two globular halves gripping the delicate helix like a pair of soft pliers dreamed up by Claes Oldenburg, one side red and the other yellow. Some workers in the lab described this as "the Pac-Man grip," but a more apt analogy was that the enzyme wrapped its arms around the DNA helix like a stiff-armed dancer, one arm high along the back, the other low around the waist from the other side, pulling it tight, even bending it a little—and then suddenly, without warning, cleaving it in two. You would have to blow up this picture to about two hundred thousand times its original size for it to be as large as the period at the end of this sentence.

There is a famous picture of Watson and Crick posing next to their model of DNA, a metal contraption meant to represent the double helix but looking like a spiral staircase fashioned out of Bunsen-burner holders. All that modeling, all the tinkering and rearranging, is now done in computers, which have revolutionized not only the speed of X-ray crystallographic work, but the clarity with which three-

James Watson *(left)* and Francis Crick pose in front of their three-dimensional, pre-computer model of the structure of DNA. (Cold Spring Harbor Laboratory Archives, from J. D. Watson, *The Double Helix,* Atheneum, New York, 1968)

dimensional structure can be seen. When Judson viewed the metal-and-wire model of hemoglobin in 1968, he wrote: "The trick was to ignore [the support rods] totally, though they obscured almost everything else, and concentrate on where the colored cables led." With modern computer graphics, all the support rods and stays are removed; indeed, any distracting part of the structure itself can be removed at a touch.

In a small room informally known as the Inner Sanctum, Rosenberg and his coworkers can manipulate their molecular structure on the screen as if they were turning it in their hands, simply by twisting a few knobs. By flipping a switch, Rosenberg can make the screen jitter with double images; then, viewed through stereopticon viewers, the whole model assumes vivid dimensionality. What we see, in the most intimate detail attainable by human ingenuity, is one of the routine, but in no way random, acts of violence in the natural world—DNA inserting its neck into the guillotine of an enzyme. Rosenberg achieved a resolution of three angstroms; at the time, it offered twice as much detail as other structure groups.

It was while piecing together the three-dimensional map in late 1983 that Rosenberg's group first noticed a startling feature. As described in a preliminary communication to *Nature* in 1984, the DNA seemed to contort itself to allow the enzyme to have its whack. In the words of the researchers, it *kinked.* Indeed, as they assigned more and more atoms to their proper place according to the electron density

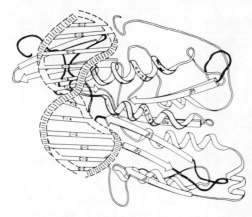

The stiff-armed dancer: by solving the three-dimensional structure, the University of Pittsburgh team created a schematic "map" to show how one arm of the enzyme *Eco* RI wraps around the double helix of DNA before chopping it in two. (J. Rosenberg)

map, they succeeded in choreographing a mortal molecular ballet. The double helix cricked its neck, as it were, and that allowed the blade of the enzyme to slip in and do the dirty deed.

When the image of the interaction is called up on the computer screen and examined closely, you can see swords being unsheathed at the atomic level. The protein wraps around the DNA in such a way as to bring several hydrogen bonds from the protein in close proximity to hydrogen bonds holding the DNA helix together. Hydrogen bonds are supple girders, strong enough to hold the two strands of the double helix together, but weak enough to allow it to split apart so that it can perform its two essential tasks: dividing in two and migrating into germ cells (egg or sperm) so heritable information can be passed on to offspring, and temporarily and partially splitting so as to dispense its coded instructions to the rest of the cell. When the protein *Eco* RI wraps its mitts around DNA, the hydrogen bonds fairly groan and the integrity of the DNA molecule wavers. By the time Rosenberg's group had dotted every atomic *i* and crossed every allosteric *t,* the collaboration had determined the position of nearly five thousand atoms. So intimate was their view of the molecules that, in a stunning analysis of their flickering three-dimensional image, they were able to identify sixteen specific hydrogen bonds—sixteen electrostatic tendrils reaching in like tentacles from the enzyme—that used their infinitesimally small charge of electricity at the atomic level to weaken the bonds of the double helix and ultimately undo it. That was chief among the revelations when the group published a full account of the cocrystal's structure in *Science* in December 1986. After nearly ten years, the long drought was over. In recognition of the prodigious feat, *Science* ran a

rare accompanying commentary that celebrated the Rosenberg structure as "a milestone in modern molecular biology."

The implications were clear to biologists, but perhaps not to the
public at large. What made it a milestone? And why was it so important?

In the homeostatic hum that keeps life going in lumpen bacteria
as well as in humans, there is a continuous, life-sustaining conversation
between DNA and proteins, such as the one described in the chapter
on fate maps. Genes are not turned on all the time, nor do they
produce the same quantity of material all the time. Sometimes genes
are turned off, or suppressed; and sometimes their output is stepped
up, or enhanced; and both these functions, as well as simply turning
them on, are accomplished by proteins interacting with DNA. The
effort to look at cocrystals like the DNA–*Eco* RI complex represents
the initial attempt to eavesdrop on a frozen moment of that conversation. It is an important one.

Proteins that recognize discrete patches of DNA do so with astonishing precision. DNA's information is encoded in a limited four-letter
chemical alphabet, a sequence of bases known as A's and T's and G's
and C's; in humans the sequence adds up to 3 billion letters. *Eco* RI
zeroes in on a single, specific six-base sequence, GAATTC. It is as if
GAATTC provides an identifiable landmark along the seemingly monotonous linear landscape of the DNA molecule, something geographically distinct and recognizable, because the enzyme lands on that spot,
and cuts there and nowhere else. It makes a mistake one in 10 million
times, and a good thing, too, because mistakes would be lethal to the
bacterium, a form of biochemical hara-kiri. "How the protein says
'Here, and not there,' " says Rosenberg, "is the bottom line with this
thing."

How do proteins say "Here, and not there"? It is a question of
surpassing importance, not only to bacteria—which live if they chop
up invading viruses and die if they don't—but also to human beings.
At a crucial moment in human development (to cite one of countless
examples), we suddenly manufacture a protein that finds and sup-
presses the gene for fetal hemoglobin, which is useful to fetuses but not
to infants; this protein somehow turns on the gene for the adult form
of the protein. Researchers do not yet understand how this process of
recognition works in humans, which is why they study bacteria and
viruses. In the case of *Eco* RI, which not only recognizes DNA but cuts
it, the Pittsburgh group has found that there are two independent
"reading events," both of which have to say "Go" before severance

occurs. The enzyme cuts one strand of the DNA helix, then stops for one-fortieth of a second to ask itself if it should cut through the second strand and make the deed irrevocable. Rosenberg likens it to the "Delete" function on many word-processing programs; evolution has built into this biological program a step where the enzyme asks itself, "Do you really want to do this?" That type of mechanism may not occur in humans, but the fact that such exquisite engineering goes into simple, one-celled creatures argues that nature believes recognition is a fundamental molecular process necessary for the development, growth, and survival of the organism, be it bacterial or human.

What John Rosenberg's protein structure suggests, and what other X-ray crystallographers are looking at as well, is that there may be some general rules to this kind of recognition. Do those hydrogen bonds recognize a particular geography in the sequence of DNA letters, and is there a whole new code waiting to be broken? Brian Matthews of the University of Oregon, writing in a recent *Nature* article, argued that such a code may not exist. "I think Brian's point," says Rosenberg, "is that he was looking for something very simple to put on a small piece of paper and explain everything with a few very simple rules. There've been enough examples now that it's not going to be a few simple rules that one could put on the back of a postcard. On the other hand, I don't think that means there aren't rules. At a certain level, it almost *has* to be true. I mean, the information is encoded in the molecules."

Those rules elude researchers at the moment. With the aid of the national supercomputer center at nearby Carnegie-Mellon University, however, the Rosenberg group continues to pursue them. They have had to revise portions of the structure, but they are moving ahead on making "before" and "after" pictures of *Eco* RI at work, hoping to clarify the exact sequence of events, hoping, too, to get closer to some straightforward explanation for the way proteins cruise DNA and seize hold of the correct sequence. They would even like to make a movie of the interaction, something now possible with the use of supercomputers. When he is asked if the answer lies in the near future, John Rosenberg pauses for a moment and then gives the quintessential reply of the X-ray crystallographer: "We'll just have to wait and see."

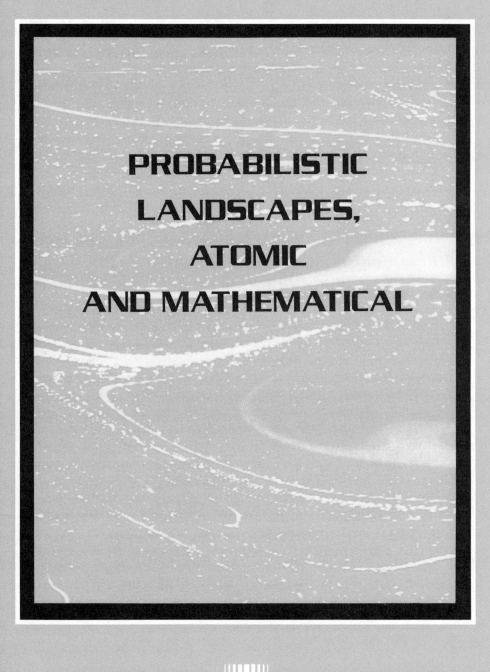

PROBABILISTIC
LANDSCAPES,
ATOMIC
AND MATHEMATICAL

12. "Here One Saw Little Hills"

MAPPING ATOMIC SURFACES
WITH SCANNING PROBE MICROSCOPES

||||||||||

> ... nature hath adapted the eyes of the
> Lilliputians to all objects proper for
> their view: they see with great exactness,
> but at no great distance.
>
> —Jonathan Swift,
> "Travels by Lemuel Gulliver"

Randall Feenstra, as sober and casual as could be in khaki slacks and sport shirt, acted as if nothing was unusual as he moved around the small ground-floor laboratory. It was a scene that, in another time and another context, might have been of greater interest to clinical psychologists than to solid-state physicists. As if tiptoeing through a linoleum minefield, Feenstra took tiny, timid, perversely infirm footsteps across the lab. Each Hush-Puppied foot brushed the floor as though Feenstra traversed some thin and brittle membrane, fragile as a soap bubble, through which he might suddenly plunge and disappear without a moment's warning into the big blue yonder.

"You can breathe," he told me generously. "But you can't move around."

I asked him if I could talk. "Acoustic vibrations," he replied, "are not a problem for me."

He had been up and tiptoeing since 5 A.M., a grown man reduced to moon-walking pantomine, and yet he spoke calmly and confidently about what he was up to. He said he could see atoms. He said he could perceive pits in the skin of a piece of metal, holes many times smaller than a wavelength of light. He said he could look at an invisible speck of matter and see valleys, depressions, rounded knolls, the rigorous yet beautiful discipline with which nature assembles itself into larger and larger structures. To have heard a scientist make any of these claims a mere ten years earlier, indeed to have seen scientists anywhere similarly tiptoe with exaggerated delicacy across their laboratory floors, would have been to demand a suspension of disbelief more appropriate to the theater than to science. In 1990, though, science and art have colluded in an unexpected technology as powerful as it is beautiful, and Randy Feenstra's dainty, slow-motion footsteps that morning belied the giant, rapid strides that physicists have taken in the last decade in their ability to see the topography of atoms.

Feenstra, a researcher at IBM's Thomas J. Watson Research Center in Yorktown Heights, New York, was tiptoeing around a versatile new type of microscope that has brought us, like scientific tourists, to scenic overlooks that peer out over the microcosmos. Standing at the edge of these fantastic atomic vistas, we can make out landscapes so minute that the hummocks and rolling hills are nothing less than atoms, the valleys nothing less than gaps in electron shells. It is a device so sensitive that a heavy footfall, an indiscreet cough, even the warming beam of a flashlight (to say nothing of the construction crew marching up and down the hallway outside Feenstra's lab this particular morning) will blur its vision as surely as fingerprints on eyeglasses.

The instrument itself is deceptively simple. It sits on a black-enamel table, inside a vacuum chamber that faintly resembles a deep-sea diver's helmet, with its heavy bolts and thick windows. Inside that chamber, a needle sharpened to a point that measures exactly one atom in width rides across a prepared surface of a semiconducting material called germanium, feeling out its contours by using a black-magic trick, called "tunneling," dragged out of the bag of quantum mechanics. Unlike a phonograph, where the needle is stationary and the record moves, the probing tip of this microscope roams over a stationary sample, which is mounted vertically; and like a lethargic electron struggling to etch an image on a television screen, data from the probe inches across a computer monitor behind Feenstra, line by deliberate line, until the atomic dermis of germanium's semiconducting skin begins to rise in relief. Atoms bulge out, emerge paired like dumbbells, grow in neat, repetitive rows: the orderly face that germanium turns to the world. If this image turns out to be as popular as a similar portrait of gallium arsenide, taken by Feenstra and colleague Joseph A. Stroscio in late 1986 (see color illustration), it will no doubt appear in many technical and semipopular publications, becoming as ubiquitous as pinups in gas stations.

"Oh, something happened there." Feenstra spoke without alarm, even though a big burp of current bloated the signal on his oscilloscope. The image on the screen went flat. "An atom," he announced, "jumped on the tip."

One way to measure progress in any area of mapping and visualization is by the perfectly flat inflection with which the astonishing is pronounced: *an atom jumped on the tip.* Feenstra, though, has earned his phlegmatic delivery. He has been taking images with the scanning tunneling microscope (STM) for eight years, which in this fast-moving field puts him somewhere between pioneer and sage ("In terms of taking STM data," he says, "I've probably taken more than anyone else"). Just out of Caltech at the end of 1982 with an expertise in semiconductors but with nothing specific to do, he was hired by IBM. Just about that time, a couple of IBM researchers in Zurich had developed this funny new microscope, and the company wanted people to use it. No one, not even Feenstra, leapt at the opportunity.

"They had been trying to get people interested in working on STM," Feenstra recalls, "and they couldn't find anyone to do it, half because people didn't believe it." Feenstra numbered himself among the skeptics. He couldn't even bone up on the literature; there were hardly any papers yet. But not having anything better to do, he finally agreed to go to Zurich in December of 1982, learned the technique, came back to Yorktown Heights, and built his own microscope, the same one he was tiptoeing around this day, seven years later. It rapidly converted its doubters—so rapidly that in 1986 those two IBM researchers in Zurich, a former rock musician and composer named Gerd Binnig and a fatherly physicist named Heinrich Rohrer, traveled to Stockholm to pick up their Nobel prizes.

"Oh," Feenstra said again, looking up. A faint rumble passed by the laboratory. "Oh," he said with a grimace, "that was a wheelbarrow."

The scanning tunneling microscope is a classic example of the accidental progression from pure scientific curiosity to an unimagined and novel technology of measurement, all the more remarkable because it was invented in the commercial sector without the slightest promise of providing commercial return. In answering an exceedingly narrow scientific question, the device added new and unexpected acuity to human vision. Binnig and Rohrer did not set out to invent a way to see atomic landscapes. Binnig, born and raised in Germany, bass guitarist and singer of Frankfurt's own Soft Pops while pursuing his Ph.D. in physics, began working at IBM's Zurich Research Laboratory in 1978 and had become interested in studying the energy states of atoms; Rohrer, Swiss by birth and paternal in temperament, had for many years studied magnetic fields and superconductivity. They set out, in the late 1970s, to address a very basic question: what does the electronic structure of a semiconductor like silicon look like?

The question implies practical import, although Binnig insisted in a recent interview that the two researchers "never thought about applications for IBM." Silicon is the parchment and paper of the electronic age, the thin leaves upon which a computer chip's microcircuits are etched, and as microcircuits have grown smaller and smaller, the *surface* of silicon and other semiconductors has grown more and more interesting, not least because atoms nestle and bunch and squeeze together in different configurations on surfaces than inside a semiconductor; not only the topography but also the electronic character of the surface atoms is different, and those differences can wreak havoc on microchip performance. Yet that is not what motivated Binnig and Rohrer. Surfaces are scientifically challenging. Surfaces are so bewitchingly complex, in fact, that Binnig and Rohrer have been known to invoke the famous curse of physicist Wolfgang Pauli, who once cried, "The surface was invented by the devil!"

With no background in either surface science or microscopy, Binnig and Rohrer began their quest in the autumn of 1978, and they brought so little prior knowledge to the task that, as they later recalled, their naïveté "probably gave us the courage and lightheartedness to start something which should 'not have worked in principle,' as we were so often told."

To appreciate the problem of "seeing" atoms, consider the limitations of more traditional microscopes. In optical microscopes light waves must be smaller than the object they seek to illuminate, just as a rubber ball must be thrown against a wall larger than it in order to bounce back. But light waves fall between 4,000 and 7,000 angstroms in length (the angstrom, a measure of wavelength, equals one-ten-billionth of a meter), and an atom typically measures about three angstroms in diameter, so shining a light on an atom is like trying to bounce a tennis ball off a poppy seed. Anything smaller than 4,000

Said Gerd Binnig *(left)* of the first silicon image, "This appeared to me as the unsurpassable highlight of my scientific career and therefore, in a way, its end." Heinrich Rohrer *(right)* whisked his awed colleague away to a village in the Swiss Alps to write their landmark paper. (IBM Research)

angstroms simply doesn't offer a "wall" big enough for light waves to bounce back from, and bouncing back is just another term for reflection, the way in which objects are visually captured.

Or consider the electron microscope, invented in the 1930s. Electron microscopes form an image when a beam of electrons is fired at the target. Since electrons are smaller than atoms, electrons can indeed bounce off atoms and thereby define them. But there are drawbacks to the method, not the least of which is that electron beams can travel only through a vacuum and so the object under study must similarly be in a vacuum. The smaller the target, the higher the energy of the electron beams—the result being that you basically zap the very object you want to scrutinize.

As early as 1972, physicists had toyed with the idea of "tunneling" as a way to examine surfaces, and Binnig and Rohrer—working with colleagues Christoph Gerber and Edi Weibel at IBM's Zurich Research Laboratory—began toying with the idea of trying to use tunneling technology to do spectroscopy (that is, to measure the electronic state of surface atoms). Binnig describes it as "feeling the 'color' of those atoms." Relying on physical intuition as well as immense engineering skill, they created a mechanical device that would allow them to "see" not by the usual bounce of reflection, but by using an electric current as a kind of tactile organ. By passing a current between an experimentally manipulated scanning probe and the surface of the material under study, they could "feel" the topography by small variations in the current, which relied on the strange effect of quantum physics called tunneling.

The term "tunneling" is a bit of a misnomer for how the effect works in this kind of microscopy. The nuclei of atoms are surrounded by shells of electrons that almost look like clouds or, more appropriately, atmospheres; they are, according to quantum theory, mists of probability that never burn off. Physicists have demonstrated the mathematical probability that an electron might be at any energy level within that atmospheric cloud at any time. When the probe tip of the scanning tunneling microscope comes close to the surface of a material, the atmospheric cloud of electrons buzzing around its single atom begins to overlap the clouds of the surface atoms. That overlap provides not so much a tunnel, however, as an electronic riverbed that connects the two atmospheres. Ordinarily, an electron would not have sufficient energy to jump from its familial atmosphere to another. But when a small current is applied and the two atomic atmospheres have been made suddenly and artificially contiguous with the approach of the needle, there is a path—a *tunnel*—of escape.

Yet "flow" more accurately captures the physics at work than tunneling, because that is exactly how the scanning microscope's probe tip "feels" the atomic landscape it scans: the flow of electrons. Binnig and Rohrer realized that by applying just two or three volts of current through the probe tip as it scanned the surface of silicon, for example, they could detect an electron cloud whenever the tip overlapped the cloud from an atom of silicon; the proximity would align riverbeds, as it were, so that electrons could flow from one substance to another, and a small stream of current would trickle through the tip. Perhaps the key aspect of the entire technique was that the current was exquisitely sensitive to distance. The diameter of an atom is about three angstroms; retracting the probe tip from one to three angstroms' distance from the surface corresponded to a thousandfold drop in the flow of current. The microscope records these drops and spikes of current as the probe tip scans an atomic landscape, and the peaks and troughs of current correspond to peaks and troughs of topography (during actual operation a sensitive feedback mechanism, adjusting to these fluctuations every millisecond, keeps the current steady by moving the needle higher or lower over the landscape). A computer converts those adjustments, which are essentially distance measurements, into a three-dimensional image of the atomic surface.

It took Binnig and Rohrer about two years to refine these ideas and engineer the contraption that would allow them to test this unique application of tunneling. Their efforts were a corporate secret, though

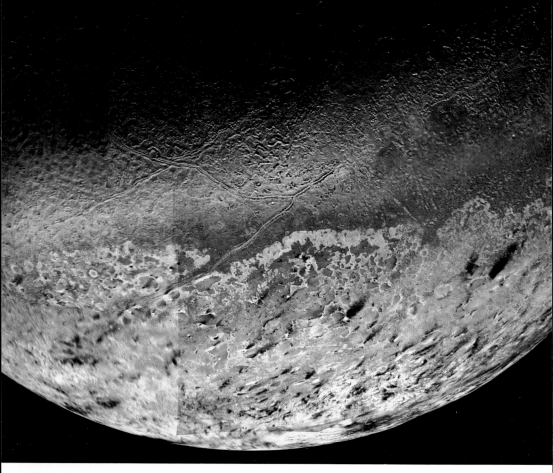

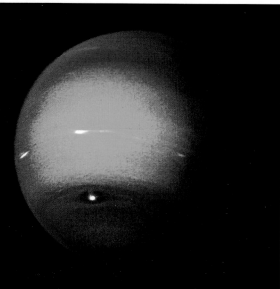

Voyager: The "cantaloupe" terrain of Neptune's moon Triton, in a photomosaic image by *Voyager 2 (above)*. The false-color image of Neptune *(left)* reveals the haze surrounding the gaseous planet; regions that appear white or red are reflecting sunlight before it reaches clouds of methane, which absorbs the light. *(chapter 1)*

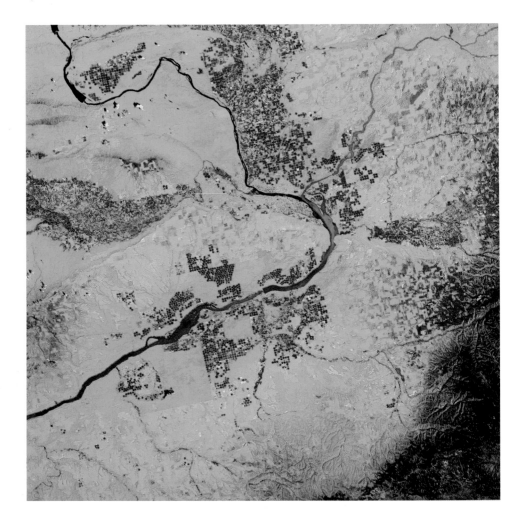

Landsat: "We now procured...a sketch of the Columbia.... They drew it with a piece of coal on a robe; and afterward transferred to paper, it exhibited a valuable specimen of Indian delineation." On Oct. 16, 1805, Lewis and Clark came down the Snake River *(upper right)* and arrived at the Columbia; on July 5, 1984, Landsat's Thematic Mapper "delineated" this satellite view of the Snake coming into the Columbia River in the state of Washington. *(chapter 2)* EARTH OBSERVATION SATELLITE CO., LANHAM, MD.

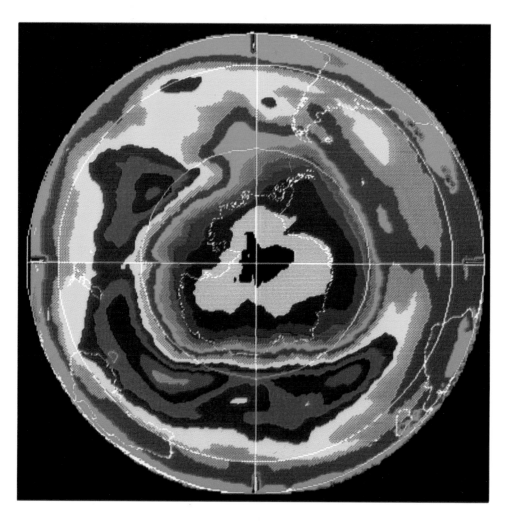

Ozone: The hole in the ozone layer over the South Pole, first reported in 1985, provoked even greater global concern with this Oct. 5, 1987 map of Antarctica, which charted the lowest value of ozone ever recorded up to that time (low values in black, pink, and purple). The data was collected by NASA's Total Ozone Mapping Spectrometer (TOMS) aboard the *Nimbus 7* satellite. *(chapter 6)* NASA/GODDARD SPACE FLIGHT CENTER

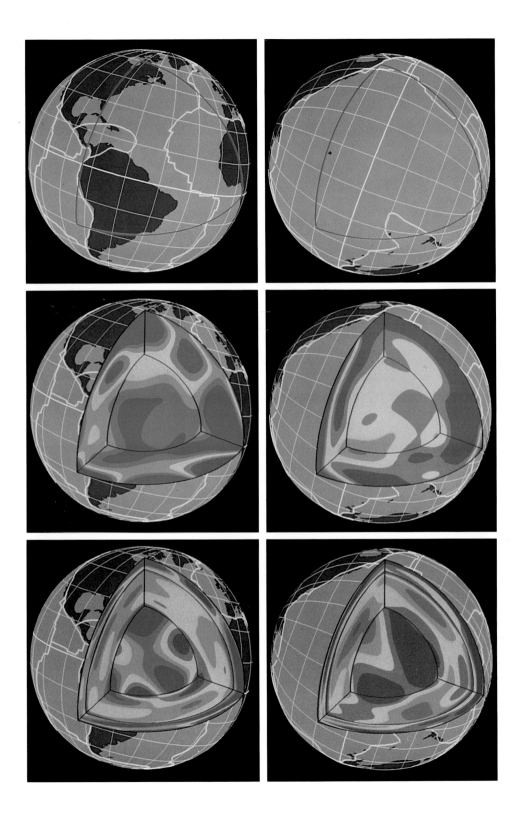

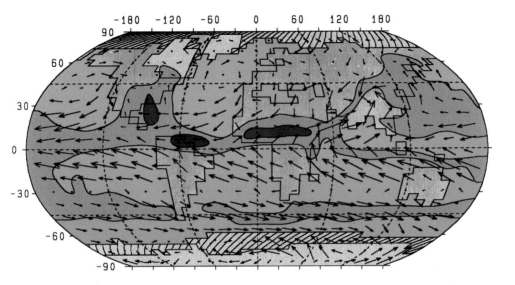

Paleoclimate: Using fossil pollen data, packrat detritus, and paleolithic data, a group of paleoclimatologists called COHMAP has recreated the earth's climate since the peak of the last Ice Age, 18,000 years ago *(above)*. This map, on a Robinson projection, shows typical July climate 9,000 years ago; note the ice sheet over North America and increased monsoon activity in parts of North Africa and South Asia (dark green marks 8 millimeters of precipitation per day, light green marks 4 millimeters per day, and arrows represent surface winds). *(chapter 5)* P. BEHLING/COHMAP

Core and Mantle: With a technique known as seismic tomography, geophysicists map the earth's core and mantle *(left)* by measuring the travel times of earthquake waves. Cutaway maps of the Atlantic and Pacific oceans, to a depth of 550 and 2,890 kilometers, show the two oceans to be quite dissimilar (blue represents cold, dense, sinking material, while orange represents hot, buoyant, rising material). *(chapter 4)* © 1987 AAAS/A. DZIEWONSKI

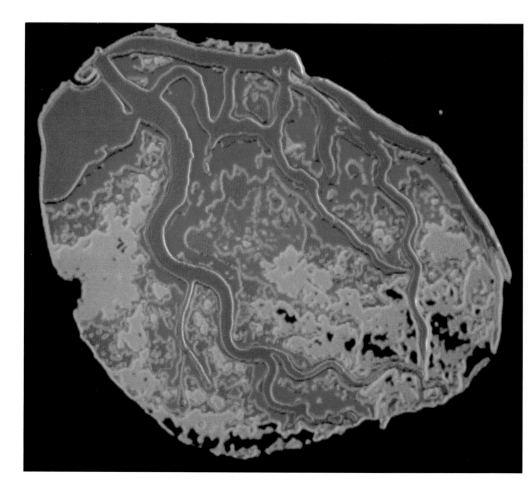

Anatomy: A color-enhanced image of the heart *(above)*, with coronary arteries in red, obtained by digital subtraction angiography (DSA), one of numerous new techniques of anatomic cartography, including computed tomography (CT) scans, sonograms, and magnetic resonance imaging (MRI). *(chapter 7)* © HOWARD SOCHUREK

Brain: This false-color autoradiographic map of a guinea pig brain *(right)* shows receptors for the active ingredient in marijuana. The seahorse-like structure is the hippocampus, where memories are encoded; red indicates the highest density of receptor, followed by pink, blue, and green. *(chapter 8)* M. HERKENHAM/NATIONAL INSTITUTE OF MENTAL HEALTH

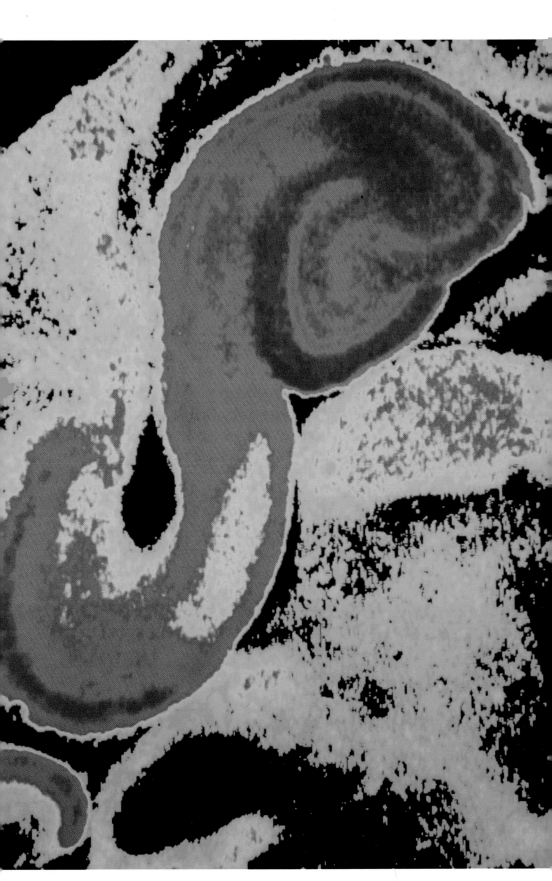

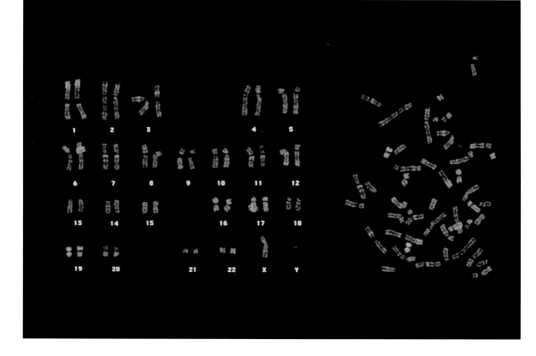

Gene: Genetic cartography, first attempted in 1913, has exploded since 1980. Molecular biologists can map pieces of DNA to their proper location on a chromosome with the use of visible markers. In the illustration, the human gene for a blood protein called beta globulin has been mapped (red fluorescing dots) to chromosome 11, one of twenty-three pairs that make up the human genetic territory. *(chapter 9)* D. WARD/
YALE UNIVERSITY

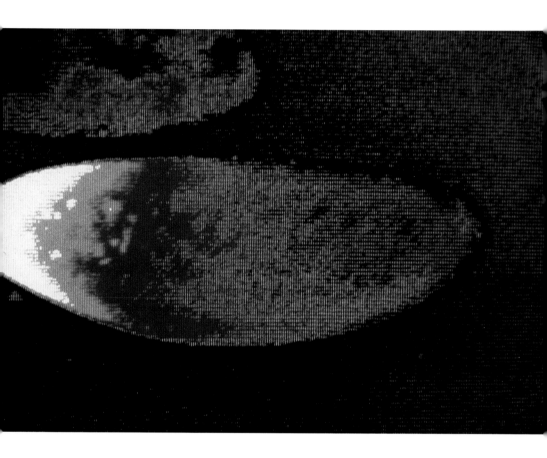

Fate Map: Fate map of a fruit fly egg moments after fertilization. Yellow indicates the highest concentration of a protein that appears in the region of the egg destined to become the head of the organism. *(chapter 10)* C. NÜSSLEIN-VOLHARD/© 1988 *Cell*

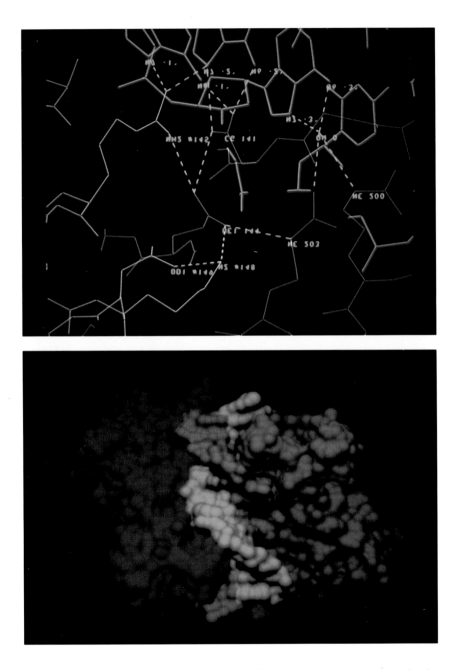

DNA-Protein: X-ray crystallographers create electron density maps *(top)* to plot the exact location of atoms in biological molecules. With such maps, University of Pittsburgh researchers plotted the location of more than four thousand atoms, producing a three-dimensional structure *(bottom)* that shows the interaction between DNA's double helix (in blue and green) and an enzyme (in orange and yellow) that wraps around and cuts it. *(chapter 11)* J. ROSENBERG/© 1986 AAAS

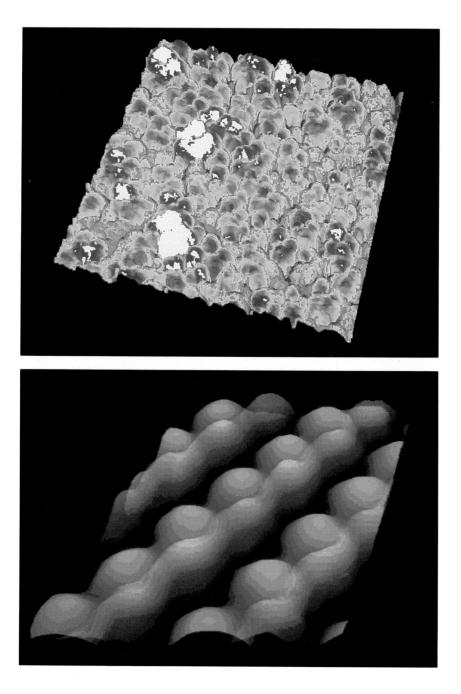

STM: With the use of scanning probe microscopes and a trick of quantum mechanics, physicists can measure the location of individual atoms and recreate the three-dimensional surface topography of chemical elements and compounds. This is the surface of spattered gold *(above)* and gallium arsenide *(below)*. *(chapter 12)* IBM RESEARCH

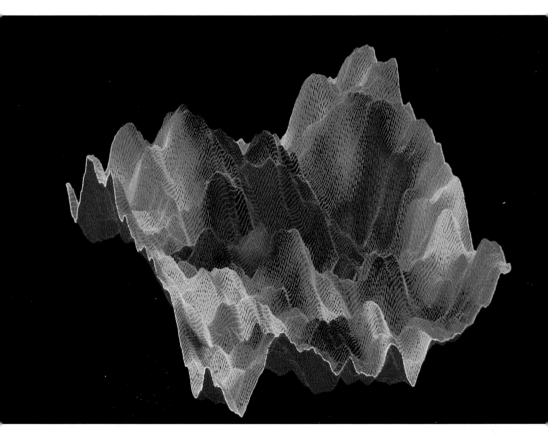

PI: By plotting "trends" in the first one million digits of the mathematical constant pi, David and Gregory Chudnovsky created a fractal landscape they call a "pi-scape"— an example of the kind of numerical cartography they hope may enhance analysis of certain problems in number theory. *(chapter 13)* D. AND G. CHUDNOVSKY

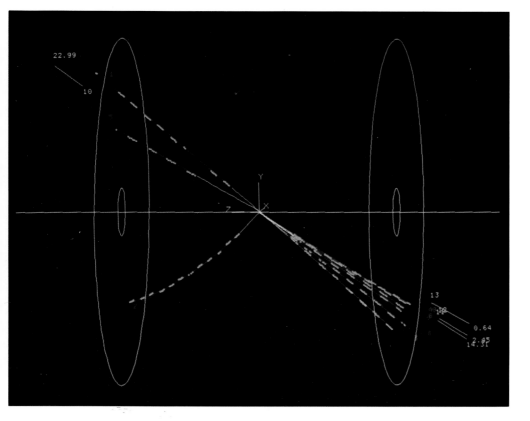

Atom: By creating a "blank map" of the Interaction Point, where atomic particles collide in modern accelerators, physicists trace the mass, charge, and trajectory of short-lived subatomic shrapnel (pink in the illustration) and use the information to construct current models of the atom. The tracks in this image mark the creation of the first Z particle, in 1989, at the Stanford Linear Accelerator Center. *(chapter 15)* SLAC

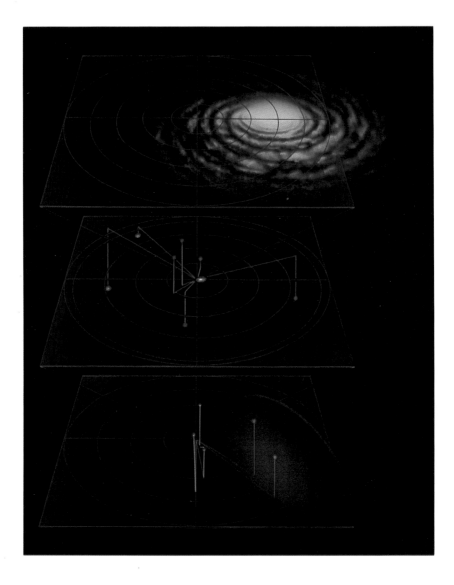

Milky Way: Since the mid-1970s, radio astronomers have detected and mapped concentrations of carbon monoxide (white, red, and yellow, in decreasing order of intensity) in the Milky Way *(below)*, revealing the location of giant molecular clouds where stars form in our galaxy. *(chapter 16)* T. DAME AND P. THADDEUS

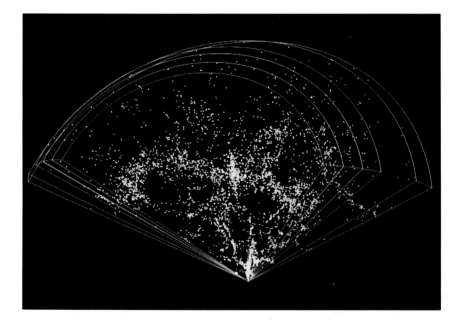

Great Wall: The Harvard-Smithsonian Center for Astrophysics redshift survey of galaxies in the northern celestial hemisphere of the universe has revealed filaments, bubbles, and, arching across the middle of the sample above, an uninterrupted structure 500 million light-years long called the "Great Wall." It is the biggest "thing" ever mapped, and one of the biggest challenges to prevailing theories about galaxy formation. *(chapter 18)* SMITHSONIAN ASTROPHYSICAL OBSERVATORY

Great Attractor: These three maps *(left)* show the scale of the Great Attractor relative to the Milky Way. In the top tier, our sun lies at the center of the grid, approximately two-thirds from the center of the swirling Milky Way; the map measures 50 kiloparsecs (about 160,000 light-years) on a side. The sun and Milky Way lie at the center of the second map, surrounded by the galaxies that form the Local Group; the scale is one megaparsec (about 3.2 million light-years) on a side, twenty times larger than the first map. On the bottom map, the scale is 100 times greater still, each side measuring 100 megaparsecs (about 326 million light-years) per side, with the Local Group in the center and five superclusters in the vicinity. Maps of peculiar velocity show that all the superclusters are streaming toward a single point, dubbed the Great Attractor and marked by the purplish disk in the bottom map. *(chapter 17)* "NEWTON"/KYOIKUSHA; D. BURSTEIN

Lakes of Wada: These mathematical charts of the "Lakes of Wada" reveal a topological (and perhaps philosophical) paradox about boundaries. Beginning in the upper left corner and moving right, row by row, each subsequent image enlarges a portion of the previous "map," and close examination shows that if you are on the boundary between two different fates (where fates are represented by different colors), you are on the boundary of all possible fates. The "fates" in this case are four possible behaviors of a dynamic physical system—specifically the motion of a pendulum. *(chapter 14)* © 1990 JAMES A. YORKE not in the customary sense. "Not a secret to other physicists in the department," Binnig explains. "They of course were aware. But higher management didn't know for about two years." The fear, he said, was that if the tunneling concept was not immediately successful, management people would become "tense and jump on everything that might be wrong." Quietly, Binnig and Rohrer and their colleagues prepared their initial device, using custom-blown glassware, "lots of Scotch tape," and a needlessly complicated superconductor that levitated the whole apparatus. On the night of March 16, 1981—"hardly daring to breathe from excitement, but mainly to avoid vibrations," they later noted—they first tested the tunneling concept and proved that the variations in electrical current indeed mirrored topography. Their initial success was in hand. The first word of the new instrument appeared in an in-house IBM "Activity Report" that same month. The inventors went public with their results at a scientific meeting in Los Angeles in August of 1981. In effect, they announced a scientific revolution. Nobody came.

Rohrer tried to interest IBM researchers in the United States, with no success; Bell Laboratories was aware of the technology early on, Binnig recalls, but chose not to pursue it. "Most reactions were benevolent, some enthusiastic, and two even anticipated the Nobel Prize," they later recalled, "but the STM was apparently still too exotic for any active outside engagement." Their first paper on the tunneling technique, Binnig says, was turned down by the prestigious *Physical Review Letters.*

So they returned to Zurich and started asking other scientists what the most famous unsolved problem in surface science was. "People told us it was the silicon seven-times-seven [7 × 7]," Binnig remembers. "So we said, 'Okay, then we'll solve this one, and then people will believe the technique.'" The surface of silicon was famous because its atoms arranged themselves in a repetitive diamond-shaped pattern. That repeating pattern, known as the "unit cell," was unusually large and for that reason fascinated surface scientists. "It was simply the most famous surface structure at the time," Binnig says. "Why is it so complicated? Silicon is interesting for technological reasons. Everyone knew it, and everyone wanted to know how it forms and what it looked like."

So they worked out some kinks in their technique over the summer of 1982, and by that fall managed to capture an image of surface science's golden grail—silicon 7 × 7. Binnig, enchanted with the image, could not stop looking at it. "I expected a much simpler struc-

Steps to success: this stepwise relief of silicon's 7 × 7 structure proved to doubters that scanning tunneling technology worked. Two diamond-shaped unit cells are clearly visible in the atomic landscape. (IBM Research)

ture," he said in an interview years later. "Here one saw little hills, and the hills formed a complicated pattern with this symmetry. I knew it was real, not an artifact. Because of this symmetry. We like symmetry. If something is symmetrical, it is very pretty. This was complicated but regular, extremely surprising and pretty." Years later, Binnig was pressed to explain why he found the topographic image so compelling. "If you see a beautiful woman," he replied after a considerable pause, "it's also hard to explain why she is pretty. You just know she is."

Binnig continued to stare at the image for one week. "It was like entering a new world," he remarked later. "This appeared to me as the unsurpassable highlight of my scientific career and therefore, in a way, its end." Sensing Binnig's reaction, Heinrich Rohrer "whisked" his colleague away to a small village in the Swiss Alps, where the two wrote a landmark paper on the 7 × 7 surface of silicon. By that time, their very first paper showing images produced by STM—the surface landscapes of gold and of a calcium-iridium-tin alloy—had appeared in the July 5, 1982 issue of *Physical Review Letters.* Although the authors noted that these first STM pictures "should give a taste of its fascinating possibilities," only a handful of researchers seemed interested in second helpings. In one of those nonessential but telling details that seemed to bespeak all of science's initial diffidence, the journal misspelled Binnig's name on that first landmark paper.

For several years, Binnig and Rohrer were the only scientists in the world who could get the microscope to work at atomic resolution. They began to hear rumors that other scientists had wagered cases of champagne in the belief that their spectacular STM images were nothing more than computer simulations. If there was a turning point in

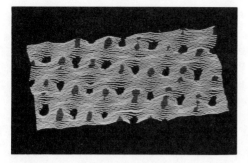

"Hilltops" formed by carbon atoms rise three angstroms—three ten-billionths of a meter—above the valleys in a landscape of graphite. (IBM Research)

terms of acceptance, it occurred in 1985, when other researchers using STM finally achieved a similar degree of expertise. Randall Feenstra came first to the rescue, with his breathtaking image of gallium arsenide. Calvin Quate of Stanford University, perhaps the most enthusiastic early disciple, followed with an image of platinum. The beat of successes reached a crescendo at the March 1985 meeting of the American Physical Society in Baltimore, when Paul Hansma of the University of California–Santa Barbara showed what atomic graphite looked like and the Soviet physicist J. Golovchenko showed the atomic lay of the land when germanium was deposited on silicon. As the images were projected on a screen, the inventors thrilled to the reaction. As they later exulted, "One could have heard a pin drop in the audience." That silence symbolized the end of scientific resistance, to say nothing of champagne wagers.

Rarely has a new scientific tool been so rapidly embraced and so readily adapted to so various a range of applications as the scanning tunneling microscope then became. *Scientific American* quickly invited Binnig and Rohrer to write a history of its invention. "The ability of the microscope to resolve both topography and electronic structure," they wrote in 1985, "will make it useful to investigators in physics, chemistry, and biology." This was classic understatement: scientific visualization at the atomic level has been completely revolutionized by STM and its emergent technological cousins. A cottage industry has cropped up, in California and elsewhere, selling the microscopes for anywhere from $10,000 to $200,000. With unusual ease and breathtaking resolution, scientists have been able to see the beautiful moors of atoms on the surface of silicon, to espy islands of germanium floating on a wavy sea of silicon, to detect the telltale coils of DNA, to watch the miracle of fibrinogen organizing itself into a blood clot in atomic detail, and, with a robotic device called the "magic wrist," actually to "feel" the bumps and canyons of atomic landscapes in their fingertips (see color illustration).

Binnig and Rohrer foresaw many of these new applications, but they foresaw unique problems, too. "In all the foregoing applications," they warned, "it is vital that the imaging process not destroy or even alter the object." Several colleagues at IBM's Almaden Research Center in San Jose failed to heed the warning—at first by accident, then increasingly by design—so that by 1990 it had become possible to use the scanning tunneling microscope not merely to see atoms, but to pick them up and move them around like pawns on the ultimate miniature chessboard. Many newspapers heralded the result of these labors in their pages when in 1990 a group of scientists at Almaden reported that they had managed to drag xenon atoms across a surface of nickel and arrange them in a nonrandom pattern that, surprisingly, resembled the letters IBM.

We are not so far removed from those pious but grandiose days when the worthiness of a new technology like the telegraph was announced to the world with the likes of "What hath God wrought"; now, when we acquire the ability to write with atoms, like gods, what is the first thing we write? A corporate logo. Social historians may mull over the significance of that, just as historians of technology will be kept busy tracing all the descendants of the original scanning tunneling microscope.

By 1990 it had become clear that the most important aspect of Binnig and Rohrer's prototype was not the tunneling concept per se, but rather the architecture of the instrument—not the particulars of the needle, as it were, but the phonograph itself. Its engineering allowed scientists, with complete precision, to move a probe up and down, left and right, forward and back, in increments of one angstrom—that is, about one-third the diameter of an atom at each step—with a simple tap of a keyboard key. This ability to bring *any kind* of probe tip close to a material and scan its surface at a distance of mere angstroms has given surface microscopists the same versatility of bandwidth that astronomers enjoy when they view the cosmos with X rays and visible light and gamma rays.

Just as the phonograph needle has given way to the laser reading head for compact discs, atomic microscopists have proved unusually inventive in changing the reading head of the scanning tunneling microscope, and in so doing have opened the way for an explosion of devices that are just now beginning to change the way we measure, study, and ultimately see atomic surfaces. "In fifty or a hundred years, as people are still interested in these developments, my feeling is that the scanning tunneling microscope will be known primarily for the microscopes it inspired," says Paul Hansma. "It will be known as the predecessor of the atomic force microscope and other scanning probe microscopes."

Between 1985 and 1990 alone, a second generation of scanning machines arrived in the laboratory, and virtually no signal of physical measurement resisted application. The tiny forces between atoms? The atomic force microscope, developed in 1985 by Binnig and colleagues at IBM along with Calvin Quate of Stanford University, depends not on tunneling, but uses an infinitesimally small probe to detect and measure the minute forces that exist between electrons. With this device scientists were able to visualize nonconducting surfaces (which, ironically, eliminated even the need for tunneling). Friction? The friction force microscope (1987) detects the snags and catches of friction at the atomic level as the tip is dragged across the surface of graphite. Magnetism? The magnetic force microscope (also 1987), developed by Yves Martin and H. Kumar Wickramasinghe of IBM, measures and maps the magnetic field on computer discs down to twenty-five-nanometer resolution. Static electricity? The electrostatic force microscope (1988) uses an electrically charged tip to detect static electric charges that develop when two surfaces rub or touch. Temperature? The scanning thermal microscope maps temperature variation by in effect dragging a tiny thermometer over any surface; researchers hope to be able to take the temperature of individual living cells. Sound waves? Calvin Quate at Stanford, as venerable a figure in the field as Binnig and Rohrer, has developed the scanning acoustic microscope, which applies something like sonar on a nanometer scale to map surfaces. Even living things can be measured.

Paul Hansma, who built his first models of STMs out of rubber bands, soda straws, Styrofoam, screws, glue, and a bit of wood in his Santa Barbara home, has led STM expeditions into biological landscapes. He has mapped the surface of cells, mapped the landscape of DNA, and has designed yet another STM spinoff, the scanning ion-conductance microscope (1989), in order to chart the landscape of cell membranes where nerve impulses are triggered, or inhibited, by the flow of such ions. Hansma has already astounded colleagues by using the atomic force microscope to produce a movie showing how blood proteins rally at the molecular level to form clots. As a reminder that new technologies of measurement and new cartographic enterprises

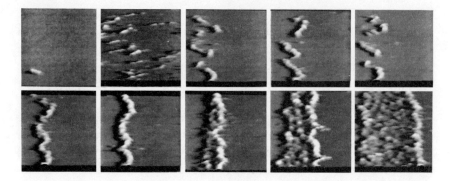

Biology in action: a succession of atomic force microscope images over an eight-minute period shows the protein fibrinogen gathering to form a blood clot. (University of California and Stanford University)

have a habit of finding and enhancing each other, Hansma's group at Santa Barbara has most recently concentrated its efforts on using the atomic force microscope to discern the chemical letters that make up the rungs on DNA's double helix, to the point where such a device could be used to decipher the genetic text in the massive project to map the human genome. "It's certainly a long, long, long, long way to go to do it with complete confidence," Hansma says, "but I think it will be possible to sequence DNA with the scanning probe microscope."

It is a long, long way, too, from the days in the 1960s when Paul Hansma's high school science teacher declared, not without good reason, that human beings would never be able to see atoms, that all our vision and all our artfulness would never bring us to the parapet overlooking that invisible landscape. All that changed in 1981. "It was true," Hansma said recently, "that, in the same way that those beautiful photos of the earth taken from space, when you see the blue disk against the black sky, had an impact, an emotional impact, it was the same thing with these surfaces. Everybody knew these surfaces had atoms, and how they were packed. But to see them was enlightening in a way beyond words."

13. One Picture, Worth Billion Bytes

A FRACTAL MAP OF PI AND
THE FUTURE OF CARTOGRAPHY

||||||||||

Humility alone designs
Those short but admirable Lines,
By which, ungirt and unconstrain'd,
Things greater are in less contain'd.
Let others vainly strive t'immure
The *Circle* in the *Quadrature*!
These *holy Mathematicks* can
In ev'ry Figure equal Man.
　　　　　—Andrew Marvell,
　　　　　　"Upon Appleton House,
　　　　　　to My Lord Fairfax"

When you pay a visit to the Chudnovsky brothers, you are not merely dropping in on a charmingly odd couple of Old World mathematicians, although that would not be an unreasonable first impression. David Chudnovsky, the elder brother, typically meets you at the door and leads you down a long, narrow corridor faintly seeded with the odors of dust and perspiration, past sedimentary piles of books and files and past the wheelchair, into an unlikely laboratory for the future of cartography: a dark room in an eighth-floor apartment in a prewar building on Manhattan's Upper West Side, a room that would overlook 120th Street if it weren't for the blinds that seem always to be drawn. It is a cozy, enclosing den of intellectual toil, one long wall of the room blank save for a large wiring diagram (for a computer the Chudnovskys recently invented) and two small framed portraits, both of Andrei Sakharov (whose scientific papers they recently edited). It seems like a cluttered office, but it seems even more like a makeshift and disheveled electronic brain that has burst out of its architectural housing and spilled into what once must have been a living room, its memory and its synapses cobbled together from four or five monitors, a few central processing units, data storage packs, cables crisscrossing the parquet floor, and of course the telephone lines, metallic axons of modern computer networks, linking this electronic monastic cell and its nimble-minded homebodies with the most powerful computing machines in the world, which the Chudnovskys use to explore the imaginary terrain of pure numbers.

Then Gregory enters the room, haltingly, leaning on a cane. He wears slippers and blue sweatpants. He looks slightly pale, and his hair is disheveled. He does not immediately strike you as the most powerful and creative mathematician alive in the world today, as some of his colleagues maintain. In fact, he looks barely able to keep up a conversation. But then he begins to talk about numbers, about their shape and feel, their very particular topography. As he talks, the color slowly returns to his face.

In a few short hours, David and Gregory Chudnovsky will conversationally flit from their efforts to map π, the classic mathematical constant, to the origins of the universe to "Little Fermat," a most unusual computer they hope will change the way topography of any sort makes its way from digitized numbers to a visual display. Just behind him, on a color monitor, Gregory sets in motion a simulation done on one of those old-fashioned, balky supercomputers; it shows gas and interstellar dust clouds kneading themselves into stars and filaments and galaxies. Concocted by the Chudnovskys along with Columbia astrophysicist Kevin Prendergast and M. M. (Monty) Denneau of IBM, it simulates the evolution of the cosmos, and with each vertical line scrolling across the screen—a slow metronomal backdrop to the talk—10 million years pass. It is the only clock in the room.

The simulation gives Gregory an excuse to complain, which he does at the highest intellectual level. "You see, a map is not really a true representation of a landscape, because for this you really need to see third dimension," he says, for the first of many times this day. His talk reverts often to what he calls "the mountain." It is his Everest, his metaphor for the cartographic future. It is not enough to see a two-dimensional rendering of a mountain, or its contours, or even a solid three-dimensional model that you walk around. You must, cartographically speaking, venture inside it, see its composition from the inside out and be able to see how it changes as you move through it and how the mountain itself changes with time. *"I must see the mountain!"* Gregory insists.

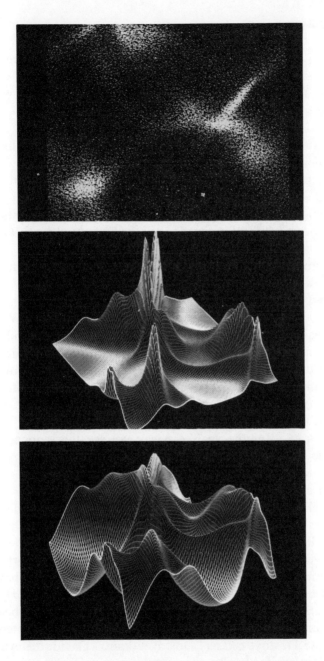

"Galaxy in a sandbox": David and Gregory Chudnovsky set up initial conditions for their computer simulation and then watch as stars, gases, and dust knead themselves into galaxies. Shown at top is a two-dimensional slice through their galaxy; landscape graphs plot the distribution of mass density for the same slice in linear *(middle)* and logarithmic *(bottom)* scales. (D. and G. Chudnovsky)

The problem with most present-day cartography, he continues, is that three dimensions can only be captured and shown as a succession of slices. The very same problem could be said about a conversation with the Chudnovskys.

GREGORY: "People are no longer satisfied with solids blocking the view of what is inside!"

DAVID: "You know, with a fantastic wine, you want to hold the glass up to the light so that the light will . . ."

GREGORY: ". . . will go through. Well, okay, this is fantastic. But not fantastic. You want to see through deep water. One of the things we would like—"

DAVID: "Also we want to see some turbulent atmosphere."

GREGORY: "*Through* turbulent atmosphere."

DAVID: "Which leads you to the Hubble telescope."

GREGORY: "But anyway, you want to see *through*. We are not really very happy with seeing a solid as an object, and with just walking around it. You see, if you really take a landscape, in order to see what is behind the mountain, unless you do contouring, you really have to basically walk around it."

DAVID: "But anyway, it's *still* bullshit because you not only want to fly through. You want to fly through *in time*."

GREGORY: "In time, yeah. Anyway, you see, this is not an unrealistic demand."

Not at all. Anyway, you get the idea.

A fellow mathematician remembers the first time he saw the Chudnovskys give a seminar. "Very strange," he recalls. "One of them would talk for three sentences, then the other talked for three sentences." They do mathematics as a team sport. David, forty-four, is good-humored and heavy-lidded, well-girthed and clean-shaven, and one quickly senses the finitude of his patience; Gregory, thirty-nine, is slender and fragile-looking, with a lean face, a pointed beard, and bright animated brown eyes that would strike even someone who hasn't read Dostoyevski as "Dostoyevskian." David, the cynical and worldly one, rolls his eyes theatrically at every naïve utterance, and lapses easily into short dismissive laughs. Gregory is a timeless naïf, though a brilliant one (he belonged to the first class of MacArthur Foundation geniuses in 1981); he lapses easily into high-pitched laughter, the kind that betrays some secret, higher plane of irony. David is considered merely an excellent mathematician by his peers; Gregory has a gift that leaves many colleagues speechless. Talking to Gregory, says one admirer, himself a member of the National Academy of Sciences, is "like watching an atomic pile glowing in the dark."

They work here in this apartment, think here, ponder the relationship of numbers here, paint mathematical landscapes here, recreate the universe here. They do everything here partly because, to their considerable stupefaction and that of many contemporary mathematicians, they do not have jobs, or offices to go to. They do everything here partly because of a politically motivated mugging that took place on a street in Kiev in 1977. And they do everything here because Gregory Chudnovsky cannot really go anywhere else. He has myasthenia gravis, an autoimmune disorder that causes overwhelming muscular fatigue, and so he ventures only with difficulty out of the apartment, where his allergies to grass compound his problems. What is true of all mathematicians in a sense has been physiologically imposed upon the Chudnovskys: homebound, deskbound, forced to use their imaginations as vehicles of transport to an unusual degree, they have specialized in number theory, that most abstract branch of pure mathematics where one studies the nature and quality of numbers—whether they are random, or rational, or transcendental. Of late, mathematicians have begun to explore those qualities graphically, as when the Chudnovskys recently expressed pi as a fractal landscape. Consequently, they spend a lot of time in this dark room thinking, talking, and dreaming about mapping data in new ways as well as optimizing ways of seeing the information inherent, but often buried and invisible, in the pattern of numbers.

"Your brain is superbly conditioned to process extremely efficiently this visual information," David says at one point. "I mean, the bandwidth of our visual perception is . . ."

". . . is *staggering!*" Gregory says.

"It beats *anything* which was invented by man so far," David continues. "Because it's not only row and capacity, but how is this reprocessed. As they say, one picture is worth thousand words. I think it is a *mild* understatement."

A *thousand* words? Integers, like allergens, set off a reaction in Gregory. He will not let the number be. "Actually," he says, after a moment's thought, "a thousand words, it's only couple of kilobytes of information. While the eye, in a second, can process practically gigabytes of information. *Billions* of bytes of information."

"So it's basically very stupid," David says, "to handicap us by not using this channel." He says this as if some arbitrary or capricious authority had blindfolded them in order to impede their progress. It is in any event an odd context for the word "handicap," implying that the most unpleasant and intractable problems they face are not medical and economic, but mathematical. Still, on the plane of imagination, where they spend most of their time, the Chudnovskys clearly feel no disadvantage. They recall a bit of mathematical oral folklore, a comment attributed to David Hilbert, one of the great mathematicians of the twentieth century. Someone once asked Hilbert what had become of one of his former students.

"He lacked imagination," David says, quoting Hilbert's famous retort. *"And this is why,"* chimes in Gregory, *"he became a poet!"* And the two Chudnovsky brothers laugh uproariously.

In his delightfully cranky and erudite book *A History of Pi,* Petr Beckmann calls the history of pi "a quaint little mirror of the history of man." That may overstate the case, but the roster of thinkers who have devoted some portion of their considerable intellects to π reads like a Who's Who of mathematics: Archimedes, Euclid, Fibonacci, Descartes, Newton, Leibniz, Euler, Ramanujan, and von Neumann, to say nothing of Albrecht Dürer and Leonardo da Vinci and Dante.

The allure of the number, and the tedium that attends its various computations, stems from the magical fact that pi represents the ratio of the circumference of a circle to its diameter, whether that circle is the size of an electron cloud or a polka dot or the disk of the sun or the mouth of a black hole. Because the circle is one of nature's fundamental forms, this simple ratio becomes an integral part of all sorts of calculations, from the number of bricks Roman engineers needed to build the dome of the Pantheon to the quantum spin of an electron to the homework problems solved by schoolchildren. And yet the number we all learned in geometry, conveniently shortened to 3.1416, is nonetheless an *approximation*, whether rendered in five digits or five million.

The story is probably apocryphal, but the Greek sage Archimedes is said to have been sketching a circle in the sand at the time of his demise in Syracuse in 212 B.C., bristling—so the tale goes—at being interrupted by a Roman soldier. The soldier promptly ran his sword through Archimedes, making him the most celebrated casualty of the Second Punic War. The story is not out of character, however, for Archimedes was among the earliest to become obsessed by this crucial ratio (not until the eighteenth century, it seems, did a writer dub it "pi"). He realized that upper and lower limits of the ratio could be

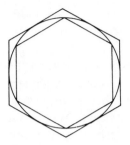

Archimedes approximated the value
of pi by "surrounding" a circle with
inscribed and circumscribed polygons.
(Petr Beckmann, *A History of Pi,*
Golem Press, Boulder, Colo., 1971)

obtained by constructing a many-sided figure, or polygon, outside and inside the circumference of a circle, converging on it from both directions. With a polygon of ninety-six sides, Archimedes proved that this ratio falls somewhere between 22/7 and 223/71—that is, between 3¹/₇ and 3¹⁰/₇₁. He spelled out this proof in the short treatise *The Measurement of the Circle.* Ever since, mathematicians have cut their teeth on this endlessly expanding number, prompting mathematics historian Carl Boyer to remark, "We should bear in mind that accuracy in the value of π is more a matter of computational stamina than of theoretical insight."

No one improved on Archimedes' solution for fifteen hundred years. Many tried. Computing pi was among the earliest and most international of mathematical brotherhoods. Around 470 A.D., Tsu Ch'ung-chih in China proposed a value of 355/113; it turned out to be one of the best approximations for a thousand years, though that did not stop Hindu, Indian, and Muslim mathematicians from taking estimable cracks at it. In 1593 the Frenchman François Viète outdid Archimedes by computing a 393,216-sided polygon inside a circle; that Herculean effort gave a value of pi correct to all of nine digits. Ludolph van Ceulen of Holland had pushed the envelope to 35 digits by the time he died in 1610, and the last three digits, published posthumously in 1621, were carved into his tombstone; a Polish Jesuit, Adamas Kochanski, nudged the value further; and in 1674 Gottfried Wilhelm von Leibniz—credited along with Newton as having invented the calculus—proposed a novel infinite series to give a value for pi.

The ensuing era, according to Petr Beckmann, belonged to "the digit hunters." In the early eighteenth century, John Machin calculated pi to 100 decimal places, and in 1873, William Shanks of England after twenty years of work computed it to 707 places. By the twentieth century, students dumbly recited a mnemonic device: "How I want a drink, alcoholic of course, after the heavy lectures involving quantum mechanics." The number of letters in each word—

3.14159265358979—equals the value of pi to 15 places. A venerable value, that one, for it had first been established by the Arab mathematician al-Kashi in the fifteenth century.

William Shanks was comfortably dead, buried, and beyond the touch of mathematical mortification when it was discovered, shortly after World War II, that he had made a mistake in the 527th place of his computation. Soon after, the computer era of pi began. Whereas it took Shanks fifteen years to stagger 707 places, the prototype postwar computer, ENIAC, took pi to 2,037 places in seventy hours, an expedition led by none other than John von Neumann in September of 1949. By 1958 computers took a hundred minutes to do 10,000 places; three years later, a computer took pi to 100,265 places in less than nine hours. With more powerful computers came more powerful computations. In 1973, Jean Guilloud and M. Bonyer of France broke the million-digit barrier and in the 1980s, with the advent of supercomputers, the pace of progress increased with dizzying speed—2 million places in 1981, 8 million the following year. A. William Gosper struck a blow for enlightened math and limited power when he took pi to 17 million digits on a Symbolics workstation in 1985. In 1988 the tenacious Japanese researcher Yasumasa Kanada attained 201 million digits. With supercomputers, there developed, as the Chudnovskys acknowledged in a 1989 paper, "a race for leadership in these computations, where the performance of algorithms and supercomputers is measured in tens of millions of digits of *pi* computed using a given algorithm in a given supercomputer."

But to what end? You obviously don't need to know pi to 1 million digits to lay out a traffic circle. Why the fuss? Several reasons, actually. First, calculations of pi are to a powerful supercomputer what a test track is to a race car: a way to put a new machine through its paces, check its power, work out its bugs, find out how fast it is. Second, it challenges mathematicians to construct new and more efficient algorithms by which pi can be calculated, and this has led to a perhaps underappreciated branch of mathematics tailored specifically to clever algebraic uses of computers, a skill the Chudnovskys seem to possess in bewildering abundance. Using an IBM-developed electronic blackboard called Scratchpad, they created a unique algebraic formula that "converges"—or zeroes in—to the value of pi faster than any previous approach.

Finally, pi has always been of interest to number theorists because it looks and smells like a random number. Random numbers betray no pattern in the sequence of their digits (this very unpredictability makes them useful for secret codes). "Normal" numbers, which fall some-what short of being random, do betray a pattern; each digit between 0 and 9, for example, appears with roughly 10 percent frequency. "Normalcy" is an issue of great interest in the field of number theory, and number theory was of consuming interest to a couple of young Ukrainian mathematicians back in the 1970s. Their path to pi, though, was littered with obstacles, the least of which were mathematical.

"All mathematicians," says Lipman Bers, former chairman of the mathematics department of Columbia University, "were aware of the situation."

Not until July 24, 1977, however, did the "situation" become known to a larger public in the United States, and only then by virtue of one of those brief items in the *New York Times* that teeter between news and filler. Soviet dissident Andrei Sakharov informed Western reporters in Moscow of a vicious unprovoked attack upon an elderly couple of refuseniks in the Ukraine. Early one evening, on a quiet street in Kiev across from a cinema and a candy store, unidentified thugs assaulted Volf and Malka Chudnovsky in an attack that had all the earmarks of KGB intimidation. Mr. Chudnovsky, then seventy, was beaten severely; Mrs. Chudnovsky, then sixty-seven, was taken to a local hospital emergency room, where doctors told her that X rays were negative when in fact she had suffered a broken arm and collar-bone. Their son Gregory was not injured in the attack. That was because he was home, bedridden and in grave condition.

Indeed, it was Gregory's deteriorating health that prompted the family to apply for an emigration visa. At the urging of a prominent Soviet mathematician, I. M. Gelfand, the Chudnovskys had applied in January 1977 for passage to Israel in hopes of obtaining better medical treatment for Gregory. Not only did officials in the Kiev passport office turn down their request; the authorities stripped all four Chud-novskys of their teaching posts shortly after they applied to leave. The elder Chudnovskys, both civil engineers and senior university profes-sors, lost their jobs. So did David, then a senior research fellow at the Ukrainian Academy of Sciences, and Gregory, a research fellow at Kiev State University. The Chudnovskys believe their home was bugged, their phone tapped. They were frequently called in for ques-tioning.

When Gregory remained unable to obtain the Swiss-made medi-cine for his illness, Moscow dissidents took up the cause of the Chud-novskys and mounted a publicity campaign, joined by scientists and

"Why waste all the time with instruments when you could predict it theoretically?" asks Gregory Chudnovsky *(left)*. "We are working on it," says David Chudnovsky. (D. and G. Chudnovsky)

mathematicians in the West. Gregory had published significant work by the age of sixteen, and his reputation as a number theorist had spread to the United States. One of his collaborators, the Russian-speaking mathematician Edwin Hewitt of the University of Washington, alerted American authorities and enlisted the aid of the late Senator Henry Jackson in getting the Chudnovskys out of Russia. Lipman Bers, then at Columbia, contacted the Chudnovskys while in Kiev, telling them "they weren't forgotten." "We thought the important thing was to get them out because we were concerned for their lives," adds Herbert Robbins, another Columbia professor. And so when in August 1977 the Chudnovskys finally received permission to leave the Soviet Union and made their way to Austria, there was a telegram awaiting them in Vienna that said there were positions for them at Columbia. Naturally, they believed it.

After a six-month layover in Paris, the family arrived in New York in February of 1978. Bers and Robbins found an apartment for them on 120th Street; local Jewish relief organizations provided food and furnishings. Only then did the Chudnovskys learn the unfortunate truth: there were no jobs for them at Columbia, just nonsalaried titles of "senior research scientist." Since 1978 they have survived on grants (some quite considerable) and the salaries of their wives. "We have never succeeded in getting them jobs anywhere," admits Robbins. "Sources of support for the whole family have been: each of the boys got a Guggenheim fellowship for a year, Gregory got a MacArthur Fellowship for five years, and they have had a certain amount of part-time consulting work at IBM. As for the rest, they've been supported through government research contracts administered through Columbia University but they're not on the faculty."

"I consider it the biggest scandal in the mathematics community right now," says Richard Askey, a mathematician at the University of Wisconsin. "Gregory has knowledge that nobody else in the world has. He needs to have a teaching position, and he needs to have students to whom he can pass that knowledge on, and it's an absolute crime that he doesn't." To search for comparable mathematical intellects, Askey is forced to suggest names like Carl Ludwig Siegel, Yuri Linnik, Srinivasa Ramanujan, and N. H. Abel; those names probably don't ring bells in most lay ears, but if the subject were violin playing instead of number theory, comparable names would be Perlman, Heifetz, Menuhin, and Stern.

Mathematicians without portfolio, academics without an academy, the Chudnovskys have nonetheless functioned—grudgingly, kvetchingly, one suspects even despondently—as productive scientists. They work out of the apartment on West 120th street, which they share with their mother (Volf Chudnovsky died in 1985 of heart disease, a condition his sons believe was related to the beating he suffered in 1977). They organize high-powered scientific meetings, such as a symposium on "Computers and Mathematics" in June of 1989, sponsored by MIT. They publish regularly. And they remain gifted mathematicians whom, as if stained by the religious or political prejudices they thought they'd left behind in the Soviet Union, no one will hire.

The adjective that crops up again and again whenever other mathematicians attempt to describe Gregory Chudnovsky's work is "deep." He likes deep problems. He is a deep thinker. He has a taste for deep, exceedingly difficult problems, such as diophantine equations, named after the Greek mathematician Diophantos. These demanding calculations can reveal what makes numbers different from each other, and it was partly with a diophantine approach that the Chudnovskys, around 1984, began seriously to think about pi.

Some mathematicians would argue that the expansion of π to millions of digits is not a deep problem. But in mathematics *how* you get there is often as important as what you end up with, and the great breakthrough achieved by the Chudnovskys is that they constructed a new algorithm, or set of instructions, especially well tailored to the computer determination of pi, and although their method will not put an end to ever-more-dizzying totals, it may forever dominate the race to reach those totals. In the past, in order to compute π to 53 or 53 million or 530 million digits, mathematicians always had to start from scratch each time, because the computations were "floating point" calculations—at the end of each operation, they rounded off rather than saved the decimal, and that was enough to throw off any subsequent expansion. By using this new approach, the Chudnovskys didn't round off numbers and lose valuable information along the way. The formula, elephantine as well as diophantine, looked like this:

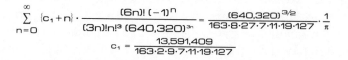

$$\sum_{n=0}^{\infty} (c_1 + n) \cdot \frac{(6n)! \, (-1)^n}{(3n)! n!^3 \, (640,320)^{3n}} = \frac{(640,320)^{3/2}}{163 \cdot 8 \cdot 27 \cdot 7 \cdot 11 \cdot 19 \cdot 127} \cdot \frac{1}{\pi}$$

$$c_1 = \frac{13,591,409}{163 \cdot 2 \cdot 9 \cdot 7 \cdot 11 \cdot 19 \cdot 127}$$

The Chudnovskys publicly presented this complex equation at a meeting in 1985, hoping that someone else would actually grind out the results. No one took the bait. And so, beginning in December of 1988, they began the thankless task of computing π on their own. Their biggest problem was getting access to the right kind of computer.

"Not fun" is how David summarizes the experience; in two hours of talk marked by plenty of rolling eyes and exaggerated sighs, the biggest were reserved for the saga of pi. They had to cajole colleagues, write imploring letters and fire off faxes, appeal for support from the National Science Foundation (with success), wheedle computer time from corporations, and, more difficult still in the costly world of computer real estate, beg for invaluable electronic warehouse space in which to store their hundreds of millions of pi digits. "It's an extremely inefficient way of doing things, frankly, because of course you count computer time in seconds, but *your* time, real physical time, is really hours or days . . ." Gregory laments. "Or *months!*" David says.

It took nine months in real time to do the computations. After much negotiating they received about 40 hours on a Cray 2 supercomputer at the Minnesota Supercomputer Center and about 100 hours on an IBM 3090-VF at IBM's Thomas J. Watson Research Center in Yorktown Heights, New York. Those 140 hours, however, were won fifteen minutes here, twenty there, on the Fourth of July and New Year's Eve, almost always in the middle of the night. Many sessions ended on abrupt, sour notes. The hard disk would simply crash, taking all of pi with it, like some errant kite augering into the ground and dragging with it that gaudy, endless, and now irretrievable tail of digits. Sometimes the work simply disappeared. David likens the entire ordeal to doing mathematics at a laundromat. "When you do your laundry, you share the dryer," he says. "If you come too often, the machine won't be available until everybody else is done. Or the next day you come and maybe you find what you left."

"Or maybe you *don't* find what you left!" Gregory adds. He seems to find this very funny.

Oh, they put the computers through their paces, all right. "It's almost the equivalent of a full physical," David explains. "It's like a stress test. You run it on the treadmill until it drops dead. And in many cases, I regret to say, we were successful." Crashed disks and vanishing data were nothing compared to more subtle, nearly invisible glitches. "The dreadful thing is not that the data are lost, but when the data are crap!" David says. "If a single bit is flipped and you don't know that?" More rolled eyes and sighs. They spent 90 percent of their supercomputer time on verification. Typically, they figured out a way to double-check their results so thoroughly that they reduced the probability of an uncorrected error at any step to less than one in 10^{290}—one followed by 290 zeroes.

By September of 1989, they had their answer, sort of. The Chudnovskys had computed π to 1,011,196,691 digits. Yes, that's more than 1 billion digits. In this typeface their version of pi would stretch approximately 1,580 miles. Printed out by computer, the stack of paper would reach as high as a twelve-story building. But quantity is not the goal. What the Chudnovskys are after is much bigger. They want to know what makes a number random.

That, in a sense, is the more interesting part of the exercise, for the Chudnovskys believe that converting sequences of numbers into graphic images, or maps, affords unique possibilities of mathematical analysis. Number theory thrives on finding patterns in numbers, and the conversion of pi's digits into a landscape was an experiment to see if such visual images provided topographical clues to global patterns. "The usefulness of this information is only based on its physical, spatial correlations," says Gregory. "*Not* in this idiotic long sequential display of it."

So they created a picture of π, a landscape measuring 1,000 digits by 1,000 digits, to search for clues to pi's unique numerical character. They did it by taking strings of pi's digits, summing them and averaging that sum to get a mean value, and then plotting each next digit against the average of all the digits that preceded it. Called a "random walk," the two-dimensional terrain that emerged is more popularly known as a fractal landscape. When a digit is above the mean, the landscape rises slightly; when below, it dips toward a valley. As they walked through the first one million digits of π, they created a pleasantly hilly landscape—just what you would expect from a fairly random sequence. They called it a "pi-scape" (see color illustration).

"In the case of pi," Gregory says, holding a postcard of the pi-scape, "if your numbers are really random, you just want to see them, to observe them. And you *plot* them on a graph, a one-dimensional graph. What you would be seeing is a jiggle. You know, it goes from zero to nine, a *totally random* jiggle. It's basically what people like to say is noise, random noise. Well, it is true in the sense that each individual digit is really random. But as with any nontrivial physical process, there is a global relationship.

"So in this particular case what you try to describe is the relationship in the string of characters. You're building this landscape potentially moving, pointing up or down, creating these hills and valleys. And now we are watching a global behavior of the digits. If an individual digit is, you know, one or zero, it will only *slightly* move the landscape. It's only when suddenly all digits would be zero, you would start seeing a phenomenally flat valley. If all digits will suddenly become nine, *or* if you will see the repetition of zero-nine, zero-nine, zero-nine, you will start seeing something absolutely interesting in the global behavior." They are still analyzing the data ("It's like with the flight of a planetary probe, first you collect a data base," David explains), but they have begun to see hints of what Gregory calls "nontrivial" global behavior in π. The problem is, ahem, that 1 billion digits aren't enough. "The data base, I hate to tell you, is very inadequate," David explains.

"You see that there are differences between the frequencies of the digits," Gregory says. "But Jesus, we can't put it in a quantitative way. And here, unfortunately, unless intuition suggests something, we have no way of conjecturing what this relationship may be except by analysis of data." It will take, they think, another 9 billion digits. In the meantime, they are swearing off fractal maps. "With the pi-scape," Gregory says, "you could take it and compare it with a bunch of other generic ones, and it would very mildly differ in its general appearance. It's almost like saying, 'Once you have seen one Grand Canyon, you've seen them all'!"

Two billion years have flown by, just like that, on the simulated galaxy grinding away in the background. "Cheap!" Gregory shrugs, waving the postcard showing the pi-scape. "That's why landscapes in fact are cheap imitations of what we really want to do. . . . A map is not really a true representation of a landscape, because for this you

Soul of a unique machine:
"Little Fermat" is designed
to do speedy, "big-numb"
calculations of equations used by
seismic tomographers, climate modelers,
and other number-crunching mappers.
(D. and G. Chudnovsky)

really need to see third dimension. And that is still done on paper. What I really want is to be able to assess three-dimensional information in all directions, and to be able to reconstruct the depths, and in this way avoid this artificial landscape representation."

When the Chudnovskys talk about historical precedents for the kind of cartography they would like to perfect, they do not speak the dialect of Martin Behaim's globe and Ptolemy's maps. They refer instead to the Musée des Plans-Reliefs, on the fourth floor of Les Invalides in Paris, a curious collection of scale models. One after another, row upon row, these three-dimensional models represent the frontier fortresses and towns that dotted France's borders, a practice initiated by Louis XIV in the seventeenth century. The models break out of the plane of two dimensions. They represent a topographical data base. They can be viewed from north or south, inside or out.

Fittingly, the Chudnovskys have turned to seventeenth-century France and its greatest mathematician for inspiration in their daunting quest to recreate three-dimensional landscapes. After all the obsequious pleas for computer time for their pi-scape, after all the wee-hour workdays and the lost data, the Chudnovskys decided to solve that problem. With Monty Denneau of IBM (who designed IBM's most powerful parallel computer, the GF11) and Saed G. Younis, a graduate student at MIT, they created a computer unlike anything ever built before, the aforementioned Little Fermat, named after Pierre Fermat, the amateur mathematician credited with founding number theory.

The diminutive in the name is something of a misnomer. "It's *big*, it's *big!*" Gregory cries.

Most personal computers operate on 16 bits; Little Fermat runs on 257, which allows it to do number theory, perform operations on large numbers with greater precision, and in general crunch the big numbers that turn up in scientific problems related to imaging, modeling, and three-dimensional dynamics—things like magnetic resonance imaging, CT scans or any kind of tomography, and climate or galaxy models. The unique "dialect" of this computer is based on one of mathematics' most famous numbers: the Fermat number $2^n + 1$, where $n = 2^x$—in this case, $2^6 + 1$. It is designed not only to carry out sophisticated scientific computing of complex physical systems, such as climate, but to visualize data in more sophisticated ways. In David's words, it is "sort of a graphic engine with a very different geometry."

The challenge Little Fermat must overcome is subtle but significant. Assuming (as they do) that this cartographic future will be powered by supercomputers, or by novel computers like Little Fermat, the Chudnovskys envision maps not merely as graphic displays of information, but as graphic *storage* devices. All maps, to a certain extent, represent a process of subtraction, a boiling down of all possible information to essential information. A map of waterways will subtract highways as nonessential; a highway map doesn't bother with every creek and marsh. One of the problems with the "galaxy in a box" simulation is that in order to model galactic behavior in three dimensions, the Chudnovskys have created a grid of 100 cells by 100 cells by 100 cells; that's 1 million cells times how ever many conditions and effects they wish to simulate, and the system nearly chokes on the amount of information that needs to be processed. But everything needs to be included because no one knows what information is expendable and what isn't. The Chudnovskys believe that reduced, essential data can be *stored* not as twelve-story stacks of numbers, but as an *image*—*if* you have determined the difference between all possible information (what they call "dense" data) and necessary information ("sparse" data). Oddly enough, this has parallels with a track of work in neurobiology suggesting that this may be how human memory works, too. John Allman, the Caltech psychobiologist, has constructed a model of human memory in which past experience is stored in the visual cortex as a kind of map; visual information is reduced to essential geometries, lodges in the cortex, and becomes what he calls a form of "implicit memory."

What this is all about, ultimately, is more than pi-scapes or landscapes or flying through mountains. The Chudnovskys want to mathematically create nature in a box, want to throw out unnecessary details and fiddle with the rest, somehow tease out the secrets of nature by creating a picture of it in a computer and making that picture so sophisticated that it engages heretofore untapped potential in the human eye and brain to discern information. And they, better than most, understand the terrible mathematical and imaging complexities of modeling space in three dimensions, to say nothing of predicting behavior.

"Let me give you a simple example," says David, pacing back and forth in a corner of the room. "Let us look at a model problem. We have a baseball game. The Yankees versus Dodgers, the Redskins versus whatever." He shrugs, as bewildered by the names as most people are by Fermat numbers. "We are dealing with a very limited chunk of space. And very limited number of players. It's not millions of galaxies over thousands of light-years. We are dealing with, say, fifty-four players."

"And very simple rules," Gregory says.

"Very simple rules. You have all the records. You must mention all the records, many of them. And we have just to predict what is going to happen in two minutes." David pauses. *"And in hell you can predict what's going to happen!"*

"You can't!" says Gregory. "You have to watch the game to know its outcome."

"Very explicit, and simple."

"At least in baseball game, we know that we are interested only in predicting a number," Gregory continues. "The score or something. In the case of galaxies, we are really studying this dense new phenomenon. Or any other new phenomenon. And we have to observe all the information. We have to be able to see it. We need some kind of map, or simple ways of representing this as a map, so the information can be easily stored, on tape, and in a *very,* very precise, small, and short form. And it cannot be really done in a couple of numbers; this is really not a score anymore.

"On the other hand, if you look on the whole continent of North America, just in the simple piece on the map, well, *it's a very good and efficient representation!*" he squeals. "You would be very happy to be able to have such a very nice and simple form of representation now of the three-D universe. So instead of keeping this unbelievable amount of unnecessary and too-detailed information, you would be able to see it. And I mean, this slice is a perfect representation! Just by flipping these pages—I mean, this is all we would ever be able to see on the telescope. No telescope will show as a three-D. So this is basically like flipping pictures, you know, on the evolution of the galaxy."

Four billion years have sped by since the conversation began, galaxies forming and dissolving and reforming again; it is time to go. Gregory continues to talk about "the mountain." "You want to see what is *inside*," he says. Such representations, David adds, will require new algorithms for transforming data, and he predicts there will be a lot of hardware problems. When last seen, David has his hand in a central processing unit, holding a circuit together with a Band-Aid. In their dark, overcrowded, underfunded laboratory, in their bewildering unemployability, in this room where the blinds seem always drawn, it is as if they are trying to map and model the world without ever seeing it, an impression reinforced by Gregory when he asks, "Why waste all the time with instruments when you could predict it theoretically?" And David says simply, "We are working on it."

14. The Lakes of Wada

A MAP OF
CHAOS AND DESTINY

||||||||||

Mathematics, after all, is more
than an art form.

—Seki Takakazu, Wasan mathematician,
written on student diploma in 1704

A number of years ago, long before the airwaves of science crackled with talk about chaos and strange attractors and odd boundaries, James A. Yorke, a mathematician at the University of Maryland, engaged in an exercise that only by the most generous interpretation could be considered a thought experiment. He tried to think up the four most disparate personalities of his time and ken—the four people in the world most *unlike* each other. It didn't start out as a mathematical exercise (and Yorke stiil doesn't think of it as such); if anything, the real motivation fell somewhere between idle speculation and interior decorating. Yorke was interested in hanging pictures of these four personalities on his office wall. After thinking about it for a while, he ended up with Albert Einstein (no stranger to laboratory walls); Mao Zedong; Theda Bara, the silent-film vamp; and Humphrey Bogart. One might quibble with the diversity of the choices (beginning with gender), but in Yorke's mind, they represented four distinct, antipodal, mutually exclusive destinies. Nothing to do with mathematics, of course, to say nothing of physical law. The pictures went up on his office wall, and Yorke went back to his specialized world of nonlinear differential equations and phase space and Rayleigh-Bénard instabilities, blissfully unaware that his thought experiment with four fates might have been working steadily away at his subconscious and that he might be in the midst of a creative process once described by Jules Henri Poincaré, the great French mathematician, as "long, unconscious prior work."

Now, many years later, only the pictures of Einstein and Bara have survived the various moves and relocations and redecorations at the Institute for Physical Science and Technology, over which Yorke presides as director. "They just cleaned the place while I was gone," he said, in part to explain why he couldn't find what he was looking for one day and in part to suggest what might have happened to the missing images of Bogart and Mao. The point is (as Yorke would say), his work has caught up with his imagination. One of the seminal figures in developing the theory of chaos, Yorke with his colleagues has designed and charted a kind of mathematical map of physical destinies. How many destinies? Four.

How do you mathematically chart destiny? Perhaps the best way to hint at what the map shows—and why it is so startling for philosophical as well as physical reasons—is to refer by analogy back to Yorke's foursome of opposites. Let us suppose there is some crucial early juncture, or set of influences, where destiny is sealed. In mathematics and in physical systems, they are called "initial conditions"; biologists less manageably might call them nature (as opposed to nurture). In Yorke's experiment a million different sets of initial conditions were entered into a computer, and all those initial conditions produce but one of four fates, which can be plotted on a two-dimensional chart like geographical coordinates on graph paper. One can even imagine entire regions of initial conditions that lead to one basin of fate or another, with borders between them: a kind of abstract geography. Yorke began to examine these boundaries mathematically and discovered a very curious thing. He discovered that if your fate hovers on the boundary between Einstein and Mao, poised to slide into one destiny or another, you are actually straddling the boundary of all four fates. You are equally likely to become not only Einstein or Mao, but also a wild-eyed vamp or a tough-guy actor. Mathematically speaking. And since mathematics often speaks a language that anticipates quirky but demonstrable aspects of physical reality, from Ein-

stein's non-Euclidean curvature of space-time to the frothing worm-
holes suggested by quantum mechanics, this peculiar and unexpected
conclusion has rather startling implications in topology, to say nothing
of scientific prediction.

Yorke didn't work out the problem using Einstein and Mao, of
course. His team used something better because it is real, sort of. They
used a pendulum that exists only inside a computer. By studying a
mathematical map that plotted both the initial conditions and the fate
of their pendulum, they discovered this perplexing property of boundaries. There is a topological term that applies to a boundary of this
type; it is said to be an "indecomposable continuum."

Yorke shies away from the word "map." It has a very specific
connotation in mathematics, one that is related but a bit different from
this particular exercise. He prefers the word "chart." But the nature of
boundaries, not so much geographical as dynamical, revealed by the
computer experiment results in a phenomenon known as the "Wada
property," and to those of us rooted to customary geographical intuition, the Wada property is decidedly bizarre. It says that in a territory
with three or more regions, each point on the boundary between any
two regions is actually on the boundary of all regions.

"One of my ideas, one of my *approaches*," Yorke was saying, "is
to take mathematical ideas and try to find applications of them in the
real world."

For someone who studies the nature of boundaries both mathematical and physical, James Yorke spends a lot of time defying them.
Trained at Columbia and the University of Maryland, he has modeled
the spread of venereal disease for epidemiologists, exposed flaws of
mathematical logic in gasoline-rationing plans drawn up by bureau-
crats during the 1978 oil crisis, and dipped into the strange boundary
world of topology. He is also famous for his role in spreading the
gospel about nonlinear physics in the 1960s and 1970s. It would be
stretching a point to call him the father of chaos, but he did get to name
the baby, in a famous 1975 paper with Tien-Yien Li entitled "Period
Three Implies Chaos." This dense sequence of equations confirmed the
emerging message of nonlinear systems: certain physical systems be-
have in a way that is nonperiodic, unpredictable, indeed "chaotic."

As one of the early protagonists of chaos, he occasionally speaks
with a pioneer's arrogance, even though it comes in a package with
rounded edges; Yorke is soft-spoken, patient, a tad portly, and, as one
collaborator puts it, "oozing with ideas." And he is not averse to

staking out a few intellectual boundaries of his own. "In mathematics," he says, "there are a lot of bright people working really hard. And the best way to approach what they do is to assume that they're all wrong, and we have to discover *how* they're wrong. If you realize that they're doing it wrong, you have a chance to find a better way. For example, mathematicians are locked into theorem-proof, theorem-proof. It's the *only way.* It's the air they breathe. But even if only ten percent of what they are doing is wrong, that gives you a pretty good edge. You can find new directions." He describes himself as a "part-time mathematician. The other part is, I do what I want to do." What he really does, in the words of one colleague, is "social mathematics."

Mathematics and physics have traditionally had an odd, arms-length but often confirmatory relationship. "Mathematics," the physicist Paul Dirac once remarked, "can lead us in a direction we would not take if we only followed physical ideas by themselves." Yorke has followed his nose down those paths, and it has led him to a terrain of mathematics quite distinct from classical physics—a terrain, in fact, whose exploration has been accompanied over the past century by a genre of mathematical maps. These maps trace nothing less than the departure of the physical world from classical physics.

With classical physics, scientists could study the physical motions of the planets and their moons, record the numbers, and derive physical laws from the equations that explained those numbers, as did Newton; or, one could examine and interpret numbers on a page within the mathematical lanes prescribed by those laws and infer the existence of something that had escaped scientific notice, as Leverrier and John Couch Adams did when they independently predicted the existence of the planet Neptune in the nineteenth century on the basis of perturbations in other planetary orbits. Those are tidy examples from a time when physics was classical and tidy. Such tidy systems, because they operated outside the damping effects of friction, were said to be "conservative"; a planet orbiting the sun, for example, *conserved* its energy, nearly repeating the same orbit again and again, and a class of equations called Hamiltonians explained those conservative behaviors.

That ability to tame cause and effect with equations, to not only explain but *predict,* inspired a certain mathematical hubris, nowhere more apparent than in the pronouncements of the eighteenth-century French mathematician Pierre Simon de Laplace. "The present state of the system of nature," he wrote in 1776, "is evidently a consequence of what it was in the preceding moment, and if we conceive of an intelli-

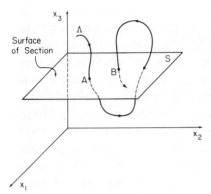

Numerical maps: at the turn of the century, French mathematician Henri Poincaré developed a form of mathematical mapping in which the solutions to functions would intersect a surface (S), just like racehorses intersecting the plane of the finish line. If the functions were reiterated again and again, the record of their intersections with the surface would form a distinct pattern. Such mathematical patterns are called Poincaré maps. (J. Yorke/© 1987 AAAS)

gence which at a given instant comprehends all the relations of the entities of this universe, it could state the respective positions, motions, and general affects of all these entities at any time in the past or future." Give me all the initial conditions, he said, expressing the conceit that lies at the heart of all science, and I can predict the future. From there it was a mere hop, skip, and philosophical jump to a much broader conclusion: that everything in the world was predetermined, and free will did not exist. Heavy implications indeed for a set of equations.

Other aspects of the physical world, however, do not abide the tidy side of Newtonian rules. Water surging and burbling against a midstream boulder, cream spreading in a cup of black coffee, smoke rising from a cigarette—all are everyday examples of dynamic physical systems that, literally and figuratively, don't walk a straight line. They are said to be "nonlinear." Unlike frictionless systems, they never "settle down" into a steady, repetitive behavior. Instead of being conservative, they are said to be "dissipative." They exhibit unpredictable behavior. As much as it can be explained, nonlinearity is explained by a class of formulas known as differential equations. Since one object of the physical sciences is to predict future behavior, it was discovered that these formulas described nonlinear behavior by a series of iterations, which have been aptly described by scientist and author Douglas R. Hofstadter as "mathematical feedback loops": you solved the equation for one value, took the result, and plugged it back into the equation.

Among the first to observe this was Poincaré, who may be said to be the spiritual godfather of chaos, and also the inspiration for mathematical maps. At the turn of the century, Poincaré showed that if one plotted the points at which an orbit or trajectory intersected a flat plane in three-dimensionai space, and continued to repeat (or iterate) those intersections, the points would build up into a distinct pattern (the idea has been likened to mapping the points where a racehorse intersects the plane of the finish line if it continues to run around the track for many laps). That pattern came to be called a Poincaré map, and it showed that a small change in initial conditions created patterns, or two-dimensional maps, that departed markedly from the previous initial conditions. As Poincaré noted in 1903, ". . . it may happen that small differences in the initial conditions produce very great ones in the final phenomena. A small error in the former will produce an enormous error in the later. Prediction becomes impossible, and we have the fortuitous phenomenon." By examining these nonlinear systems mathematically, Poincaré began to repeal Laplace's determinism.

Mathematicians, to cite Dirac once again, "must follow up [a] mathematical idea and see what its consequences are, even though one gets led to a domain which is completely foreign to what one started with." In this century alone, mathematics has led us to quite foreign domains in our notions of physical time, space, and predictability, thanks to relativity and the uncertainty principle. Nonlinearity and its mathematics, first intuited by Poincaré, have led to another foreign domain: chaos. This intellectual journey has been charted by maps, and its vehicle of discovery has been an unusual instrument of measurement: the computer.

Mathematical maps have played a crucial role in elucidating the paradoxical laws of chaos, and essential to their creation has been the wider availability and increasing power of computers, which have allowed mathematics to become an experimental science. In describing the origins of chaos theory, Douglas Hofstadter noted in *Scientific American* that "the style of exploration is entirely modern; it is a kind of experimental mathematics, in which the digital computer plays the role of Magellan's ship, the astronomer's telescope and the physicist's accelerator. Just as ships, telescopes and accelerators must be ever larger, more powerful and more expensive in order to probe ever more hidden regions of nature, so one would need computers of ever greater size, speed and accuracy in order to explore the remoter regions of mathematical space." (Yorke, mulling over this remark, says, "I'm just thinking about Magellan's trip, and realizing that he got killed on it.")

The evolution of chaos theory, not surprisingly, closely followed the evolution of the computer, and so it began to take off in the early

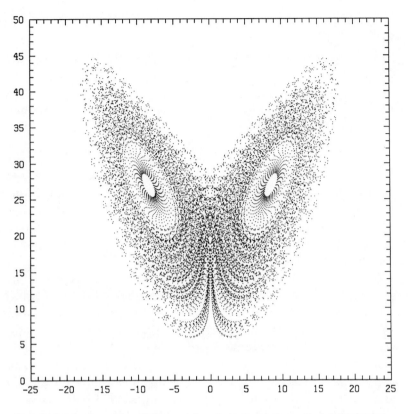

Regularity in the midst of chaos: using the new mathematical mapping permitted by computers, Edward Lorenz of MIT was the first to detect pattern in chaos. This is one of many versions of the famous "Lorenz butterfly." (Edward N. Lorenz)

1960s, when a meteorologist at MIT named Edward Lorenz used, and mapped, differential equations to model the weather. He quickly realized that the system never settled down, never permitted certain prediction; and that initial uncertainty was mirrored in the map of the iterations, which assumed the shape of beautiful, looping confusion known now as the Lorenz butterfly. The Lorenz butterfly was a picture of Poincaré's intuition, and when James Yorke saw the paper, he immediately realized the power of the picture in conveying something new and profound about physics. He sent it to everyone he knew, including a mathematician at the University of California at Berkeley named Stephen Smale. Smale had previously plotted out a set of differential equations that resulted in another famous map: the Smale

The beauty of a mathematical stutter: by
reiterating a mathematical equation again and
again, workers at the University of Maryland
record a pattern known as an Ikeda map,
which relates to the behavior of an electromagnetic
field. (© 1990 James Yorke)

horseshoe. To mathematicians, and later to physicists, the message implicit in those maps was both troubling and exciting. Each looping line was a noose around Laplacian notions of predictability, and yet each graphic representation suggested that there was some sort of mathematical regularity to chaos. And as computers got more powerful, so, too, did the graphic evidence of chaos.

While everyone, scientists included, reflexively tosses around the word "revolution" like pocket change to describe new theories (which might be great) and novel ideas (which might truly be new), some people—Yorke among them—suggest that the *mechanisms* of scientific inquiry in themselves create bigger revolutions, albeit stealthier ones that are more difficult to identify and categorize. Before about 1975 mathematicians typically created their maps and charts on the old-style green-striped computer paper, studying shaded patterns where X's represented one state and O's the other. "People would study which letters had the most ink," Yorke recalled, "so as to figure out how to get the shading as interesting as possible." It took two days to create the crudest picture. Ed Lorenz's Royal McBee computer could barely spit out its first butterfly.

"Computers before around 1975 were particularly good at investigating in detail something you basically understood already, okay?" Yorke says. "Getting more information. But if you had a phenomenon you *didn't* understand, the idea of trying one thing and then another thing was so difficult, the turnaround time was so slow, that you couldn't *play* with ideas. Now the turnaround time is *seconds*."

And that, Yorke believes, is the ultimate revolution. "People interested in hype have said that chaos is one of the three revolutions in twentieth-century physics, along with relativity and quantum mechanics. And some people"—his inflection perhaps casts Yorke with this latter lot—"disagree with that. . . . The *real* revolution in physics, if you want to take a broader view, is the computer. And it didn't start in 1950. It's really much more modern. . . . The idea of being able to represent the world in a computer is one thing. Then you have to get the information out, in this graphical way of charting the world." (An example of such a chart is the Ikeda map done by Yorke and his colleagues showing points generated by a mathematical expression.)

Those charts made chaos impossible to ignore. Chaos lives up to its name, if for no other reason than because it is inherently confusing. In a very strict mathematical sense, chaos refers to a nonrandom order in the midst of seeming disorder. On the one hand, it offers mathematical support for the idea that the behavior of a dynamic system over time—the motion of a pendulum or the weather—becomes so complex so quickly that there's no way to predict where it is finally going to end up. On the other hand, mathematicians have identified a kind of mathematical determinism at the heart of chaotic systems, which leads them to conclude that *some* of this chaotic behavior is actually predictable. That is the tease and paradox of chaos: predictably random, it is nonetheless randomly predictable.

Some physicists would probably like to keep chaos locked up in a box, because the infuriating thing about nonlinear dynamics is that it applies to *real* physical things. Yorke walked over to a cabinet behind his desk to illustrate the point. He pulled out a small plastic case with a handle, set it on his desk, and opened it up. This is among the most dubious of exercises for a mathematician, but among the most necessary and useful for nonmathematicians: show-and-tell.

Opening the case, Yorke extracted a C-clamp and two lengths of brushed metal, one orange and the other red. Crossing the room, he began to assemble these components and attach them to the edge of a table. It took about three minutes, and he stopped occasionally to take a tug from a diet Coke. When he finished, a funny-looking pendulum swung from the clamp. This is not the classic pendulum, the weighted object suspended from the ceiling and swinging back and forth. This is a double-jointed pendulum that swings, like a gymnast on the high bar, around a horizontal axis. For those of a certain age, it recalls a very common, and very cheap, toy from the 1950s in which a double-jointed trapeze artist can be made to buckle and flip forward and backward.

The pendulum, as James Gleick wrote in *Chaos: Making a New Science,* is "the laboratory mouse of the new science." Yorke's experiments study the behavior of a pendulum, but the pendulum he uses in his experiments is fictional. It swings back and forth in a computer. There are precise equations that describe the motions of a "forced damped pendulum" such as this (that is, one free to swing 360 degrees around the bar, but slowed down by friction); they take into account inertia, friction at the pivot, gravity, and several forms of torque that occur when force is applied. Beginning around 1986, Yorke and two colleagues, Celso Grebogi and Edward Ott, simply plugged hundreds of thousands of different initial conditions into these equations. The computer did the rest. (If nothing else, sophisticated computer programs have saved poor graduate students from the ignominious task of flipping a pendulum a million times.)

Yorke began to chart the behavior of this fictive pendulum. In the initial experiment, the pendulum, depending on how it was set in motion, would settle into one of two simple behaviors, or fates: it might flip clockwise or it might flip counterclockwise. Very simple. Two variables, or initial conditions, affected the ultimate fate of the pendulum: the angle at which the arm stood at the moment of release (the x), and the velocity at which it was traveling (the y). These initial conditions, the x and y, have the quality of geographical coordinates on a two-dimensional plane, such as a piece of paper; they can be translated into a specific point on this two-dimensional grid, and Yorke's computer logged each set of initial conditions and plotted each one of those points. Each point—each set of initial conditions, each x and y—produced a specific, unvarying destiny. If you released the arm at fifteen degrees and at a velocity of two meters per second, for example, it would always, without exception, arrive at the same inevitable fate. If you assigned a different color to each of these two fates, you thereby added a third dimension to the map: blue for clockwise, red for counterclockwise. The combination of coordinates for a system and its state (or fate) produces a map of what is called "phase space."

Yorke plotted out all the points, blue and red, and ended up with a striking two-tone swirl of phase space. Certain provinces of his map were rich in one color only, deep pools of red or slanting arms of blue. In chaos theory these are called basins of behavior. Just as water inevitably drains into one water basin or another, so initial conditions lie in one basin of behavior or another. By the time some five hundred thousand points were plotted, each assigned a color depending on the eventual behavior of the pendulum, Yorke was left with a magnificently marbled computer map of possible pendulum behaviors. It had all the grainy elegance of Florentine paper. The chart ended up on the cover of the October 30, 1987 issue of *Science,* and that cover went up on the wall of Jim Yorke's office. Right across from the pictures of Albert Einstein and Theda Bara, high on the opposite wall.

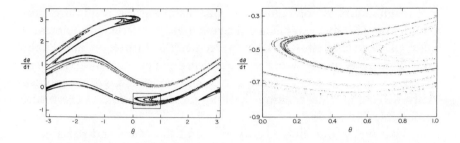

Destiny on the boundary: the behavior of an imaginary pendulum, plotted out in a chart *(left),* revealed that when the pendulum teetered between two physical fates, it actually rested on the border of all possible fates, as close examination of boxed boundary area *(right)* revealed. (J. Yorke/© 1987 AAAS)

The Maryland researchers then repeated their computer experiment, with a twist. By decreasing the force of the imaginary push to the pendulum, they introduced new fates. Under these new initial conditions, the pendulum would not always receive enough of a push to flip over. It would instead characteristically wobble lopsidedly on one side of vertical or the other. Two more fates, two more colors (yellow and green), one more map richer and more complex still in the swirl of its mingled destinies. It, too, went up on the wall.

Scientific maps and computer visualizations, like art, have the power and richness to disclose different messages over time. You live with them; you observe them out of the corner of your eye; you ignore them, fruitfully. After a while, if you're lucky and observant, you begin to see them all over again. They change their story. They contradict your assumptions. They surprise you. They reveal meaning, stingily, over time. Harold Urey, the Nobel Prize–winning chemist who later switched to astronomy, once remarked of a large map of the moon that filled a wall of his office, "You have to look at that picture for a year before you start to understand it."

Yorke began to understand. He stared at the *Science* cover on his wall, he glanced at it, he ignored it. If there is such a thing as visual osmosis, he experienced it. "You start seeing features there even months after you've been looking at it, features that you hadn't previously appreciated." The computer-generated picture revealed "basins of attraction"—two or four sinks of behavior—for the forced damped pendulum. Analyzing the image, Yorke and his colleagues reached the conclusion—this is the inherent conundrum of chaos—that you could not reach definitive, predictive conclusions about the pendulum's behavior. Laplace had established the rule that knowledge of the present state of a system allowed one to predict the future. "Chaos," the Maryland researchers wrote in the *Science* paper, "adds a basic new aspect to this rule: small errors in our knowledge can grow exponentially with time, thus making the long-term prediction of the future impossible."

That was a tidy little conclusion, and the Maryland researchers felt pretty good about it. Then, one time when Yorke was describing the work at a meeting, someone stood up and asked if the solid-color regions in the map of phase space were connected—a question about boundaries. Yorke and his colleagues hadn't thought about that. As Yorke puts it, "People tend to ask complicated questions, and the real art is to be able to ask simple questions." So the Maryland mathematicians asked a few simple questions, crossed the boundary into topology, and discovered that somebody had already done essentially the same experiment, and created the same map—without a computer, without a pendulum, without chaos, without colors, and nearly a century earlier.

No one seems to know much about the mysterious "Mr. Wada." He appears only in a cryptic footnote to a 1917 paper about continuous sets that appeared in a Japanese mathematical journal, a footnote that in its entirety reads: "This was informed to me by Mr. Wada." As far as Yorke or anyone else seems to know, he is not to be confused with the Wasan mathematician Yasushi Wada, although "Mr. Wada's" unusual example suggests that such confusion would not be philosophically out of line.

Modern historians have described the Japanese school of mathematics known as Wasan as "more of an art form than a field of scholarly inquiry." It was established in the seventeenth century and intellectually shaped by Seki Takakazu, who died in 1708. Wasan represented the kind of mathematics that preceded the influence of Western mathematics in Japan. Wasan was among the purest of intellectual inquiries, and its practitioners did not presume that their work connected with, or illuminated, either philosophy or any of the natural sciences. It emphasized the puzzlelike qualities of mathematics, and was a leisure activity pursued by samurai, peasants, and merchants. Indeed, in publishers' catalogues from the period, books about Wasan are listed in the same section with flower arranging and the tea ceremony. And yet one of the leading Wasan mathematicians, Yoshita

Kurushima, is said to have found "Euler's function" before Euler and "Laplace's expansion" before Laplace.

The latter-day Mr. Wada explored a fascinating problem in topology, the mathematics of complex sets. The problem begins with simple geography and quickly attains abstract and wild ramification. Here is the situation he envisaged (like a certain television mogul, we will take the liberty of colorizing Wada's black-and-white cartoon to make it more vivid, as did Yorke in a recent paper).

Wada proposed the existence of an island in the middle of an ocean of red water. The island possessed two round lakes, equal in size, in its interior; one lake was blue, the other green. An industrious master builder, Wada decided to construct a series of very precise mathematical canals on the island. He built one canal that connected the ocean to the interior, its red waters snaking through the island in such a way that no point of land was more than an arbitrary unit of distance from the red canal (it could be one mile or one "wada"; the unit makes no difference). Next, Wada and his imaginary corps of engineers built a second, narrower channel from the blue lake, plotting its path in such a way that any point of remaining land was no more than one-half "mile" from blue water. Next Wada dug a canal from the green lake, and plotted this very waterway in a path that snaked through the remaining land, such that it was never more than one-quarter "mile" from any point of remaining land.

Now Wada was a perfectionist, so he went back to the red canal, and lengthened it a little so it was within one-eighth of a mile of all remaining land; and then lengthened the blue by one-sixteenth of a mile, and the green by one-thirty-second of a mile, and so on. Indeed, he went back and by turns lengthened each canal an infinite number of times, and by the time he had finished, the only land that remained was lines—the boundaries, in effect, between the different canals.

The red and blue and green canals left a very pretty swirl of three colors. From a mathematical—and, more pertinently, a topological— point of view, you would be left with a surveyor's nightmare and a delightful paradox. Wada proved that any point on the boundary between two canals must lie on the boundary between all three. If the point teetered between two colors, it had to touch all three, without exception. This odd subdivision in the real estate of mathematics went by the name of the "Lakes of Wada." Kunizo Yoneyama cited it in his 1917 article in the English-language *Tohoku Mathematical Journal*. And then it was almost totally forgotten, a fate that seems equally to apply to Mr. Wada.

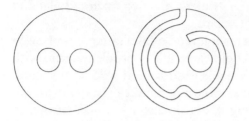

Construction of the Lakes of Wada, first described in 1917, produces a mathematical map with exactly the same topological properties as the physical map of pendulum behavior. "These basins of Wada," James A. Yorke says, "tell us how strange reality is."

The Lakes of Wada, of course, had no more relevance to the real world than those advertisements of Arizona lake sites. They simply represented an interesting topological exercise. They lay there, one more brainteaser in a dusty book, for decades. And then Jim Yorke kept staring at a picture on his office wall, and kept thinking, and the Lakes of Wada—weird, implausible, counterintuitive maps about the nature of physical reality—began to seem not so much like an aberration. They began to seem real.

Yorke vaguely remembers having heard of the Lakes of Wada at some point, but he was reminded of the example when he began to collaborate with a topologist, Judy Kennedy, to help make sense of the patterns. For some reason most of the people who study this type of topology seem to come from either the American South or Poland; Kennedy studied at Auburn in her native Alabama, though she now teaches at the University of Delaware. To Kennedy, who knew of the Wada example, "the whole thing seemed very Japanese. . . . It reminded me of Oriental painting." With a little work, Kennedy and Yorke found that their pendulum chart had a lot in common with Wada's mysterious canals.

"Now the mathematicians who investigated this property were looking at a very peculiar kind of figure, and Wada's conception was obviously a labored construction," Yorke says now. "But what we have found is that in the studies of the pendulum, this Wada behavior necessarily occurs without any construction on our part. We just look and see this chart, and that chart is showing us a Wada construction."

Twirling and tweaking his pendulum in a Floating Point Systems 264 computer, running it on his own custom-made program, coloring in the results with the help of a Cray supercomputer, Yorke began processing the data from roughly five hundred thousand computer-generated pendulum fates and dipping into his computer palette to assign a color to each of the four separate behavioral fates. The computer image would inch across the screen, composing this multicolor map. A few years ago, it took a week to create and process one of the images out in California; now it takes twenty minutes to extrude one from a desktop DEC unit in Yorke's office.

Like good topologists, they zeroed in on the boundaries. To see if the Wada property held up, Yorke and Kennedy zoomed in on one section of the map and kept blowing it up. They made 216 maps, each one enlarging a portion of boundary from the previous map, each one showing the same boundary in greater and greater detail (see color illustrations). The last image had magnified the border one hundred thousand times from the initial map. At each successive enlargement, the colors alone betrayed the muddy, crossed destinies. "This'll show you what we saw," Yorke said, spreading a visual synopsis of the results on the carpet in his office—some two dozen images, each a blowup of the one before. Some of the swirls resembled those "paint-ings" one does by squirting colors on a spinning turntable; some looked like the rings of Saturn. It was a mathematician's abstract version of Antonioni's film *Blow-Up,* except that instead of discovering a perpetrator, they discovered a paradox.

"One of the ideas is, if you're given a velocity and a starting angle for the pendulum, but not *exactly,* one possibility is that you're well into one of these basins, and then you know what basin you're in. But if you're simply near the boundary, you have *no* information as to what basin you will end up in. You cannot reduce it. You cannot say, 'Well, at least here the boundaries were between the colors red and blue.' Instead, once you're near blue and red, you must also be near green and yellow." To profane the conclusion in more popular terms, if you're on the cusp of becoming either Einstein or Mao, you must be equally close to becoming Theda Bara or Humphrey Bogart. "Looking at the pictures is what told us that these properties exist. And without making these pictures, people had no idea of what these things looked like," Yorke said.

Staring down at the pictures covering his office floor, Yorke was asked if this peculiar boundary property had any resonance beyond the imaginary landscape of Wada. Could you say anything about *non-mathematical* fate, about destinies in general, on the basis of these pictures?

"Well . . ." Yorke began tentatively, which is about the only way physicists generalize, at least about something as peculiar as Wada's lakes. "Well, what you would expect philosophically, or naïvely, is that if you had four different possible fates, and you knew a lot about your state, you could probably figure out what your fate was. Well, we agree with that. But if you were in a borderline case, then you would expect, probably, to be able to tell which of the two fates you have. You would cut the list down to two. Whereas what we're saying here is that it's possible that if you can't pin it down to one fate, then you have *no* idea. All fates remain possible."

The question was reframed and asked again: could that idea be generalized to something more than the behavior of a fictitious pendulum?

Jim Yorke paused quite a while; the ghost of Laplace haunts every mathematical utterance along these lines. "Well," he said finally, "what we are saying is not that this is always the case. That's certainly not true." A pause, then in a voice more conspiratorial than scientific, more whisper than pronouncement: "But this is a likely possibility."

The Lakes of Wada, mathematical mirages for nearly a century, came fully to life in May of 1990, when James Yorke and Judy Kennedy addressed a meeting in Los Alamos, New Mexico, with the title "Non-linear Science: The Next Decade." They described their work. They reviewed Wada's work through the lens of chaos and strange attractors, and rechristened them the "basins of Wada." They showed a movie, their Wada version of *Blow-Up*.

For all its popular cachet, chaos and its spin-offs still don't get respect in some quarters—not always from the precinct of pure mathematics, not from scientists peering with bewilderment from other disciplines, not from cultural observers. Vivian Sobchack, a film scholar at the University of California-Santa Cruz, attacked chaos theory in a recent issue of *Artforum* as "yet another historically specific manifestation of the logic that informs post-Modern cultural production—a logic based on paradox, recursivity, multiplicity, a simultaneous fetishizing and trivializing of difference, and a consequent homogenization of populations that are actually heterogeneous into a totalized 'mass' culture." With enemies like that, Yorke suggests in reply, we must be doing something right.

They are. The Lakes of Wada experiment is emblematic—both thematically and graphically—of the changes visualization has wrought in mathematics and physics. And Yorke believes that all kinds of *strange* charts, with all sorts of unlikely connections to physical nature, are going to come out.

"My view is that there are very strange, *very* strange concepts that we find hard to fathom, which are quite applicable to reality. And we have to discover these strange relationships. Things so strange that you can't imagine them. Like the idea of four regions and the boundary having this Wada property. We are all limited in imagination. We are able to look out a little further, but we don't know what to look at. And five hundred years from now, our concepts of reality will be *extremely* different—different in ways that we can't imagine. Just like Einstein, sitting in a patent office, had the imagination to reimagine the universe, we should be spending more time on the more difficult aspects of the field, and looking for the more meaningful ideas. These basins of Wada tell us how strange reality is."

15. Stiff Tracks

THE CARTOGRAPHY OF
SUBATOMIC PARTICLES IN DETECTORS

‖‖‖‖‖

I am happy to eat Chinese with
theorists, but to spend your life
doing what they tell you is
a waste of time.

—Samuel Ting,
physicist

With trepidation and embarrassment as a science writer, I begin this chapter with an unusual confession: I have always found the world of particle physics a bit like a Russian novel-in-progress, with too many oddly named characters and not enough plot resolution in sight. Never more so, I suppose, than one morning in 1990 when I brought my car to a halt in a parking lot located just east of the Sand Hill Road exit of Interstate 280 in Northern California, about forty minutes south of San Francisco. I paused to look at the lovely California countryside, and tried to reconcile this view with the fact that everything within sight line and earshot—the rolling hillside nearby, its residual geometry suggestive of a long-ago orchard; all the profuse vegetation, from scrub oak and wildflowers to daisies and goldenrod; that light pole in the parking lot; the mountains to the east, rising irregularly toward Mount Diablo; the trucks laboring up Sand Hill Road from Palo Alto; the campanile of the nearby Stanford campus; an airplane on final descent to San Francisco International Airport and the air through which it flew; and a bird beating its wings in the thick, invisible, buoyant batter of air molecules closer by; that same batter bearing the voices of several Spanish-speaking gentlemen gathered purposively around a lawnmower; the lawnmower itself, and the lawn itself, and every lumbering annelid making its way between blades of grass—all of these things, animate and not, were at their very essence confections of quarks and leptons and all the other peculiarly named protagonists in the seeming fiction known as subatomic physics. And all the things around me—birds and planes and gardeners and sounds—reflected the essence of the research that took place a few feet beneath this bucolic setting.

I was standing just outside the Stanford Linear Accelerator Center (SLAC), where in a below-ground chamber the fundamental particles of matter that conspire to compose this pastoral and quotidian beauty are daily smacked together in an effort to identify the subvisible brick and mortar out of which is built everything we see and experience, including a past that leads back to the creation of the universe and the creation of these very particles.

In this panorama around me, too, I could discern, or at least infer, the four fundamental forces of nature that physicists are trying to unify. First was the electromagnetic force, in the form of light waves bathing my retina with the California countryside. Next came gravity, pulling on that jumbo jet. The protons and neutrons of every atom composing every object within eyesight, and the quarks of which they were made, were held together by something called the strong force. And finally, in the ground beneath my feet, I presumed the existence of the odd atom of rare earth in the dirt, firing off random particles as part of its normal radioactive decay, reflecting a process called the weak force.

The weak force turned out to be strong enough to attract me to Northern California. The weak force, like the other three forces of nature, is transmitted by ghostly particles known collectively as gauge bosons, particles that invisibly enforce the physical rules governing subatomic commerce. Light has its photons, gravity its gravitons, the strong force its gluons—all particles that act almost like physical accountants, balancing local accounts in such fundamental interactions as isospin and conservation of energy and conservation of charge. In the case of the weak force, these particles are known as W-plus, W-minus, and Z-zero, and here in Palo Alto and elsewhere, great effort (to say nothing of taxpayer expense) attended the study of those Z particles. To hear physicists talk, Z particles may provide the missing characters and resolve the unresolved conflicts in this Russian novel of the sciences, may in fact be a way to take steps toward the ultimate goal of physics: a simple, straightforward, elegant, and universal Theory of Everything (an equation for the universe that would fit, as one physicist predicted, on a T-shirt).

Then again, according to Wolfgang Pauli, the late physicist and curmudgeon, it may not turn out to be that simple. "If a theoretician says 'universal,' " he once remarked, "it just means 'pure nonsense.' "

The problem for me—and possibly for other lay observers—is that particle physics' genealogy chart has always seemed hopelessly confusing. To Democritus it was simply "atoms and void." To modern physicists it is—well, here's an example from Michael Riordan's eminently readable *The Hunting of the Quark*:

> Leptons and quarks come in distinct "generations," each with four members. The first generation contains the electron and its neutrino, plus the up and down quarks; the second includes the muon, its own neutrino, plus the strange and charmed quarks. Quarks appear in three different colors, while leptons are colorless. All these spin-½ matter particles interact with one another by swapping another family of twelve spin-1, force-carrying particles that are intimately related by gauge field theory: a photon carrying the electromagnetic, the W and Z particles carrying the weak, and the eight colored gluons carrying the strong force.

I suppose if you had to sum up *War and Peace* in one paragraph, it would sound similarly incoherent. On the other hand, University of Michigan physicist Martinus J. G. Veltman once mused that there seemed to be so many particles that "it is amazing a person can even see the stars on a clear night!"

In any event, I had come to SLAC for a reason. I had seen computer-generated graphics that recorded the collisions between atomic particles in laboratories like this one, and the pictures struck me as nothing less than a kind of subatomic cartography, a brief geographic sketch of colliding matter in an exquisitely well-defined and calibrated spatial domain—quite possibly the best-defined, most scrupulously measured and monitored three-dimensional space in the history of civilization, or at least this side of angels on pins. And so I wondered if one might be able to view particle physics as an increas-

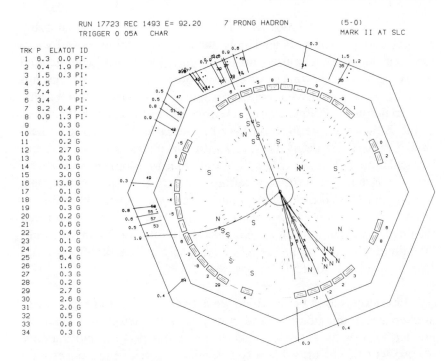

RUN 17723 REC 1493 E= 92.20   7 PRONG HADRON   (5-0)
TRIGGER 0 05A   CHAR   MARK II AT SLC

TRK P ELATOT ID
1   6.3 0.0 PI-
2   0.4 1.9 PI·
3   1.5 0.3 PI·
4   4.5   PI-
5   7.4   PI·
6   3.4   PI-
7   8.2 0.4 PI·
8   0.9 1.3 PI-
9   0.3 G
10   0.1 G
11   0.2 G
12   2.7 G
13   0.3 G
14   0.1 G
15   3.0 G
16   13.8 G
17   0.1 G
18   0.2 G
19   0.3 G
20   0.2 G
21   0.6 G
22   0.4 G
23   0.1 G
24   0.2 G
25   6.4 G
26   1.6 G
27   0.3 G
28   0.2 G
29   2.7 G
30   2.6 G
31   2.0 G
32   0.5 G
33   0.8 G
34   0.3 G

Searching for Zs: the particles last a trillionth of a trillionth of a second, but their disintegration etches lines on the blank map of the detector and their tracks are captured permanently by computers. (SLAC)

---

ingly sophisticated exercise in map interpretation. The physicists didn't make these maps. The particles did. Physicists merely spent billions of dollars to provide the blank paper.

The particle of the hour turned out to be the aforementioned Z-zero particle. One of those ghostly gauge bosons, it was first glimpsed in 1983 at the European Laboratory for Particle Physics, known as CERN, by a group headed by Carlo Rubbia. The particle was peculiar enough, rare enough, heavy enough, and important enough to incite fevered construction of new machines costing tens, even hundreds of millions of dollars, both here at Stanford and abroad. Why so much money for such tiny particles? The official reason was that, with enough power, these machines could create many Z particles; and with enough Z particles, physicists could pin down once and for all the subatomic genealogy chart of the physical world. The more ambitious reason was that they might stumble upon a particle known as the Higgs boson.

Proposed in the 1960s by a mild-mannered University of Edinburgh physicist named Peter Higgs, the enigmatic Higgs boson was a theoretical particle conjured up to tie up a loose end in unification theories ("So loose is this loose end," wrote *Nature* in 1983, "that it is not even clear whether the Higgs mechanism is a particle or a 'mathematical fiction'—a fudge factor"). It is the ultimate prey to be snatched in the Z factories, because on very rare occasions—or so it is theorized—Z particles decay fleetingly into the Higgs particle, and this particular particle may explain the nature of mass. Some people believe it is the last major particle awaiting capture. It is one of the main reasons the United States and other nations may spend $8 billion to build the superconducting super collider in Texas. "When I consider the huge sums going for this," Higgs said not long ago in an interview, "the lifetimes spent on the search, I can't help but think: 'Good heavens, what have I done?' "

Physics has long been a dialogue between theory and experiment, mathematical imagination and nuts-and-bolts detection. Theorists predict, experimentalists see; theorists can still perform cutting-edge science with chalk on a blackboard, while experimentalists can "do physics" only by building the largest and most expensive tools in the history of science, monstrous machines capable of capturing ineffably brief events. For most of the twentieth century, it seems the theorists have kept a decade or so ahead of the experimentalists, who, in addition to tackling the difficulties of subatomic visualization, must also negotiate the perils of public funding, political debate, and fine-scale engineering, any one of which is enough to set a project a decade behind schedule. For all that, experimentalists stay close to the ground, and the field goes nowhere without them. "You have to remember that theoretical physicists are parasites," Howard Georgi, a theoretical physicist, once remarked. "The people that do the real work are experimenters."

From the moment in 1895 when Wilhelm Roentgen noticed the ghostly shadows that X rays cast on photographic film, one could idiosyncratically view the progress of particle physics over the ensuing century as the creation of increasingly sophisticated maps of the trajectories left by atomic particles in transit. So the task of the experimentalists has been to design a quantifiable geography, a blank but booby-trapped landscape, upon which particles leave unambiguous and measurable signatures. This is not the standard way of explaining particle physics, of course, especially since it slights theory. But it allows the history of particle detection to be told as a succession of increasingly refined graphics.

Particles, whether hurled out of modern accelerators or dribbling off a chunk of radium or, like cosmic rays, zipping by unpredictably from the sun or a supernova, leave a trail as they plow through matter. They leave wakes, they create ions, they decay and disintegrate. As physicists have graduated to finer and finer scales of measurement, the frames about their maps, and the particles passing through them, have become tinier, shorter-lived, and better-defined. This process of stalking the atom can be said to have begun little less than a century ago, when in 1897 J. J. Thomson identified some negatively charged "corpuscles" boiling off a cathode-ray tube in a vacuum; they would become known as electrons. A decade later a rough-edged Kiwi named Ernest Rutherford initiated a set of experiments that can be seen as the rough-edged prototype of modern nuclear physics experiments: he did not simply create a collision, he surrounded it with an experimentally controlled geography of measurement that allowed him to infer secrets about the interior of the atom.

As a source of particles, Rutherford and his assistants, Hans Geiger and Ernest Marsden, used a small bit of radium that unleashed a spray of alpha particles. Unlike particles in today's accelerators, these particles were not whipped up to great speed and high energy; they were simply shed during radium's radioactive decay, nonetheless zipping along at thousands of miles per hour. To measure the degree of scattering, Rutherford placed a thin foil of gold near the radium. Some of the alpha particles managed to hit the foil. Rutherford expected that most of the alpha particles would pass straight through the foil, but he hoped some would be deflected, for that would give clues to the atomic structure of the gold. To detect any deflections, the experimenters placed a phosphorescent screen made out of zinc sulphide, which would display a brief flash of light whenever hit by one of the alpha particles. At first, they placed the screen behind the foil, as a backdrop. But Rutherford made a crucial experimental decision—a geographic one, if you will. It was his idea to place the screen *in front of* the target as well; this allowed them to detect any particles that hit the gold foil and bounced straight back. That is exactly what happened—not often, just once in eight thousand times, but that was often enough to startle even a gruff and skeptical intellect like Rutherford's. Rutherford is said to have professed shock at this ("It was almost as if you fired a fifteen-inch shell at a piece of tissue paper and it came back and hit you!" is his famous remark), but in fact he had anticipated some type of scattering.

The alpha particles bounced back because they had struck something hard in the gold foil; that "something hard" turned out to be the nucleus of gold atoms, as Rutherford formally proposed in 1912. It would take decades for the rest of this initial model to assume its familiar configuration—not until 1920 did Rutherford place the proton in the nucleus and not until 1932 would James Chadwick discover the neutron, in effect completing the first-draft architecture of the atom as a hard nut of protons and neutrons surrounded by a nearly empty mist of electrons. It bespeaks the power of visualization that this defunct model, outdated now by half a century of high-powered parsing of the atom, still persists as a cultural icon recognizable in everything from corporate logos to neon signs to the symbol of the equally defunct Atomic Energy Commission.

With those very first experiments, Rutherford, Geiger, and Marsden essentially invented particle physics's two-word vocabulary for exploring the atom: *collisions* occurred whenever beams of particles could be focused on (and later hurled at) a target, and *detectors* surrounded these collisions with a spatial domain within which the paths of decomposing particles could be visualized, analyzed, and characterized.

Another word of geographical flavor is *tracks,* and it entered the scientific vocabulary with the discovery of the first sophisticated detector: the cloud chamber. Discovery more than invention seems to capture the process undertaken by Charles T. R. Wilson, for during an 1894 visit to the Ben Nevis Meteorological Observatory in Scotland he had marveled at the optical effects of the sun interacting with cloud formations, such as the corona, and rushed back to the Cavendish labs in Cambridge to try to imitate them. By 1895 he had created a dust-free chamber filled with moist, water-saturated air, and with the quick increase of volume provided by a piston, he could mimic cloud formation and even precipitation. In a detour so typical of great scientific discoveries, Wilson one day decided out of curiosity to observe the effects of X rays passing through his man-made cumuli. One thing led to another, and by 1911 he had managed to photograph "little wisps and threads of clouds" that formed when X rays streaked through the artificial clouds. What happened was this: As a ray—cosmic ray or X ray—passed through the supersaturated water vapor, it knocked electrons off the water molecules in its path, creating ions; and ions were

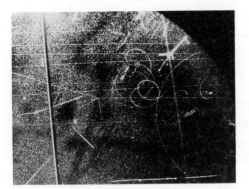

Atomic particles first left "tracks" a century ago when C. T. R. Wilson noticed "little wisps and threads of clouds," like the ones at left, in his cloud chambers. (Brookhaven National Laboratory)

seeds around which water condensed, producing a visible line much like the condensed-water trail left by a jet airplane high in the sky. The line followed a particular trajectory through the volume of the chamber. Wilson called it a "track," and so they have been called ever since.

With magnets and electrodes, experimenters make these particles bend and curve, and take pictures of their trajectories; from these images they can deduce the physical characteristics of particles, such as charge (positive or negative), mass, and life-span. In August of 1932, using a cloud chamber in the Caltech laboratory of Robert Millikan, Carl Anderson detected the track of a particle that seemed to curl in a magnetic field in exactly the opposite way that an electron does. This particle turned out to be the positron, the positively charged equivalent of the electron. A surprising trajectory thus led physics into the age of antiparticles (as theorists in 1928 had predicted it would). Poring over the fuzzy cloud chamber pictures like hunters reading animal tracks in melting snow, physicists continued to bag new prey: mesons, kaons, and other increasingly exotic seedlings of matter.

As detectors improved, scientists turned to the collisions and tried to figure out how to make them bigger, better, and more energetic. Until the late 1940s, physicists essentially took what nature gave them. Since cosmic rays and radioactive decay were the only sources of energized particles, physicists mounted expeditions to mountaintop observatories, hauling their cloud chambers up the Alps and the Pyrenees and Pikes Peak, the better to capture those rare cosmic rays. But they wanted ever-harder, ever-more-explosive collisions, and that need ushered in the era of the man-made colliders.

Particle accelerators—"atom smashers," to employ a term

fraught with the everyman awe of the time—marked a decisive change in nuclear physics. Maturing as the technology did after the conclusion of World War II, the era of atom smashers began principally as an American adventure. The science required big machines; big machines required large budgets and supportive bureaucracies; and high-energy physicists became almost overnight a strange army of egghead pilgrims, scurrying to collect data at the sites of these huge technological shrines.

The era began at Berkeley, where in 1930, Ernest O. Lawrence's group at the University of California built the first circular accelerator, known as a cyclotron; the guts of the prototype, a four-inch magnet, fit in the palm of one's hand. The cyclotron gave circulating electrons a kick of energy each time around the track, so that when they finally were routed toward a collision, they had accumulated great energies— energies that sounded even more impressive than they were because they were measured in a vanishingly small unit known as the electron volt. With larger and larger models, Lawrence's cyclotrons attained energies of 80,000 electron volts, then 1 million, then about 10 million. In 1949 the Berkeley group built its "Synchrocyclotron" and promptly discovered its first particle, the neutral pion.

The names of these machines somehow capture the optimism and omnipotence with which technology was deified in postwar America— an etymology of awe-inspiring, can-do, technological brawn. Brookhaven National Laboratory on Long Island had its Cosmotron (1952). Berkeley had the Bevatron (1955), the "BEV" coming from "billion electron volts." In 1960 the Europeans joined the parade with a 28-GeV machine at CERN, the Proton Synchrotron in Geneva. The Fermi National Accelerator Laboratory (Fermilab) in Illinois would later build its Tevatron. And in 1966, Stanford University went on-line with its own linear accelerator. Unlike in biology or chemistry or any of the earth sciences, if you wanted to do an experiment in particle physics, you had to go to Berkeley or Geneva or Palo Alto or Long Island or Chicago, or, in later years, to Hamburg or Russia. There were about half a dozen places on earth to which physics' pilgrims migrated; and given the size, complexity, and expense of these structures, it is not frivolous to see them, as Fermilab's Robert Wilson once suggested, as twentieth-century echoes of the Gothic cathedrals of the Middle Ages: they reflected the cultural theology of their time, required political (and, to a degree, social) consensus for their construction, involved economic sacrifice of a communal rather than private sort, and promised eternal answers to fundamental questions. If God

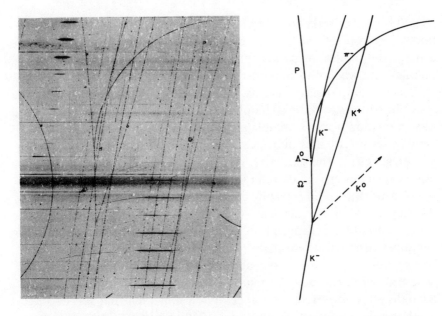

Beer did not inspire the invention of the bubble chamber, but it did figure in
its testing. The bubble chamber image *(left)* and the schematic map interpretation *(right)* proved the discovery of the omega-minus particle, which
disintegrates after one ten-billionth of a second. (Brookhaven National Laboratory)

is in the details, then particle detectors became the ultimate altars of
science.

With high-energy nuclear physics came the need for more sensitive detectors. The cloud chamber could no longer handle the job.
With the more powerful particles, it would need to be one hundred
yards high to measure tracks accurately. In 1952, Donald Glaser of the
University of Michigan solved the problem by inventing the bubble
chamber. Glaser's device operated on a principle almost exactly the
opposite of Wilson's: whereas liquid droplets formed tracks in the gas
of the cloud chamber, bubbles of gas formed tracks in the liquid of the
bubble chamber. The liquid had to be stable, with low surface tension,
high vapor pressure, and yet be maintained on the very edge of boiling;
into this edgy liquid, usually supercooled hydrogen or diethyl ether,
would fly a particle, creating its trail of ions and igniting a linear burst
of boiling—that is, a thin track of bubbles. (It is not true that Glaser
got the inspiration for this discovery from watching beer bubbles rise
in a mug, but it is true that he tested the idea by firing particle rays at

heated bottles of soda and beer.) Bubble chambers served as the work-horse detectors of the 1950s and 1960s, and as sprays of particles generated by collisions passed through the liquid, they created paths of bubbles that when photographed revealed tracks, trajectories, strange curlicues, telling disintegrations.

The prototype bubble chamber was but a few cubic centimeters in size, providing a mere thimble's worth of data, but as the chambers grew in sensitivity and dimension, they gave physicists a superb geo-graphical edge in the sense that they offered more volume, and thus a more capacious spatial domain in which to visualize tracks; a ten-day accelerator run would typically generate 1 million images for analysis. As they came into wider use—Luis Alvarez lashed a six-foot-long, five-hundred-liter hydrogen bubble chamber to Berkeley's Bevatron—volunteer armies of "scanners" were recruited among students and housewives to pore over photographs of tracks in search of telltale footprints of particles. In just such a way, Nicholas Samios's team at Brookhaven discovered a "strange" baryon in 1964 that set the stage for the prediction of quarks. Between 1950 and 1970, aided immensely by these new forms of visualization, physicists identified more than a hundred new subnuclear particles. Enrico Fermi, in a comment that strikes sympathetic vibrations far outside the field, once complained, "If I could remember the names of all these particles, I'd have become a botanist instead of a physicist."

And still the garden grew. In 1964 theorist Murray Gell-Mann proposed the existence of an entirely new beast of a subatomic particle and chided the experimenters by saying, "Why don't you look for them experimentally if you want them to be real?" Ten years later, using the new generation of detectors, Burton Richter of Stanford and Samuel Ting of MIT did just that. But Gell-Mann was the one who named it. He called it the quark.

The very fact that quarks could be predicted and then found gave physicists a great deal of confidence. Physicist Leon Lederman, winner of the Nobel Prize and former director of Fermilab, wrote in a 1981 article for *GEO* magazine that the goal of particle physics "is nothing less than a complete, consistent, and unified theory that fully explains how the universe works. Once perfected, such a theory will enable scientists to understand the functioning and history of our cosmos right back to the fireball that started it all, to account for all the observations and measurements in the present, and to predict how the universe will evolve in the future.

"There is a widely held belief," he added, "that total success is close at hand."

This confidence stemmed from the fact that, beginning in the early 1970s, physicists availed themselves of the revolution in electronics to construct an entirely new genre of detector. Before, they had been intercepting just part of what was exploding outward. By the 1970s, to use a crude analogy, they arranged for their collisions to take place inside huge metallic cans, stuffed with layers of detectors so sensitive that the entire volume of space within became a kind of geographical entity—a blank three-dimensional map that, with each collision, was instantly etched with the tracks of decaying particles, traveling at a measurable speed, heading in a measurable direction.

By the time the dust settled, briefly, at the end of the 1970s, physicists believed the universe could be explained with twenty-four particles: leptons, six in all, were the light and swirling particles typified by the electron and its cousins, while the quarks, also six in number, combined in various ways to form protons and neutrons, the heavier particles in the nucleus. And since theory demanded that each and every quark and lepton have its antimatter particle, there were twelve antiparticles as well, from the positron to the antiquark. It would be fruitless here to provide biographies of all these particles, from the tau neutrino to the charmed quarks (there are several superior book-length histories describing these discoveries, including *The Second Creation* by Robert Crease and Charles Mann and *The Hunting of the Quark* by Michael Riordan); suffice it to say that the electron, the electron neutrino, and up and down quarks make up every bit of matter humans can see, feel, taste, and smell.

The other families—at least two, maybe more—were like unseen relatives, yet they attracted the most attention. They lived at high energies, vanished almost immediately, and were archaic in the sense that they promised to reflect the nature of matter at the beginning of the universe. Indeed, the energies required for their formation occurred only during, or shortly after, the Big Bang, and so experimentalists aspired to nothing less than modest, short-lived emulations of the Big Bang in their detectors. In one such collision, as predicted, Carlo Rubbia's team at CERN discovered that first Z-zero particle in 1983, setting off a new frenzy of anticipation and competition.

The Z "particle" is not a constituent of matter. Rather, it is a bearer of force—a gauge boson, one of several ghostlike particles that impart the four known forces. If we imagine gravity as a force that holds the moon in orbit around the earth, physicists argue, there must be a very brisk traffic between the two objects in the form of a particle called the graviton that carries this force back and forth; unfortunately, the graviton is one of those characters yet to make an appearance. The weak force is carried by three "intermediate vector bosons": W-plus, W-minus, and Z-zero. Of these three, the Z particle attracted great attention because physicists realized it might provide an avenue to the answer of even bigger, more fundamental questions. One had to do with being able to impose a rigorous mathematical population control on the number of atomic families. The other involved the potential for detecting that enigmatic, possibly nonexistent particle known as the Higgs boson. The Higgs particle might explain nothing less than why things are heavy, why they have mass.

The future in a sense was already mapped out, not only by the scientific hunt for the Higgs but in very broad and predictive cartoons of interaction known as Feynman diagrams. They tell physicists what to look for. "Now some people are looking for some very odd signature that would indicate something strange is going on," said Michael Riordan of SLAC, sketching out the Feynman diagram on the blackboard in his office. It looked like this:

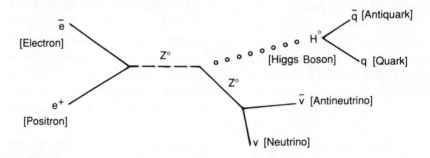

"This is the Holy Grail of physics," he said. "This is a Nobel Prize–winning signal."

As scientists routinely do, they hailed the Z particles as the Rosetta stones and Holy Grails of the decade. And so commenced the race to build accelerators that would become known as "Z factories." Nearly a decade after Leon Lederman wrote that the answer was near at hand, Stanford physicist John Rees dusted off that optimistic sentiment in a *Scientific American* article published in 1989. "Physicists," he wrote, "believe they are on the verge of having a complete theory of matter."

The race to create a Z factory turned high-energy physics into, as one Nobel Prize–winning physicist later put it, "a soap opera—like *Dallas*." As in other scientific disciplines, the battle could be seen to represent (among other things) the slow transition from an American-dominated postwar field of endeavor to one where the international community played an equal, sometimes dominant, role. In 1981 the fourteen-nation European consortium at CERN approved $1 billion for construction of a state-of-the-art Large Electron-Positron collider (LEP), scheduled to be completed by 1989 and designed to produce Z particles in abundance. In an ill-disguised attempt to steal CERN's thunder, a Stanford group headed by Burton Richter won funding for a "cheap," $115 million machine, a new type of accelerator—a bargain-basement Z factory, as it were. The race was on.

Travelers on Interstate 280 south of San Francisco are familiar with the original structure of the Stanford Linear Accelerator; it is that long, square-shaped structure that looks like a luge run and descends a little more than two miles through hills and under the highway near Palo Alto. When it was originally conceived and constructed in the 1960s, electrons were hurled down the length of this tube at nearly the speed of light until they struck a stationary target, producing great flares of fragments and significant physics.

But in the particle physics game, higher energy grants experimenters access to a new atomic landscape in which they can discover new and different tracks, and so, in the late 1970s, Richter proposed a radical new architecture of collision to get more energy: he wanted to channel the speeding particles into a newly built add-on at the bottom of the linear accelerator run—two curving, caliperlike arms extending on either side, one bearing electrons, the other positrons, bending these two beams around until they collided head-on, producing a flash of energy. As in any collision, from protons to Porsches, the amount of energy released increases when it is head-on; because of quantum physics, head-on collisions of particles briefly increase the energy by a factor of ten. In the case of the Stanford Linear Collider (SLC), as the beast would be called, particles hitting each other head-on could reach energies approaching 90 billion electron volts—the predicted energy at which Z particles formed.

Simply by creating the head-on collision, the Stanford mechanism upped its energy capacity to the neighborhood where Z particles lived, briefly. The ground rules for attaining higher energy levels follow Einstein's famous equation about energy and mass, $E = mc^2$. Einstein showed that energy (E) equals mass (m) times the speed of light

The most elaborate instruments of measurement on earth: electrons and positrons are hurled down the two-mile-long linear accelerator at Stanford *(left)* before colliding inside huge detectors like the recently retired Mark II *(right)*. (SLAC)

squared (c²). Put another way, energy and mass are two forms of the same thing, so when a powerful accelerator upped the value of E in the equation, that inevitably increased the likelihood of creating and finding particles with a higher m, or greater mass, as well. The Z-zero particle had great mass. In fact, it was predicted to be the heaviest known particle.

But massiveness carries a considerable experimental price. The heavier the particle, the shorter the lifespan. Z-zero particles, coalescing out of the pure energy of the collision, vanished in 10^{-25} seconds—a trillionth of a trillionth of a second. The Stanford group used a sensitive detector, called the Mark II, to pick up the Z. "The maps we make are of how it decays, which is a way to work back to what it was before it decayed," says Riordan. It worked like this.

Imagine for a moment that you are a Northern California electron. At the westernmost end of what Stanford people call "the world's longest building," you are sent flying down the luge run in a copper vacuum tube four inches in diameter. Along the way you pass more than 240 booster stations known as klystrons, which, drawing on the power that runs SLAC's monthly electric bills up to about $1 million, whip you up toward the speed of light. Each klystron generates a wave of electromagnetic energy, and like any good California electron, you surf on the crest of this wave. You are not alone. Something like 50 billion electrons gather in bunches, typically some 120 bunches per second, each about the size of a flea (one-tenth of a millimeter across, less than a millimeter long), all surfing down this four-inch copper tube. By the time you reach the Beam Switchyard at the bottom of the two-mile pike, you have been roused to an energy of about 50 billion electron volts. Powerful magnets at the switchyard steer you and an adjacent lane of positrons into opposite directions, and guide you around the curving arms. As an electron, you take the northern arm; positrons come up from the south. A series of magnets tug and squeeze and pack you into a tight, "luminous" beam. After the whole trip, lasting all of a hundredth of a millisecond, you are destined to meet inside the Collider Experiment Hall, at that wonderful rendezvous spot called the Interaction Point, traveling nearly at the speed of light. With any luck, you are about to disintegrate into a Z particle. And since time slows down when you are traveling at the speed of light, this is a good moment to hop off the wave and view what happens next from the outside.

When I first set foot in the Collider Experiment Hall, I couldn't help but think of one of those scenes from an old James Bond movie where the protagonists cross some innocent-looking threshold, leaving behind a bucolic rural landscape of orchards and cows and, passing suddenly from light to shade, enter a technoscuro lair of nefarious activity—technicians scurrying around in hard hats, that queer fluorescent lighting, some odd menace in the sheer diabolic size of the machinery. At Stanford you get that same feeling: you step into a squarish, mustard-colored building of corrugated metal, surely one of the least ambitious architectural statements on the West Coast, and discover a huge pit, about seventy feet deep, lined with poured concrete and lead bricks, cold in the eerie light, a theater of activity that belongs to engineers and technicians as much as physicists. And there, in the middle of it all, sits the detector. It is the kind of postmodern monument that Francis Picabia would have loved, the Tangle as architecture. (At the time of my visit, the Stanford center was breaking in its new Stanford Large Detector [SLD], a $60 million, 3,500-ton descendant of Glaser's bubble chamber, to replace the 1,800-ton Mark II, built in the late 1970s and originally used to track results in another collider called SPEAR.)

When electrons and positrons come together at the Interaction Point, their beams less than a human hair in width, the head-on collisions produce flares and streaks and metamorphizing trajectories that last for mere fractions of a second. In this case such a collision might produce a Z particle, but it would instantly decay into two quarks or two leptons; those second-order particles would travel a millimeter or two, and last one-trillionth of a second (10^{-12} second, or a picosecond). The idea behind the detector is simply to swaddle the Interaction Point with seven million pounds of hardware, costing tens of millions of dollars, in order to discern a short-lived particle traveling about the length of a hyphen in this typeface.

The detector itself is immense, about thirty feet long and thirty feet high, yet it can accurately pinpoint the location of particle tracks to less than fifty microns—that is, one-twentieth of a millimeter. The entire volume of the detector bristles with trip wires to snag a passing particle, a series of instruments working outward, like a succession of innervated sleeves, from the narrow beam pipe.

First come three .3-millimeter-thick "barrels" of microetched silicon, each about the size of an elongated soda can; silicon detector modules, arranged like barrel staves, sense the ions produced when a particle passes through, determining its position to an accuracy of five microns. Then comes a pressurized gas drift chamber, filled with carbon dioxide and a pinch of ethane and bristling with detection wires; as charged particles fly from the collision, they knock electrons off the molecules of gas, and those electrons drift to tiny sense wires, marking the trajectory of the particles as they fly outward from the Interaction Point. A larger drift chamber follows, an office-sized space filled with argon gas and crisscrossed by more detection wires. The workhorse of the detector, this chamber records the pathways and energies of all the particles bearing electrical charge. Next, the energy of electrons, positrons, and photons is measured when they hit a layer called the calorimeter, strips of lead interspersed with liquid argon; the octagonal end caps do much the same. Time-of-flight counters on the perimeter measure the time, in billionths of a second, for shrapnel from the initial collision to reach the outer part of the detector. And four 8-inch-thick plates of iron, stacked like layers of puff pastry on the sides and top with detectors sandwiched in between, arrest the passage of all but the highly penetrating particles called muons.

Finally, the detector not only detects the path of particles; it perturbs them. A magnetic field around the Interaction Point bends the path of charged particles. Low-energy particles produce slow, loopy tracks; high-energy particles, by contrast, produce "stiff tracks." All the information recorded within the detector—location of the path, speed, direction, bend, by-products—is geographic, and from this three-dimensional subatomic picture of disintegration come clues to the mass, charge, and character of particles coalescing out of these modest simulations of the moment of creation.

Perhaps the most unheralded part of the process involves what might be called map interpretation—the computer analysis of the tracks. Coils of piping, thick lariats of multicolored cable, stiff dreadlocks of wire carry reports from 50,000 separate channels, 50,000 subatomic listening posts, to a bank of computers upstairs. With 50,000 streams of information pouring in per collision (the new Stanford detector will have 200,000), and 120 potential collisions per second, the Stanford computers have to be able to collate all that information, render it into a three-dimensional landscape of tracks, and compare that image instantaneously with the idealized trajectories that theorists predict should exist when Z-zero particles are created. The computers are programmed to predigest this information in a few milliseconds (considered slow by state-of-the-art standards); they are programmed to ask themselves, "Does this look like a Z particle?"; they are programmed, if the answer is yes, to save the data, which is otherwise discarded, before the next wave of 50,000 bits comes crashing into the computer; and they were programmed, later on, to fill the control room with a bagpipe ditty while one of those hiccupy mechanized computer voices bleated to all within earshot, "A wur-thee event, a wur-thee event . . ."

It was no secret to the physics community that the Stanford group had aspirations to steal a noteworthy event, perhaps even a Nobel Prize, out from under the noses of the Europe-based scientists and their bigger, costlier, more conventional machine at CERN. The CERN machine could generate more than 200 GeVs (billion electron bolts) of energy; it featured four detectors; CERN had assembled an astonishing army of eighteen hundred technicians, engineers, and researchers to search for the Z. Stanford's gamble, a one-shot deal, hinged on how quickly they could work out the bugs in their novel design and get on with the production of Z-zero particles. It was a gamble, too, because once CERN's LEP accelerator was up and operational, it would probably sandblast the Stanford machine with Z particles. And that is why the gaffes, the delays, the setbacks, and the problems that beset the SLC ate away at their brief time advantage. There were heat waves and brownouts; equipment failures and tuneups; only 30 percent of the new klystrons worked at first, and many of them had the disconcerting habit of blowing out their windows from the intense energy. Originally scheduled to produce its first Z's in May of 1988, the SLC had, nearly a year later, produced none.

Burton Richter's growing impatience was nicely captured by writer Charles Mann, who sat in on a June 1988 meeting at SLAC at which Richter, baggy-eyed and volcanically silent, listened to a litany of costly setbacks, from human error to failures of hardware. When SLAC's program deputy ventured the opinion that the group was getting "close enough to proceed as if we were going to start for real," Richter's frustration spilled out. "Not *as if*," he said. "We *are* starting. It is real. We can't wait anymore on this. From now on, if something goes wrong, work around it. You can't do science waiting for everything to work right. I want us to start taking data at 4 P.M."

Despite those marching orders, data was a long time coming. At 7:30 in the morning of April 12, 1989, a postdoc in physics at Caltech named Barrett Milliken—an SLC collaborator—turned on his computer and began to look over data collected the day before. Milliken was one of the so-called fire-eaters—a group combing through the data in search of the first Z-zero particle. Five hundred miles south of the Interaction Point, he found it. Entering SLAC's IBM 3090 computer from his office in Pasadena, he called up data stored on a magnetic tape that had been mislabeled the day before and hadn't been analyzed. He found two possible events. The first turned out to be junk, but the second event looked promising. Indeed, Milliken latched on to this particular collision because the computer had reconstructed the image, or map, of its outcome, and its stiff tracks and particular geometry visually matched expectations. Exactly twenty-four hours earlier, at 7:32 A.M. on April 11, unbeknownst to everyone and everything, including the computers programmed to recognize these "wurthee events," an electron had collided with a positron *just so,* and, in their mutual annihilation, had created a Z-zero particle. In 10^{-25} second, as predicted, the Z had decayed into two heavy quarks. These quarks, in turn, produced jets of subatomic shrapnel. The Z and quarks didn't leave tracks, but the jets did, telltale signatures, one hitting the north end cap, the other the south. Sitting there on Milliken's computer screen was the trajectory inscribed by Stanford's first Z-zero particle (see color illustration).

Milliken reported the discovery to SLAC just before 8 A.M. It bespeaks the deliberate, Old World pace of modern physics that, although great effort was taken to keep the event secret until it could be confirmed, even among the team in Palo Alto, Richter received a congratulatory computer message from a physicist in Rome by 10 A.M.,

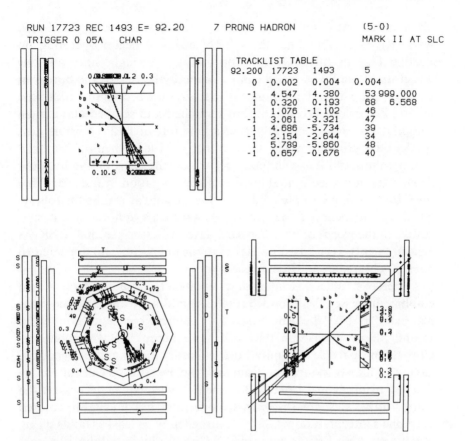

RUN 17723 REC 1493 E= 92.20   7 PRONG HADRON   (5-0)
TRIGGER 0 05A   CHAR   MARK II AT SLC

"A wur-thee event . . .": on April 11, 1989, the Mark II detector produced maps like the sequence above to display the creation of SLAC's first Z particle. In the blank map of the detector, disintegrating particles carve tracks that betray their charge, mass, and nature; computerized analysis produces views of the shrapnel from the top, side, and end cap. (SLAC)

less than two hours after he'd been told in strictest confidence about the possible Z. "The significance of the event is not that it represents a revolution in science," Richter told colleagues. "It's that the machine we struggled so hard to make work is starting to perform as it's supposed to." A realist, Richter also said, "One leaf does not make a laurel wreath."

The sentiment was shared in Geneva. Having become a ruthless and in some ways sloppy field, where the headlong rush for priority of discovery has effectively retired professional etiquette, particle physics observed a controversial conclusion to this first round of the Z-zero wars. Right on schedule, the CERN machine began operating on Bastille Day in July of 1989 (appropriately enough, since all four detectors of the Swiss-based campus actually lay across the border in France), and within ten minutes of start-up, the accelerator produced its first Z particle. While Stanford scratched and scraped and almost conjured up each event, Z particles flew out of LEP collisions like sparks off a grinding wheel. On October 12, 1989, when the Stanford group announced its preliminary results on the basis of five hundred Z particles, it caused a double dose of consternation in Europe. First, the CERN group had planned to announce similar results the following day, and believed the timing of Stanford's announcement suggested, in the words of one, "hockey player's tactics"; second, CERN's measurements were based on eleven thousand events and appeared to offer much greater statistical reliability.

CERN's official leader and unofficial loose cannon, Carlo Rubbia, dismissed the Stanford results, confiding to an Italian newspaper that "at best the Americans will confirm our data, coming in second place—a position they will never accept." But Rubbia, the ultimate antiparticle to Emily Post, is hardly a paragon of decorum, having ruthlessly scooped colleagues in the past (the epic of rude glory that led to his Nobel Prize is documented with equal ruthlessness in Gary Taubes's *Nobel Dreams*). Competition has inevitably colored everyone's interpretation: "SLC is finished now, at least as far as trying to compete with LEP is concerned," CERN physicist John Ellis told *New Scientist.* Indeed, Stanford continued to experience bad luck with its accelerator; that the delicate machine lay just over the hill from the epicenter of the October 1989 Loma Prieta earthquake didn't help. When operations resumed in January of 1990, Stanford officials reported a "steady trickle" of Z particles; at LEP it was more like a roaring torrent, some five hundred thousand particles in about six months.

When the rivalry subsides, the record will show that both groups agreed that the energy of the Z-zero particle was approximately 91.10 GeV. That means that when collisions occurred between particles at exactly 91.1 billion electron volts, this newest and heaviest of atomic particles to date—fated to exist but a fraction of a second—was created.

The first returns from Geneva and Palo Alto were, however, essentially experiments that resulted in "no" answers. No new neutrinos turned up, meaning that only three families of matter exist in the universe. No new particles or surprises appeared to unravel the Standard Model. Most important, no Higgs bosons turned up.

The theory of everything, and the tracks it leaves in the next generation's $500 million detectors, will have to await completion of the superconducting super collider around the year 2000. "There is bound to be growing impatience with the static state of affairs we seem to have encountered," SLAC physicist James D. Bjorken wrote recently, not exactly echoing the optimism of a decade earlier.

While waiting for the theory of everything to be achieved, we might in the meantime amuse ourselves with Lucretius's "humanitarian" model of the atom, a reminder to ourselves, and perhaps the physicists, of how strange this noble quest can be. "What of those atoms that specifically compose the human race?" Lucretius asked in *On the Nature of the Universe*. "Presumably they are not merely sentient, but also shake their sides with uproarious guffaws and besprinkle their cheeks with dewy teardrops and even discourse profoundly and at length about the composition of the universe and proceed to ask of what elements they are themselves composed." As long as they're laughing with us, and not at us.

ASTRONOMICAL
AND COSMOLOGICAL
LANDSCAPES

16. Star Noise

A MAP OF MOLECULAR

CLOUDS IN THE MILKY WAY

||||||||||

My guide and I came on that hidden road
to make our way back into the bright world;
and with no care for any rest, we climbed—
he first, I following—until I saw,
through a round opening, some of those things
of beauty Heaven bears. It was from there
that we emerged, to see—once more—the stars.

—Dante,
Inferno

In the early 1970s, an astronomer at the Goddard Institute of Space Studies in New York named Patrick Thaddeus shattered centuries of precedent in the field of astronomy and bucked a trend dating all the way back to Galileo when he decided that, in order to proceed on a modest project to map the entire Milky Way, he simply did not need and in fact refused to use a larger telescope made available for his research. He wanted a small one. In an era made conspicuous by bigger, more sophisticated, and (need it be added?) more expensive telescopes, Thaddeus insisted on a small and relatively inexpensive instrument, which he and his colleagues proceeded to build from scratch. They planned to aim the telescope, nicknamed the "Mini," at a spectacular confection of dust and stars in our galaxy known to professional astronomers as M42, but more familiar to amateur stargazers as the Orion Nebula. They would build up a view of this region point by point. And they would, at the end of it all, have a map.

Thaddeus, a man of certifiably utopian optimism, thought the project could be completed in five or six years.

Now, nearly twenty years later, that same telescope sits atop the roof of a prim brick building in a section of Cambridge, Massachusetts, known as Observatory Hill, still functioning, still adding points of radio signals to the overall map. It has been torn apart and refitted and put together again several times, and has been transplanted from New York to New England and rebuilt again, and cloned, too, its twin now sitting on a mountaintop in Chile. And it has been dedicated, as single-mindedly as its operator, day and night for these past two decades, to no less a task than mapping the location of giant molecular clouds in the Milky Way, which to hear Thaddeus and other astronomers talk, are the glittering prizes of our galaxy. They are the places where stars form, a process in which all of astronomy is keenly interested.

Few of us have the time or inclination to ponder the nature of stars, where they form and how they come to be, which if nothing else reflects an impoverished curiosity about our own atomic genealogy. Every atom in our bodies, every atom shaping an unforgettable face or reddening an infected hangnail, every atom of every thread of DNA in each of the 100 trillion cells we trundle about each day—every one of those atoms save hydrogen was exhaled at some earlier point in the history of the universe by an exploding star. And if that ancestry fails to move us, we might at least remember that our fragile and privileged ecological niche in an extremely vast and inhospitably frigid cosmos depends on the proximity of one particular star, the sun, which is gentle enough to warm an orchid yet variable enough to touch off ice ages, distant enough to spare us the roar and force of its inferno, dependable enough that we can set our circadian clocks against it and get up each day to ponder such mysteries as the origin of stars. Stars do not just happen. They result from complex astrophysical processes; they are milky accretions of dust and gas that ignite into luminous beacons of light, light conceived in a manner as mysterious and miraculous as the birth of a pearl, and the evolution of these cosmological jewels occurs only in special birthing places, and only under the right conditions. Any effort to identify those birthing grounds, often referred to as "stellar nurseries," sends astronomers down a path of celestial cartography, and it is a path that has been traveled with singular success by radio astronomy in the post–World War II era.

The Milky Way has proved to be an immensely fertile region in which to explore the origins of star formation, and Patrick Thaddeus makes for an especially felicitous tour guide to these star-sotted precincts, partly because he takes the mapper's craft seriously, seeing himself very much in the tradition of the sixteenth-century cartographers; partly because his upbringing in a utopian community in northern Delaware has imbued Thaddeus—nearing sixty years old now, with burning eyes and a prow for a chin—with an independent, almost swashbuckling small-science style; and partly because he always seems ready with an apt metaphor for explaining the arcana of his profession, whether it's the klystron on his superheterodyne receiver (the "cat's whisker") or the telescope itself, which he frequently calls his "paintbrush."

Thaddeus came of scientific age just as astronomy found it had more than one set of eyes through which to view the universe. For twenty centuries or more, astronomy lived through the naked eye and what that eye could perceive through telescopes—visible light. But light is nothing more than electromagnetic radiation within a particular range of wavelengths, and to switch metaphors, optical astronomy was like a primitive radio with a very narrow receiving band, condemned to pick up only a few stations. Much of twentieth-century astronomy, to continue the analogy, has been devoted to building a bigger, more sensitive radio, able to pick up more stations on either side of the narrow visible range; the music of the spheres has turned out to be quite different, and quite a bit more raucous, than expected.

"Until the war, astronomy was confined to about an octave, or factor of three, in wavelength, centered on the visual," Thaddeus explains. His voice is hoarse, and he speaks with a characteristically hectic, erudite locution. "And what we've done since then is just *explode* across the whole spectrum, so that now astronomy goes from very, very long radio wavelengths, meters and tens-of-meters long, down to gamma rays. And so to a great degree what we've been doing is just explode into these empty regions of frequency space, and in many ways we're still really just doing the survey work. Finding out what's there, and doing the basic mapping. Every time you go to a new wavelength band, the general rule is that you find a completely different aspect of nature in that information."

That information has changed the way we view the heavens. The artifacts that decorate Thaddeus's office at the Harvard-Smithsonian Center for Astrophysics bridge the antipodes of stellar cartography: in one corner, an old celestial dome, representing the fixed ceiling of stars as they appeared to everyone from Aristotle to young Edwin Hubble, and pinned to the wall across the room, contoured molecular maps of nebulae, their topographic swirls looking like lariats flung out over the vast limbs of interstellar space. "Basically, we're fixed to one point in the universe that we're looking at. And in the first order, what one should do is make maps." That is exactly what Thaddeus and some twenty doctoral students have done for the past two decades. Thaddeus's vessel of exploration is that modest little rooftop telescope; it is one small part of the age's collective technological retina that makes Thaddeus believe we are living through the greatest period in the history of astronomy.

"I used to say it was *comparable* to the age of Newton," he says, shaking his head. "But now I have to say to my students this is by far the best, most fruitful period of all."

Back in the 1950s, when Thaddeus began graduate school, there was a perennial question on the standard qualifying exam for astronomy that succinctly captures the enthusiasm with which the old guard greeted radio astronomy. "Name two ways," the question went (this is Thaddeus's recollection), "in which optical astronomy will *always* be superior to radio astronomy."

Radio astronomy grew, fitfully, out of one of the most serendipitous discoveries in the history of science. In 1929, according to the oft-told tale, Bell Laboratories asked one of its engineers, Karl Guthe Jansky, to investigate the source of static that bedeviled the company's newly introduced overseas telephone service. A physicist by training and a college hockey star at the University of Wisconsin, Jansky built a movable antenna near the Bell Labs complex in Holmdel, New Jersey, by 1930 and began to search for a source of the mysterious static.

He identified three possible sources for the signals. He quickly realized that two were related to the electricity generated by nearby or distant thunderstorms. The third, however, was another order of beast. It was, in Jansky's words, "a very steady hiss type static, the origin of which is not yet known." By 1933 he had concluded that the hiss came from outer space—a startling assertion that promptly landed on the front page of the May 5, 1933 *New York Times* under the headline NEW RADIO WAVES TRACED TO CENTRE OF THE MILKY WAY (Thaddeus remembers hearing that the static was played on the radio following the *Times* article, sounding to many listeners like "a hissing radiator"). Two years later Jansky reported that the strongest source of "star noise," as he called it, seemed to originate in the direction of the constellation Sagittarius. Since the Milky Way represented a service area well beyond Bell's obligations, Jansky was not encouraged by his superiors to pursue the discovery, and few other astronomers seemed excited by the find either.

"It is a most extraordinary affair that no one took any notice of Jansky's discovery," Sir Bernard Lovell has noted. More extraordinary still is the fact that it took an amateur astronomer to push radio astronomy one giant step closer to respectability. Indeed, it took someone temperamentally unafraid of bucking the system to pursue radio astronomy at that time, and Grote Reber had the right temperament; a radio engineer with the exaggerated, Thomas Hart Benton–like features of the midwestern prairie, Reber was independent-minded to the point of crankiness, once crediting his success to the fact that "there were no self-appointed pontiffs looking over my shoulder giving bad advice."

An electrical engineer by training and an amateur radio operator, Reber lived in Wheaton, Illinois, with his mother (who, by coincidence, turned out to be the seventh- and eighth-grade teacher of a young man named Edwin Hubble), and on a vacant lot next door to their home on West Seminary Avenue this extraordinary self-taught astronomer not only built his "peculiar contraption"—a 31.4-foot, paraboloid-shaped steerable radio antenna, the world's first, and granddaddy of all backyard satellite dishes—but discovered the Milky Way's hiss at a wavelength of 2.4 meters. Despite local interference, including the electrical ignition systems of passing cars, he painstakingly pinpointed the origin of the "star noise" in the Milky Way and reported the results in the *Astrophysical Journal* in 1940.

You would think these intriguing, enigmatic signals would have electrified the astronomical community, but they suffered that most dismal of academic fates: they fell in the crack between disciplines. Radio engineers viewed the waves as a minor nuisance and astrophysicists viewed the idea of radio waves from space as, according to Reber, "at best a mistake and at worst a hoax." His neighbors viewed the antenna as a death ray, and professional astronomers were hardly less skeptical; on one occasion, editors from an academic journal, paying a site visit, had to forgo a demonstration when they discovered Mrs. Reber's laundry lines strung from the big dish. But unlike most other innocent scientific curiosities, Reber's work did not come to a halt during World War II, and he published the very first radio maps of the Milky Way in 1944. They showed that the radio signals covered a large part of the galaxy, not just isolated spots.

The war gave particular impetus to radio astronomy, not least

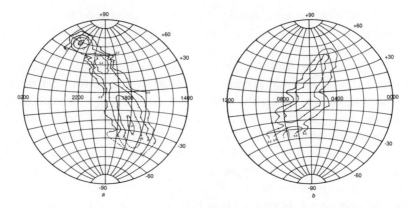

"There were no self-appointed pontiffs looking over my shoulder giving bad advice," says amateur astronomer Grote Reber, who in 1944 published radio astronomy's very first maps, pinpointing sources of "cosmic static" in the Milky Way, in the *Astrophysical Journal*. (G. Reber)

because many scientists acquired expertise in radar and related technologies; nor does it seem in retrospect accidental that the field came to be dominated by the war's victors—the English in particular (much relieved, no doubt, to detect galaxies and not Messerschmitts with their antennae), but also the Canadians, the Dutch, the Australians, the French, and, finally, the Americans. Immediately after the war, radio astronomers began to describe a different cosmic domain. In 1946, Arthur Covington of Canada detected radio signals from the sun; they ultimately would reveal sunspot activity. In 1948, Martin Ryle of England discovered the first radio galaxy, located in the area of Cygnus A, proving that galaxies signed the sky in other than visible light. Some years later, astronomers at Jodrell Bank in England detected pulsating bursts of radio signals, which came to be known as pulsars—the steady beat of a collapsed star.

And yet there was a charmingly haphazard evolution to this great revolution, nowhere more apparent than in the establishment of Britain's pioneering Jodrell Bank Radio Observatory. Symbol of the new astronomy, it got its start because astronomer Bernard Lovell obtained permission from a horticulturalist to set up two trailers full of war-surplus radar equipment at the University of Manchester's botany research station, which happened to lie twenty-five miles south of Manchester on eleven muddy acres of farmland called Jodrell Bank. Indeed, the siting of the first permanent buildings was determined not by architects or committees or, God forbid, the scientists; a crucial equipment truck got irretrievably mired in the mud in 1946, and everything was built around it. Yet within a decade, Jodrell Bank housed the world's largest radio telescope and found itself on the receiving end of some of the young science's most spectacular discoveries.

Like prospectors' pans, those huge antenna dishes slowly swished through the sky in search of treasure and came up with quasars, radio stars, radio jets, interstellar masers, and other strange beasts. Where once the universe had appeared a peaceable kingdom, populated by grazing stars and quiescent galaxies, it suddenly took on a violent, explosive, radiative personality. Hot, frothing, spewing, spiraling, percussive, racked and roiled by titanic forces—the universe no longer spoke in just light. It spoke in many tongues, loudly.

In the time-honored tradition of graduate students, a young astronomer named A. Edward Lilley proposed, in the early 1950s, that these new radio telescopes could be used to look for molecules in space, and he was told to excise such speculative rubbish from his thesis if he wanted a Ph.D. from Harvard. But in fact during the war, the Dutch astronomers H. C. van de Hulst and J. H. Oort predicted that a single atom of hydrogen, H_1, would give off a detectable radio signal under certain circumstances, and in 1951 Lilley and H. I. Ewen discovered the first evidence of such a radio signal. Within the decade scientists had produced the first sky surveys of H_1.

The allure of atoms, and ultimately molecules, swirled around the central mystery of stellar evolution. Hydrogen and helium account for more than 99 percent of all matter in the universe; hydrogen gas in particular, in the form of the molecule H_2, serves as the cosmic clay for many astrophysical creations, from galaxies to stars and certainly the newly discovered quasars and pulsars as well. The problem is that neither helium nor hydrogen gas betrays its whereabouts with radio waves. Helium, an inert gas, almost never forms molecules. Molecular hydrogen (H_2) is electromagnetically catatonic, so stable that its electrons simply resist any form of excitation and thus emit no radio chirp, no "star noise," to be picked up. The great excitement in 1951 was that atomic hydrogen, H_1, *did* crackle over the air waves. When hydrogen's lone electron jumped from one energy state to another, as quantum physics insisted it must, it shed an infinitesimally faint, low-frequency buzz that zipped across trillions upon trillions of miles of space. Much of that space is obscured by clouds of gas and dust, but radio waves (and infrared radiation, too) pass with equanimity through the murk and muck, dazzling astronomers lucky enough to have sensitive receivers tuned to the proper wavelength of twenty-one centimeters. The problem was, atomic hydrogen (H_1) wasn't molecular hydrogen (H_2), and it was the clouds of *molecules* that aroused the most interest, because stars form out of those gaseous, invisible molecules.

At about this time, Patrick Thaddeus began to get interested in astronomy. Born in Wilmington, Delaware, in 1932, Thaddeus grew up in the town of Arden, a utopian community dedicated to the economic principles of social reformer Henry George and among whose earliest settlers were Thaddeus's grandparents. His father, trained as a chemist, became a writer and sometime contributor to H. L. Mencken's *Smart Set*; his mother was a political activist. He graduated from the University of Delaware in 1953, promptly won a Fulbright Fellowship, and ended up at Columbia University, where he studied radio physics in the laboratory of Charles Townes, who would go on to win a Nobel Prize in 1964 for discovering the maser.

Soon after, Townes moved on to the University of California at Berkeley, where he shook up the world of radio astronomy with a series of experiments reported in 1968. Using a technique known as microwave spectroscopy, physicists shine radio waves through tubes filled with the gas of a particular molecule; if that particular molecule (ammonia, for example) absorbs radio energy at a particular frequency, researchers will see a dip in the energy of radio waves coming out the other end of the tube, and that dip betrays an extraordinarily sharp and precise frequency, or resonance, line. These dips in signal are known as spectral lines, and they are as unique to each molecule—such as water (H_2O) or ammonia (NH_2)—as fingerprints to a person. Townes and his Berkeley team tuned the receiver of their radio telescope to the frequency of the known radio waves for water and other molecules, and then pointed their antenna dish at the sky like some inverse divining rod. And yes, they found water in outer space.

"They didn't have a very good reason for doing it," Thaddeus admits now, "but they looked for ammonia and water. And they found them! And that is really what uncorked the bottle in many ways. From 1968 on, people realized that you could detect these stable molecules, and the place to do it was the short radio wavelengths in the millimeter waveband." Two years later the key molecule of radio astronomy was identified, and given Karl Jansky's original work in radio astronomy, the discovery fittingly came at the hands of three scientists at Bell Labs. Arno Penzias, Robert Wilson, and Keith Jefferts detected the presence of carbon monoxide, CO, in 1970 from Kitt Peak National Observatory in Arizona. Odorless and tasteless, without color or conspicuous chemical personality, CO hummed its molecular song at a wavelength of 2.6 millimeters—about the width of a matchstick. The molecule itself seemed as bland in space as it did on earth; as far as anyone knew, it didn't form stars, it didn't fuel galaxies, it wouldn't even flare if you held a torch to it. But to radio astronomers, it did something much more valuable. Carbon monoxide turned out to be a fellow traveler to molecular hydrogen, the true object of the hunt. Just as a biologist stains a cell to see its internal structure, astronomy now had a stain that would reveal the location of molecular hydrogen and, it was hoped, the location of star formation itself.

Wherever you saw CO, there was H_2. Indeed, astronomers began to see vast clouds, tens and then hundreds of light-years across, in the Milky Way. Robert Wilson of Bell Labs was the first to report a phenomenon that everyone else, to their considerable surprise, would quickly discover for themselves: the molecules of CO "just kept on going." As MIT astronomer Alan Barrett has remarked, "From that time on, molecular astronomy mushroomed." So, too, did those funny-looking mushroom-shaped telescopes.

The state of the technology, however, held up the gold rush. "In the beginning," Thaddeus says, "we just didn't have an instrument. There was a period of time when nobody could make any progress, because they didn't have the telescope parts. So initially the bottleneck was instrumentation." For a short time, beginning around 1972, Thaddeus's group at Columbia joined a consortium including the University of Texas (which maintained a sixteen-foot radio telescope), Bell Labs, and Harvard. That initial collaboration made clear, unfortunately clear in Thaddeus's mind, the drawbacks of radio maps.

A radio telescope does not take pictures; it measures the intensity of radio signals from a single point (in this, radio astronomers have more in common with Georges Seurat than with Galileo). You focus on one spot, measure it, move the beam slightly, take another measurement. After hundreds and thousands of dots, you can plot it all out as some quantitative pointillist vision. "In our first run down there," Thaddeus recalls, "we looked for CO in the nearest and biggest clouds to the sun, the Orion Nebula and the Horsehead Nebula. I said to the students, 'Don't think about the map of the completed area. . . . Undersample the thing. Go out and find a place where you find zero.'" And so the students kept mapping outward from the centers of these landmark clouds, looking for an edge or boundary or limit where CO levels dropped to zero, and like Wilson, they found that CO billowed

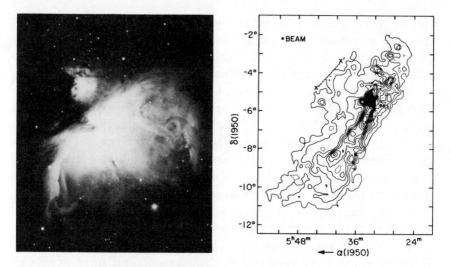

"We were dealing with a very big thing," Patrick Thaddeus recalls, "much bigger than we had thought." Optical view of the Orion nebula *(left)* compared to a map of carbon monoxide *(right),* where clouds of CO extend well beyond the dark contours of the nebula itself. (NOAO; P. Thaddeus)

onward and outward. "It was clear," Thaddeus says now, gesturing at some of those first few maps, "that we were dealing with a very big thing, much bigger than we had thought." That was when Thaddeus started thinking about changing the size of his paintbrush.

Science—and mapmaking for that matter—often succeeds or fails on the basis of fateful decisions that turn on trivial facts, and in the mid-1970s Thaddeus found himself laying his scientific future on the line, against a metric ruler. He knew that the radio wavelength of H_1 was 21 centimeters, little more than half a foot; CO's was 2.6 millimeters, about a hundred times narrower. He knew that to build a radio telescope that would map atomic hydrogen with the necessary resolution, he would need an antenna, as he puts it (the idiom dates the speaker), "as large as a battleship." CO, on the other hand, could be mapped to a similar degree of accuracy using a much smaller antenna because its wavelength was so much smaller. He ended up building a telescope that was about one-eighth the size of Grote Reber's prairie extravaganza.

"We were in the position of the guy who is trying to paint a barn with a quarter-inch brush," Thaddeus remembers. A radio telescope "sees" with its "beam," and the beam can be likened, although in inverse fashion, to the area of light illuminated by one of those small flashlights with a twistable cap that produce a circular beam of light either large and diffuse or narrow and sharp. Radio telescopes *receive* waves the way those flashlights emit waves of light, and the bigger the telescope, the narrower its beam; Thaddeus realized that using a sharp, narrow beam on the Milky Way would be like trying to construct a street map of Manhattan using a microscope. "From these initial observations and the underlying data, we immediately said that what we've got to do is to build a special-purpose telescope which is not too big, which has good receivers, and that is an adequate match for the job of putting your arms around big things. And is the right size of paintbrush for the galaxy we found."

Abandoning the Texas consortium did not displease Thaddeus. He didn't like the idea of sharing telescope time. He liked to run his own program. He liked to tinker, "know what's under the hood," as he put it, of his machinery. Starved though they were for telescope time, the Columbia group decided to design a customized radio telescope with a four-foot aperture—a shutter, if you will, slightly larger than a card table. Fortunately, the wavelength for CO was ever so slightly above the point where the greenhouse gases in the earth's atmosphere throw up a veillike blanket of molecules that block out smaller radio waves. He found some mechanical help and set out to build this unique telescope, tiny by the standards of contemporary astronomy, to commence his search for CO. He was not alone. Bell Labs, under Robert Wilson, put together a formidable team; and Thomas Phillips, then at IBM and now at the California Institute of Technology, would go on to invent a quantum superconducting receiver that pried the faintest, most distant signals from the sky. With their superheterodyne receivers, their klystrons, their "cat's whiskers," these astronomers all tuned their receivers to the Milky Way.

It is a minor wonder of modern astronomy that Thaddeus could install this telescope in 1975 on the roof of Pupin Hall, the physics building at Columbia University, which is fifteen stories above and a few footsteps off the Great White Way of Broadway and all the tumult and noise and light of Gotham, and operate it in complete serenity. Just as light pollution is the bane of optical astronomy, static is the bane of radio astronomy, but Thaddeus's telescope operated at wave bands around a millimeter or two, well below the frequencies of radar and radio and television and people popping popcorn in their microwaves. "If you live in New York City, if you were to put on a

The right "paintbrush" for the job: Thomas Dame, Patrick Thaddeus, and E. Samuel Palmer *(left to right)* with their small and serviceable radio telescope. (Steve Seron/Harvard-Smithsonian Center for Astrophysics)

receiver, you'd discover La Guardia radar and television and radio and microwave ovens and all these things, a tremendous cacophony," Thaddeus says. "But if you tune your receiver down—down, down, down, down, down—all of a sudden the cacophony becomes deathly quiet. We operated this telescope of ours down there, in New York City, for ten years or so before we came to Harvard, and we during that whole time did not hear a *single peep* from the environment. The great metropolis was as quiet, as I used to say, as the day Henry Hudson sailed up that river." In that virginal radio silence, as still and serene as pre-Columbian America, they began to map the raucous and violent star births muffled and hidden within the ubiquitous molecular clouds of the Milky Way.

Mapping *anything* in the Milky Way is not a trivial exercise. Our galaxy is a thick pancake of dust and gas and billions of stars measuring 100,000 light-years (roughly 5.9×10^{17} miles) in diameter and 1,000 light-years thick, with a slight bulge at the center; and we sit, like a middling blueberry, about two-thirds of the way out from the center. Anytime we try to look along the plane of the pancake, we are trying to pierce a batter not only pocked by 100 billion stars, but obscured by thick clouds of smoke and dust. Therein lay the great advantage of carbon monoxide. It's not simply that the densest clouds, where stars form, prevent light from escaping; they warm up as gravitation begins to stir the gas and dust, and as the temperature rises, the spectral line of H_1 gets obscured. So CO becomes the lone clue to star formation.

The Thaddeus group, like Wilson's team at Bell Labs, started with obvious targets, landmarks familiar to even the most casual of backyard astronomers—the great Horsehead Nebula and the famous Orion Nebula, a region of star formation so rich and brilliant it resembles a string of firecrackers bursting white and hot within clouds of its own

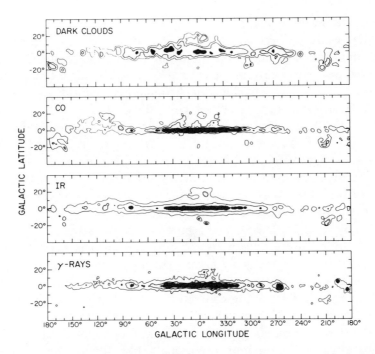

Four slices of the Milky Way: the plane of our galaxy betrays different contours when viewed *(top to bottom)* as dark clouds, clouds of carbon monoxide, infrared radiation, and gamma ray emissions. (T. Dame and P. Thaddeus)

luminous and ignited gunpowder. Again and again, they were surprised by the sheer *extent* of carbon monoxide: it went on and on and on. Only slowly did it dawn on them that they were trying to map the boundary of the largest objects in the galaxy. These giant molecular clouds were tens of thousands of light-years across; they contained the mass of more than 1,000 suns.

In 1979 the Columbia group received money from the National Science Foundation to build a copy of the Columbia telescope to operate in Cerro Tololo, Chile, where it could map the southern skies. In a series of papers published in the *Astrophysical Journal* beginning in 1980, the Thaddeus group mapped swatches of the Milky Way along the galactic plane (where the equator basically traces the plane that cuts through the middle of the pancake). Finally, in 1987, Thomas M. Dame, who has worked with Thaddeus for more than a decade and who moved with him to Massachusetts when the telescope moved to Harvard-Smithsonian, gathered all these regional maps together, smoothed the data, integrated the borders, and produced a panoramic, 360-degree map of the entire Milky Way galaxy. This composite survey, built up out of thirty-one thousand measurements of CO spectra, covered nearly one-fifth of the entire sky. It was made into a poster; if you visit almost any astronomy department in the world, you are likely to see it on somebody's wall (see color illustration).

To the unschooled eye, the survey looks like a topographical map of a long river canyon, with a thick, especially steep rise of CO emission toward the center of the galaxy. Radio measurements of velocity graphically show that these molecules, the clouds they trace, the whole core of the Milky Way, is swirling around the center, which is indeed what one would expect of a spiral galaxy like ours. And though we do not enjoy what could be called a bird's-eye view of the galaxy, Dame and Thaddeus were nonetheless able to plot an overview of the galaxy's molecular clouds as if you were staring down at a petri dish, with our sun as the central spore, surrounded by colonies of dust and stars. All those thick, fermenting confections of molecules and dust—Coal Sack, Vela Sheet, Chamaeleon, Taurus, the Aquila Rift, to name a few—looked like buildings in the blueprint for an industrial park. And industry was not an inappropriate metaphor, for as Thaddeus says, "Molecular clouds are the factories where star formation is occurring in the galaxy, and in other galaxies."

"If you'd have said twenty years ago that all star formation occurs in molecular clouds, people wouldn't have known what you meant," says Thaddeus. Molecular clouds had not been discovered, or their significance appreciated. "Star formation was a dubious subject, and in trying to explain star formation, people in a sense were trying to do Hamlet without the Prince of Denmark." Carbon monoxide supplied radio astronomers with the missing character. Moreover, Thaddeus maintains, it delivers on the promise raised, but never delivered, by atomic hydrogen.

"If you make a map in twenty-one centimeters [of atomic hydrogen]," he argues, "it does not delineate star formation at all. It's one of the big disappointments of twenty-one-centimeter astronomy. The atoms did not seem to peak up around areas where stars form. But if you look at CO, it really is the Holy Grail. *Wherever* there's a peak in CO, wherever the CO is dense, wherever there's molecular gases, there's star formation." That, says Thaddeus, is the "central dogma" of star formation.

These factories abound throughout the galaxy. The molecular maps show where stars form, but they don't instantly suggest *how* stars

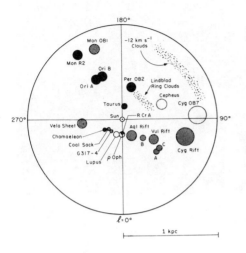

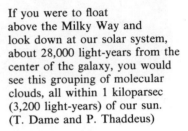

If you were to float above the Milky Way and look down at our solar system, about 28,000 light-years from the center of the galaxy, you would see this grouping of molecular clouds, all within 1 kiloparsec (3,200 light-years) of our sun. (T. Dame and P. Thaddeus)

form. The standard explanation has been that stars aborning, beginning with a twitch of gravitation, begin to suck in gas and dust until they reach a critical density that triggers nuclear fusion; like a cigarette lighter, these sunlike stars suddenly flick on, usually within the densest region of molecular clouds. According to a recent hypothesis advanced by Charles J. Lada of the University of Arizona and Frank H. Shu of the University of California at Berkeley, as gas and dust are gravitationally drawn toward the core of the forming star, some material begins to accrete in a disk and bulge out, like a spinning sphere striving to become a pancake. The in-swirling material contributes something called angular momentum, making the protostar spin more rapidly, like the oft-cited skater going into a tuck position, and physics suggests that at a certain point the angular momentum should become so great that it would tear the incipient star apart before it had a chance to ignite. But in the early 1980s, radio astronomers observed "lobes" of gas flying off at supersonic speed from the north and south poles of new stars; Lada and Shu now argue that these lobes represent stellar winds that in effect draw off some of that angular momentum, like huge vents, and thus preserve stability. Intense study, using every electromagnetic dialect discernible to astronomy, from gamma ray to infrared to submillimeter wavelengths, is under way to pin this down.

Indeed, since the late 1960s molecular surveys of the heavens have produced spectacular maps. The group at Bell Labs under Robert Wilson is well along in mapping the galaxy called M31, more popularly

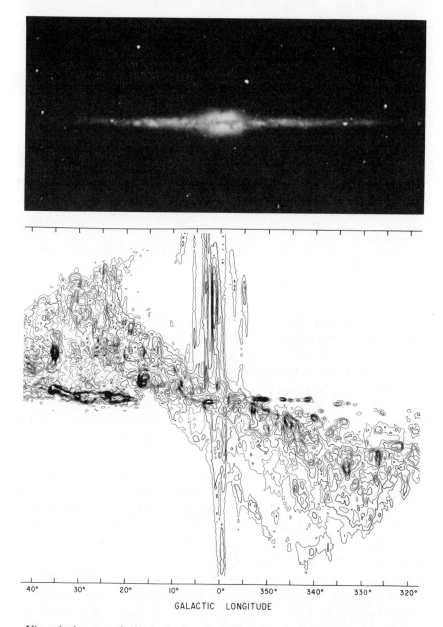

GALACTIC   LONGITUDE

Viewed edge-on, spiral galaxies like the Milky Way are flat disks with a bulge
in the center (*top,* near infrared image). But the disk is spinning, and this
"longitude-velocity map" of molecules in the galactic center *(bottom)* betrays
the motion. Molecular clouds of CO at left of center are moving away from
the earth, while clouds at right of center are coming toward the observer.
(NASA/COBE Science Working Group; T. Dame and P. Thaddeus)

known as the Andromeda galaxy. Some of the most impressive new mapping work has been done by Caltech's Tom Phillips, who has pushed the technology into the submillimeter range and has achieved greater distance by using an array of radio antennas, a technique known as interferometry (Phillips has mapped the galaxy M82, and has even discovered a hint of fractal dimension in molecular clouds, having mapped self-similar structure in large and small portions of molecular clouds in Perseus, Taurus, and Auriga). These radio surveys suggest where to look next, and by what means to peer inside the swaddling clouds surrounding protostars, so that we might finally witness, and perhaps understand, the birth of stars themselves.

There is one aspect of Patrick Thaddeus's work on the star-forming process that distinguishes it from that of most of his fellow astronomical cartographers, and it involves an unusual chemical dialogue he promotes between discoveries in an underground laboratory at Harvard and outer space. In a large room in the basement of Pierce Hall, Thaddeus and his colleagues send Jovian two-thousand-volt bolts of lightning through vacuum tubes filled with gaseous mixes of primordial material. The idea is to create novel, exotic, even nonterrestrial organic chemicals. They isolate these new compounds in the laboratory, analyze them to determine their spectral lines, and then tune a large millimeter-wave dish (Thaddeus uses one in Spain) like a radio to those wavelengths to see if they can detect these same molecules in star-forming regions of the sky. Remarkably, dozens of complex molecules—ninety at last count—have been detected in the molecular clouds. Molecules in space are not rare. They are astonishingly abundant, and Thaddeus's group has accounted for roughly one-quarter of the molecules identified since the early 1970s, including the first carbon ring ever detected in space. The discovery of carbon rings raised the eyebrows even of biologists, because the biochemistry of living things uses as its fundamental brick that same versatile, tough, adaptable carbon ring.

If the idea of firing electricity into a broth of organic chemicals sounds vaguely familiar, it should. In 1953, in one of the landmark experiments in twentieth-century biology, Stanley L. Miller and Harold Urey of the University of Chicago set off sparks in a flask containing organic ingredients such as ammonia, methane, hydrogen, and water. When they poked through the soup afterward, they found the large molecules known as amino acids, which function as the building blocks of life. This, went the argument, is how life on earth might have developed, and consequently the Miller-Urey experiment has sometimes been called the "origin-of-life" experiment.

Thaddeus has taken that primordial soup and in effect flung his soup bowl at the densest clouds in the galaxy. The Milky Way teems with these molecules. "Half are things you can get in a chemical stockroom," says Thaddeus, rummaging around his office for the latest census, a veritable shopping list of ingredients. "Methanol, ethanol. There's alcohols, aldehydes, organic acids, and esters," he says, scanning the list. "But then coexisting with this are these wonderful methyl formate molecules, things that I've specialized in, which are either very poorly known or completely unknown in the terrestrial laboratory. Some of these things were found in space before they were found in the lab."

The preponderance of these molecules in galactic clouds raises some interesting chemical questions about star formation. Thaddeus argues—and here the maps are merely platforms for speculation—that diffuse gases, such as are found in molecular clouds, become dense and ultimately gravitationally unstable, and that molecules are a bellwether of these changes. When their density reaches a critical point, dramatic physicochemical changes take place. Just as ice is a different phase of water, although both are chemically identical, the atoms in molecular clouds recombine to form molecules. Atomic hydrogen, H_1, combines to form H_2. Carbon and oxygen unite, forming the telltale CO that "stains" the clouds for radio astronomers to map. Other atoms combine, too, to form what Thaddeus refers to as "this wonderful, mysterious bestiary, this compost heap of molecules." This compression and phase change is an intermediate step, he believes, because neither CO nor carbon rings survive the temperatures of nuclear burning, once a cloud's fuse is lit. In other words, the formation of molecules may be an essential, if short-lived, transitional step critical to the formation of stars. "The message of this is very clear and overwhelming: that in space, as on earth, when nature wants to synthesize big things, it avails itself of the remarkably subtle and constructive properties of the carbon bond," says Thaddeus.

When this crusade began, when it first became clear back in the early 1970s that astronomers could begin to paint in the dimensions of molecular clouds, few astronomers viewed it as a long-term task. Thaddeus, for example, believed he would pack it in after six or seven years. "What's happened is, as we put our arms around this beast," he says now, "he just gets bigger and bigger and bigger." Just so, the list of molecules to look for gets longer and longer: ammonia, formalde-

hyde, acetylene, silicon dicarbide. They finally have their Prince of
Denmark, and many bit players too, but the drama of understanding
star formation appears still to be in the first act. "It's like, you know,
landing at Plymouth Rock," Thaddeus says, recalling an earlier band
of utopians, "and never setting foot inland."

17. The Great Attractor

A MAP OF PECULIAR
MOTIONS AND THE LARGE-SCALE
FLOW OF GALAXIES

||||||||||

> But even those stars that are
> motionless, or because of their
> speed keep equal pace with the rest
> of the universe and seem not to
> move, are not without rule and
> dominion over us.
>
> —Seneca

"Have you ever seen the Milky Way from the southern hemisphere?"

Alan Dressler intends it as a straightforward question, but it quickly becomes a lesson in cosmic geography. He is standing in his office on a bright summer day in Pasadena, surrounded by his computers and his histograms and his Hubble flow charts, an office located less than a thousandth of a light-second east of Hollywood and that other star system that shouts its name with so much neon and so much candlepower that it threatens to drown out what little of the night is left to astronomers. Which is why Dressler speaks so fondly now of an observing trip to the Las Campanas Observatory in Chile back (he thinks) in 1984 when, fatigued by a long night chasing galaxies and feeling "susceptible" (his word, and a curious one to describe the everyman emotions to which he is about to confess), he staggered out of the telescope dome at four o'clock in the morning and did something astronomers don't always feel moved to do these days: he looked up at the sky. No lenses, no television monitors, no "2D-FRUTTI" photon detectors came between him and the night sky. Just Alan Dressler's Ohio-born rods and cones panning for light from a billion stars. He's a bright young astronomer, not without ego, yet the experience left him feeling a little *estranged.* He goes so far as to call it—scientists out of habit qualify even their epiphanies—"perhaps" the most vivid moment of his life.

"The southern sky is so different from the northern, it's difficult to describe," he explains. "I mean, you see the *bulge* of our galaxy and it's so big. I never experienced anything remotely like it in the north. You look up at the sky when that Milky Way is overhead, and your whole frame of reference is altered by the experience of seeing this galaxy, which is *this* big"—Dressler stretches his arms as wide as they will go, a spontaneous (if not peer-reviewed) unit of measure—"and dominates the whole sky. And your frame of reference on the earth, that completely disappears. You sort of say, 'Here I am off on this little world, you know, out at the edge, standing off at some funny angle.' Your *whole frame* is just tilted. We are now becoming familiar with a much larger galactic or extragalactic environment."

It has become a cliché to point out that modern astronomers no longer have time for the humbling distraction of actually looking at the stars, so deeply engrossed are they in the TV monitors electronically lashed to their huge eyepieces, to the computers that later decant and make sense of the streams of data, but Alan Dressler's little epiphany south of the equator can be seen as exemplary, in an unintended way, of the kind of healthy cosmological estrangement currently under way because of recent and traumatic rearrangements in astronomy's frame of reference. These unsettling developments, alas, further erode our romanticized but flawed mythologies about Great Men and Their Telescopes. Most of us still think of astronomical achievement in terms of the discovery of "objects"—the newest planet, the nearest nebula, the most distant quasar, the first black hole. All irrelevant, Alan Dressler would argue. "The hardest thing to explain to people is that that kind of discovery, the naming of objects, has absolutely no relevance to what's going on in modern astronomy. It's like discovering trees. Trees in a forest don't have names. You can go out and say, 'I discovered this tree.' So what? There are that many galaxies, that many stars." In the last half century, with more sophisticated telescopes and more efficient technology, astronomers have stopped acting like gardeners, tending individual trees in the cosmos, and begun to act more like foresters, surveying vast tracts of stars and clusters and galaxies.

And once they started looking at the forest instead of the trees, they began to see amazing, unexpected things.

Dressler and six other colleagues, known collectively as the "Seven Samurai," embarked on one such survey about a decade ago. As seems almost standard for such endeavors, they set out to do something else. They set out to measure the physical properties of certain galaxies. They ended up creating a map of galaxies in movement, a forest on the run, as it were. They did this by recording the movements of galaxies that fraternize in clusters, which have been fittingly likened to "megalopolises of stars." And by meticulously plotting the movements of these galaxies, the Seven Samurai have uncovered evidence—like some thinly scrawled, inconceivably large X in the middle of a treasure map—suggesting that there is a huge concentration of matter orchestrating the dance of a million galaxies around it, an enormous cosmic lodestone. They call it the "Great Attractor."

The Great Attractor is so large that it is hard to see. It does not deposit any photons on optical telescopes, leaves no bark of static for radio telescopes to detect. That is in part because it itself is a forest of galaxies, incredibly dense and unimaginably large, lying off at a distance of 150 million light-years, in the direction of the Hydra-Centaurus supercluster (see color illustration). Our galaxy, the Milky Way, is caught in the tug of this Great Attractor, and so are we, hurtling—though we'd never know it—toward this mysterious mass at a speed of 370 miles per second. Even friendly skeptics seem intrigued.

"Let's put it this way," says John Huchra, an observer at the Harvard-Smithsonian Center for Astrophysics. "Everybody is pretty certain that there's something out there, and everybody is certain that they know what it is, although nobody agrees on what that is. Whether that something is simply the confluence of the Hydra-Centaurus clusters plus the associated garbage that goes along with it, or whether there's really an invisible mass and invisible galaxies hidden in the invisible galactic plane—it's going to be hard to tell."

Hard, yes. Impossible? Not according to Alan Dressler. That is what is occupying him on this hot summer day.

"I should have these data out in another month," he is saying. "If the whole analysis doesn't fall flat on its face . . ." It is late August 1989, and the main pressure weighing upon Dressler is not so much a time deadline as credibility. Some astronomers have questioned the preliminary Great Attractor data, thought it a bit thin, even argued that certain measurements in the optical range might be subject to too much error. In order to refute those objections, the forty-three-year-old Dressler—who with his light curly hair, high forehead, and soft, fleshy smile recalls a high-minded version of Harpo Marx—sits at his desk doing the grunt work of astronomy, staring into the black hole of a computer screen, in this case measuring the rotation curves of galaxies in an attempt to answer precisely the questions raised by Huchra and other critics. A map is only as good as the data points out of which it is built, and this is the workshop where each measurement, recorded months ago on chilly nights in another hemisphere, is inspected and weighed and sanded and smoothed, made as reliable as possible or marked down as damaged goods.

A DEC Microvax computer hums beneath Dressler's workstation; a small Sony videocassette, about the size of a paperback whodunnit, holds the raw data from a recent weeklong session in Chile which, Dressler hopes, will fall into place on his increasingly detailed map in such a way that it will turn the Great Attractor hypothesis into a *fait accompli.* "I've been very fortunate in the past," he says, "and if I get lucky again, it won't be long. But it could be that doing it in the optical will turn out to be much less reliable and I'll sort of panic and just go back to . . ." The sentence trails away, replaced by hasty taps on the computer keys. It is the unassured, wavering voice of science that rarely if ever finds its way into journals or newspapers; it is the way scientists talk when they are alone with their data.

The search for the Great Attractor is founded upon measurements of large-scale flows in the universe, and it works something like this. Imagine you wake up to find yourself in a boat that seems to be drifting through the Gulf Stream in a dense fog (the fog being a not inappropriate metaphor for the confusion of astronomers about this point until the mid-1970s). You know you are moving but you're not sure about the direction. The fog begins to lift slightly, and you see a taut towrope fastened to the bow—something is pulling you off at an angle from the Gulf Stream current. The fog lifts a little more, and you can make out another boat in front pulling you along (with binoculars, you can even make out the name: Local Group). The fog begins to lift even more, with two startling developments. First, you can make out the shoreline for the first time, which gives you a frame against which you can gauge your speed. Second, as the fog lifts further, you notice a rope leading from the boat in front of you; it too is being yanked along. With your binoculars, you notice a still larger boat pulling the boat that is pulling you (you can even make out the name: Local Supercluster). As the sun breaks through the fog and you can see even farther, you pick up your most powerful binoculars and look again. Sure enough, something is pulling the Local Supercluster; it is so far away that you can't make it out, except for the taut rope leading toward it. In astronomy, the direction of the rope indicates direction of flow, and the pulling is done by gravity, not towboats. Alan Dressler and his colleagues have observed an analogous situation in the universe. Instead of the flow of boats relative to an ocean current, they have measured the flow of galaxies relative to the expansion of the universe; instead of a tugboat in the ocean, the huge pulling force seems to be a dense and extensive clump of matter far beyond a supercluster of galaxies called Hydra-Centaurus. Galaxies in our neighborhood are streaming toward that one part of the sky at the heady clip of about four hundred miles a second.

In order to figure out exactly where they are headed, and how fast, the data must be strained through the computer. "The idea is that if you measure the rotation of a galaxy, you're measuring something about its mass," Dressler is saying. "And then you're supposed to know how bright it is, and that should tell you how far away it is." In order to make those measurements, astronomers must observe galaxies optically (to see how bright they are) and spectroscopically (to see how fast they are moving); the combination of those two measurements results in the ability to fix the location of the galaxy in three-dimensional, extragalactic space. Dressler is this afternoon processing and refining measurements for some 120 spiral galaxies; he took spectral measurements on the hundred-inch telescope at Las Campanas while Sandra Faber, one of the original samurai and Dressler's graduate advisor at the University of California-Santa Cruz, took optical measurements on the forty-inch telescope. One by one, the points get positioned on a map, a galactic flow chart.

Do galaxies actually *flow*? Yes. We have known that about as long as we've known about galaxies themselves, which is only about sixty-five years, though these cloudy conglomerations, containing 100 billion or more stars, had been observed and contemplated for centuries. In 1924 the American astronomer Edwin P. Hubble proved that certain star-rich regions known then as "nebulae" lay outside the Milky Way, and thus was the era of galaxies born. Hubble's discovery complemented an earlier, but inexplicable, observation by other astronomers, who had noticed a displacement of spectral lines in the light from certain nebulae. These lines shift when the object observed is in motion (relative to the observer); most of those nebulae turned out to be galaxies, and their spectra all seemed to drift to the red end of the spectrum. This so-called redshift indicates movement away from the observer, just as a shift to the blue end indicates movement toward the observer. Hubble correlated the degree of redshift with distance, and this gave astronomers a way to measure and therefore map the distribution of galaxies in three dimensions.

What caused the movement? Hubble provided the startling answer in 1929, when he showed not only that all galaxies were hurtling away from the Milky Way and each other, but that their speed corresponded to distance: the greater the redshift (and thus velocity), the greater the distance. This uniform ratio of speed to distance demanded a uniform force big enough and primordial enough to create space and time and everything in it, from naked hydrogen atoms to vast galaxies moving through the universe. Georges Lemaître, a Belgian priest and theoretician, hypothesized that the universe began as a "cosmic egg," which then exploded in a conflagratory fireball that hurled a mist of protomatter outward in all directions, an expansion of space-time fabric that continues to this day. The initial explosion came to be known, derisively at first, as the Big Bang (astronomer Fred Hoyle, as skeptics often do in astronomy, provided the name that stuck). Controversial at first, the notion of a single explosive initiating event had gained wide acceptance by the late 1930s, and gained almost unassailable credibility in 1965 when, as described in the previous chapter, workers at Bell Labs in New Jersey accidentally discovered what is called the microwave background—a radio hiss in all directions of the sky that marks the faint, ubiquitous, unvarying echo of the Big Bang. Writing in *Scientific American* several years ago, Dressler noted that, taken as a whole, this sequence of observations "represented a change in world view in every way as fundamental as the Copernican revolution; the notion of a static universe was by then as well established as the geocentric universe had been in the 15th Century."

What made Hubble's observations so persuasive was that the data could be reduced to a graph with that feature so beloved of scientists—a straight line. The line established that direct relationship between the velocity of a galaxy and its distance from us; known as a Hubble diagram, the graph showed that the velocity at which a distant galaxy recedes from an observer (its "recession velocity") was equal to its distance (estimated by how bright it appeared to astronomers) multiplied by a constant number. This number is known as the "Hubble constant" (determinations of the number have turned out to be anything but constant, but that is another story). This dull little graph nonetheless rewrote cosmology, for it implied a number of startling

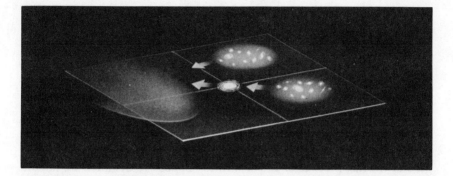

The Milky Way *(center)* is caught in the gravitational tug of a huge overdense mass known as the Great Attractor *(left)*, as is the Perseus-Pisces supercluster *(lower right)* and the Coma supercluster *(upper right)*. Peculiar motions, indicated by arrows, suggest the location of gravitational lodestones in the universe. ("Newton"/KYOIKUSHA)

things—that the universe is expanding in a uniform, *constant* manner; that, calculating backward from current rates of expansion, the Big Bang must have occurred some 10-to-20 billion years ago; and that, given the cosmic egalitarianism with which the Big Bang dispensed matter, all mass in the universe should be distributed fairly evenly, with few clumps and voids. One can think of this expansion of space fabric—Dressler grows visibly grouchy at its mention, though he has used it like everyone else—as carrying galaxies apart just as raisins in a baking cake are carried apart by the expanding dough.

But there was one small wrinkle in this smooth expanding universe, and as is so often the case, major new discoveries were found hidden in the folds of those annoying wrinkles. Certain nearby galaxies—the raisins in the spreading dough—seemed to have other motions independent of the general expansion. Imagine a cake confected by Alice in Wonderland Bakeries, where the raisins, in addition to expanding, drifted sideways, as if attracted to each other. Movements that depart from Hubble's predicted path and speed of expansion are called "peculiar motions." It was as if the raisins, even while expanding, were tugged toward each other to make bigger clumps of raisins. Since no movement is gratuitous or incidental, some force had to be acting on these galaxies. The fact is that no one could imagine, much less measure, such motions for decades. Finally, in the 1970s, the first tentative measurements could be made, and for the second time in the century, a part of the universe was set in motion. Galaxies did not just move away from each other outwardly; they moved *peculiarly*.

If it's painful to break an egg to make an omelet, you can imagine how disturbed some astronomers became when they were asked to break the "cosmic egg." Something theoretically akin to that kind of heresy occurred when peculiar motions were systematically observed for the first time in the mid-1970s. Allan R. Sandage, like his mentor Hubble before him and like Dressler later on, was affiliated with Mount Wilson Observatory in Pasadena, California. A dominant figure in postwar astronomy, Sandage did not believe that galaxies departed in any significant way from that nice straight line on Hubble's graphs. Peculiar motions were nothing more than unreliable measurements, random noise; that was Sandage's opinion, and the opinion of one of the giants in the field counted for a lot. The universe according to Sandage expanded in a nice, smooth, reassuringly *uniform* way in every direction. An oft-used metaphor described galaxies as spots painted on a balloon: as the balloon inflated, the spots expanded and grew apart. Peculiar motions implied another prop from Wonderland: a balloon on which the spots *moved.* This became a matter of intense disagreement, and for a rather good reason: at stake was nothing less than the way the universe had formed and evolved.

A great conundrum of modern cosmology is understanding how galaxies, great forests of light and matter, managed to organize themselves out of the uniform distribution of matter; or, put another way, how do you build a mountain of light out of clouds of dust and mists of atoms? Mass attracts mass, but in a universe of uniformly distributed matter, no grain of sand, no hopped-up atom of hydrogen would seem to have more gravitational charisma than any other grain or atom in terms of attracting other atoms and initiating the slow, accretionary, momentous growth into galaxies. So what gave? The original theory would have to give, or at least bend a little. There would have to be tiny wrinkles in the fabric of the expansionary universe, and these wrinkles—tiny voids in some cases, tiny clumps in others—would act as topological seeds around which, allowing billions of years for gravity's glacial work speed, would form galaxies, and then clusters, and then superclusters, and so on. But in order for all that to happen, you would have to see a little wiggle or wobble in Edwin Hubble's straight line, and that became an issue as fraught with the sociology of broken cosmic eggs as with science.

"There was a guy who sat in that office over there for many, many years," says Dressler, nodding in the direction of Allan Sandage's second-floor office at the observatory headquarters in Pasadena, "who argued fairly persuasively that all departures from a smooth Hubble flow would be very small. He had some data nearby showing that galaxies were not moving around in all directions, that they moved very coherently. He didn't consider the possibility that they could all be moving coherently together but much in excess of what their velocity should be at any given place. He was only sort of looking at the noise, the random sort of swimming around. And when he proved that the random noise was small, he generalized that result to believe that there were no large-scale motions. That clearly was a mistake. But that expectation carried a lot of weight. And I think it discouraged people from spending what at those times were very difficult years of work to get rather poor measurements that nobody would believe."

That exact fate befell Vera Rubin and W. Kent Ford, Jr., of the Carnegie Institution of Washington and two colleagues in the mid-1970s. Using complicated and (to hear some astronomers tell it) not entirely convincing measurements, they reported that the Milky Way, our galaxy, had a peculiar velocity of about 500 kilometers per second. In other words, the Milky Way was hurtling about 370 miles per second off the plumb of the Big Bang. Rubin in fact had suggested the same thing way back in 1950, but her data had been even sketchier, the reaction even chillier. The new work, reported in 1975, still met with considerable skepticism. The effect seemed too large. "People didn't believe it," Dressler recalls, "because they really didn't believe the technique." The surprising result was consigned, fellow samurai David Burstein would write later, to that "astronomical 'limbo' reserved for controversial results of uncertain reliability."

That was 1975. Within a year, everything changed—except the disbelief. New measurements of the cosmic background, that soft antique hiss of the Big Bang, provided an outer frame to all the other motions, just as a shoreline provides a frame against which to gauge a river or ocean current. The Local Group, a gang of about twenty galaxies including the Milky Way and its nearest neighbor, the Andromeda galaxy, possessed its own peculiar motion. In other words, twenty supposedly independent galaxies were not toeing the Hubble line, either, and took an almost choreographed, unison step off course. With the new frame of reference, this movement could be measured, and it was indeed significant—600 kilometers a second. "In 1975 no one believed it was possible to move that fast," Burstein recalls. "By 1976 it was possible, but the Rubin and Ford movement was perpendicular to the cosmic background radiation." So people still disbelieved the result. But something was afoot.

Astronomers began to look for the unexplained, unseen, unidentified source responsible for its movement. Attention at first focused on the Local Supercluster, a group of galaxies in and around the Virgo cluster, about 40-to-80 million light-years from the Milky Way. A group of first-rate surveyors including the late Marc Aaronson (University of Arizona), John Huchra (Harvard-Smithsonian Center), Jeremy Mould (Caltech), Paul Schechter (Mount Wilson/Las Campanas), and R. Brent Tully (University of Hawaii) mapped several hundred spiral galaxies around the Local Supercluster and detected a pattern of velocities consistent with the presence of some massive gravitational attractor in Virgo—a so-called region of overdensity. By 1983, however, it had become apparent that the Local Supercluster alone did not impart sufficient "kick," as Dressler puts it, to account for all the peculiar motions in the Local Group. Calculations produced a new set of "velocity vectors"—directions in which moving bodies or clusters are headed—and, like arrows, these pointed toward the next closest supercluster, known as Hydra-Centaurus. Intrigued, researchers went on to map the peculiar motions around this supercluster.

In retrospect, Rubin and Ford's work opened up a Pandora's box of possibilities. The suspicion grew that these strange motions reflected a large concentration of matter with strong gravitational effects, just as iron filings twisting and curling on a piece of paper might reflect the presence of a large but unseen magnet underneath. These peculiar motions appeared especially pronounced in nearby galaxies with smaller redshifts, which proved to be a technical godsend, since the measurement of distant galaxies would introduce too much error into the calculations. So astronomers began to realize that by plotting the velocities of nearby galaxies, they might be able to infer the location of the "unseen magnet"—the mass exerting these powerful gravitational effects.

It was as if someone had pushed a button on a fantastic machine. With the cosmic background radiation as a fixed outer "wall," you could suddenly see galaxies, gangs of galaxies, even millions of confederated galaxies set in motion. More important, you could finally measure that motion against a fixed background. This animated swirl of movement updated that seventeenth-century mechanical object d'art known as the armillary sphere, which brought the Copernican revolution into the royal court and the Victorian parlor, delighting monarchs as well as children by showing the motions of the planets as they circled the sun. A modern galactic armillary sphere would look like this: The Milky Way falls toward its neighbor, the Andromeda galaxy, at 300 kilometers a second. These two galaxies, and another twenty or so that make up the Local Group, are moving toward the center of the Local Supercluster, a vast conglomeration of galaxies in the direction of Virgo. "And then *that* whole structure is part of yet a bigger, overdense structure," Dressler explains. The supercluster, too, has a peculiar motion. It is egged on by a still larger, still more distant, still mostly invisible attracting mass.

There is something zenlike about the computational exercise Dressler is performing at the moment: in order to see the forest of galaxies better, you must subtract trees from the sky. In a little room in Pasadena, working on a television image of the sky, Dressler patiently moves his cursor around a bright star in the vicinity of a galaxy listed in his logs as SPS 391, one of the 130 galaxies measured. Having corralled it, Dressler pauses momentarily, then pushes the DELETE button. The star disappears from the screen. Its light will no longer distort the very precise measurements he needs for the brightness of the nearby galaxy. Point by point, erasure by erasure, Dressler must tidy up the sky around each galaxy he measures; must determine if he is seeing the galaxies, barely more than specks, face-on (as if you were looking into a mirror) or edge-on or at some angular stage in between; must use sophisticated computer programs like the one called CASSANDRA, or invent new ones, to objectify the measurements and make them even more accurate.

"Now here's one with a great big redshift," Dressler is saying. "Because it's spinning very rapidly, it's likely to be a very luminous galaxy that would be predicted to be traveling well over three thousand kilometers a second. It's a very, very massive system and therefore the stars are really whipping around. So there should be a good correlation now between this speed and the fact that the galaxy is very bright, and that should tell us how far away it is." Dressler lines up the galaxy for measurement. He describes this work as "a pattern-recognition game that you can do very easily with your eye. But you *don't* want to do that. You want it to be objective. You want to make use of statistics and get the lines centered very accurately. So I had to teach the program how to be smart about it." The computer is educated to analyze the data objectively; out of 120 galaxies, the computer considers only 60 or 70 as "class-A observations." The rest are given less weight. These are particularly crucial measurements because Dressler is now

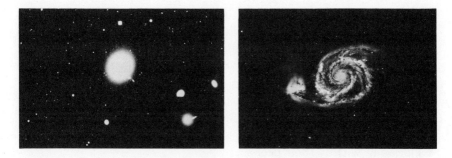

The Seven Samurai began their survey by measuring elliptical galaxies (like M87, *left,* in Virgo), but then added spiral galaxies (like M51, *right,* known better as the Whirlpool galaxy) to fill in the map more precisely. (NOAO)

trying to chart the region on the far side of the Great Attractor, showing that the galaxies on that side are falling back, not traveling with the same giddyap as the Hubble flow.

If it sounds as if one samurai is doing the work of seven, the fact of the matter is that Dressler came late to the consortium. In the late 1970s, a group of four astronomers—Sandra Faber at UC-Santa Cruz, Roberto Terlevich (now at the Royal Greenwich Observatory in England), David Burstein (now at Arizona State University), and Roger Davies (now at Oxford University)—decided to take a quick look at the structure of about two dozen elliptical galaxies. Unlike our Milky Way, with its spiraling arms, elliptical galaxies are dense, roundish, beehives of matter chock-full of stars, and they tend to congregate in the crowded core of clusters. Of perhaps greater astronomical (to say nothing of cartographical) importance, the four astronomers developed a new technique to estimate distance that made elliptical galaxies easier to measure than spirals. The purpose of the initial study had hardly anything to do with departures from the smooth Hubble flow; mostly, they wanted to see if there was a connection between the luminosity of these galaxies and their internal structure (there wasn't). "I seem to have a knack for doing things for the wrong reasons," Faber admitted later in an interview in *Origins: The Lives and Worlds of Modern Cosmologists,* "and this was no exception." "If you're a good astronomer," Burstein explains, "you do the right things for the wrong reasons."

The original four collaborators decided to increase their sample to more than five hundred galaxies, and they needed help to do it. They recruited a reluctant Alan Dressler to join the collaboration in 1980 because he had telescope time in the southern hemisphere. That same year, Donald Lynden-Bell, a theorist at Cambridge University, became so excited at the prospect of applying the new distance formula to a large sample of galaxies that he volunteered to join the group as an *observer*. About a year later, Gary Wegner of Dartmouth University, an expert in photometry, joined the collaboration. The group now numbered seven. Later, Lynden-Bell would even suggest a name, the Pleiades, but in astronomy, groups are always named (and often with disparaging wit) by their peers.

"And then we just spent *years* collecting data, sorting through it, trying to understand it," says Dressler, "before we got anywhere close to sitting down and looking at the result." Between 1983 and 1987, meeting once or twice a year, for one or two weeks at a stretch, the seven researchers would discuss the results. "We always came with great plans that we were going to *finally* get to look at the things we wanted to know," Dressler remembers, "and we always wound up spending the whole time mucking through the details." This is the unglamorous earthbound part of astronomy. It has nothing to do with the poetic firmament and everything to do with niggling over the reliability of every point on a map, reducing margins of error, deciding which measurements are questionable and which are keepers. Over two years Lynden-Bell refined the formula for calculating distance, and it seemed to work well. Too well. "We were starting to see some funny things in the data," recalls Burstein, who wrote a letter in early 1985 to alert the group, "in that galaxies were not where everyone thought they were supposed to be. We were getting *odd* answers."

By the summer of 1985, they could not ignore the evidence that something very . . . *peculiar* was going on. The seven collaborators had by then boiled down their data to 385 reliable measurements of both elliptical and spiral galaxies; they had measured both their distance and their peculiar motions. The survey took in a volume of several hundred million light-years centered on us but extending well beyond the Hydra-Centaurus Supercluster. Faber recalls that Dave Burstein was the first to characterize the nature of the beast. "Look at this," he told the group, holding a quick plot of the data. "There's a whole region in Centaurus, and it's moving at a thousand kilometers a second." When they saw these first big "bulk" deviations from the Hubble flow in their sample, they were stunned.

They knew something was going on, Burstein recalls; they just didn't know what. Burstein recalls an "electric moment" one morning at a meeting in July at Dartmouth, when all seven astronomers realized

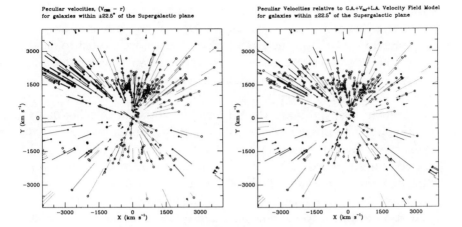

Peculiar velocities, $(V_{\underline{\ }} - r)$
for galaxies within ±22.5° of the Supergalactic plane

Peculiar Velocities relative to G.A.+V$_{\underline{\ }}$+L.A. Velocity Field Model
for galaxies within ±22.5° of the Supergalactic plane

A map of peculiar motion in the supergalactic plane *(left),* where open circles represent approaching galaxies and closed circles represent receding galaxies, shows coherent mass streaming toward a distinct focal point in the upper left quadrant. When the Great Attractor is removed as a possible gravitational lodestone *(right),* galaxies no longer display coherent flow. (D. Burstein/ Institute of Physics)

they'd all noticed the same effect. "We all looked at each other and said, 'We've got something here!' But we decided that before we said anything about it, we better figure out what it is we got." In order to figure that out, they began to draw some maps.

"When we first met at Dartmouth and measured these motions, we didn't know where they were in the sky," Dressler says. "When I got back to Pasadena, I started making an all-sky map. I started out with a Mercator projection on the sky and marked each galaxy with an *X* or *O*, whether it was moving away from us or toward us. And I think that was the first time we saw all these *X*'s on one side and all the *O*'s on the other." A second map in effect squashed the celestial sphere into a plane, so that velocity could be plotted. What they began to create, in those first crude plots, was a map of mass—a map that used the effect of gravity, in terms of the motions of galaxies streaming toward a gravitational nexus, to pinpoint the location of a surprisingly large attracting mass.

The "map" crystallized over the next five months, culminating in a meeting in November and December in Pasadena. As they computed the velocities of these various galaxies and plotted them out, they got their first peek at pattern. Not only had they zeroed in on the right cosmic neighborhood; they discovered that the whole neighborhood was *moving,* en masse, in a single bulk flow at a tremendous speed and in a direction clearly off the Hubble flow. "When we started to make maps," Dressler says, "we made the conceptual leap of seeing that this was a kind of global behavior, that it was something more than a chaotic local phenomenon."

Velocity maps, frankly, do not have the grandeur of other maps. Color-coded in a minimalist way, they initially appear uninformative to lay eyes. Galaxies moving away from us, because they are "red-shifted," are depicted as red circles, and their direction of motion is indicated with a red line—a short one if they are moving slowly, a longer one if their velocity is high. Galaxies moving *toward* us have their spectra shifted to the blue end, and thus are depicted in blue (or as open circles). When some ninety-seven elliptical galaxies were plotted on a map centered on the Hydra-Centaurus Supercluster, five other large clusters appeared to be falling toward the sixth central mass—the Hydra-Centaurus Supercluster.

"And what the group eventually found," Dressler says, "was that it was moving *away* from us at five hundred kilometers per second. In other words, we were moving in that direction and it was moving even *faster* in that same direction. That was the result of this bigger motion." Galaxies in every direction, for hundreds of millions of light-years, were fellow travelers with the Milky Way in this mass streaming. "It was a total shock to us," Faber remarked at the time. It suggested that an even greater mass than suspected, lying at an even greater distance, orchestrated the peculiar motions of millions of galaxies. "That's when I sort of became convinced that there was something really interesting going on," Dressler says. What made their maps truly revealing is that by plotting motions they were indirectly tracing the location of mass and not merely light, as in optical astronomy, and this gave them a novel cartographic way to probe one of cosmology's more perplexing paradoxes—that approximately 90 percent of the matter in the universe is invisible. The distribution of galaxies traces mass, Dressler once dryly remarked, "with all the precision of a finger painting." But motion induced by gravitational attraction betrays the location of mass, visible or hidden, and their mapped galaxies were like arrows, all pointing toward an invisible concentration of mass.

Having convinced themselves that the bulk motion was real, they were ready to go public in the first week of January 1986. Faber would disclose the result while accepting a prize from the American Astronomical Society. Davies and Burstein traveled to Houston to bask in the reaction. They expected trumpets, hosannas, wreaths of laurel dropping out of the sky. To accommodate the expected media crush, they even prepared a press release. Unfortunately, that was the same meeting at which Harvard researchers revealed that the universe had the texture of bubbles (see next chapter), a revelation that dominated press coverage. Even more unfortunately, very few of the astronomers who could truly appreciate the implications of the discovery were at the meeting. Most of them were planning to attend another meeting in Kona, Hawaii, the following week. So it fell to David Burstein to go to Kona and deliver a piece of news that slapped cosmology upside the head: that vast tracts of galaxies, dozens of light-years across, flowed in a single coherent motion toward some unseen conglomeration of matter. Burstein found the reaction more to form: he remembers the stunned audience of knowledgeable peers, the gape-mouthed disbelief of those in the front row, remembers it indeed as "the Woodstock of extragalactic astronomy." Dennis Overbye, describing the reaction in *Lonely Hearts of the Cosmos,* writes, "The afternoon dissolved in pandemonium. I felt that I was watching forty lava tubes simultaneously erupt."

When the group reported the same results at a July 1986 workshop in Santa Cruz, they finally got christened. Amos Yahil of the State University of New York at Stony Brook, a friendly skeptic of the theory, had Japan on his mind from a recent trip, and offhandedly referred to the collaborators as the "Seven Samurai" in his talk. "It was one of those nicknames that immediately caught on," Yahil admits, "to the point that it's now a standard reference in the literature."

By the spring of 1987, the Seven Samurai had realized that there was more to this phenomenon than just a bulk motion. There was a discernible acceleration in the motion, suggesting not only the existence of this large unseen mass, but its proximity. At first, they called it the New Supergalactic Center and the VMO—the Very Massive Object. "But Dressler knew that if we called it that, it would be curtains," Burstein says. "Alan always liked catchy names." And so it was Dressler who sat at a press conference in April 1987, and—on the spur of the moment, he says—invented a name for this unseen mass that has proved to have great marquee value. He called it the "great attractor." The term appeared in the first few papers in lowercase; as confidence in the data grew, the phrase began to appear as the Great Attractor.

Not everyone was convinced by the data at first, so as early as 1986, Dressler and Sandra Faber began to use telescopes at Las Campanas, in Chile, to double-check their results, repeating all their measurements on one telescope for the spectroscopy and on another for the photometry, in order to get greater uniformity. When Dressler plotted these additional measurements, he managed to fill in the skimpy back-side of the picture. The galaxies between us and Hydra-Centaurus were rushing away; the galaxies on the far, far side of Hydra-Centaurus, though small in number, appeared to have slowed up, as if falling back toward the supercluster. "There it was," he says now. "It was clearly a confirmation of what we'd done. . . . You know, it could have come out to be, well, not quite as good as the first result and we'd have to go back and think. . . . But it just came out dead-on."

There, in another dull array of dots on a piece of paper in a room in Pasadena, lay the evidence for an array of matter so immense, so sprawling, that its mass equaled 5×10^{16} solar masses—it was 50,000,000,000,000,000 times as massive as our sun, which in turn is about 300,000 times as massive as the earth. The Milky Way, that smear of 100 billion stars that so awed Dressler, is to the Great Attractor as a pebble is to a Mack truck. No one had ever seen the thing, Dressler would later explain, not only because the plane of the Milky Way obscured part of it, but also because it simply took up such a large amount of space. And without the cosmic background radiation as a frame, the swirl of movements made it difficult to detect. "Imagine what it would be like to be in an amusement park ride like the Tilt-a-Whirl, and you don't know that you are in it," Burstein says. "It's very confusing to figure out where you are."

When our grandparents looked up at the night sky in their child-hood and adolescence, not so very long ago, the largest "structures" within view and ken were age-old, hand-me-down mental constructs, the constellations, perhaps Draco or even something smaller but famil-iar, like the Big Dipper. They did not know about galaxies, had never heard of a quasar. They certainly couldn't wrap their minds around something as large, or a concept so strange, as the Great Attractor. It is almost as difficult to comprehend as to explain. Alan Dressler helps us try.

The Great Attractor, he says, represents a concentration of matter that is, paradoxically, incredibly massive but incredibly diffuse. "Now what makes it a *great* attractor," Dressler continues, "is that with that much mass, it *dominates* the motion of galaxies over a really big region. It would appear that it dominates the motions over a region of hun-dreds of millions of light-years, and that's so much bigger than people thought mass fluctuations would be." Standard theory, again, argues that with the even distribution of matter flung out by the Big Bang, such large areas of mass would not have been able to form. Yet data builds to support the Great Attractor; in 1990 astronomers at Rutgers University, allegedly attempting to shoot down the Great Attractor thesis, instead reported independent measurements that seemed to confirm its existence. Furthermore, it may not be the only such mass. Amos Yahil, with collaborators Michael Strauss and Marc Davis of UC-Berkeley, has used data from the Infrared Astronomical Satellite (IRAS) survey to plot redshifts from more than two thousand galaxies, and they have found a large, attractorlike object in the opposite part of the sky, in the direction of the Perseus-Pisces Supercluster. And a group at the Harvard-Smithsonian Center for Astrophysics in Cambridge, in mapping the entire universe in three dimensions, has found the largest structure ever seen (see next chapter).

"The Great Attractor's significance is simply this," says Dressler. "Looking for the motions of galaxies enables you to tell the largest sort of organized, lumpy structures, and the first tries to do this—the very first peeping out, you might say—has shown a rather large structure dominating a very large area, and that went contrary to expectations. So the point is not that it's unique. Undoubtedly, there are other great attractors. But it's awfully significant that the first time you look out at something, how common it is."

Whether the Great Attractor turns out, improbably, to be one of a kind or merely the first of many such dense regions, the evolving map of peculiar motions suggests that the universe is a more complex and perhaps odder place than we have known in the past. Just as the earth rotates on its axis, just as the planets revolve around the sun, just as the sun joins that swirl around the center of the Milky Way, just as the Milky Way in turn is tugged by nearby galaxies, and the Local Group by the Local Supercluster, the entire chain is under the influence of this incomprehensibly massive object called the Great Attractor, all caught in a cosmic, slow-motion version of crack-the-whip. In a universe thought only recently to have significant motions in but one direction—outward—and a speed limit imposed on these motions every bit of the way by the Hubble constant, the Seven Samurai have placed us in a universe of wayward motions and contrary flows, slow bends and unexpected eddies, all a bit reminiscent of a big river, and all the motion due to gravity sticking its finger in the current and giving it a whirl. As Alan Dressler realized that night in Chile, we do indeed stand off at some funny angle, but we now know we are also in gravitational thrall, always moving, hurtling without sensation toward some as-yet-unknown destination.

"And discovering that only happens once," Dressler says. "You know, in the same way that the earth was sort of discovered once, when those guys in the fifteenth and sixteenth centuries got to sail around the world and found the continents and where all the other people were living—it sort of knit it all together. I think we're going through that age now for the universe. It's sort of like being on the fringe of a continent. I think of these superclusters as continents, and we are *just* on the fringe of one and see just the beach. And now, I think, we've started to map into the hinterland."

18. The Universe According to John Huchra

BUBBLES, VOIDS,
THE GREAT WALL, AND, PERHAPS,
THE DEATH OF THE BIG BANG

||||||||||

Everywhere being nowhere,
who can prove
one place more than another?

We come back emptied,
to nourish and resist
the words of coming to rest:

*birthplace, roofbeam, whitewash,
flagstone, hearth,*
like unstacked iron weights

afloat among galaxies.

—Seamus Heaney,
"The Birthplace"

The mere mention of the word, or any of its derivatives, brings a gentle snort from John Huchra. Indeed, his face inflates, much as the universe he has spent so many years observing is presumed to have done aeons ago. The words that typically inspire his disdain are: *theory, theorize, theoretical.* In the world of cosmology, where to subscribe to a theory on the origin of the universe seems to involve the rites of religion as much as the rigors of science, Huchra is probably its most resolute atheist, and almost surely its most good-natured. He is a hunter-gatherer of map points. One of astronomy's nomads, he travels light and wanders widely, from hemisphere to hemisphere along earth's more mundane terrestrial coordinates, for a night or two of telescope time, weather permitting, and a chance to roam the celestial latitudes and push a little deeper into the visible universe. He stalks data in order to measure and map it. Ask him if he would prefer an open universe or a closed one, with hot dark matter or cold, with chopped nuts or candy sprinkles—he says he doesn't care. And he means it. In a field thick with theorists, he is what in astronomy passes for an "experimentalist." He just looks.

And on this September night in Arizona, having just journeyed from an observatory in Chile to Tucson by way of airport lounges in Lima, Miami, and Dallas, Huchra sits in the control room of the Multiple Mirror Telescope (MMT) atop Mount Hopkins in southern Arizona, a bottle of aspirin and a can of Dr Pepper by his right hand, George Winston music drizzling out of the stereo, his trademark floppy brown hat drooping over a television monitor that in turn shows a ghostly galaxy that unleashed this very light about 60 million years ago. A self-proclaimed "swamp rat" from Jersey City, New Jersey, a blue-collar astronomer if ever there was one, blind in one eye until he got a cornea transplant several years ago, John Huchra views the world through thick glasses, yet his two minimally functional eyes have been on the receiving end of more photons emanating from more galaxies than probably any other person in all the history of humans peering with curiosity at the night sky. And that is why, by talent and temperament, he is probably the preeminent cartographer in this, astronomy's preeminent era of mapping.

"Surveys are not the most important thing in astronomy," Princeton University astrophysicist Jeremiah Ostriker likes to say. "They are the *only* thing." That is why about a hundred nights a year you will find the forty-two-year-old Huchra at one telescope or another, logging measurements with edgy enthusiasm, talking a blue streak in between, as down-home as a country-and-western song, brainy as a precocious child; you get the feeling that if there weren't bad weather, he might never take a day off. The more data, the better the sample. Data talks. It converses in patterns. Get enough measurements, properly taken, and they begin to form a picture; if you get a clear enough picture and if you are an experimentalist, as is Huchra, one of the sweetest pleasures in life is to kill off a theory with the sheer contradictory power of your data. The map is simply a picture of the corpse.

It has taken about ten years of gathering data, but Huchra and his colleagues at the Harvard-Smithsonian Center for Astrophysics are en route to undoing 18 billion years or so of cosmology. What he is doing, in these dreary nightlong marathons of measurement, is sticking pins in the model of the Big Bang, or at least puncturing some major assumptions that derive from it about the origin of the universe and how it has evolved. What enabled the Harvard group to challenge this popular model was a survey—astronomers prefer the word "survey" to "map"—of galaxies in a slice of overhead sky.

In between measurements this September night, Huchra talks about the "Great Wall." Back at the Center for Astrophysics in Cambridge, Massachusetts, where he is professor of astronomy, Huchra and his longtime collaborator, Margaret J. Geller, have identified a structure, a gauzy sprawl of galaxies in the northern celestial sky so large and uninterrupted that it is the largest *thing* that humans have ever laid eyes on. Larger than a galaxy, than a group of galaxies, than a supercluster of galaxies, it stretches all across the sky, at least 500 million light-years long (our galaxy, the Milky Way, measures about 100,000 light-years across; the Great Wall could swallow 5,000 Milky Ways, each with its 100 billion stars, like so many goldfish). Though its exact mass remains uncertain, it has landed like a ton of bricks on some cherished theories about the evolution of galaxies and other large-scale structures in the universe. Just as some maps encapsulate or embellish theory, this map looks as if it might demolish some. Huchra says he doesn't care one way or another. But he says that with a mischievous smile.

Every time astronomers discover something new, something different, a collective sigh blows through the community as if, finally, the largest of the Chinese boxes has been found and the puzzle is finally complete. Then a year or two later, somebody finds something that looms larger, recedes faster, lies more distant, appears to have a quirkier pattern. Experience has made both Huchra and Geller reluctant about jumping to conclusions. "Here's a bit of personal philosophy," says Huchra, a compulsive ad lib philosopher, in between measurements. "The two most important sentences to learn in the English language are 'I don't know' and 'I am wrong.' If you learn to speak those words without trepidation, life will be much easier." Shortly thereafter, he is asked to explain exactly what the Great Wall means. At peace with his ignorance, Huchra says he doesn't know. It is not the job of an experimentalist, he would argue, to say what theoretically might be the case. But it does fall within the job description, he would add, to point out what can't be true. And he does allow, under questioning, that the implications of the Great Wall, followed to their logical conclusions, seem to imply that something is seriously, and perhaps fatally, wrong with prevailing theory about how galaxies form and perhaps even how the universe began and evolved. A once-fashionable theory that predicted something called cold dark matter,

for one, seems mortally stricken with inconsistency as a result of this
and other recently published surveys, and for the first time in modern
memory one even hears grumbles that perhaps the Big Bang itself is
beginning to outlive its usefulness as a theory. What has brought
cosmology to this richly promising moment of crisis is the unprecedented amount of mapping that has occurred in astronomy over the
past ten years, and how those maps have in nearly every case flown in
the face of theory.

"I've been known to get telescope time on anything that doesn't
move."

Huchra makes this assertion while standing in the kitchen of the
MMT building, stirring a grim ragù of onions, cream, and particles of
pasta in a pot even as the building itself is whirling around (it rides on
a steel rail and all four stories rotate, rather than just the telescope, to
line up on celestial targets). The universe, too, seems to work like this:
motions within motions, stirrings within stirrings. Huchra is merely
one of many contemporary astronomers trying to measure enough
celestial objects to discern pattern in all this flow. Wearing blue jeans,
a blue-checked Western shirt (tails out), moccasins, and a beard, he
always seems slightly out of breath, a small man who seems bigger than
he really is because of his enthusiasm and bluster and brash sense of
humor. He has been known to open talks at conferences by showing
the following slide:

NO THEORY ZONE

$$E = mc^2$$

At a meeting several years ago at the Vatican, he took it upon himself
to remark that "the theorists seem to be running a little rampant again
and it's about time for those of us who are observers to rein them in
a little and bring them at least a little closer to reality." That is Huchra:
a walking reality check. He can get away with this because, as many
others in the field concede, he is very good at collecting data. Speaking
of the Harvard-Smithsonian survey, Princeton's Ostriker says, "In
conception and execution, it's absolutely first-rate. It's been very accurately compiled. No one goes back and looks at the galaxies and finds
anything different." No, because Huchra is quick, efficient, reliable.

And he is hardly the only cosmic cartographer who is quick, efficient, and reliable, either. The Center for Astrophysics survey is merely one of numerous mapping projects under way at places like Cornell, UC-Berkeley, the State University of New York at Stony Brook, Caltech, the University of Hawaii, and elsewhere. Galaxies weren't even known as a separate astrophysical beast until the 1920s, but Princeton and the University of Chicago have now begun a joint effort to map 1 million of them by the year 2000. This explosive growth in mapping stems from yet another technological revolution: the ability to detect many more photons, which in turn permits accurate and rapid measurement of redshifts, which determines the velocity of galaxies, which in turn implies their distance. That chain of hard-won mathematical relationships was constructed in the first half of this century (a superb account can be found in Timothy Ferris's *The Red Limit*), and it has allowed these new maps to overcome the great conceptual constraint of all astronomy prior to 1900. That constraint, stated baldly, was that the sky fit over the world like the lid of a pot—static, without dimension, immovable—because there was no way to measure distance.

Astronomy's first redshift survey was completed in 1925. Unfortunately, it came before the true significance of redshifts was known, and almost before the existence of galaxies had been established. Early in the nineteenth century, chemists discovered that any source of light—starlight or candlelight, it made no difference—could be directed through a slit and prism in such a way that the light would be broken down into a series of vertical lines; these lines, known as spectra, offered a kind of fingerprint of the chemicals contained in the material. If you throw a dash of common table salt (sodium chloride) into a candle flame, you will see a characteristic orangish color revealed by sodium and you will see a characteristic pattern of vertical lines; in the furnace of a star or galaxy that burns sodium, such as our sun, those same colors and that same telltale pattern of lines appear. Each species of atom, from hydrogen to platinum, produces a particular spectral palette and leaves a particular spectral signature.

In the middle of the nineteenth century, astronomers borrowed this trick from the chemists and, attaching the same slit-and-prism apparatus to a telescope, routinely measured the spectra of stars and thus learned of their chemical composition. The physicist Christian Doppler, in the meantime, had noticed that the characteristic pattern of vertical lines shifted to the right or left, toward the red or blue ends of the spectrum, when the object was moving at high velocity away from or toward the observer. It was one of those subtle observations that have nonetheless underscored much twentieth-century astronomy. In astronomical spectra, those shifts indicated movement by the celestial object, and the spectrum of an object moving away was said to be "redshifted." The estimable Vesto Slipher of Lowell Observatory in Arizona, a man so fastidious that he would spend entire nights at the telescope without loosening his tie, began a redshift survey of objects called spiral "nebulae" and by 1925 had accumulated redshifts for forty-five spirals. This was the first hint of a rustle of movement in the celestial dome, but the full significance of these measurements awaited brilliant insights from another quarter.

At the time Slipher began his redshift survey, astronomy was racked by a debate about the size of the universe. The question centered on those same spiral "nebulae." Did they lie within our own galaxy, the Milky Way, or did they exist outside it as "island universes" unto themselves, as the philosopher Immanuel Kant had improbably predicted way back in 1755? Harlow Shapley of Mount Wilson Observatory in California was the first to introduce a little breathing room to the overhead dome. Between 1914 and 1920, Shapley mapped the stars in globular clusters—luminous spheres drippingly rich with stars—and figured out a novel way to establish their distance. With this three-dimensional map of globular clusters, he concluded that they lay at the center of the Milky Way, a brilliant and incisive deduction; unfortunately, he went on to drastically overestimate the diameter of the Milky Way at 250,000 light-years, and that error led others to misgauge the size and thus the very nature of the universe. Arguing without sufficient evidence that spiral nebulae were not galaxies, Shapley suggested that the entire known universe fell within the bounds of the Milky Way. Just as Ptolemy fixed the earth at the center of our solar system, the influential Shapley placed the earth's galaxy, the Milky Way, at the center of the cosmos, its lone geographic cell.

In 1919, as Shapley was publishing his work on globular clusters, an astronomer named Edwin Hubble arrived at Mount Wilson. Hubble, a Rhodes scholar and amateur pugilist, set out to investigate the enigmatic spiral nebulae. Using the hundred-inch telescope on Mount Wilson, and employing the astronomical yardstick worked out by Shapley and ultimately improving on it, Hubble showed by 1924 that certain spiral nebulae were nongalactic—that is, they lay outside the Milky Way. This seemingly modest observation had enormous cosmological implications; the Milky Way, Hubble implied, was not the only galaxy in town. With patient observation and the Atlas-like shoulders

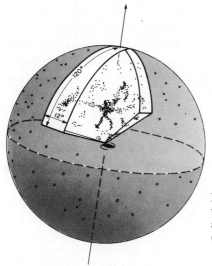

Plot of the celestial sphere,
with the Milky Way in the center
and the first map slice rising above it.
(Smithsonian Astrophysical Observatory)

of Intellect, Hubble heaved the dome of the sky deep into space. Galaxies existed outside our own. The universe was much larger than we had thought.

To this great conceptual breakthrough, Hubble added one crowning achievement. Building on the work of Vesto Slipher and others, he puzzled over the curiously displaced spectra of those spiral galaxies, now known to lie far beyond the Milky Way, and discovered that virtually all of them had shifted to the red end of the spectrum. Through painstaking calculations, he deduced—the reality emerged over the course of several years—that a redshifted spectra meant motion. The shift represented the slight elongation of light waves reaching observers on earth from a star or galaxy that *was moving away from the earth.* This was the light equivalent of the way an ambulance's sound waves become more elongated (and the sound of the siren lower) after it has passed by. Redshifts betrayed galaxies on the move. Redshifts also provided a measure of movement; the larger the redshift, the greater the distance. It was not enough that Hubble invented a universe with multiple galaxies; he also set these galaxies in motion. The entire universe was expanding outward. In several decades, with the help of the new generation of telescopes, Hubble and Slipher and Shapley and others had blown the fixed celestial dome, the astronomy of two dimensions, clear out of the sky.

And that is where the matter stood *theoretically* in 1929. Astronomers were poised to push through to the other side of the "celestial dome" of the ancients, push deep into a vast new frontier, into the third dimension. Except they couldn't quite do it. They didn't have the technology to do it, and they wouldn't for decades. Redshifts proved so onerous to measure that between 1912 and 1956, only about six hundred were catalogued. In the 1930s, for example, it could take ten nights of observation to obtain a single spectrum. The problem, in a word, was photons.

"Photons," Huchra was saying, between bites of his dinner, "are the name of the game."

Photons are the *lingua franca* of astronomy. X-ray astronomers build false-color maps with X rays, which are exceedingly energetic photons; radio astronomers construct pictures with radio waves, which can also be considered photons. The Hubble Space Telescope, if its blurred vision is fixed, and other astronomical eye pieces in use or on the drawing board will revolutionize the capture of signals in virtually all the photonic tongues in which the universe speaks. The history of optical astronomy can be boiled down to a simple maxim: the ability to see distant or faint objects depends on the ability to capture photons, the fundamental particles of light, after they've boiled off the surface of stars and galaxies and quasars and zoomed through the cosmos at 186,000 miles per second, and then strike John Huchra's rebuilt eye and retina, or ours—eight minutes later if they've left our sun, 12 billion years later if they started out from the most distant of quasars.

Human eyes make poor collectors of astronomical photons. We can discern only the brightest objects in the sky, down to about the sixth magnitude, and we retain photons on our retinas for only a tenth of a second or so; like windshield wipers, the eyes sweep away residues of light before faint sources can build up into a more coherent image. We began to rectify part of the problem in 1609, when Galileo placed a concave lens behind a convex lens and pointed it heavenward for the first time. His telescope gathered and focused more photons from distant stars and planets, but did not allow faint sources to build up. Similarly, the concave mirrors of reflecting telescopes, invented by Isaac Newton, allowed the construction of larger—but not necessarily more efficient—gatherers of photons. The problem was that something like 99.5 percent of the photons escape detection. Astronomers tried attaching photographic plates to the back ends of mammoth telescopes, and still those plates registered about one-half of 1 percent of the photons reaching the plate, to say nothing of photons lost at each reflection and each glass-air surface within the telescope. Only the brightest of objects or the longest of exposures made pretty pictures. Huchra argues that there was "no real significant change in detector technology" from 1917, when the hundred-inch reflecting telescope on Mount Wilson in California went into operation, until the 1960s.

As long as photographic plates captured only 0.5 percent of the photons hitting a telescope, as they did into the 1960s, redshifts for all but nearby objects were impossible to record. But then the Carnegie Institution of Washington, which runs observatories on Mount Wilson in California and Las Campanas in Chile, adapted a technology used by the military in Vietnam for its night-vision scopes to create what was called a "Carnegie tube." Only a few Carnegie tubes were made, but these few made the point: similar to a photocathode tube, they captured 15 to 20 percent of the photons. Astronomers lucky enough to have one gathered thirty or forty *times* as much light as their peers.

Still, even the best Carnegie tubes missed 80 percent of the photons. In the early 1970s, realizing this, several astronomers—James Gunn of Princeton and Stephen A. Shectman of Caltech get most of the conceptual credit here—had the idea of attaching an exquisitely sensitive silicon chip to the bottom of the photocathode tube. Where once the photons hit photographic plates and toppled a halide crystal or two, they would now be amplified in the photo tube before striking one of the chip's tiny light-sensitive squares, generating an electronic signal. Shectman converted this idea into a practical measuring tool for astronomy. Employing a silicon chip known as a Reticon, smaller than a dime and divided into a grid of squares (contemporary models, for example, have 2,048 squares), he wired each square to be independently capable of firing an electronic pulse when hit by a photon, and the photons piled up like snowflakes into a measurable spectrum; later, with more sophisticated sensors, those impulses were amplified, retained electronically until an actual image built up, and then processed by computer, whereupon the image would appear on a television monitor. Gone was the eye piece. Gone was the drudgery of plunging photographic plates with chill fingers into developer. Gone, too, was the night sky: astronomers watched it all on TV.

Called a charge-coupled device (or CCD), this kind of back-end accessory now allows astronomers to capture up to 70 percent of the photons. "One photon that is detected coming in," explains Huchra, "will produce a million out the back end." The speed, accuracy, and improved seeing of the CCDs testify to a new technology of measurement that has completely changed optical astronomy in the last ten years. Put another way, from the time of Galileo to 1925, galaxies were an unknown entity; from 1925 to roughly 1975, redshift measurements of galaxies numbered perhaps fifteen hundred; but with the CCDs in place since the mid-1970s, tens of thousands of redshifts have been measured; and in cosmic cartography, redshifts are the only route to obtaining the third coordinate—distance—in a three-dimensional map. Thus the new imaging technologies have allowed large-scale mapping projects that would have been impossible a generation earlier. And they have led to another of John Huchra's philosophical tenets. "I have a rule," he announced over his shoulder, rushing up the stairs to the control room with his uneaten dinner, "which is you should never waste any time not collecting photons."

The powerful new detectors meant astronomers could measure the redshifts of fainter, more distant galaxies, and by the mid-1970s it for the first time became reasonable to contemplate making a large-scale survey of the sky. The first two dimensions, right ascension and declination, were the celestial equivalents of latitude and longitude. The third dimension was velocity, as betrayed by redshifts; and if you knew the velocity of a galaxy as it receded from earth, you could estimate its distance. Not *perfectly*; that is one of the shortcomings of the method. But well enough to get a decent three-dimensional picture of the distribution of galaxies. The time was ripe to mount large surveys; Princeton astrophysicist P. James E. Peebles, one of the leading theorists in the field, began to push for the creation of broad redshift surveys in the mid-1970s.

Enter Huchra. In 1975, Huchra was a graduate student at Caltech—"the dumbest of the best," he likes to say. Born in Jersey City two days before Christmas in 1948 and raised in nearby Ridgefield Park, he remembers his hometown as poor, predominantly Catholic, and unkind to the bright or the small. His parents, both born in the United States, were raised in rural Poland before returning to America in their teens. His father was a freight conductor for the railroad, his mother a bookkeeper.

Huchra may be, after Hubble, optical astronomy's most accomplished martial artisan, having achieved considerable success as a scholastic wrestler. "I was a little bit of an outcast," he says of his school days. "In that part of the world, it was not good to be small and not good to be smart, and the interesting thing was that I was both small and smart, and that got me into a lot of trouble. Here's another bit of personal philosophy: There are three types of kids in high school. There are the jocks, the hoods, and the nerds. And if you're a nerd, you're in big trouble. So I became a jock. I went out for the wrestling team and wrestled ninety-eight pounds. And I never lost a match."

Still, he had time to read, and if there were a book award given purely on the basis of career influence, surely George Gamow's *One, Two, Three . . . Infinity* would win in science, for it captivated Huchra as it did many other physicists and astronomers of his generation (how ironic, though, that Huchra's work has begun to cast doubt on Gamow's pet theory, the Big Bang). He ended up studying physics at MIT, dabbled in X-ray astronomy, graduated in 1970, and did his graduate work at Caltech, where he studied a subspecies of the cosmic zoo known as Markarian galaxies and discovered an asteroid, which he named Asmodeus, after a Christian archdemon infamous for lechery. In September of 1975, his thesis virtually complete, Huchra stumbled into one of those warps of coincidence that in retrospect turn out to be a definitive fork in the road. Set to leave for Australia, where he had accepted a position at a state-run observatory, Huchra got a telephone call telling him that the Australian government had collapsed, that a hiring freeze had been instituted, and that he no longer had a job. "I carefully neglected to turn in my thesis," Huchra says, "until I could apply for jobs again."

As it turns out, a North Vietnamese postdoctoral fellow at Caltech named Trinh Thuan was at that very moment hatching plans to launch one of the most ambitious redshift surveys yet attempted: to measure redshifts for eleven hundred galaxies brighter than fourteenth magnitude in what was known as the Zwicky catalogue (during the 1960s, the legendary Caltech astronomer Fritz Zwicky, who among other things used to do one-armed push-ups on the floor of Caltech's faculty dining room, had mapped the northern hemisphere as part of what was known as the Palomar Sky Survey). Thuan's collaboration included Caltech astronomer Wallace Sargent, a radio astronomer named Gillian Knapp (now at Princeton), and Huchra, who described himself as "a real infantryman in the optical observational game, because I'd probably spent more time playing with telescopes and taking spectra and doing all of that kind of stuff than anybody else, and had a reputation, even then, for being pretty careful about data." The group got time at four telescopes and measured redshifts for approximately six hundred galaxies before the collaboration began to

The CfA maps don't answer any questions, but they pose some tough ones. Geller: "Every survey we do seems to contain a structure as big as the survey." Huchra: "The standard Big Bang may be just plain wrong." (Steven Seron/ Smithsonian Astrophysical Observatory)

dissolve. Huchra, meanwhile, found a job in August of 1976. The Harvard-Smithsonian Center for Astrophysics, normally a bastion of theoreticians, decided to hire a token observer that year.

Even as the wheels were coming off the Caltech collaboration, Huchra found two new collaborators to keep the project rolling. Margaret Geller and Marc Davis, both out of Princeton, had been indoctrinated by James Peebles with the idea that the time was ripe to do redshift surveys. Born in Ithaca, New York, Geller too was raised in New Jersey, where her father worked as an X-ray crystallographer at Bell Labs; a forceful, no-nonsense extrovert interested in becoming either a mathematician or an actress, she ended up studying physics as an undergraduate at UC-Berkeley and then survived the high-powered but male-dominated graduate program in astrophysics at Princeton. At about the time the redshift survey got under way, she frankly admits to experiencing a frustration and disillusionment that had her entertaining thoughts of getting out of the field entirely. "I decided that if I could not get a position in astronomy that I felt I merited, then I would get out," she recalls. "Then the Smithsonian job came through, and things began to change."

At Harvard, Huchra, Geller, and Davis planned an even more ambitious mapping project. They expanded their sample to include all galaxies in the Zwicky catalogue to 14.5 magnitude; adding that 0.5 in magnitude bumped their workload up from eleven hundred to about twenty-four hundred galaxies. Then Huchra and colleagues Dave Latham and John Tonry souped up the machinery of the sixty-inch telescope on Mount Hopkins in Arizona, outfitting it with one of the new-fangled CCD photon detectors, upgrading the computer software, and fine-tuning the spectrograph. By March of 1978, they were ready to take measurements, and by 1981 they had measured redshifts for twenty-four hundred galaxies.

The results, while interesting, were inconclusive. They hadn't gone deep enough. The distribution of galaxies appeared to be random, with a few filaments and blobs, which is what everyone expected to see; but in a universe of 1 billion galaxies, twenty-four hundred data points formed not so much a map as a few smashed bugs on a windshield. They needed more data, but reality intervened. Davis took a job at UC-Berkeley (where he has gone on to spearhead an infrared survey of galaxies). Huchra and Geller, meanwhile, were derailed by a bugaboo of university life that discriminates, increasingly, against work that requires patience and time. Maps require years of work to compile, yet scientists are expected to publish frequently. So Huchra and Geller spent the next several years looking at clusters of galaxies. "We were working on clusters because you could do a cluster and write it up and get it over with," Huchra admits. "Whereas big surveys can take two or three years before you begin to see really [anything . . .] All the time, in the back of our minds, I think, was the idea that we would expand the survey a little deeper."

The large-scale structure of the universe appeared so confusing to cosmologists by the early 1980s that many would have subscribed to the exasperation of Alfonso the Wise, the thirteenth-century Castilian king who remarked of the Ptolemaic worldview, "Had I been present at the Creation, I would have given some useful hints for the better ordering of the universe."

With more groups launching mapping projects, the universe as it was "ordered" in these surveys began to look terribly confounding. Some saw Swiss cheese, others saw "spongy" material; still others saw filaments and knots. The night sky became a high-stakes Rorschach test for every theory. And everything revolved around a central mystery in cosmology: how did galaxies, huge luminous maelstroms of matter, form? How did they precipitate out of the even distribution of matter that appeared in the sky?

The standard theory grew out of the implications of Hubble's great discovery, that the universe expanded evenly. Theoreticians argued that gravity—the straw that stirs the cosmological drink— would not have had enough time from the Big Bang to form clumps of galaxies. That view posed no problem for several decades because nobody was in a position to measure unusual densities and see any clumps. You could only see what the technology permitted you to see.

The first crack in the smooth wall of the universe came in the 1950s, when Gérard de Vaucouleurs of the University of Texas argued—mostly to deaf ears—that the Milky Way belonged to a Local Super-cluster of galaxies, and thus there were larger confederations of matter than mere galaxies. Then, in the 1970s, astronomers began to detect some voids and filaments. With each new jolt of data, theorists struggled to keep up (to hear the observers tell it, they struggled to keep up the way ambulance chasers do). Then, quite unexpectedly, much more serious gaps began to appear in the supposedly smooth distribution of matter.

A huge hole in the theory appeared in 1981, measuring approximately 300 million light-years across. That was the size of a large void that appeared in the sky near the constellation Boötes, according to Robert Kirshner (then at the University of Michigan, now at Harvard-Smithsonian) and his colleagues. Not a black hole, not a dust cloud, just more or less empty space. According to the Standard Model, some five thousand galaxies should have been milling about in something that size. The Boötes void was a real pea in the smooth mattress of the standard model. If the Big Bang, like some spherical shower head, sprayed matter in all directions with even distribution, and the universe was reckoned to be 10 or 15 billion years old, physics could not explain how gravity could dig such an enormous hole. Were other parts of the universe similarly pitted and pocked? Was matter distributed evenly or unevenly? Margaret Geller remembers thinking at the time, "That must be the only void in the universe. It must be very rare." It was precisely these questions that a redshift survey was uniquely capable of answering.

And so several groups of astronomers—Huchra and Geller among them—sat down to design sky surveys that might provide some reliable answers. Kirshner's group attempted to map a large part of the sky; they measured thin, small regions within it, an approach likened to sticking knitting needles through a ball of yarn. Marc Davis and his group at UC-Berkeley opted for something called "randomly selected sparse sampling"; they would randomly measure and map every third or fifth galaxy in the sky. Huchra and Geller wanted a sample both labor-saving and quickly informative. "The strategy Margaret and I adopted, for several reasons, was to do dense sampling," Huchra explains. "I mean, do *everything* in the sample. But instead of trying to do the whole thing at once, do them in strips. It has two advantages. Advantage number one, from purely a technical point of view, is that telescopes don't like to move. The less you move a telescope, the better

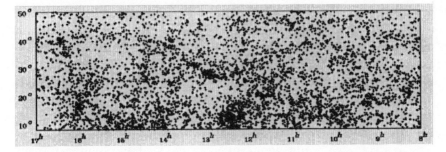

Viewed head-on, as if one were standing at the point of a wedge of pie and looking into the slice, galaxies occasionally congregate in small clumps, but the view is two-dimensional and minimally informative. (Smithsonian Astrophysical Observatory)

it is. So if you just let the telescope wiggle back and forth a little bit while the earth rotates and you catch the galaxies as they go around, it's a very efficient way of doing these kinds of surveys. And the second advantage is that if you do a strip survey, you can in one year get a survey that has at least one big dimension [whatever redshift you get to, plus the angular dimension on this point and along the length of this strip]. So you can look for big structures."

Somewhat less deliberation, Huchra says, went into the decision about what slice of the sky they would first tackle: "The one that went straight overhead in Tucson."

To say the group had no expectations is to politely downplay their utter and misplaced faith in prevailing theory. "We decided to do this strip," Geller says flatly, "to show that there weren't any other voids." The Harvard-Smithsonian group began taking measurements in 1984 (this essentially meant Huchra; Geller, the theorist, rarely showed up at the observatory). A dervish of nervous energy and hectic efficiency in the control room, Huchra set out to measure fifteen thousand galaxies. He could measure redshifts for as many as fifty galaxies on his dusk-to-dawn runs, and figured that, combining his own observations with data compiled by others, he could get three thousand done in one year.

If you happen to stand in your backyard some evening, you can get a sense of where Huchra trained his electronic cross hairs. The slice passed through what is called the Coma cluster, a thick clot of stars located in the constellation Coma Berenices in the northern sky, not far from the Big Dipper. It may at first be difficult to visualize the

three-dimensional shape of the surveyed area. Imagine yourself floating over a baseball field. If the earth is home plate and Huchra's
telescope is pointed north toward center field, he was able to measure
all the galaxies that fell within the first and third base lines (the Harvard-Smithsonian survey was actually a little broader, but geometri-
cally similar). But the field itself represents only a flat, two-dimensional
slice of the universe; for the third, wedgelike dimension, imagine the
trajectory of a low, hard, line drive that clears the fence for a home run.
The first Harvard-Smithsonian survey included all the volume of space
from the playing field up to the plane of that home run's trajectory.

Within that wedge, the Harvard-Smithsonian group measured
584 new redshifts in a sample that contained eleven hundred galaxies
with a magnitude of 15.5. Most of the data was in hand by the late
spring of 1985, but it wasn't until June of that year, very curiously, that
they bothered to see what the map looked like.

"Normally, when you're doing something like this, you plot the
data up every day," Huchra says. "Every time you get a new redshift,
you make a plot and see what it looks like. Well, we were so sure that
it wasn't going to look any different from what we had seen in the
shallower surveys that we didn't plot the data up until we'd collected
it all, right? *Very strange.* Normal experimentalists aren't so weird. We
gave the stuff to a graduate student of ours, Valérie de Lapparent. She
plotted it up after we'd gotten the last redshift. And damned if there
wasn't a real strange distribution."

Strange indeed. De Lapparent, a student from the University of
Paris, at first refused to believe what she saw on her computer screen.
Looking straight up into the mapped slice, as if standing on home plate
and looking through clouds of gnats attracted by the lights, the view
looked pretty random: a few clumps here and there, but mostly a
monotonous smear of galaxies like a rich star field. But that was the
two-dimensional view, with no depth. When the slice was viewed from
the side, as if one hovered like a pop-up over the baseball field, the
"randomness" descrambled itself. Suddenly, there were clumps and
voids. There was architecture, there were sheets and round shapes.
There even appeared to be a kind of stick figure, a galactic homunculus, in the Coma cluster. The map shocked them all. They saw sinewy
masses of galaxies on the one hand, great empty holes and galactic
voids on the other. What had looked like filaments in two dimensions
resolved into the intersection of thin, bubblelike sheets of galaxies
surrounding voids in three dimensions. Bubbles—frothy, foamy bubbles! And one of the bubble-voids was nearly as large as the Boötes

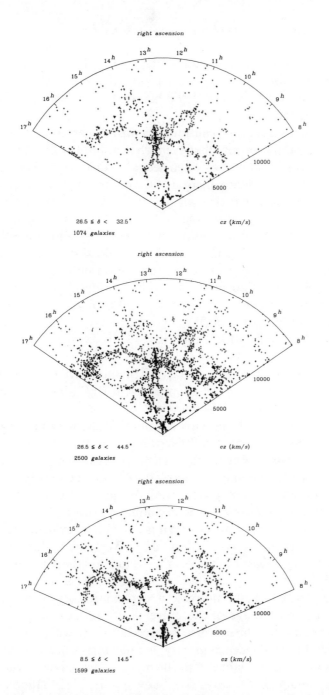

Huchra thought the printer was malfunctioning when he saw the first slice of 1,074 galaxies *(top)* with its filaments, voids, and a little stick-figure homunculus. As more slices were added *(middle and bottom),* it appeared that galaxies formed in thin sheets on the surface of bubbles surrounding large voids. (Smithsonian Astrophysical Observatory)

void. "Frankly, we were all pretty damned astonished," Huchra remembers. "Because, like I was saying, it was *not* what we expected to see. Not by a long shot." "Flabbergasted" is the word Geller uses to describe the moment.

There resides in the cautious scientist's heart a reservoir of paranoid uncertainty so great that even when a freshly minted map contradicts expectations (as it so often seems to do), researchers reflexively doubt not the standard theories of strangers that hold sway at the moment, but rather their own hard-won data. "The first thing that came to my mind," says Huchra, "was, 'Oh, shit, is my data good enough?' Because by definition, when you see something you don't expect, the first thing you say is, 'Did we do something wrong?' You go through, you check the data, and there's nothing wrong with the plotting routine. You know, the ink cartridge hasn't fallen off the paper plotter or something like that. And then you say, 'Well, yeah, it *is* real. What does it mean?'"

Finally, a job fit for a theorist.

"I've always thought of galaxy formation as like seeing the end of a movie and wondering what happened earlier," Margaret Geller says. "And a *lot* of things could happen."

The story line of that movie is nothing less than the origin of the universe, and by the mid-1980s, a pretty good title for it would be *The Search for Omega*. Omega is the astrophysical symbol for the mean mass density of the universe—or, simply put, the average amount of matter (or mass) in any given chunk of the entire universe. For theorists, *The Search for Omega* is becoming a horror film.

Omega is important because it is one of the key mathematical legs upon which current theories about the universe are built. Cosmologists use three key measures to form a picture of the Big Bang and its aftermath: the amount of matter in the universe (suggested by omega), the speed at which the universe is expanding (keyed to the Hubble constant), and the age of the universe. If omega is larger than one, theory argues that the universe is "closed": space will curve in on itself because of the influence of gravity, parallel lines will converge (a paradox known as the "flatness" problem), and the universe will not continue expanding in the way first discovered by Edwin Hubble, but will snap back into something known informally as the Big Crunch. If omega is less than one, the universe is "open": theory argues that there is simply not enough matter upon which gravity can build the larger structures we see through our telescopes—galaxies, quasars, and so on.

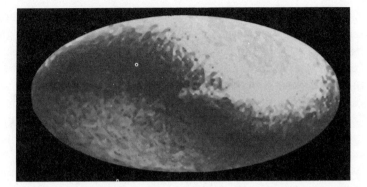

How did the universe get to be so lumpy and bubbly from so smooth a beginning? Two sets of maps have put cosmology between a rock and a hard place. The Huchra-Geller maps imply much more galactic structure than astronomers expected, while NASA's new maps of the cosmic background radiation *(above)* imply that at its very beginning, the universe was extremely smooth. (NASA/COBE Science Working Group)

So theorists have proposed a complicated, "inflationary" model of the universe that begins with all matter compressed into a highly dense 10^{-43}-centimeter "singularity"; it explodes in the Big Bang, inflates exponentially before the universe has aged a single second, and then slows again to a steadier expansion. For the universe to work that way, however, omega very conveniently must equal exactly one. The problem is that galactic surveys, for the first time, are producing lots of data about omega, and omega doesn't seem to equal one. In fact, it appears to be well less than half that.

To accommodate all these odd conditions of the universe, cosmologists add "parameters." These could be likened to subtheories that explain problems, but to the cynical or skeptical, adding parameters might be likened to adding spices to mask a failing stew. One vexing problem is that the observed mass in the universe amounts to only 10 percent of what is needed to form galaxies; the other 90 percent has been considered "missing matter," and most recently has been believed to take the form of the aforementioned cold dark matter. Cold dark matter, in turn, requires the existence of yet undiscovered subatomic particles that account for all that missing mass—a light neutrino is one candidate, axions are another.

That is why the Harvard-Smithsonian map left everybody in a quandary (not for nothing did Geller begin titling her talks "Bubble,

Bubble, Toil and Trouble"). Evidence for a smooth distribution of matter from the Big Bang is quite solid; if anything, it has grown stronger in 1990 with the results of a separate mapping project called the Cosmic Background Explorer (COBE), which has confirmed that the Big Bang left a perfectly homogeneous microwave background—a perfectly uniform echo of radiation, with no apparent wrinkles, no subtle clumps. The redshift survey offers equally strong, but utterly contradictory evidence. Bubbles are not random, nor are they rare. As Geller remarked at the time, "It now turns out that this type of structure is very common, but we couldn't see it before because we hadn't looked at a large enough volume of the universe. We probably are sitting on the surface of a bubble. We can't see the other bubbles until we look deep enough."

What it meant, in a broader sense, was big trouble for the Standard Model. Gravity has always been cast as the sculptor of galaxies and large-scale objects in the universe. If, as had been argued, the universe began with an even distribution of matter, then you might expect to see galaxies form when dust and matter cooled and coalesced into ever-larger congregations of gas (the bottom-up theory) or when large conglomerations of pancakelike accretions broke down into galaxies (the top-down theory). No model made provisions for suds and bubbles, with the possible exception of a 1981 theory floated by astrophysicists Jeremiah Ostriker of Princeton and Lennox Cowie, then of Johns Hopkins University; they suggested that when the universe was quite young, perhaps a billion years after the Big Bang, massive stars rapidly formed, rapidly burned themselves out and then, fueled by massive collapse, exploded into supernovas whose shock waves formed concussive shells. These concussions bunched gases and matter into shapes resembling bubbles. The topological resemblance was right, but the scale seemed off; the size of the Harvard-Smithsonian bubbles were ten times larger than those blown by supernovas.

De Lapparent, Huchra, and Geller published their first slice in *Astrophysical Journal* (*Letters*) in March 1986. For the first time, the universe took on this sudsy, bubbly, foamy texture. Critics howled, and continue to. The Harvard-Smithsonian team has continued to measure slices of the sky adjacent to the first, and with each additional slice, the picture has become more complex, but hardly more comforting to the theorists. They still find the foamy architecture. "We can slice and dice both vertically and horizontally, and we do find some bubbles," says Huchra. But the bubbles have receded, like a sinkful of subsiding suds, in the presence of something even more puzzling, something called—well, let's let John Huchra describe what happened after he measured or compiled more than ten thousand redshifts and, in 1989, at the suggestion of colleague Massimo Ramella, made some plots of the whole sky. "Instead of just looking at a cone diagram, we decided to look at the *whole thing,* all the way around! So we did that in the spring of 1989, and what did we find?" Huchra pauses here, and laughs; it is nothing less than a cosmic chuckle. "Something that went all the way around! A pretty humongous structure."

They called it the Great Wall. It's not exactly a sheet of galaxies or a long filament, but a curling, discursive surface that extends a hundred degrees and goes from one side of the sky to the other. It lies at a redshift distance of approximately eight thousand kilometers a second, though it wanders nearer and farther, like a snake (see color illustration). Its volume is bigger than the much-heralded void in Boötes, though it is much more spread out. Its mass is equal to the Great Attractor. Its meaning? Huchra refuses to theorize. He prefers instead to raise a cautionary, more uncomfortable point.

"What we're trying to do," he says, "is to somehow come up with a big enough chunk of the universe that we think is representative, a problem known as defining a fair sample. And what is representative is often dependent very much on what you think the model is. And in fact one of the things that was very surprising about the 1986 results, the bubble stuff, was that it showed that what we *thought* was representative wasn't. One of the things that's sort of interesting about this Great Wall business is that once again, when people had begun to be happy with one set of sizes, we look a little deeper, we look a little harder, and then all of a sudden there's a new level, a new layer." As Margaret Geller likes to point out, drawing conclusions about the universe on the basis of the small and incomplete Harvard-Smithsonian survey is like inferring all varieties of earthly geography, the Alps and the oceans and Great Salt Lake, when you've only mapped an area the size of Rhode Island. There is a danger of jumping to conclusions, a danger nicely articulated by *Nature* writer David Lindley, who observed in 1988, ". . . the human eye is notorious for finding orderly patterns in the most random of data, and when some cosmologists declare that galaxies are 'obviously' arranged in filaments or knots or loops, like the fabric of a coarse-meshed net flung on the sky, others have countered that the whole thing is a web of delusion invented by hopeful minds."

Pessimistic, perhaps, but pessimism is as useful a tool as a computer in making sense of galaxy distribution. These new maps do not provide answers; if anything, they demonstrate the inadequacy of all the questions that have been posed before them, and have rendered even more tentative and wobbly the conclusions that can comfortably be held about the universe. Cosmological surveys, in a metaphoric sense, have begun to resemble the maps from a story by Jorge Luis Borges, where the map keeps growing as big as the territory it purports to map. Geller made the point at a 1988 cosmological conference hosted by the Vatican in this way: "It's sobering that every survey we do seems to contain a structure as big as the survey. Thus it's rather difficult to derive statistics we can trust. The errors and uncertainties in the statistics we generally use are probably larger than we have thought."

Another way of putting it is that astronomers haven't found a big enough frame to put around their picture of the cosmos; it would be like trying to grasp the meaning and beauty of Fra Angelico's *Annunciation* in a version that cropped out the archangel Gabriel. Astronomers may be cutting off important parts of the cosmological picture in a similar way because they do not know the adequate frame, or fair sample, to use. That uncertainty in turn undermines the values of omega and other crucial constants required for a mathematical understanding of the big picture. "That is the problem," Huchra says. "The more we find out, the more we realize that we *don't* really have a good idea of what a fair sample is. And yet there's always a set of people who say, 'Ha! This is it! We've done it. Now it's okay. Now we can calculate all these things.' And it's all copacetic. And you know, there's the optimistic viewpoint and the pessimistic viewpoint, and I've learned—and Margaret's learned—that the pessimistic viewpoint is more likely to be correct."

The current maps have dumped a lot of messy questions into the laps of theorists. How do you build the universe that has suddenly appeared in the surveys? If it starts out so smooth, how does it get so clumpy? "How did it get from one state to another?" asks Ostriker, reflecting the current dilemma among theoreticians. "What theory do we have to explain this? We don't have any good theories. We have a lot of theories, but we don't have any *good* ones. The theories keep getting surprised by the surveys."

If Huchra and Geller seem reluctant to say what bubbles and the Great Wall prove, they are not reluctant about saying what the new redshift maps *disprove*. The appearance of bubbles, voids, and great cosmic walls, in Geller's words, "pose a serious challenge for all current models of galaxy distribution." Moreover, the large-scale clustering of galaxies seen in the Geller-Huchra map poses serious challenges for at least parts of the Standard Model. As more and more of the universe becomes measurable, the key mathematical legs upon which the model is built look wobblier and wobblier. The Hubble constant, once thought to be 50, now looks like it might be 80 or 90; the age of the universe, according to measurements done by Huchra a decade ago, looks to be about 13 billion years, not enough time for gravity to whip up the suds and sculpt the great walls that appear in the maps; and all their measurements to date imply that omega equals something like 0.3, way below the Golden One.

"Those values are inconsistent," Huchra says. His voice has grown uncharacteristically quiet. It is quite late, but that is not the only reason; it is the quietness of shock, the sense of finding oneself bereft of some cherished intellectual keepsake. "In fact, you can't have those in almost *any* universe, they're so inconsistent. There are those of us who think that it's a finite chance that the cosmological model may just be plain wrong. The standard Big Bang may be just plain wrong."

There, it is said.

Just about the time every schoolboy knows the world began with the Big Bang, there are a few voices rising to challenge and even dismantle the model. "Not very many," Huchra admits. "But the numbers are getting to be larger all the time." In a 1989 essay called "Down with the Big Bang," *Nature* editor John Maddox observed, "In all respects save that of convenience, this view of the origin of the Universe is thoroughly unsatisfactory." In a letter to the *New York Times* in 1990, mathematician and cosmology gadfly I. E. Segal made much the same point in saying "the big bang is a charming literary conception, but is it science?" Segal answered his own question by concluding that the theory is just barely good enough to be worth the effort that will be necessary to prove it wrong.

"It's probably the case," Huchra will say later, "that the very basic parts of the Big Bang are more or less correct and will stick around for a while as the foundation of any new theory—the microwave background and its temperature, for example, and the expansion of the universe. But the more pertinent details, such as exactly how old is the universe supposed to be, how did we get from smooth to lumpy, how did galaxies and quasars really form without making small bumps in the cosmic background—all are problems that almost require that the simple model be discarded."

This is what is at stake in the wee hours of the morning, when you've stayed up all night and run through all the Windham Hill tapes and want to shag a few more photons from deep space, win one more data point for the map, and so around 5:40 A.M., with dawn starting to dirty the sky with light, John Huchra keeps pushing. "I'm going to try one more," he announces.

"Another one?" says his incredulous colleague, Frank Low. "*Mamma mia!* I like the way you close."

"C'mon," chides John Huchra, lining up another galaxy with his well-traveled, reconstructed eye. "This is *science!*"

"Elephants for Want of Towns"

THE MAP AS
FALLIBLE OBJECT

||||||||||

Give me a map; then let me see how much
Is left for me to conquer all the world . . ."

—Christopher Marlowe,
Tamburlaine

In the lives of emperors there is a moment which
follows pride in the boundless extension of the
territories we have conquered, and the melancholy
and relief of knowing we shall soon give up any
thought of knowing and understanding them. . . . It is
the desperate moment when we discover that this
empire, which had seemed to us the sum of all
wonders, is an endless, formless ruin, that
corruption's gangrene has spread too far to be
healed by our scepter, that the triumph over
enemy sovereigns has made us the heirs of
their long undoing.

—Italo Calvino,
Invisible Cities

Science is the only self-correcting
human institution, but it also is a
process that progresses only by showing
itself to be wrong.

—Allan Sandage,
astronomer

Reading a map represents a profound act of faith. Faith in the map-maker, in technologies of measurement (and the science that underlies them), in the *idea* of the map—that the unique mosaic of boundaries and symbols corresponds to real space in what we like to call the real world. That is why a map attributed to Giacomo Gastaldi in the early 1560's represents a profound act of betrayal.

Gastaldi, official cosmographer to the Venetian Republic, perpetrated one of geography's most infamous fictions: the "Strait of Anian," a navigable body of water that purportedly stretched across the North American continent, linking Hudson Bay with the Pacific Ocean. Nowadays any schoolchild knows, or should know, that no natural body of water links the Atlantic and Pacific Oceans, but that was unknown to Gastaldi's contemporaries and later cartographers who perpetuated the fiction (including Zaltieri, whose 1566 map marks the earliest dated appearance of the strait), and it was unknown to the explorers who searched for this mythical "Northwest Passage" for two centuries, a record of courage and futility culminating in Alexander Mackenzie's journey up eleven hundred miles of river in 1789, a journey that wended its way teasingly westward before taking an icy turn north to the Arctic Circle. We now know that river as the Mackenzie. Mackenzie originally gave it another name; he called it Disappointment.

The Gastaldi map, not just in its errors but in its influence on human affairs, can be seen as emblematic of the disappointments and dangers that can lurk in any map. On the most fundamental level, Gastaldi's map was geographically wrong. On the level of imperial ambition, the idea implicit in it—the existence of a Northwest Passage and thus swift access to the riches of the Orient—elicited nothing less than geopolitical lust in the British Admiralty, which dangled the astonishing sum of £20,000 as a reward for any lucky explorer who could find the fabled waterway. And in terms of social impact, the map emboldened one glory-seeking explorer after another to thrash through the North American wilderness in search of the Pacific and Mammon, an ethic that in one form or another seems to persist to this day.

With centuries of distance and historical hindsight, we can see that error and bias, exploitation and colonialism, self-serving centrism and ecological harm can so easily be read into the subsoil of old maps that they may as well be listed with symbols and explained in the legend. In maps we trust, but maps are fallible, in their execution and in their use. Even accurate maps in the wrong hands can become dangerous objects, and that is surely as true of our technologically precise modern maps—maps of chromosomes and brain peptides, of the earth's resources and the terrains of nearby planets—as of old maps. In the preceding pages, we have read a great deal about the heroic efforts of men and women charting the new geographies of our twenty-first-century world. These new maps, too, may conceal dangers

The road to disappointment: the earliest dated appearance of the fictitious Strait of Anian is in this 1566 map by Bolognini Zaltieri. (Rare Book Division, New York Public Library, Astor, Lenox and Tilden Foundations)

and disappointments no more obvious to us than Gastaldi's fictions were apparent to Mackenzie.

Like any powerful tool, a map can be misused. That the price of such misuse can be extremely dear is apparent in what arguably is the most transforming discovery ever to appear on a map. The social historian Tzvetan Todorov has estimated that, as a result of the Spanish discovery of the New World, 70 million people lost their lives through such collateral forms of damage as religious persecution, xenophobic massacre, and Europe's first major export to the New World, the epidemic. It would be foolish to ascribe that unspeakable tragedy, larger than the Holocaust, larger than the number of American casualties in all the wars the United States has ever fought, to the maps that charted the New World; but it would be equally foolish to ignore the intricate weave of social and cultural nerves that connect discovery, exploration, and mapmaking. The map is the game board upon which human destinies are played out, where winning or losing determines the survival of ideas, cultures, and sometimes entire civilizations. Science has brought twentieth-century societies to the verge of another New World, its exotic geographies taking shape on chromosomes and in the solar system and deep space, its first erratic and uncertain shorelines appearing on hundreds of new maps. Since the information encoded in maps, which we may call "map knowledge," has historically become a form of power and a tool for the expression of political and economic ideologies, looking at the lies and biases and sobering tales told by old maps may serve as a first step in helping us identify patterns of error and bias, in mapmaker and map-reader alike, that can influence the way we look at and use these new maps. Since these are the maps that are cartographically sketching out the boundaries of our collective future, nothing less than the future rests in our ability to read them wisely, responsibly, and with enlightened distrust.

IMAGINARY GEOGRAPHY

Error runs like a river, spidery and blue, through the history of cartography. Historians like Carl Wheat and William Goetzmann speak of "hypothetical geography" or "imaginary geography," by which they mean the way many early cartographers took artistic liberty in depicting features which, as modern scientists would say, were not supported by the data. Simply put, they made things up.

In his book *The Mapmakers,* John Noble Wilford devotes an entire chapter to the geography of imagination and mythology that arose during the Dark Ages, "a millennium without a significant advance in the mapping of the world," as he puts it. Early maps of Africa and Asia are veritable zoological gardens superimposed on the earth, with animals and fishes gamboling over vast savannahs of geographical ignorance. It was precisely such capricious cartography that invited Jonathan Swift's dismissive observation about the cartographic trade:

> So Geographers in *Afric*-Maps
> With Savage-Pictures fill their Gaps;
> And o'er uninhabitable Downs
> Place Elephants for want of Towns.

Whether elephants or islands, these fictive landmarks merely reflected the act of imagination within the craft of cartography, an imagination that flourishes especially at the boundary between the known and the unknown in maps old and new.

Some medieval maps thoughtfully insert traditional compass points to aid pilgrims in their journey to Paradise; others locate a Christian kingdom in Africa or the Far East ruled by the fabled Prester

The estimable British cartographer John Speed, as did many others, depicted California as an island in this 1627 world map, nearly a century after exploration proved otherwise. (from *Decorative Maps*, Crescent Books, New York, 1989)

John, a fictional ally that Christendom conjured up in dark and distant lands, a perfect cartographic invention to keep the infidel at bay in Europe. The initial temptation is to scoff at such invention as wishful science. Yet it may turn out that theoretical astrophysicists have in a sense invented the modern cosmological equivalent of Prester John by predicting the existence of an as-yet-unidentified and increasingly dubious entity called cold dark matter to explain the distribution of "invisible" mass in the universe and rescue prevailing theories about its origins and evolution.

Some errors, as Swift implies, come at the hands of bad mapmakers. As early as 1539, when Francisco de Ulloa sailed the Gulf of California, evidence suggested that California was not an island, a fact decisively confirmed by Juan Cabrillo in 1542. How, then, explain that as late as the 1740s, maps by popular British cartographers such as Overton, Kitchin, and Bowles & Son managed to ignore two centuries of knowledge and depicted California as an island? Some errors originate with the explorer-mappers themselves. James Cook missed the mouth of the Columbia in 1778, just as Lewis and Clark missed one of its largest tributaries, the Willamette, when they sailed past in 1805. Some errors are interpretative rather than graphic: Lewis and Clark convinced themselves that the head of the Missouri River marked "an essential point in the geography of the western world." How many Americans know that the name of this essential point is Three Forks, Montana?

Imaginary cartography, the geography of convenient omission and wishful inclusion, is obviously not an archaic phenomenon. The Italian astronomer Giovanni Schiaparelli erred on the side of wishful inclusion when he limned in dozens of canals on his map of Mars in the late nineteenth century, as did Percival Lowell in the early twentieth century, whereas the U.S. Geological Survey errs on the side of convenient omission when it leaves out the locations of nuclear waste dumps on its official topographic maps. As recently as 1988, the Soviet Union's chief cartographer admitted that for fifty years maps of the USSR, on orders of the secret police, included such peculiar geomorphic perversities as vanishing rivers, wayward lines of latitude and longitude, and towns that hopped across the steppes, all cartographic inventions made apparently in an effort to disorient aerial bombardiers and ground-level snoops (the *New York Times* article reporting these revelations noted that leaders of the Russian Revolution in 1917 appreciated the ideological power of maps, for they believed that "cartography should be used for economic advancement, propaganda, and military needs"). Lest imaginary cartography be smugly added to the posthumous sins of Marxism, it has been suggested, most recently in Mark Monmonier's *How to Lie with Maps,* that map publishers insert fictitious features—a river, a road, a town—in order to trap copyright violators. Whether communism or capitalism, economic imperatives apparently exonerate cartographic fictions.

To the old examples of mistaken data we can add a thoroughly modern technological pitfall, namely the parameters and models by which computers are programmed to receive and analyze data. The classic recent example involves the failure of a NASA computer to detect evidence of a hole in the ozone over Antarctica for about five years; the low readings fell outside the range of values considered plausible by the NASA scientists who programmed the computer. In another celebrated instance, British meteorologists failed to predict the devastating October 1987 storm that ravaged England because the cyclone was smaller than the grid point resolution on their computer

Like many cartographic fictions, Percival Lowell's 1903 globe showing canals on Mars was the product of insufficient scientific rigor and excessive scientific enthusiasm. (Lowell Observatory)

maps. A computer, and a computer model, inherits all the limitations and errors of judgment of its programmers—something to bear especially in mind in conjectural computer maps, such as projections of future climate and global warming, that cannot independently be checked against ground truth. A flaw in the program will produce nothing more than an extremely fancy and expensive form of imaginary cartography.

Fiction nonetheless has played a decisive role in mapmaking and discovery. The Ptolemaic atlases that began to recirculate in the fifteenth century, with their underestimated versions of the world's circumference, nourished Columbus's ill-reasoned belief that Asia could be reached by sailing west, and Columbus's selection of data—a process essential to the creation of any map, even a map carried in one's head—piled one error upon another. Wilford provides a hilarious catalogue of the wrong choices and "nimble arithmetic" Columbus used to estimate the distance to Japan prior to his trip. With willful precision, he selected every estimate that coincided with his personal bias, a conveniently short oceanic crossing, and then set sail upon this sea of calculated error, forever changing the course of history.

Such blatant examples of selection bias clearly belong to the more imprecise and "unscientific" past. Or do they? A recent remark by an astronomer about two influential cosmologists in contemporary astronomy suggests that a small string of imprecision can still add up to larger truths. The first cosmologist, according to this observer, "always does things the right way, but never seems to get the right answer," while the second cosmologist "*never* does things the right way, and always seems to get the answer that pans out in the end." Allan

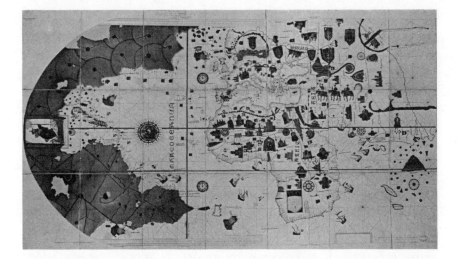

Even cartography has moments of heroism: Columbus made crew members swear that he had discovered the Asian mainland, but the first map to include the New World, by Juan de la Cosa around 1500, depicted Cuba as an island. (Map Division, New York Public Library, Astor, Lenox and Tilden Foundations)

Sandage, the dominant cosmologist in postwar astronomy, recently told an interviewer, "I have kind of changed from a pure observer, hoping to see the absolute, to a mystic believer in beauty."

Mysticism, accident, bias, serendipity—they are not words typically associated with the cartographic enterprise, but perhaps scientific intuition is just a short step, after all, from imaginary geography. "Even blind sailing," Lewis Mumford once wrote, "may open up territory more effectively than reliance on a well-drawn chart that reveals only the mapmaker's own preconceptions."

PROJECTION AND PREJUDICE

Even when the data is sound, when maps are not wrong or incomplete or even imaginary, they can (and often do) mislead. Cartographic choices, some scientific and some merely decorative, can have subtle but far-reaching social consequences. Why is north at the top of maps? Ptolemy put it there because that part of the world was better known— to Greek cartographers, that is. Yet twelfth-century Arab cartographers like Idrisi put south at the top. Cultures sophisticated enough to

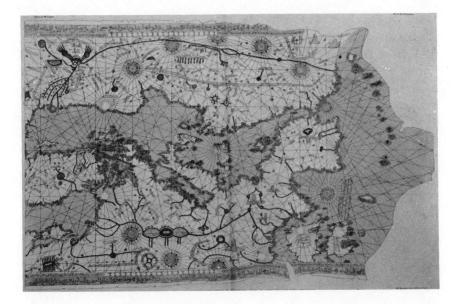

Why is north at the top? Ptolemy put it there, according to map historians, because that part of the world was best known. To Arab cartographers like Mohammed Ebn-Aly Ebn-Ahmed, however, south looked just fine at the top, as in his 1009 map of Europe. (Map Division, New York Public Library, Astor, Lenox and Tilden Foundations)

produce maps tend to produce ethnocentric geography. Babylonia, Greece, Jerusalem, China, Persia, and Turkey have all marked the geographic center of their worlds. When ethnocentric geographies conflict, like the cultures that create them, they symbolize the clash of real cultures and powers, and the outcome of the clash can be read in the next generation of maps. The Ptolemaic maps, with north at the top and Europe in the center, reflect geopolitical power. The *type* of population—European, Caucasian, wealthy, educated—enforces a kind of bias in the organization of the geographical world, just as religious maps of the Dark Ages put east at the top, where Paradise was presumed to lie.

That cultural values and social bias seep into cartography is readily apparent in the way southern continents and latitudes were depicted by medieval European cartographers. Aside from the popular and scientifically indisputable truth that the African interior was too hot to be habitable, many medieval maps bore the mark (and visual vignettes) of the Roman grammarian and fabulist Gaius Julius Solinus. As if the

Dark Ages needed any more darkness, Solinus's book *Polyhistor* described tales of horse-footed men and one-eyed hunters in the East, griffons in Asia, one-legged men in India; the Africa of Solinus's imagination teemed with menacing hyenas and deadly cockatrices and ants as big as mastiffs. And onto maps of the Middle Ages pranced that bestiary of ignorance. John Noble Wilford quotes from a note in a 1761 map by Claude Buy de Mornas to the following effect:

> "It is true that the centre of the continent is filled with burning sands, savage beasts, and almost uninhabitable deserts. The scarcity of water forces the different animals to come together to the same place to drink. Finding themselves together at a time when they are in heat, they have intercourse with one another, without paying regard to the differences between species. Thus are produced those monsters which are to be found there in greater numbers than in any other part of the world."

Cosmas, an influential sixth-century monk, argued that any peoples living in the southern hemisphere "could not be of the race of Adam."

Other map historians have indulged these maps as historical curiosities, or simply as works more artful than accurate, and not as geographically informational. It is also useful to see them as culturally *disinformational.* For centuries the relentless, vivid, and visually powerful message was that terra incognita is a place inhabited without exception by freaks and monsters—a powerful, thousand-year lesson taken to heart by the time of the great discoveries in the fifteenth and sixteenth centuries. The residue is painfully evident in the journals of explorers from Columbus to Lewis and Clark, with their befuddled asides about the inferior habits and inexplicable value systems of "savages." It is not hard to see these biases, perpetrated in the name of science (or at least the science of geography), having resurfaced in the cultural and racial prejudices that persist in northern European cultures; the prejudices engendered toward people of African origin seem especially clear. Maps not only shape worldviews and cultural values; they perpetuate those values in powerful visual vignettes. When the values are discriminatory, a map's underlying social message leaves as lasting a mental imprint as the shapes of the continents do on our memories.

Biases, and their social messages, can lie hidden within the most mathematical, most neutral aspects of the mapmaking craft. When you hold a map in your hand, you are coming to grips with cartography's

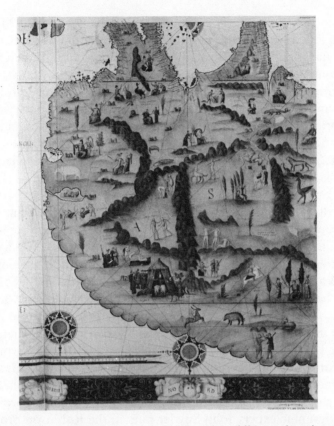

Elephants, dog-headed men, and natives burning children: these images of Asia appeared in Descalier's 1546 world map prepared for Henry II. (Map Division, New York Public Library, Astor, Lenox and Tilden Foundations)

most obvious bias: the size and format of the map itself. It can be crude, as in the ancient portolans used by medieval mariners, maps whose very irregularity of shape followed the neck and flanks of the particular calf or goat upon whose pelt they happened to be drawn; or it can be subtle, as in the widely accepted but nonetheless arbitrary use of 8½-by-11-inch paper or a computer screen as the appropriate frame or boundary of a mapped territory. If the portolan goatskins amuse us, future generations may view our efforts to reproduce Einstein's space-time curvature on a computer screen as similarly quaint.

Some cartographic errors are intrinsic to the discipline; to make a map of the earth is to transfer, futilely, information from a three-dimensional sphere to a two-dimensional plane. Gerhardus Mercator is justifiably hailed for his method of "projecting" the spherical earth onto a flat map in 1569, a mathematical solution that much abetted oceangoing navigation; nonetheless, on Mercator's projection, Greenland is nine times larger than all of South America, and historians of cartography have noted that this navigational convenience came at a social price. The Mercator projection places Europe at the center of the world and exaggerates its size, while relatively diminishing the extent of Africa, the Americas, and the southern hemisphere in general. It is not trivial to suggest that the "North-South debate" begins with this projection. One historian of cartography cites the Mercator projection as an example of the "geopolitical prophecy" of colonialism.

By correcting one distortion, projections inevitably create another, and the historical evolution of map projections is like a mathematical shell game that always seems to cheat the southern hemisphere. In the Van der Grinten projection, used by the National Geographic Society between 1922 and 1988, some parts of the globe were wildly out of scale; Greenland, long the bane of cartographers because its high latitude incurs spatial exaggeration, was 554 percent larger than actual size, the United States 68 percent larger. On the Robinson projection, which improves considerably upon Van der Grinten, the Greenland exaggeration is only 60 percent. Less wrong, but wrong nonetheless. Africa, significantly, is 15 percent *smaller* on the Robinson projection. As cartographic expert John Snyder puts it, the Robinson projection was selected because it offered "the best combination of distortions."

Why does it matter? Such errors can have an impact out of all proportion to their size, as the American Cartographic Association well understands. "A poorly chosen map projection can actually be harmful," the association recently noted. "We tend to believe what we see, and when fundamental geographical relationships, such as shapes, sizes, directions, and so on, are badly distorted, we are inclined to accept them as fact if we see them that way on maps."

And yet the recent controversy over the projection championed by Arno Peters, a German historian, revives this debate and in some ways sharpens the issues. Peters argues that the Mercator projection has promoted the "Europeanization of the earth," and that the customary practice in atlases of using many different scales to show different parts of the world is literally belittling to Third World nations. Terry Hardaker, chief cartographer of the *Peters Atlas,* goes further. He has written that other map projections offer "the equivalent of peering at Europe and North America through a magnifying glass and then

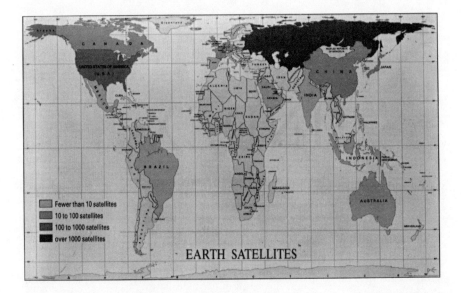

EARTH SATELLITES

Fewer than 10 satellites
10 to 100 satellites
100 to 1000 satellites
over 1000 satellites

"Wet ragged long winter underwear hung out to dry on the Arctic circle," or a more egalitarian way of viewing the world? The controversial Peters projection puts Europe in its place, and includes thematic maps showing which countries possess high technology such as earth satellites. (From *Peters Atlas of the World,* © 1990, Akademische Verlagsantalt; reprinted by permission of HarperCollins Publishers, Inc.)

surveying the rest of the world through the wrong end of a telescope."

The Peters atlas has been attacked as ideological propaganda, as cartographically misleading, as merely a clever repackaging of the century-old Gall equal-area projection; Arthur Robinson has likened its elongated landmasses to "wet, ragged, long winter underwear hung out to dry on the Arctic Circle." From an aesthetic point of view, Robinson is right: the Peters projection leaves much to be desired. But the philosophy underlying it focuses attention on a critical issue in cartography—scientific and mathematical choices, even sound ones, carry profound social and political implications. The prime meridian, 0 degree longitude on any map, runs through Greenwich, England, because the "center" of the world coincided with the eminence of the British Empire; yet if the prime meridian passed through the densest population area on earth, according to map theoretician Mark Monmonier, 0 degree longitude would pass through India or East Pakistan (at what is now 63 degrees east) and North America would lie split on the margins of the world map. Such cartographic choices can pit purely scientific accuracy against social accuracy, a choice in which cartography by definition must come down on the scientific side and yet a choice that embodies a philosophical conflict which currently animates discussions about twentieth-century science and, by extension, twentieth-century scientific mapping, as we shall see shortly.

Finally, cartographers have roundly attacked Arno Peters for setting up Mercator as a straw man. The Mercator projection is four hundred years old, they point out, and many better projections have been developed, so Peters's approach is more propaganda than science. It is a point well taken, but it is not taken far enough. As even Arthur Robinson admits, the Mercator projection, four centuries after its creation, is *still* the most widely used map projection in the world. Its continued use suggests not only that cartographers have failed in their mission as propagandists for a more accurate vision of the world, but that maps can be appropriated and used for the wrong reasons, gaining an inertia of acceptability almost impossible to reverse. Peters, the historian, may be more sensitive than cartographers to the fact that mapmakers ultimately do not control the way their maps are used, and map abuse, even more than pure cartographic error or bias, can lead us down a path with harrowing social consequences. This has been historically true of old maps, as we shall see, and it has the potential to be true about the new scientific cartography as well.

SCIENTISTS AND CONQUISTADORS

It is all well and good to blame cartographers for their errors, great and small. But the path of progress in cartography, like all of science, is paved with mistakes. How maps, right or wrong, come to be *used* marks the point where science stops and the socialization of knowledge begins, a transition fraught with temptations of economic and political self-interest. Such use and abuse provides a new landscape in which to observe an old dilemma: the uses and abuses of technology.

Maps are not merely made; they are read. More to the point, they are read in different ways by different temperaments and intellects. If we look back at the geographic-cum-cartographic upheavals of the sixteenth century, we can discern all the different ways in which the newly minted map of the world could be seen. If you were a European monarch like Charles V, for example, looking at the New World, you would see intriguing new possibilities of empire and colonization, and also a suddenly larger game board upon which the geopolitical struggles of the sixteenth century would be played. If you were a merchant adventurer, you would see new natural resources to exploit, new trade routes to ply, a new geography in which markets and commodities could be paired. If you were the pope, you would see herds of lost souls awaiting conversion, new outposts where missionaries could be dispatched to spread the church's word. If you were an explorer, you would be attracted to those mysterious blank spots just beyond the bounds of knowledge; the map would tell you where your next step should be. All these perspectives converge on a single thematic point, and one that applies no less to modern scientific terrains than to old: shortly after a spatial domain has been mapped, there is a tendency to impose upon it an overlay of values, whether economic or ideological or religious. *Every map presages some form of exploitation.*

Imagine the decisive philosophical conversion that must have transfixed and seduced the minds of those first map-readers in the era of empire who, by studying that most empirical of pictures, the map, could from its abstract two-dimensional symbolic geography exert policy and power over a real domain. Geopolitics, after all, is impossible without a cartographer, and that exercise of control over a distant domain marks a watershed in political power, confirming the notion that maps are not merely pictures of the world, but depictions of a world that can be shaped, manipulated, acted upon.

Maps invite action. Exploration, conquest, occupation, exploitation, administration, and organization—action seems always inflicted upon the bare outlines of a map, and the action can take many forms: a military campaign or a vacation, a dispute over property boundaries or a claim staked by a mining enterprise, dreams of a slave republic or the movement of the scalpel toward a hidden lesion of the brain. Moreover, maps by their very nature depersonalize and abstract the effects of action taken at a distance, a detachment as fundamental and philosophically far-reaching as the detachment customarily ascribed to airmen viewing cities and towns through a bombsight, physically and conceptually removed from the consequences of the actions they are about to take. The sum total of decisions that lead to the finger on the bomb release start, and end, with a map.

Thinking about the act of exploration inevitably leads to thoughts of its concomitant activity, mapping, and that conceptual coupling prompts an uncomfortable and perhaps surprising question about the combined fruits of exploration and mapping: does the curiosity that drives exploration and discovery invariably lead to some sort of imperialism?

Tension has always existed between the interests of scientists who pursue pure knowledge and the interests of monarchs who pursue the goals of empire, but few anecdotes surpass Louis XIV's plaintive and somehow menacing remark in 1682 to Jean Dominique Cassini after the Italian-born cartographer completed the most meticulously measured and scientifically precise map of its day, a map whose only shortcoming was that France turned out to be smaller than previously believed. "I paid my academicians well," said Louis, "and they have diminished my kingdom." One hears in that lament both imperative and expectation: that maps, by some privileged right of their commissioning elites (kingdoms, countries, corporations) are meant to *expand* and *empower,* not contract and diminish. (It also makes explicit who works for whom.)

Although it is not customary to view "admirals of the ocean sea" like Columbus and twentieth-century scientists as brethren, both are explorers and both return from their exploits with maps, and social analyst Lewis Mumford implied just such a kinship in *The Pentagon of Power.* "To become the 'lords and possessors of nature,' " Mumford writes, "was the ambition that secretly united the conquistador, the merchant adventurer and banker, the industrialist, and the scientist, radically different though their vocations and their purposes might seem." One of the best means of possessing nature is to map its domains, and it does not distort Mumford's intent to suggest that the creation of a map is the first step in acquiring suzerainty over a particular geography or domain. The history of exploration, as Louis XIV and every other head of state well knew, is a long, uninterrupted lesson about the geopolitical and economic perquisites that attend first possession.

Map historian J. B. Harley refers to cartography as the "science of princes," and it is a characterization that applies to modern mapmakers as well. From the expeditions financed by Spain and Portugal in the fifteenth century to experiments sponsored by the National Science Foundation last year, there exists a tradition of what might be called "mercenary geographers." In the context of contemporary science, the term strikes the ear harshly; but in the context of the history of exploration and mapping, there is compelling and overwhelming evidence that "explorers," terrestrial or intellectual, must align their professional and personal ambitions with wealthy and powerful nations, which can afford the expeditions (or, in the modern analogue/ idiom, the "experiments") that chart and stake a claim to new territories. In the past those territories were literally geographic and peopled; today, they are figurative and uninhabited landscapes. None-theless, they are landscapes that can be charted, producing maps upon which human destinies can unfold in less than benign ways.

The great expeditions of discovery, and the maps that arose from them, ultimately served the interests of royal houses, nation-states, powerful trading companies, religious doctrines, political ideologies. As J. B. Harley and David Woodward make clear in their *History of Cartography,* mapmaking served as an "intellectual weapon" for its commissioning elites: "with the religious elite of dynastic Egypt and of Christian medieval Europe; with the intellectual elite of Greece and Rome; and with the mercantile elite of the city-states of the Mediterranean world during the late Middle Ages." And what do those elites do with the maps in their possession?

To borrow a concept from contemporary cartography, they engage in "thematic mapping." In exchange for the papal bulls that recognized Spain's claims of territories discovered and conquered during the explorations of the fifteenth century, King Ferdinand and Queen Isabella agreed to the Pope's insistence that the conquered territories must conform to the dictates of Roman Catholicism. An overlay of religion, in short, was instantly superimposed, by agreement between the political and ecclesiastical elites of Europe, upon the map of the New World. In just such a fashion, territories not only are discovered, but are *configured,* or recast, in the image of the conquerors. History is not only written by winners: winners redraw the maps.

History does not stint with examples of the tragic consequences of these ideological overlays. Cabral discovered Brazil in 1500, and within two years, Portuguese vessels sailed back to Europe laden with "brazilwood." One might arguably date the initial destruction of the tropical rain forest to 1502 (a process lamentably accelerated by a more recent mapping project, the Radar Amazon initiative of the 1970s).

In 1502, on his fourth voyage to the New World, Columbus landed off the north coast of present-day Honduras and thus became the first European to encounter Mayan civilization; he stumbled upon an advanced culture which, even in decline, had independently achieved linguistic and mathematical sophistication, a culture capable of creating calendars, predicting eclipses, and tracking the movement of planets. But the map that grew out of this discovery wasn't configured to preserve Mayan religion; to those who refused to convert to Catholicism, Ferdinand's gentle suasion included the threat to "enter your lands and make slaves of your wives and children," and in 1562, the priest Diego de Landa of Izamal, in the name of the same God that granted Spain deed to these foreign lands, burned all the Mayan codices. Sixty years after the coastline of Central America first appeared as a shaky line on a hand-drawn map, the sum total of Mayan culture and civilization lay in irretrievable ruin, literally wiped off the very map that betrayed its existence to European monarchs in the first place.

Magellan's discovery of the Philippines in 1521 sketched a thin line across the Pacific that would ultimately become the nine-thousand-mile "track of the Manila galleons," and so remunerative was this trade route—silks and other goods coming from the Orient to Mexico and then Europe, the silver of Acapulco sent back to Manila to pay for the goods—that when, in 1603, Chinese settlers in Manila were perceived as stirring local unrest, the Spaniards and their allies summarily killed more than twenty thousand of them. Less than a century after Magellan's discovery of the Philippines, the map of Manila—its values shaped as much by the trading houses of Europe as by local geography—had no place for ethnic dissidents.

Even later explorations, such as the expedition of Lewis and Clark in 1804–1806 to traverse and map the American West, occurred during an epoch which Goetzmann associates with "the rage for scientific discovery as a new excuse for adventure and more subtle imperial conquest." In reading Lewis and Clark's *History,* one is struck by the slow ecological disaster that has transformed the virginal land they so earnestly and innocently mapped. The discoverers constantly describe plenitudes and abundances that no longer exist: "Immense numbers of buffalo," so numerous that dozens crowd into rivers and drown in a matter of minutes as the herd comes to drink; "vast numbers of otter and beaver"; "almost impentrable thickets of small pine"; a landscape "so infested by the prickly pear that we could scarcely find room to lie down at our camp"; elk, deer, antelope, wild horses, and mules "as numerous as the grass of the plains"; "almost inconceivable" numbers of salmon, swimming in waters of the Columbia "so clear that they can be readily seen at the depth of 15 or 20 feet"; and, of course, Native Americans, including the Shoshone, Clatsop, and others. They are all gone.

It is not that Lewis and Clark were men of conspicuous ill will, nor was Columbus or Magellan; it is that the domains that explorers chart, and the maps they produce, open up territories to interests that view them differently, interests that inevitably consume, exhaust, and extinguish the resources that are discovered, be they gold deposits or stands of timber or dispensable human cultures. The maps serve as the ground plan, the blueprint, the graphic agenda for subsequent exploitation. It is impossible to escape the genocidal irony in the words of Meriwether Lewis when he one day lectured three Shoshone chiefs on the importance of keeping their word: "If you wish the whites to be your friends, to bring you arms, and to protect you from your enemies, you should never promise what you do not mean to perform." From the Native American point of view, history is the map of broken promises.

Writing in 1759 about the expeditions encouraged by Prince Henry the Navigator, who instigated the first great age of discovery in the fifteenth century, Samuel Johnson reached the conclusion that "much knowledge has been acquired, and much cruelty been committed: the belief of religion has been very little propagated, and its laws have been outrageously and enormously violated. The Europeans have scarcely visited any coast but to gratify avarice, and extend corruption; to arrogate domination without right, and practise cruelty without incentive. Happy had it then been for the oppressed if the designs of Henry had slept in his bosom, and surely more happy for the oppressors."

To repeat: "Surely more happy for the oppressors." That grim benediction may hold special resonance for those of us in the late twentieth century who are about to occupy a world staked out by these new scientific geographies. To twist the oft-quoted idiom of George Santayana, those who believe history repeats itself are condemned to miss all the ways in which history unfolds in subtly different ways from the past. The better question raised by cartography's sobering past may be the following: can we acquire modern map knowledge without, to paraphrase Johnson, inventing and committing new, equally modern and unimagined cruelties?

"IN WAR, MEN THINK OTHERWISE . . ."

Do our curiosities and explorations in pure science hold analogous dangers of imperialism such as we have seen associated with mapping in earlier ages of great discovery? What dangers may lay hidden in the computer-generated maps in geophysics or biology or astronomy? Analogy makes for poor prophecy, but it is a useful way to train our ears and eyes for warning signs. The analogy travels best over short distances—that is, most easily to mapping endeavors connected to traditional geography.

Consider remote-sensing maps created by satellite. In 1972, two months before the launch of the first Landsat satellite, the United

Nations Scientific Subcommittee on the Peaceful Uses of Outer Space met in New York, and the Swedish delegate set off sharp disagreement when he asked the United Nations to take steps to protect small nations without space programs from economic exploitation by larger countries with access to remote-sensing data about mineral deposits, for example. The United States opposed the measure, and it did not pass. It seemed to be one more forgettable vote by an obscure subcommittee of a marginally influential organization; and yet it helped reconfigure the globe, in terms of synoptic technology, as surely as the popes reconfigured it with their papal bulls.

Was the concern of the Swedish representative warranted? "I would not go so far as to say those fears have been realized," says Ade Abiodun, a member of the Nigerian mission to the U.N. and an expert on space applications. "But to the extent that prices have become higher, yes, the flow of information has become limited." Landsat used to provide Third World nations with satellite data at no cost; but the Reagan administration privatized the operation in 1985, and the EOSAT Co., along with the French-based SPOT satellite system, abandoned the practice. "EOSAT and SPOT will not give the information for free," Abiodun says, "so there has been a slowdown in information exchange." It is not simply that access to information in this information-driven age can pit the private sector against sovereign but information-poor nations; it is that when such maps are in effect made available to the highest bidder, they threaten to make of every territory a map of two domains, the haves and the have-nots.

And what of the haves? Many commercial applications of Landsat data speak as much of exploitation as of empowerment, and it is by no means clear who has benefited most from this. Remote sensing from outer space has promoted oil drilling and the wholesale clear-cutting of forests—not inherently evil activities, but activities that perpetuate certain economic imperatives, including the ideology that internal combustion—despite pollution, fears of global warming, and the geopolitical and military costs imposed on consumer nations—is the best, most efficient form of energy. "Leading companies in the forest industries," reads a brochure published by Landsat in 1987, "were quick to use the synoptic coverage of Landsat to help site mills, determine the optimum position for haul roads and survey timber stands for pests and general health. Oil and gas companies embraced this new look at the Earth, and soon became a consistent user of Landsat data." If the aim was to shepherd earth's finite natural resources, it is ironic to read in this same brochure that "oil and mining industries are the largest [private] purchasers of Landsat data." Alexander von Humboldt, the father of modern geography, recognized the ecological implications even while mapping South America: "In this paradise of the American forests, as well as elsewhere, experience has taught all beings that benignity is seldom found together with power." Knowing as he did that maps empower, von Humboldt could well appreciate the unprecedented power of satellite mapping, and also the dangers if that power belonged more to exploiters rather than conservators.

Consider space exploration and our ongoing mapping of the solar system. "Someday," reads a recent issue of the Planetary Society's *Report,* "humans will plant flags of their earthly nations on the surface of Mars. Whose flags will they be?" Here is an even more pertinent question: who can think of flags fluttering over unsettled territories without imagining conflict? New frontiers represent the possibility of reenacting all the romanticized antics of earlier frontier expansion: territoriality, lawlessness, confrontation, exploitation. We already possess maps of our moon, Venus, Mars, Mercury, Saturn, Jupiter, Uranus, and Neptune, in addition to many planetary moons. These maps not only provide scientifically useful data, but plant the seed for return trips, which are being planned. And we have now arrived at the moment of initial, almost fanciful discussion about space colonies on other planets, of mining operations on distant satellites. On the one hand, such missions seem too futuristic or improbable; on the other, astronomers in 1991 published a map of the moon pinpointing the richest deposits of titanium, a metal ore of high strategic value. If maps presage action, will we someday see steam shovels and bulldozers strip mining on the moon? Will a war be fought, fifty or five hundred years from now, over mineral rights to Miranda, or over attempts to colonize Mars? Will the radar maps of Venus so recently sent back by Magellan contain information that will set off another space race decades hence?

Consider climate maps. Global warming has focused a great deal of public attention on the scientists who model climate, but the father of the field envisioned something much more ambitious—and ominous—than mere knowledge for knowledge's sake. John von Neumann, whose record as a scientific visionary needs no elaboration, realized that when scientists understood climate well enough to predict it, they would probably understand it well enough to control it, too, and as early as the 1950s he suggested that such manipulation would not necessarily be benign. "The most constructive schemes for climate control," he wrote, "would have to be based on insights and techniques that would also lend themselves to forms of climatic warfare as yet unimagined." He admitted that "to make a new ice age in order to annoy others, or a new tropical, 'interglacial' age in order to please everybody is not necessarily a rational program." But in the same breath he conceded that "the very techniques that create the dangers and the instabilities are in themselves useful, or closely related to the useful."

Consider genetic maps. In this realm of biology, the first of the unsettling scenarios is already upon us. Biologists have begun to assemble a complete map of all human genes, a conquest of territory that legitimately promises great advances in both interventive and preventive medicine. Although keenly aware of potential social and legal dangers, however, not all biologists have appeared nearly so keen to ensure legal safeguards, so busily have they been adding new genes to the map. No legislation is in place to date to protect abuses of the map knowledge, as it were, and these abuses have already begun to occur. *Wall Street Journal* reporters Jerry Bishop and Michael Waldholz, in their book *Genome,* describe an internal insurance-industry document circulating in 1989 that suggests that companies may want to refuse coverage to any individuals who refuse to submit to genetic testing. They also report the first instances of insurance companies refusing to insure newborn children brought to term if fetal tests disclose that the children will be born with genetic disorders. A similar policy, outside the protective mantle of responsible business practice, would be identified for what it is: for-profit eugenics.

The genetic map may also reinvent invasion of privacy at the molecular level. It is not difficult to imagine a future in which health insurance companies and life insurance companies demand tests for thousands of genetic disorders, as they demand now for a handful; nor is it hard to imagine, finally, that an individual's private map of genetic destiny will be entered irretrievably into a data base shared by the industry at large and containing information that may be viewed in an entirely different and perhaps more ominous medical light ten or twenty years in the future.

Just as political ideologies have been imposed on terrestrial maps, social and philosophical ideologies may quickly slip into place once the genetic map territory is conquered. Eugenics, of course, is a troubling possibility. Chromosome mapping may also, in a pervasive and insidious way, promote a kind of sociological stratification based on genetic notions of normalcy. Each human being possesses roughly half a dozen recessive disease genes—six or so genes which, if paired with similarly recessive genes from a spouse, can result in a child that inherits a genetic disease. One can imagine a society increasingly sensitized and socialized to the idea of genetic inferiority, where the "right" genes will be normal genes, and "carriers"—those who possess recessives, even though they themselves do not manifest disease—suffer all the stigma associated with imperfection and "deviancy." They will be polluters of the gene pool. In a society already less than sympathetically disposed toward the handicapped, the infirm, the ill, or the merely cosmetically imperfect, medical ethicists like Neil Holtzman and Dorothy Nelkin legitimately raise the possibility that we may inadvertently be cultivating a biological underclass.

Consider other biological landscapes, like the mammalian brain. Research on the map of the cannabinoid receptor, described in an earlier chapter, was sponsored in part by a pharmaceutical company, which raises the question "Will drug companies ultimately control aspects of human behavior simply because they control proprietary knowledge about how some region of the brain is chemically organized and how it responds to patented forms of therapeutic stimulation?" The answer is: they already do. It simply promises to become a more pervasive problem.

During the years that Hoffman–La Roche owned the exclusive patent for Valium, the company earned countless billions in sales, even as the drug became widely recognized as one of the most overprescribed and abused pharmaceuticals in the modern pharmacopoeia. Brain maps clearly don't cause drug abuse, any more than the goldfields near Sutter's Mill, when they appeared on maps of California, caused human greed; they merely increase the geographical odds that one will find the other. The discovery of new anatomical territories, like the molecular receptor upon which Valium works, opens up that same territory to the possibility of therapy and abuse. In just the past two decades, some fifty brain receptors have been identified and mapped. Each receptor is an opportunity for therapy and treatment, but also for abuse, and each raises the possibility that future generations will succumb to ever-new pharmacological tyrannies of sedation or stimulation.

Consider our molecular fate maps in the field of embryology. Will our growing knowledge of the fertilized egg and its shifting, determinative geography during the crucial early minutes and hours of gestation tempt us to tamper with and augment certain regions? Experiments have already shown that fruit-fly embryos can be manipulated in such a way that, with an injection of protein early in development, the embryo will develop with two heads or no head. That was not the aim of the experimentation, but it raises another geographic, though highly speculative and long-range, question: could microinjections of homeotic proteins or genetic manipulation of developmental genes enhance certain gross physical characteristics such as heft or height or size of brain?

Consider the maps that emerge from physics and astronomy. These maps outline territories that pose more difficult conjectural exercises. With scanning probe microscopes, for example, physicists can now arrange atoms, move them at will, spell out corporate logos, and think about designing machines at the atomic level. The optimist sees enormous possibilities for microengineering; the pessimist fears that such engineering may be put to the service of microscopic weaponry and surveillance. Inhalable sensors, no larger than germs, might allow surveillance of convicted felons or political dissidents.

Consider mathematical maps. As mathematician James Yorke says, "Five hundred years from now, our concepts of reality will be *extremely* different." Just as Heisenberg's uncertainty principle has sometimes been generalized, often recklessly, to forgive the fundamental uncertainties of human relationships and social responsibility, James Yorke's Wada chart showing the unpredictability of a pendulum's behavior may be one of those narrow academic ideas, like deconstruction, that spread into the mainstream and color our way of thinking about the everyday world and how we function in it.

These are questions that are obviously hard to answer; it is hard even to know if they are framed correctly. But the history of cartography suggests that questions need to be asked, and with a certain amount of urgency, before the overlays of ideology and commerce slip quickly and firmly into place.

Finally, scientists—our quantifiers, our mapmakers—must acknowledge that pursuit of knowledge requires sponsorship, and that its sponsors have historically appropriated and corrupted the knowledge won by science. Nuclear weapons, and the insidious nuclear fear that has suffused every layer of political, social, and psychological life for the past half century, is an example that requires no elaboration. But subtler, less dramatic examples occur all the time. Particle accelerators received government funding in the 1950s not only because of the basic knowledge that physicists sought, but because U.S. lawmakers were led to believe during the Cold War years that particle physics might provide insights leading to the construction of particle-beam death

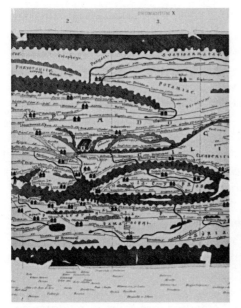

The map as a form of control: Romans invented the road map (like the third-century Peutinger table, *left*) as a tool to maintain military supremacy. (Map Division, New York Public Library, Astor, Lenox and Tilden Foundations)

rays and radiation bombs, an illusion that physicists like E. O. Lawrence were only too eager to foster in Red-baiting congressional testimony.

The military has always been closely associated with the cartographic enterprise for obvious reasons of strategic advantage, intelligence, and security; the road map, after all, sprang as a concept from the desire of Roman generals to consolidate control of territory, and the Persian Gulf war saw an unprecedented use of satellite maps and imagery to assist activities ranging from strategic planning to guidance of Cruise missile sorties to the ensuing bomb-damage assessments, including perhaps the ultimate device in personal cartographic orientation in this age of beepers and Walkmans: a pocket-sized electronic device linked to a satellite that provided exact latitude and longitude information to soldiers in real time.

Like other sponsors or patrons of exploration, the military has extracted a price for its support. Ever since the Padrón Real, the secret master chart compiled by the Spanish in the sixteenth century, that price most often has been to classify data or information as secret. Military specialists bitterly opposed the idea of a civilian satellite like Landsat, and the Navy refused to release the gravity anomaly data from the Seasat and Geosat satellites for many years, delaying the creation of new maps of the ocean floor. The military is also heavily involved in funding that purest of intellectual pursuits, mathematics: the National Security Agency supports work in number theory because of its implications for coding and security, and the Defense Advanced Research Project Agency (DARPA) has supported studies of chaos, including the Lakes of Wada work.

The astronomer Carl Sagan recently expressed the belief that the Apollo moon program, and its attendant exploration, was merely a peripheral benefit of military strategy. "Apollo was not mainly about science," Sagan wrote in 1989. "It was not even mainly about space. Apollo was mainly about ideological confrontation and nuclear war. . . ." Vehicles of exploration can, with only slight modification, become vehicles of destruction. "The same technology that transports a man to the Moon," Sagan noted, "can carry a nuclear warhead halfway around the Earth." The same technology that creates new instruments of measurement may create new instruments of violence, repression, exploitation. And it poses an interesting question. Would astronomers and planetary scientists, for example, have renounced exploratory trips to the moon and Neptune and Mars if, by doing so, they were convinced that no ballistic missiles would have been developed? The question is almost certainly unfair and naïve; yet it reanimates, in the cartographic sphere, the enduring conflict between scientific imagination and social consequence. "To the extent that the scientist's capacity for pursuing truth depends upon costly apparatus, institutional collaboration, and heavy capital investment by government or industry," Mumford wrote, "he is no longer his own master." That dilemma, that potential loss of control, speaks to the very heart of potential social harm in the new cartography. Who controls the information? Who ultimately becomes master of the map?

The great danger represented by the role of the military (and, by extension, the state) in scientific research in general, and in the capture of new scientific "territories" more specifically, can be neatly summarized in a letter that appeared in the January 12, 1922 issue of the journal *Nature*. The letter came from a German chemist named Fritz Haber, who had helped convert the "benign" technology used to make synthetic dyes into the rather less benign technology for manufacturing the poison gases used in World War I.

"In war," Haber wrote in self-defense, "men think otherwise than they do in peace." To restate the problem in its broadest and most ominous syntactic implications, one can think of Haber's sentence as the template for all possible perversions of modern exploration and technocartographic knowledge. In commerce, men think otherwise than they do in science. In affairs of state, men think otherwise than they do in science. In monarchies and dictatorships and even self-described democracies, men think otherwise than they do in science.

Here may lie the ultimate potential for abuse of the map. Map knowledge arises from an admirable intellectual context—scientific curiosity; yet once the map has been completed, cartographers ancient or modern never retain control of the territory. Charles V and Louis XIV, Suleiman and Hitler, Prince Henry and Lyndon Johnson, Ferdinand and Bismarck, Stalin and Kissinger—they are always looking over the shoulders of their explorers and cartographers, tempted by annexation, bombardment, or economic dominations every bit as oppressive as military occupations. The territory, literally and figuratively, is ceded to the powers that be. In a 1955 essay entitled "Can We Survive Technology?" John von Neumann wrote, "Technology—like science—is neutral all through, providing only means of control applicable to any purpose, indifferent to all."

Neutrality is not the crucial issue here; it is the indifference. Cartography is a discipline built upon the premise of boundaries, and yet the boundary between war and peace, or between commerce and science, or between benign and harmful applications of technology, appears so slender and subtle, so easily and painlessly traversed, that the passage seems both invisible and irrevocable. Considering all the harm and human suffering that have historically accrued when that boundary has been breached in the past, and considering the many new boundaries that may just as painlessly and invisibly be breached as a result of the revolution in mapping currently under way, indifference no longer seems a defensible posture for science to take. The central issue becomes one of control: is there a way to control the context in which map knowledge is used?

"THE MAP IS NOT THE TERRITORY . . ."

Maps typically represent such a powerful form of knowledge, such a quantitative and authoritative picture of the world, that when two maps interpret the same territory in a radically different way, there is suggested nothing less than two cultures of knowledge clashing over the same domain. Something very much like that occurred in a recent land dispute in Australia. An aboriginal artist, claiming to be ancestral "owner" of a geographical/mythical site in the Western Desert, sued a mining company for the right to receive potential royalties from a

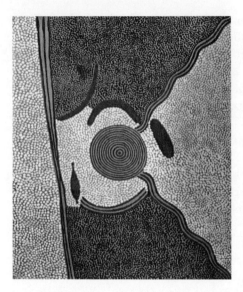

Mapping the spiritual domain: Aboriginal dream paintings, such as *Possum Dreaming at Kurningka,* by Tim Leura Tjapaltjarri, use cartographic symbols to sustain important myths and celebrate a creation story that does not start with the Big Bang. (South Australian Museum/ Aboriginal Artists Agency Ltd.)

proposed mining venture, on the grounds that the Dreaming tracks depicted in his paintings also represented the seams of mineral deposits, and that therefore his depiction constituted prior ownership.

The Australian conflict spotlights the least obvious, but perhaps most significant, limitation of data-based, quantitative maps: they encode only one form of knowledge. Among the oldest "maps" extant are those aboriginal song-lines of Australia, where the ancestral myths of creation have been transposed in dream paintings so rich and precise in their geographic detail that they merge mythology and cartography. Peter Sutton, an Australian art historian, writes: "As maps of political geography—only one of their many roles—these works are conservative statements about relationships between people and land, relationships sanctioned by the Dreaming. They present, and reinforce, not merely order but a particular order. It is therefore appropriate that they be schematicized, rather like a subway map or a circuit diagram, compressing the unruly facts of geography into a semblance of the balance, unity, and reciprocity desired of human relations." Inspired by similarities between the Dreaming and the *Metamorphoses* of Ovid, Bruce Chatwin wrote in *The Songlines*: "And it struck me, from what I now knew of the Songlines, that the whole of Classical mythology might represent the relics of a gigantic 'song-map': that all the to-ing and fro-ing of gods and goddesses, the caves and sacred springs, the sphinxes and chimaeras, and all the men and women who became nightingales or ravens, echoes or narcissi, stones or stars—all could be interpreted in terms of totemic geography."

That distinction recalls a persistent theme in Lewis Mumford's later work. He argued with erudite passion that science and technology's emphasis on quantitative measurement tended to marginalize and ultimately diminish a more humanistic calibration of reality and experience, notably art, culture, religion, and myth. This may at first seem far removed from the province of maps, but maps derive from, and in fact represent a visual image of, quantitative measurements—readings, data, numbers—filtered according to the subtractive parameters of science. And an increasingly popular school of thought, associated most prominently and recently with postmodernist theory (but in reality dating back at least to the American transcendentalism of the last century), challenges the *narrowness* of the assumptions upon which science—and by extension its cartographic version of the world—is based. It is perhaps best summarized in the well-known caveat attributed to Alfred Korzybski and more recently popularized by Gregory Bateson: "The map is not the territory."

The old debate that casts technology and humanism in adversarial roles can be revisited via the scientifically based map. There is a tradition as old as Thoreau and as recent as Mumford and Jacques Ellul, with plenty of kibitzers along the way, that challenges the narrow aperture of science's lens, and one needn't subscribe to the entire program to appreciate some of its insights and to see it as a reaction to the very scientific indifference confessed by von Neumann. Precisely at a moment when new technologies of measurement allow scientists to explore, map, and thereby *capture* more new physical ground than ever before, historians are calling attention to all the things that reductionism discards—all the values left out of the map.

Mary Hesse of Cambridge University, speaking at a 1989 conference entitled "The End of Science?" said: "Clearly, the whole imperialist aim of theoretical science to be the royal and single road to knowledge has been a profound mistake. Perhaps we should be looking in another direction. Scientific theory is just one of the ways in which human beings have sought to make sense of their world by constructing schema, models, metaphors and myths. Scientific theory is a particular kind of myth that answers to our practical purposes with regard to nature. It often functions as myths do, as persuasive rhetoric for moral and political purposes." Another philosopher, Sandra Harding of the University of Delaware, argued that we find ourselves in a particular historical moment when it is possible to repudiate the fundamental assumptions embraced by the "modern West" and the "elites" within it that share those same assumptions. "More science in a socially regressive society," she said, "will increase the social regression. It will increase the movement of the resources from the many to the few."

Lest these sound like trendy temper tantrums thrown on the fringes of historiography, consider the words of J. B. Harley, coeditor of the University of Chicago Press's definitive, multivolume *History of Cartography*. In a superb essay entitled "Maps, Knowledge, and Power," he writes: "The way in which maps have become part of a wider political sign-system has been largely directed by their associations with elite or powerful groups and individuals and this has promoted an uneven dialogue through maps. The ideological arrows have tended to fly largely in one direction, from the powerful to the weaker in society. The social history of maps, unlike that of literature, art, or music, appears to have few genuinely popular, alternative, or subversive modes of expression. Maps are preeminently a language of power, not of protest."

Henry David Thoreau anticipates many of these sentiments by more than a century. He makes a distinction between the *kinds* of knowledge worth having, I believe, in the famous remark: "It is not worth the while to go round the world to count the cats of Zanzibar." The cats of Zanzibar are just one more increment of measure; and perhaps, Thoreau says, their number constitutes data not worth knowing.

Thoreau's is a particularly valuable perspective because it matured during the final splurge of mapping during what William Goetzmann calls the "second great age of discovery," and because he exemplified the nineteenth-century self-educated man, combining self-directed curiosity with skepticism and a fierce intellectual independence. Remarkably well informed about the latest developments in exploration and science, including the exploits of Frobisher and Franklin and Mungo Park, Thoreau at the same time philosophically analyzed, and ultimately attacked, the implicit value of certain among those explorations. He sees terrestrial exploration as digressive, a diversion from an interior mapping of self he calls "home-cosmography." Then, like so many of us, he reverts to the vocabulary and metaphor of cartography, but arrives at an altogether different destination:

What does Africa,—what does the West stand for? Is not our own interior white on the chart? black though it may prove, like the coast, when discovered. . . . Be rather the Mungo Park, the Lewis and Clarke [sic] and Frobisher, of your own streams and oceans; explore your own higher latitudes . . . be a Columbus to whole new continents and worlds within you, opening new channels, not of trade, but of thought. Every man is the lord of a realm beside which the earthly empire of the Czar is but a petty state, a hummock left by the ice.

Thoreau then goes on to say:

. . . it is easier to sail many thousand miles through cold and storm and cannibals, in a government ship, with five hundred men and boys to assist one, than it is to explore the private sea, the Atlantic and Pacific Ocean of one's being alone.

With this metaphor Thoreau extends the purview of mapping, of geography, and of knowledge to the self and solitude and the soul. How thoroughly modern! Like that of other geographers, Thoreau's ultimate aim is to achieve some sort of orientation, but his approach to mapmaking seeks spiritual orientation in the erratic compass of a world already become modern and bewildering. It is not merely a clever semantic argument; it argues the importance, in any age of exploration, of a different and perhaps complementary kind of exploratory expedition, and thus a different, complementary kind of knowledge. Its coordinates, much trickier to determine even than latitude with an astrolabe or longitude without a clock, are faith, self-reliance, self-sacrifice and the commonweal, the nature of knowledge, social responsibility, morality, wisdom. Not a single one of those destinations, each one desirable and essential to civilized life, can be mapped by standard coordinates of latitude and longitude. They are, as Thoreau's nineteenth-century contemporary Herman Melville once put it, "not down on any map; true places never are."

MAPPING UTOPIA

Historians and scientists as diverse as William Goetzmann, Thomas P. Hughes, and Bruce Murray (the former director of NASA) have detected, and lamented, precisely these philosophical challenges to scien-

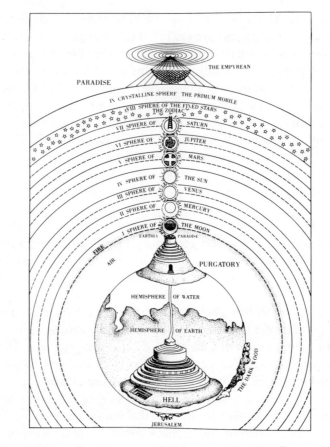

Dante's *Paradiso*: unlike other maps of the heavens, the units of measurement in this universe include intellect, honor, virtue, and love. (From J. J. Callahan, "The Curvature of Space in a Finite Universe," © 1976 by Scientific American, Inc. All rights reserved)

tific thought in contemporary society. Goetzmann speaks of two ends of the "cultural spectrum," one of which he defines as having "a voracious appetite for new information" and the other of which he defines as following a "tradition of defensive folk culture." At a symposium sponsored by the Planetary Society, he said, "We need Voyagers and Vikings and yes, even our tragic Challengers, to avoid falling backward into a solipsistic, self-absorbed culture." Hughes verges on the elegaic, speaking of "an era of technological enthusiasm in the United States, an era now passing into history."

If the new science-wary historians are saying that scientific explorations (and the maps that inevitably result) are too dangerous, too

freighted with the potential for social subjugation and suffering even
to pursue, then the argument is not only unrealistic but fatally extreme;
such a conclusion reflects fear rather than conviction, a contraction of
human curiosity, a shrinking of our mission. If, however, the arguments are heard as a warning about the limitations of scientific indifference as described by von Neumann, heard, too, as a legitimate effort
to shape the context in which map knowledge is understood and used,
then they initiate a different and perhaps more effective dialogue about
the way citizens and scientists themselves might actively defend the
borders of map knowledge from ideological encroachment and corruption. That would require a scientific community willing to play an
active role in controlling the uses of technology, but it would also
require a society willing to do the hard work of distinguishing between
legitimate technological danger and a more superstitious and sometimes irrational distrust of technology. (In this regard, I would say the
scientists have come further than society.)

How can we reconcile our belief in and need of exploration, and
the cultural exhilaration that maps inspire, with the menace and danger we see written into so many of them? If history is a map with
ideological and economic overlays, how can we defend these new maps
from similar invasions that will surely continue to emerge at the end of
the twentieth century?

"To ask in advance for a complete recipe would be unreasonable," von Neumann opined. "We can specify only the human qualities required: patience, flexibility, intelligence." As scientists
themselves like to say, those conditions are necessary but not sufficient
in the face of such rapid and irrevocable change. It is tempting to
recapitulate the hope articulated by Lewis Mumford in the 1930s that
modern society would be able to benefit from modern technology and
be able to minimize its dangers if it was managed and controlled by
reform-oriented social scientists and enlightened civic leaders. Yet
Mumford gave up on the idea by the 1960s as hopelessly naïve.

Half a century later, for better and for worse, with a hole in the
ozone layer and a burgeoning greenhouse effect and a war recently
fought to defend our right to pour gasoline down the bottomless gullet
of an earlier technological invention, it's clear that society has not
quite developed the knack for contesting, much less controlling, the
imperial nature with which economics and politics embrace, glorify,
and enshrine new technologies and, by extension, the territories that
new technologies conquer; modern society seems to lack the technical
understanding, the economic leverage, and perhaps even the intellec-

tual resolve to shape its direction and future. Ellul, according to Thomas Hughes, did not doubt that technology would rise to the occasion and provide solutions to problems like air pollution and urban congestion; his great fear, however (and one we would do well to bear in mind), is that new technologies and the systems they engender "would simply deny us the essential moral choices." These are dilemmas that crowd the margins of almost any map we might admire, regardless of its information, regardless of its beauty.

For all these reasons, we need to view maps warily. We must see not only the information they purvey, but the biases they may conceal, the ideologies they may preserve, and the abuses they may invite. We must not simply be dazzled by the technology, dazzling though it inarguably is, but be ever aware of the map's inherent fallibility. A healthy distrust of maps may be as essential to our survival and well-being as maps themselves undeniably are.

In the past we have not resisted the temptation to convert these simple and elegant maps of the physical world, won by human courage, ingenuity, and sweat, into thematic maps with our overlays of ideology, religion, culture, empire, economic domination, and exploitation. As if suffering from an addiction, we give in to the impulse to impose values upon the map. Our mission, perhaps, is to understand that if we are to contest or condition the uses to which a map is put, whether it is a genetic map or a planetary map or a map of the earth's interior, we must do so soon after it is made.

It is impossible to look at a map of the world from the sixteenth century, the century that most resembles ours in the degree of exploration and intellectual ferment, without seeing it as a record of failed dreams. It is impossible to contemplate these modern maps, of atoms and chromosomes and galaxies, without sensing that same promise and without fearing that same past.

The maps created by twentieth-century scientists during this latest and perhaps greatest era of discovery in the history of civilization represent dreams as yet unspoiled, one more shot at one more New World, and as we attempt to revise and reshape our worldview on the basis of the territories we are now discovering and exploring, we would do well to bear in mind not only the cartographic imperative to fill in the blank spaces on the map, but also a countervailing imperative to inhabit those spaces with wisdom and equality and a generous spirit, remembering the injunction of that home-cosmographer Oscar Wilde, who once remarked, "A map of the world that does not include Utopia is not worth even glancing at."

GENERAL SOURCES AND NOTES

LATITUDE, LONGITUDE, INFINITUDE

GENERAL SOURCES

Rudolf Arnheim, "The Perception of Maps," in *New Essays on the Psychology of Art,* University of California Press, Berkeley, 1986; Leo Bagrow, *History of Cartography,* revised and enlarged by R. A. Skelton, 2nd ed., Precedent Publishing, Chicago, 1985; Daniel Boorstin, *The Discoverers,* Random House, New York, 1983; Lloyd A. Brown, *The Story of Maps,* Dover, New York, 1949, 1979; Italo Calvino, *Six Memos for the Next Millennium,* Harvard University Press, Cambridge, 1988; Robert P. Crease and Charles C. Mann, *The Second Creation,* Macmillan, New York, 1986; Timothy Ferris, *Coming of Age in the Milky Way,* Anchor/Doubleday, Garden City, N.Y., 1988; George Gamow, *One, Two, Three . . . Infinity,* Dover, New York, 1961, 1988; William H. Goetzmann, *New Lands, New Men: America and the Second Great Age of Discovery,* Viking, New York, 1986; Richard L. Gregory, *Eye and Brain: The Psychology of Seeing,* 4th ed., Princeton University Press, Princeton, N.J., 1966, 1990; Robert Harbison, *Eccentric Spaces,* Godine, Boston, 1977, 1988; J. B. Harley and David Woodward, eds., *History of Cartography,* University of Chicago Press, Chicago, 1987; Homer, *The Odyssey,* Robert Fitzgerald, trans., Anchor/Doubleday, Garden City, N.Y., 1963; Horace Freeland Judson, *The Search for Solutions,* Johns Hopkins University Press, Baltimore, 1987; Wallace I. Matson, *A New History of Philosophy* (2 vols.), Harcourt Brace Jovanovich, San Diego, 1987; Philip Morrison and Phylis Morrison, *The Ring of Truth: An Inquiry into How We Know What We Know,* Random House, New York, 1987; Arthur H. Robinson and Barbara Bartz Petchenik, *The Nature of Maps,* University of Chicago Press, Chicago, 1976; Edward R. Tufte, *The Visual Display of Quantitative Information,* Graphics Press, Cheshire, Conn., 1983; Edward R. Tufte, *Envisioning Information,* Graphics Press, Cheshire, Conn., 1990; John Noble Wilford, *The Mapmakers,* Knopf, New York, 1981.

NOTES

p. 3 Epigraph: Hideki Yukawa, quoted in Crease and Mann, op. cit., p. 159.

p. 3 "art with a purpose": L. Brown, op. cit., p. 32.

p. 5 "a representation . . .": *Encyclopaedia Britannica,* 11th ed., Cambridge University Press, Cambridge, 1910, vol. 17, p. 629.

p. 6 "a graphic representation . . .": Robinson and Petchenik, op. cit., p. 16.

p. 7 On the "whirlwind tour": Sources include Charlene M. Anderson, "Planetary Maps: Passports for the Mind," *The Planetary Report,* vol. 10, Nov.–Dec., 1990, pp. 12–19; Voyager 2 Handbook, NASA/Jet Propulsion Laboratory, Pasadena, 1989; COHMAP, *Science,* Aug. 26, 1988, pp. 1043–1052; V. Norwood, personal interview; Malcolm W. Browne, "The Wanderings of a Gigantic Iceberg Uncovers Polar Currents," *New York Times,* Oct. 16, 1990, p. C4; P. Jouventin and H. Weimerskirch, "Satellite Tracking of Wandering Albatross," *Nature,* vol. 343, Feb. 22, 1990, p. 746; Crease and Mann, op. cit.; J. J. Quattrochi et al., "Mapping Neuronal Inputs to REM Sleep Induction Sites with Carbachol-Fluorescent Microspheres," *Science,* vol. 245, Sept. 1, 1989, pp. 984–986; R. Bianchi et al., "Remote Sensing of Italian Volcanoes," *EOS,* vol. 71, Nov. 13, 1990, p. 1789; J. F. Asmus et al., "Computer Enhancement of the *Mona Lisa,*" *Perspectives in Computing,* vol. 7, Spring 1987, pp. 11–22. This last, modestly titled study describes how workers created a digitized color transparency of the painting, and then analyzed it using digital image-processing techniques originally developed to process remote-sensing images obtained from space, such as Landsat maps.

p. 7 "Atlas, or cosmographical . . .": J. Wilford, op. cit., p. 85. For background on the origins of the word "atlas," see Wilford, pp. 85–86, and L. Brown, op. cit., pp. 164–167.

p. 8 "geography is facts": L. Bougainville, quoted in W. Goetzmann, op. cit., p. 42.

p. 9 "The transition from . . .": W. Heisenberg, quoted in Michael Riordan, *The Hunting of the Quark,* Simon & Schuster, New York, 1987, p. 38.

p. 11 The accomplishments of *Voyager 2,* as well as its historical context in mapping, is described by William H. Goetzmann, "Voyager Retrospective: A Symposium on Exploration," *The Planetary Report,* vol. 9, no. 6, Nov.–Dec. 1989, pp. 6–9; I am also indebted to Victor McElheny for a summation and analysis of Goetzmann's remarks.

p. 11 "It was like being . . .": T. Mutch, quoted in Bruce Murray, *Journey into Space,* Norton, New York, 1989, p. 162.

p. 11 On distance scales: See M. Mitchell Waldrop, "The Farthest Galaxies: A New Champion," *Science,* vol. 241, Aug. 19, 1988, p. 905; on atomic scale, see Howard Georgi, quoted in Crease and Mann, op. cit., p. 36; on biological scale, see Stephen S. Hall, "James Watson and the Search for Biology's 'Holy Grail,' " *Smithsonian,* February 1990, pp. 41–49.

p. 11 "almost always in . . .": Francis Crick, *What Mad Pursuit,* Basic Books, New York, 1988, p. 35.

p. 12 On the role of computers in the visualization of data: Robert S. Wolff, "Visualization 101: A Tour Guide of Basic Concepts," *Computers in Physics,* May–June, 1990, pp. 260–265; Thomas Levenson, "At the Speed Limit," *Atlantic,* March 1990, pp. 40–46; David Bjerklie, "The Electronic Transformation of Maps," *Technology Review,* April 1989, pp. 54–63.

p. 12 The original computer-assisted map appeared in J. G. Charney et al., "Numerical Integration of the Barotropic Vorticity Equation," *Tellus,* November 1950, pp. 237–254.

p. 13 "Aesthetic qualities . . .": Roger Penrose, quoted in John Horgan, "Quantum Consciousness," *Scientific American,* Nov. 1989, pp. 30–33.

pp. 13–14 On cartographic movies: See, for example, Marcia Barinaga, "Biology Goes to the Movies," *Science,* vol. 250, Nov. 30, 1990, pp. 1204–1206.

p. 14 "mediators between . . .": J. B. Harley, *History of Cartography,* op. cit., p. 1.

p. 14 "The forest goes on . . .": Patrick Thaddeus, Harvard-Smithsonian Center for Astrophysics, Cambridge, Mass., personal interview, Sept. 14, 1989; "Finding your way . . .": ibid.

pp. 15–16 "Mathematical equations . . .": Arthur H. Robinson, "The Uniqueness of the Map," *American Cartographer,* vol. 5, no. 1, 1978, pp. 5–7.

p. 16 "Large areas of constant . . .": R. L. Gregory, op. cit., p. 68.

p. 16 "feature maps": Anne Treisman, "Features and Objects in Visual Processing," *Scientific American,* November 1986, pp. 114–124. Treisman writes: "Certain aspects of visual processing seem to be accomplished simultaneously (that is, for the entire visual field at once) and automatically (that is, without attention being focused on any one part of the visual field). Other aspects of visual processing seem to depend on focused attention and are done serially, or one at a time, as if a mental spotlight were being moved from one location to another" (p. 114).

p. 16 Other mapping work involving the visual system of the brain includes Richard Durbin and Graeme Mitchison, "A Dimension Reduction Framework for Understanding Cortical Maps," *Nature,* vol. 343, Feb. 15, 1990, pp. 644–647. A review of recent work is Michael P. Peterson, "The Mental Image in Cartographic Communication," *Cartographic Journal,* June 1987, pp. 35–41.

pp. 16–17 "We live in a noisy . . .": John Allman, Dept. of Psychobiology, California Institute of Technology, Pasadena, telephone interview, Feb. 4, 1991. Allman believes the topographical organization of the brain may have developed by the same mechanism of gene duplication discovered by E. B. Lewis and described in chapter 10.

pp. 18–19 "our brains seem to . . .": Alan Gevins, quoted in Rick Weiss, "Shadows of Thoughts Revealed," *Science News,* Nov. 10, 1990, p. 297; "We have found . . .": Walter J. Freeman, "The Physiology of Perception," *Scientific American,* February 1991, pp. 78–85.

p. 19 "there is the infinitely . . .": Hannah Arendt, *The Human Condition,* Anchor/Doubleday, Garden City, N.Y., 1959. Apropos of pattern recognition, Arendt also notes: "In any event, wherever we try to transcend appearance beyond all sensual experience, even instrument-aided, in order to catch the ultimate secrets of Being, which according to our physical world view is so secretive that it never appears and still so tremendously powerful that it produces all appearance, we find that the same patterns rule the macrocosm and microcosm alike, that we receive the same instrument readings. Here again, we may for a moment rejoice in a refound unity of the universe, only to fall prey to the suspicion that what we have found may have nothing to do with either the macrocosmos or the microcosmos, that we deal only with the patterns of our own mind, the mind which designed the instruments and put nature under its conditions in the experiment . . ." (p. 260).

p. 20 "My approach is . . .": Alan Dressler, Observatories of the Carnegie Institution of Washington, Pasadena, Calif., personal interview, Aug. 28, 1989.

p. 21 "Our immediate neighborhood . . .": Edwin Hubble, quoted in Allan R. Sandage, "The Red Shift," *Scientific American,* September 1956, p. 182.

p. 22 On international collaborations in astronomy: Rosat, launched in 1990, has surveyed the central region of the Large Magellanic Cloud (*Nature,* Feb. 14, 1991, p. 579); Granat, launched in the spring of 1990, recently found evidence suggesting a small black hole near the center of the Milky Way (*Science,* Jan. 11, 1991, p. 166); the European Southern Observatory's proposed Very Large Telescope, using self-correcting optics, would have fifty times the light-gathering power of the Hubble Space Telescope, and ten times that of the 200-inch Hale Telescope at Palomar (*New York Times,* July 20, 1990, p. A12).

pp. 22–23 On Mission to Planet Earth: Bob Davis, "U.S. Climate Satellites Weather Criticism," *Wall Street Journal,* March 22, 1990, p. B1.

p. 23 Jesuit map: Described in David McCracken, "Our Worldly Passion for Maps," *Chicago Tribune,* Jan. 12, 1990, p. 3 ("Friday" section). The map is in the collection of the Newberry Library in Chicago.

p. 25 On galactic surveys: John Huchra, interview (see chapter 18, "The Universe According to John Huchra").

p. 26 no practical value: Galileo, quoted in Morrison and Morrison, op. cit., p. 136.

p. 26 "The solar system . . .": Carolyn Porco, press briefing, Jet Propulsion Laboratory, Pasadena, Calif., Aug. 22, 1989.

p. 26 "An unmapped discovery . . .": J. Wilford, op. cit., p. 62. See Wilford on the Vinland discoveries and lack of a map, pp. 61–63.

p. 27 "Now when I was . . .": Joseph Conrad, *Heart of Darkness,* Norton, New York, 1988, p. 11.

1. "WE DO PRECISION GUESSWORK"
GENERAL SOURCES

Book-length accounts of *Voyager 2*'s Grand Tour include William Burrows, *Exploring Space,* Random House, New York, 1991; Henry S. F. Cooper, *Imaging Saturn,* Holt, Rinehart, & Winston, New York, 1982; Joel Davis, *Flyby: The Interplanetary Odyssey of Voyager 2,* Atheneum, New York, 1987; Mark Littmann, *Planets Beyond: Discovering the Outer Solar System,* Wiley Science Editions, New York, 1988 (a good history of planetary exploration by the historian at the Space Science Institute in Baltimore); Bruce Murray, *Journey into Space: The First Thirty Years of Space Exploration,* Norton, New York, 1989; and *The Voyager Neptune Travel Guide,* JPL Publication 89-24, edited by Charles Kohlhase, National Aeronautics and Space Administration, Pasadena, Calif., 1989.

The book-length, blow-by-blow accounts of planetary encounters suffer, in my opinion, from the same problem as the scientific press conferences sponsored by the Jet Propulsion Laboratory during the flybys: the stories and explanations change so much each day that the tale becomes confusing and tedious. In some respects magazine summaries are clearer and more effective. Among treatments of *Voyager 2* written with both accuracy and flair, there are: James R. Chiles, "Flying on a Wing and a Prayer, Voyager Heads for a Last Rendezvous," *Smithsonian,* Sept. 1988, pp. 42–53; June Kinoshita, "Neptune," *Scientific American,* Nov. 1989, pp. 82–91; William I. McLaughlin, "Voyager's Decade of Wonder," *Sky & Telescope,* July 1989, pp. 16–20; Kathy Sawyer, "Keeping Voyager 2 on Course for 12 Years, 4½ Billion Miles," *Washington Post,* Aug. 14, 1989, p. A3 (specifically about the navigational team); and John Noble Wilford, "Flight to Jupiter Is Set for Sunday," *New York Times,* Feb. 25, 1972, p. 7 [Launch of *Pioneer 10*]; "Voyager 2 Finds Rings at Neptune (But Not All the Way Around It)," *New York Times,* Aug. 12, 1989, p. 1; "Uncannily Precise, Voyager Bears Down on Neptune," *New York Times,* Aug. 24, 1989, p. A–14.

Amid the veritable torrent of reports about the Neptune encounter, particularly reliable and edifying coverage has consistently been produced by J. Kelly Beatty in *Sky & Telescope*; Jonathan Eberhart in *Science News*; Mark Washburn in *Air and Space*; and John Noble Wilford in the *New York Times.*

NOTES

p. 31 Epigraph: John Keats, from "On First Looking into Chapman's Homer," *Selected Poems and Letters,* Barnes & Noble, New York, 1966, p. 25.

p. 32 "I think it's a great . . .": Carl Sagan, quoted in "Voyager Retrospective: A Symposium on Exploration," *Planetary Report,* vol. 10, Nov.–Dec. 1989, p. 6.

p. 32 On early navigation: Samuel Eliot Morison, *Admiral of the Ocean Sea: A Life of Christopher Columbus,* Little, Brown, & Co., Boston, 1942, pp. 183–196.

pp. 33–34 Description of B-plane: The author was privileged to attend the Aug. 19, 1989 meeting. Some notes derive from "Nav H TCM B20 Tweak Results Meeting," Aug. 19, 1989, briefing papers prepared for meeting.

p. 34 "There's some risk . . .": Bradford Smith, quoted in John Noble Wilford, "Voyager 2 Finds Rings at Neptune (But Not All the Way Around It)," *New York Times,* Aug. 12, 1989, p. 1.

p. 35 "We really diddled around . . .": Donald Gray, speaking at TCM B20 meeting, Aug. 19, 1989.

p. 36 "I have bad news . . .": Anthony (Tony) Taylor, speaking at same meeting; "We're going to advertise . . .": ibid.

p. 37 "Okay, so it's four . . .": Edward Stone, speaking at same meeting.

p. 37 "the final movement . . .": Edward Stone, press conference, Jet Propulsion Laboratory, Aug. 21, 1989.

p. 37 "This is the last . . .": Norman Haynes, press conference, JPL, Aug. 21, 1989.

p. 37 "No, but if you happen . . .": Robert Cesarone, navigation team, Jet Propulsion Laboratory, Aug. 19, 1989.

pp. 37–43 Background about the Grand Tour trajectory: Much of this account is based on an interview with Gary A. Flandro, Pasadena, Calif., Aug. 25, 1989. The key paper is G. A. Flandro, "Fast Reconnaissance Missions to the Outer Solar System Utilizing Energy Derived from the Gravitational Field of Jupiter," *Astronautica Acta,* vol. 12, no. 4, 1966, pp. 329–337. For additional information, see also Mark Littmann, *Planets Beyond: Discovering the Outer Solar System,* Wiley Science Editions, New York, 1988, which includes a section written by Flandro describing his work at JPL during the summer of 1965. The official JPL-NASA version of the *Voyager 2* Grand Tour trajectory, edited by Charles Kohlhase, tends to emphasize the contributions of Michael Minovitch over those of Flandro. Minovitch, according to the guide, "created a revolution in planetary mission design" in 1961 with gravity-assist, and showed how it could be used to derive energy bursts at each planetary flyby. It goes on to say that Minovitch in 1962 "graphically illustrated" a Jupiter-Saturn-Neptune tour for 1976. Gravity-assist was first applied in 1974, when *Mariner 10* picked up energy from Venus on its way to Mercury.

p. 38 "I thought they'd just . . .": G. Flandro, interview.

p. 40 "We realized that you can . . .": ibid.

p. 40 Michael Minovitch's two papers were: "Determination and Characteristics of Ballistic Interplanetary Trajectories Under the Influence of Multiple Planetary Attractions," Technical Report No. 32-464, Jet Propulsion Laboratory, Pasadena, Calif., Oct. 31, 1963, and "Utilizing Large Planetary Perturbations for the Design of Deep Space, Solar Probe, and Out-of-Ecliptic Trajectories," Technical Report No. 32-849, Jet Propulsion Laboratory, Pasadena, Calif., Dec. 15, 1965.

p. 40 Minovitch's "Gravity Thrust and Interplanetary Transportation Networks," a fascinating paper delivered at the AAS Symposium in Boston (May 25–27, 1967), describes a fleet of gigantic "space liners" up to 1,000 yards across engaged in "never-ending" journeys around the inner planets, powered by gravity-assist in so efficient a manner that "trip costs will be within reach of ordinary people." See Michael Minovitch, "Gravity Thrust and Interplanetary Transportation Networks," in Robert D. Enzmann, ed., *Use of Space Systems for Planetary Geology and Geophysics,* based on AAS Symposium, Boston, Mass., May 25–27, 1967.

p. 40 "He was around . . .": G. Flandro, interview; "The thing that really . . .": ibid.

p. 42 "It was the early days . . .": G. Flandro, interview.

pp. 42–43 The source for the costs of Apollo and the space shuttle is John Pike, Federation of American Scientists; the two figures are in 1990 dollars and, given the vagaries of accounting for such large projects, must be considered approximate.

p. 43 The Minovitch patent is described in Edmund Andrews, "New Ideas for Travel in Space," *New York Times,* Nov. 25, 1989, p. 32.

p. 43 "If *Voyager 1* had failed . . .": Andrey Sergeyevsky, former trajectory chief, *Voyager 2,* personal interview, Jet Propulsion Laboratory, Pasadena, Calif., May 30, 1989.

p. 43 "some black sack . . .": Homer, *The Odyssey,* Anchor/Doubleday, Garden City, N.Y., p. 210. Of all the language with geographic-metaphoric resonance in Homer's long map-poem, perhaps my favorite phrase is Athena saying to Odysseus, "Stranger, you must come from the other end of nowhere" (p. 237).

p. 44 For background on how the Grand Tour trajectory was actually designed, perhaps the best summation is Andrey B. Sergeyevsky, "Voyager 2: A Grand Tour of the Giant Planets," paper delivered at the AAS/AIAA Astrodynamics Special Conference, Lake Tahoe, Nev., Aug. 3–5, 1981. For an account of how the various obstacles at Neptune were anticipated, see R. J. Cesarone et al., "Mission Design Challenges Posed by the Voyager 2 Neptune Encounter," paper presented at AAS/AIAA Astrodynamics Specialist Conference, Kalispell, Mont., Aug. 10–13, 1987.

p. 44 "You never really return . . .": A. Sergeyevsky, interview.

p. 44 "If everything goes just . . .": R. Cesarone, trajectory chief, *Voyager 2* Neptune encounter, personal interview, Pasadena, Calif., May 23, 1989.

p. 44 "What that meant . . .": ibid.

p. 45 "So then you launch . . .": ibid.; "When you know where . . .": ibid.; "We got a new . . .": ibid.

p. 47 "That bought us . . .": ibid.

p. 47 "alarming": Mark Ryne, personal interview, Aug. 24, 1989.

p. 47 "At that point . . .": A. Taylor, personal interview, Aug. 24, 1989.

p. 47 For background on the problematic radio transmissions, a good account is Richard P. Laeser, William I. McLaughlin, and Donna T. Wolff, "Engineering Voyager 2's Encounter with Uranus," *Scientific American,* Nov. 1986, pp. 36–45.

p. 48 "Now we hold . . .": A. Taylor, interview.

p. 48 "Jesus, right in the middle!": ibid.

p. 50 The map of the heliopause was anticipated in an interesting paper by Robert J. Cesarone, Andrey B. Sergeyevsky, and Stuart J. Kerridge, "Prospects for the Voyager Extra-Planetary and Interstellar Mission," presented at AAS/ AIAA Astrodynamics Specialist Conference, Lake Placid, N.Y., Aug. 22–25, 1983, vol. 45, AAS microfiche series. This is a fascinating, futuristic look at what the interplanetary space probes—not just the two *Voyagers,* but also *Pioneer 11*—might encounter once they leave the solar system. Cesarone, interestingly, has gone on record as saying that he believes future generations will have the capability of retrieving *Voyager 2,* so that "within a couple hundred years, they'll be sitting in the Air and Space Museum."

p. 50 "That would be . . .": R. Cesarone, interview.

p. 51 "I must tell you . . .": G. Flandro, interview.

2. GROUND TRUTH

GENERAL SOURCES

S. A. Drury, *Image Interpretation in Geology,* Allen & Unwin, London, 1987; David S. Simonett, "The Development and Principles of Remote Sensing," in Robert N. Colwell, ed., *Manual of Remote Sensing,* 2nd ed., American Society of Photogrammetry, Sheridan Press, Falls Church, Va., 1983, pp. 1–35; Thomas M. Lillesand and Ralph W. Kiefer, *Remote Sensing and Image Interpretation,* 2nd ed., John Wiley & Sons, New York, 1987; Pamela E. Mack, *Viewing the Earth: The Social Construction of the Landsat System,* MIT Press, Cambridge, Mass., 1990; Christopher Mueller-Wille, *Images of the World: An Atlas of Satellite Imagery and Maps,* Rand McNally, Chicago, 1983; Robert S. Rudd, *Remote Sensing: A Better View,* Duxbury Press, North Scituate, Mass., 1974; Doug Stewart, "Eyes in Orbit Keep Tabs on the World in Unexpected Ways," *Smithsonian,* Dec. 1988, pp. 70–81; John Noble Wilford, "Mapping from Space," in *The Mapmakers,* Knopf, New York, 1981.

NOTES

p. 52 Epigraph: Montaigne, from "On Physiognomy," *Essays,* Penguin, New York, 1958, p. 311.

pp. 52–53 On the New York Bight incident: Described in C. T. Wezernak, "Water Quality Monitoring Using ERTS-A Data," Report on the Preliminary Data Analysis, Environmental Research Institute of Michigan, Ann Arbor, April 1973, plus Norm Roller, ERIM, telephone interview, Feb. 14, 1990; and Enrico P.

Mercanti, "ERTS-1: Teaching Us a New Way to See," *Astronautics & Aeronautics,* Sept. 1973, pp. 36–63. The Mercanti article notes that the Bight image was recorded about fourteen hours after the dumping, which put the dumping at approximately 7:30 P.M.

p. 54 "a new way to look": James C. Fletcher, "ERTS-1: Toward Global Monitoring," *Astronautics & Aeronautics,* Sept. 1973, p. 32.

p. 55 Colwell background: Robert Colwell, telephone interview, Jan. 20, 1990; Robert N. Colwell, "Some Practical Applications of Multiband Spectral Reconnaissance," *American Scientist,* March 1961, pp. 9–36.

p. 56 "Just as our musical . . .": R. N. Colwell, ibid., p. 34.

p. 58 The role played by the agricultural community in developing Landsat has been overshadowed by NASA's more obvious role. In addition to Colwell's work at the University of California, a group at Purdue University spearheaded by Ralph Shay, and the University of Michigan group, pushed developments in the early 1960s. Shay chaired an influential National Academy of Sciences committee that not only endorsed the idea of remote sensing, but pushed for multispectral analysis.

p. 58 Account of the first Michigan symposium found in "Proceedings of the First Symposium on Remote Sensing of the Environment," Infrared Laboratory, Institute of Science and Technology, University of Michigan, March 1962. The first symposium was attended by about seventy scientists; the IST's study program was sponsored by the Office of Naval Research, and funded by the Army, Navy, and Air Force, substantiating the military's interest in remote sensing. In his summational remarks, Walter H. Bailey of the Office of Naval Research openly acknowledged the "problem of security of classification."

p. 58 "This came up . . .": Walter Bailey, Office of Naval Research, remarks in *Proceedings,* p. 109.

p. 58 Fischer's participation was limited. As he told the symposium, the USGS was "new to the sophisticated sensing field." Yet Fischer is credited, by several sources, as the person who suggested the idea of a civilian remote sensing satellite—that is, Landsat.

p. 59 On satellite and space vehicle photography: a good review is Paul D. Lowman, Jr., "The Evolution of Geological Space Photography," in Barry S. Siegal and Alan R. Gillespie, eds., *Remote Sensing in Geology,* Wiley, New York, 1980; and Wilford, op. cit. It bears emphasizing that the orbital missions followed the Michigan symposia, and that the spectral imaging community was pursuing a technology much more information-rich than straightforward photography.

p. 59 "Since the physiological effects . . .": Wilford, op. cit., p. 338.

p. 59 On the opposition within NASA: See Richard D. Lyons, "Satellite-Borne Dowsing Rod to Be Orbited in Spring," *New York Times,* Feb. 4, 1972, p. 11, an excellent account of the bureaucratic opposition to Landsat. Among other evidence, Lyons cites letters between the Interior Dept. and NASA that "clearly indicate that NASA officials, including [NASA chief James E.] Webb were lukewarm to the EROS program, partly because they wanted a long period of experimental flights, partly because they did not want to invest funds at that time, and partly because of the problems created by the Apollo fire that killed three astronauts." Former Interior Secretary Stewart L. Udall attributed delays in the program to the "blindness and footdragging" of NASA.

p. 59 "There was a lot of pressure . . .": A. Colvocoresses, United States Geological Survey, Reston, Va., telephone interview, Oct. 24, 1989.

p. 60 "NASA may have had . . .": Mack, op. cit., p. 58.

p. 60 The Pecora background comes from the Landsat 15th anniversary booklet (EOSAT, 1987); obituaries in the *New York Times* (July 20, 1972, p. 36) and the *Washington Post* (July 20, 1972, p. B-6); and widow Wynn Pecora, Washington, D.C., telephone interview, Jan. 18, 1990.

p. 60 The Sept. 20, 1966 press conference was described in "Sensing Satellite to Study Earth Resources," *New York Times,* Sept. 21, 1966, p. 1. In a press release, Udall said, "Project EROS is based upon a series of feasibility experiments carried out by the U.S. Geological Survey with NASA, universities, and other institutions over the past two years. It is because of the vision and support of NASA that we are able to plan project EROS."

p. 60 Unlike NASA's objective, Interior's aim was operational and environmental. Udall said, "The time is now right and urgent to apply space technology towards the solution of many pressing natural resources problems being compounded by population and industrial growth."

p. 60 "The next day . . .": W. Pecora, interview.

p. 61 "NASA was the reluctant . . .": R. Mroczynski, EOSAT Co., Lanham, Md., telephone interview, Jan. 16, 1990.

p. 61 Background on the debate between scanners and television cameras: David Landgrebe, Purdue University, West Lafayette, Ind., telephone interview, Sept. 25, 1989; R. Mroczynski, op. cit.; "Hughes Multispectral Scanner System for ERTS Goddard Space Flight Center," promotional brochure, Hughes Aircraft Company, El Segundo, Calif., circa 1972, and Hughes promotional data, ca. 1968. For Norwood paper, see Virginia T. Norwood and Jack C. Lansing, Jr., "Electro-Optical Imaging Sensors," in Robert N. Colwell, ed., *Manual of Remote Sensing,* pp. 335–367.

p. 61 "We were pushing a scanner . . .": Virginia Norwood, Hughes Co., El Segundo, Calif., personal interview, Aug. 29, 1989; "No woman in our . . .": ibid.; "People thought it . . .": ibid.; "The blue band . . .": ibid.

p. 64 "Mapmakers like myself . . .": A. Colvocoresses, letter to author, Oct. 30, 1989. A related issue in the debate was pure imaging versus overall information. "The mappers wanted to have good photographic products," Richard Mroczynski recalls. "Arch Park [of the Department of Agriculture] was interested in developing digital processing technology. So it was the image makers versus the people who wanted information, and you can tell who won the battle by the band numbers." Bands 1, 2, and 3 were on the imaging RBVs, bands 4, 5, 6, and 7 on the digitized MSS.

p. 64 "People were so . . .": V. Norwood, interview.

pp. 64–65 "When Landsat was . . .": D. Landgrebe, interview.

p. 65 "a new era of . . .": Boyce Rensberger, "An Earth-Exploring Satellite Is Orbited," *New York Times,* July 24, 1972, p. 1. ERTS-1 was originally scheduled to be launched in May. A launch on July 20 was scrubbed because of engine trouble, and the following day by "technical difficulties" (*New York Times,* July 22, 1972, p. 9).

p. 65 According to Robert Colwell, Landsat's artful orbit was designed over beers by Fischer, Park, and John DeNoyer.

p. 65 The demise of the return beam vidicons is described in Lillesand and Kiefer, op. cit., p. 540, who observe that "RBV operations were plagued with various technical malfunctions." Donald Lowe (in "Acquisition of Remotely Sensed Data," Barry S. Siegel and Alan R. Gillespie, eds., *Remote Sensing in Geology,* Wiley, New York, 1980) writes: ". . . it was originally thought that the vidicon with reseau marks would yield better geometric accuracy for cartographic purposes than the MSS. However, the geometric accuracy of the scanner was much better than anticipated. When the format is computer adjusted with ground control points, the images meet 1:250,000 map accuracy standards. Because the radiometric quality of the MSS data is much superior to the RBV, the RBV system of Landsat is not turned on but serves as a backup sensor. . . ."

p. 65 "But if ERTS had not . . .": Allen Watkins, EROS Data Center, Sioux Falls, S.D., telephone interview, Feb. 8, 1990.

p. 67 "Sophisticated in program . . .": William Pecora, quoted in Landsat Anniversary Booklet (1987), p. 33.

p. 67 "Our first discovery . . .": Paul Lowman, quoted in J. N. Wilford, "Satellite Takes a Portrait of New York Area," *New York Times,* Sept. 12, 1972, p. 26.

p. 67 For CIA and Dept. of Defense use of Landsat data, see Mack, op. cit., p. 131.

p. 69 "the mania for commercialization . . .": John Pike, Federation of American Scientists, telephone interview, May 20, 1991.

p. 70 "2 Oppose Shift on Photo Satellites," *New York Times,* Nov. 16, 1989, p. B12. On Landsat's latter-day difficulties: Eliot Marshall, "Landsat: Cliff Hanging, Again," *Science,* Oct. 20, 1989, pp. 321–322; E. Marshall, "Landsats: Drifting Toward Oblivion?" *Science,* Feb. 24, 1989, p. 999; and N. Mitchell Waldrop, "Imaging the Earth (I): The Troubled First Decade of Landsat," *Science,* March 26, 1982, pp. 1600–1603.

p. 70 The stereo mapping satellite, according to Alden Colvocoresses, "is well within state-of-the-art, and not that expensive to build and fly." A consensus on the basic design has been reached by the USGS and the eighty-nation International Society of Photogrammetry and Remote Sensing. The technology is protected by a U.S. patent called Mapsat.

p. 70 "We should start looking . . .": Walter Schirra, quoted in Lyons, op. cit., p. 11.

p. 70 "We should send a man . . .": V. Norwood, interview.

3. THE HIDDEN CRUCIBLE

GENERAL SOURCES

Marcia Bartusiak, "Mapping the Sea Floor from Space," *Popular Science,* Feb. 1984, pp. 80–85; Stephanie Bernardo, "The Seafloor: A Clear View from Space," *Science Digest,* June 1984, pp. 44–49, 103; William Glen, *The Road to Jaramillo: Critical Years of the Revolution in Earth Science,* Stanford University Press, Stanford, Calif., 1982; and J. Tuzo Wilson, "Continental Drift," *Scientific American,* April 1963, pp. 86–100.

NOTES

p. 71 Epigraph: William Butler Yeats, from "Byzantium," *The Collected Poems of W. B. Yeats,* Macmillan, New York, 1956, p. 244.

p. 71 Work on *Geos-3* data is described in W. F. Haxby and D. L. Turcotte, "On Isostatic Geoid Anomalies," *Journal of Geophysical Research,* vol. 83, no. B11, Nov. 10, 1978, pp. 5473–5478.

p. 72 Background on early mapping of ocean floor: "Charts and the Haven-Finding Art," in Lloyd Brown, *The Story of Maps,* Dover, New York, 1979; "Two Roads to Discovery: An Intellectual Drama," in William H. Goetzmann, *New Lands, New Men,* Viking, New York, 1986; and "Mountains of the Sea" in John Noble Wilford, *The Mapmakers,* Knopf, 1981.

pp. 74–75 Background on continental drift: There's no dearth of sources, but one of the best brief synopses—as well as a wonderfully instructive chapter in the role of outsiders in the history of science—is A. Hallam, "Alfred Wegener and the Hypothesis of Continental Drift," *Scientific American,* Feb. 1975, pp. 88–97. Between 1912 and the 1960s, Hallam writes, "Wegener's theory had at best been neglected, and it had often been scorned." The main objection to Wegener's hypothesis was that he did not explain what force could be moving the continents.

p. 75 "The continents would plow . . .": Xavier Le Pichon, "The Birth of Plate Tectonics," in *1985–1986 Lamont-Doherty Geological Observatory Yearbook,* Palisades, N.Y., 1986, pp. 53–61. This is a superbly compact account, written by an insider who backed the wrong horse, of the revolution in the 1950s and 1960s that resulted in general acceptance of plate tectonics as a theory.

p. 75 "God does not play . . .": Einstein's famous line is quoted in Abraham Pais, *"Subtle Is the Lord . . .": The Science and the Life of Albert Einstein,* Oxford University Press, Oxford, 1982, p. 440.

p. 75 "explanation which explains . . .": Harold Jeffreys, quoted in Le Pichon, op. cit., p. 53.

p. 76 "a wound that never . . .": Heezen, quoted in K. C. Macdonald, *Nature,* vol. 339, May 18, 1989, pp. 178–179.

p. 76 The famous Vine and Matthews paper was published in *Nature* (vol. 199, Sept. 7, 1963, pp. 947–949) and made the point by showing that the earth's shifting magnetic pole had magnetically "stamped" the emerging crust at the mid-ocean rifts, so that there was a symmetric pattern of magnetic stripes on either side of the rift.

p. 76 "completely ignored": Le Pichon, op. cit., p. 57. This pertains especially to discussions at Lamont-Doherty, but Le Pichon goes on to say: "It is significant that neither Vine, nor Matthews, nor [Lawrence] Morley, nor anybody else considered any follow-up to these two papers during the two following years." Henry Frankel, in a twenty-fifth-anniversary commentary in *Nature,* agreed that the paper "attracted little immediate attention" ("From Continental Drift to Plate Tectonics," *Nature,* vol. 335, Sept. 8, 1988, pp. 127–130).

p. 77 "It was very obvious . . .": J. Tuzo Wilson, telephone interview, Feb. 12, 1990. Wilson published the basic outline of plates and plate tectonics in *Nature* in 1965, vol. 207, July 24, 1965, p. 343. The "Wilson cycle" of supercontinent formation and separation is described in R. Damian Nance, Thomas R. Worsley, and Judith B. Moody, "The Supercontinent Cycle," *Scientific American,* July 1988, pp. 72–79.

pp. 78–79 Background on Seasat: G. H. Born et al., "Seasat Mission Overview," *Science,* vol. 204, June 29, 1979, pp. 1405–1406, plus accompanying reports on specific Seasat missions.

p. 79 In *Journey into Space,* Bruce Murray describes the Seasat failure thusly: "A new and (as we discovered) untested rotating electrical connection was required on Seasat where the large electrical current from the movable solar panels passed into the spacecraft bus. That connection on Seasat short-circuited after three months in orbit and brought the mission to a catastrophic end" (p. 127). Seasat, however, successfully tested the side-viewing, or synthetic aperture, radar (SAR) that would later be used on the Magellan mission to map Venus.

p. 79 "everything worked beautifully . . .": William F. Haxby, Lamont-Doherty Geological Observatory, Palisades, N.Y., personal interviews, Feb. 16, 1989, and Feb. 12, 1990.

pp. 79–80 On Seasat security issues, see "Seasat-A: Concern and Questions," *Science News,* Oct. 21, 1978, p. 280.

pp. 79–80 The security debate over release of the Seasat data was replayed several years later with a new mapping technology. The coordinated use of a wide-beam sonar scanner called Seabeam on the surface and a satellite system known as the Global Positioning System allows maps of unprecedented detail and precision to be made of U.S. coastal waters. When the National Oceanic and Atmospheric Administration announced plans to do just that in 1984, the Navy persuaded the White House to issue an order curtailing their release subject to Pentagon review. The Navy finally relaxed its position in the spring of 1989. For an account, see Colin Norman, "Navy Relents in Battle Over Mapping Sea Floor," *Science,* April 7, 1989, p. 25.

p. 80 "I simply expected . . .": W. Haxby, interview; "The shape of the ocean . . .": ibid.; "There are gravity . . .": ibid.

p. 81 "Why don't you . . .": W. Haxby, quoted by John LaBrecque, telephone interview, Feb. 15, 1990.

p. 81 "He produced a map . . .": J. LaBrecque, ibid.; "Suddenly, we had . . .": ibid.

p. 82 "created a sensation": Walter Sullivan, "Ocean Floor Maps Given New Detail," *New York Times,* Dec. 26, 1982, p. 18.

p. 82 "extremely subjective": Charles Drake, Dartmouth University, telephone interview, March 9, 1990; "First of all . . .": ibid.

p. 83 "The progress toward . . .": W. Haxby, interview.

p. 83 The actual Haxby map, described at the AGU meeting in December of 1982, became available in 1985, as described in William F. Haxby, "Gravity Field of World's Ocean (Color Map)," National Geophysical Data Center, NOAA, Boulder, Colo., Rpt. MGG-3, 1985. See also Peter W. Sloss, "Global Marine Gravity Field Map," *EOS,* vol. 68, no. 39, Sept. 29, 1987, pp. 770, 772.

p. 83 Good popular accounts, in addition to Bartusiak and Bernardo, are: Steve Olson, "The Contours Below," *Science 83,* July–Aug. 1983, pp. 38–41, and Richard F. Pittenger, "Exploring and Mapping the Seafloor" [Map of Arctic Ocean], *National Geographic,* Jan. 1990, p. 61A.

p. 85 "In this part . . .": W. Haxby, interview. The work is described in William F. Haxby et al., "Digital Images of Combined Oceanic and Continental Data Sets and Their Use in Tectonic Studies," *EOS,* vol. 64, no. 52, Dec. 27, 1983, pp. 995–1004. See also S. C. Cande, J. L. LaBrecque, and W. F. Haxby, "Plate Kinematics of the South Atlantic: Chron C34 to Present," *Journal of Geophysical Research,* vol. 93, no. B11, Nov. 10, 1988, pp. 13,479–13,492, and John L. La-

Brecque, "The USAC Aerosurvey: Accelerating the Exploration of the Antarctic," *Lamont-Doherty Geological Observatory Yearbook,* Palisades, N.Y., 1987, pp. 52–59.

p. 85 "Generating maps was . . .": W. Haxby, interview.

pp. 85–87 Background on Geosat: Chet Koblinsky, "Geosat vs. Seasat," *EOS,* vol. 69, no. 44, Nov. 1, 1988, p. 1026; and David C. McAdoo and David T. Sandwell, "Geosat's Exact Repeat Mission," *EOS,* Nov. 15, 1988, p. 1569.

p. 86 "This is the tip . . .": W. Haxby, interview. The peculiar structures in the South Atlantic have been described in the abstracts W. F. Haxby, "The Gravity Field of the Weddell Sea from Geosat/ERM Altimeter Data," Lamont-Doherty Geological Observatory, and W. F. Haxby, "Organization of Oblique Sea Floor Spreading into Discrete, Uniformly Spaced Ridge Segments: Evidence from Geosat Altimeter Data in the Weddell Sea."

p. 86 "are distinct in character . . .": W. Haxby, abstract.

p. 86 "When you see . . .": W. Haxby, interview.

p. 87 "In the last ten . . .": ibid.

4. A PARTICULAR DISCONTINUITY

GENERAL SOURCES

The best general source on the interior of the earth is Bruce A. Bolt, *Inside the Earth: Evidence from Earthquakes,* W. H. Freeman and Co., San Francisco, 1982.

For magazine-length treatments, there are: Don L. Anderson and Adam M. Dziewonski, "Seismic Tomography," *Scientific American,* Oct. 1984, pp. 60–68; Raymond Jeanloz, "The Earth's Core," *Scientific American,* Sept. 1983, pp. 56–65; D. P. McKenzie, "The Earth's Mantle," *Scientific American,* Sept. 1983, pp. 67–78; Raymond Siever, "The Dynamic Earth," *Scientific American,* Sept. 1983, pp. 46–55; Stephanie Weisburd, "Seismic Journey to the Center of the Earth," *Science News,* vol. 130, July 5, 1986, pp. 10–11; and "Core Questions," *Scientific American,* Feb. 1987, pp. 60–61.

NOTES

p. 88 Epigraph: Jules Verne, *Journey to the Center of the Earth,* Penguin, New York, 1965, p. 180.

p. 89 Background on the Macquarie Island earthquake: William Ward Maggs, "Labor Pains at Subduction's Birth," *EOS,* June 13, 1989, p. 650; Barbara Romanowicz and Goran Ekstrom, "Macquarie Earthquake of May 23, 1989: The Largest Strike-Slip Event in More Than 10 Years," *EOS,* July 11, 1989, p. 700; and Kevin McCue, "Earthquake Update" (letter to editor), *EOS,* Jan. 2, 1990, p. 3.

p. 91 "See, that's the point!": Adam Dziewonski, Department of Earth and Planetary Sciences, Harvard University, Cambridge, Mass., personal interview, March 6, 1990.

pp. 91–95 Background on the early history of seismological research: this section owes much to Bolt, op. cit. See also Cliff Frohlich, "Deep Earthquakes," *Scientific American,* Jan. 1989, pp. 48–55.

pp. 91–92 "The disturbances noticed . . .": E. von Rebeur Paschwitz, quoted in Bolt, op. cit., p. 8.

p. 92 "It is not unlikely . . .": John Milne, quoted in Bolt, op. cit., p. 8.

p. 93 "Of all regions . . .": R. D. Oldham, "The Constitution of the Interior of the Earth, as Revealed by Earthquakes," *Quarterly Journal, Geological Society,* vol. 62, August 1906, pp. 456–475. Reviewing the work of Milne, Oldham, Moho-rovičić, and others, Bolt (p. 13) makes the following cogent point: "It seems strange that no Nobel Prizes in physics (instituted in 1901) are awarded even today for discoveries of structure within our planet but are for those within the minute world of the atom."

p. 95 "If the internal . . .": A. M. Dziewonski and J. H. Woodhouse, "Global Images of the Earth's Interior," *Science,* vol. 236, April 3, 1987, pp. 37–48. Among other virtues, this paper offers a spectacular gallery of cartographic images prepared by Woodhouse.

p. 95 "a playground for mathematicians": R. D. Oldham, op. cit., p. 456.

p. 96 "often lacked copying . . .": Barbara A. Romanowicz and Adam M. Dziewonski, "Global Digital Seismographic Network: Research Opportunities and Recent Initiatives," American Geophysical Union, 1987, pp. 99–110.

p. 96 "an inward-looking telescope": Don L. Anderson, quoted in Walter Sullivan, "Seismic Networks Aim to Take the Pulse of Earth," *New York Times,* Dec. 27, 1988, p. 17 (National ed.).

p. 96 "And then I think . . .": A. Dziewonski, interview.

p. 96 A. M. Dziewonski, B. H. Hager, and R. J. O'Connell, "Large-Scale Heterogeneities in the Lower Mantle," *Journal of Geophysical Research,* vol. 82, no. 2, Jan. 10, 1977, pp. 239–255. As an indication of their caution, the authors noted, "We do not hope to provide here all the answers; to a large extent this is an initial feasibility study" (p. 239).

p. 96 "large doses of skepticism": A. Dziewonski, interview.

p. 97 "For the first time . . .": ibid.

p. 97 "To the first order . . .": Raymond Jeanloz, Dept. of Geophysics, University of California, Berkeley, Calif., personal interview, March 19, 1990.

p. 97 The early, 150-kilometer upper-mantle map, and many others in the journey to the center of the earth, are described in the 1987 Dziewonski and Woodhouse *Science* paper.

p. 97 Early papers in seismic tomography include Goran Ekstrom and Adam M. Dziewonski, "Evidence of Bias in Estimations of Earthquake Size," *Nature,* vol. 332, no. 6162, March 24, 1988, pp. 319–323; Bradford H. Hager et al., "Lower Mantle Heterogeneity, Dynamic Topography, and the Geoid," *Nature,* vol. 313, no. 6003, Feb. 14, 1985, pp. 541–545; and J. H. Woodhouse and A. M. Dziewonski, "Seismic Modelling of the Earth's Large-Scale Three-Dimensional Structure," *Philosophical Transactions of the Royal Society of London,* A 328, 1989, pp. 291–308.

p. 98 "The rock is like . . .": R. Jeanloz, interview.

p. 100 "Then you might ask . . .": ibid.

p. 100 "We did not expect . . .": A. Dziewonski, interview.

p. 100 "a particular discontinuity": ibid.; "This argument has been . . .": ibid. For a summation on the positions in the ongoing debate about the upper and lower mantle, a good reprise is Richard A. Kerr, "A Generational Rift in Geophysics," *Science,* vol. 248, April 20, 1990, pp. 300–302.

p. 101 "I would say . . .": A. Dziewonski, interview; "The Pacific Basin . . .": ibid.

p. 102 The Olson proposal is contained in Peter Olson, Paul G. Silver, and Richard W. Carlson, "The Large-Scale Structure of Convection in the Earth's Mantle," *Nature,* vol. 344, March 15, 1990, pp. 209–215. Acknowledging the work of Dziewonski and Woodhouse, Olson et al. write, "The images from global seismic tomography . . . may be interpreted in terms of cold downwelling and warm upwelling regions, confirming that large-scale subsolidus convection is ubiquitous in the mantle" (p. 209). They also point out that upward-welling regions are not contiguous. A popular account of the argument can be found in Walter Sullivan, " 'Graveyard' Fuels Geological Debate," *New York Times,* May 8, 1990, p. C-1.

p. 102 "Everyone now agrees . . .": Peter Olson, Johns Hopkins University, telephone interview, Jan. 2, 1991.

p. 103 "most dramatic . . .": Andrea Morelli and Adam M. Dziewonski, "Topography of the Core-Mantle Boundary and Lateral Homogeneity of the Liquid Core," *Nature,* vol. 325, no. 6106, Feb. 19, 1987, pp. 678–683.

p. 103 "It's a very remote . . .": A. Dziewonski, interview; "enormous coincidence": ibid.

p. 104 General background on the core-mantle boundary: Richard Monastersky, "Meeting of Mantle, Core No Longer a Bore," *Science News,* Dec. 10, 1988, p. 373; Thorne Lay, "Structure of Core-Mantle Transition Zone: A Chemical and Thermal Boundary," *EOS,* Jan. 24, 1989, pp. 49–59. Work in geomagnetic mapping is described in Jeremy Bloxham and David Gubbins, "The Evolution of the Earth's Magnetic Field," *Scientific American,* Dec. 1989, pp. 68–75.

p. 104 "If we compare . . .": A. Dziewonski, interview.

p. 104 "Once you get close . . .": A. Dziewonski, interview; "In some sense perhaps . . .": ibid.

p. 104 "First of all . . .": R. Jeanloz, interview.

p. 105 "There's probably some good . . .": A. Dziewonski, interview.

p. 105 "While it may take . . .": Morelli and Dziewonski, op. cit., p. 683.

5. PLAUSIBLE FORTUNES

GENERAL SOURCES

John Imbrie and Katherine Palmer Imbrie, *Ice Ages: Solving the Mystery,* Enslow, Short Hills, N.J., 1979 (an excellent, understandable account of the CLIMAP project and the dynamics of solar insolation); Bill McKibben, *The End of Nature,* Random House, New York, 1989; Stephen H. Schneider and Randi Londer, *The Coevolution of Climate and Life,* Sierra Club Books, San Francisco, 1984 (good history on climate modelling); and Warren M. Washington and Claire L. Parkinson, *An Introduction to Three-Dimensional Climate Modelling,* University Science Books, Mill Valley, Calif., 1986.

NOTES

p. 106 Epigraph: Sir Arthur Conan Doyle, *The Complete Sherlock Holmes,* Doubleday, Garden City, N.Y., 1930, p. 13.

p. 106 "We don't call them . . .": Warren Washington, Climate and Global Dynamics Division, National Center for Atmospheric Research, Boulder, Colo., telephone interview, Oct. 9, 1990.

p. 107 "end of nature": B. McKibben, op. cit., p. 8 ("I believe," McKibben writes, "that without recognizing it we have already stepped over the threshold of such a change: that we are at the end of nature"); *The Infinite Voyage* reference in Robert M. White, "The Great Climate Debate," *Scientific American,* July 1990, pp. 36–43.

p. 107 "more powerful hurricanes . . .": Daniel Lashof, "A Net Saving," letter to the editor, *New York Times,* Dec. 8, 1989, p. A-38.

p. 107 ". . . just as Marxism . . .": Warren T. Brookes, "The Global Warming Panic: A Classic Case of Overreaction," *Forbes,* Dec. 25, 1989, pp. 96–102.

p. 108 "could well spell . . .": ibid.

p. 108 "painfully short": T. P. Barnett, "Beware Greenhouse Confusion," *Nature,* vol. 343, Feb. 22, 1990, pp. 696–697.

pp. 109–110 Kutzbach background: John Kutzbach, Center for Climatic Research, University of Wisconsin, Madison, personal interview, May 30, 1990.

p. 109 "This was a cave . . .": J. Kutzbach, interview; "strong personal identification": ibid.

pp. 109–110 For background on Bryson, see William J. Broad, "A 30-Year Feud Divides Experts on Meteorology," *New York Times,* Oct. 24, 1989, p. C-1.

p. 110 Background on Kutzbach research: William Booth, "On Ancient Supercontinent Pangaea, the Summers Were Sizzlers," *Washington Post,* May 29, 1989, p. A-3; J. E. Kutzbach and R. G. Gallimore, "Pangaean Climates: Mega-monsoons of the Megacontinent," *Journal of Geophysical Research,* vol. 94, no. D3, March 20, 1989, pp. 3341–3357; and W. F. Ruddiman and J. E. Kutzbach, "Forcing of Late Cenozoic Northern Hemisphere Climate by Plateau Uplift in Southern Asia and the American West," *Journal of Geophysical Research,* vol. 94, no. D15, Dec. 20, 1989, pp. 18,409–18,427.

p. 110 Background on carbon-14 dating: This technique, first applied in 1947, allows scientists to date samples reliably back 30,000 years. The ability to date with such precision derives from the fact that all living things, plant or animal, incorporate a radioactive form of carbon known as carbon-14 into their tissues while alive; once dead, however, the organisms of course no longer incorporate C-14 from the environment. Since it has a steady decay rate whereby half of it decays every 5,730 years, one can work backward to date samples. Recent work suggests that other methods of dating, such as measuring the ratio of uranium to its breakdown product, thorium, may be more accurate (see Malcolm W. Browne, "Errors Are Feared in Carbon Dating," *New York Times,* May 31, 1990, p. A-21).

pp. 110–111 Background on L. F. Richardson: Washington and Parkinson, op. cit., pp. 3–5; Lewis F. Richardson, *Weather Prediction by Numerical Process,* Cambridge University Press, 1922 (Dover reprint, New York, 1965); Schneider and Londer, op. cit., pp. 210–212. Schneider and Londer in fact describe the role of maps in Britain's Meteorological Office and early weather predictions, where field observations were telegraphed to the main office and "set in their places upon a large scale map" (p. 210). In his preface, Richardson describes how part of his manuscript was lost during the battle of Champagne and turned up "some months later under a heap of coal." A pacifist as well as a scientist, Richardson wrote *Arms and Insecurity: A Mathematical Study of the Causes and Origins of War.*

p. 111 "disproportionately cumbersome . . .": J. von Neumann, memorandum to O. Veblen, March 26, 1945, in John von Neumann, *Collected Works, Volume VI: Theory of Games, Astrophysics, Hydrodynamics, and Meteorology,* A. H. Taub, ed., Pergamon Press, New York, 1963, p. 357.

p. 111 "was searching around . . .": Joseph Smagorinsky, former director, Geophysical Fluid Dynamics Laboratory, Princeton, N.J., telephone interview, Jan. 25, 1991.

pp. 111–112 For additional background on von Neumann and the Meteorological Research Group at the Institute for Advanced Study, see Ed Regis, *Who Got Einstein's Office?*, Addison-Wesley, Reading, Mass., 1987, pp. 97–122; J. Smagorinsky, "The Beginnings of Numerical Weather Prediction and General Circulation Modeling: Early Recollections," in Barry Saltzman, ed., *Advances in Geophysics: Theory of Climate*, Academic Press, New York, 1983, pp. 3–37.

p. 112 "It may be of interest . . .": J. G. Charney, R. Fjörtoft, and J. von Neumann, "Numerical Integration of the Barotropic Vorticity Equation," *Tellus*, vol. 2, no. 4, Nov. 1950, pp. 237–254 (p. 245). They may even have been prettifying the data. Smagorinsky, in a memo to the chief of the Weather Bureau, claimed that ENIAC required "36 hours for a 24 hour forecast" (Smagorinsky, op. cit., p. 10).

p. 112 GFDL background: J. Smagorinsky, op. cit., pp. 25–37. It is fitting that GFDL ended up back in Princeton because one of von Neumann's last projects at the Institute for Advanced Study was a long and detailed proposal for a general circulation research group, which ultimately became GFDL.

p. 112 Syukuro Manabe and Richard T. Wetherald, "The Effects of Doubling the CO_2 Concentration on the Climate of a General Circulation Model," *Journal of the Atmospheric Sciences*, vol. 32, 1975, pp. 3–15.

p. 114 "cry-wolf history": R. M. White, op. cit., p. 41.

p. 115 "Do you think . . .": J. von Neumann, quoted in J. Smagorinsky, op. cit., p. 29.

p. 115 "We in a sense . . .": J. Kutzbach, interview; "That involved these new . . .": ibid.

p. 116 Background on CLIMAP: CLIMAP Project Members, "The Surface of the Ice-Age Earth," *Science*, vol. 191, March 19, 1976, pp. 1131–1137. W. Lawrence Gates of the Rand Corp. then tested the results on a computer model, the results reported in W. L. Gates, "Modeling the Ice-Age Climate," *Science*, vol. 191, March 19, 1976, pp. 1138–1144. These two papers clearly provided a model for the subsequent COHMAP project.

p. 116 "She's got some fantastic . . .": T. Webb, quoted by J. Kutzbach, interview. For an example of paleolake studies, see F. Alayne Street-Perrott and R. Alan Perrott, "Abrupt Climate Fluctuations in the Tropics: The Influence of Atlantic Ocean Circulation," *Nature*, vol. 343, Feb. 15, 1990, pp. 607–612.

p. 117 Background on the origins of COHMAP: Interviews, plus Herbert E. Wright, Jr., "Introduction" (draft chapter for manuscript in press), and John E. Kutzbach and Thompson Webb III, "Late Quaternary Climatic and Vegetational Change in Eastern North America: Concept, Models, and Data," in L. K. Shane and E. J. Cushing, eds., *Quaternary Landscapes*, University of Minnesota Press, Minneapolis, in press.

p. 117 "Right around that time . . .": J. Kutzbach, interview.

p. 117 "Mapping was second nature . . .": Thompson Webb III, Dept. of Geological Sciences, Brown University, Providence, R.I., telephone interview, Jan. 25, 1991.

pp. 117–118 For a discussion of the pollen, paleolake, and rat midden data used by COHMAP, see COHMAP Members, "Climatic Changes of the Last 18,000 Years: Observations and Model Simulations," *Science*, vol. 241, Aug. 26, 1988, pp. 1043–1052. A more popular treatment of middens, if that's not a contradiction in terms, is Jared Diamond, "Pack Rat Historians," *Natural History,* Feb. 1991, pp. 24–29.

p. 119 "It really is a time . . .": J. Kutzbach, interview.

p. 119 For actual maps, see COHMAP Members, op. cit.

p. 120 "If you visualize . . .": J. Kutzbach, interview, ibid.

p. 122 "Orbital insolation," as the phenomenon is called, was first proposed by Croll in the nineteenth century; the hypothesis was substantially proven by Milankovitch in 1920. For a highly readable account of the geophysics underlying these discoveries, see Imbrie and Imbrie, op. cit.

p. 122 "Everything else being . . .": J. Kutzbach, interview.

p. 122 "It's the only way . . .": Herbert E. Wright, Jr., University of Minnesota, telephone interview, Jan. 30, 1991.

p. 122 "Our ability to chart . . .": J. Kutzbach, interview. Kutzbach makes many similar points in an essay intended for lay readers, "Historical Perspectives: Climatic Changes Throughout the Millennia," in R. S. DeFries and T. F.Malone, eds., *Global Change and Our Common Future,* National Academy Press, Washington, D.C., 1989.

p. 123 "Mathematical climate models . . .": S. Schneider, "Climate Modelling," *Scientific American,* May 1987, pp. 72–80 (p. 72).

p. 123 "We're all in shambles . . .": Robert Cess, State University of New York at Stony Brook, telephone interview, March 3, 1990. Cess's assessment of climate models was published as R. D. Cess et al., "Interpretation of Cloud-Climate Feedback as Produced by 14 Atmospheric General Circulation Models," *Science,* vol. 245, Aug. 4, 1989, pp. 513–516. A more general treatment is Warren M. Washington, "Where's the Heat?" *Natural History,* March 1990, pp. 66–72.

p. 123 "The Rocky Mountains are . . .": W. Washington, interview.

p. 124 "No 'smoking gun' evidence . . .": Warren M. Washington and Thomas W. Bettge, "Computer Simulation of the Greenhouse Effect," *Computers in Physics,* May–June, 1990, pp. 240–246. More detailed versions of these results appear in W. M. Washington et al., "Computer Simulation of the Global Climatic Effects of Increased Greenhouse Gases," *International Journal of Supercomputer Applications,* vol. 4, no. 2, Summer 1990, pp. 5–19; and W. M. Washington and G. A. Meehl, "Climate Sensitivity Due to Increased CO_2: Experiments with a Coupled Atmosphere and Ocean General Circulation Model," *Climate Dynamics,* vol. 4, pp. 1–38, 1989.

p. 124 "Climate models do not . . .": S. Schneider, *Scientific American,* op. cit., p. 80.

p. 125 "You can argue . . .": J. Kutzbach, interview.

p. 126 "In an ideal world . . .": ibid.

6. THE HOLE IN THE ROOF OF THE SKY

GENERAL SOURCES

There is no dearth of material about the hole in the ozone layer. For up-to-date book-length accounts, see Robert H. Boyle and Michael Oppenheimer, *Dead Heat: The Greenhouse Effect,* Basic Books, New York, 1990; John Gribbin, *The Hole in the Sky,* Bantam, 1988; and Fred Pearce, *Turning Up the Heat: Our Perilous Future in the Global Greenhouse,* The Bodley Head, London, 1989. James

Lovelock, *The Ages of Gaia: A Biography of Our Living Earth,* Norton, New York, 1988, contains considerable detail on atmospheric sciences.

For background on the chlorofluorocarbon theory, two good sources are Lydia Dotto and Harold Schiff, *The Ozone War,* Doubleday, Garden City, N.Y., 1978, and Paul Brodeur, "In the Face of Doubt," *New Yorker,* June 9, 1986, pp. 70–87. Two good historical summations appearing in magazines are Richard S. Stolarski, "The Antarctic Ozone Hole," *Scientific American,* Jan. 1988, pp. 30–36, and Joe Farman, "What Hope for the Ozone Layer Now?" *New Scientist,* Nov. 12, 1987, pp. 50–54.

NOTES

p. 127 Epigraph: Joseph Conrad, *Heart of Darkness,* Norton, New York, 1988, p. 12.

p. 127 Background on the backscatter ultraviolet instrument provided by Arlin Krueger, NASA Goddard Space Flight Center, Greenbelt, Md., telephone interview, Feb. 4, 1991.

p. 128 The original chlorofluorocarbon paper was Mario J. Molina and F. S. Rowland, "Stratospheric Sink for Chlorofluoromethanes: Chlorine Atom-Catalysed Destruction of Ozone," *Nature,* vol. 249, June 28, 1974, pp. 810–812. Accounts of their early work are summarized in Brodeur, op. cit.

p. 128 "The work is going . . .": F. Sherwood Rowland, quoted in Boyle and Oppenheimer, op. cit., p. 44.

p. 129 "It was as if . . .": A. Krueger, interview; "Able to map all . . .": ibid.

p. 130 Background on the early work of the British Antarctic Survey: Joseph Farman, British Antarctic Survey, Cambridge, England, telephone interview, Feb. 11, 1991. There are also accounts in Farman, *New Scientist,* and Gribbin, op. cit., pp. 107–117, and Pearce, op. cit., which borrows heavily from the *New Scientist* story.

p. 131 "It was a fairly old . . .": J. Farman, interview; "things were getting . . .": ibid.

p. 131 Krueger suggested in an interview that the production people on the NASA project did not communicate the drop in ozone values to the scientific team; "Production people are interested in numbers," Krueger said, "not in geophysics. But we definitely knew what was going on by 1984." NASA's first report, however, did not appear until 1986, in R. S. Stolarski et al., "Nimbus 7 Satellite Measurements of the Springtime Antarctic Ozone Decrease," *Nature,* vol. 322, Aug. 28, 1986, pp. 808–811.

p. 131 "Satellites get so . . .": J. Farman, interview.

p. 132 "That should have . . .": A. Krueger, interview.

p. 132 "the least complex . . .": J. Lovelock, op. cit., p. 28.

p. 132 Background on CFCs: Among a wealth of sources, see Boyle and Oppenheimer, op. cit.; Brodeur, op. cit.; and Dotto and Schiff, op. cit.

p. 132 The chemical scenario was proposed in J. C. Farman et al., "Large Losses of Total Ozone in Antarctica Reveal Seasonal ClO_x/NO_x Interaction," *Nature,* vol. 315, May 16, 1985, pp. 207–210.

p. 133 "Because of the reviewing . . .": J. Farman, interview.

p. 134 "Why did Joe Farman . . .": A. Krueger, interview; "There was this wealth . . .": ibid.

p. 134 "Most of us were . . .": Robert Watson, NASA, Washington, D.C., telephone interview, March 8, 1991.

p. 135 Background on the Montreal protocol: A good summation of the terms, and of the politics behind the accord, can be found in Kiki Warr, "Ozone: The Burden of Proof," *New Scientist,* Oct. 27, 1990, pp. 36–40.

p. 135 "Well, I suppose . . .": A. Krueger, interview.

p. 136 The GAO report is described in Christopher Anderson, "Too Much of a Good Thing," *Nature,* vol. 349, Feb. 14, 1991, p. 553. According to the GAO audit, the funding for data maintenance has dropped from $27 million in 1983 to $21 million in 1989, even though currently operational satellites generate an additional one thousand new data tapes every day.

p. 136 Background on data demands of Earth Observing System: Jeff Dozier, "Looking Ahead to EOS: The Earth Observing System," *Computers in Physics,* May–June, 1990, pp. 248–259.

p. 137 The ozone–jet stream connection is described in Arlin J. Krueger, "The Global Distribution of Total Ozone: TOMS Satellite Measurements," *Planetary Space Science,* vol. 37, no. 12, 1989, pp. 1555–1565.

p. 138 The sulfur dioxide–ozone connection is described in A. J. Krueger, "Sighting of El Chichón Sulfur Dioxide Clouds with the Nimbus 7 Total Ozone Mapping Spectrometer," *Science,* vol. 220, June 24, 1983, pp. 1377–1379.

p. 138 "We still have ten . . .": J. Farman, interview.

7. VESALIUS REVISITED

GENERAL SOURCES

Perhaps the best technical overview of all the new technologies can be found in Lee Sider, ed., *Introduction to Diagnostic Imaging,* Churchill Livingstone, New York, 1986. Several good popular summaries exist, including Frederic Golden, "Diagnostic Wizardry," *Los Angeles Times Magazine,* Oct. 8, 1989, p. 19; Robin Marantz Henig, "The Inner Landscape," *New York Times Magazine,* April 17, 1988, pp. 59–60; "L.C.H.," "Imaging Revolution Is Pushing Forward," *Medical World News,* March 26, 1990, pp. 34–35; Howard Sochurek, "Medicine's New Vision," *National Geographic,* Jan. 1987, pp. 2–41; and Rob Taylor, "Evolutions: Brain Imaging," *Journal of NIH Research,* vol. 2, May 1990, pp. 103–104.

NOTES:

p. 141 Epigraph: John Donne, from "Hymne to God My God, in My Sicknesse," *Poetical Works,* Oxford University Press, Oxford, 1987, p. 336.

p. 141 Accounts of Roentgen's discovery can be found in Stanley Joel Reiser, *Medicine and the Reign of Technology,* Cambridge University Press, Cambridge, 1978, pp. 58–68 (with many amusing anecdotes about the early use of X rays), and Robert P. Crease and Charles C. Mann, *The Second Creation,* Macmillan, New York, 1986, pp. 10–11; of magnetic resonance in Paul C. Lauterbur, "Cancer Detection by Nuclear Magnetic Resonance Zeugmatographic Imaging," *Cancer,* vol. 57, no. 10, May 15, 1986, pp. 1899–1904; of Damadian's role in Partain et al., *Nuclear Magnetic Resonance Imaging,* W. B. Saunders Co., Philadelphia, 1983, p. 37; of Prichard in F. Golden, *Los Angeles Times Magazine,* p. 19; of Allman in Mora et al., "*In Vivo* Functional Localization of the Human Visual Cortex Using Positron Emission Tomography and Magnetic Resonance Imaging," *Trends in*

Neuroscience, vol. 12, no. 8, Aug. 1989, pp. 282–284; and the GE anecdote in H. Sochurek, op. cit., p. 31.

pp. 142–143 To appreciate the changes these new technologies have wrought, Reiser quotes a physician in 1899 bemoaning the fact that medicine was "gradually relegating hearing to a lower intellectual plane than sight" (p. 68).

p. 143 Sources for the catalogue of devices are: Earl Ubell, "When Your Head Starts Pounding," *Parade,* March 11, 1990, pp. 4–5; Randall Black, "Ultrasound Catheter Images Arteries from Inside Out," *UCI News* (press release), March 17, 1990; Richard L. Popp, "Echocardiography," *New England Journal of Medicine,* vol. 323, July 12, 1990, p. 101; John Rennie, "Anatomical Cartography," *Scientific American,* September 1990, p. 170; James Gleick, "Brain at Work Revealed Through New Imagery," *New York Times,* Aug. 18, 1987, p. C1; and Wendy L. Wall, "Medicine's 'Magic Bullets' Add a New Dimension to Imaging," *Wall Street Journal,* Aug. 14, 1987, p. 17.

p. 144 The dates on Mercator come from Lloyd Brown, *The Story of Maps,* Dover, New York, 1979, pp. 158–159; the *Encyclopaedia Britannica* (14th ed., 1968) and Sherwin Nuland both place Vesalius in Louvain between 1536, when he left the university in Paris, and 1537, when he left for his historic stay at the university in Padua.

p. 144 For descriptions of the ambience surrounding medieval and Renaissance dissections, see C. D. O'Malley, *Andreas Vesalius of Brussels, 1514–1564,* University of California Press, Berkeley, 1964; "The Reawakening: Andreas Vesalius and the Renaissance of Medicine" in Sherwin B. Nuland, *Doctors: The Biography of Medicine,* Knopf, New York, 1988, pp. 61–93.

p. 144 For two unusual but interesting views, see H. V. Morton, *A Traveller in Italy,* Dodd, Mead & Co., New York, 1964, pp. 315–319, on dissections; and Johann Wolfgang von Goethe, *Italian Journey,* North Point Press, San Francisco, 1982, p. 54. Goethe likened the famous anatomical theater at Padua (built *after* Vesalius's tenure, and the oldest in existence) to "a kind of high funnel," and observes that "such a cramped school is unimaginable even to a German student. . . . The anatomical theater, in particular, is an example of how to squeeze as many students together as possible."

p. 145 "epitomizes the confluence . . .": S. Nuland, op. cit., p. 62.

pp. 145–146 For general background on diagnostic imaging techniques, I am grateful to Dr. Jeffrey Weinreb, professor of radiology and director of the Magnetic Resonance Imaging Section of New York University Hospital. A good textbook survey of techniques, though somewhat technical and short on anecdote, is Sider, op. cit.

p. 146 Background on CT scans: Sider, op. cit., pp. 21–31; Allan M. Cormack, "Early Two-Dimensional Reconstruction and Recent Topics Stemming from It," *Science,* vol. 209, Sept. 26, 1980, pp. 1482–1486; Godfrey N. Hounsfield, "Computed Medical Imaging," *Science,* vol. 210, Oct. 3, 1980, pp. 22–28 (the latter two articles are the remarks made by Cormack and Hounsfield in accepting their Nobel prizes, and provide some of the best anecdotal background on the development of CT scans); G. N. Hounsfield, "Computerized Transverse Axial Scanning (Tomography): Part I, Description of System," *British Journal of Radiology,* vol. 46, 1973, pp. 1016–1022; Suzanne Fogle, "Sir Godfrey's CAT," *Journal of NIH Research,* vol. 2, May 1990, pp. 82–86; and William R. Hendee, *The*

Physical Principles of Computed Tomography, Little, Brown, Boston, 1983, pp. 1–7.

    p. 147 "an impact that is . . .": W. Hendee, op. cit., p. 1.

    p. 147 The very first CT scan, described by Hounsfield to Fogle, op. cit., uncovered a brain tumor in a female patient.

    p. 147 Among the ironies of the CT scan development, according to Hounsfield (in Fogle, op. cit.), is that EMI experienced financial difficulties before it could exploit the invention; similarly, when he came to the United States for the first time to describe the technology, Hounsfield was so short of cash that he took to staying overnight with people he met on the street. Barely seven years later, he would win his Nobel.

    p. 148 Background on ultrasound: Sider, op. cit., pp. 10–21; "Imaging Revolution Is Pushing Forward," *Medical World News,* March 26, 1990, pp. 34–35; Matthew Hussey, *Basic Physics and Technology of Medical Diagnostic Ultrasound,* Elsevier, New York, 1985.

    p. 148 Background on angiography and nuclear medicine: Sider, op. cit., pp. 31–36.

    pp. 149–150 Background on PET scans: Council on Scientific Affairs, "Positron Emission Tomography—A New Approach to Brain Chemistry," *Journal of the American Medical Association,* vol. 260, Nov. 11, 1988, pp. 2704–2710; Milt Freudenheim, "Will Hospitals Buy Yet Another Costly Technology?" *New York Times,* Sept. 9, 1990, p. F5; "Scanning the Receptors in Human Brains," *Science News,* vol. 123, June 25, 1983, p. 406; "PET Scans Brain Pathways," *Science News,* vol. 124, Sept. 24, 1983, p. 196; Jeanne D. Talbot et al., "Multiple Representations of Pain in the Human Cerebral Cortex," *Science,* vol. 251, March 15, 1991, pp. 1355–1358; B. Bower, "Epileptic PET Probes," *Science News,* vol. 133, April 30, 1988, pp. 280–281.

    p. 151 "That's all outside . . .": Jeffrey Weinreb, M.D., Magnetic Resonance Imaging Section, New York University Hospital, New York, N.Y., personal interview, Feb. 7, 1991; "I can't tell . . .": ibid.

    p. 151 Background on nuclear magnetic resonance: Sider, op. cit., pp. 36–38; Paul C. Lauterbur, "Cancer Detection by Nuclear Magnetic Resonance Zeugmatographic Imaging," *Cancer,* vol. 57, May 15, 1986, pp. 1899–1904; C. Leon Partain et al., *Nuclear Magnetic Resonance Imaging,* W. B. Saunders Co., Philadelphia, 1983; Stewart C. Bushong, *Magnetic Resonance Imaging: Physical and Biological Principles,* C. V. Mosby Co., St. Louis, 1988; Sonny Kleinfeld, *A Machine Called Indomitable,* Times Books, New York, 1985; Donald P. Hollis, *Abusing Cancer Science: The Truth About NMR and Cancer,* Strawberry Fields Press, Chehalis, Wash., 1987.

    p. 151 The initial NMR paper was R. Damadian, "Tumor Detection by Nuclear Magnetic Resonance," *Science,* vol. 171, March 19, 1971, pp. 1151–1153. This is not the place to revive the debate over who thought of what first in the MRI field; it seems to be a dispute exacerbated by personalities on both sides. Damadian was exceedingly aggressive about claiming credit, making extravagant claims for his body scanner during a press conference in 1977. Lauterbur, on the other hand, saw his original *Nature* submission turned down in 1973 because it was so reticent to make any scientific claims. Be that as it may, even Kleinfeld, generally sympathetic to Damadian's version of events, describes Lauterbur's thoughts about imaging in 1971 and writes, "Unlike Lauterbur, however, Damadian was not at this time thinking about making pictures with an NMR machine" (Kleinfeld, op. cit., p. 61).

p. 152 "However, even normal . . .": P. Lauterbur, *Cancer,* p. 1899. Lauterbur made the remark during a 1985 speech accepting the Kettering Prize of the General Motors Cancer Research Foundation.

pp. 152–154 P. C. Lauterbur, "Image Formation by Induced Local Interactions: Examples Employing Nuclear Magnetic Resonance," *Nature,* vol. 242, March 16, 1973, pp. 190–191. The fact that Lauterbur did not reference Damadian's 1971 paper did nothing to allay Damadian's perception that he wasn't receiving sufficient credit.

pp. 152–153 Lauterbur begins his brief *Nature* paper with the following sentence: "An image of an object may be defined as a graphical representation of the spatial distribution of one or more of its properties." A narrow but not bad definition of a map.

pp. 152–153 *Nature*'s rejection of the original Lauterbur paper is described in Hollis, op. cit., pp. 145–148.

p. 153 Damadian's disastrous 1977 press conference is described in Lawrence K. Altman, "New York Researcher Asserts Nuclear Magnetic Technique Can Detect Cancer, But Doubts Are Raised," *New York Times,* July 21, 1977, p. A18. Hollis also refers to the incident at some length.

p. 154 "In general, the advantages . . .": J. Weinreb interview; "Assuming cost does not . . .": ibid.; "Nobody has a clue": ibid.

8. "THE BRAIN IS WET"

GENERAL SOURCES

William F. Allman, *Apprentices of Wonder: Inside the Neural Network Revolution,* Bantam, New York, 1989; Richard Bergland, *The Fabric of Mind,* Viking, New York, 1986 (written by a neurosurgeon, this book provides an insightful sociohistorical analysis of how neuroscience becomes wedded to its paradigms); David H. Hubel, "The Brain," *Scientific American,* Sept. 1979, pp. 26–35; Robert Kanigel, *Apprentice to Genius: The Making of a Scientific Dynasty,* Macmillan, New York, 1986 (discusses the discovery of the opiate receptor as well as offering a good take on the sociology of the neurosciences); Robert Ornstein and Richard F. Thompson, *The Amazing Brain,* Houghton Mifflin, Boston, 1984 (illustrated by David [*The Way Things Work*] Macauley, this book provides an imaginative and interesting visual tour of brain architecture); and Steven Rose, *The Conscious Brain,* Knopf, New York, 1974.

NOTES

p. 155 Epigraph: Santiago Ramón y Cajal, quoted in Fernando Reinoso-Suárez, "Cajal: A Modern Insight in Neuroscience," in *Ramón y Cajal's Contribution to the Neurosciences,* Elsevier, Amsterdam, 1983, p. 4.

p. 155 The metaphor of the brain as an add-on edifice is beautifully rendered, in David Macauley's drawings as well as in words, in Ornstein and Thompson, op. cit.

p. 156 "It is not too strong . . .": S. Rose, op. cit., p. 65.

p. 156 Herkenham's work on the cannabinoid receptor was first described at the annual meeting of the Society for Neuroscience in November of 1988. The principal paper is M. Herkenham et al., "Cannabinoid Receptor Localization in Brain," *Proceedings of the National Academy of Sciences,* March 1990, pp. 1932–1936. Other coverage includes Rick Weiss, "Marijuana's Brain Receptors Mapped," *Science News,* Nov. 26, 1988, p. 350; the *High Times* article is in press; and Sandra J. Ackerman, "Marijuana Receptor: Pinpointing the Brain's 'Pot Holder,' " *The Journal of NIH Research,* May 1990, pp. 36–38.

p. 156 On July 21, 1990, eighteen months after Herkenham presented his data at the neurosciences meeting in Toronto, the *New York Times* reported on its front page that the marijuana receptor had been "discovered"; what in fact had happened was that the marijuana receptor had been *cloned*—that is, genetically isolated, recreated, and characterized.

p. 157 "that facilitates forgetting . . .": Sam Deadwyler, Bowman Gray School of Medicine, Wake Forest University, Winston-Salem, N.C., telephone interview, May 29, 1991.

p. 158 "We still don't have . . .": Miles Herkenham, National Institute of Mental Health, Bethesda, Md., personal interview, April 17, 1989.

pp. 158–160 Background on neuroanatomy: Rose's *The Conscious Brain* remains remarkably clear, literate, and well illustrated, while Ornstein and Thompson is more fun. Also, Ronald E. Kalil, "Synapse Formation in the Developing Brain," *Scientific American,* December 1989, pp. 76–85.

p. 159 The Greek meaning of the term *synapto* is described by William S. Haubrich, *Medical Meanings: A Glossary of Word Origins,* Harcourt Brace Jovanovich, San Diego, 1984, p. 236; the provenance of the term is described by Henry Alan Skinner, *The Origin of Medical Terms,* 2nd ed., Hafner, New York, 1970, p. 394, which cites Fulton's *Physiology of the Nervous System.* Although widely credited with coining the term "synapse," Sherrington (according to Skinner) favored the term "syndesm."

p. 159 Work on the squid axon, and other research, revealed how the nerve cell translates chemistry into electrical impulses that can be passed along. The inside of a nerve cell is slightly negative in charge, while the outside of the membrane is slightly positive. The difference, about seventy to a hundred millivolts, however, is separated by an equally slight membrane, only one-millionth of a centimeter thick. When a nerve cell "fires," its internal chemistry changes electrical character. During the passage of an "excitatory" message, neurotransmitters arriving at a synapse provoke local changes in the membrane; channels in the membrane open, allowing positive ions of sodium (Na^+) to pour into the cell, while potassium ions (K^+) pour out separate channels. The net effect is that the cell interior becomes momentarily positive and sets off an electrical wave that induces similar local changes along the membrane. The sum of those local changes, one after another, is the passage of an electrical impulse the length of a cell, to *its* synapses, which may release neurotransmitters and reiterate the process.

p. 162 "I would hate to . . .": M. Herkenham, interview; "I was sort of . . .": ibid.; "I became interested . . .": ibid.

p. 163 Background on the psychopharmacological revolution: A short treatment is Solomon H. Snyder, "Medicated Minds," *Science 84,* November 1984, pp. 141–142. A book-length treatment that describes the discovery of the opiate receptor in some detail is R. Kanigel, op. cit., pp. 153–226.

p. 163 "God presumably did not . . .": Candace Pert, quoted in Stephen S. Hall, "A Molecular Code Links Emotions, Mind, and Health," *Smithsonian,* June 1989, pp. 62–71 (p. 67).

p. 164 "This allowed us . . .": Michael Kuhar, Johns Hopkins University, Baltimore, Md., telephone interview, Feb. 8, 1990. In 1983, Kuhar and his group at Johns Hopkins took autoradiography one step further when they discovered that receptors could be mapped in living organisms with the use of positron emission tomography (PET) scans. The first map showed dopamine receptors in the brain of a baboon.

p. 164 "my holes fit . . .": M. Herkenham, interview. This interaction is also described in Kanigel, op. cit., pp. 207–208.

p. 165 "I called her up . . .": M. Herkenham, interview; "So Candace and I . . .": ibid. They described their technique in M. Herkenham and C. Pert, "In Vitro Autoradiography of Opiate Receptors in Rat Brain Suggests Loci of 'Opiatergic' Pathways," *Proceedings of the National Academy of Sciences,* vol. 77, Sept. 1980, pp. 5532–5536.

p. 165 The two "cover story" articles were: M. Herkenham and C. Pert, "Mosaic Distribution of Opiate Receptors, Parafasicular Projections and Acetylcholinesterase in Rat Striatum," *Nature,* vol. 291, June 4, 1981, pp. 415–418, and S. P. Wise and M. Herkenham, "Opiate Receptor Distribution in the Cerebral Cortex of the Rhesus Monkey," *Science,* vol. 218, Oct. 22, 1982, pp. 387–389.

p. 165 "striking concordance": Herkenham and Pert, *Proceedings,* p. 5532.

p. 166 "There were immunochemists . . .": M. Herkenham, interview.

p. 167 "a new concern": M. Herkenham and C. Pert, "Light Microscopic Localization of Brain Opiate Receptors: A General Autoradiographic Method Which Preserves Tissue Quality," *Journal of Neuroscience,* vol. 2, Aug. 1982, pp. 1129–1149 (p. 1147).

p. 167 "And to some people . . .": M. Herkenham, interview.

p. 167 The paper comparing hippocampi is Stafford B. McLean et al. "Distribution of Opiate Receptor Subtypes and Enkephalin and Dynorphin Immunoreactivity in the Hippocampus of Squirrel, Guinea Pig, Rat, and Hamster," *Journal of Comparative Neurology,* vol. 255, Jan. 22, 1987, pp. 497–510.

p. 167 "It's hard to imagine . . .": M. Herkenham, telephone interview, Dec. 12, 1989.

p. 167 The original "mismatch" paper was Richard B. Rothman et al., "Visualization of Rat Brain Receptors for the Neuropeptide, Substance P," *Brain Research,* vol. 309, 1984, pp. 47–54. Michael Kuhar at Johns Hopkins says he had noticed some opiate receptor mismatches in the 1970s, but he did not publish anything on mismatches as a phenomenon until 1985; he has been somewhat more reluctant than Herkenham to ascribe significance to it. In an interview (Kuhar, op. cit.), however, he said, "My feeling is that mismatches are great in magnitude, and in frequency, and therefore is likely to be a real phenomenon."

p. 168 "Maps were published . . .": M. Herkenham, interview. Reviews of the literature include M. Herkenham, "Mismatches Between Neurotransmitter and Receptor Localizations in Brain: Observations and Implications," *Neuroscience,* vol. 23, Oct. 1987, pp. 1–38; and M. Herkenham, "Mismatches Between Neurotransmitter and Receptor Localizations: Implications for Endocrine Functions in Brain," in K. Fuxe and L. F. Agnati, *Volume Transmission in the Brain: Novel Mechanisms for Neural Transmission,* Raven Press, New York, 1991, pp. 63–87.

p. 168 "We're talking millimeters . . .": M. Herkenham, interview.

p. 168 "until recently . . .": Deborah M. Barnes, "The Receptor Mismatch Controversy," *Science,* vol. 239, Jan. 8, 1988, pp. 142–143. In the article Kuhar is quoted as saying, "I believe that mismatches exist, but I worry that Herkenham's conclusions about their significance might be premature and based on incomplete data."

p. 169 "It's the myth . . .": M. Herkenham, interview.

p. 170 Robert Jastrow, *The Enchanted Loom: Mind in the Universe,* Simon & Schuster, New York, 1981. Jastrow writes that "a bold scientist will be able to tip the contents of his mind and transfer them into the metallic lattices of a computer" (p. 166), in part because both operate "on little pulses of electricity traveling along wires . . ." (p. 165).

p. 170 "I said that there . . .": M. Herkenham, interview.

p. 170 F. O. Schmitt, "Molecular Regulators of Brain Function: A New View," *Neuroscience,* vol. 13, no. 4, pp. 991–1001, 1984.

p. 171 "You have the opportunity . . .": F. O. Schnitt, Massachusetts Institute of Technology, telephone interview, Dec. 12, 1989.

p. 171 Background on the molecular mind-body connection: The principal paper is C. B. Pert et al., "Neuropeptides and Their Receptors: A Psychosomatic Network," *Journal of Immunology,* vol. 135, Aug. 1985, pp. 820–826s; another is C. B. Pert, "The Wisdom of the Receptors: Neuropeptides, the Emotions, and Bodymind," *Advances,* vol. 3, Summer 1986, pp. 8–16. This section is also based on remarks made by Pert at the UCLA School of Medicine Conference on Psychoneuroimmunology, Lake Arrowhead, Calif., March 12, 1988.

p. 171 For more popular accounts, see Hall, *Smithsonian,* op. cit., and R. Kanigel, "Where Mind and Body Meet," *Mosaic,* Summer 1986, pp. 52–60. A good book-length treatment for lay readers is Steven Locke and Douglas Colligan, *The Healer Within,* Dutton, New York, 1986.

pp. 171–172 "Neuropeptides and their . . .": Pert et al., *Journal of Immunology,* p. 820s.

p. 172 "Can thinking go . . .": R. Bergland, op. cit., p. ii.

p. 172 "I would like to subscribe . . .": M. Herkenham, interview.

9. A MOST UNSATISFACTORY ORGANISM

GENERAL SOURCES

Jerry E. Bishop and Michael Waldholz, *Genome,* Simon & Schuster, New York, 1990 (a good up-to-date account on human gene mapping); Robert Cook-Deegan, "The Human Genome Project: Formation of Federal Policies in the United States, 1986–1990," in K. E. Hanna, ed., *Biomedical Politics,* National Academy of Sciences Press, Washington, D.C., 1991; Stephen S. Hall, *Invisible Frontiers: The Race to Synthesize a Human Gene,* Atlantic Monthly Press, New York, 1987 (a popular history on the origins of genetic engineering); Horace Freeland Judson, *The Eighth Day of Creation: Makers of the Revolution in Biology,* Simon & Schuster, New York, 1978 (magisterial history of molecular biology);

Mapping Our Genes, Office of Technology Assessment, Washington, D.C., 1988; James A. Peters, ed., *Classic Papers in Genetics,* Prentice-Hall, Englewood Cliffs, N.J., 1959; *Report of the Committee on Mapping and Sequencing the Human Genome,* National Research Council, National Academy Press, Washington, D.C., 1988.

Leslie Roberts of *Science* has consistently produced excellent backgrounders on the human genome project and genetic mapping in general.

NOTES

p. 174 The account of the much-reported Alta meeting is reconstructed from interviews with participants, accounts in the scientific and popular press, and papers originating out of the discussion. A particularly thorough discussion can be found in Bishop and Waldholz, op. cit., pp. 49–68.

pp. 176–177 Background on hemochromatosis: Kerry Kravitz, M.D., psychiatrist, Mountain View, Calif., telephone interview, Jan. 28, 1991; Mark Skolnick, Dept. of Medical Informatics, University of Utah Medical Center, Salt Lake City, telephone interview, Jan. 9, 1991; David Botstein, Dept. of Genetics, Stanford University School of Medicine, Stanford, Calif., personal interview, March 20, 1990.

p. 177 For a popular treatment, see Terry Monmaney, "Iron Man," *Discover,* July 1989, pp. 63–65; for the scientific paper that resulted, K. Kravitz et al., "Genetic Linkage Between Hereditary Hemochromatosis and HLA," *American Journal of Human Genetics,* vol. 31, 1979, pp. 601–619. Part of the confusion over whether the disorder was dominant or recessive stemmed from the fact that some individuals develop mild forms of iron retention when they inherit a single copy of the defective gene, which would suggest the dominant mode; Kravitz's computerized linkage analysis was able to distinguish these "false positives" from the people who inherited *both* copies of the defective gene, which decisively indicated that the disease was recessive.

p. 177 "Man is one of . . .": A. H. Sturtevant, "Social Implications of the Genetics of Man," *Science,* vol. 120, Sept. 10, 1954, pp. 405–407.

p. 177 "It requires indeed . . .": Gregor Mendel, "Experiments in Plant-Hybridization," originally published in *Verh. naturs Ver. in Brunn, Abhandlungen,* vol. IV, 1865, translated by the Royal Horticultural Society of London and republished in *Classic Papers in Genetics,* pp. 1–20.

p. 178 T. H. Morgan work, "Sex Limited Inheritance in Drosophila," *Science,* vol. 32, 1910, pp. 120–122. As is spelled out in greater detail in the following chapter, Morgan embarked on his genetics studies with the expectation of disproving Mendel!

p. 179 A. H. Sturtevant, "The Linear Arrangement of Six Sex-Linked Factors in *Drosophila* As Shown by Their Mode of Association," *Journal of Experimental Zoology,* vol. 14, 1913, pp. 43–59. Perhaps the most important sentence of this remarkable paper is its conclusion, in which Sturtevant argues that his results "strongly indicate that the factors investigated are arranged in a linear series, at least mathematically."

p. 179 "As a sophomore . . .": D. Botstein, interview. In accepting an award recently, Botstein summarized the early history of linkage mapping; the remarks have been published as D. Botstein, "1989 Allen Award Address: The American

Society of Human Genetics Annual Meeting, Baltimore," *American Journal of Human Genetics,* vol. 47, Dec. 1990, pp. 887–891.

p. 181 For a description of cloning and other developments in the recent history of recombinant DNA, see Hall, op. cit., or Jeremy Cherfas, *Man-Made Life,* Pantheon, New York, 1982.

p. 183 "So I listened . . .": D. Botstein, interview; "And then I said . . .": ibid.

p. 185 "It took a while . . .": M. Skolnick, op. cit.

p. 185 "By dinner . . .": D. Botstein. Skolnick has argued that he perceived the significance of the RFLP idea for human genetics more than the others; Botstein says, "Neither [Ron] Davis nor I were prepared to turn our labs into a search for human polymorphisms. We had other fish to fry."

p. 186 Botstein et al., "Construction of a Genetic Linkage in Man Using Restriction Fragment Length Polymorphism," *American Journal of Human Genetics,* vol. 32, May 1980, pp. 314–331.

p. 186 "My initial response . . .": From Ray White, "1989 Allen Award Address: The American Society of Human Genetics Annual Meeting, Baltimore," *American Journal of Human Genetics,* vol. 47, Dec. 1990, pp. 892–895.

p. 186 "opened up tremendous . . .": Victor McKusick, Johns Hopkins School of Medicine, Baltimore, Md., telephone interview, Jan. 18, 1991; "at most two dozen . . .": ibid.

p. 186 "The history thereafter . . .": D. Botstein, interview.

p. 187 "People reacted the same . . .": ibid.

p. 187 The figure for NIH expenditures on the Huntington's gene was provided by Sandra O'Connor of NIH and refers specifically to National Institute of Neurology funding for the search for the gene.

p. 187 "What they do . . .": D. Botstein, interview.

p. 187 Apropos of the split between molecular biology and human genetics, Botstein is probably the most outspoken in suggesting that the NIH study sections that approve grants did not function in their customarily wise and efficient manner. Botstein said in an interview, "To say that the human genetics community as a *group* was hostile to this idea is an understatement." The view appears to be substantiated in Cook-Deegan, op. cit.

p. 188 Victor McKusick, a respected member of the human genetics community, says: "There may be something to that. It may be that the NIH study sections might not have looked too favorably on what might have looked at that time like a fishing expedition. . . . With the retrospectoscope, it's easy to see that this was a winner, but that wasn't clear to us at the time."

p. 188 "shopped the idea": D. Botstein, interview.

p. 188 On the Collaborative Research effort: Helen Donis-Keller, Collaborative Research, personal interview, Bedford, Mass., Feb. 16, 1988; Botstein, interview; H. Donis-Keller et al., "A Genetic Linkage Map of the Human Genome," *Cell,* vol. 51, Oct. 23, 1987, pp. 319–337.

p. 190 "premature and presumptuous": R. White, quoted in Richard Saltus, "Mass. Firm's Genetic Map Said to Aid Health Care," *Boston Globe,* Oct. 8, 1987, p. 1; "It is a very useful . . .": R. White quoted in Leslie Roberts, "Flap Arises Over Genetic Map," *Science,* vol. 238, Nov. 6, 1987, pp. 750–752. Other contemporary accounts of the dispute: David Stipp, "Genetic Map That Could Speed Diagnosis of Inherited Disease Touches Off Dispute," *Wall Street Journal,* Oct. 8, 1987,

p. 33; Marcia Barinaga, "Critics Denounce First Genome Map as Premature," *Nature,* vol. 329, Oct. 15, 1987, p. 571; and Harold M. Schmeck, Jr., "New Map of Genes May Aid in Fighting Hereditary Diseases," *New York Times,* Oct. 8, 1987, p. A1.

p. 190 "A map is a map. . . .": H. Donis-Keller quoted in Roberts, op. cit., p. 751.

p. 190 For background on the Santa Cruz meeting, see Stephen S. Hall, "Genesis: The Sequel," *California,* July 1988, pp. 62–69.

p. 190 "Most people thought . . .": D. Botstein, quoted in Hall, op. cit., p. 63.

p. 190 "There was perhaps a consensus . . .": R. Sinsheimer, quoted in Hall, op. cit., p. 65.

p. 191 On the official start of the genome project: See Stephen S. Hall, "James Watson and the Search for Biology's 'Holy Grail,' " *Smithsonian,* Feb. 1990, pp. 41–49. An update on the genome project appeared in J. Claiborne Stephens et al., "Mapping the Human Genome: Current Status," *Science,* Oct. 12, 1990, p. 237, which is notable for their definition of a map, surprisingly close to the Robinson-Petchenik version noted in the opening essay: "A map is a representation of the relationships among landmarks organized according to a defined coordinate system."

p. 191 On fluorescent chromosome mapping: Peter Lichter et al., "High-Resolution Mapping of Human Chromosome 11 by in Situ Hybridization with Cosmid Clones," *Science,* Jan. 5, 1990, pp. 64–69.

p. 191 On the breast cancer work: M. Skolnick et al., "Inheritance of Proliferative Breast Disease in Breast Cancer Kindreds," *Science,* vol. 250, Dec. 21, 1990, pp. 1715–1720.

p. 191 "clinicians doing diagnoses . . .": M. Skolnick, interview.

10. HEAD STUFF AND TAIL STUFF

GENERAL SOURCES

Embryology and developmental biology have, regrettably, never received popular treatment in book-length form. The following are good summaries that at least give a taste of the excitement that has animated the field in the past decade.

Shannon Brownlee, "The Lord of the Flies," *Discover,* April 1987, pp. 26–40; Philip De Jager, "Homeo Box Genes: Of Mutants and Morphogenesis," *Yale Scientific,* Fall 1988, pp. 5–8; Walter J. Gehring, "The Molecular Basis of Development," *Scientific American,* Oct. 1985, pp. 153–162; Stephen S. Hall, "The Fate of the Egg," *Science 85,* Nov. 1985, pp. 40–49; Ben Patrusky, "A Biological Rosetta Stone," *Mosaic,* vol. 18, no. 3, Fall 1987, pp. 26–35; B. Patrusky, "Development in the Embryo: A Matter of Position," *Mosaic,* vol. 18, no. 4, Winter, 1987–1988, pp. 36–48.

NOTES

p. 193 Epigraph: "The Fly," from *The Poetical Works of William Blake,* Oxford University Press, London, 1913.

p. 194 Description of E. B. Lewis's office based on visits in 1985 and 1989.

p. 194 "The early experimenters . . .": E. Lewis, California Institute of Biology, Pasadena, Calif., personal interview, March 7, 1985, and Aug. 23, 1989.

p. 195 "If one of us died . . .": Michael Levine, Dept. of Biology, Columbia University, New York, N.Y., personal interview, Sept. 26, 1989. Levine has subsequently moved to the University of California-San Diego.

p. 195 The Blake drawing was on the cover of *Mechanisms of Segmentation,* a Supplement of *Development,* vol. 104, The Company of Biologists Limited, Cambridge, England, 1988; the Blake drawing to which Lewis referred, *What Is Man!,* originally appeared as the frontispiece to *For Children: The Gates of Paradise* and is dated May 17, 1793. Below a later version appear the lines:

> The Suns Light when he unfolds it
> Depends on the Organ that beholds it.

From David Bindman, *The Complete Graphic Works of William Blake,* Thames and Hudson, London, 1978.

p. 196 "It's an incredible . . .": E. Lewis, interview.

p. 196 "The fertilized germ . . .": C. Darwin, quoted in *Isaac Asimov's Book of Science and Nature Quotations,* Isaac Asimov and Jason A. Shulman, eds., Weidenfeld & Nicolson, New York, 1988, p. 104.

p. 197 "a sort of stuff . . .": T. H. Morgan, quoted in Peter A. Lawrence, "Background to *Bicoid,*" *Cell,* vol. 54, July 1, 1988, pp. 1–2. The "stuff" Morgan presciently referred to is obviously some sort of protein gradient, a supposition that would be proven nearly a century later by Nüsslein-Volhard. As for Morgan and his various "stuff," he confessed, "I do not pretend that this explains anything at all, but the statement covers the results as they stand."

p. 197 On Morgan's skepticism about Mendel and Darwin: See Garland E. Allen, "T. H. Morgan and the Split Between Embryology and Genetics, 1910–1935," in T. J. Horder, J. A. Witkowski, and C. C. Wylie, eds., *A History of Embryology,* Cambridge University Press, Cambridge, 1986, pp. 113–146.

p. 198 "You see, primitive . . .": E. Lewis, interview.

p. 198 Bateson as founder of genetics: William Bateson, *Material for the Study of Evolution,* 1894, and *Encyclopaedia Britannica,* 14th ed., 1968, vol. 3, pp. 273–274.

p. 198 It has been the custom at least since the 1920s to write fruit-fly mutation genes in italics. Furthermore, dominant mutations (like *Antennapedia*) are capitalized, while recessive mutations (like *bithorax*) are not. Groups of related genes, known as complexes, are not italicized, but often are capitalized. There has been some effort recently to change some of these rules, but the above-mentioned system prevails in the literature through 1990.

p. 198 The *Antennapedia* mutant was first observed by Bateson, op. cit.; the *bithorax* mutation was first described in C. B. Bridges and T. H. Morgan, *Carnegie Institution of Washington Publication No. 327,* vol. 137, 1923, p. 152.

p. 199 "No books, practically": E. Lewis, interview, for this and family background.

p. 199 "much more of an artist's . . .": M. Levine, op. cit., interview.

p. 199 Gerald M. Rubin, "*Drosophila melanogaster* as an Experimental Organism," *Science,* vol. 240, June 10, 1988, pp. 1453–1459.

p. 200 Background on *star:* E. Lewis, interview; Edward Novitski, University of Oregon, Eugene, Ore., telephone interview, Feb. 20, 1990.

p. 200 The first chromosome maps were published in Calvin B. Bridges, "Salivary Chromosome Maps, with a Key to the Banding of the Chromosomes of *Drosophila Melanogaster," Journal of Heredity,* vol. 26, Feb. 1935, pp. 60–64.

p. 200 On "multiple alleles": E. B. Lewis, "Pseudoallelism and Gene Evolution," *Cold Spring Harbor Symposia on Quantitative Biology,* vol. 16, 1951, pp. 159–174. The paper set out the evolutionary question answered twenty-seven years later by Lewis's *Nature* paper: where do new genes come from? They come, he suggested in this landmark 1951 paper, "from pre-existing genes."

p. 201 "The whole basis . . .": E. Lewis, interview.

p. 202 "But that's probably . . .": ibid.

p. 202 "It was quite nice . . .": E. Lewis, interview. The professor to whom he refers, of course, was A. H. Sturtevant.

pp. 202–206 E. B. Lewis, "A Gene Complex Controlling Segmentation in *Drosophila," Nature,* vol. 276, Dec. 7, 1978, pp. 565–570. According to folklore, the editors of *Nature* requested that Lewis make the paper a little less complicated, and Lewis, feeling it wouldn't be worth the trouble, made noises about withdrawing it.

p. 206 "innovative analysis"; "intellectual inspiration"; and "The successes . . .": P. W. Ingham, "The Molecular Genetics of Embryonic Pattern Formation in *Drosophila," Nature,* vol. 335, Sept. 1, 1988, pp. 25–34. This is perhaps the best recent review of the role genes play in fruit-fly development and of the work that has grown out of Lewis's 1978 paper.

p. 206 "Molecular biology put . . .": M. Levine, interview.

p. 207 "Somehow I lost . . .": ibid.

p. 209 "What was striking . . .": M. Levine, interview. "To see molecules . . .": William McGinnis, Yale University, New Haven, Conn., telephone interview, Oct. 23, 1990; "That really left . . .": Levine, interview.

p. 209 "They were predominantly . . .": M. Levine, interview.

p. 210 W. McGinnis et al., "A Conserved DNA Sequence in Homeotic Genes of the *Drosophila* Antennapedia and Bithorax Complexes," *Nature,* vol. 308, Mar. 29, 1984, pp. 428–433; and Matthew P. Scott et al., "The Molecular Organization of the *Antennapedia* Locus of *Drosophila," Cell,* vol. 35, Dec. 1983, pp. 763–776.

p. 210 See also Michael Akam, "A Common Segment in Genes for Segments of *Drosophila," Nature,* vol. 308, Mar. 29, 1984, pp. 402–403. These discoveries touched off a frenzy described by *Science* magazine (April 11, 1986) as "Homeomadness."

p. 210 "These are the genes . . .": M. Levine, interview; "It was just . . .": ibid.

pp. 211–212 The achievement of C. Nüsslein-Volhard is discussed in Lawrence, op. cit., and Ingham, op. cit. Key papers in this lovely body of work include: C. Nüsslein-Volhard et al., "Determination of Anteroposterior Polarity in *Drosophila," Science,* vol. 238, Dec. 18, 1987, pp. 1675–1681; W. Driever and C. Nüsslein-Volhard, "A Gradient of *Bicoid* Protein in Drosophila Embryos," *Cell,* vol. 54, July 1, 1988, pp. 83–93; and Driever and Nüsslein-Volhard, "The *Bicoid* Protein Determines Position in the Drosophila Embryo in a Concentration-Dependent Manner," ibid., pp. 95–104.

p. 213 "Our justification for . . .": M. Levine, interview.

p. 213 For background on the emerging links between the insect and vertebrate homeobox genes, see Michael Akam, "Wondrous Transformation," *Nature,* vol. 349, Jan. 24, 1991, p. 282, and Eddy M. De Robertis et al., "Homeobox Genes and the Vertebrate Body Plan," *Scientific American,* July 1990, pp. 46–52. A recent paper has even suggested a link between the homeotic genes first seen in insects and a congenital human disorder known as DiGeorge's syndrome; see O. Chisaka and M. Capecchi, "Regionally Restricted Developmental Defects Resulting from Targeted Disruption of the Mouse Homeobox Gene *hox*-1.5," *Nature,* vol. 350, April 11, 1991, pp. 473–479.

p. 213 "It's remarkable how . . .": E. Lewis, interview.

11. A SAGA OF LOW CUNNING

GENERAL RESOURCES

Francis Crick, *What Mad Pursuit: A Personal View of Scientific Discovery,* Basic Books, New York, 1988; Horace F. Judson, *The Eighth Day of Creation: The Makers of the Revolution in Biology,* Simon & Schuster, New York, 1979 (among its many virtues, offers a highly detailed history of the development of X-ray crystallography, including an exhaustive account of Max Perutz's work on hemoglobin); Max Perutz, "The Birth of Protein Engineering," *New Scientist,* June 13, 1985, pp. 12–15; James D. Watson, *The Double Helix: A Personal Account of the Discovery of the Structure of DNA,* edited by Gunther S. Stent, Norton, New York, 1980 (a critical edition of the entertaining and best-selling account of X-ray crystallography's greatest triumph).

NOTES

p. 215 Epigraph: Ovid, *Metamorphoses,* Penguin, London, 1955, p. 106.

p. 216 Background on restriction enzymes: Jeremy Cherfas, *Man-Made Life,* Pantheon, New York, 1982, pp. 26–60 (an in-depth discussion of the original discoveries of these enzymes); Stephen S. Hall, *Invisible Frontiers,* Atlantic Monthly Press, New York, 1987, pp. 58–63.

p. 216 The phenomenon of restriction was first described, but not explained, in the early 1950s by Salvador Luria and Mary Human. The first restriction enzyme was isolated by Matthew Meselson and Robert Yuan of Harvard, who published the results as "DNA Restriction Enzyme from *E. coli,*" *Nature,* vol. 217, 1968, pp. 1110–1114.

p. 216 Background on *Eco* RI: J. Hedgpeth et al., "DNA Nucleotide Sequence Restricted by the RI Endonuclease," *PNAS,* Nov. 1972, pp. 3448–3452.

p. 217 "Almost all aspects . . .": F. Crick, op. cit., p. 61.

p. 217 Background on X-ray crystallography: Virtually nothing of a popular treatment exists on the subject, but Crick returns to the theme frequently in his autobiography, and the third section of Judson's book (pp. 493–604) gives the field as literate and lengthy a discussion as it is likely to get.

p. 219 "The object is to . . .": L. Bragg, quoted in Judson, op. cit., p. 530.

p. 219 "It's a bit like . . .": M. Perutz, quoted by John Rosenberg, Dept. of Biological Sciences, University of Pittsburgh, Pittsburgh, Pa., personal interviews, April 21, 1986, and Nov. 13, 1989.

p. 220 "He was very evangelical . . .": ibid.

p. 220 "You have to be . . .": Alexander Rich, Massachusetts Institute of Technology, Cambridge, Mass., telephone interview, Feb. 15, 1990; "And there he was . . .": ibid.

p. 220 "For a very long . . .": J. Rosenberg, interview; "What keeps you going . . .": ibid; "Sisyphus is . . .": ibid.

p. 221 "something like three-dimensional . . .": ibid.

p. 221 The reason that *Eco* RI did not cut the DNA into pieces during the experiment was that the cocrystals were grown in an absence of magnesium ions, which are necessary for the enzyme's cutting function.

p. 222 "You have to have . . .": J. Grable, University of Pittsburgh, personal interview, April 21, 1986; "They don't all . . .": ibid.

p. 223 "Everybody copes with . . .": J. Rosenberg, interview.

p. 223 "Growing a crystal . . .": J. Rosenberg, interview.

p. 224 "Then, if you are . . .": ibid.

p. 225 "incomprehensible Greek stuff . . .": J. Rosenberg, interview; "On a conventional . . .": ibid.

p. 227 "That was a very . . .": J. Rosenberg, interview.

pp. 229–231 Background on kinked DNA: Christin A. Frederick et al., "Kinked DNA in Crystalline Complex with *Eco* RI Endonuclease," *Nature,* vol. 309, May 24, 1984, pp. 327–331.

p. 230 The complete structure of the cocrystal was described in Judith A. McClarin et al., "Structure of the DNA-*Eco* RI Endonuclease Recognition Complex at 3 A Resolution," *Science,* vol. 234, Dec. 19, 1986, pp. 1526–1541.

p. 231 "a milestone in modern . . .": Helen M. Berman, "How *Eco* RI Recognizes and Cuts DNA," *Science,* vol. 234, Dec. 19, 1986, pp. 1482–1483.

p. 231 "How the protein says . . .": J. Rosenberg, interview.

p. 232 Background on possible recognition code: See Brian Matthews, "No Code for Recognition," *Nature,* vol. 335, 1988, p. 294. For a quick review of other cocrystal projects, see Jean L. Marx, "A Crystalline View of Protein-DNA Binding," *Science,* vol. 229, Aug. 30, 1985, pp. 846–848.

p. 232 "I think Brian's point . . .": J. Rosenberg, interview.

p. 232 On the revised structure: Youngchang Kim et al., "Refinement of *Eco* RI Endonuclease Crystal Structure: A Revised Protein Chain Tracing," *Science,* vol. 249, Sept. 14, 1990, pp. 1307–1309.

12. "HERE ONE SAW LITTLE HILLS"

GENERAL SOURCES

It is too soon for a general history of the scanning tunneling microscope to appear for other than a technical audience, but there have been an abundance of good magazine-length popular and semipopular treatments, among which: Gerd Binnig and Heinrich Rohrer, "The Scanning Tunneling Microscope," *Scientific American,* Aug. 1985, pp. 50–56; Paul K. Hansma and Jerry Tersoff, "Scanning Tunneling Microscopy," *Journal of Applied Physics,* vol. 61, Jan. 15, 1987, pp. R1–R23; and James Trefil, "Seeing Atoms," *Discover,* June 1990, pp. 54–60.

The best single source on the history of STM development is recounted by Binnig and Rohrer in their lecture accepting the 1986 Nobel Prize in physics, which I have consulted a great deal for this account. It was later published as Gerd Binnig and Heinrich Rohrer, "Scanning Tunneling Microscopy—From Birth to Adolescence," *Reviews of Modern Physics* (hereafter *RMP*), vol. 59, no. 3, July 1987, pp. 615–625.

NOTES

p. 235 Epigraph: Jonathan Swift, "Travels by Lemuel Gulliver," in *The Portable Swift,* Penguin, New York, 1977, p. 255.

p. 235 "You can breathe . . .": Randall Feenstra, IBM Thomas Watson Research Division, Yorktown Heights, N.Y., personal interview, Aug. 24, 1990.

pp. 236–237 Background on Feenstra work: Described in R. M. Feenstra, "Scanning Tunneling Microscopy," in V. Bortolani, N. H. March, and M. P. Tosi, eds., *Interaction of Atoms and Molecules with Solid Surfaces,* Plenum, New York, 1990, pp. 357–379. The gallium arsenide work appeared as R. M. Feenstra et al., "Atom-Selective Imaging of the Ga As (110) Surface," *Physical Review Letters,* vol. 58, March 23, 1987, pp. 1192–1195. The germanium work, submitted to *Physical Review Letters,* shows how atomic surfaces become disordered as they are heated.

pp. 236–237 In revealing the atomic identity of both gallium and germanium, Feenstra bridged a chemo-political rift described by essayist Primo Levi. Gallium, he wrote, "was isolated in 1875 by the Frenchman Lecocq de Boisbaudran; *cocq* (today written *coq*) means 'cock,' and Lecocq baptized his element *gallium.* A few years later, in the same mineral examined by the Frenchman, the German chemist Winkler discovered a new element. Those were years of great tension between Germany and France; the German assumed gallium to be a nationalistic homage to Gaul and baptized his element *germanium* in order to even the score" (P. Levi, "The Language of Chemists (II)," in *Other People's Trades,* Summit, New York, 1989, pp. 119–120).

p. 237 "Oh, something happened . . .": Feenstra, interview; "In terms of . . .": ibid.

p. 237 "They had been trying . . .": ibid.

pp. 237–238 Background on early STM development is based on Binnig and Rohrer, *RMP.* The account is primarily technical, with a good list of references, but it contains many delightful personal asides about the process of scientific discovery. "Our narrative," they write, "is by no means a recommendation of how research should be done; it simply reflects what we thought, how we acted, and what we felt" (p. 615).

p. 238 "never thought about . . .": Gerd Binnig, University of Munich, telephone interview, Dec. 3, 1990.

p. 238 "The surface was . . .": Wolfgang Pauli, quoted in Binnig and Rohrer, *Scientific American,* p. 50.

p. 238 "probably gave us . . .": Binnig and Rohrer, *RMP,* p. 615.

p. 239 "feeling the 'color' . . .": G. Binnig, interview.

p. 241 "Not a secret . . .": ibid.; "tense and jump . . .": ibid. This view is substantiated in their Nobel remarks; Binnig and Rohrer offer their experience as an argument for "a more relaxed attitude towards doing science" (*RMP,* p. 615).

p. 241 "hardly daring to breathe . . .": Binnig and Rohrer, *RMP,* p. 618.

p. 241 "Most reactions were . . .": ibid., p. 619.

p. 241 "People told us . . .": G. Binnig, interview; "It was simply . . .": ibid.; "I expected a much . . .": ibid.

p. 242 "If you see . . .": ibid.

p. 242 "It was like . . .": G. Binnig, quoted in Binnig and Rohrer, *RMP,* p. 620.

p. 242 "should give a taste . . .": G. Binnig et al., "Surface Studies by Scanning Tunneling Microscopy," *Physical Review Letters,* vol. 49, no. 1, July 5, 1982, pp. 57–61.

p. 242 Champagne rumors: Binnig and Rohrer, *RMP,* p. 622, confirmed by Binnig in interview.

p. 243 "One could have heard . . .": Binnig and Rohrer, *RMP,* p. 623.

p. 243 "The ability of the microscope . . .": Binnig and Rohrer, *Scientific American,* p. 54.

p. 243 A cottage industry: Dollar amounts cited come from V. Richard Sheridan and Wendy Wilson Sheridan, "Scanning Tunneling Microscopy: A Breakthrough in Imaging," *The Scientist,* June 12, 1989, p. 18.

p. 244 "In all the foregoing . . .": Binnig and Rohrer, *Scientific American,* p. 56.

p. 244 Background on the STM's ability to move atoms: D. M. Eigler and E. K. Schweizer, "Positioning Single Atoms with a Scanning Tunneling Microscope," *Nature,* vol. 344, April 5, 1990, pp. 524–526. The authors advert to the long-term significance of their experiment in the first paragraph, noting that "the possibilities for perhaps the ultimate in device miniaturization are evident."

p. 244 For more popular accounts, see Mark Dowie, "Brave New Tiny World," *California,* Nov. 1988, p. 90; Malcolm W. Browne, "2 Researchers Spell 'I.B.M.,' Atom by Atom," *New York Times,* April 5, 1990, p. B11.

p. 245 "In fifty or a hundred years . . .": P. Hansma, Dept. of Physics, University of California, Santa Barbara, Calif., telephone interview, Sept. 25, 1990.

p. 245 Background on STM derivatives: H. Kumar Wickramasinghe, "Scanning Probe Microscopes," *Scientific American,* Oct. 1989, pp. 98–105 (an excellent review of these second-generation machines); June Kinoshita, "Sons of STM," *Scientific American,* July 1988, pp. 33–35; and Robert Pool, "The Children of the STM," *Science,* vol. 247, Feb. 9, 1990, pp. 634–636. I am indebted to Paul Hansma for the suggestion of referring to the entire class of instruments as "scanning probe microscopes," for that is what they have all become.

p. 245 Background on biological applications: P. K. Hansma et al., "Scanning Tunneling Microscopy and Atomic Force Microscopy, Application to Biology and Technology," *Science,* vol. 242, Oct. 14, 1988, pp. 209–216.

p. 246 "It's certainly a long . . .": P. Hansma, interview.

p. 246 "It was true . . .": ibid.

13. ONE PICTURE, WORTH BILLION BYTES

GENERAL SOURCES

Petr Beckmann, *A History of Pi,* Golem Press, Box 1342, Boulder, Colo. 80306, 1971; Ivars Peterson, *The Mathematical Tourist,* Freeman, New York, 1988, and *Islands of Truth,* Freeman, New York, 1990.

NOTES

p. 247 Epigraph: Andrew Marvell, from "Upon Appleton House, to My Lord Fairfax," in *The Poems of Andrew Marvell,* Routledge & Kegan Paul, London, 1952, p. 81.

pp. 247–248 Background on Chudnovsky apartment: Gregory and David Chudnovsky, New York, N.Y., Aug. 8, 1990, and Oct. 15, 1990.

p. 248 Background on "galaxy-in-a-box" simulation: D. V. Chudnovsky et al., "Supercalculations on GF11: A Case Study of Galaxy Code," *Proceedings of Supercomputing '89,* vol. II, pp. 8178–8182. For a more popular treatment, see Ivars Peterson, "From Dust to Dust," *Science News,* vol. 135, Jan. 14, 1989, pp. 24–25.

p. 248 "You see, a map . . .": G. Chudnovsky, interview; *"I must see . . .":* ibid.

p. 250 "People are no longer . . ." and ensuing dialogue: G. and D. Chudnovsky, interview.

p. 250 "Very strange": Richard Askey, Dept. of Mathematics, University of Wisconsin, Madison, telephone interview, Oct. 12, 1990.

p. 250 On MacArthur Foundation: see Kathleen Teltsch, "Foundations to Support 21 as 'Geniuses' for 5 Years," *New York Times,* May 19, 1981, p. A1. Other 1981 fellows included Stephen Jay Gould, Robert Coles, Joseph Brodsky, Robert Penn Warren, and John Imbrie (of the CLIMAP project described in chapter 5).

p. 251 "like watching an atomic . . .": Herbert Robbins, professor emeritus, Dept. of Mathematics, Columbia University, telephone interview, Sept. 25, 1990.

p. 251 "Your brain is . . ." and ensuing dialogue: D. and G. Chudnovsky, interview.

p. 252 "He lacked imagination . . .": David Hilbert, as quoted by D. Chudnovsky, interview.

p. 252 "a quaint little mirror . . .": P. Beckmann, op. cit., p. 3.

p. 252 On Archimedes and pi: ibid., pp. 62–72; *Encyclopaedia Britannica,* 11th ed., 1910, vol. 2, pp. 368–369; E. J. Dijksterhuis, *Archimedes,* Princeton University Press, Princeton, N.J., 1938, pp. 30–32; Plutarch, "Archimedes," in James R. Newman, ed., *The World of Mathematics,* Simon & Schuster, New York, 1956, pp. 180–185.

p. 252 The name "pi" is attributed to the writer William Jones in 1706, according to *Historical Topics for the Mathematics Classroom,* National Council of Teachers of Mathematics, Reston, Va., 1989, pp. 148–154.

p. 253 "We should bear . . .": Carl B. Boyer, *A History of Mathematics,* 2nd ed., Wiley, New York, 1989, p. 228.

pp. 253–254 Background on calculations of pi: P. Beckmann, op. cit.; Boyer, op. cit.; Dario Castellanos, "The Ubiquitous Pi," *Mathematics,* vol. 61, no. 2, April 1988, p. 67; Tom Waters, "Pi in the Sky," *Discover,* Jan. 1990, pp. 76–77.

p. 253 "How I want . . .": Boyer, op. cit., pp. 272–273.

p. 254 The first computerized value of pi was reported in N. C. Metropolis, G. Reitwiesner, and J. von Neumann, "Statistical Treatment of Values of First 2,000 Decimal Digits of *e* and of *pi* Calculated on the ENIAC," *Mathematical Tables and Other Aids to Computation,* vol. 4, 1950, pp. 109–111.

p. 254 For the recent history of computed values of pi, see D. V. Chudnovsky and G. V. Chudnovsky, "The Computation of Classical Constants," *Proceedings of the National Academy of Sciences,* vol. 86, Nov. 1989, pp. 8178–8182; T. Waters, op. cit.

p. 254 "a race for leadership . . .": D. Chudnovsky and G. Chudnovsky, *Proceedings,* p. 8178.

p. 255 "All mathematicians . . .": Lipman Bers, former chairman, Dept. of Mathematics, Columbia University, telephone interview, Sept. 25, 1990.

p. 255 Background on Kiev mugging: "Sakharov Reports Beating of Couple Asking to Leave," *New York Times,* July 24, 1977, p. 5 (the attack occurred on July 22, 1977); D. and G. Chudnovsky, interview; "Ailing Mathematician Said to Get Permission to Leave Soviet Union," *New York Times,* Aug. 23, 1977, p. 11.

p. 256 "We thought the . . .": H. Robbins, interview.

p. 256 "We have never succeeded . . .": ibid. Columbia University, as is customary at other universities, takes its share of "overhead costs" out of the Chudnovskys' government grants.

p. 257 "I consider it . . .": R. Askey, interview.

p. 257 Background on unemployability: When asked why no one will hire the Chudnovskys, no compelling reason is mentioned, although there are some obviously complicating circumstances. Because of Gregory's physical condition, for example, both brothers need to work at the same place, and Gregory is unable to handle a full teaching load. Another possible reason, according to Herbert Robbins, is that one Chudnovsky paper did not adequately cite another mathematician's work (a standard which, if employed in biology, for example, might leave hundreds unemployed overnight). R. Askey suggests that Gregory Chudnovsky published several claims in analytical number theory in a Soviet journal that were not backed by proofs, and other mathematicians claimed he was "wiping out all the work for the graduate students of those other professors."

p. 258 Formula for pi: D. and G. Chudnovsky, *Proceedings,* p. 8180.

p. 258 "Not fun": D. Chudnovsky, interview; "It's an extremely . . .": G. Chudnovsky, interview.

pp. 258–259 "When you do your laundry . . .": D. Chudnovsky, interview.

p. 259 Background on the pi computation: "At the Limits of Calculation, Pi to a Billion Digits and More," *Focus* (Newsletter of the Mathematical Association of America), vol. 9, no. 5, Oct. 1989, pp. 1–4; Michael Vitez, "A Billion Slices of Pi," *Philadelphia Inquirer,* Oct. 2, 1989, p. 1E; T. Waters, op. cit.; I. Peterson, *Islands of Truth,* pp. 178–186.

p. 259 "It's almost the equivalent . . .": D. Chudnovsky, interview; "The dreadful thing . . .": ibid.

p. 259 "The usefulness of . . .": G. Chudnovsky, interview.

p. 260 "In the case of . . .": G. Chudnovsky, interview.

p. 260 "It's like with the flight . . .": D. Chudnovsky, interview; "The data base . . .": ibid.

p. 260 "Cheap!": G. Chudnovsky, interview; "It's big . . .": ibid.

p. 261–262 Background on Little Fermat: D. V. Chudnovsky et al., "A Design of General Purpose Number-Theoretic Computer," *Proceedings of the Third International Conference on Supercomputing,* edited by L. P. Kartashev and S. I. Kartashev, vol. II, International Supercomputing Institute, 1988, pp. 498–499; Ivars Peterson, "Little Fermat," *Science News,* vol. 138, Oct. 6, 1990, pp. 222–223.

p. 262 For Allman theory: See description in opening essay.

p. 262 "sort of a graphic . . .": D. Chudnovsky, interview.

p. 263 "Let me give you . . .": ibid.; "At least in baseball . . .": G. Chudnovsky, interview.

p. 264 "You want to see . . .": G. Chudnovsky, interview; "Why waste all . . .": ibid.; "We are working . . .": D. Chudnovsky, interview.

14. THE LAKES OF WADA

GENERAL SOURCES

James P. Crutchfield et al., "Chaos," *Scientific American,* Dec. 1986, pp. 46–57; James Gleick, *Chaos: Making a New Science,* Viking, New York, 1987 (the best general treatment of chaos and how it was discovered); Ivars Peterson, *The Mathematical Tourist: Snapshots of Modern Mathematics,* W. H. Freeman, New York, 1988.

NOTES

p. 265 Epigraph: Seki Takakazu, quoted in *Dictionary of Scientific Biography,* C. C. Gillispie, ed., Scribners, New York, 1978, p. 745.

p. 266 "long, unconscious prior work": Henri Poincaré, "Mathematical Creation," in James R. Newman, ed., *The World of Mathematics,* Simon & Schuster, New York, 1956, pp. 2041–2050 (p. 2045).

p. 266 "They just cleaned . . .": James A. Yorke, director, Institute for Physical Science and Technology, University of Maryland, College Park, Md., personal interview, Sept. 6, 1990, and telephone interview, Oct. 19, 1990.

p. 267 "One of my ideas . . .": J. Yorke, interview.

p. 267 On "naming the baby": Tien-Yien Li and James A. Yorke, "Period Three Implies Chaos," *American Mathematical Monthly,* vol. 82, 1975, pp. 985–992; "chaotic": ibid., p. 986.

p. 268 "In mathematics . . .": J. Yorke, interview.

p. 268 Gleick, op. cit., pp. 65–69: Gleick tells the amusing anecdote of how Yorke's name came to be associated with Edward Lorenz's pioneering work and thus the origins of chaos. He sent a copy of Lorenz's landmark 1963 paper to Stephen Smale with his address label pasted in the corner. Smale, Gleick writes, "made many photocopies of 'Deterministic Nonperiodic Flow' and thus arose the legend that Yorke had discovered Lorenz" (p. 67).

p. 268 "Mathematics can lead . . .": J. Dirac, quoted in Robert P. Crease and Charles C. Mann, *The Second Creation: Masters of the Revolution in 20th Century Physics,* Macmillan, New York, 1986, p. 77.

p. 268 "The present state . . .": Laplace, quoted in Crutchfield et al., op. cit., p. 48.

p. 269 "mathematical feedback . . .": Douglas R. Hofstadter, "Strange Attractors: Mathematical Patterns Delicately Poised Between Order and Chaos," *Scientific American,* Nov. 1981, pp. 22–43.

p. 270 ". . . it may happen . . .": Poincaré, quoted in Crutchfield et al., op. cit., p. 48.

p. 270 "must follow up . . .": Crease and Mann, op. cit., p. 77.

p. 270 "the style of exploration . . .": D. Hofstadter, op. cit., pp. 22–24.

p. 270 "I'm just thinking . . .": J. Yorke, interview.

p. 271 Lorenz work: The benchmark paper is Edward Lorenz, "Deterministic

Nonperiodic Flow," *Journal of the Atmospheric Sciences,* vol. 20, 1963, pp. 130–141; see also Gleick, op. cit., pp. 11–31.

pp. 271–272 Smale horseshoe: see Gleick, op. cit., pp. 45–53.

p. 272 "People would study . . .": J. Yorke, interview; "Computers before around . . .": ibid.; "People interested in . . .": ibid.

p. 273 "the laboratory mouse . . .": Gleick, op. cit., p. 39.

pp. 273–275 On the pendulum experiment: Celso Grebogi, Edward Ott, and James A. Yorke, "Chaos, Strange Attractors, and Fractal Basin Boundaries in Nonlinear Dynamics," *Science,* vol. 238, Oct. 30, 1987, pp. 632–638.

p. 275 "You start seeing . . .": J. Yorke, interview.

p. 276 "Chaos adds . . .": Grebogi et al., op. cit., p. 637.

p. 276 "People tend . . .": J. Yorke, interview.

p. 276 "This was informed to . . .": Kunizo Yoneyama, "Theory of Continuous Set of Points (not finished)," *Tohoku Mathematical Journal,* vols. 11 and 12, Tokyo, 1917, pp. 43–158 (p. 60).

p. 276 On Wasan lore: Shigeru Nakayama, "Japanese Scientific Thought," in *Dictionary of Scientific Biography,* pp. 744–756; *Kagaku Gijutsushi Jiten (The Dictionary of the History of Science and Technology),* Kobundo, 1983; *Iwanami Sogaku Jiten (Iwanami's Dictionary of Mathematics),* 3rd ed., Iwanami Shoten, 1986. (I am grateful to Yukako Kornhauser for locating, translating, and bringing the Wasan material to my attention.)

p. 276 "more of an art . . .": S. Nakayama, op. cit., p. 744.

pp. 277–281 On the Lakes of Wada: Described in John G. Docking and Gail S. Young, *Topology,* Dover, New York, 1961, pp. 143–145, and expanded upon in Judy Kennedy and James A. Yorke, "Basins of Wada," in press. The Kennedy and Yorke paper describes the work on indecomposable continuums. The original Wada example as given in *Topology* is for *two* canals; Yorke and Kennedy adapted it to three in their "Basins" paper, and it is so described here.

p. 278 "the whole thing . . .": Judy Kennedy, Dept. of Mathematics, University of Delaware, Newark, telephone interview, Oct. 17, 1990.

p. 278 "Now the mathematicians . . .": J. Yorke, interview.

p. 279 "This'll show you . . .": J. Yorke, ibid.; "One of the ideas . . .": ibid.; "Looking at . . .": ibid.

p. 280 "Well, what you . . .": J. Yorke, interview; "Well, what we . . .": ibid.

p. 280 "yet another . . .": Vivian Sobchack, "A Theory of Everything: Meditations on Total Chaos," *Artforum,* Oct. 1990, pp. 148–155.

p. 281 "My view is . . .": J. Yorke, interview.

15. STIFF TRACKS

GENERAL SOURCES

Robert P. Crease and Charles C. Mann, *The Second Creation: Makers of the Revolution in 20th Century Physics,* Macmillan, New York, 1986 (an excellent account of the history of particle physics in this century); Michael Riordan, *The Hunting of the Quark: A True Story of Modern Physics,* Simon & Schuster, New York, 1987; Gary Taubes, *Nobel Dreams: Power, Deceit, and the Ultimate Experiment,* Random House, New York, 1986.

Shorter treatments include David Dickson, "New Machine Sparks Rivalries at CERN," *Science,* vol. 244, June 16, 1989, pp. 1257–1260; Charles C. Mann, "Armies of Physicists Struggle to Discover Proof of a Scot's Brainchild," *Smithsonian,* March 1989, pp. 106–117; and Christine Sutton, "The Making of a Particle Machine," *New Scientist,* July 8, 1989, pp. 60–64.

NOTES:

p. 282 Epigraph: Samuel Ting, quoted in Crease and Mann, op. cit., p. 236.

p. 284 "If a theoretician . . .": ibid., p. 236.

p. 284 "atoms and void": Democritus, quoted in Wallace I. Matson, *A New History of Philosophy,* vol. 1, Harcourt Brace Jovanovich, New York, 1987, p. 53.

p. 284 "Leptons and quarks . . .": Riordan, op. cit., p. 323.

p. 284 "it is amazing . . .": Martinus J. G. Veltman, "The Higgs Boson," *Scientific American,* Nov. 1986, pp. 76–84; for other background on the Higgs boson, see C. Mann, *Smithsonian,* and Stephen Budiansky, "Moving into the Higgs Sector?" *Nature,* vol. 304, July 21, 1983, p. 210.

p. 286 "So loose is . . .": Budiansky, op. cit., p. 210.

p. 286 "When I consider . . .": Peter Higgs, quoted in C. Mann, *Smithsonian,* p. 117.

p. 286 "You have to remember . . .": H. Georgi, quoted in Crease and Mann, op. cit., p. 36.

pp. 287–288 "It was almost as . . .": Ernest Rutherford, quoted in Riordan, op. cit., p. 24.

p. 288 "little wisps and threads . . .": Charles T. R. Wilson, "On the Cloud Method of Making Visible Ions and the Tracks of Ionizing Particles," *Nobel Lectures in Physics, 1922–1941,* Elsevier, Amsterdam, 1965, pp. 194–217 (these are Wilson's remarks in accepting the 1927 Nobel Prize in physics). Other background on cloud chambers: Crease and Mann, op. cit., pp. 88–91; C. Henderson, *Cloud and Bubble Chambers,* Methuen & Co., London, 1970.

p. 290 Background on cyclotrons: Crease and Mann, op. cit., pp. 256–259; Ernest O. Lawrence, "The Evolution of the Cyclotron," in *Nobel Lectures in Physics, 1922–1941,* p. 430.

pp. 291–292 Background on bubble chambers: Donald A. Glaser, "Elementary Particles and Bubble Chambers," *Nobel Lectures in Physics, 1942–1962,* Elsevier, Amsterdam, 1964, pp. 529–553.

p. 292 "If I could remember . . .": Enrico Fermi, quoted in Riordan, op. cit., p. 69.

p. 292 "is nothing less . . .": Leon Lederman, "The Heart of the Matter," *GEO,* July 1981, pp. 10–30.

p. 293 Background on families of particles: Gary J. Feldman and Jack Steinberger, "The Number of Families of Matter," *Scientific American,* Feb. 1991, pp. 70–75.

p. 294 "Now some people . . .": Michael Riordan, SLAC, Stanford, Calif., personal interview, March 20, 1990; "This is the Holy . . .": ibid.

p. 294 "Physicists believe they are . . .": John R. Rees, "The Stanford Linear Collider," *Scientific American,* October 1989, pp. 58–65.

p. 295 "a soap opera . . .": Carlo Rubbia, quoted in Roland Pease and David Lindley, "Is the End of Particle Proliferation at Hand?" *Nature,* vol. 341, Oct. 19, 1989, p. 555.

p. 295 Background on LEP: Stephen Myers and Emilio Picasso, "The LEP Collider," *Scientific American,* July 1990, pp. 54–61; Christine Sutton, op. cit.

p. 295 Background on the Stanford accelerator: Ian Anderson, "A Production Line for Particle Physics," *New Scientist,* May 19, 1988, pp. 56–60; Gary Taubes, "Slacking Off," *Discover,* Jan. 1989, pp. 58–59.

p. 296 "The maps we make . . .": M. Riordan, interview.

p. 296 For descriptions of the Mark II detector, and detector technology in general, I have relied heavily upon accounts published in SLAC's excellent quarterly newsletter, *Beam Line,* in particular Kathy O'Shaughnessy, "The Mark II Detector at the SLC," *Beam Line,* Sept. 1988, pp. 3–9, and remarks by John Jaros.

p. 300 "close enough to proceed . . .": C. Mann, *Smithsonian,* p. 114; "Not *as if* . . .": Burton Richter, quoted, ibid.

p. 300 On the discovery of SLAC's first Z particle: A richly detailed account is Michael Riordan, "The SLC Makes Its First Z⁰ Particles," *Beam Line,* April 1989, pp. 3–5.

p. 301 "The significance of the event . . .": Burton Richter, quoted ibid., p. 5.

p. 302 "hockey player's tactics": C. Rubbia, quoted in Pease and Lindley, op. cit., p. 555; "at best the Americans . . .": C. Rubbia, quoted ibid.

p. 302 "SLC is finished . . .": John Ellis, quoted in David Dickson, "European Physicists Narrow Down the Neutrinos in the Universe," *New Scientist,* Oct. 21, 1989, p. 27.

p. 303 "There is bound . . .": J. D. Bjorken, "The New Physics: Where Is It?" *Beam Line,* Spring 1990, pp. 1–6.

p. 303 "What of those atoms . . .": Lucretius, *On the Nature of the Universe,* Penguin, New York, 1951, p. 89.

16. STAR NOISE

GENERAL SOURCES

Marcia Bartusiak, *Thursday's Universe,* Times Books, New York, 1986; Bart J. Bok and Priscilla F. Bok, *The Milky Way,* 5th ed., Harvard University Press, Cambridge, 1981; Nigel Calder, *Violent Universe,* Viking, New York, 1969; Thomas H. Dame, "The Molecular Milky Way," *Sky & Telescope,* July 1988, pp. 22–27; Nick Scoville and Judith S. Young, "Molecular Clouds, Star Formation, and Galactic Structure," *Scientific American,* April 1984, pp. 42–53; W. T. Sullivan III, ed., *The Early Years of Radio Astronomy,* Cambridge University Press, Cambridge, 1984; Gerrit L. Verschuur, *The Invisible Universe Revealed: The Story of Radio Astronomy,* Springer-Verlag, New York, 1987.

NOTES

p. 307 Epigraph: *The Divine Comedy of Dante Alighieri,* Canto XXXIV, *Inferno,* translated by Allen Mandelbaum, University of California Press, Berkeley, 1980, p. 320.

p. 309 "Until the war . . .": Patrick Thaddeus, Harvard-Smithsonian Center for Astrophysics, Cambridge, Mass., personal interview, Sept. 14, 1989.

p. 310 "Basically we're fixed . . .": P. Thaddeus, interview; "I used to say . . .": ibid.; "Name two ways . . .": ibid.

pp. 310–311 On the Karl Jansky experiment: G. Verschuur, op. cit., pp. 209–211; and Kenneth Kellermann and B. Sheets, eds., *Serendipitous Discoveries in Radio Astronomy,* NRAO, Green Bank, W.Va., 1983 (a superb source of anecdotal recollections of the early days of radio astronomy).

p. 310 "a very steady hiss . . .": Jansky quoted in Verschuur, pp. 209–210; "New Radio Waves Traced to Centre of the Milky Way," *New York Times,* May 5, 1933, p. 1.

p. 310 "star noise": K. Jansky, quoted in G. Verschuur, op. cit., p. 211. In his preface to *Serendipitous Discoveries,* Ken Kellermann, director of the National Radio Astronomy Observatory, lends credence to one of the lingering suspicions about Jansky's work when he says that Jansky's boss at Bell Labs "apparently did not encourage Jansky to pursue this line of research."

p. 311 "It is a most extraordinary . . .": Bernard Lovell, *Voice of the Universe: Building the Jodrell Bank Telescope,* Praeger, New York, 1968, 1987 (rev.), p. 21.

p. 311 On Grote Reber work: G. Verschuur, op. cit., pp. 78–81; B. Lovell, op. cit., pp. 21–22; Grote Reber, "Radio Astronomy Between Jansky and Reber," in *Serendipitous Discoveries,* pp. 71–78. Reber *had* read Jansky's paper.

p. 311 On the Hubble connection: "Wheaton was a small place at [the] turn of [the] century. Each teacher took two grades. Mother (Harriet Grote) was at bottom of totem pole, so she got the two least desirable, 7th and 8th. John Hubble, Edwin's father, moved to Wheaton about 1898, so Edwin passed through her hands 1901 & 1902. He graduated from Wheaton High class 1906, and University of Chicago class 1910. She picked him out as a bright boy and watched his progress with considerable interest." (Grote Reber, letter to author, May 22, 1991).

p. 311 Grote Reber, "Cosmic Static," *Astrophysical Journal,* vol. 91, June 1940, pp. 621–624.

p. 311 "at best a mistake . . .": G. Reber, *Serendipitous Discoveries,* p. 76.

p. 311 The first map of radio astronomy, by the estimate of K. Kellermann (telephone interview), appeared in G. Reber, "Cosmic Static," *Astrophysical Journal,* vol. 100, Nov. 1944, pp. 279–287.

p. 312 "There were no . . .": G. Reber, *Serendipitous Discoveries,* p. 75.

p. 312 On the origins of Jodrell Bank: B. Lovell, op. cit., pp. 1–22.

p. 314 On Thaddeus background: P. Thaddeus, interview.

p. 314 "They didn't have . . .": ibid.

p. 315 "just kept on going . . .": Robert Wilson, in *Serendipitous Discoveries,* p. 287.

p. 315 "From that time on . . .": A. Barrett, "The Beginnings of Molecular Radio Astronomy," in *Serendipitous Discoveries,* p. 286.

pp. 315–325 On the Milky Way mapping project: The summary paper is T. Dame et al., "A Composite CO Survey of the Entire Milky Way," *Astrophysical Journal,* vol. 322, Nov. 15, 1987, pp. 706–720. Two more popular accounts are T. Dame, op. cit., and E. Samuel Palmer, "Unveiling the Hidden Milky Way," *Astronomy,* Nov. 1989, pp. 32–40.

p. 315 "In the beginning . . .": P. Thaddeus, interview; "In our first run . . .": ibid.

p. 316 "We were in the position . . .": ibid.

p. 317 "From these initial . . .": ibid.; "If you live . . .": ibid.

p. 320 "Molecular clouds are the factories . . .": P. Thaddeus, interview; "If you'd have said . . .": ibid.; "If you make a map . . .": ibid.

p. 320 On theories of star formation: Charles J. Lada and Frank H. Shu, "The Formation of Sunlike Stars," *Science,* vol. 248, May 4, 1990, pp. 564–572. For a less technical discussion, there are Ivars Peterson, "The Winds of Starbirth," *Science News,* June 30, 1990, pp. 408–409, and Rudolph E. Schild, "A Star Is Born," *Sky & Telescope,* Dec. 1990, pp. 600–602.

pp. 321–323 On submillimeter radio mapping: Thomas G. Phillips and David B. Rutledge, "Superconducting Tunnel Detectors in Radio Astronomy," *Scientific American,* May 1986, pp. 96–102. The work on self-similarity is reported in E. Falgarone and T. G. Phillips, "The Self-Similar Structure of Molecular Clouds," paper presented at the Conference on Submillimeter and Millimeter Wave Astronomy, Kona, Hawaii, October 1988, Caltech Submillimeter Observatory Astrophysics Reprint #109.

pp. 323–324 For an excellent review of current thinking on the origin of life, see John Horgan, "In the Beginning . . ." *Scientific American,* Feb. 1991, pp. 116–125.

p. 324 "Half are things . . .": P. Thaddeus, interview; "The message of this . . .": ibid.; "What's happened is . . .": ibid.

17. THE GREAT ATTRACTOR

GENERAL SOURCES

David Burstein, "Large-Scale Motions in the Universe: A Review," *Reports on Progress in Physics,* vol. 53, April 1990, pp. 421–481; Alan Dressler, "In the Grip of the Great Attractor," *The Sciences,* Sept.–Oct. 1989, pp. 28–34, and "The Large-Scale Streaming of Galaxies," *Scientific American,* September 1987, pp. 46–54; Dennis Overbye, *Lonely Hearts of the Cosmos,* HarperCollins, New York, 1991 (an insightful and entertaining look at cosmology).

NOTES

p. 326 Epigraph: Seneca, quoted in D. Boorstin, *The Discoverers,* p. 20.

p. 326 "Have you ever . . .": Alan Dressler, staff astrophysicist, Observatories of the Carnegie Institution, Pasadena, Calif., June 5, 1989, and August 28, 1989.

p. 327 "The southern sky . . .": ibid.; "The hardest thing . . .": ibid.

p. 328 "Let's put it . . .": John Huchra, Harvard-Smithsonian Center for Astrophysics, interview, Sept. 30, 1989.

p. 328 "I should have . . .": A. Dressler, interview.

p. 329 "I've been very . . .": ibid.

p. 329 On galaxy flow: Dressler has provided two excellent backgrounders for lay readers on the history of galactic flows in *The Sciences* and *Scientific American* (see "General Sources"). On galaxy formation, see Thanu Padmanabhan, "How Galaxies Pull Themselves Together," *New Scientist,* June 3, 1989, pp. 56–59.

p. 330 "The idea is . . .": ibid.

p. 331 "represented a change . . .": A. Dressler, *Scientific American,* op. cit., p. 46.

p. 333 "There was a guy . . .": A. Dressler, interview.

p. 334 On Sandage and the Hubble flow: See Allan R. Sandage, "The Red-

Shift," *Scientific American,* September 1956, pp. 170–182; and Overbye, op. cit. Sandage's career forms the heart of *Lonely Hearts.*

p. 334 On Rubin work: See Marcia Bartusiak, "The Woman Who Spins the Stars," *Discover,* Oct. 1990, pp. 88–94.

p. 334 "People didn't believe . . .": A. Dressler, interview; "astronomical 'limbo' . . .": D. Burstein, op. cit., p. 429.

p. 334 "In 1975 no one . . .": D. Burstein, Dept. of Physics, Arizona State University, Tempe, telephone interview, Jan. 30, 1991.

p. 336 "And then *that* . . .": A. Dressler, interview.

p. 336 "Now here's one . . .": A. Dressler, interview; "a pattern-recognition . . .": ibid.

p. 337 On origins of Seven Samurai: D. Burstein, interview.

p. 337 "I seem to have . . .": Sandra Faber, quoted in Alan Lightman and Roberta Brawer, *Origins,* Harvard University Press, 1990, p. 332.

p. 337 "If you're a good . . .": D. Burstein, interview.

p. 338 "And then we just . . .": A. Dressler, interview; "We always came . . .": ibid.

p. 338 "We were starting . . .": D. Burstein, interview; "Look at this . . .": D. Burstein, quoted by Faber in Lightman and Brawer, op. cit., p. 334. Faber discusses the Seven Samurai collaboration on pp. 332–335.

p. 338 "electric moment": D. Burstein, interview; "We all looked . . .": ibid.

p. 340 "And what the group . . .": A. Dressler, interview. For an example of a color velocity map, see A. Dressler, *Scientific American,* p. 53.

p. 340 "It was a total . . .": S. Faber, quoted in James Gleick, "Galaxies Reported Moving at High Speed," *New York Times,* Dec. 2, 1986, p. C1.

p. 340 "That's when I . . .": A. Dressler, interview. Dressler recalled in an interview that in preparing the group's first paper in the fall of 1986, he mistakenly used an incorrect mathematical sign that suggested that galaxies in the Hydra-Centaurus Supercluster were flowing *toward* the Local Supercluster, as the group had expected; upon discovering the incorrect sign, Dressler discovered that the H-C galaxies were flowing *away* from the Local Supercluster at even greater speed, suggesting the existence of the huge concentration of mass accounting for the attraction.

pp. 340–341 Background on Houston and Kona: D. Burstein, interview. For such significant results, they didn't receive major attention in the lay press for nearly a year (for example, Gleick, op. cit.).

p. 341 Among good treatments for lay readers are: Shawna Vogel, "Star Attraction," *Discover,* Nov. 1989, pp. 20–22; "Astronomers Home In on the Great Attractor," *New Scientist,* Dec. 9, 1989, p. 26; Liz Glasgow, "The 'Great Attractor' Comes with Strings Attached," *New Scientist,* Sept. 30, 1989, p. 31; Philip J. Hilts, "Far Out in Space, a Giant Discovery," *New York Times,* Jan. 12, 1990, p. A22; and Ivars Peterson, "Looking Well Beyond the Great Attractor," *Science News,* vol. 135, April 15, 1989, pp. 230–231.

p. 341 "the Woodstock . . .": D. Burstein, interview.

p. 341 "The afternoon dissolved . . .": D. Overbye, op. cit., p. 412. The drama of the Kona meeting is well captured by Overbye.

p. 341 The main papers in the Seven Samurai canon are: A. Dressler et al., "Spectroscopy and Photometry of Elliptical Galaxies: I. A New Distance Estimator," *Astrophysical Journal,* vol. 313, Feb. 1, 1987, pp. 42–58; A. Dressler et al., "Spectroscopy and Photometry of Elliptical Galaxies: A Large-Scale Streaming Motion in the Local Universe," *Astrophysical Journal* (Letters), vol. 313, Feb. 15, 1987, pp. L37–L42; D. Lynden-Bell et al., *Astrophysical Journal,* vol. 326, March 1, 1988, pp. 19–49; and A. Dressler, "The Supergalactic Plane Redshift Survey: A Candidate for the Great Attractor," *Astrophysical Journal,* vol. 329, June 15, 1988, pp. 519–526.

p. 341 In addition, Dressler has written two useful reviews: "Large-Scale Structure in the Universe," presented at the 14th Texas Symposium, Dallas, Dec. 1988 (perhaps Dressler's best single exposition of the Great Attractor idea and its cosmological implications); and "The Great Attractor: Do Galaxies Trace the Large-Scale Mass Distribution?" *Nature,* vol. 350, April 4, 1991, pp. 391–397. See also N. Kaiser, "Where Is the Great Attractor?" *Nature,* vol. 338, April 13, 1989, pp. 538–539.

p. 341 "It was one . . .": Amos Yahil, State University of New York at Stony Brook, personal interview, Sept. 11, 1989.

p. 341 "But Dressler knew . . .": D. Burstein, interview.

p. 342 "There it was . . .": A. Dressler, interview.

p. 342 "Imagine what it . . .": D. Burstein, interview. Along these same lines, Burstein says, "If you think of the universe as a jigsaw puzzle of 100,000 pieces, we have a few hundred pieces, and they are by no means contiguous. That's what makes it fun."

p. 342 "Now what makes . . .": A. Dressler, interview.

p. 343 "The Great Attractor's . . .": A. Dressler, interview.

p. 344 "And discovering that . . .": ibid.

18. THE UNIVERSE ACCORDING TO JOHN HUCHRA
GENERAL SOURCES

Marcia Bartusiak, *Thursday's Universe,* Times Books, New York, 1986 (a good all-around primer for lay readers on the latest developments in astronomy and cosmology); Timothy Ferris, *The Red Limit: The Search for the Edge of the Universe,* 2nd ed., Quill, New York, 1983 (a superlative introduction to twentieth-century cosmology); George Gamow, *"One Two Three . . . Infinity: Facts and Speculations of Science,* Dover, New York, 1947 (the classic that launched the careers of dozens of astronomers); Margaret J. Geller, "Mapping the Universe: Slices and Bubbles," in James Cornell, ed., *Bubbles, Voids, and Bumps in Time: The New Cosmology,* Cambridge University Press, Cambridge, 1988, pp. 50–72; Richard Preston, *First Light: The Search for the Edge of the Universe,* Atlantic Monthly Press, New York, 1987 (good descriptions of astronomers in action); Vera C. Rubin and George V. Coyne, S.J., eds., *Large-Scale Motions in the Universe,* Princeton University Press, Princeton, N.J., 1988; Joseph Silk, *The Big Bang,* W. H. Freeman, New York, 1989.

NOTES

p. 345 Epigraph: Seamus Heaney, "The Birthplace," *Station Island,* Farrar Straus & Giroux, New York, 1985.

p. 346 "Surveys are not . . .": Jeremiah Ostriker, astrophysicist, Princeton University, Princeton, N.J., telephone interview, Feb. 16, 1990.

p. 347 "Here's a bit . . .": John Huchra, professor of astronomy, Harvard-Smithsonian Center for Astrophysics, personal interview, Sept. 30, 1989 (Mount Hopkins, Ariz.).

p. 348 "I've been known . . .": ibid.

p. 348 "the theorists seem . . .": J. Huchra in Rubin and Coyne, eds., op. cit., p. 581.

p. 348 "In conception and execution . . .": J. Ostriker, interview.

pp. 349–352 The Princeton-Chicago collaboration, known as the Digital Sky Survey, will chart the three-dimensional location of 1 million galaxies and 100,000 quasars, and provide two-dimensional coordinates for another 100 million galaxies. Because the data will be digitized, it will be instantly available to all researchers.

p. 352 On spectra and redshifts: Ferris, op. cit., gives a superb account of the early work leading up to Hubble's dramatic breakthrough.

p. 352 "Photons are the name . . .": J. Huchra, interview.

p. 352 For recent developments in optical telescopy, see Stephen P. Maran, "A New Generation of Giant Eyes Gets Ready to Probe the Universe," *Smithsonian,* June 1987, pp. 41–53.

p. 353 "no real significant . . .": J. Huchra, interview; "One photon that is . . .": ibid.

p. 354 "I have a rule . . .": ibid.

p. 354 "the dumbest of . . .": J. Huchra, interview; Huchra family background, ibid.; "I was a little . . .": ibid.

p. 355 "I carefully neglected . . .": ibid.; "a real infantryman . . .": ibid.

p. 356 Background on M. Geller: Margaret Geller, theoretical astrophysicist, Harvard-Smithsonian Center for Astrophysics, Cambridge, Mass., personal interview, Sept. 6, 1988.

p. 356 "I decided that if . . .": M. Geller, interview.

p. 357 The original 2,400 galaxies were published in J. P. Huchra et al., *Astrophysical Journal Supplement,* vol. 52, June 1983, pp. 61–87.

p. 357 "We were working on . . .": J. Huchra, interview.

p. 357 "Had I been present . . .": Alfonso the Wise (1221–1284), quoted in *The Oxford Dictionary of Quotations,* 3rd ed., Oxford University Press, Oxford, 1979, p. 3.

p. 357 On cosmological theories in the early 1980s: See Joseph Silk, Alexander S. Szalay, and Yakov B. Zel'dovich, "The Large-Scale Structure of the Universe," *Scientific American,* October 1983, pp. 72–80.

p. 358 Boötes's void was reported in Robert P. Kirshner et al., "A Million Cubic Megaparsec Void in Boötes?" *Astrophysical Journal,* vol. 248, Sept. 1, 1981, pp. L57–L60. Bartusiak, op. cit., provides a good review of large-scale surveys in the chapter "Celestial Tapestry."

p. 358 "That must be . . .": M. Geller, interview.

p. 358 "The strategy Margaret and I . . .": J. Huchra, interview; "The one that went . . .": ibid.

p. 359 "We decided to do . . .": M. Geller, interview.

p. 360 "Normally, when you're doing . . .": J. Huchra, interview.

pp. 360–361 The first slice was reported in Valérie de Lapparent, M. J. Geller, and J. P. Huchra, "A Slice of the Universe," *Astrophysical Journal* (Letters), vol.

302, March 1, 1986, pp. L1–L5 (this is the original "bubbles" paper). Expanded slices were reported in J. Huchra et al., "The Center for Astrophysics Redshift Survey," in J. Audouze et al., eds., *Large-Scale Structures of the Universe,* IAU, 1988, pp. 105–112.

p. 360 De Lapparent's reaction is described in Marcia Bartusiak, "The Bubbling Universe," *Science Digest,* Feb. 1986, pp. 64–65.

p. 362 "Frankly, we were all . . .": J. Huchra, interview; "Flabbergasted": M. Geller, interview.

p. 362 "The first thing . . .": J. Huchra, interview.

p. 362 "I've always thought . . .": M. Geller, interview.

pp. 362–364 Background on omega and cosmological theory: An up-to-date summary is John Horgan, "Universal Truths," *Scientific American,* October 1990, pp. 108–117.

p. 364 On the Cosmic Background Explorer: See David Lindley, "An Excess of Perfection," *Nature,* vol. 343, Jan. 18, 1990, p. 207.

p. 364 "It now turns out . . .": M. Geller, interview.

p. 364 "We can slice . . .": J. Huchra, interview; "Instead of just looking . . .": ibid.

p. 365 The "Great Wall" is described in Margaret J. Geller and John P. Huchra, "Mapping the Universe," *Science,* vol. 246, Nov. 17, 1989, pp. 897–903. Popular accounts of this work include: Jeff Hecht, "Cosmic Contradictions Trouble the Astronomers," *New Scientist,* Dec. 2, 1989, pp. 34–35; A. McKenzie, "Cosmic Cartographers Find 'Great Wall,'" *Science News,* vol. 136, Nov. 25, 1989, p. 340; and N. Mitchell Waldrop, "Astronomers Go Up Against the Great Wall," *Science,* Nov. 17, 1989, p. 885.

p. 365 "What we're trying . . .": J. Huchra, interview.

p. 365 ". . . the human eye is . . .": David Lindley, "Reading Tea-leaves in the Sky," *Nature,* vol. 334, Aug. 25, 1988, p. 647.

p. 366 "It's sobering that . . .": M. Geller, in Rubin and Coyne, eds. op. cit., pp. 594–595.

p. 366 "That is the problem . . .": J. Huchra, interview.

p. 366 "How did it get . . .": J. Ostriker, interview.

p. 366 "pose a serious . . .": M. Geller, interview.

p. 367 "Those values are inconsistent . . .": J. Huchra, interview; "Not very many . . .": ibid.

p. 367 "In all respects . . .": John Maddox, "Down with the Big Bang," *Nature,* vol. 340, Aug. 10, 1989, p. 425. Two other alternative views are Anthony L. Peratt, "Not with a Bang," *The Sciences,* Jan.–Feb. 1990, pp. 24–32, and H. C. Arp et al., "The Extragalactic Universe: An Alternative View," *Nature,* vol. 346, Aug. 30, 1990, pp. 807–812. See also John Noble Wilford, "The Big Bang Survives an Onslaught of New Cosmology," *New York Times,* Jan. 21, 1990, p. 5 ("The Week in Review").

p. 367 "the big bang is . . .": I. E. Segal, "The Unscientific Charm of the Big Bang" (letter to the editor), *New York Times,* May 4, 1990, p. A34.

p. 367 "It's probably the case . . .": J. Huchra, letter to author, May 4, 1991.

p. 368 "I'm going to try . . .": J. Huchra, interview.

p. 368 "Another one?": Frank Low, interview; "C'mon . . .": J. Huchra, interview.

"ELEPHANTS FOR WANT OF TOWNS"

GENERAL SOURCES

Gregory Bateson, *Mind and Nature: A Necessary Unity,* Dutton, New York, 1979; Lloyd Brown, *The Story of Maps,* Dover, New York, 1979; Jacques Ellul, *The Technological Society,* Vintage, New York, 1964; Michel Foucault, "Questions on Geography," in Colin Gordon, ed., *Power/Knowledge: Selected Interviews & Other Writings,* Pantheon, New York, 1980; William H. Goetzmann, *New Lands, New Men,* Viking, New York, 1986; O. B. Hardison, Jr., *Disappearing Through the Skylight: Culture and Technology in the Twentieth Century,* Viking, New York, 1989; J. B. Harley, "Maps, Knowledge, and Power," in Denis Cosgrove and Stephen Daniels, eds., *The Iconography of Landscape,* Cambridge University Press, Cambridge, 1988, pp. 277–312; J. B. Harley and David Woodward, *The History of Cartography, Volume One: Cartography in Prehistoric, Ancient, and Medieval Europe and the Mediterranean,* University of Chicago Press, Chicago, 1987; Thomas P. Hughes, *American Genesis: A Century of Invention and Technological Enthusiasm,* Viking, New York, 1989; Meriwether Lewis and William Clark, *The History of the Lewis and Clark Expedition,* edited by Elliott Coues, Dover, New York, 1893; Jean-François Lyotard, *The Postmodern Condition: A Report on Knowledge,* University of Minnesota Press, Minneapolis, 1984; Mark Monmonier, *How to Lie with Maps,* University of Chicago Press, Chicago, 1991; Phillip C. Muehrcke, *Map Use: Reading, Analysis, and Interpretation,* 2nd ed., JP Publications, Madison, Wis., 1986; Lewis Mumford, *The Myth of the Machine: The Pentagon of Power,* Harcourt Brace Jovanovich, New York, 1964, 1970; Raymond H. Ramsay, *No Longer on the Map: Discovering Places That Never Were,* Viking, New York, 1972; Peter Sutton, ed., *Dreamings: The Art of Aboriginal Australia,* George Braziller/Asia Society, New York, 1988; Henry David Thoreau, *Walden and Other Writings,* Bantam, New York, 1962; John Noble Wilford, *The Mapmakers,* Knopf, New York, 1981.

NOTES

p. 369 Epigraphs: Christopher Marlowe, *Tamburlaine,* Part II, *The Complete Works of Christopher Marlowe,* vol. I, Cambridge University Press, Cambridge, 1973, p. 216; Italo Calvino, *Invisible Cities,* Harcourt Brace Jovanovich, New York, 1974, p. 5; and Allan Sandage, quoted in Alan Lightman and Roberta Brawer, *Origins,* Harvard University Press, Cambridge, Mass., 1990, p. 82.

pp. 369–370 On the Gastaldi map: W. Goetzmann, op. cit., pp. 97–101. Ramsay (op. cit., p. 124) agrees that it was an Italian invention, but attributes the idea to *Jacopo* Gastaldi in 1562, with the first map being done by Bolognini Zaltieri in 1566. The original Gastaldi map has never been authoritatively identified and is described by map historian Rodney Shirley as "lost."

p. 371 Todorov figure: cited in Gary Wills, "Goodbye, Columbus," *New York Review of Books,* Nov. 22, 1990, pp. 6–10. Todorov discusses the thesis in *The Conquest of America: The Question of the Other,* Harper & Row, New York, 1984.

p. 372 "imaginary geography": W. Goetzmann, op. cit., p. 100; Carl I. Wheat, "Mapping the American West, 1540–1857," *Proceedings of the American Antiquarian Society,* vol. 64, April 21, 1954, pp. 19–27; R. V. Tooley, "Geographical Oddities, or Curious, Ingenious, and Imaginary Maps and Miscellaneous

Plates Published in Atlases," *Map Collectors' Circle,* vol. 1, no. 1, 1964, pp. 1–22; and Ramsay, op cit.

pp. 372–373 On medieval maps: J. N. Wilford, "The Topography of Myth and Dogma," in *The Mapmakers,* pp. 34–55; "a millennium without . . .": ibid., p. 34.

p. 372 "So geographers . . .": Jonathan Swift, "On Poetry: A Rhapsody," *The Portable Swift,* Penguin, New York, 1948, 1988, p. 541.

pp. 373–374 On California as an island: R. V. Tooley, "California as an Island," *The Map Collectors' Circle,* vol. 1, no. 8, 1964. As Tooley points out, Father Eusebio Kino crossed from the mainland to the Baja Peninsula in the late seventeenth century and thus had firsthand knowledge of the local geography, but his map of circa 1705 showing California as connected to the mainland was roundly denounced, especially by European mapmakers—as if their maps assumed greater credibility than the actual geography!

p. 374 "an essential point . . .": Lewis and Clark, op. cit., p. 444.

p. 374 Apropos of computer modeling of data, cartography expert Phillip Muehrcke points out that the absence of any subset of relevant information can produce completely distorted and misleading results in an expert information system, which can be likened to a complex computer model (telephone interview, April 25, 1991).

p. 374 On maps of Mars: John Noble Wilford, *Mars Beckons,* Knopf, 1990, pp. 21–24; the nuclear-waste-dump aspect is mentioned in J. B. Harley, op. cit., p. 289.

p. 374 On Soviet cartography: Bill Keller, "Soviet Aide Admits Maps Were Faked for 50 Years," *New York Times,* Sept. 3, 1988, p. 1; "cartography should be . . .": Robert Pear, "In the West, Map Makers Hail Shift in Soviet Stance," *New York Times,* Sept. 3, 1988, p. 4.

p. 375 "nimble arithmetic": J. N. Wilford, *The Mapmakers,* p. 64.

p. 375 On Columbus's data selection: Wilford, *The Mapmakers,* pp. 61–66. Wilford shows that by manipulating units of measure, Columbus estimated the distance between the Canary Islands and Japan to be 4,300 kilometers when the real distance was closer to 15,000 kilometers. As Wilford puts it, "Columbus had in his own mind reduced Earth to a size more congenial to his plan of action" (p. 65).

p. 375 "always does things . . .": John Huchra, Harvard-Smithsonian Center for Astrophysics, interview, Sept. 30, 1989.

p. 376 "I have kind of . . .": A. Sandage, quoted in Lightman and Brawer, op. cit., p. 83.

p. 376 "Even blind sailing . . .": L. Mumford, op. cit., p. 110.

pp. 377–378 On medieval maps and Solinus: Wilford, *The Mapmakers,* pp. 34–35. L. Brown also discusses Solinus and includes illustrations of the monsters.

p. 378 "It is true . . .": de Mornas, quoted in Wilford, *The Mapmakers,* p. 35; "could not be . . .": Cosmas, quoted ibid., p. 37.

pp. 379–380 On map projections: "Matching the Map Projection to the Need," American Cartographic Association, Bethesda, Md., 1991; Wilford, *The Mapmakers,* pp. 73–85; John Noble Wilford, "The Impossible Quest for the Perfect Map," *New York Times,* Oct. 25, 1988, p. C1; M. Monmonier, op. cit., pp. 115–118.

p. 380 "geopolitical prophecy": J. B. Harley, op. cit., p. 290.

p. 380 "the best combination . . .": John P. Snyder, consultant, United States Geological Survey, telephone interview, April 25, 1991.

p. 380 "A poorly chosen . . .": quoted in Wilford, "The Impossible Quest," op. cit.

p. 380 "Europeanization of the earth": Arno Peters, *Peters Atlas of the World,* Harper & Row, New York, 1990, p. 3; "the equivalent of . . .": T. Hardaker, in *Peters Atlas,* p. 6.

p. 381 "wet, ragged, long . . .": Arthur H. Robinson, "Arno Peters and His New Cartography," *American Cartographer,* vol. 12, no. 2, 1985, pp. 103–111. For other aspects of the Peters debate, see John Loxton, "The Peters Phenomenon," *Cartographic Journal,* vol. 22, Dec. 1985, pp. 106–108; and M. Monmonier, op. cit., pp. 96–98. None of these treatments is kind to Peters.

p. 384 "I paid my academicians . . .": J. D. Cassini, quoted in Philip and Phylis Morrison, *The Ring of Truth,* Random House, New York, 1987, p. 128.

p. 384 "To become the 'lords . . .": L. Mumford, op. cit., p. 78. The quote within the quote refers to a remark by Descartes.

p. 384 "science of princes . . .": J. B. Harley, op. cit., p. 281.

p. 385 "with the religious elite . . .": J. B. Harley and D. Woodward, op. cit., p. 506.

p. 385 On the discovery of Brazil: "Portugal-Brazil: The Age of Atlantic Discoveries," exhibition, New York Public Library, 1990.

p. 385 On Mayan discovery: Wilbur E. Garrett, "La Ruta Maya," *National Geographic,* Oct. 1989, pp. 424–479; "enter your lands . . .": ibid., p. 447.

p. 386 On Magellan: Eugene Lyon, "Track of the Manila Galleons," *National Geographic,* Sept. 1990, pp. 5–37.

p. 386 "the rage for . . .": W. Goetzmann, op. cit., p. 9.

p. 386 "Immense numbers . . .": Lewis and Clark, op. cit., pp. 382, 380, 451, 707, 428, 569, 641.

p. 387 "If you wish . . .": Lewis and Clark, ibid., p. 549.

p. 387 "much knowledge has been . . .": Samuel Johnson, quoted in G. Wills, op. cit., pp. 6–10.

pp. 387–388 On U.N. meeting: Kathleen Teltsch, "Space Plans Frustrate the 'Have-Nots,' " *New York Times,* May 14, 1972, p. 15.

p. 388 "I would not go . . .": Ade Abiodun, Chief of Space Applications, Outer Space Division, United Nations, telephone interview, July 25, 1991.

p. 388 "Leading companies in . . .": "Landsat," Earth Observing Satellite Co., 1987 (brochure published by Eosat on the occasion of Landsat's fifteenth anniversary), p. 13; "oil and mining industries . . .": ibid., p. 17; on Landsat prices, see "Landsat Data Commercialized," *EOS,* Jan. 22, 1991, p. 33.

p. 389 "In this paradise . . .": Alexander von Humboldt, quoted in Mumford, op. cit., pp. 15–16.

p. 389 "Someday humans will . . .": *The Planetary Report,* Sept.–Oct. 1990, p. 3; on titanium map, see "Lunar Prospecting from Earth," *Sky & Telescope,* June 1991, p. 576.

pp. 389–390 "The most constructive . . .": John von Neumann, "Can We Survive Technology?" *Fortune,* June 1955, p. 106; "to make a new ice . . .": ibid., p. 108; "the very techniques . . .": ibid., p. 151.

p. 390 On genetic maps: see Jerry Bishop and Michael Waldholz, *Genome,* Simon & Schuster, New York, 1990; S. S. Hall, *Smithsonian,* February 1990, pp. 40–49. On genetics and insurance: Bishop and Waldholz, op. cit., pp. 290–300; on social implications, see Neil A. Holtzman, *Proceed with Caution,* Johns Hopkins University Press, Baltimore, 1989, and Dorothy Nelkin and Laurence Tancredi, *Dangerous Diagnostics: The Social Power of Biological Information,* Basic Books, New York, 1989.

p. 392 "Five hundred years . . .": James A. Yorke, personal interview, Sept. 6, 1990.

pp. 392–393 On E. O. Lawrence testimony: Robert Crease and Charles Mann, *The Second Creation,* Macmillan, 1986, p. 258.

p. 394 "Apollo was not . . .": Carl Sagan, "The Gift of Apollo," *Parade,* July 16, 1989, pp. 4–7; "The same technology . . .": ibid., p. 5.

p. 394 "To the extent . . .": L. Mumford, op. cit., p. 123.

p. 394 "In war men think . . .": F. Haber, "Chemical Warfare" (letter to the editor), *Nature,* vol. 109, Jan. 12, 1922, p. 40. Haber's remark came in response to a book review. Thomas Hughes recounts the episode in *American Genesis,* pp. 115–116.

p. 395 "Technology—like science . . .": J. von Neumann, *Fortune,* p. 151.

pp. 395–396 On Aboriginal art: The mining dispute is mentioned in Christopher Anderson and Françoise Dussart, "Dreaming in Acrylic: Western Desert Art," in P. Sutton, ed., op. cit., p. 139.

p. 396 "As maps of political . . .": Peter Sutton, "The Morphology of Feeling," ibid., p. 80. Redolent of the subtractive processes that occur in traditional cartography, Sutton adds: "What we are suggesting here is that much Western Desert art produces a finite design by subtraction—even quotation—from a potentially infinite grid of connected places/Dreamings/people, in which real spatial relationships are literally rectified and represented by connected roundels in what Nancy Munn calls a site-path framework" (p. 84).

p. 396 "And it struck me . . .": Bruce Chatwin, *The Songlines,* Viking, 1988, p. 117.

p. 397 "The map is not . . .": G. Bateson, op. cit., p. 30; Bateson adds, "Science *probes*; it does not prove" (p. 30).

p. 397 "Clearly, the whole . . .": Mary Hesse, quoted in "Does Ideology Stop at the Laboratory Door? A Debate on Science and the Real World," *New York Times,* Oct. 22, 1989, p. E24.

p. 398 "More science in . . .": S. Harding, quoted ibid.

p. 398 "The way in which . . .": J. B. Harley, "Maps, Knowledge, and Power," p. 300.

pp. 398–399 "It is not worth . . .": Henry David Thoreau, op. cit., p. 342; "What does Africa . . .": ibid., p. 341; "it is easier to sail . . .": ibid., p. 342.

p. 399 "not down . . .": Herman Melville, quoted in P. Muehrcke, op. cit., p. 387.

p. 400 "cultural spectrum": W. Goetzmann, remarks at "Voyager Retrospective: A Symposium on Exploration," Pasadena Civic Auditorium, Aug. 23, 1989. Some of the remarks, in slightly different form, appear in *The Planetary Report,* vol. 9, no. 6, Nov.–Dec. 1989, pp. 6–9.

p. 400 "an era of technological . . .": T. P. Hughes, op. cit., p. 1.

p. 401 "To ask in advance . . .": J. von Neumann, *Fortune,* p. 152.

p. 402 "would simply deny . . .": T. P. Hughes, op. cit., p. 452.

p. 402 "A map of the world . . .": O. Wilde, quoted in Richard Ellmann, *Oscar Wilde,* Knopf, 1988. I am grateful to Joseph McElroy for bringing this quotation to my attention.

ACKNOWLEDGMENTS

Just as many invisible hands go into the making of a map, so too have many invisible hands helped in the making of this book, and it is a special pleasure to make their contributions more visible—to put them on the map, as it were.

The veracity and virtue of any book about science depend critically upon the cooperation and patience of the scientists themselves. I am grateful to the following researchers, who gave generously of their time to sit through interviews, dug up illustrations, and who cheerfully (and almost always promptly) answered tedious follow-up questions: John Allman, Richard Askey, Gerd Binnig, David Botstein, David Burstein, Robert Cesarone, David and Gregory Chudnovsky, Alden Colvocoresses, Alan Dressler, Adam Dziewonski, Joseph Farman, Randall Feenstra, Gary Flandro, Margaret Geller, William Haxby, Miles Herkenham, John Huchra, Arlin Krueger, John Kutzbach, Michael S. Levine, E. B. Lewis, Virginia Norwood, Thomas Phillips, John Rosenberg, Andrey Sergeyevsky, Mark Skolnick, Joseph Smagorinsky, Anthony Taylor, Patrick Thaddeus, Warren Washington, Jeffrey Weinreb, Amos Yahil, and James Yorke.

For steering me to the right people, handling logistics, tracking down illustrations, or otherwise keeping me on a straight rhumb, I wish to thank Ron Beck of the EROS Data Center; Pat Behling of the University of Wisconsin; Dan Brocious of the Whipple Observatory in Arizona; Susan Cooper of Cold Spring Harbor Laboratory; Kevin Corbley of Eosat Co.; Robert Finn of Caltech; Lynn O'Dell of NYU Hospital; Gerald Present of IBM's Thomas J. Watson Research Center; Michael Riordan and Nina Stolar at Stanford Linear Accelerator Center; Ellen Seufert and Jesse Katz of NASA–Goddard Space Flight Center; Janet Sillas of Brookhaven National Laboratory; and Alan Wood of the Jet Propulsion Laboratory. A special thanks to Kate

Anderson for some wonderful photographs, and to Joe McNally for cheerfully making the best of the usual bad situation.

I wish to thank the Rockefeller Foundation for supporting me as a resident at the Bellagio Study and Conference Center, and for their hospitality and good company it is a special pleasure also to thank Francis and Jacqueline Sutton, Gianna Celli, and the entire staff at Bellagio. It was my good fortune at Bellagio to consort with a worldly and sometimes seditious cohort of scholars who, in addition to humoring my nighttime rambles to Bar Sport and Caffè Maxim, provided a critical and astute audience against which to test the premises of this book. Some lent direct help; others influenced and inspired in ways they might never have imagined, so I would like to thank Gilles Barbedette, Cornell and Kay Fleischer, Roderick and Marjorie Home, John Deutch, Richard Close and Marisha Chamberlain, Scott Ely and Susan Ludvigson, Denise and Philip Sherrard, Lee and Cheryl Siegel, Harold and Pamela Silver, Walter Wetherell, Kate Metropolis, Chris Quigg, Robert Cahn, Hortense Calisher, Curtis Harnack, Anne Williams, and especially Wallace Matson, who showed all of us how close both cartography and philosophy are to stand-up comedy.

Having benefited from many expert readers who agreed to referee portions of the manuscript, I hereby absolve them of all responsibility for any errors that remain and thank them for the many they spotted ahead of time: Anthony Taylor, David Landgrebe, Jeffrey Weissel, Raymond Jeanloz, Thompson Webb III, Joseph Farman, Jeffrey Weinreb, John B. Penney, Jr., Michael Levine, Kerry Kravitz, David Botstein, Paul Hansma, Herbert Robbins, James Yorke, Patrick Thaddeus, David Burstein, and John Huchra. Alice Hudson of the Map Division of the New York Public Library not only reviewed several chapters for cartographic content, but provided a rich bounty of sources, suggestions, and inspiration.

I am especially grateful to those who read individual chapters and whose suggestions forced me toward greater readability: Jamie Diamond, Steve Fishman, Cornell Fleischer, June Kinoshita, Thomas O'Neill, and Philip Sherrard. Those saddled with the more substantial task of reading larger parts of the manuscript deserve more substantial thanks: they are Kevin Dolan (with whom it is becoming a pleasant tradition to review manuscripts in Section 44 of the upper deck at Shea Stadium on Opening Day) and Charles Mann (who, were it not for his tiny handwriting, would be an almost perfect reader). Nelson Smith, in addition to dragging me out to Fanelli's when I threatened to disappear into the horse latitudes of composition, read earlier drafts and thus traveled a bumpier road, thus deserving heartier thanks.

Acknowledgments in the scientific literature are filled with allusions to "useful discussions," and this project has introduced me to the significance of the phrase. Several early discussions were more than useful: they were crucial in convincing myself that this was an idea worth pursuing; so I wish to thank Alan Friedman, Walter Gilbert, and Victor McElheny for their early enthusiasm and support. Among the earliest and most enthusiastic people was my agent, Melanie Jackson, who saw potential in this idea from the very beginning, and gently nudged me in the right direction.

My good fortune abounds in my colleagues at Random House, beginning with my editor, Becky Saletan, whose energy, enthusiasm, savvy, and intelligence are everywhere present in the final product. I would also like to thank Harold Evans for his early interest and enthusiasm, Bob Scudellari and Oksana Kushnir for their commitment to enterprising design, Fred Wiemer for excellent copy editing, and Bill Piersol for flawlessly fielding my every yelp for help.

Finally, a few idiosyncratic and spiritual debts to pay: to David Woodward, who a decade ago generously agreed to review a manuscript about Italian mapmakers by a young writer he'd never heard of, nor heard from again (until now), but whose enthusiasm for maps seems to have rubbed off in a lasting manner; to the friends who lent sustenance and spare beds and the right word of encouragement at the right moment along the way (Steve and Carolyn Rubenstein; Jerry and Linda Roberts; Jamie Diamond; Ann Friedberg and Howard Rodman; Larry Sulkis and Margareta Schiappa; Yukako and Alan Kornhauser; Richard Klug and Kate Stearns; Christopher Winner; John Thorn; Thea Lurie and Mickey Friedman; and B. K. Moran); to Eric Schrier and the gang at In Health, who challenge me with good assignments and who have patiently indulged the deferred projects caused by this book; to Jim Leyland, for making the long summer of 1990 not quite so long (and for showing that you can find intellectual and moral inspiration in the oddest corners of the globe, including a locker room); to Virginia Stern, a home-cosmographer, who has helped map some interior landscapes; to Barbara Ellmann and Joseph McElroy, who provided more meals and more food for thought than could ever be repaid; to the Team of Central Park, for humoring this aging third baseman and for good bonhomie year round; to Mindy Levine, for thoughtful and close reading of the text as well as patience and understanding about that endless purgatory known as "almost finished"; and to my parents, who had the wisdom and faith to turn this boy loose on a map with an abundance of blank space, which is to say without too many boundaries staked out in advance, or areas off-limits to exploration.

INDEX

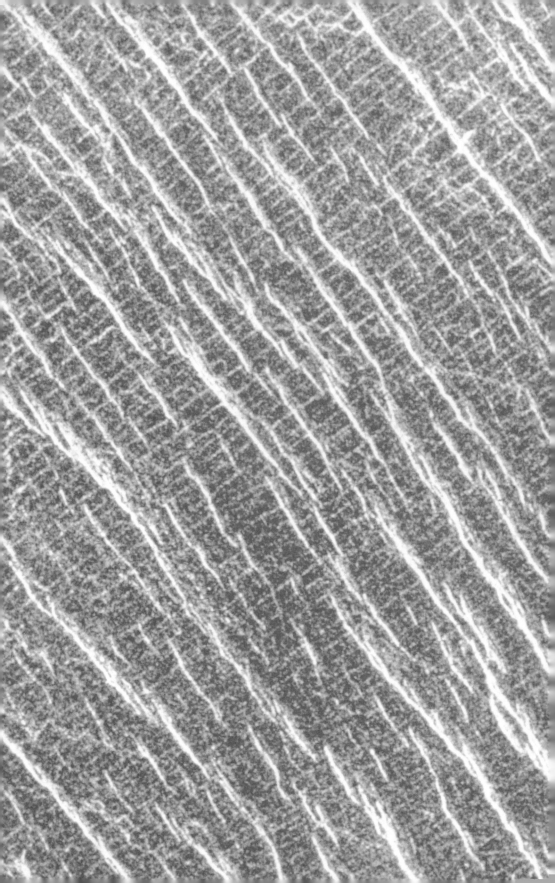